Elizabeth Gund  country's first quality and valu Of all her bool popular, re-appearing editions, of which this is the tenth. She is also the author of *England by Bus & Coach* (Sphere); *Running your own Bed and Breakfast* (Piatkus) for people who want to start doing this themselves; and of about 40 other books.

Staying Off the Beaten Track regularly reaches the best-seller listings. It is a book for all seasons.

VOUCHERS WORTH £18

(by courtesy of the houses concerned)

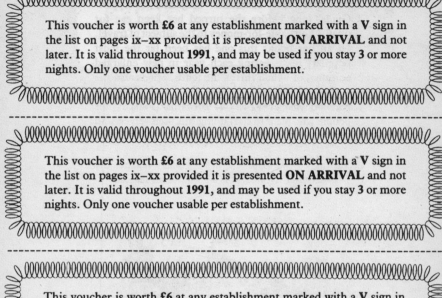

This voucher is worth **£6** at any establishment marked with a **V** sign in the list on pages ix–xx provided it is presented **ON ARRIVAL** and not later. It is valid throughout **1991**, and may be used if you stay **3** or more nights. Only one voucher usable per establishment.

This voucher is worth **£6** at any establishment marked with a **V** sign in the list on pages ix–xx provided it is presented **ON ARRIVAL** and not later. It is valid throughout **1991**, and may be used if you stay **3** or more nights. Only one voucher usable per establishment.

This voucher is worth **£6** at any establishment marked with a **V** sign in the list on pages ix–xx provided it is presented **ON ARRIVAL** and not later. It is valid throughout **1991**, and may be used if you stay **3** or more nights. Only one voucher usable per establishment.

THE NEXT EDITION

Using an out-of-date edition can lead to costly disappointments. A new edition appears early every November, updated, with fresh entries added, some deleted and others revised, and with vouchers valid for the next year. Make sure you are not using an out-of-date edition by ordering a copy in advance from your bookshop; or by post (£7.95) from Explore Britain, Alston, Cumbria, CA9 3SL (UK and BFPO only). There is an order form on page 379. *Overseas readers*: Apply to your nearest British Tourist Authority office.

New in 1992: many new entries for Avon; Beds; Berks; Bucks; Cambs; Cumbria; Devon; Hants; Herts; Kent; Norfolk; Northants; Northumberland; Oxon; Somerset; Surrey; Sussex; Warwicks; Wilts; Worcs; Yorks.

STAYING OFF THE BEATEN TRACK

ELIZABETH GUNDREY
with WALTER GUNDREY

*A personal selection of moderately priced
guest-houses, inns, small hotels, farms and country houses
in England and Wales*

10th EDITION
1991

Edited by Jacqueline Krendel

ARROW

To Andrew, with love

Arrow Books Limited
20 Vauxhall Bridge Road, London SW1V 2SA

An imprint of Random Century Group

London   Melbourne   Sydney   Auckland
Johannesburg and agencies
throughout the world

First published in Great Britain 1982
by Hamlyn Paperbacks
Second edition 1983
Third edition 1984
Fourth edition 1985
Fifth edition 1986
Arrow edition (Sixth edition) 1986
Seventh edition 1987
Eighth edition 1988
Ninth edition 1989
Tenth edition 1990

Set in Linotron Plantin by
Rowland Phototypesetting Limited
Bury St Edmunds, Suffolk
Printed and bound in Great Britain by
The Guernsey Press Co. Limited, Guernsey, C.I.

Front cover picture: **Upper Green Farmhouse**, Oxfordshire
Back cover: **Upton House**, Worcestershire

British Library Cataloguing in Publication Data
Staying off the beaten track – 10th ed. (1991)
1. Great Britain. Hotels & inns
647.944101

ISBN 0-09-961400-6

The author and publishers would like to thank all those
owners who allowed us to use their drawings. Additional
line drawings by David Mostyn, Peter Gregory, Matthew
Doyle, Nicole Tedder, Jeremy Ford, Leslie Dean, Pat
Gundrey and Elizabeth Gundrey

CONTENTS

COUNTIES OF ENGLAND

SCOTLAND

NORTHUMBERLAND

TYNE AND WEAR

CUMBRIA

DURHAM

CLEVELAND

NORTH YORKS

LANCS

WEST YORKS

HUMBERSIDE

MANCH.

SOUTH YORKS

MERSEYSIDE

CHESHIRE

DERBY

NOTTS

LINCS

STAFFS

LEICS

NORFOLK

SHROPS

W. MID

WARWICK

NORTHANTS

CAMBS

SUFFOLK

HEREFORD AND WORCESTER

BEDS

FOR WALES SEE PAGE 353

GLOS

OXON

BUCKS

HERTS

ESSEX

LONDON

AVON

WILTS

BERKS

SURREY

KENT

HANTS

SOMERSET

WEST SUSSEX

EAST SUSSEX

DORSET

DEVON

CORNWALL

0   50
miles

N

	A	B	C	D	E	F	G	H	J	K
1										
2										
3										
4										
5										
6										
7										
8										
9										
10										
11										
12										
13										
14										

L

C

	A	B	C
13			
14			

Bude

Launceston

Camelford

Padstow

Yeo

Liskeard

Fowey

St Agnes

St Austell

Looe

Truro

St Ives

Isles of Scilly

The hotels and houses in England appear in alphabetical order, followed by those in Wales. However, for convenience in locating them, they are grouped in the following list according to counties. On the left is the nearest town (sometimes distant), with its map reference (see page vii), followed by the house or hotel and its nearest village.

Establishments marked with a V will accept the discount vouchers from page ii. Other discounts to readers are described in the text.

NOTE: The houses in this book have been personally visited by Elizabeth (or in some cases Walter) Gundrey. **At most of them you may stay for as little as £10–£18 (for bed-and-breakfast)** although their best rooms may cost more, and their prices may rise in high season. But owners, and prices, can change overnight; so check before you book. At many places, you can dine or lunch without staying: see entries under **'Dinner'**.

COMPLAINTS: We will investigate if you have first taken the matter up with the owners, who are normally anxious to put right anything that is wrong.

Acknowledgments

We acknowledge with much appreciation the assistance of the rest of the 'Staying Off the Beaten Track' team (Jacqueline Krendel, Jonathan May, Jennifer Christie and – last but far from least – Andrew Cockburn); of editor Jan Bowmer and her colleagues at Arrow Books; and of all the proprietors of houses.

Elizabeth and Walter Gundrey

COUNTY LIST OF HOUSES & HOTELS

Nearest town	Map ref. (see p. vii)	Address		Page
AVON				
Bath	F.11	(Avonside, see Wiltshire)		12
		(Bradford Old Windmill, see Wiltshire)		30
		Oldfields		234
		The Orchard, Bathford		235
		Paradise House		240
		Parkside		303
		(Pickford House, see Somerset)		249
		Somerset House	V	291
		Strathavon	V	303
Bristol	F.11	Dornden, Old Sodbury	V	94
BEDFORDSHIRE				
Bedford	J.10	Church Farm, Roxton		59
		The Grange, Ravensden		122
BERKSHIRE				
Hungerford	G.11	Marshgate Cottage, Marshgate		183
Maidenhead	H.11	Inverlodden, Wargrave		155
Newbury	G.11	St Mary's House, Kintbury		278
Reading	H.11	Boot Farm, Bradfield		28
		Bridge Cottage, Woolhampton		28
BUCKINGHAMSHIRE				
Aylesbury	H.10	Foxhill, Kingsey		115
		Poletrees Farm, Brill		253
		Wallace Farm, Dinton	V	321
Beaconsfield	H.11	Old Jordans, Jordans		215
High Wycombe	H.11	White House, Widmer End		339
Milton Keynes	H.10	Richmond Lodge, Mursley	V	267
CAMBRIDGESHIRE				
Cambridge	J.9	(Chiswick House, see Hertfordshire)		56
		Coach House, Dry Drayton	V	71
		Old Rectory, Swaffham Bulbeck	V	281
		Seven, Chesterton		281
		The Watermill, Hildersham		327
Ely	K.9	The Black Hostelry		25
		Old Egremont House		25
		Spinney Abbey, Wicken	V	325
		Warden's House, Wicken		325
Huntingdon	J.9	Millside Cottage, Houghton		189
CHESHIRE				
Chester	E.7	Castle House		50
		Duddon Lodge, Tarporley		97
		Hatton Hall, Hatton Heath		135
		Newton Hall, Tattenhall		135
Macclesfield	F.7	Golden Cross Farm, Siddington		119
		Hardingland Farmhouse	V	133
Nantwich	F.7	Burland Farm, Burland		44

Nearest town	Map ref. (see p. vii)	Address		Page
CORNWALL				
Bude	C.12	(Leworthy Farmhouse, *see* Devon)		166
		Manor Farmhouse, Crackington Haven		178
		Old Borough House, Bossiney		207
		Rosebud Cottage, Bossiney		207
Camelford	C.13	St Christopher's, Boscastle	V	275
Launceston	C.13	Fleardon Farm, Lezant		109
		Hurdon Farm, Hurdon	V	153
		Winnacott Farm, North Petherwin		109
Liskeard	C.13	Old Rectory, St Keyne		224
Looe	C.13	Coombe Farmhouse, Widegates	V	76
		Slate House, Bucklawren		76
Padstow	B.13	Old Mill, Petherick		216
(Plymouth, Devon)	C.13	Cliff House, Kingsand	V	69
St Agnes	B.13	Rose-in-Vale Hotel, Mithian		272
St Austell	B.13	Anchor Cottage, Mevagissey	V	185
		Marina Hotel, Fowey		182
		Mevagissey House, Mevagissey	V	185
St Ives	A.14	Old Vicarage, Parc-an-Creet	V	231
Truro	B.14	Tregony House, Tregony	V	312
		Trewerry Mill, Trerice		313
CUMBRIA				
Ambleside	E.4	Blea Tarn House, Little Langdale		27
Brampton	F.3	Abbey Bridge Inn, Lanercost		2
		Hare and Hounds Inn, Talkin		134
		Hullerbank, Talkin	V	134
Cockermouth	E.4	Link House, Bassenthwaite Lake		168
		Low Hall, Brandlingill		174
		Owl Brook, High Lorton	V	174
Grasmere	E.4	Tongue Ghyll		27
Millom	E.5	Foldgate Farm, Corney	V	111
		Whicham Old Rectory, Silecroft		336
Penrith	F.4	Bradley Foot, Ousby	V	31
		The Gatehouse, Melmerby	V	31
		The Mill, Mungrisdale		187
		Prospect Hill Hotel, Kirkoswald	V	261
Wigton	E.4	Friar Hall Farm, Caldbeck		116
		High Greenrigg House, Caldbeck		141
Windermere	E.5	The Archway	V	9
DERBYSHIRE				
Ashbourne	G.8	(Beechenhill Farm, *see* Staffordshire)		296
		Old Orchard, Thorpe	V	218
		(Stanshope Hall, *see* Staffordshire)		296
Bakewell	G.7	Rock House, Alport		269
Belper	G.8	Shottle Hall Farm, Shottle		286
Buxton	G.7	Biggin Hall, Biggin-by-Hartington		23
		The Hall, Tideswell		131
		Milne House, Millers Dale		190
(Sheffield, West Yorkshire)	G.7	Cryer House, Castleton		89
		Highlow Hall, Hathersage		145

Nearest town	Map ref. (see p. vii)	Address		Page

LEICESTERSHIRE

(Grantham, Lincolnshire)	H.8	Peacock Farm Guest-House, Redmile	V	242
Market Harborough	H.9	Wheathill Farm, Shearsby	V	335
Melton Mowbray	H.8	Home Farm, Old Dalby	V	151
		Saxelbye Manor House, Saxelby		280
Oakham	H.8	Rutland Cottages, Braunston	V	274

LINCOLNSHIRE

Grantham	H.8	(Peacock Farm Guest-House, see Leicestershire)		242
Lincoln	H.7	Carline Guest-House		319
		The Grange, East Barkwith		123
		Manor House, Potterhanworth		180
		Penny Farthing Inn, Timberland	V	180
		Village Farm, Sturton-by-Stow		319
Louth	J.7	Hoe Hill, Swinhope	V	147
Maplethorpe	K.7	Rookery Farmhouse, Castle Carlton		271
Spalding	J.8	Guy Wells, Whaplode		130

LONDON

Hampstead	J.11	Avoca House Hotel		11
		Buckland Hotel		11
Hornsey	J.11	Middle House		186

NORFOLK

Cromer	L.8	Cley Mill, Cley-next-the-Sea		68
Diss	L.9	Greenacres Farm, Wood Green		222
		Lodge Farm, Fersfield	V	172
		Old Rectory, Gissing	V	222
Fakenham	K.8	Cobblers, South Creake		73
		Holland House, Docking		73
		Old Bakehouse, Little Walsingham	V	205
King's Lynn	K.8	Crown Inn, Downham Market	V	88
Norwich	L.8	Glavenside, Letheringsett		126
		Grey Gables	V	126
		Kimberley Home Farm, Wymondham		157
		Regency House, Neatishead	V	266
Swaffham	K.8	Corfield House, Sporle		77
		Hall Farm, Castle Acre		77
Thetford	K.9	Cedar Lodge, West Tofts		53
		College Farmhouse, Thompson		75

NORTHAMPTONSHIRE

(Banbury, Oxon)	G.10	Rectory Farm, Sulgrave		264
Brackley	H.10	Walltree House Farm, Steane	V	323
Corby	H.9	Castle Farm, Fotheringhay	V	49
		Ship Inn, Oundle	V	285
Kettering	H.9	Dairy Farm, Cranford St Andrew		90
		Wold Farm, Old		347
Oundle	J.9	The Maltings, Aldwincle		176
Towcester	H.10	Old Wharf Farm, Yardley Gobion		233

Nearest town	Map ref. (see p. vii)	Address		Page
SURREY				
Dorking	J.12	Bulmer Farm, Holmbury St Mary		41
		Crossways Farm, Abinger		87
(Gatwick, West Sussex)	J.12	Chithurst Farm, Smallfield	V	57
		(Water Hall Farmhouse, see West Sussex)		326
Guildford	G.12	Clandon Manor Farm, East Clandon		64
		Hazelgrove, West Horsley		64
Hampton Wick	J.11	Chase Lodge	V	54
Haslemere	H.12	(Deerfell, see West Sussex)		93
		Town House		93
SUSSEX (EAST)				
Hailsham	K.12	Cleavers Lyng, Herstmonceux	V	67
Hastings	K.12	105 High Street	V	67
Rye	K.12.	Old Vicarage	V	232
		(Tighe Farm, see Kent)		310
		Western House		332
(Tunbridge Wells, Kent)	K.12	Newbarn, Wadhurst		198
Winchelsea	K.12	Country House		81
		Winchelsea Tea Room		81
SUSSEX (WEST)				
Chichester	H.12	Easton House, Chidham		98
		Old Rectory, Chidham		98
		St Hugh's, Boxgrove		276
		White Barn, Bosham		337
		Whyke House		341
Gatwick	J.12	Water Hall Farmhouse, Charlwood		326
(Haslemere, Surrey)	H.12	Deerfell, Blackdown Park	V	93
Haywards Heath	J.12	Old Cudwells Barn, Scaynes Hill		208
		Old Place, Ansty		220
Horsham	J.12	Brookfield Farm Hotel, Plummers Plain		35
		Churchgate, Billingshurst		162
		Lannards, Billingshurst		162
		Westlands, Monk's Gate		35
Midhurst	H.12	Cumbers House, Rogate		350
		Woodmans Green Farm, Woodmans Green		350
Petworth	H.12	River Park Farm, Lodsworth		268
Worthing	J.12	Gratwicke House		125
		Racehorse Cottage, Nepcote	V	263
		Rock Windmill, Washington		270
		Upton Farmhouse, Sompting		125
TYNE & WEAR				
Newcastle-upon-Tyne	G.3	Beecroft, Woolsington	V	18

Billiard-room at Stone House Hotel (see page 299)

WALES

Nearest town	Map ref. *(see p. 353)*	Address		Page
CLWYD				
(Oswestry,	E.8	Bwlch y Rhiw, Llansilin	V	377
Shropshire)		Wynnstay Inn, Llansilin	V	377
Ruthin	E.7	Eyarth Station, Llanfair-Dyffryn-Clwyd		364
(Welshpool,	E.8	Bron Heulog, Llanrhaeadr-ym-Mochnant	V	354
Powys)		Glyndwr, Pen-y-Bont-Fawr		354
DYFED				
Aberystwyth	D.9	Brynarth Farmhouse, Lledrod	V	369
		Pantyfedwen, Pontrhydfendigaid		369
Cardigan	C.10	Broniwan, Rhydlewis	V	356
		Hendre Farm, Llangrannog		370
		Park Hall, Cwmtydu		370
Carmarthen	C.10	Cwmtwrch, Nantgaredig	V	360
		Fferm-y-Felin, Llanpumsaint		360
Fishguard	B.10	Mount Pleasant Farm, Penffordd		373
		Tregynon, Gwaun Valley	·	373
GWENT				
Abergavenny	E.10	The Cloisters, Llanvihangel Crucorney	V	359
Pontypool	E.10	Ty'r Ywen, Trevithin		376
GWYNEDD				
Bala	D.8	Dewis Cyfarfod, Llandderfel		362
		Melin Meloch	V	362
Barmouth	D.8	Llwyndû, Llanaber		367
Betws-y-Coed	D.7	Royal Oak Farmhouse		374
		Ty Gwyn	V	374
Caernarfon	C.7	Bronant, Bontnewydd		355
		Tŷ'n Rhos, Llanddeiniolen		375
Conwy	D.7	Cefn, Tyn-y-Groes		358
Dolgellau	D.8	Herongate, Arthog	V	367
Menai Bridge	D.7	Plas Trefarthen, Brynsiencyn,		
		Isle of Anglesey		371
POWYS				
Brecon	E.10	Old Rectory, Aberyscir		368
Llandrindod Wells	E.9	Argoed Fawr, Llanwrthwl		357
		Bwlch Coch, Llanwrthwl		357
		Ffaldau, Llandegley	V	365
Machynlleth	D.8	Talbontdrain, Uwychygarreg	V	372
Newtown	E.9	Highgate Farm, Betws Cedewain		366
Welshpool	E.8	(Bron Heulog, *see* Clwyd)		354
		Burnt House, Trelydan	V	363
		Cyfie Farm, Llanfihangel		361
		Dysserth House, Powis Estate	V	363
		(Glyndwr, *see* Clwyd)		354

THE 10th ANNIVERSARY

In the competitive world of accommodation guides, it is gratifying that *Staying Off the Beaten Track* not only has annually increased its sales for ten years but is now regularly in the bestseller lists. To mark the tenth edition, many proprietors are offering – in the tenth month of the tenth year (October 1991) – presents to or special parties for SOTBT readers staying with them then: see page xxvii.

Ten years ago, the (then) little book was a one-woman operation and the kitchen table was my desk. Although my brother now collaborates with me, and I have a number of assistants for paperwork and for much of the regular re-inspecting which goes on, the personal touch which makes the book different from so many remains unchanged. Every house is visited by me (or, mainly in the north, by Walter Gundrey) before it can be accepted for inclusion. Every reader's letter is read by me, with its contents considered carefully and acted upon appropriately. It is because I believe in the need for considerable, personal, behind-scenes care that I took the decision to confine the coverage of the book to England and Wales.

A Decade of Change . . .

During these ten years I have seen many changes. The volume of traffic on even 'B' roads has become quite unpleasant in some of the most popular counties, especially at peak periods (I myself try to avoid travelling in July–August and at Bank Holidays). It is more difficult to get truly 'off the beaten track' unless you know where to go: therefore you will find plenty of advice on this in my book now.

Prices have inevitably gone up (see page xxix), but so have standards of b & b accommodation, increasingly used – and run – by people of discrimination. I refer to the quality and style of furnishings, owners' individuality and level of taste, and standards of cooking (good plain cooking and lighter, healthier food in particular – with emphasis on organically-produced and home-grown produce – often being preferrred to gourmet food). There is more about meals on page xxiv.

The national tourist boards have improved their inspection and registration systems in recent years. However, I believe that demanding more and more facilities has some unfortunate and inflationary effects: by pressuring proprietors to include extras which not all visitors want, in order to qualify for an extra symbol to display, costs are pushed up. For example, one proprietor was required by an inspector to clutter up a narrow landing with an electric shoe-polisher costing hundreds of pounds and to replace (even in no-smoking bedrooms) all his attractive wicker wastebins with tin ones. Have you ever thought just how many pounds per night are added to your bill for an en suite bathroom, 'free' toiletries, bedside telephone, other electric gadgetry, and credit card facilities? (Yet none of these hotel-style extras would you expect when staying as a friend in a private house – which is what, in fact, most b & b houses are.) These, too, are things that have multiplied in the last ten years. The reason why you find no mention in this book of official 'merit marks' of various kinds is that some excellent places have none, either because they do not fulfil all such requirements of the tourist boards or motoring organizations, or because they do not want to pay a substantial charge to be inspected. Yet, in my experience, many of these are superior to those which do qualify for such recognition while lacking the sort of ambience I want, as do readers like the one who wrote to me as follows:

'We stayed on a dairy farm; we had powdered milk on the tea tray, microwaved breakfast, which had been placed in the Rayburn to dry out although we were down on time. All through the meal the television was on – and this was tourist board approved!'

Other noticeable trends include the spread of 'no-smoking' houses and, alas, of 'no children' ones – the latter a direct result of the increasing number of parents unable to keep their offspring in check. If you want to avoid the presence of children, this is another reason not to travel in the peak periods or to seaside resorts when schools are on holiday.

Such labour-savers as foil-wrapped butter, powdered milk on bedroom tea trays, carton orange-juice and portion-packs of jam continue to increase: I constantly campaign against these but, even at some of the houses in this book, they continue in use. Towels (for the bath) under four feet long, bedside lamps so low that one cannot read in bed, limp pillows: they still occasionally occur, as do elderly mattresses (for which there is no possible excuse). Readers should – at the start of their stay – ask for better whenever they encounter such things.

I regret the increasing insistence on en suite bathrooms even in houses where only two or three bedrooms are let. The disastrous result has often been that once well-proportioned bedrooms have been ruined, and made pokey, by the installation of (usually) a cramped shower; and with the bed-and-breakfast price inflated as a consequence. Television, too, is a doubtful benefit, killing conversation whether it is in a sitting-room or in bedrooms (again, adding to b & b prices).

The readership of the book today includes a wide spectrum of professions, and many readers use it for business as well as holiday travel. The now considerable feedback I get from readers and proprietors alike is very helpful in showing me where readers most want to go, what are the most popular types of accommodation, what price limits I should set, and so forth. Proprietors help me to collect county-by-county statistics about SOTBT visitors (which is one reason why they like you to tell them whether it was from this book that you heard about them). This tenth edition is thus much more closely tailored to readers' needs as I perceive them than the early editions were. From the first three editions, only two dozen houses remain in the book today.

The habits of readers (and of other people too) have changed. Not only is there a trend towards many short breaks in the year, and touring rather than stay-put holidays, but also towards early spring and late autumn travelling. There is at least

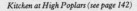

Kitchen at High Poplars (see page 142)

a good chance of excellent weather then, colours and scenery are at their best, there are fewer other travellers about, and there is plenty to do under cover if it does rain. For another big change in the last decade has been the increase in both the quantity and quality of 'sights' available to visitors, from many more stately homes and museums on the one hand to experiential or interpretative shows such as open farms, underwater viewing, countryside exhibitions, craft demonstrations and so forth. In this edition, there is much more information given about these, particularly the newest or less well-known sights, as well as those in areas you might wrongly suppose are of limited interest; and ones run by local people on a small scale and featuring themes of genuine local interest.

. . . and Changeless Scenes

There will, however, never be any man-made sight which, in my opinion, can compare with the simple pleasure of enjoying the open countryside which, despite constant threat, still remains unspoilt. Even for those who cannot appreciate it by the best means of all – walking – there is a great deal to enjoy in what are, for England and Wales, quite ordinary scenes even outside such famous areas as the Cotswolds or West Country.

From last year's journeys I remember with especial delight the descent to the Elan Valley in Wales. At every turn there were stupendous views, with the summer's heather still in bloom. On the lower slopes, oak glades and tracts of bracken with mossy boulders descended to a valley where, amid sunlight and leafy shade, stonecrop and ferns were growing from the drystone walls and one could pick blackberries, rosehips and hazelnuts among the last of the year's butterflies.

In Norfolk – a complete contrast – I recall lowland countryside so tranquil that baby rabbits played in the gorse-fringed road ahead of us and partridges crossed it at a leisurely stroll. Adjoining it is another underrated county, Lincolnshire – perhaps at its best in spring when the scudding clouds in blue skies are reflected in the many dykes that drain the land, and the fields of the bulb-growing districts are brilliant with daffodils or tulips – road verges too. Villages are picturesque, and this is an outstanding area for gardeners who want to go home laden with purchases from the many nurseries.

Inland Dorset is less frequented by tourists than its justly celebrated coast, but I found it a region of great beauty, and with many stately homes or small unspoilt villages and inns to visit. The scenery is varied: chalk streams meander through secretive valleys. Some parts, by contrast, are all stone and thatch. There are lush pastures in the Vale of Blackmoor, wild moorland further south, few major roads to disturb the peace, and market towns – including Dorchester itself – which retain some of the character that Hardy described in so many novels or poems. Many lanes must still be very much as he saw them.

At the well-hidden little Border village of Llanfair-Waterdine in Shropshire, the most distinguished resident is John Hunt who – on being offered a peerage after his conquest of Everest in 1953 – chose the title of Lord Hunt of Llanfair-Waterdine. On his return in 1953 he had been drawn home in a pony-trap by villagers. Waving his ice-axe aloft, he said: 'This is the moment I longed for most, the welcome of my own people'. It is easy to understand his affection for this remote spot on the globe, once you have visited it.

And everywhere there are associations with history, legend or literature (sometimes all three together) to be traced. Take Tintagel, for instance, with all its Arthurian associations. The story goes that an early Duke of Cornwall (Prince

Charles is the present duke) incarcerated his wife in the sea-lashed castle there, to protect her from King Uther's lustful pursuit. But Merlin by magic gave Uther the appearance of the duke so that he got past the guards, seduced the duchess and thus begat Arthur. (That the site was indeed inhabited by a 5th- or 6th-century leader was indicated when imported pottery of that period was dug up, a luxury only such a household might have afforded.) But Tennyson told the story differently:

> 'And down the wave and in the flame was borne
> A naked babe, and rode to Merlin's feet,
> Who stoopt and caught the babe and cried "The King!
> Here is an heir for Uther!"'

Facts, folk memories or a poet's fancy: what does it matter which speaks loudest to a wondering visitor today?

Looking Back

In the preamble to the first edition, I described how the book had begun – as a mere offshoot from my other work as a travel writer who herself needed to find good, inexpensive places at which to stay. (Now SOTBT occupies all my time.) I had found no accommodation directory of much use – either because prices of places recommended were too high, or because the gradings, symbols and bald text were insufficient to tell me whether or not I would enjoy the places listed.

I determined therefore to set a price limit, and to describe each house I recommended as fully and vividly as I was able. And also to rely on my own judgment and taste, rather than that of unknown members of the public writing in, or of 'inspectors' qualified only to count or measure without evaluating that elusive quality, ambience. It seemed essential, too, to indicate what the environs of each place were like – just as decisive a factor when choosing where to go for a holiday or short break – as well as to show a picture of the house itself.

I continue to follow those principles since they are evidently what has attracted so many readers. However, each edition has altered slightly so that the tenth is very different from the first (and four times as full), many of the changes being in response to what I learn about readers' preferences. I greatly value comments which may help me to improve future editions still more – please keep on writing!

Through regular newsletters and meetings, I try to influence proprietors to provide what readers want.

Good Food

Standards of freshly cooked meals in the home have been getting steadily higher over the years while those in some public eating-places have gone down, particularly in many inns and pubs owned by brewers who impose standard menus throughout their chains ('chef's own pâté' that is identical at each, and certain dishes which are a sure sign that mass-produced frozen items are on offer – ubiquitous Mississippi mud pie and cod Kiev are two examples).

You do not have to be a gourmet to value the difference between bulk-produced restaurant meals and fresh food cooked specially for you (often using produce straight from the garden) which is the norm at the small houses which predominate in this book. Although it is invidious to do so, I suggest the following as examples of round-England tours which anyone who values good food would undoubtedly enjoy, staying at different SOTBT houses on the way.

The first is for those who appreciate the best of English cookery. Travelling from south to north: Isles of Scilly, **Coastguards**; Cornwall, **Coombe Farmhouse**; Dorset, **The Beehive**; Wiltshire, **Enford House**; Sussex, **Country House**; Kent, **Barnfield**; Suffolk, **Buttons Green Farm**; Northants, **Castle Farm**; Warwickshire, **Brookland**; Shropshire, **Fitz Manor**; Lancashire, **Clay Lane Head**; Cumbria, **Gaisgill Farm**; North Yorkshire, **Bramwood**; County Durham, **Grove House**.

And the second, for those who want somewhat more elaborate dishes on the menu: Cornwall, **Manor Farmhouse** (Crackington); Devon, **Wavenden**; Somerset, **Claybatch Farmhouse**; Wiltshire, **Church House**; Oxfordshire, Elm **Farmhouse**; Essex, **Elm House**; Norfolk, **Grey Gables**; Shropshire, **Birches Mill**; Cheshire, **Burland Farm**; Northumberland, **Coach House**.

But, as I said, this is an invidious choice, for there are so many others I might have picked out – as readers can see for themselves as they read in the following pages about, for instance, the salmon pies at **Cwmtwrch**, pork with apple and ginger at **Ty Gwyn**, the celery and lemon soup at **Dewis Cyfarfod** (all these are in Wales); or the chicory-stuffed chicken with blue cheese sauce at **Woodmans Green Farm**, filet Chateaubriand at **Windmill House**, and the pavlova topped with lemon curd and Jersey cream at **White Barn**. Compose your own gastronomic tour – for the options are legion!

Increasingly SOTBT proprietors are willing to provide (particularly for elderly visitors or single women who do not want to go out to inns or restaurants, and those conscious of the drink-drive laws) light suppers, or else a share of the family meal. They do not always want this mentioned in the book, but it is worth enquiring if this is what you prefer. I have found some of these 'light suppers' superior to many a restaurant meal, and at far less cost. I recall, for instance, particularly enjoying a help-yourself kitchen supper of courgette soup, smoked chicken with an imaginative salad, and cheese with grapes.

The old kitchen dining-room at Old Jordans (see page 215)

And the Next Decade?

'Attila the Tourist' is the way some people, concerned for the environment, see the growth in tourism – too many people on the move, causing wear and tear at the most popular sites (whether landscapes or historic buildings), and giving rise to more and bigger hotels, car and coach parks, caravan sites, Disney-type pleasuregrounds, and so forth. The problem is likely to become a really big issue during the 1990s.

In *Staying Off the Beaten Track* I have always urged readers to explore areas where the crowds do not go, at seasons when they are not on the move, and to stay in small houses, inns or farms which are already an integral part of the local scene, involving no big concentration of visitors in any one spot, no traffic congestion, no great new building blots on the landscape. 'B & b', unlike cottages taken out of the housing stock to provide self-catering holidays, does not deprive communities or lead to rural depopulation. Visitors help to sustain rural employment: staff in pubs and petrol stations, for instance, and growers of local produce as much as domestic workers employed in the houses themselves.

If travel does, as they say, broaden the mind – often an arguable proposition – it involves getting to know other people in their own homes or workplaces, making one's own small and personal discoveries, and lingering in one area rather than hurtling from one famous sight to another. You have only to buy one of the Ordnance Survey *Landranger* maps (they cover Britain in microscopic detail, about 1 inch to 1 mile) to realize how much there is to discover in a short radius of where you are staying, without need to add your own quota of pollution and congestion to main roads and over-popular areas. A much more relaxed way of doing things, too. Readers sometimes write to me saying such things as:

> 'We use your book to steer us towards areas that we might have missed. For instance, we enjoyed the area near Leek, Staffordshire, which we would have missed otherwise'.

That said, it is a fact that without tourists much conservation work would not take place – canals or gardens restored, old buildings converted into craft workshops, watermills working again, and so on. Rightly deployed, tourism can in fact help to keep the countryside alive in years to come.

There is much comment now about stress-related illness and the need for adequate holidays. Rather than long-haul trips which only add to stress, frequent short breaks at an easy pace are better.

Fireplace at Tudor Farmhouse Hotel (see page 314)

CELEBRATING THE 10th EDITION
GIFTS AND PARTIES IN OCTOBER

Readers staying at certain houses during the 10th month of the 10th year – that is, October 1991 – will get a pleasant surprise, namely a small present to celebrate this anniversary year.

What it is will vary from house to house. It may be a bottle of wine at dinner or a home-produced gift to take home: a cake, preserves, pâté, confectionery or a pot-plant, for instance; or a local speciality such as cheese, sausages, wine, a corn dolly, lavender-bags or a local guidebook. One proprietor plans to give each SOTBT guest a pottery pig, another a caddy of tea, and a third a sack of potatoes!

Houses at which such 10th anniversary gifts will be offered to SOTBT visitors in October are indicated in the text by an asterisk (★).

Also in celebration of 'the 10th month of the 10th year', about 20 SOTBT proprietors are organizing special celebratory luncheons or dinners for readers during October 1991 – accommodation does not have to be booked too if not required. For exact dates, menus and prices please contact the following houses (telephone numbers and descriptions are in the text of the book).

AVON, **Somerset House**; DERBYSHIRE, **Shottle Hall**; DEVON, **Wavenden**; ESSEX, **Elm House**; GLOUCESTERSHIRE, **Windrush House**; HEREFORD-SHIRE, **The Haven**; KENT, **Wallett's Court**; LEICESTERSHIRE, **Peacock Farmhouse**; LINCOLNSHIRE, **Guy Wells**; LONDON, **Avoca Hotel**; NOR-FOLK, **Grey Gables**; NORTHUMBERLAND, **Coach House**; SHROP-SHIRE, **Upper Buckton**; SOMERSET, **Claybatch**; STAFFORDSHIRE, **Pethill Bank**; SUFFOLK, **Pipps Ford**; SUSSEX, **Brookfield**; WARWICK-SHIRE, **Lansdowne House**; WILTSHIRE, **Stratford Lodge**; WORCESTER-SHIRE, **Old Parsonage**; WALES: NORTH, **Ty Gwyn**; WALES: SOUTH, **Cwmtwrch**.

YOU AND THE LAW

Once your booking has been confirmed – orally or in writing – a contract exists between you and the proprietor. He is legally bound to provide accommodation as booked; and you are legally bound to pay for this accommodation. If you are unable to take up the booking – even if through sickness – you still remain liable for a very substantial proportion of the charges (in addition to losing your deposit).

If you have to cancel, let the proprietor know as soon as possible; then he may be able to re-let the accommodation (in which case you would be liable to pay only a re-letting cost or forfeit your deposit).

(A note to American readers. It may be an acceptable practice elsewhere to make bookings at several houses for the same date, choosing only later which one to patronize; but this way of doing things is not the British practice and you are legally liable to compensate any proprietors whom you let down in this way.) Phone if you are going to arrive late.

You can insure against having to cancel, and a special 15 per cent discount on this has been negotiated for readers. Details are on page 379.

HOW TO HAVE A GOOD TIME

As the readership of this book grows so also does the diversity of readers' tastes. My detailed descriptions are meant to help each one pick out the places that suit him or her best; but I still get readers who write to complain about bar or carpark noise at inns (so why pick an inn rather than a house without a bar?), the presence of dogs (why go to a house with the code letter **D**, meaning dogs accepted, or to a farm where dogs are almost certainly kept?) and so forth. Light sleepers should avoid rooms overlooking, for instance, a market square: not all entries in this book are rural.

Some people have very particular requirements; and it is up to them to discuss these when telephoning to book. Many hosts in this book are more flexible than big hotels, and all are eager to help if they can. I have in mind such things as: a bad back, needing a very *firm mattress* (I carry a folding bedboard from the Back Shop – tel: 071 935 9120); special *dietary* requirements, and *allergies* to feather pillows or animals; a strong preference for *separate tables* rather than a shared dining-table – or vice versa; *fewer courses* than on the fixed menu; *twin beds* rather than double beds – or vice versa; freedom to *smoke* – or freedom from it; a particular wish for *electric blanket*, *hot water-bottle*, etc. or a dislike of *duvets*; the need to arrive, depart or eat at *extra-early* or *extra-late* hours; an intention to pay by *credit card* (this should not be taken for granted, particularly at small guest-houses). Houses which ordinarily do not admit non-residents to dine may nevertheless permit you to invite a friend – just ask.

The code letters that appear after the name of each house will help you identify houses suitable for children, dogs, handicapped people, users of public transport, etc.: for full explanation, see page xxxiv.

Please also use the 'how to book' checklist on page xxix when telephoning.

Take the trouble to get free booklets about the area before you set off. Every habitual traveller should keep a copy of the booklet of local Tourist Information Centres issued free by the English Tourist Board (Thames Tower, Blacks Road, London W6; tel: 081-846 9000) for this purpose. These centres can tell you about guided tours or country walks, coach tours, events and much else. It's best to stay at least 2–3 days: you cannot possibly appreciate an area if you only stay overnight (prices per night are often less, too, if you stay on). The vouchers on page ii are usable for 3-night stays.

There is another, important component in having an enjoyable experience: congenial company. I am struck by the number of readers who comment that, when they stay at a *Staying Off the Beaten Track* house, they find other visitors – from the same source – very agreeable company because they are compatible people. (Just occasionally there is an exception: the one who keeps aloof, or who loudly complains about trivia, for instance.)

When to go? Seaside resorts or other places suitable for children will be at their busiest (and dearest) in July–August and during half-term holidays (especially, in late May, which is also a bank holiday period). Other peak periods are, of course, Easter, Christmas, New Year and the bank holiday in late August. (The bank holiday in early May is not usually a peak, because it comes rather soon after Easter, but much depends on the weather.) There are local peaks, too (the Gold Cup races at Cheltenham or the regatta at Henley, for instance, are apt to fill hotels for miles around), and local troughs (Brighton, a conference centre, is least busy in high summer). Houses which do *not* take children tend to have vacancies in July and August. In holiday areas, travel on any day other than a summer Saturday if you can. Make ferry, Motorail or coach/train reservations well in advance if travelling at such periods.

And one final tip on ensuring that you get all that you hope for: at the end of each season, throw away *Staying Off The Beaten Track* and get next year's edition (you can soon recoup its cost through using the fresh set of accommodation vouchers it contains). Here's why this is so important. A reader wrote to me as follows: 'The house was dirty; room smelt damp; toilet-seat wobbly and stained; under-pillows had no cases; grubby carpets . . . (etc.)'. The house had changed hands years ago, and been dropped from my book as a consequence; but the reader was using an out-of-date edition. Prices change, so do telephone numbers and much else. Change of owner or grossly inflated prices are the two most common reasons why I drop houses; a third is that I find somewhere better – or of better value – nearby.

TELEPHONING TO BOOK: A CHECKLIST

Book well ahead: many of these houses have few rooms. Further, at some houses, rooms (though similarly priced) vary in size or amenities: early applicants get the best ones. Mention that you are a reader of *Staying Off the Beaten Track*. Telephoning is preferable to writing to enquire about vacancies, and, in many cases, the best time is early evening.

1. Ask for the owner by the *name* given in this edition. (If there has been a change, standards may differ.)
2. Specify *your precise needs* (such as en suite bathroom, if available), see page xxviii. (Do not turn up with children, dogs or disabilities if you have not checked that these are accepted or provided for.) Elderly people may wish to ensure that their room is not on the second floor.
3. Check *prices* – these, too, can change (particularly after spring). Ask whether there are any bargain breaks.
4. Ask what *deposit* to send (or quote a credit card number).
5. State your intended *time of arrival*, and what *meals* are wanted. (If you should then be late, telephone a warning – otherwise your room may be let to someone else. It is inconsiderate to arrive late for home-cooked meals prepared especially for you.)
6. Ask for precise instructions for *locating the house*: many are remote. Better still, ask for a brochure with map to be posted to you. Check where to park.
7. Few proprietors expect visitors to stay out of the house in the daytime; but if you want to stay in, check this when booking.

> **At houses where dinner is not served, a light supper can often be obtained (if ordered in advance), ranging from sandwiches to family 'pot luck'. (Packed lunches too.)**

PRICES

This book came into being to provide a guide to good accommodation at prices suited to people of moderate means. That remains its policy.

In the current edition are houses at which (with few exceptions) it is possible to stay, at the time of publication, for as little as £10 – £18 for b & b – that is, per person sharing a double room: singles, see below. (However, for the best room in the house, or later in the year, you may well be asked for more. **Check when booking**.)

The prices are as quoted to me when the book was in preparation during 1990. But sometimes unexpected costs force proprietors to increase their prices subsequently: becoming liable for VAT or business rates, for instance.

In the case of houses charging a minimum of £19 or so, I have included only those where there are significant discounts to be had, bargain breaks, etc.

A 'bargain break' is usually a 2- or 3-day booking including dinners, at a discount; sometimes at low season only.

You can see from the text data when price rises occur. For instance, in the Isle of Wight few proprietors raise prices until summer (if then), while in the Lake District and Yorkshire Dales many put them up in spring.

Inclusive terms for dinner, bed-and-breakfast (particularly for a week) can be much lower than those quoted here for these items taken separately. Most houses in this book have bargain breaks or other discounts on offer, some exclusive to readers. Only a minority raise prices at the peak of summer.

SINGLES

Travelling alone may not be much fun. For the single person of 30–75, Travel Companions can help by bringing together like-minded people. You fill in a detailed questionnaire and, for a fee of £35, they promise to find you a minimum of three compatible Travel Companions for you to meet before you decide to travel. Where and when you then go on a holiday or for a short break is up to you, whether 'off the beaten track' in this country or abroad. For details send a stamped addressed envelope to: Travel Companions, 110 High Mount, Station Road, London NW4 3ST. Tel: 081 202 8478. (Even when travelling alone, single people may find more company in houses that have a shared dining-table, a bar, and no TV. As my descriptions indicate, some owners mingle more with their guests than others do.)

READER PARTICIPATION

1 It would be very helpful if you will let me know your opinion of places from this book at which you have stayed. Please post this to: Elizabeth Gundrey, 19 Fitzjohns Avenue, London NW3 5JY (no phone calls please!). **If you wish for an acknowledgment please enclose a stamped addressed envelope.**

Names of establishments

Your comments (with date of stay)

2 Please tell me if (and when) it has proved hard to find a vacancy at houses of your choice – but see note overleaf.

3 If you find other places you think I should visit, for possible inclusion in a future edition, please will you send me your description (including price and address), with brochure. **No expensive places, please.** See overleaf.

Your name and address (capitals): _____

_____

Date: _____ Occupation (optional): _____

Proprietors wishing to apply for inclusion: see page 380.

THANK YOU . . . to those who send me details of their own finds, for possible future inclusion in the book. Do not be disappointed if your candidate does not appear in the very next edition. I never publish recommendations from unknown members of the public without verification, and it takes time for me to get round each part of England and Wales in turn.

Inevitably, there is a time-lag between my visits and the appearance of what I write in book form. The details you send are always filed, under counties, until such time as I go to the county in question; and then they are a very great help, although there is never enough space for all of them to be used. Please, however, do not send details of houses already featured in many other guides, nor any that are more expensive than those in this book.

It is unreasonable to expect to find vacancies at short notice. A reader wrote to me on 6 February 1990, saying 'We stayed at five houses recommended in *Staying Off the Beaten Track* and would have stayed at more had we not been phoning ahead only one day or so at a time. An amazing number of your houses were fully booked even at this time of year.' And from one proprietor came this comment: 'So many people rang at very short notice that I just could not accommodate them, as most of my regular visitors book well in advance. I must have refused over 50 enquirers.' Another said: 'On just one day, I refused 17.'

Entrance hall at Bron Heulog, Wales (see page 354)

SOMETHING SPECIAL ON THE THAMES

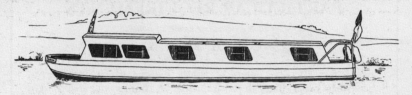

Taking to the water for bed and board is a most tranquil way to achieve a really different weekend or short holiday.

Azure sky; and a white-gold sun lighting up the autumn tints. Sapphire flash of a kingfisher, grey flight of a heron, snowy swans. These were the colours of the Thames in November when, with friends, I booked onto *Waterjoy* for a few days of cruising, gourmet food and good wines. Scarcely another boat was moving on the river and through its locks, unlike the busy summer months.

Waterjoy sleeps four people, plus skipper/chef Ron Trott and his wife Bridie. It departs from Chertsey (near the M4 and Heathrow – from which visitors can be fetched by car) for Runnymede (Magna Carta) and Windsor (castle) – further if you go for more than two days. The boat is 45 feet long and 12 feet wide. Warmth, comfort and service are all you could wish. There are two wc/showers; and attention to detail is notable – flowers in each cabin, tea and newspapers brought to you in bed, video and cassette recorders, champagne and other wines or brandy in abundance (all included in the price).

Ron and Bridie have spent all their working lives in the catering trade and are now using their expertise to ensure that the guests on *Waterjoy* are given a service they will remember long after they return home. Meals are outstanding in both quality and quantity – for instance, king prawns flambéed in brandy, fillet steaks, pavlovas, a help-yourself buffet eaten on deck or a barbecue on the riverbank, smoked salmon, rack of lamb, lemon bavarois. . . . All enjoyed against a backdrop of, for instance, Windsor Great Park or the 15th-century chapel of Eton College seen across the watermeadows; or else by candlelight, with the moon reflected on the lapping waters outside.

At the usual price of £112 a head for a weekend, this is good value. And for SOTBT readers (using the following coupon) there is a big discount of £100 off any booking for four people. For a brochure or to book, telephone 071-609 3669 or 0932 567700. (Or write to Ron Trott at Rosian, Laleham Reach, Chertsey, Surrey.)

£100
WATERJOY

This coupon is worth £100 towards payment for any booking for four people (minimum 2 days) on Waterjoy.

PARTICULAR REQUIREMENTS
(see code letters after names of houses)

C D H PT S X

Code letters after the names of houses indicate which ones are (in alphabetical order) likely to prove suitable for families with *children* (**C**), *dogs* (**D**) or *handicapped people* (**H**); and for those who, being without a car, depend upon *public transport* (**PT**). (In the case of children, a minimum age is sometimes stipulated, in which case this has been indicated by a numeral: thus **C**(5) means children over 5 are accepted.) **S** indicates those that charge singles no more, or only 10% more, than half a double (except, possibly, at peak periods). Some accept visitors at *Christmas* (**X**), but do not necessarily provide Christmas meals.

In most cases, places that accept *children* (**C**) offer reduced rates and special meals. They may provide cots, high chairs and even baby-listening; or games and sports for older children. Please enquire when booking. And do not expect a toddler to be regarded as a (free) baby. Many houses have cards, games, Scrabble etc. – just ask. (And also such things as irons, hair-dryers, maps, gumboots and bicycles.) Families which pick establishments with plenty of games, swimming-pool, animals, etc., or that are near free museums, parks and walks, can save a lot on keeping youngsters entertained. (Readers wanting total quiet may wish to avoid houses coded **C**.)

For *dogs* (**D**) a charge is rarely made, but often it is a stipulation that you must ask before bringing one; and the dog may have to sleep in your car, or be banned from public rooms.

Handicapped people vary in their needs. Wherever I have used the code letter **H**, this indicates that not only is there a ground-floor bedroom and bathroom but that these, and doorways, have sufficient width for a wheelchair, and that steps are few. For precise details, ask when booking.

It is not necessary to have a car in order to get off the beaten track because public transport is widely available: hotels indicated by the code **PT** have a railway station or coach stop within a reasonable distance, from which you can walk or take a taxi (quite a number of hosts will even pick you up, free, in their own car). The symbol **PT** further indicates that there are also some buses for sightseeing, but these may be few. Ask when booking.

Some hotels and even farms offer special Christmas holidays; but, unless otherwise indicated (by the code letter **X** at top of entry), those in this book will then be closed.

ALPHABETICAL DIRECTORY OF HOUSES AND HOTELS IN
ENGLAND

Prices are per person sharing a double room, at the beginning of the year. You may be quoted more for the best rooms, particularly after spring.

*Indicates October gifts
for readers (*see page xxvii*)

ABBEY BRIDGE INN

C(5) **PT S X**

Lanercost, Cumbria, CA8 2HG   Tel: 06977 2224

North of Brampton. Nearest main road: A69 from Haltwhistle to Brampton.

5 **Bedrooms.** £17–£20. Some have own bath/shower/toilet. Tea/coffee facilities. Views of garden, country, river. No smoking.
Dinner. A la carte, at 7–8pm. Vegetarian or special diets if ordered. Wine can be ordered. No smoking. **Light suppers** available.
2 **Sitting-rooms.** With open fire, central heating, TV. **Bar.**
Small garden

Where two rivers converge to the sound of rushing water, there is an old hump-backed bridge of red sandstone built in the time of James II. The traffic ignores it, hurrying across over a modern bridge further along. From it you can see part-ruined Lanercost Priory, or leave it to walk along riverside paths. Right here, Mr and Mrs Arthur run the Abbey Bridge Inn. Its name has been changed at least five times – once, when the reforming Countess of Carlisle made it 'dry', it was called the Temperance Hotel.

It's a snug place to stay, particularly when log fires are blazing in the lounges, or after a day's strenuous walking in the Border hills. The bedrooms are simply furnished. The Arthurs' first achievement was the renovation of what was once a blacksmith's forge, dating back to the 17th century, where meals (other than breakfast) are served to residents and non-residents. It is a barn-like building with gnarled rafters and white-painted walls. The bar (with real ale) and sitting-area downstairs are made cosy by a big iron stove. Up a specially made wrought-iron spiral staircase is a gallery where one eats beneath wrought-iron chandeliers with flickering electric candles. You can have either very good bar snacks; or a dinner including home-made pâté, venison and a fruity dessert, for instance.

Drinks or coffee can be enjoyed sitting under sun-umbrellas on the old bridge itself; or in the garden, frequented by the Arthurs' Great Dane. Across the way they have created, in an ancient stone building, a crafts centre with tea-room beneath it.

As well as scenic walks or drives, and the beautiful priory, there is plenty to do or see in the area: 14th-century Naworth Castle, Hadrian's Wall with Roman forts, the Saxon church at Over Denton, and historic villages like Gilsland and Bewcastle with Roman remains. Bewcastle has a decorated stone cross which is one of Britain's greatest Saxon treasures. In the river at Corby Castle on the way to Carlisle are salmon-traps built by 12th-century monks and still in use today. The road from Brampton to Alston is particularly attractive, running alongside the River South Tyne, with views of the northernmost Pennines. There is a good garden centre at Hexham. The new 'dig' at Birdoswald Roman fort is near the inn, a particularly interesting site (with interpretation centre) where one can see the dig in process.

Readers' comments: A wonderful stay. Very high standard, excellent food, thoroughly to be recommended. Exceptional interest in the well-being of guests; outstanding value for money. Well ordered; Mrs Arthur gives a warm welcome and caters for guests as individuals. Quite wonderful. Glorious!

ABBEY HOUSE

Monk Soham, Suffolk, IP13 7EN   Tel: 072882 225
North-west of Woodbridge. Nearest main road: A1120 from Stowmarket to Yoxford.

3 Bedrooms. £15–£17 (less for 6 nights). Prices go up in May. All have own bath/toilet. Tea/coffee facilities. Views of garden, country. Washing machine on request.
Dinner. £10 for 4 courses and coffee, at 7.15pm (except on Sundays). Vegetarian or special diets if ordered. Wine can be brought in. **Light suppers** if ordered.
1 Sitting-room. With open fire, central heating, TV.
Large garden
Closed from mid-December to mid-January inclusive.

'Fish, fish, do your duty!' the rector who lived here in the late 19th century used to admonish the inhabitants of his ponds (still there), which had originally provided Friday food for monks at the abbey (long vanished). This and other anecdotes of his life at Abbey House are in a book by his son which Sue Bagnall shows her visitors. It was he who planted the huge oaks, beeches and limes in the grounds. The architect was Teulon, a high Victorian gothicist.

Sue and her husband have made the old mansion comfortable and have furnished it with antiques, keeping the atmosphere informal. Among fine old features they have restored is a magnificent cast-iron fireplace in the dining-room. Colours are soft (pale buff or shell pink, for instance). Sue, a former nurse, cooks traditional English meals (using their own meat and vegetables) such as artichoke soup, steak-and-kidney pie, lemon ice cream and cheeses.

Guests are welcome to look at the livestock which includes Jersey cows (calves sometimes), sheep, pigs, turkeys, chickens, ducks, black swans and peafowl. In the large garden, there is croquet and a swimming-pool.

The Norfolk Broads are within reach; historic Norwich; bird reserves along the coast; old-fashioned seaside towns like Southwold; Lowestoft with its sands and its busy fishing port. At nearby Snape Maltings there are annual concerts, part of the Aldeburgh music festival.

Other sights include Somerleyton and Helmingham halls, Framlingham and Orford castles, Bressingham Steam Museum (with gardens), the Otter Trust, wildlife or farm parks, Saxtead windmill, rural crafts, vineyards and inns.

Readers' comments: Delightful.

Nearby is **MONK SOHAM HALL** (tel: 072 882 358), a very pleasant Tudor farmhouse where in addition to other bedrooms Gay Clarke has created, in a beamed ground-floor room opening onto garden and moat, a bedroom and bathroom fully equipped for disabled people. There is also a games room and lawn tennis. From £15 to £16.

rear view

ALEXA HOUSE   C H PT
26 Ripon Road, Harrogate, North Yorkshire, HG2 2JJ   Tel: 0423 501988
On A61 from Leeds to Ripon.

13 Bedrooms. £18–£21 (less for 7 nights or for 2 outside summer). Prices go up at Easter. Bargain breaks. All have own bath/shower/toilet. Tea/coffee facilities. TV. Views of garden. No smoking. Washing machine on request.
1 Sitting-room. With central heating, TV, record-player. Bar.
Small garden

Dating from 1830, this house is typical of many such solidly built and handsome private homes which later became small hotels in Yorkshire's famous spa town. It has been furnished by Marilyn Bateson with an eye to her guests' comfort (generous armchairs in the bedrooms, for instance) more than to elegance.

In the cheerful breakfast-room, Marilyn recently uncovered a pink-and-white marble fireplace, and added silver chandeliers. As to dinner, she gives visitors a street map with nearby recommended restaurants marked on it.

Behind the house are some small new rooms (very neatly designed) ideal not only for visitors wanting quiet, but also for disabled guests – with sitz baths and grab-rails, for instance. (Marilyn was once a teacher of physically handicapped children, and understands what is needed.)

A clerical visitor wrote to Marilyn after his first stay: 'I have never fared better since I once spent a weekend at Balmoral. Both hostesses proved to be most charming and kind, but I think you have the edge over HM for you did not feel disposed to discuss my sermon with me!'

Elegant Harrogate is full of shops selling antiques and other luxuries. Its award-winning gardens and flowery parks are famous; it has a large, modern entertainments centre; and it is an ideal centre from which to explore the Yorkshire Dales and such famous sights as Fountains Abbey, Ripon Cathedral, Harewood House, Harlow Car gardens and, of course, the city of York as well as Bolton Abbey, Ripley Castle, Newby Hall and Knaresborough, where you can go to what is possibly Britain's oldest tourist sight: since 1630, visitors have been beating a path to Old Mother Shipton's cave and the petrifying well where anything left under the dripping water ultimately turns to stone. The ruined castle here is on a high cliff above the river.

There are few counties that have more stately homes. Not only the world-famous ones but also, for instance, Broughton Hall at Skipton which has been lived in by the same family since 1597. Skipton Castle, too, is still a home – one of the best-preserved mediaeval castles in England – but Hazlewood Castle, Tadcaster, now belongs to Carmelite friars (its chapel dates back to 1286) and Spofforth Castle is just a picturesque ruin. Swinsty Hall (Elizabethan) is owned by a musician, who plays on his collection of early pianos when he shows visitors round. Bramham Hall (Queen Anne) at Wetherby has been described as a miniature Versailles. At 17th-century East Riddleston Hall (NT) by the River Aire a colossal barn houses a collection of farm wagons. What variety!

Readers' comments: Every comfort, and super food. Courteous welcome, we had an excellent time – our stay surpassed all others. Excellent food and facilities. Well furnished, comfortable; quieter at the back. Will return whenever possible; refreshingly friendly atmosphere, staff happy to please.

4

ALFOXTON COTTAGE   S

Holford, Somerset, TA5 1SG   Tel: 027874 418
West of Bridgwater. Nearest main road: A39 from Bridgwater to Minehead.

3 Bedrooms. £13 (less for 4 nights). Prices go up in June. Views of garden, country. No smoking. Washing machine on request.
Dinner. £14 for 4 courses and coffee, at 7pm. Non-residents not admitted. Wine can be ordered or brought in. No smoking.
1 Sitting-room. With open fire, central heating, piano, record-player. No smoking.
Small garden
Closed from December to February inclusive.

The cottage is truly remote, right up in the Quantock Hills with views across the Bristol Channel to Wales. You may believe you are never coming to it as you follow twists and turns up the small wooded lane to the top of the hill.

This little house is now the home of Richard and Angela Delderfield who started Little Byres in Sussex (in previous editions of this book). Rooms are small and low but pleasantly furnished – for instance, bamboo or velvet bedheads; a grandfather clock and flounced armchairs by the log fire in the white sitting-room, from which a door leads to the garden, woods, a trickling stream, donkeys and chickens.

Angela's cooking is one of the main attractions of staying here. She sometimes serves as a starter prawns in a creamy sauce containing whisky, or perhaps chilled lettuce soup. Chicken breasts will be stuffed with cashew and brazil nuts, raisins, herbs and lemon juice. Into her salads may go unusual ingredients such as spinach, sunflower seeds or hot crisp bacon with slivers of avocado. She makes flans of rhubarb and lemon, rum and almonds, or orange and almonds.

All round the cottage are the Quantock Hills and pretty hamlets, the very first area of Britain to get official designation as an area of outstanding natural beauty. Alfoxton House (now a hotel) was tenanted by Wordsworth and his sister in 1797. They frequently walked here on their way to visit Coleridge who was busy writing *The Ancient Mariner* and *Kubla Khan* at Nether Stowey (his cottage now belongs to the National Trust). Some of Wordsworth's best poems, the *Lyrical Ballads*, were inspired by the Quantocks. The area is ideal for walking and for wildlife-spotting (red deer roam here) and wildflowers are abundant. Within a short drive are Exmoor, Dartmoor, the fenland known as the Somerset Levels, and the coast – including Watchet's active little harbour, cliffs and sands (Cleeve Abbey's Norman remains are in this direction). There are idyllic finds to be made up many a secluded lane – for instance, East Quantoxhead's cottages around a duckpond. Nether Stowey has a ruined castle, prehistoric earthworks, two mediaeval mansions and a stream; beyond it is Stogursey with priory church and castle. Let Wordsworth have the last word about Alfoxton:

> 'Through primrose tufts, in that green bower,
> The periwinkle trailed its wreaths;
> And 'tis my faith that every flower
> Enjoys the air it breathes.'

Readers' comments: A wonderful establishment. A lovely home in a beautiful area. Very hospitable, food and service excellent. Friendly and genuine people. Truly gifted cook. Delightful hostess.

17 Market Place, Lavenham, Suffolk, CO10 9RH   Tel: 0787 247168
North-east of Sudbury. Nearest main road: A134 from Sudbury to Bury St
Edmunds.

3 Bedrooms. £15.50. Tea/coffee facilities.
TV. Washing machine on request.
Dinner. £10 for 3 courses and coffee. Non-
residents not admitted. Vegetarian or special
diets if ordered. Wine can be brought in.
Light suppers if ordered.
1 Sitting-room. With open fire, central heating, TV.
Small garden

In the Middle Ages, Suffolk grew rich on wool and woollen cloth. As a result, and
in Lavenham above all other villages, the country is full of splendid mediaeval
churches and the houses of wealthy merchants.

This house, built in 1482 – the year before Richard III became King – is one of
the finest, its name taken from the adjoining Angel Inn to which it was once
connected by the round-arched doorways you can still see in its large entrance hall.

To the left of this are the sitting- and dining-rooms, with log fire, beams and
quaint carved figures decorating one of the doorways. Here and upstairs are
blue-and-white Delft tiles, and views of the informal, brick-walled cottage garden
at the back (only one bedroom overlooks the market square and its old preaching
cross – busy by day but quiet once the throngs of day-visitors have gone). Beyond
an oak-panelled door in the hall are narrow stairs and passages leading to pretty
bedrooms.

Although there are a number of eating-places in Lavenham, Maureen Bourne
will prepare dinner if this is ordered in advance, cooking such dishes as deep-fried
mushrooms (served with cucumber and mint yogurt), chicken breasts in orange
sauce, and summer pudding.

Just across the square is the town's great half-timbered Guildhall which houses a
museum of wool history. The resplendent Wool Hall where merchants traded is
now part of the big Swan Hotel, which has notable music recitals. The church
owes much of its splendours to benefactions made as atonement by a cloth-
merchant (who, in the reign of Henry VII, got rich by giving short measure and
other sharp practices): in return he had his coat-of-arms carved 36 times on the
high tower. Constable went to the grammar school in Lavenham; Shilling Street is
named for a Flemish weaver who taught the English clothmaking skills (Jane
Taylor, who wrote 'Twinkle, Twinkle, Little Star' lived here in the 18th century);
Prentice Street is lined with cottages where apprentices lodged. One wanders
through lanes of colourful, half-timbered and lopsided houses little changed since
the 15th century, some embellished with symbols of the crafts once carried on in
them (for instance, the comb of St Blaise – a patron of clothworkers because he was
tortured with wool-combs). With the introduction of machine-weaving (powered
by coal, which is not found in this region), prosperity deserted Lavenham – which
is why, fortunately for us, its ancient buildings were never replaced with 18th- or
19th-century 'improvements'.

For explanation of code letters (**C, D, H, PT, S, X**) see page xxxiv.

APPLETREE COTTAGE

12 Shitterton, Bere Regis, Dorset, BH20 7HU   Tel: 0929 471686
South of Blandford Forum. Nearest main road: A35 from Dorchester to Poole.

rear view

2 Bedrooms. £13.50–£14.50 (less for 4 nights). Prices go up in April. TV. Views of garden, country. No smoking. Washing machine on request (at a small charge).
Light suppers if ordered the day before. Vegetarian diets. Wine can be brought in. No smoking.
1 Sitting-room. With open fire, central heating, TV, piano. No smoking.
Garden
Closed from mid-December to mid-January.

This is a real Hansel-and-Gretel style cottage – thick cob (clay) walls and thatched roof, with honeysuckle clambering round the pink front door. It was built in the 17th century and was a tiny inn when the little lane outside was a coaching road.

Inside, all ceilings are low, and walls slope. The breakfast-table is in the sitting-room, which has silky patchwork cushions on the velvet armchairs gathered around the inglenook with log stove. The very modern bathroom (its chocolate-brown suite includes a bidet) is also on the ground floor. Bedrooms have sprigged wallpapers, beams and board doors, and overlook the pretty garden with flagstone steps leading to the lawn. For evening meals, Beryl Wilson recommends two inns in the hamlet, especially the Royal Oak, although she will provide two-course snack suppers.

Bere Regis is where the d'Urbervilles are buried and 'Tess' was filmed here. Hardy re-named it Kingsbere ('a little one-eyed, blinking sort o' place') and here the story begins with old Farmer Durbeyfield boasting, 'Under the church of that there parish lie my ancestors – hundreds of 'em – in coats of mail and jewels, in gr't lead coffins weighing tons and tons. There's not a man in the county of South Wessex that's got grander and nobler skillentons in his family than I.'

Bere is about half way between Poole and Dorchester, the environs of which are described elsewhere in this book. Lulworth Cove, T. E. Lawrence's cottage, Hardy country, good walks, pretty villages like Milton Abbas, a parachute club, seaside resorts and mellow old towns are all within easy reach as well as Bovington Tank Museum, Corfe Castle, Kingston Lacy house (and garden). Garden-lovers will enjoy Abbotsbury, Compton Acres, Athelhampton, and Galtons garden centre. The area has many antique shops, and pick-your-own farms. Two events which attract visitors from all over the country are the Blandford Great Steam Fair in September and the tank battle, fair and open day at Bovington Camp in July.

The county town of Dorchester now has a dinosaur museum with animated models, as well as traditional local history and military museums. Another new attraction is a reconstruction of Tutankhamun's tomb with facsimiles of all the treasures. You can visit the Old Crown Court (just as it was when the Tolpuddle Martyrs were condemned to transportation), Maumbury Rings (a 'coliseum' where Romans watched gladiators), and – by appointment – a local brewery at work. Near here is Palladian Came House, noted for its fine plasterwork and great Victorian conservatory. Southward lies Owermoigne with a working cider museum.

Readers' comments: An enjoyable holiday. Very pretty.

APSE MANOR

C(6) **D H PT X**

Apse Manor Road, Whiteley Bank, Isle of Wight, PO37 7PN
Tel: 0983 866651
West of Shanklin. Nearest main road: A3020 from Shanklin to Newport.

rear view

7 Bedrooms. £19–£21 (**SOTBT readers only**). Prices go up at Easter. Bargain breaks. All have own bath/shower/toilet. Tea/coffee facilities. TV. Views of garden, country.
Dinner. £8 for 5 courses (with choices) and coffee, at 7pm. Non-residents not admitted. Vegetarian diets if ordered. Wine can be ordered. No smoking.
1 Sitting-room. With open fire, central heating. Bar.
Large garden

Until recently, this fine Tudor mansion was a farmhouse but it has since been renovated – Sue Boynton will show you her albums of 'before' and 'after' pictures as you sit by the log fire blazing in a huge inglenook that was one of the features uncovered and restored. This is in a great room with coffered ceiling and stone-mullioned windows.

A corridor, still with a long row of bells to summon servants, leads to bedrooms which have flowery wallpapers and light colour schemes; one suite has a four-poster. The main entrance hall serves as a bar – you help yourself and write down what you have taken.

The choices at dinner by candlelight may include plaice goujons or home-made pâté to start with; pork cooked with cider, apples and cream; then perhaps crème caramel or profiteroles and cheeses. Sue, who used to do large-scale catering, says she much prefers cooking for smaller numbers to higher standards, often using produce straight from the garden.

The surroundings are attractive, from the flowerbeds by the drive, with cupid statues here and there, to the stone verandah with view of a stream below.

Readers' comments: Very comfortable and well appointed. Friendly hosts, strongly recommended. Delightful.

★ About a mile northward is **THE GRANGE**, Alverstone; an immaculate guest-house where Geraldine Watling provides good home cooking (tel: 0983 403729). From £16.50 to £18.
Readers' comments: Effortless efficiency. Relaxed and happy atmosphere. Imaginative cooking. Warm and welcoming. Excellent accommodation, wonderful food.

★ THE ARCHWAY
College Road, Windermere, Cumbria, LA23 1BY Tel: 09662 5613

C(12) **PT S X**

Nearest main road: A591 from Kendal to Ambleside.

5 Bedrooms. £18 (less for 7 nights). Prices go up at Easter. Bargain breaks. Most have own bath/shower/toilet. Tea/coffee facilities. TV. Views of garden, country. No smoking.
Dinner. £12.50 for 3 courses and coffee, at 6.45pm. Non-residents not admitted. Vegetarian or special diets if ordered. Wine can be ordered or brought in. No smoking.
1 Sitting-room. With open fire, central heating. No smoking.
Small garden

The Windermere-Ambleside axis is the heart of the Lake District, for which many first-time visitors head. The Archway is in a side road close to the centre of Windermere (and conveniently near the railway station). It is in a Victorian terrace typical of those in Lake District towns, built of the green slate much used for houses hereabouts, and stands above road level behind a sloping garden.

A big semicircular arch divides the sitting-cum-dining room, which has stripped pine chairs and tables at one end and, at the other, cretonne-covered settees and chairs near a large and handsome fireplace. Walls are painted dusty pink – pinks are evidently the Greenhalghs' favourite shades; there are books everywhere; and on the walls here and throughout the house are prints, posters, Victorian engravings and other pictures, all chosen with a discriminating eye – not surprisingly, since Tony Greenhalgh has a degree in the history of art.

Each bedroom, as well as its pictures, has a patchwork quilt. Views from most are of the Lake District mountains across a roofscape of green slates.

Anthony and Aurea, who share the cooking, are enthusiasts for food and wine. Breakfast could include home-made muesli and yogurt and American pancakes or, more conventionally, kippers, Cumberland sausage or black pudding; each breakfast order is freshly prepared. Dinner might be cream of watercress soup or vegetable terrine; roast lamb with home-made rowanberry jelly; and such a pudding as franzipani tart or bread-and-butter pudding – sweets are a speciality.

Windermere, which takes its name from the lake (the largest in the Lake District) by which the town has grown up, is a bustling place overlooked by famous peaks such as Scafell Pike, Great Gable, and Crinkle Crags. The lake itself offers sailing and waterskiing to the strenuous, cruises in variety to the less energetic. A car ferry across it (busy in the summer) is a short cut to Hawkshead (rigorously preserved by the National Trust) and Beatrix Potter's Far Sawrey; beyond is Coniston Water of *Swallows and Amazons* fame. On Belle Isle, Windermere's largest island, is a circular Palladian mansion open to the public. Off the lakeside road to Ambleside are the National Park visitor centre, Hayes's famous garden centre, and Wordsworth's Dove Cottage.

Book well ahead: many of these houses have few rooms. Do not expect dinner if you have not booked it or if you arrive late.

9

★ **ASHEN COPSE**   **C S**

Coleshill, Wiltshire, SN6 7PU   Tel: 0367 240175

North-east of Swindon. Nearest main road: A361 from Swindon towards
Faringdon.

2 Bedrooms. £13–£16 (less for 7 nights). Prices go up at Easter. Some have shower/ toilet. Views of garden, country. No smoking.

1 Sitting-room. With open fire, central heating, TV. No smoking.

Large garden

If you approach from the Faringdon direction there are panoramic views to the north of the road (and to the south the National Trust's celebrated stone barn at Great Coxwell – almost cathedral-like in its grandeur). A long, well-surfaced drive leads through pheasant woods to the 300-year-old house built of stone and brick; and around lie the 600 acres of the Hoddinotts' beef and arable farm (with a few pet lambs and a pony): all is owned by the National Trust. In this peaceful place, birdsong is usually the only sound.

It is an ideal house to bring children for a country holiday as there is a particularly good family room separate from the rest – very big and light, with its own shower-room, and with windows on each side: one overlooks a lawn with magnolia, lilac and cherry trees (at their best in late spring) and the other the farmyard where calves and chickens are often to be seen. By the staircase to the other room are row upon row of colourful rosettes won at pony shows by the Hoddinotts' daughter every year since she was eight. From this bedroom you can look beyond the small swimming-pool (unheated) to the famous Uffington White Horse cut into the chalk of the hills and the prehistoric Ridgeway Path striding across the high horizon. Every room is immaculate; paintwork sparkling-white.

Pat serves breakfast only: the Radnor Arms is recommended for dinner.

This is good walking country. From Ashen Copse there is a footpath all the way to Great Coxwell Barn, built by monks in the 13th century and one of the most impressive in Europe. Another goes all round Badbury Clump (site of an Iron Age fort), which is prettiest at bluebell time and from which there are fine views.

In the vicinity are attractive villages such as Highworth (17th-century houses and distant views), Buscot with a National Trust mansion of 1780 containing art treasures and water-gardens running into a lake, Kelmscott (Tudor manor house where William Morris lived), Lechlade celebrated for its statue of Old Father Thames, old bridge and river locks, and picturesque Ashbury, worth a visit for the 14th-century brasses in its church and for 17th-century Ashdown House (the prehistoric site known as Waylands Smithy is near here).

In this direction, too, are the great gardens of Pusey House which would take all day to explore fully; and of Kingston Lisle, surrounding a fine manor house.

Readers' comments: Attractive house, pleasant welcome and attention.

10

AVOCA HOUSE HOTEL
43 Belsize Park, London NW3 4EG   Tel: 071-722 7777

C PT S X

50 Bedrooms. To SOTBT readers only, £26.50 for dinner, bed and breakfast (min. 2 nights): this may go up after March. (Normally b&b only is £35.) All have own bathrooms. Tea/coffee facilities. Remote-control, satellite and other, TV; video films. Laundry service.
Dinner. A la carte or £7.50 for 3 courses (some choices) and coffee, at 6.30 – 9.30pm (not on Sundays, so the SOTBT rate is less then). Lunches. Vegetarian or special diets if ordered. Wine can be ordered. **Light suppers.**
3 Sitting-rooms. With central heating, TV, piano. **Bars.**

Once Belsize Park was exactly that: a park ('the most noble that ever I saw', Pepys wrote in his diary). The stately mansion to which it belonged (home, later, of Prime Minister Spencer Percival, who was assassinated in the House of Commons in 1812) was entirely surrounded by farm lands. Development took place about 1850, a good period of architecture; so the quiet streets of this area (between Hampstead and St John's Wood) are now lined with handsome villas – flights of steps lead up to big porticoes, wide windows have classical pediments above, inside are handsome panelled doors. The house next door to the Avoca (41) became the home of Jerome K. Jerome after *Three Men in a Boat* brought him fame and fortune.

The hotel, owned by the Dillons but run by a manager, consists of five such houses converted to provide rooms comfortably furnished in conventional hotel-style, with thick carpets and good bathrooms (sizes differ).

In the dining-room, there is the choice of an à la carte menu (with such selections as seafood cocktail or melon, steak or cutlets) or a very inexpensive table d'hôte (typically, soup, beef bourguignonne and four gâteaux). The hotel also has a little bistro overlooking the small garden with birds, squirrels, and barbecue (and carpark): I had excellent and ample salmon mayonnaise (£5.25).

The hotel caters mainly for businessmen midweek; however, all the receptionists are trained to give tourist information, make theatre bookings, etc. Close by are Swiss Cottage Underground station (the Jubilee line takes you to Piccadilly in about 15 minutes) and plenty of bus routes direct to Oxford Street and other parts of central London. M1, M40 and M4 are easily reached.

In adjoining Buckland Crescent are similar houses, one of which is now a good guest-house, the **BUCKLAND HOTEL** (tel: 071-722 5574; manager, Rosalind Charters) which has comfortable and well-equipped rooms with showers, TV etc; a sitting/breakfast-room; and a garden at the back. £22. (As in most London houses, garden-facing rooms are quieter.)

11

AVONSIDE

Limpley Stoke, Wiltshire, BA3 6EX   Tel: 0225 722547

South of Bath (Avon). Nearest main road: A36 from Bath to Warminster.

2 Bedrooms. £16–£18 (less for 4 nights). Prices go up in April. Tea/coffee facilities. Views of garden, country, river. Washing machine on request.
Dinner. £10.50 for 3 courses with aperitif and coffee, at 7.30pm. Non-residents not admitted. Wine can also be brought in.
1 Sitting-room. With open fire, central heating, piano.
Large garden

A typical English country house, built of honey-coloured Bath stone, the Challens' secluded home stands on the banks of the River Avon: walks along it (or the nearby Kennet & Avon Canal) and coarse fishing are among the attractions of staying in this very scenic area.

Ursula has furnished the sitting-room with tangerine or pale lime armchairs, oriental rugs and antiques that show up well against walls painted peach, on which hang many paintings by Peter who, after serving as a major in the Gurkhas, turned to a completely different career as an artist. Through the bay window is a serene view of the well-kept lawn and landscaped grounds, with tennis and croquet.

Other rooms are equally pleasing, with attractive wallpapers and leafy views. The Challens treat visitors as if they were house guests, offering them pre-dinner drinks (no extra charge). Typical of the kind of meal Ursula serves: avocado pâté; roast lamb with quince jelly and vegetables from the garden; a brûlée of brown sugar, cream and yogurt over raspberries. Alternatively, visitors can go out to the excellent Nightingales restaurant in the village or to the Hop Pole inn.

At Bradford-on-Avon several steep roads converge downhill to the mediaeval bridge with domed chapel on it. It takes time to discover all Bradford's handsome houses, Saxon church, vast tithe barn and old inns. A few miles away is Bath, and, northward, such other lovely spots as Corsham, Lacock (mediaeval abbey, and museum of photographic history) and the Chippenham-Calne area. Garden-lovers head for Stourhead, antique-hunters for Bath. Malmesbury (on a hill almost surrounded by the River Avon) has its famous Norman abbey and handsome stone houses from the 17th and 18th centuries lining its streets and market square. Longleat, Dereham Manor and the historic American Museum are popular.

Readers' comments: Wonderful people, very friendly. Elegant; lovely meals. The Challens make one feel like their house guests. Excellent accommodation and food. A place of peace and comfort.

When writing to me, if you want a reply please enclose a stamped addressed envelope.

★ **BANK COTTAGE**   C(6) S
Bryher, Isles of Scilly, TR23 0PR   Tel: 0720 22612

rear view

5 Bedrooms. £15.75. Prices go up in May. Some have own shower/toilet. Tea/coffee facilities. TV. Views of garden, country, sea. **Dinner.** £8.50 for 4 courses and coffee, at 7pm. Non-residents not admitted. Vegetarian or special diets if ordered. Wine can be ordered. **Light suppers** if ordered. **1 Sitting-room.** With central heating, TV. Bar. **Small garden** with badminton. **Closed from November to mid-March.**

Even a millionaire might have a long search before finding somewhere to stay in quite such an idyllic situation as this little guest-house on Rushy Bay. Visitors here have a superb sandy beach (right outside) virtually all to themselves: when I was there, I encountered only one other couple on the golden, sunny sands. And beyond it is one of England's most beautiful seascapes, dotted with 22 islets.

Mac Mace works as a diver: sometimes diving for lobsters and crabs or for archaeological finds, including Spanish doubloons, on the many nearby wrecks; sometimes for sea urchins, the decorative shells of which are exported by the thousand. He and his wife Tracy take a few guests in their cottage (built at least 300 years ago, but with later additions). The rooms are simple, with low ceilings and thick walls to keep winter's gales at bay. Bedrooms are cheerful and bright.

Many visitors are content just to sit all day in the colourful garden (facing south-west) to enjoy the view of the bay, sheltered by the pink-flowered escallonia hedges; or they can accompany Mac when he is setting nets or fishing. The sunsets are outstanding. A gate opens onto the beach, but although the climate is warm here, the sea is not. The garden is at its most colourful in early summer (fuchsias, flowering cherries, tulips and arum lilies abound); the islets are best in late spring, when they are smothered in pink sea-thrift.

Vegetables and loganberries are home-grown, rolls home-baked, eggs from the Maces' hens. A typical meal cooked by Tracy may start with fish or fish pâté, followed by a roast or casserole. Tracy particularly enjoys making puddings like banana mousse or sherry trifle and her vegetarian meals are imaginative. Sometimes meals are served outdoors, using the granite barbecue.

Visitors arriving by boat from St Mary's are met and their baggage taken up for them by tractor or Landrover. The boats provide a service throughout winter (which can be mild and sunny, or with dramatic storms), but less frequently. Up to Easter, there are very few visitors; but even in summer Bryher is never crowded.

Readers' comments: Wished we could stay for ever! Felt completely at home; happy and relaxed atmosphere. Comfortable room, excellent food. Simply delighted, a marvellous time. Nothing is too much trouble. Excellent food and accommodation, good hosts. Now a regular and much-loved destination.

13

BANK VILLA
C(5) D

Masham, North Yorkshire, HG4 4DB Tel: 0765 89605

North-west of Ripon. Nearest main road: A6108 from Ripon to Leyburn.

7 **Bedrooms.** £14.50 (less for 7 nights). Prices go up in March. Some have own shower. Views of garden, country.
Dinner. £12 for 3 courses, at 7.30pm. Non-residents not admitted. Vegetarian or special diets if ordered. Wine can be ordered.
2 **Sitting-rooms.** With central heating, TV.
Large garden
Closed from November until Easter.

Good food is the principal attraction at Bank Villa, where Phillip Gill (former administrator of York's arts festival) is an inspired cook.

The villa is a late Georgian stone house set back from the busy road, with a steep terraced garden behind it (where there is a sunny summerhouse in which to sit). Here are grown fruit and vegetables for the kitchen.

Dinner is served in a pleasant room – pretty 'Old Colonial' china and rush mats on the pine tables contrast with the deep raspberry walls. Phillip cooks, and his partner Anton serves, such delicious menus as spinach-and-cheese soufflé as a starter, smoked pork cooked with Calvados, and iced Drambuie parfait.

Bedrooms, too, are attractive but not smart, many with floral wallpapers and pine furniture, and some with a glimpse of the River Ure at the foot of the hill.

Masham, a little market town, has a church with interesting features; and, in mid-July, a traction-engine and steam fair. The town stands at the foot of Wensleydale, in an area of great historic as well as very varied scenic interest: within a few miles are two abbeys, three castles, one cathedral and a stately home, as well as the spa towns of Harrogate and Ripon. There are scenic roads, markets, the sight of racehorses exercising, waterfalls, a beautifully restored Georgian theatre (at Richmond) and fine gardens.

Bedale, which has had a market since the 13th century, is a town of pleasing buildings with a very fine church. Don't miss Fountains, finest of all the Yorkshire abbeys. Other nearby sights are Newby Hall, Ripon's cathedral, Middleham Castle, Brimham Rocks and Harlow Car gardens.

If you visit Ripon, you can hardly miss the big inscription over the market square: 'Except ye Lord keep ye cittie, ye Wakeman waketh in vain'. And if you are there at 9pm, you will see and hear the wakeman (i.e., watchman) blowing his buffalo horn and wearing a frock coat, a cocked hat, white gloves and a silver badge on his arm. The office dates back to Alfred the Great, who gave the city its first charter and a horn in AD 886. The wakeman was there to keep an all-night watch for Viking raiders, and he had to blow the horn to let the citizens know that he was on duty. The nocturnal patrol ceased centuries ago, but the horn-blowing continues. The wakeman's house, built in 1250, is now the city's tourist information centre. Below the cathedral is a Saxon crypt, all that remains of Ripon's first Christian church, which was destroyed by those same raiders, and in it is a fine monument to a wakeman of the past.

Readers' comments: A great start to our stages to Scotland: we'll be back. Food as good as in the priciest restaurants. Energetic, cheerful and efficient.

14

BARK HOUSE

D

Oakford Bridge, Devon, EX16 9HZ   Tel: 03985 236
North of Tiverton. Nearest main road: A396 from Exeter to Minehead.

6 Bedrooms. £18–£26 (less for 7 nights). Some have own bath/shower/toilet. Tea/coffee facilities. TV. Views of garden, country, river. No smoking. Washing machine on request.
Dinner. £12.50 for 4 courses (with choices) and coffee, at 8pm. Non-residents not admitted. Vegetarian or special diets if ordered. Wine can be ordered. No smoking.
Light suppers if ordered.
1 Sitting-room. With open fire, central heating. No smoking.
Large garden
Closed in January and February.

In a wooded valley through which runs the River Exe is a stone building of unusual origin. It was once used as a tannery, the oak bark for which was brought from Exmoor Forest. (From powdered oak bark, rich in tannin, were made vats of liquor in which to soak hides – the tanning process. At Colyton this process is still in use.) Today, it has been handsomely converted; and Pauline and Douglas West provide visitors with complete comfort. Books, good pictures, thick Berber carpets, antiques, pot-plants and the flicker of a cheerful log fire set the scene.

In the dining-room brown and pink tablecloths contrast with white walls; around the tables are either pews or Windsor chairs. Every bedroom is different. No. 1 has a bow window with window-seat from which to enjoy the tranquil view; no. 4, art nouveau nymphs on the ceiling – however did *they* get there! No. 6 is a huge family room with its own ancient arched door to a rock garden with pool, and leaded casements.

Dinner may begin with smoked salmon mousse or fish chowder or eggs en cocotte (there are several choices at every course). With a daube of beef will be served potato galette and other vegetables. The fresh peach Melba has an orange-and-raspberry sauce. Because the Wests once lived in Provence, Pauline has many recipes from the region. (Breakfast is continental. English breakfast extra.)

From Bark House there is a particularly scenic route over moors to Minehead in Somerset. Both Exmoor and the sea are near; and so are Exeter, Taunton and Barnstaple, all described elsewhere. The area has a great many stately homes to visit, such as Knightshayes (NT), and gardens (Killerton); as well as churches and castles. Dunster village and Dartington are other popular outings. South Molton, a market town, has a number of good 18th-century buildings and fine views; North Molton likewise (derelict copper mines here); Swimbridge, a particularly rich church; outside Rose Ash is pretty Cuckoo Mill Bridge.

Readers' comments: Beautiful setting; excellent cooking; friendly and cheerful hosts. Have stayed four times. Charming hotel and surroundings. Very comfortable.

15

★ **BARNFIELD FARM** C S
near Charing, Kent, TN27 0BN Tel: 023371 2421
North-west of Ashford. Nearest main road: A20 from Maidstone to Ashford.

4 Bedrooms. £16–£18 (less for 7 nights). Tea/coffee facilities. TV. Views of garden, country, river. No smoking. Washing machine on request.
Dinner. £9 for 3 courses and coffee, at 7pm. Non-residents not admitted. Vegetarian or special diets if ordered. Wine can be ordered/brought in. No smoking. **Light suppers** if ordered.
2 Sitting-rooms. With central heating, TV, record-player. No smoking.
Large garden with tennis.

This historic farmhouse was built about the time of the Battle of Agincourt (1415). It is so remarkable that sometimes coachloads of overseas visitors come to see it; and even individual visitors are given a tour round by Martin Pym, who grew up here, or his wife Phillada.

One steps into a large hall, where the oak framework of the house is exposed to view (draped with hop bines) and a cask holding shepherds' crooks stands in one corner – for outside are sheep pastures, with arable fields beyond. The main sitting-room has an exceptionally large inglenook where logs blaze in front of a Cromwellian fireback; the original pot-hooks, soot-blackened, are still in place. Along one beam hangs a set of handbells, on which Christmas is rung in every year. The dining-room, too, has an open fire and ancient beams, with one especially fine door (linenfold panels contrasting with intricately carved foliage), made from a church chest. There is another sitting/dining-room for guests' use, comfortably furnished with deep cretonne armchairs, plenty of books and – like every room in the house – attractive objects.

The bedrooms are equally agreeable, and in two one can see the construction of the house very clearly: massive treetrunks, rough-hewn to shape, curve up to support the roof. Some overlook the River Stour on its way to Canterbury.

Some of the furnishings were made by Martin's grandmother – for instance, a screen of Victorian scraps in one room, and an intricate embroidery commemorating two Pyms who died in the First World War in another. An old linen-press, chests, rocking-chairs – at every turn of the wandering corridors there is something interesting to see. Outside are lawns, herbaceous borders surrounding a pool guarded by four stone owls, and a lake visited by ducks and Canada geese.

Phillada serves such meals as egg mayonnaise, casseroled lamb cutlets and apple fool with shortbread – loading a hot-tray on the sideboard so that guests can help themselves to as much as they wish.

The most popular sights in the vicinity are Leeds, Chilham and Dover castles, Canterbury Cathedral, and Godinton Park. (Bicycles on loan.)

At Charing are remains of the archbishop's palace where Henry VIII stayed en route to the Field of the Cloth of Gold (1520), and from Charing Hill are views across the Weald.

Readers' comments: Enjoyed our stay very much; a warm welcome. Unobtrusive but charming hostess. Delightful house and garden. Excellent meal. Nicely secluded position. Kindly welcome.

BARROW HILL FARM

C(8) D S

Ramsdean, Hampshire, GU32 1RW   Tel: 073087 340
West of Petersfield. Nearest main road: A272 from Petersfield to Winchester.

rear view

3 Bedrooms. £15–£17 (less for 4 nights). Some have own bath/shower/toilet. Tea/ coffee free. TV. Views of garden, country. No smoking. Washing machine on request. **1 Sitting-room.** With open fire, central heating, TV. No smoking.

Large garden
Closed from November to February inclusive.

A nearby hill with prehistoric burial-mound gives this beef- and dairy-farm its name. In the opposite direction it has a view of equally ancient Butser Hill, a windswept height well worth a visit.

The tile-hung house itself is beautifully furnished, with Victorian antiques shown at their best against well-chosen colour schemes and fabrics. The beamed sitting-rooms are divided by a see-through fireplace, and on the sills of the big windows all round is a profusion of pot-plants. Breakfast is served at a large oval table of mahogany in the dining-room. Bedrooms are excellent.

Everything is immaculate, outside as well as in, from carefully trained roses climbing up flint walls to the smooth lawns where one can sit to enjoy the setting sun amid the scent of catmint or lavender. Old chimney-pots have been used for planting petunias and lobelias. There are mementoes of Beatrix Potter – the very plates to be seen in the Tiggy-Winkle drawings; Mary's great-aunt was the little girl illustrated in the story.

Mary Luff serves only breakfast, recommending local inns (or Langish House Hotel) for other meals, including those at East Meon, described elsewhere.

Petersfield's 18th-century streets are pleasant; and at Greatham Mill is a lovely garden. All around are hills, woods and tranquil valleys of great beauty: a very agreeable area to explore by car or on foot. Jane Austen's home at Chawton and Gilbert White's at Selborne are only a few miles away. The Queen Elizabeth Country Park is an area of superb scenery. Beyond it is the Sir George Staunton Conservatory, a tropical rainforest under glass.

In green valleys amid the South Downs you will find churches that go back to Saxon times, flint-walled houses, and prehistoric burial mounds. To the south are woodlands, remnants of the once-great Forest of Bere, and then comes Portsmouth Harbour. Despite heavy traffic on roads into the port, this is well worth a visit – to see Nelson's *Victory*, Henry VIII's *Mary Rose* and his Southsea Castle, and – the newest attraction – a big D-Day show.

Readers' comments: Excellent, very comfortable. A pleasant welcome. Huge, comfortable room. Excellent breakfast. A most generous and cheerful hostess.

★ BEECROFT   C PT

Middle Drive, Woolsington, Tyne & Wear, NE13 8BS   Tel: 091 2861009
North-west of Newcastle-upon-Tyne. Nearest main road: A696 from
Newcastle to Ponteland.

2 Bedrooms. £14–£15 (less for 5 nights). Prices go up in April. Bargain breaks. Tea/ coffee facilities. TV. Views of garden. No smoking. Washing machine on request. **1 Sitting-room.** With open fire, central heating, TV, record-player. No smoking.	**Small garden** **Closed from December to February inclusive.**

Newcastle's airport was built on what was once the great Woolsington estate, of which John Beattie's grandfather was head gamekeeper.

This 17th-century sandstone lodge was his home, and John remembers seeing game hanging and pheasant chicks being reared here. No longer, alas – though there remain the bees that give the house its name and which provide honey for breakfast. John also produces leeks (for which Northumberland is famous – in early September, growers compete at leek shows throughout the county).

All bedrooms are on the ground floor. From the house there are pleasant woodland walks to Woolsington Hall and its lake.

This is obviously a very useful stopover for people using the airport to go to Europe or Canada (the Beatties give free lifts to and from the airport). But it deserves a lingering stay, not least to visit Newcastle itself, ¼ hour by bus. No one driving through this city's one-way maze can guess at its hidden splendours: it needs to be explored on foot. It has some really exceptional Georgian streets.

I recommend starting at the old Blackfriars monastery, which has a particularly imaginative museum explaining the city's history, crafts and a good café. Downhill are Dean Street (antiques, crafts and bistros), the cathedral, castle (where Northumbrian pipes are played – different from Scottish bagpipes), quays (markets and a lighthouse museum). All Newcastle's museums are exceptionally good: the Joicey (historical – particularly good on Bewick), the Laing art gallery, the Hancock (natural history) and the Museum of Science and Engineering. Another bus will take you to Gateshead (for the finest park in the north and an excellent art gallery), the metro to Jarrow (where Bede's monastic times are vividly brought to life again). In the Eldon Square shopping centre, Marks & Spencer's first 'penny bazaar' has been recreated. To the east of the city, near Stocksfield, is the birthplace of Thomas Bewick; northward is Morpeth with a bagpipe museum.

Prices are per person in a double room at the beginning of the year.

Osmington, Dorset, DT3 6EL   Tel: 0305 834095
North-east of Weymouth. Nearest main road: A353 from Weymouth towards
Wareham.

4 Bedrooms. £14–£17.50 (less for 3 nights).
Prices go up in March or April. Bargain
breaks. Some have own shower/toilet. Tea/
coffee facilities. TV. Views of garden, country. No smoking. Washing machine on
request.
Dinner. A la carte or £6.50 for 3 courses and
coffee, at 7.45pm. Non-residents not admitted. Vegetarian or special diets if ordered.
Wine can be brought in. No smoking. **Light
suppers** sometimes.
1 Sitting-room. With open fire, central heating, TV. No smoking.
Small garden
Closed in January.

Mary Kempe's father was Lord of the Manor at Osmington; and this little
thatched stone cottage was the holiday home of her childhood. While the manorial
lands passed into other hands, she was pursuing an academic career at the
universities of Nairobi and London: the former accounts for the presence of
African crafts in the old cottage, which is now her permanent home.

It is tucked away – in a pocket-handkerchief garden – down a lane leading to
countryside of great beauty, with some lovely walks; to the south fine coast scenery
lies only a mile away (shingle beaches closest, sandy ones a little further).

The friendly sitting-room is a place of books and watercolours, lead-paned
windows and old cretonne-covered sofas or chairs. Breakfast is served in the big,
cork-floored kitchen warmed by a stove (you can buy jars of Mary's home-made
jams). She produces, on certain nights only, imaginative dinners with many dishes
based on traditional local recipes and produce – for instance, Martlemas (or
Michaelmas) beef, which is marinaded in wine and vinegar then rubbed with
spices before being baked, or Wessex chicken in a cider sauce. Before this might
come Dorset pâté or a soup of carrots or lentils; and after it apple hedgehog,
blueberry pie or buttered oranges. Or you can eat well at the nearby Smugglers'
Inn. (Ask Mary for an excellent leaflet on where to buy Dorset local foods to take
home.)

Birdwatchers go out from here to spend days at Radipole Lake, the Fleet or
Studland nature reserve. Others tour the Thomas Hardy sites. Osmington, being
roughly midway between Poole at one end of Dorset and Lyme Regis at the other,
is a good centre from which to explore all parts of the county: see details elsewhere
in this book. Further afield, one can visit such beauty-spots as Lulworth Cove and
the Purbeck Hills; T. E. Lawrence's cottage at Clouds Hill; and picturesque
villages like Wool which has *Tess of the d'Urbervilles* associations. Kingston Lacy
House and gardens (National Trust) and Corfe Castle are also popular destinations. Nearby are good nurseries and garden centres, too.

To the attractions of a traditional seaside resort, Weymouth has in recent years
added a Sea Life Centre; an outstanding butterfly farm; and a brewery converted
into museum, restaurants and shops.

Readers' comments: Superb; delightful haven of peace; a marvellous hostess. One
of the best meals we have ever sampled.

BELLS

37 Bridewell Street, Clare, Suffolk, CO10 8QD   Tel: 0787 277538
West of Sudbury. On A1092 from Long Melford to Clare.

2 **Bedrooms**. £15. Prices go up at Easter.
TV. No smoking.
Dinner. £9.50 for 3 courses and coffee, at
7pm. Non-residents not admitted. Vegetarian or special diets if ordered. Wine can
be brought in. No smoking. **Light suppers** if
ordered.
1 **Sitting-room**. With central heating. No
smoking.
Small garden

This small but historic house (once three cottages in a terrace) is filled with
antiques, paintings that include family portraits which go back to the 18th
century, all kinds of Victoriana and a great many books. At the back is a little
paved garden frequented by the Bells' three cats and their dogs. Around the
dining-table are ladderback chairs and a pine settle. Bedrooms, too, are cottage-
like in their furnishings.

For many years, the Bells used to run a restaurant in nearby Cavendish, so
cooking here is above average: Gillian serves such meals (if ordered in advance) as
fish mousse, chicken provençale and raspberries with home-made ice cream.

Clare is a place to explore on foot, to enjoy all the details of its ancient houses –
plasterwork decoration, exuberant inn signs, the old priory. It is close to
Cavendish, Sudbury and other attractive places in Suffolk such as Kentwell Hall
and gardens, Long Melford (good for antique-hunting), Clare country park, the
Colne Valley steam railway, Gainsborough's house, Hedingham Castle and
Melford Hall. Bury St Edmunds and its abbey gardens are worth a leisurely visit,
and so is Lavenham (both described elsewhere in this book); as well as Beth
Chatto's garden, Constable's Flatford Mill, and Cambridge.

The area has several out-of-the-ordinary museums – at Cotton, one devoted to
mechanical music, for instance; at Mildenhall, the Mildenhall Treasure and RAF
memorabilia under one roof; the big National Horseracing Museum at Newmarket (you can also go on conducted tours of the National Stud here) and a
particularly fine clock museum in Bury St Edmunds.

In nearby Callis Street is the **SHIP
STORES** (tel: 0787 277834). Miles
from the sea, this one-time inn was
originally called the Sheep, not the
Ship. Now it is a small shop run by
Colin and Deborah Bowles, with a few
simply furnished bedrooms and an upstairs sitting-room for guests. Secrets
in this building, 400 years old, have
been uncovered: fireplaces long
boarded up, and the original brick floor
downstairs, for instance. It is a place of
low beams, creaking floors, undulating
roof and pink-plastered front: full of
character, but very modest (as are its
prices). In the breakfast-room there is

solid elm furniture locally made; and
anyone who wants an out-of-the-
ordinary breakfast (pâté? sardines?
beans?) is welcome to select from the
stock in the grocery. £12.

Readers' comments: A beautiful, charming and superbly run establishment.

BERE MARSH HOUSE

C(6) D S

Shillingstone, Dorset, DT11 0QY Tel: 0258 861133
North of Blandford Forum. Nearest main road: A357 from Blandford Forum to
Sturminster Newton.

2 **Bedrooms.** £12–£14 (less for 3 nights).
Prices go up in April. Some have own bath/
toilet. Tea/coffee facilities. TV. Views of
garden, country, river. Washing machine on
request.
Dinner. £10 or £12 for 4 courses (with
choices) and coffee, from 7.30pm. Vegetarian or special diets if ordered. Wine can
be ordered. **Light suppers** if ordered.
2 **Sitting-rooms.** With open fire, central
heating, TV, piano, record-player. Bar.
Conservatory.
Large garden
Closed in January.

It is the food which brings most visitors here, for in the restaurant James and
Felicity Roe serve gourmet meals. In the past, Felicity used to cook directors'
lunches in London and then worked at the celebrated Peacock Vane hotel on the
Isle of Wight during its heyday.

There's a breakfast-room with dried flowers overhead, a conservatory with
grapevine (meals are sometimes served here), armchairs surrounding a log stove in
the hall of the 18th-century house. In the garden are a tennis court, summer-house
overlooking a rock garden in a dell and a big vegetable garden. Beyond are far
views over good walking country.

As to the meals, the Roes operate a sensible system. Although their repertoire is
very considerable, they let the first party to book dinner choose the menu for that
night, for all comers: that way, they can provide dishes from freshly bought and
cooked ingredients and (there being no waste) at a very reasonable price. So it pays
to make your reservation and study their list of dishes well in advance. Most dishes
are such classics as mushrooms à la grecque, boeuf Stroganoff and crème brûlée.

There are plenty of good drives around here. For instance, one might go via
Sturminster Newton and Mere (which has a 16th-century inn that was a Royalist
stronghold during the Civil War) to visit the world-famous landscaped gardens
and lake of Stourhead and the 18th-century mansion itself (full of art treasures).
Alternatively, via Shaftesbury (described elsewhere) one could drive to Tollard
Royal on a road of hairpin bends that is an outstanding scenic route with superb
views when you get to the top. Along the way, lynchets can be seen – narrow
terraces constructed on the steep hillsides to make cultivation possible. This is part
of Cranborne Chase, for a thousand years a royal hunting forest: at Tollard Royal
the hunting-lodge of King John has been carefully preserved (the village church is
also worth a visit, particularly for its effigy of a knight in armour; and also Larmer
Grounds park when it is open – there are oriental temples and a wooden theatre).

Other places of interest in the vicinity include the 15th-century manor house at
Purse Caundle; Sherborne for its golden abbey and two castles; and Longburton in
the church of which is a remarkable painted and canopied tomb.

Southward lie Dorchester and the seaside resort of Weymouth, both described
elsewhere. To the numerous attractions of the latter, new enterprises are constantly being added – as varied as a diving and shipwreck centre and another for
shire horses, a Victorian coastal fort recently restored and a 7-acre waterlily and
fish farm.

21

BICKLEIGH COTTAGE

S PT

Bickleigh, Devon, EX16 8RJ   Tel: 088 45 230
South of Tiverton. On A396 from Exeter to Tiverton.

9 Bedrooms. £15–£19.50 (less for 7 nights). Some have own bath/shower/toilet. Tea/coffee facilities. View of garden, country. **Dinner.** £8.50 for 4 courses and coffee, at 7pm. Non-residents not admitted. Vegetarian or special diets if ordered. Wine can be ordered. No smoking. **Light suppers.**

3 Sitting-rooms. With central heating, TV. **Large garden** **Closed from mid-October to the end of March.**

Built about 1640 and later extended, this very picturesque thatched cottage has been run as a small hotel by the same family for over 50 years. It stands on a road by the banks of the River Exe, with a foaming weir a few yards downstream: everyone's ideal of a typically Devonian beauty-spot.

The rooms downstairs are full of antiques such as old chests and carved oak chairs, as well as a collection of blue glass and other interesting trifles including articles of Honiton lace made by Mrs Cochrane, which are for sale. The bedrooms are more simply furnished, though one has a four-poster bed. For total quiet, ask for a river-facing room (there are several). Outside is a pretty riverside garden with a fish-pool and glasshouses containing a collection of cacti and succulents.

Meals are of plain home cooking, a typical menu being smoked mackerel, roast lamb, pineapple meringue and cheeses.

A good day's outing via Tiverton (which has a castle) would be along the Exe Valley (visiting opulent Knightshayes Court, lavishly designed by William Burges in 1869 amid beautiful gardens) to Dulverton – old woodlands giving way to open moors as you travel towards Exmoor. In Dulverton are mediaeval lanes and an ancient bridge, tempting shops, weavers' workshops and Exmoor's interpretation centre. There are good walks in Eggesford Forest on the way to the steep village of Lapford, in the church of which are outstanding Tudor woodcarvings. Crediton's stately church once had cathedral status (built of red sandstone, it has stained glass windows depicting the life of its patron St Boniface). In the vicinity are other stately homes, such as Fursdon (Fursdons have lived in it from the 13th century to the present day) and Bickleigh Castle which, among other unusual exhibits, has espionage gadgets invented by the original of 'Q' in the James Bond novels. Bickleigh's watermill houses a craft centre. At South Molton (northward) you can see an exhibition of cider-making, and the Quince Honey Farm with bees busily at work. If you follow the path in the Great Western Canal Country Park you will see (or can take a trip on) horse-drawn canal barges.

Readers' comments: Delightful. A favourite place. Beautiful position, good meals. Delightful cottage and scenery.

BIGGIN HALL   C D X

Biggin-by-Hartington, Derbyshire, SK17 0DH   Tel: 029 884 451
South of Buxton. Nearest main road: A515 from Ashbourne to Buxton.

12 Bedrooms. £15–£20 (less for 5 nights). Prices go up at Easter. Bargain breaks. All have own bath/shower/toilet. Tea/coffee facilities. TV. Views of garden, country. Washing machine on request.
Dinner. A la carte or £12.50 for 4 courses (with choices) and coffee, at 7pm. Non-residents not admitted. Vegetarian or special diets if ordered. Wine can be ordered. No smoking. Light suppers if ordered.
2 Sitting-rooms. With open fire, central heating, TV, piano, record-player. Bar. No smoking in one.
Large garden

Charles II was on the throne when this handsome stone house with leaded windows was built, and it has changed little since his day (modern comforts apart). Logs blaze in the great stone fireplace, with cretonne-covered chairs grouped around on a quarry-tiled floor. Another sitting-room has one wall of bookshelves, and glass doors opening onto the garden where children can play on the swing. Upstairs, one oak-panelled room has an oak-panelled half-tester bed (pink lilies on its blue draperies) and another a spectacular four-poster under the exposed beams – its bathroom is huge, carpeted and even equipped with a bidet. There are other rooms in an 18th-century stone annexe which are all equipped with fridges and microwaves. The Hall's owners, the Moffetts, used to be antique dealers.

In the dining-room (oriental rugs on flagstones, rush chairs, flowers on each table) breakfast is (unless you pay a little extra) continental-style, but this includes a choice of cereals, fruits and juices followed by home-made brioches, croissants and jams. In winter, cooked breakfast, packed lunch and mulled wine are free.

Evening meals may comprise a home-made soup, roast lamb with fresh vegetables, and queen of puddings, followed by cheese, fresh fruit and coffee.

In front of the house is a small stone-walled garden with poppies and peonies, and an old laburnum bowing low over its iron gates. A serene spot (slightly marred by telephone wires and a bright green plaque) in which to take one's tea or coffee.

Biggin is near the centre of the Peak District, 1000 feet up where the air is pure and fresh. Scenery is the main attraction here, but most visitors also go to see sights like the spa town of Buxton and varied attractions in or near it such as a museum with walk-through caves and barrows; the old lime kilns in Miller's Dale; the Micrarium – insects under 40 microscopes; country park with view from 1500 feet up, interpretation centre and a cave with stalactites; and a steam railway centre.

Northward are the great peak of Kinder Scout and Glossop where you will find another railway, a heritage centre and a scenic group of five reservoirs. On the way is Chapel-en-le-Frith with its sanctuary for owls and otters.

Westward lies Matlock, to the more famous attractions of which have been added craft workshops in Caudwell's mill (water-powered) where you can take tea while enjoying the lovely view; two country parks particularly suitable for children (High Tor: caves, views – and Gulliver's Kingdom: royal cave, dinosaur trail, etc.); a big aquarium; and the wildlife park at Riber Castle.

Readers' comments: A wonderful weekend; warmly greeted, gorgeous furniture. The Moffetts are friendly, humorous and jovial. Warm and welcoming.

BIRCHES MILL

C(11) **D S X**

Clun, Shropshire, SY7 8NL   Tel: 05884 409
West of Ludlow. Nearest main road: A488 from Knighton to Bishops Castle.

3 Bedrooms. £13–£16.50 (less for 3 nights mid-week). Prices go up in March. Bargain breaks. Views of garden, river. Washing machine on request.
Dinner. A la carte or £9 for 3 courses (with choices) and coffee, at 7.30pm. Vegetarian or special diets if ordered. Wine can be brought in.
1 Sitting-room. With central heating, TV.
Large garden

On the secluded valley banks of a trout river stands a 17th-century, ivy-covered watermill, its working days long over. Now it is the home of Avis and Peter Ades, beautifully converted to provide accommodation for guests. The sitting-room still has the old flagged floor and stone walls, but now with a thick Indian carpet, and deep leather armchairs drawn up around the fire. Glass doors open onto waterside lawns. The loudest sounds are the slow tick of a grandfather clock within and the frothing weir without. There is a large rock garden (with plants for sale – primulas are a speciality), and all around grow fritillaries, ragged robin, crocuses and orchids. This is an area particularly rich in wildflowers. (The miller's cottage is used as an annexe. It has its own TV, armchairs and tea-making facilities.)

In the beamed dining-room there is still an old range in the stone fireplace. Here Avis serves, on handsome Royal Worcester porcelain, meals using organically-grown produce. The choice is wide and her standards are high. There might be a choice of rabbit pâté or onion soufflé soup to start with, and then saddle of lamb accompanied by an onion marmalade. (Guests can also select dishes from an interesting vegetarian menu.) Puddings such as apple pie or brandied prunes (with cream) are followed by cheeses. You can buy some of her jams and marmalade to take home.

Attention to detail is evident in everything from freshly squeezed orange juice at breakfast to the lace or crochet trimmed bedlinen. Altogether there is something idyllic about this isolated spot, the old mill and the Ades' hospitality.

The south (hilly) part of Shropshire is particularly beautiful: A. E. Housman country.

In addition there are some notable buildings to visit, particularly the castles which testify to the unsettled times along the Welsh/English border. Thirteenth-century Stokesay Castle is outstanding, Clun Castle houses a local history museum, Norman Hopton Castle is a picturesque shell and Ludlow Castle an even more impressive ruin. (Ludlow also has historic houses to visit, galleries of crafts and paintings, a superb church with exceptional early glass and carvings, and a history museum: a guide will take you on a walk if you wish.) In the direction of Cleobury Mortimer are the Clee Hills where you can drive to a viewpoint over 1700 feet high, and also Mawley Hall (18th-century). Or head towards Shrewsbury, in which direction is the very popular Acton Scott farm museum where you can see heavy horses at work and other Victorian farming techniques in action.

Readers' comments: Cared for with consideration, in most congenial surroundings. Very comfortable, many amenities; the peace is so special; delicious cooking. Intend to return. Comfort standards are high, dinners most interesting. Courteous, friendly and helpful.

24

THE BLACK HOSTELRY
C D PT

Firmary Lane, Cathedral Precincts, Ely, Cambridgeshire, CB7 4DL
Tel: 0353 662612 (Closed for alterations until May 1991.)
Nearest main road: A10 from Cambridge to Ely.

2 Bedrooms. £18. Bargain breaks. Each has own bath/shower/toilet. Tea/coffee facilities. TV. Views of garden. Washing machine on request.
Small garden

Once Ely Cathedral was at the heart of an extensive network of community services run by monks. Among these was a big infirmary for the sick, and a hostel for travelling monks of the black-robed Benedictine order. Here the Vice-Dean and his wife, Sylvia Green, now have their home.

Some visitors have a suite (sitting/breakfast room and bedroom) distinguished by tremendous Norman arches with dogtooth decoration and carved stone corbels. The great fireplace is 15th-century; the elegant painted panelling (pale green and gold), 18th-century. The bedroom overlooks lawns and vegetable garden, a cedar and an ancient mulberry tree. Through a tiny doorway with pointed arch is the narrowest bathroom I have ever come across (the toilet is downstairs). Furnishings are old-fashioned.

There is another bedroom with bigger bathroom; and guests accommodated here take their breakfast downstairs in the vaulted undercroft with pointed lancet windows, at a Tudor refectory table with 'melon-bulb' legs (which was once used by the Dean and Chapter of the cathedral).

The city still has an 18th-century air, with a particularly attractive riverside walk linking its quays, and also a nature trail with not only birds to be seen but also a fine view of the cathedral. Ely has one of Europe's most glorious cathedrals, a multiplicity of pinnacles and spires outside, lofty vista within, and over the crossing a tremendous octagon from which light flows down.

★ What **OLD EGREMONT HOUSE** lacks in history (it is 'only' three centuries old) it makes up for in the attractive furnishings with which Sheila Friend-Smith has filled it; in the lovely garden; in the fine view of the cathedral; and in moderate prices. One bed-sitting room has a cream carpet and beribboned duvet, sprigged wallpaper and stripped pine furniture. There are armchairs from which to enjoy a view of the winding flower garden; from the other bedroom one sees the neat vegetable garden, and the tennis lawn. The house is full of lovely things to look at: Jeremy's collection of

rear view

clocks, pretty Portuguese tiles in bathrooms, embroideries from Jordan and stone-rubbings from Thailand. Breakfast is served at a big mahogany table; for dinner Sheila recommends The Old Fire Engine, a few minutes' walk away. (The house is at 31 Egremont Street, tel: 0353 663118.) From £15 to £17.

BLACKWATER HOTEL   C D PT X

Church Road, West Mersea, Essex, CO5 8QH   Tel: 020638 3338
South of Colchester. Nearest main road: A12 from Colchester to Chelmsford.

7 Bedrooms. £18.50–£30 (less for 5 nights). Prices go up in February. Bargain breaks. Some have own bath/shower/toilet. Tea/coffee facilities. TV. No smoking. Washing machine on request.
Dinner. A la carte or £16 for 3 courses (with choices) and coffee, from 7pm. Vegetarian or special diets if ordered. Wine can be ordered. **Light suppers** if ordered.
1 Sitting-room. With open fire, central heating. **Bar.**
Small garden
Closed early January to early February.

The coastline here is a wilderness of creeks, islets and estuaries made colourful by the sails of small boats. A causeway now connects Mersea to the mainland, yet it still has the feel of an island with an identity all its own. There are Roman, Saxon and Norman remains – and, of course, the beds of Colchester oysters still flourish as they have done for centuries. Visitors go there, too, for all the usual seaside pleasures, for golf, sea-angling, riding or walking. At nearby Fingringhoe Wick is an outstanding bird reserve, with hides alongside its lakes.

Down a quiet side-street is the creeper-covered Blackwater Hotel. Downstairs, beams and scarlet gingham tablecloths, copper pans and strings of onions, give the dining-room the informal air of a French bistro – these touches are Monique Chapleo's style. Here and in the small sitting-room with its tub chairs there are bowls of roses and pinks. All the bedrooms are very neat and fresh: wallpaper, curtains and bedspreads in matching sprigged patterns; bedheads of cane. Outside is a lawn with seats.

The food cooked by chef Roudesli is excellent, and the wine list is good. One might start with mushrooms champenoises or fish soup, to be followed by steak and kidney pie or calves' liver with mango and shallot sauce and a pudding such as floating island or French apple flan. There is a coffee-room that serves snacks.

Although so near London, there are plenty of rural rides in this part of Essex, and many sights to see within a few miles – such as the timbered village of Coggeshall (with Paycockes, a National Trust house, and antique shops), the historic city of Colchester founded by the Romans before London, St Osyth's Priory and East Bergholt (Constable country). Maldon is very near – an old port still frequented by the great sailing-barges. Here there are also a maritime centre and a collection of vintage cars. The oyster fishery and museum can be visited (tastings, boat trips – phone 0206 384141).

Colchester deserves several revisits because in addition to its more famous features there are in or near it such other sights as Oliver's Orchard (with cider-making as well as fruit-growing to see), Layer Marney Tower with its elaborate Italianate decorations, parrot and snake-handling shows at the zoo, a big steam railway museum, Bourne Mill (NT), two nature reserves (one in the historic Roman River conservation area), and no less than seven excellent museums in the city. West Mersea itself has a good local history museum.

Readers' comments: Charming hostess, excellent dinner and breakfast superb. Excellent cuisine. A real find – quite simply, perfect; charming patronne; superb meals; I don't think we have ever enjoyed a place so much. Outstanding.

26

BLEA TARN HOUSE

CDS

Little Langdale, Cumbria, LA22 9PG   Tel: 09667 614
West of Ambleside. Nearest main road: A593 from Ambleside to Coniston.

3 Bedrooms. £12.50–£13 (less for 4 nights). Prices go up in March. Views of garden, country. Washing machine on request.
Dinner. £6.50 for 3 courses (with choices) and coffee, at 6.30pm. Vegetarian or special diets if ordered. Wine can be brought in.
Light suppers if ordered.
1 Sitting-room. With open fire, central heating.
Small garden

'It seemed a home of poverty and toil', said Wordsworth of Blea Tarn House, but it does not seem at all like that any more, for it is warm and cosy and prettily decorated, with an open fire in the corner of the guests' sitting-cum-dining room. Off it is Sheila Myers' kitchen: she likes to talk to guests while she prepares, as it might be, egg mayonnaise, roast beef, and apple or lemon-meringue pie. She serves classic country dishes, always with two vegetables (usually fresh, occasionally frozen, but never tinned) and two sorts of potatoes. In summer, there will be more in the way of salads, and in cooler weather hotpots and cobblers. Upstairs, the bedrooms are small, but they are quaint and pretty.

Electricity is supplied from a generator, but it is not on all the time – you just have to ask for it to be started (e.g. for shaving).

This is the very heart of the Lake District, for Blea Tarn House sits on its own, high above the Langdales, Great and Little, amid the scenery which has made the area such a draw for centuries – rugged and colourful, and punctuated by famous peaks. Reached by a narrow and twisting road, this is a popular beauty-spot, but it is never excessively crowded with the sightseers who can sometimes detract from such places. From the late afternoon onwards the peace and quiet are unbroken.

A field away from the house is the tarn (small lake), where you can bathe or fish.

Readers' comments: Comfortable atmosphere, friendliness, good food. Delightful cottage and situation: an experience we would not have missed for anything. Excellent: good food, wonderful views, nice atmosphere. Characterful.

TONGUE GHYLL near Grasmere (tel: 09665 571) is more spacious: a 17th-century house once the home of the county's High Sheriff. From Mrs Dixon's rooms and pretty garden (with streams) there are mountain views – a path leads up to Helvellyn. B & B only. From £14 to £15.

BOOT FARM   C(10) **PT X**
Southend, Bradfield, Berkshire, RG7 6ES   Tel: 0734 744298
West of Reading. Nearest main road: M4 (junction 12).

4 Bedrooms. £16–£17.50 (less for 3 nights). Prices go up during summer. Bargain breaks. Some have own shower/toilet. Tea/coffee facilities. TV. Views of garden, country. No smoking. Washing machine on request.
Light suppers if ordered. No smoking.
1 Sitting-room. With open fire, central heating, record-player. No smoking.
Large garden

Some of the best cream is produced on this farm, which you may enjoy at high tea, a filling and very good value meal of ham salad, omelette or Welsh rarebit followed by home-made cakes and jams. (Patricia Dawes recommends the Bladebone or the Royal Oak for those who want a full dinner.)

There is a large and very comfortable sitting-room, its pastel fabrics complementing peach walls, a log fire blazing on cold days, casements open to the garden in summer. Bedrooms are attractive and the bathroom is exceptional; toilet as well as bath has a flowery pattern. In the dining-room hand-stitched roses on tapestry chairs are part of an all-pink colour scheme.

Visitors come for the open-air theatre of Bradfield College, for the trout lakes, to ride, or for the many golf courses in the county. East Berkshire has been described under other entries; to the west lies picturesque Hungerford, famous for its scores of antique shops (many open even on Sundays). Nearby are the windswept heights of the Berkshire Downs where racehorses train, and you can walk along the prehistoric Ridgeway Path. The sites of Iron Age forts or burial mounds dot the area. The Kennet Valley is in complete contrast – fertile meadows with birch and oak woods beyond, a great area for birdwatchers. The villages here have flint-and-brick cottages roofed with thatch. In and around both Lambourn and Newbury are historic buildings (the latter has a racecourse and a theatre in a converted watermill), stately homes and pretty villages. In this area is Littlecote (stately home with a Cromwellian armoury, jousting and other sights). London, Windsor, Oxford, Pangbourne and Henley are all within easy reach.

Further south, at Woolhampton is mediaeval **BRIDGE COTTAGE** (tel: 0734 713138), so-called because it is right beside a bridge over the old Kennet & Avon Canal. Jill Thornley has furnished the house pleasantly and from its windows you can see the boats going by (or take out Jill's canoes yourself). Breakfast is served in the low-beamed kitchen or in the walled garden. For dinner there is the nearby Rowbarge Inn. £17.50.

BOUCHERS

Bentham, Gloucestershire, GL51 5TZ Tel: 0452 862373
South-west of Cheltenham. Nearest main road: A46 from Cheltenham to
Stroud.

2 Bedrooms. £10.50. TV. Views of garden,
country. No smoking.
1 Sitting-room. With open fire, central heating, TV. No smoking.
Large garden

Once a farmhouse, Bouchers is still surrounded by hayfields just beyond the
garden, where rock doves fly across the lawns to a graceful weeping willow. A
sundial on one wall declares the date of the house, 1661, and of the old cider-house
which is now Bruce's workshop.

Inside all is immaculate and very comfortable, and you will get a warm welcome
from Anne Daniels as you step through the front door straight into the big
U-shaped living-room. Here plenty of velvet armchairs are grouped round the
hearth where an open fire crackles in winter, and a grandfather clock ticks the time
away. Round the other side of the U is the dining-room, for breakfast only (visitors
eat other meals at local inns or at one of the innumerable restaurants in
Cheltenham, which is also near).

Bentham, on the edge of the Cotswolds, is close to the route south to Bath.
Gloucester with its cathedral, historic Cirencester (don't miss the Roman
museum) and the Forest of Dean are all within easy reach, as are Prinknash Abbey
and the Wye Valley. Also in the area are Slimbridge Wildfowl Trust, Westonbirt
Arboretum, Badminton House (a Palladian mansion, where the Queen is often
seen at the spring horse trials), 12th-century Berkeley Castle in its lovely grounds.
Cheltenham and Tewkesbury are both near.

The Cotswolds is a rich hunting-ground for antique collectors and there is an
illustrated guide to about 50 of its antique shops (with map, on which to base a
tour) obtainable from the Cotswold Antique Dealers Association – tel:
0386 700280. This describes the speciality of each shop, its opening hours and
(briefly) the sightseeing possibilities nearby.

Cheltenham has many such shops – and others of every conceivable kind. Its
Regency houses date from its heyday as a fashionable spa: the Duke of Wellington
regularly came here whenever rheumatism or the affairs of state got him down.
The town needs repeated visits to see everything: the birthplace of composer
Gustav Holst, the Pump Room (where you still can 'take the waters'), the elegant
Promenade and Montpelier area, 14th-century church, distinguished art gallery,
very lovely gardens and Pittville Park (costume museum). Racegoers throng here
at Gold Cup time; others come for various arts festivals.

Readers' comments: Service excellent – the sort for which you would expect to pay
double the price. Will go there again. Very satisfied.

Masons Lane, Bradford-on-Avon, Wiltshire, BA15 1QN   Tel: 02216 6842

East of Bath (Avon). Nearest main road: A363 from Bath to Trowbridge.

4 Bedrooms. £18–£25 (less for 7 nights). Prices go up in March. Bargain breaks. Some have own bath/shower/toilet. Tea/coffee facilities. TV. Views of garden, country. No smoking. Washing machine on request. **Dinner.** £15 for 2 or 3 vegetarian courses and coffee, at 8pm. Non-residents not admitted. Special diets if ordered. Wine can be brought in. No smoking. **Light suppers** if ordered.

1 Sitting-room. With open fire, central heating. No smoking.

Small garden

The Napoleonic wars brought prosperity to this area (where cloth for uniforms was woven) but with peace came depression. As a result, the baker who in 1807 had built a windmill here went broke. In 1817 the mill ceased to function, and its sails and machinery were removed. Today its stump is simply a very unusual stone house, perched on a hillside within picturesque Bradford-on-Avon. From it there is a view full of interest, overlooking a higgledy-piggledy array of old roofs.

It is now in the imaginative care of Peter and Priscilla Roberts, a much -travelled couple (engineer and teacher) who have brought back finds from the Far East, New Zealand, Tahiti and Australia which now decorate the rooms – as do pictures and mementoes of their other enthusiasms, from canal boats to whales.

Every room has its own character and shape: some are circular. In the sitting-room, William Morris sofas and furniture of stripped pine face a log fire and there are maps on the walls. One bedroom (with the best roofscape view of all, through a pair of deep-set pointed windows) has a circular bed with a spread patterned with wildflowers and butterflies. In another, there are windmill pictures, arrangements of dried flowers and tea things laid out on top of an old barrel. Draped Tahitian fabrics contrast with pieces of driftwood, and there is even a water-bed covered with a patchwork bedspread.

Their cooking, too, is eclectic (even breakfasts are imaginative, with such options as hash browns, muffins or croissants, and home-made yogurts). For dinner, you may be able to try recipes from all over the world – Thailand and Nepal, in particular. If you are offered a Thai meal you might enjoy a menu that includes eggs in a spicy coconut sauce; fresh green or purple broccoli stir-fried in sesame oil and spiced with ginger; bananas baked in citrus juices and honey, garnished with toasted almonds. Less exotic dinners are normally available too, but must be booked in advance.

There is a tiny, Victorian-style garden around the foot of the mill stump and from it one gets a good view of Bradford's notable buildings – a panorama that includes a colossal 14th-century tithe barn, river bridge with one-cell prison actually on it, and an 18th-century cloth mill. The Roberts may take you on a tour of the newly restored sail gallery.

Readers' comments: Everything you could want. Very friendly, I thoroughly enjoyed my visit.

★ **BRADLEY FOOT**   **C D S**
Ousby, Cumbria, CA10 1QA   Tel: 0768 81778
North-east of Penrith. Nearest main road: A686 from Penrith to Alston.

2 Bedrooms. £9.50 (less for 3 nights). Prices go up in April. Bargain breaks. Tea/coffee facilities. Views of garden, country. No smoking. Washing machine on request. **Dinner.** £6.50 for 4 courses (with choices) and coffee, at 6–9pm. Non-residents not admitted. Vegetarian or special diets if ordered. Wine can be brought in. **Light suppers** only if ordered.
1 Sitting-room. With open fire, central heating, TV, piano, record-player.
Small garden

With soil almost as red as that of Devon, the Eden Valley takes its name from the famous salmon river which runs between the Pennines and the Lake District into the Solway Firth. In the central stretch – the East Fellside – narrow roads little used by tourists switchback their way over streams and past woods from one quiet village to another, skirting fertile fields bounded by hedges or walls.

Bradley Foot – a 250-year-old 'listed' farmhouse – is the home of John and Meryl Durdy. They have extended the house into the attached barn, the ground floor of which is their guests' sitting-room. The big elliptical arch where once were the barn doors has been glazed to give a view of the cobbled yard with a real well in the middle. Opposite the wood stove, on one of the cream-painted rough stone walls, hangs a North African tapestry of the kind which Meryl plans to import. And on the wall of the adjoining dining-room, which is furnished with Victorian antiques, is a collection of button hooks, neatly arranged in order of size.

John Durdy was a farm manager and though he is now in the feed business, the Durdys keep a cow to supply their guests with cream and butter. Meryl grows many of the fruits and vegetables which go into meals such as celery soup, roast chicken, and blackberry pie.

Views here are striking, from the Lake District peaks on one side to Cross Fell – the highest point of the Pennine chain – on the other, with conical volcanic hills below it. This is pleasant country for undemanding walks, and there is plenty to see within relaxed motoring distance.

Readers' comments: Very pleasant and very hospitable; vast meals.

At **THE GATEHOUSE**, Melmerby, an old toll cottage on the Penrith-Alston road, Lorna Egan has two rooms, one with sunbed and television set. She serves bed-and-breakfast only, but yards away is the Shepherds' Inn for particularly good pub meals. Opposite is a well known wholefood bakery with crafts gallery. Both overlook the  village green. (Tel: 0768 81571.) £11.50 to £14.50.

★ **BRAMWOOD**   C PT S X

19 Hallgarth, Pickering, North Yorkshire, YO18 7AW   Tel: 0751 74066
On A169 from Malton to Whitby.

rear view

6 Bedrooms. £11–£15 (less for 7 nights). Prices go up in March. Bargain breaks. Some have shower. Tea/coffee facilities. No smoking.
Dinner. £7 for 3 courses and coffee, at 6.30pm. Non-residents not admitted. Vegetarian or special diets if ordered. Wine can be brought in. No smoking.
1 Sitting-room. With open fire, central heating, TV. No smoking.
Small garden

The best approach to this 18th-century guest-house is from the back, through an old archway built for coaches – racks for the horses' tack and an old forge still survive, but beyond what was once the stable yard there is now a pretty and secluded garden, with clematis scrambling up old walls and an apple tree; in one part vegetables are grown for the table.

All the bedrooms are immaculate, some of them spacious. and many have cane rocking-chairs – a nice touch. The white-and-green and cream-and-blue colour schemes downstairs are tranquil and refreshing. Ann Lane, who used to enjoy cooking 'for recreation', has put her enthusiasm to good use here, providing visitors with such meals as egg and mushroom bake, pork medallions served with sage-and-apple sauce, and Yorkshire curd tart. She finds old-fashioned puddings are very popular with guests, particularly at the end of a strenuous day's walking, cycling, birdwatching or even gliding. Her home-made chutneys and marmalades are on sale.

In the vicinity are lovely Staindale and many moorland villages tucked away which are well worth seeking. Lastingham, for instance, which has fountain and crypt dating back to the 11th century. Two hundred years ago, its inn, the Blacksmiths' Arms, was run by its curate: when the bishop objected, he said he had thirteen children to support! Thornton Dale is very picturesque: trout swim in the clear stream that curves through the village and under the little footbridges that lead to each 17th- or 18th-century house and its flowery cottage-garden. Hutton-le-Hole, which has the region's folk museum, was once a refuge for persecuted Quakers. Through the middle of its cluster of pale stone houses is a ravine carved by a stream that descends, with cascades, from the high moors near Rosedale Abbey.

This area has some of the most spectacular abbey ruins: Rievaulx, Byland, etc. In 1536 over 800 monasteries flourished in Britain; by 1540 Henry VIII had the whole lot destroyed or closed. In the north's loveliest of solitary places were sited great abbeys built in the Cistercians' heyday (the 12th century). Some were wealthy and owned vast lands, but monastic life was already in decline when Henry helped himself to their properties.

When looking round these ruins it is hard to imagine them bustling with monks, pilgrims and beggars seeking bed and board, scholars in their libraries and schools, and the comings-and-goings of any big property-owning institution – all combined with ceaseless prayer, seven church services a day, and observance of St Benedict's strict Rule (no meat, no baths, no letters, no idleness).

Readers' comments: Excellent food, friendly. Lovely rooms.

BRATTLE HOUSE

C(12) **PT S**

Cranbrook Road, Tenterden, Kent, TN30 6UL   Tel: 05806 3565
Nearest main road: A28 from Ashford to Hastings.

rear view

3 Bedrooms. £17.50–£22.50 (less for 3 nights). Bargain breaks. All have own shower/toilet. Tea/coffee facilities. Views of garden, country. No smoking. Washing machine on request.
Dinner. £12.50 for 4 courses and coffee, at 7.30pm. Non-residents not admitted. Vegetarian or special diets if ordered. Wine can be brought in. No smoking. **Light suppers** if ordered.
1 Sitting-room. With central heating. No smoking.
Large garden

Reputedly this was once the home of Horatia, illegitimate but much-loved daughter of Nelson and Lady Hamilton (who was only five when Nelson died).

The tile-hung house (parts of which date back to the 17th century) has great dignity – white marble fireplace from the 18th century; wide, panelled doors with handsome brass fittings; bay windows with leaded casements. The Rawlinsons, who are a painter and a calligrapher (Alan's pictures and examples of Maureen's calligraphy hang on the walls), have furnished the rooms in suitable style with, for instance, a pale thick carpet contrasting with the moss-green of the old, silk-weave wallcovering and many pot-plants everywhere. Armchairs grouped around a picture-window have a view of lawn, roses and trees.

Bedrooms are equally handsome. There is a very big room at the front with a window-seat, brick hearth, and draped bedheads. Another also has window-seats – from which to enjoy a view of the church where Horatia's husband was vicar, and of the preserved steam train which occasionally puffs by: a scene at its most lovely when the sun goes down. Yet another is all roses and cream (fabrics, bedlinen and wallpaper), with a little black iron grate, sloping floors, and an old brick chimney thrusting up through its bathroom.

Although the Rawlinsons are themselves vegetarian, Maureen cooks such four-course meals as brandied tomatoes, beef olives (with garden vegetables), spiced peach flambé, and cheeses. They usually dine with their guests.

Tenterden, an interesting old town itself, is in the middle of an area full of things to see and do and is an agreeable place in which to shop. Within easy reach are the castles of Chilham and Bodiam. Elegant Tunbridge Wells also has shops (antiques, books, crafts, clothes boutiques) and a new heritage centre.

Readers' comments: Excellent service. Tasty and imaginative food. Elegant, gracious house in beautiful countryside.

At the quieter end of Tenterden's High Street is **WEST CROSS HOUSE** (tel: 05806 2224), a small 18th-century guest-house with antiques in the big sitting-room and simply furnished bedrooms. Mrs May provides such meals as home-made celery soup, steak pie and home-made ice cream (order meals in advance). From £14 to £15.

BROADWATER

C D PT S

Woodbridge Road, Framlingham, Suffolk, IP13 9LL   Tel: 0728 723645

West of Saxmundham. Nearest main road: A1120 from Stowmarket to Yoxford.

5 Bedrooms. £15–£17 (less for 2 nights). Prices go up in April. Some have own bath/shower/toilet. Tea/coffee facilities. Views of garden, country. No smoking.
Dinner. £10 for 3 courses and coffee, at 7pm. Non-residents not admitted. Vegetarian or special diets if ordered. Wine can be ordered. No smoking.
1 Sitting-room. With open fire, central heating, TV, piano. No smoking.
Large garden

I came away with a case of white wine – for Broadwater is a name you will find on wine labels: it consists of a vineyard and an 18th-century house, once a shooting-lodge. You can drink the wine at dinner here, in a pleasant green-and-white room. Sheila Stocker serves such meals as courgettes in cheese sauce; fish pie containing smoked haddock and prawns; summer pudding. Vegetables and fruit usually come from the garden. Big cretonne armchairs are grouped round a log fire in the sitting-room, which has windows all round with views of woodland where nightingales sing, occasional rabbits, horses and Jacob sheep. Sheila Stocker's garden is sometimes opened to the public for charity: a 70-year-old yew hedge divides it into rose, iris and well gardens and a 'long walk'.

The bedrooms are well furnished – even the single rooms, which is not always the case – and one has a four-poster bed. One of the toilets is rightly nicknamed 'the throne room': a real museum-piece!

The most popular places to visit near here are Framlingham and Orford castles, Woodbridge, Easton Farm Park and Bruisyard vineyard. Notcutts, Helmingham and Charlsfield attract garden-lovers. In summer, music-lovers are drawn to the various recitals and concerts which form part of the annual Aldeburgh Music Festival, started by Benjamin Britten.

To the north is the old market town of Bungay, with the massive remains of a Norman castle and an aviation museum with 16 historic aircraft; while near the old-fashioned resort of Lowestoft (the other half of it is a busy fishing-port around which there are conducted tours) is East Anglia's big transport museum with working trams, etc.

Westward are the Water Garden Centre at Mickfield where there are large displays of fish; Norton's tropical bird gardens; and tropical butterflies and song-birds at Barrow.

In the opposite direction you come to a particularly scenic 'heritage' coastline, the remains of 14th-century Leiston Abbey, Leiston's 'Long Shop' of 1853 (where steam engines were produced – many now on display) and Sizewell's information centre about electricity generating. Dunwich is a village that the sea has been steadily devouring since Roman times (the story is told in its little museum), and at Orford you can see an exhibition about the current underwater explorations of the submerged buildings.

If you go further afield, you will find Thetford – its architecture begins with Saxon remains and the riverside walks here are particularly attractive.

Readers' comments: Beautiful surroundings, relaxed air, good food, and, above all, very good company.

BROOKFIELD FARM HOTEL   C D PT X

Plummers Plain, West Sussex, RH13 6LO   Tel: 0403 891568
South-east of Horsham. Nearest main road: A281 from Horsham to Brighton.

rear view

25 Bedrooms. £17.50–£30. Prices go up in October. Bargain breaks. All have own bath/shower/toilet. Tea/coffee facilities. TV. Views of garden, country, lake. Washing machine on request.
Dinner. A la carte, at 6.30–9pm. Vegetarian or special diets if ordered. Wine can be ordered.
1 Sitting-room. With open fire, central heating, TV, record-player. **Bar.**
Large garden. Swimming-pool, croquet.

Over the years, John Christian has added to and improved his farmhouse extensively, creating a busy, small hotel (his sons farm the surrounding land). Apart from the well-equipped bedrooms of differing size – one on the ground floor – and the comfortable sitting-room with its open fire and array of brass and copper, there are now several dining areas, a bar opening out to the garden, a billiards room, a sauna and small gym, and a big play area at one side for children – who can also enjoy paddle boats on the lake and riding the donkeys. There is golf-driving.

John himself travels the world (broadcasting on farming): when at home, he is a blunt but very interesting person to talk to. Carol manages the hotel for him, and although she employs several chefs, she sets high standards of home-style cooking – on various occasions I have enjoyed a filling soup with home-cured ham in it, a really good steak pie, a beautifully presented and copious prawn cocktail which puts the average restaurant offering to shame, and much else.

Travellers using Gatwick appreciate the convenience (and economy) of parking their car at Brookfield while away; and, no matter how early or late their flight, the Brookfield minibus takes them to or from the airport. Honeymooners like the four-poster suite with bubble bath for at least their first night of wedded bliss!

Readers' comments: Cheerful surroundings, friendly hospitality.

An elegant Victorian house, **WESTLANDS** on Brighton Road at Monk's Gate, has been very well furnished by Kathleen Ticktum, with much emphasis on light colours and complete comfort at moderate prices. (Tel: 0403 891383.) There is a very lovely flower garden with terrace and lily-pool (floodlit at night). A good choice for anyone who values peace, spaciousness and high standards, but only b & b provided: there are nearby inns and

hotels for meals. Parking (and taxi-service) available for visitors flying from Gatwick. £17.50 to £19. *Readers' comments:* Immaculate. Friendly.

35

BROOKLAND

C S

Peacock Lane, Middle Tysoe, Warwickshire, CV35 0SG   Tel: 029588 202
South-east of Stratford-upon-Avon. Nearest main road: A422 from
Stratford-upon-Avon to Banbury.

3 Bedrooms. £12.50 (less for 7 nights). Prices go up in March. Bargain breaks. Tea/coffee facilities. Views of garden, country. No smoking. Washing machine on request. **Dinner.** £9.50 for 3 courses (with choices) and coffee, at 7pm. Non-residents not admitted. Vegetarian or special diets if ordered. Wine can be brought in. No smoking. **Light suppers** if ordered.
1 Sitting-room. With open fire, central heating, TV, record-player.
Small garden

The first battle of the Civil War was fought nearby at Edgehill (in 1642, not long before this cottage was built), a dramatically sharp ridge on the border of Oxfordshire and a fine car-drive today. Charles I narrowly missed a defeat that could have prevented his army from moving on to London and all the long struggles which followed until he was beheaded in 1649. It is difficult to imagine such violent deeds while enjoying this tranquil spot today.

When I visited Brookland, my first impression was of flowers everywhere, butterflies thronging the tall yellow spires of verbascum, stone troughs brimming with colourful blooms. There is a little sun-lounge where one can sit under a vine to enjoy the morning sunshine, while inside grandfather clocks tick peacefully. The old stone cottage still retains many of its original features, such as the tinderbox cupboard built into an inglenook fireplace; and Topsy Trought has furnished the dining-room with carved, cane chairs in William-and-Mary style.

Topsy makes wedding- and birthday-cakes for local families, but it is Tim who does the elaborate and colourful decorations of sugar fruit and vegetables. The Troughts' niece is Rosemary Nunnely whose cooking (see **Sugarswell Farm**) so many readers of past editions of this book have praised highly; and it seems that good cooking is a family accomplishment. Topsy says her most popular meal is a peach-and-pineapple starter, gamekeeper's casserole and loganberry mousse.

As to sightseeing, most visitors head first – of course – for Stratford-upon-Avon but Warwick and its castle, Leamington Spa and Coventry (for its cathedral) are all near. This is good walking country, too, with footpaths to Edgehill.

In Stratford tourists usually start by visiting Shakespeare's well-preserved birthplace in Henley Street and his grave in Holy Trinity church beside the river and its swans. New Place is the house where he finally lived and wrote 'The Tempest' (a charming Tudor knot garden adjoins it); Hall's Croft, my favourite, was the home of his daughter and son-in-law – a doctor. There is, of course, the Royal Shakespeare Company's theatre; and in the nearby village of Shottery is his wife's childhood home, always known as 'Anne Hathaway's Cottage' even though it is a house of some size. Through it all the Avon winds its way, 'pearl-paved and with blue-eyed deeps' (in the words of Michael Drayton). Tysoe is named after the same Saxon god whose name was given to Tuesday.

Readers' comments: Outstanding. Most beautiful and interesting.

BROOKSIDE   C
Lustleigh, Devon, TQ13 9TJ   Tel: 06477 310
South of Moretonhampstead. Nearest main road: A382 from Newton Abbot to
Moretonhampstead.

3 Bedrooms. £14.50–£16.50. Tea/coffee
facilities. Views of garden, country, river.
No smoking. Washing machine on request.
Light suppers if ordered. Wine can be
brought in.
1 Sitting-room. With central heating, TV.
Small garden

rear view

A show village of the Dartmoor National Park, Lustleigh is sometimes crowded
with sightseers – but even then Brookside, well tucked away, is peaceful. It looks
across its garden to the village cricket field: the visitors' TV room upstairs has a
balcony where one can watch matches being played.

The landscaped garden is raised up on what was once a railway embankment.
Round it winds the River Wrey, and one can sit above its waters on the little bridge
across which trains once puffed their way. As a backdrop to all this are the high
moors where the famous Dartmoor ponies roam free.

One enters the old house through a combined sitting/breakfast room, which has
a great granite hearth (with wood stove) at one end. A twisting stair rises to
bedrooms which Jennifer Bell has furnished in simple cottage style. The house was
originally twin dwellings belonging to a 15th-century farm, now the Cleave Inn
(and as this serves good dinners, Jennifer provides breakfast only).

In winter, the artistic Bells run painting weekends; and also guided moorland
walks, for this is an excellent area for walking. (And for birdwatching: among 67
species spotted by one visitor were whinchats, ring ouzels, pied flycatchers,
woodwarblers and rock pipits.)

Lustleigh has an ancient history: there are prehistoric remains, King Alfred
bequeathed it to his youngest son and its church is in part 13th-century. All around
are thatched cottages and a landscape threaded with bubbling streams and
primrose paths. The road to Manaton is particularly scenic.

Also in the Dartmoor National Park is
an exceptionally pretty, 450-year-old
cottage of white walls and thatch:
CORBYNS BRIMLEY, Higher
Brimley, near Bovey Tracey (tel:
0626 833332). It has been attractively
furnished by Hazel White in a style that
is in keeping with its age. B & b and
snack suppers. Visitors may eat at the
Toby Jug, Bickington; the Rumbling
Tum, Bovey Tracey; or the Rock Inn,
Haytor Vale. From £15 to £16. *Read-*

ers' comments: Superb views, splendid
accommodation, caring proprietors;
shall return again and again.

BROWNHILL HOUSE

C PT S

Ruyton XI Towns, Shropshire, SY4 1LR   Tel: 0939 260626

South-east of Oswestry. Nearest main road: A5 from Shrewsbury to Oswestry.

3 Bedrooms. £10–£13 (less for 7 nights). Prices go up in April. Bargain breaks. Tea/coffee facilities. TV. Views of garden, country, river. Clothes-washing on request. **Dinner.** A la carte, at 6.30pm. Vegetarian or special diets if ordered. Wine can be brought in. No smoking. **Light suppers** if ordered. **1 Sitting-room.** With open fire, central heating, TV.

Large garden

It is the garden which brings most visitors here. Although when they moved in Roger and Yoland Brown had not the slightest interest in gardening, within a few years the potential of the large, steep site had converted them into enthusiasts and then experts – despite the fact that thin soil and a north-facing aspect were anything but propitious. Brambles, nettles and the remains of a scrapyard had to be cleared, and the slope terraced.

Undaunted by all this, they created an outstanding garden – or, rather, a series of gardens. By the use of steps, paths, walls and banks they have provided a variety of experiences for the visitor – here a paved walk, there wild woodland, 500 different shrubs, 20 kinds of fruit or nut, a vegetable garden with glasshouses. They visit great gardens here and abroad, coming home with new ideas: a Roman garden with pond and gazebo; a Thai miniature garden; a laburnum walk inspired by one at Bodnant; parterres, walks, follies, rock gardens, statuary and a bog garden, all contributing different scenes which unfold as one wanders around. At the foot is the River Perry (free fishing available). Plants are on sale.

As to the house itself, the bedrooms are comfortable but basic; redecorated annually. The beamed sitting-room has a huge stone fireplace. Meals are served in the large farmhouse-style kitchen, and may comprise such things as soup made from the garden's vegetables or salade niçoise, stuffed pork with a crisp crumb coating, and a compôte of garden fruit. Breakfasts are exceptional. Fruit juice will be freshly squeezed (from the Browns' own berries or peaches, for example), ten items go into the main course, bread is baked in the village and jams are home-made by Yoland. Pancakes, omelettes and home-made fishcakes are also available. (There is one drawback to Brownhill House: milk-lorries pass by in the morning, so earplugs are provided).

The curious name of the village has a simple explanation – 11 small settlements were amalgamated in about 1155. Yoland has written a lively book about the history of Ruyton XI Towns, which you can buy. She starts 200 million years ago when the red sandstone was laid down which now gives distinctive character to houses in this area. Here, Normans built a castle, water-mills and church; by the 14th century Ruyton had a weekly market (and a court) – no longer, alas; it became involved in the border wars with Wales, 15th century, and the Civil War, 17th century; Conan Doyle worked here as a doctor in 1878. Altogether, this scarcely known corner of Shropshire has had a rich and varied past.

★ **BUCKNELL HOUSE** C(12) **D PT S**
Bucknell, Shropshire, SY7 0AD Tel: 05474 248
West of Ludlow. Nearest main road: A4110 from Hereford to Knighton.

3 Bedrooms. £13–£14.50 (less for 3 nights). Tea/coffee facilities. TV. Views of garden, country. Washing machine on request. **Light suppers** if ordered. Vegetarian or special diets if ordered. Wine can be brought in.

1 Sitting-room. With open fire, central heating, TV, piano, record-player. **Large garden** **Closed in December and January.**

In the early 18th century, the clergy lived well: this huge and handsome house, honeysuckle and wisteria clambering up its walls, was a vicarage then. The vicar would have approved of the equally handsome way in which Brenda Davies has furnished it – the dining-room with Sheraton chairs and fine wallpaper; the sitting-room with big velvet armchairs, curtains of pale green silk, a large gilt mirror over the Adam fireplace, cream brocade wallpaper and alcoves of fine china; flowers everywhere. Bedrooms are just as good, with lovely country views towards Wales. All are spacious; one has antique furniture, pretty floral fabrics and wicker armchairs. The shared bathroom is huge. There are family touches everywhere.

Breakfasts here are substantial (the honey is home-produced) and Brenda is sometimes also willing to provide extremely filling light suppers (home-made soup, lasagne and salad, followed by cheese or a dessert).

The grounds (garden and water meadows) are secluded, looking across the valley of the River Teme to Wales. There are rosebeds, daffodil drive, shrubbery, croquet lawn, a hard tennis court, shooting, and fishing in the river. The Davies' also keep ducks and geese, horses and hens. The surrounding woodlands and hills are full of wildlife.

Visitors come to this part of the country to enjoy the peace, the birdwatching opportunities and the many good walks there are in the vicinity – across grouse moors and the nearby Welsh and Shropshire hills, along the Elan Valley, and the old coaching road to Devil's Bridge and Aberystwyth, where you may also spot the now-rare red kite. Both Brenda and Peter Davies were born in the area and their enthusiasm for the countryside around here is infectious. They are happy to advise on the best places to head for and there is a wealth of tourist literature in the house to browse through or buy. Some guests who stayed here were even taken by Peter on a midnight ride to see rabbits by moonlight!

Readers' comments: Wonderfully comfortable bed, breakfast an ample repast, some of the most beautiful countryside in England. Such excellence and outstanding amenities; marvellous people. Pleasant welcome. Warmth and comfort. Delightful couple; nothing was too much trouble. Looked after us splendidly.

BUCKYETTE

Littlehempston, Devon, TQ9 6ND   Tel: 080 426 638

North of Totnes. Nearest main road: A381 from Newton Abbot to Totnes.

6 Bedrooms. £12 (less for 7 nights). Prices go up in June. Some have own bath/shower/toilet. Tea/coffee facilities. Views of garden, country. Washing machine on request.
Dinner. £7 for 3 courses (with choices) and coffee, at 6.30pm. Non-residents not admitted. Vegetarian or special diets if ordered. Wine can be ordered.
1 Sitting-room. With open fire, TV, piano.
Small garden
Closed from October to March inclusive.

The curious name of this house appears in the Domesday Book and is believed to be a Saxon word meaning 'head of a spring': the spring is still there, and in use. The present building, made from stone quarried on the farm, dates from 1860. It is on a commanding site with far views, and is furnished with Edwardian pieces suited to the scale of the lofty rooms. In the sitting-room is a log fire for chilly days, and for sunny ones tall French doors open onto a wisteria-hung verandah. The peppermint-pink dining-room has particularly handsome tables, which Roger Miller himself made from timber on the estate, and pictures of theatrical costumes. Bedrooms are not elegant but comfortable.

Elizabeth Miller serves such meals as lentil soup, chicken in a crisp cheese-and-garlic coating and queen of puddings; with home-baked bread. The garden provides asparagus, strawberries and other produce. Everything about the house is solid, comfortable, unpretentious, and very English. Children are particularly welcome.

Littlehempston is well placed for a family holiday because the safe sands of Torbay are so near – as are Paignton's zoo, miniature gardens, a scenic steam railway and river trips. There are plenty of inns, theatres and concerts including those at Dartington's celebrated arts and crafts centres. Totnes has its castle and streets of ancient buildings, with interesting little shops. In the church is an especially fine rood-screen. At Buckfast Abbey the monks sell their wine and honey to visitors; Buckland Abbey was Sir Francis Drake's house. Ashburton is a pretty hill town, with all of Dartmoor beyond – its most famous beauty-spot is Dartmeet where two rivers converge and there is an old 'clapper' bridge of stones by which to cross the water, a typical Devon feature. Widecombe, of 'Uncle Tom Cobleigh' fame, still has its celebrated fair high up on the moor every September. Princetown (large, bleak and weather-beaten) is where the big Dartmoor Prison is, originally built by and for Napoleonic prisoners-of-war. Salcombe and Plymouth are described elsewhere.

The West Country has many prehistoric sites. These are well explained at the Prehistoric Hill Settlement museum near Dartmouth, which even has a reconstructed Stone Age farm. There are several vineyards in the area which welcome visitors.

Readers' comments: Amazingly good welcome. Beautifully served food. Very charming lady – I will go again.

BULMER FARM

Holmbury St Mary, Surrey, RH5 6LG   Tel: 0306 730210
South-west of Dorking. Nearest main road: A25 from Dorking to Guildford.

4 Bedrooms. £13. Bargain breaks. Some have own shower/toilet. Tea/coffee facilities. TV. Views of garden, country, lake. Washing machine on request.
1 Sitting-room. With open fire, TV, record-player.
Large garden

In the folds of Surrey's high North Downs (most of which are so scenic that they are in National Trust protection) a number of very picturesque villages lie hidden, and Holmbury is one. Near the centre stands Bulmer Farm, built about 1680. One steps straight into the large dining-room, and through this to an attractive sitting-room – a room of pink walls and old beams, chairs covered in cretonne patterned with pink poppies, logs crackling in front of the cherubs and harps of an old iron fireback in the inglenook. It opens onto the large garden.

Upstairs are attractive bedrooms with immaculate paintwork and cottage-style furnishings.

Outdoors (where chickens run free among the old rickstones), a Dutch barn is crammed with hay; across the yard is an ancient byre, the tiles of its long, wobbly roof softened with moss. David Hill will show you the lake he created a few years ago, now a haven for herons, kingfishers, Canada geese, snipe and other wildfowl.

Bed-and-breakfast only, but the area is full of inns offering good meals, such as the Royal Oak.

Some tourists find this a good area in which to stay while visiting London – train day-tickets cost very little, and the journey takes three-quarters of an hour (from Dorking).

The surrounding area of woodland and hills is one of the finest beauty-spots near the capital, truly rural, and dotted with stately homes to visit, footpaths to follow, historic churches and villages with craft shops, trout farms, antiques and the like. Dorking and Guildford (the latter with castle ruins, river trips and a good theatre) are each well worth a day's visit. The Royal Horticultural Society's gardens at Wisley are near, too, and so are Box Hill (viewpoint), Leith Hill (walks), Clandon and Polesden Lacey (stately homes). Several fine gardens open to view. Beautiful Shere has monthly antiques' fairs.

If you have children with you, they may enjoy a day at the award-winning 'World of Adventure' attached to Chessington's zoo, or at the leisure park based on a series of lakes at Thorpe Park.

You can go via pleasant lanes to reach Farnham, a largely 18th-century town at the foot of a mound with castle: the local museum has William Cobbett memorabilia, while another (at nearby Tilford) has an open-air display of old agricultural machinery. Birdworld is an exceptionally good park with exotic birds, and attached to it is Underwaterworld with unusual fish.

Readers' comments: One's every wish is catered for. So warm and friendly. Made so welcome, made to feel like one of the family.

BULMER TYE HOUSE

C S

Bulmer Tye, Suffolk, CO10 7ED   Tel: 0787 269315
South-west of Sudbury. Nearest main road: A131 from Halstead to Sudbury.

4 Bedrooms. £15. Some have own bath/toilet. Views of garden. No smoking. Washing machine on request.
Dinner (only if pre-booked). £7.50 for 2 or 3 courses and coffee (time by arrangement). Non-residents not admitted. Vegetarian or special diets if ordered. Wine can be brought in. No smoking. **Light suppers** if ordered.
3 Sitting-rooms. With open fire, central heating, TV, piano, record-player. No smoking.
Large garden

One of Gainsborough's most famous paintings is of the Andrews family whom he knew when he lived in Suffolk. It was one of their sons, a parson, who in the 18th century 'modernized' this house, most of which dates back to the reign of Elizabeth I, by putting in huge sash windows and so forth.

Today its old timbers resonate to the sound of music (played by family or guests), for Peter Owen is a maker of very fine clavichords – and of much of the interesting furniture seen in the rooms. A hexagonal table with a complex pattern of end-grain triangles is his; so is a throne-like chair of elm, its joints secured with wood pegs only; and also a dolls' house – which is in fact a scale replica of Bulmer Tye House itself. Little boxes here and there and eggs in decorative woods are his work too.

His wife is an authority on antique furniture, about which she writes articles for specialist magazines (under the name Noël Riley); so not surprisingly there are some unusual period pieces in the house. Instead of using furnishing fabrics with a traditional look, the Owens have contrasted the antiques with strong modern patterns – a Bauhaus design for curtains in one room, an Aztec-style pattern in another, in colours such as tangerine and blue. A Chinese sunshade, inverted, makes an unusual ceiling light-shade. There is a large Bechstein in one of the sitting-rooms and log fires in all three. In one bedroom, with a handsome bed, 19th-century Persian curtains and a Laura Ashley pattern co-exist happily.

The quarry-tiled kitchen is decorated in brilliant primary colours and on one wall screen-printed Spanish tiles give a *trompe l'oeil* effect. Here guests eat with the family round a huge pine table and are apt to get drawn into family life, including anything from duets to political debates. Garden produce often goes into the making of soups and of fruit puddings; wine, lemonade and elderflower cordial are all home-made and Peter bakes the bread. Some of the dishes guests enjoy most are beef-and-lentil flan, Roman cobbler (pork and mushrooms with a topping of semolina and cheese), fish pie and, for vegetarians in particular, a cheesy bread-and-butter pudding served with stir-fried vegetables. For breakfast, you will be offered home-made muesli, bread and marmalade, as well as free-range eggs (no fry-ups).

The large garden is notable for its fine trees (some are 200 years old) which include copper beeches, walnuts, cedars and yews, as well as a number of unusual plants. There is a grass tennis court.

Readers' comments: Characterful house, beautiful garden, very informal and friendly.

BURGOYNE HOTEL   C D S X

Reeth, North Yorkshire, DL11 6SN   Tel: 0748 84292
West of Richmond. Nearest main road: A6108 from Richmond to Leyburn.

11 Bedrooms. £17.50 (less for 7 nights). Prices go up in March. Bargain breaks. Some have own bath/shower/toilet. Tea/coffee facilities. TV. Views of garden, country. Washing machine on request. **Dinner.** £12 for 4 courses (with choices) and coffee, at 7.30pm. Vegetarian or special diets if ordered. Wine can be ordered. No smoking.
2 Sitting-rooms. With open fire, central heating, TV. Bar.
Small garden

Swaledale is the deepest, widest and loveliest of the Dales. When Pat and Steve Foster (both formerly RAF officers) took over the Burgoyne, they soon raised the standards of rooms in this handsome 18th-century building at the top of Reeth's steeply sloping green, with an old pump just outside.

One sitting-room has a huge arched door and triple-arched stone fireplace; the other, a stone fireplace carved with Burgoyne family crests. (The most famous of the Burgoynes distinguished himself at a vital battle of the Crimean war, when Sebastopol's fort – guarding the harbour where the Russian fleet lay – was bombarded into submission.) The bedrooms now are very pleasant – for instance, one in powder-blue and white has its shower-room in matching colours, and I liked another with a restful green and grey colour scheme: like most, it has spectacular views. The house is unusually well provided with bathrooms.

There is plenty of choice at dinner, and the dishes include some imaginative options – such as spinach roulade (with Boursin cheese filling), salmon with asparagus sauce, coffee fudge pudding and local cheeses. Vegetables, too, are out-of-the-ordinary – fennel in a sauce, Anna potatoes or peas with tiny onions are examples. With coffee, mint fudge is served.

Reeth was once a busy town, a centre for the local industries which, apart from farming, included lead-mining (the relics of this are now scheduled monuments), hand-knitting stockings (men as well as women did this) and peat-digging (the peat was used for smelting the lead). All of this is recorded in Reeth's folk museum, which takes the area's history back to prehistoric times – there are plenty of earthworks to be seen. Across the river is Grinton and the big church known as the 'Cathedral of the Dales'. All around are stone-walled pastures for the curly-horned Swaledale sheep; a Swaledale tup (ram) is in fact the symbol of the Dales National Park.

It is a short drive south from here to the next big dale: Wensleydale, which – like Swaledale itself – is fully described under other entries. Or head north into Teesdale, past the disused lead mines of Arkengarthdale and over the moors (the Tan Hill Inn is the highest in England) to Barnard Castle.

★ **BURLAND FARM** C(10) **D S**
Wrexham Road, Burland, Cheshire, CW5 8ND Tel: 0270 74 210
North-west of Nantwich. On A534 from Nantwich to Wrexham.

3 Bedrooms. £17.50. All have own bath/shower/toilet. Tea/coffee facilities. TV. Views of garden, country.
Dinner. £12.50 for 3 courses (with choices) and coffee, from 7pm. Vegetarian or special diets if ordered. Wine can be brought in.
Light suppers (served in bedrooms).
2 Sitting-rooms. With open fire, central heating, TV, piano.
Small garden

This early Victorian house, surrounded by lawn and trees, is in the pretty *cottage ornée* style that was once fashionable: windows are lozenge-paned, the gable is decorated with woodwork, hinges are of wrought iron. (The lozenge panes are to be seen elsewhere – a feature of many houses on the great Tollemache estate.)

The Allwoods' furnishings complement this well. Their huge dining-table and cupboard were made from oaks felled on the farm, and other antiques have been added, such as spindleback chairs. Colour schemes are pleasant – a pink and grey bedroom, for instance, with a white tapestry bedspread from Portugal.

Sandra likes having visitors as an excuse to use her talent for 'dinner party' cooking. She produces such meals as hot chicken mousse (served with a spring-onion sauce), pork fillet in mustard sauce, blackcurrant sorbet accompanied by home-made biscuits, and then British cheeses. (Snack suppers for late arrivals.) She usually bakes her own bread, and will make American-style muffins for breakfast if requested.

Nearby Nantwich is an old town where black-and-white Tudor houses jostle one another in picturesque streets such as Welsh Row (the carvings inside the church and on the almshouses are well worth seeing). Its prosperity was founded on salt-mining, salt having been deposited here millions of years ago when the sea covered Cheshire. 'Magpie' houses (timbers painted black and plaster white) are characteristic throughout the great plain of Cheshire, a vast area like an immense park, with cows grazing among buttercups, meres shining, tracts of woodland, and rivers flowing peacefully to the sea. This is a historic area which was well populated even before the Romans came here in strength: on hilltops with far views are traces of prehistoric forts. Throughout the county there are historic towns full of character, such as Macclesfield (hilly streets from which you can see right to the Peak District, and old silk-weaving mills), Knutsford (Mrs Gaskell's 'Cranford') and of course Chester itself, described elsewhere. Near Knutsford is the huge radio telescope of Jodrell Bank (there is a visitor centre here). Macclesfield Forest is a vast wild moor, with crags and narrow valleys; at Anderton a lift raises boats from one canal to another (Cheshire is criss-crossed with canals). Also in the vicinity are two of Europe's largest garden centres – Bridgemere Garden World and Stapeley Water Gardens.

Readers' comments: Warmly recommended, lovely airy room, superb meal.

For explanation of code letters (C, D, H, PT, S, X) see page xxxiv.

BUTCHERS ARMS   C(14)
Woolhope, Herefordshire, HR1 4RF   Tel: 043277 281
South-east of Hereford. Nearest main road: A438 from Hereford to Ledbury.

3 Bedrooms. £16.50–£20.50. Bargain breaks. Tea/coffee facilities. TV. Views of country.
Dinner. A la carte. Vegetarian or special diets if ordered. Wine can be ordered. No smoking. **Light suppers.**
Small garden

The sun streamed down from a clear blue sky onto the paved garden where I was lunching; a small stream clattered by and birds were singing. Yet it was mid-November!

The half-timbered Butchers Arms, which dates back to the 14th century, stands among fields that are far from any other building. Nevertheless its excellence is well known to scores of people who, though they live some distance away, beat a path to its door; and the bar was crowded. Even the snacks are outstanding, and the small restaurant is of gourmet standard. Breakfasts too are excellent.

William Griffiths offers a wide repertoire of rather unusual dishes to complement the straightforward Herefordshire beef steaks which are also served. From a wide selection one might, for instance, choose fried clams or a terrine made from tongue, chicken livers and brandy to start with; while main courses often include rabbit-and-bacon pie, pigeon with juniper berries and beef bourguignonne. Vegetarian dishes are imaginative.

In the bar, where an open fire crackles, you must duck to avoid low beams. Dining-room and bedrooms (quiet except over the bar) are furnished simply.

Woolhope is in the middle of a particularly scenic area: the Wye Valley and Symonds Yat are only a few miles away; so are the attractive old towns of Ross-on-Wye, Ledbury, and Hereford with its fine cathedral, big garden centre and cider museum. The Welsh borders, Black Mountains, Forest of Dean and Malvern Hills attract walkers as well as those who enjoy touring by car along traffic-free lanes. There is a falconry centre at Newent and gardens at Hergest Croft. Go in late autumn if you want to see a blaze of copper and gold foliage.

Within an easy drive of the Butchers Arms are Sufton Court, a small Wyatt mansion in Palladian style with grounds laid out by Repton; and the Edwardian gardens of How Caple, its terraces overlooking the River Wye (the church there is also worth a visit). Another garden overhanging the river is at The Weir (NT) which is open when the spring flowers are in bloom. At Much Marcle is a house, Hellens, that has been lived in by the same family since 1692 and is filled with heirloom furnishings.

Readers' comments: Pleasant comfortable room; excellent staff; food extremely good. One of the nicest holidays in years. Excellent value. Outstanding value; excellent bar meals. Excellent food and service. Highly satisfied. Very good on all points.

★ BUTTONS GREEN FARM   C D PT S

Cockfield, Suffolk, IP30 0JF   Tel: 0284 828229
South of Bury St Edmunds. Nearest main road: A1141 from Hadleigh towards
Bury St Edmunds.

3 Bedrooms. £13–£14. Bargain breaks. Tea/coffee facilities. TV. Views of garden, country. Washing machine on request.
Dinner. £7 for 3 courses and coffee, from 6.30pm. Vegetarian or special diets if ordered. Wine can be brought in. **Light suppers** if ordered.
1 Sitting-room. With open fire, central heating, TV.
Large garden
Closed from November until Easter.

Behind a big duckpond and masses of roses stands an apricot-coloured house built around 1400, the centre of an 80-acre farm of grain and beet fields. It has mullioned windows and a Tudor fireplace upstairs.

In the sitting-room, with large sash windows on two sides, a pale carpet and silky wallpaper make a light background to the antiques and velvet armchairs grouped round a big log stove. In one window is an epiphyllum which annually produces over 80 huge pink blooms. The dining-room, too, has a log-burning stove in the brick inglenook, and leather-seated chairs are drawn up at a big oak table. Here Margaret Slater serves meals with home-grown or home-made produce, her own chutneys and marmalade. Among her most popular starters are egg mayonnaise and home-made pâté. A chicken or other roast may follow and then, for instance, chocolate soufflé or raspberries and cream.

Twisting stairs lead to big beamed bedrooms with sloping floors, which Mrs Slater has furnished with flowery fabrics, pot-plants and good furniture.

The farm is only a few minutes from Lavenham, one of the county's show villages – very beautiful (but, in summer, often very crowded), with a guildhall owned by the National Trust and a spectacular church. Still further south, in beautiful countryside threaded by rivers with old bridges and water-meadows, are such other historic villages as Bures (where St Edmund was crowned King of East Anglia in 855) and pretty Kersey, full of colourful half-timbered cottages.

Readers' comments: Lovely house. Charming hosts. Good home cooking. Just perfect.

Just the other side of Lavenham is
★ Brent Eleigh and **STREET FARM** (tel: 0787 247 271), its apricot walls half-timbered, its garden well-groomed. Inside are beamed ceilings and good furnishings – big velvet armchairs, and Hepplewhite-style chairs in the dining-room, for instance. Bedrooms are spacious, immaculate and well-equipped. All have tea/coffee-making facilities. There are pleasing country views throughout. Jean Gage serves breakfast only. £16 to £17.50.

Readers' comments: Very friendly. Comfortable. Beautifully maintained, very quiet. Best b & b we've had.

46

★ CARN WARVEL
Church Road, St Mary's, Isles of Scilly, TR21 0NA   Tel: 0720 22111

5 Bedrooms. £14–£16. All have own bath/shower/toilet. Tea/coffee facilities. TV. Views of garden, country. Washing machine on request.
Dinner. £8 for 4 courses (with choices) and coffee, at 6.30pm. Non-residents not admitted. Vegetarian or special diets if ordered. Wine can be ordered. No smoking. **Light suppers** if ordered.
1 Sitting-room. With open fire, central heating, record-player. Bar.
Large garden
Closed from November to February inclusive.

If a suntrap were needed on Scilly, this 200-year-old granite house is one, tucked away down a lane and surrounded by trees. Once two cottages, it has been in its time the home of a miller and of a farrier; and a farmhouse. Downstairs, the beamed ceilings are low, and so are the doorways.

Neil and Jenny Hedges ran a guest-house in little Hugh Town before taking on the renovation of what was almost a ruin. They have carried it out very well, tucking built-in fitments into stone-lintelled fireplaces in the characterful bedrooms, leaving outcrops of granite here and there, and lining walls with pine.

The cosy sitting-room opens onto a terrace surrounded by lush garden. Here, once a week during summer, guests eat from a big help-yourself salad buffet laid out indoors, with fruit cup to accompany it. Other evening meals consist of, for instance, local prawn cocktail, roast beef, and apple pie with Cornish cream. In season, grapes come from the vine in the big conservatory.

The main attractions of the Isles of Scilly are their unspoilt beauty, mild climate, low rainfall, and pure air. Storms are brief, sunny days long. Visitors to St Mary's (the largest island) get about on foot, by bus or taxi, and with hired bicycles (it is the only island with anything that could be called traffic). Apart from scenery, there is much of interest: prehistoric remains; old fortifications; craft workshops and studios; rocks and islets to explore; subtropical plants growing wild, butterflies, and in autumn rare birds that excite ornithologists. The excellent museum tells the story of innumerable wrecks and of discoveries by underwater archaeologists. You can watch weekly races between gigs (a big rowing boat peculiar to Scilly). Regular boats ply to the off islands.

Of the off islands, St Martin's (the second largest) is particularly well provided with sandy beaches. John and Barbara Clarke holidayed on Scilly for decades before they bought ★ **GLENMOOR COTTAGE** (tel: 0720 22816), where they run a small guest-house and a gift shop. The view is panoramic, though the rooms are rather small; there is a shower but no bath. Barbara is an enthusiastic cook. A typical dinner: fresh local crab, roast

lamb and five vegetables, raspberry mousse. From £13 to £14.

Readers' comments: Good food, good accommodation.

CARNWETHERS

Pelistry Bay, St Mary's, Isles of Scilly, TR21 0NX   Tel: 0720 22415

rear view

9 Bedrooms. £17–£23. Prices go up in May. All have own bath/shower/toilet. Tea/coffee facilities. TV. Views of garden, country, sea. **Dinner.** A la carte or £10 for 4 courses (with choices) and coffee, at 6.30pm. Non-residents not admitted. Wine can be ordered. No smoking.

2 Sitting-rooms. With open fire, central heating, TV. Bar. No smoking.

Large garden

Closed from October to March inclusive.

St Mary's, the principal island in the Scillies, is only three miles long. Even its centre of action, Hugh Town, can hardly be called busy by mainland standards (though it does receive tides of day-visitors during high summer), and so it is easy to find any number of unfrequented coves or beaches close by. Pelistry Bay is one of these – sheltered from wind, calm and unspoilt. Around it are pines and ferns, coastal footpaths and nature trails.

Carnwethers is more than an ordinary guest-house (and a very good one, at that). Its owner is Roy Graham, well known in the island and beyond as an underwater explorer and photographer, and a marine archaeologist – with 30 years in the Navy before he came here. Even non-experts appreciate his library of books on maritime subjects (wrecks, shipping, fish, wildlife, boats) and his immense knowledge of Scillonian history and ecology. His illustrated lectures in St Mary's twice a week should not be missed. He has assembled a number of videos about the islands which he shows to visitors, and can advise on boating or diving.

As to the house itself, this was once a farmhouse, but has been modernized. It is still surrounded by fields. Every room is as neat as a new pin. There is a bar and lengthy list of good-value wines, a heated 30-foot swimming-pool within sight of the sea itself but sheltered by granite walls and flowering shrubs, solarium, sauna, games room (for table tennis, darts, pool, etc.) and croquet lawn.

Local produce is much used by the chef for meals: fish (obviously), new potatoes, free-range eggs, home-grown vegetables and home-made marmalade, for example. A typical meal might comprise soup or fruit juice, roast turkey, and rolypoly pudding or fudge cake. Breakfasts include options like kedgeree and kippers. The dining-room has hanging plants, a stove for cold days and views of the fields with cows, flowers or potatoes in them according to season. Here and in the sitting-room, there are pictures of ships and seascapes. Bedrooms are agreeably decorated; colours are pretty, cupboards have louvred doors.

Readers' comments: Happy, friendly atmosphere. Could not ask for more.

Nearby is **CARN VEAN** (tel: 0720 22462) in a pleasant setting of lawn and trees. Here Laurel Deason provides inexpensive accommodation and meals, as well as running a tea-garden. From £11 to £12.

CASTLE FARM

Fotheringhay, Northamptonshire, PE8 5HZ   Tel: 08326 200

North-east of Corby. Nearest main road: A605 from Peterborough to Oundle.

C S

6 Bedrooms. £14–£18.50. Prices go up in June. All have own bath/shower/toilet. Tea/coffee facilities. TV. Views of garden, country, river. No smoking. Washing machine on request.

Dinner. £8.50 for 2 courses and coffee, at 7pm. Non-residents not admitted. Vegetarian or special diets if ordered. Wine can be brought in. No smoking. **Light suppers** if ordered.

1 Sitting-room. With open fire, central heating. TV.

Large garden

In the castle that was once here, Richard III was born – later to gain an infamous and probably unjustified reputation as murderer of 'the princes in the Tower'. Here, too, in that grim keep surrounded by two moats (a maximum-security prison) Mary Queen of Scots was, after many similar imprisonments, confined at the end of her life – to be tried for conspiracy against Elizabeth I. Forget the romantic picture of the lovely young queen. Ageing, lined and bent after long years of captivity, she limped pathetically with rheumatism to her execution on a scaffold she had earlier heard being hammered together in the courtyard, leaving 'this world out of which I am very glad to go' at daybreak on a bright, wintry morning: 8 February 1587. When the executioner lifted her head away from the body (clad in the scarlet of martyrdom), its wig fell off to reveal the balding head beneath. She had wished to be buried in Catholic France; but after interment by night in Peterborough Cathedral her headless corpse was later re-interred by her son, James I, in Westminster Abbey.

Her heart had been secretly buried, however, in the mound on which the castle, now long gone, was built: part of the land belonging to Castle Farm today. The thistles that grow here are called Queen Mary's tears.

At the Victorian farm, one steps straight into Stephanie Gould's huge quarry-tiled kitchen where a pine staircase rises to spacious bedrooms that are spick-and-span, all with good views (one of them looks onto the farmyard in one direction and to the ancient church in the other). There are very good bath- or shower-rooms, and much stripped pine. The big, comfortable sitting-room, too, has a view to enjoy – of the swift River Nene beyond the lawn, and a picturesque bridge. The Goulds have now converted outbuildings to make more bedrooms.

Stephanie produces traditional meals of two courses (such as lamb navarin with three or four vegetables including, for instance, home-grown asparagus, followed by sticky pear-gingerbread) or one can eat outstandingly well at the nearby Falcon Inn.

Fotheringhay church is particularly fine, and contains interesting tombs. To the south is Oundle, famous for its public school (a delightful little town within a loop of the river, on which you can go boating). The whole area is dotted with the soaring spires of mediaeval churches rising above undisturbed woods and fields watered by the winding rivers. Once, kings hunted deer in Rockingham Forest – stretches of which still survive, together with William the Conqueror's Rockingham Castle. Southward there are some fine panoramas, numerous reservoirs that attract birdwatchers, and buildings of golden stone as fine as any in the Cotswolds.

49

CASTLE HOUSE   C D PT X

23 Castle Street, Chester, Cheshire, CH1 2DS   Tel: 0244 350354

Nearest main road: A483 from Wrexham to Chester.

5 **Bedrooms.** £18 (less for 7 nights). Prices go up in April. Bargain breaks. Some have own bath/shower/toilet. Tea/coffee facilities. TV. Views of garden. No smoking. Washing machine on request.
1 **Sitting-room.** With open fire, central heating.
Small garden

Right in the middle of the city but in a quiet by-road, this interesting house has a breakfast-room which dates from 1540 behind an 18th-century frontage and staircase. The arms of Elizabeth I (with English lion and Welsh dragon) are over the fireplace.

It is both the Marls' own home and a guest-house with modern bedrooms that are exceptionally well furnished and equipped. Bed-and-breakfast only, for Chester has so many good restaurants; but visitors are welcome to use the kitchen. Newspapers and local phone calls are free – as are evening refreshments: Cheshire cheese with a help-yourself drink from a small bar. Coyle Marl, a local business-man, is an enthusiast for Chester and loves to tell visitors about its lesser-known charms, which can be toured in a horse-drawn hansom cab if you wish.

The city is, of course, of outstanding interest – second only to Bath and York in what there is to see. It is surrounded by ancient walls of red sandstone, just outside which is a large Roman amphitheatre (more Roman and even older remains are constantly coming to light, the smaller artefacts displayed in the Grosvenor Museum). You can walk all round the top of the ramparts, a 2-mile trek. The most unique feature, however, is the Rows: here steps from street level lead up to balustraded galleries overhanging the pavements, serving a second level of small shops above the ones below. Many of the half-timbered houses have particularly fine carvings. Chester's cathedral of red stone dates back to the 14th century and its zoo is one of Britain's best.

From Chester many visitors head for Wales; but there is a nearby part of Cheshire which should not be ignored – the Wirral. This thumb of land is sandwiched between two estuaries: the Mersey on its industrial side, the Dee on its other, very scenic side – facing Wales. The climate here is so mild that spring comes earlier than in some southern counties, which is why (at Ness) there are such beautiful botanic gardens. Visit little Parkgate for shrimps, sea-birds and Nelson connections; the country park for tranquillity and views; the Victorian fort on a rock at the mouth of the Mersey; the Lady Lever art gallery, containing some of the world's most famous paintings; Port Sunlight – one of the first garden-cities; Ellesmere Port for the canal boat museum – all these are on the Wirral, as is Wallasey, a popular resort with dunes, beaches and piers, and the Voirrey Embroidery Centre, the largest in the country.

Readers' comments: Welcoming. Breakfasts absolutely first-class.

50

CATHEDRAL GATE HOTEL   C PT X
36 Burgate, Canterbury, Kent, CT1 2HA   Tel: 0227 464381

25 **Bedrooms**. £17.50–£26. Prices go up in April. Some have own bath/shower/toilet. Tea/coffee facilities. TV. Views of cathedral (some). Washing machine on request.
Dinner. A la carte for about £9 for 3 courses, at 7–9.30pm. Non-residents not admitted. Vegetarian or special diets if ordered. Wine can be ordered. No smoking.
2 **Sitting-rooms**. With central heating. Bar.

The cathedral has a great, sculpted, mediaeval gateway. Tucked beside it is a row of shops and restaurants, above part of which is this upstairs guest-house (which has direct access to the cathedral precincts).

Even in Saxon times there was some kind of hospice here; and when the martyrdom of Thomas Becket in 1170 began to bring pilgrims to Canterbury in their thousands, it was in these beamy rooms that many of them stayed.

The spacious bedrooms are reached via a maze of narrow corridors and creaking stairways which twist this way and that. All are quiet (for Burgate is now restricted to pedestrians only); and some at the top have superlative views across the cathedral precincts to the great tower and south transept – floodlit at night.

When the small hotel was taken over by Caroline Jubber and her husband, they greatly improved the bedrooms – some of them reached via a rooftop walkway – while retaining ancient beams, leaded casements and bow windows. There are now two sitting-rooms, which include a bar. Breakfast (continental, unless you pay extra) is brought to you in one of these or in your bedroom. A modest evening meal is available, as well as full afternoon teas. (Many good restaurants close by.) Bedrooms are very well equipped. Some look across undulating old roofs and red chimney-pots where chattering starlings perch. The only inconvenience is that cars have to be parked a few minutes' walk away.

It is, of course, the cathedral which brings most visitors to Canterbury: one of Britain's finest and most colourful, with many historical associations. It is the site of Becket's martyrdom (commemorated in some of the finest stained glass in the world) and houses the splendid tomb of the Black Prince, and much more.

The ancient walled city still has many surviving mediaeval and Tudor buildings, the beautiful River Stour, old churches and inns, Roman remains, a very good theatre, and lovely shops in its small lanes. The Heritage Museum is also well worth a visit to see some of the city's most important treasures.

This is a useful place to stay before or after a ferry-crossing to the continent – or as a base from which to explore the historic south Kent coast, the Cinque Ports, Dover Castle and Dover's famous Roman 'Painted House', the Minster Abbey at Ramsgate, or the Kent countryside, the garden of England.

Readers' comments: Incredible situation. Very nice people.

Prices are per person in a double room at the beginning of the year.

CAVENDISH HOUSE

Eastmount Road, Shanklin, Isle of Wight, PO37 6DN   Tel: 0983 862460

3 Bedrooms. £14–£20 (less for 7 nights). Prices go up in July/August and at bank holidays. Bargain breaks. All have own bath/shower/toilet. Tea/coffee facilities. TV. Views of garden, country.
Small garden
Closed from mid-December to mid-January.

Although this resort is full of hotels, I had difficulty in finding any with really attractive rooms. Lesley Peters' home is an exception. She has furnished the large Victorian rooms with style – Laura Ashley fabrics and well-chosen colour schemes complementing good antiques. She has made the most of handsome architectural features (for instance, picking out in blue the plasterwork vine of one ceiling and filling an old tiled fireplace with pot-plants). Every room has a table and chairs for breakfast, as there is no dining-room. For dinner, Lesley (once an air stewardess) recommends The Cottage; or you can take the nearby lift to the foot of the cliff and Osborne House Hotel where, after an excellent help-yourself buffet, prepared by Mike Hogarth, you can sit on the flowery, grass-enclosed verandah facing the sea (bedrooms available, but hardly 'off the beaten track').

Shanklin itself has sandy beaches and a particularly lovely chine (ravine) running down to the sea, and is well placed to visit the innumerable sights of the island by bus or car, or to follow the network of well-marked footpaths if you want to get out into the very lovely countryside or to follow a shoreline which can be outstandingly dramatic in parts.

There are at least 70 man-made attractions if scenery and (usually) sunshine are not enough in themselves – such things as Calbourne watermill (17th-century and still producing flour for the cakes and loaves that are on sale), unique iridescent glassware (you can watch it being made), a landscaped butterfly house with Italianate and Japanese gardens adjoining, a miniature village with real thatch and plants in the picture-postcard village of Godshill, the horse centre that has every breed from tiny Shetlands to massive shire horses, delicate Chessell porcelain (another watch-them-work opportunity), one of Palmerston's chain of great forts housing military historic exhibits, a whole 'village' of country craft studios at Arreton, a flamingo park, the chairlift at Alum Bay's multi-coloured cliffs, aquaria, a wax museum, Robin Hill's exceptionally good adventure park for children, the impressive 'world of timber' show, tropical bird gardens, a steam railway, cruises in the Solent . . . the list goes on and on. Newest of all is Water Planet at Ryde where the 'mysteries of the oceans unfold before your eyes'.

But the island is definitely not a wall-to-wall carpet of tourist attractions. There is plenty of secluded countryside (particularly to the west), and plenty of historic interest too: Roman villas at Brading and Newport, Yarmouth Castle (16th-century), stately homes (such as Appuldurcombe in a park landscaped by Capability Brown, 17th-century Arreton Manor, Morton Manor and Haseley Manor), Victorian fortifications at the Needles and elsewhere, windmills, a church at Whippingham designed by Prince Albert, and other places of interest described under other entries. There are museums devoted to geology and fossils, maritime, toys and natural history. You can visit several farms, a herb garden and vineyards.

CEDAR LODGE

West Tofts, Norfolk, IP26 5DB   Tel: 0842 878281
North-west of Thetford. Nearest main road: A134 from Thetford towards
Downham Market.

3 Bedrooms. £16–£16.50 (less for 4 nights). Bargain breaks. Some have own bath/ shower/toilet. Tea/coffee facilities. TV. Views of garden, country. Washing machine on request.

Dinner. £13 for 5 courses (with choices) and coffee, at times to suit guests. Vegetarian or special diets if ordered. Wine can be ordered or brought in. **Light suppers** if ordered.

1 Sitting-room. With open fire, central heating, TV, piano, record-player.

Large garden

Closed from Christmas Eve to late January.

Christine Collins comes from a family of gourmets. Her parents ran a restaurant in Bristol, she qualified at the Cordon Bleu Cookery School in London, and then her daughter trained with Prue Leith. So it is very largely the exceptional food which brings visitors to her home – that and the total peace and comfort.

She lives in a Colt cedar house, its timber walls of treble thickness to be warm in winter and cool in summer. Around her is Thetford Forest and its meres, and the house has large picture-windows from which to appreciate the apple-blossom in her garden and the leafy scene beyond. There is a croquet lawn and a tennis court.

Indoors, soft blues and celadon green contrast with timber walls, cork floors, and a hearth of light stone; in the dining-room, buttoned leather chairs surround a very lovely yew table, laid with silver at dinner; bedrooms are light and airy.

As to meals, a typical dinner might comprise: twice-baked soufflé (topped with cheese and cream), chicken breasts in Calvados; fruit-filled brandysnap baskets with two sauces – raspberry and apricot; and cheeses. Every year, Christine goes to France to select wines for her cellar.

Near the house is Lynford Hall (where antique fairs are held) and its arboretum; and through the forest are trails to follow. Along the road to Swaffham, where forest and heath meet, beeches and chestnuts that touch overhead give way to an avenue of pines which have been twisted by the prevailing winds into bonsai shapes.

The story of Thetford Forest goes back into antiquity. Thetford was the capital of Boadicea who led her tribe against the Romans; but long before that prehistoric men used to slash and burn clearings in which to live with their livestock. By the 18th century, however, grazing was at an end because rabbits had reduced the area to desert – there were even sandstorms. Only when pine forests were planted (between the two world wars) was erosion halted. There is a forest information centre at Santon Downham; talks, guided tours and waymarked walks with information boards (and the chance of spotting red squirrels and four kinds of deer) help to explain the forest to visitors.

Then for a totally contrasting wildlife experience, one can go a few miles to Welney's wildfowl reserve (south of Downham Market), a fenland site which attracts thousands of migrant birds in winter. An unusual feature: evening viewings (by floodlight) of the swans roosting around a lagoon. There is an observatory to watch the birds at their nests in spring; and a summer nature trail. For a more exotic experience, visit Barnham Zoo near Thetford (it has snow leopards, a monkey sanctuary and enough family entertainment for a whole day).

★ **CHASE LODGE**   **C D H PT X**
Park Road, Hampton Wick, Surrey, KT1 4AS   Tel: 081-943 1862
Nearest main road: A308 from Staines to Surbiton.

6 Bedrooms. £18.50–£22.00 (less for 3 nights). Prices go up in March. Bargain breaks. Some have own bath/shower/toilet. Tea/coffee facilities. TV. No smoking. Washing machine on request.
Dinner. £7.95 for 3 courses (with choices) and coffee, at 7.30pm. Non-residents not admitted. Vegetarian or special diets if ordered. Wine can be brought in. No smoking. **Light suppers** if ordered.
1 Sitting-room. With open fire, central heating, TV.
Small garden

This is a very handy place at which to stay in order to explore the 'royal' stretch of the Thames Valley (monarchs chose nearby Richmond, Hampton Court, Kew and Windsor for their palaces). It is only half an hour from London in one direction and from Heathrow Airport in the other. Park Road is in a quiet conservation area, a street of pretty little Victorian villas with cottage-gardens, yet only a minute or two from a railway station, buses and the excellent shops and market of Kingston.

Chase Lodge has been redecorated with interesting pieces of Victorian furniture and decorative trifles in its sitting-room and elsewhere. There are African violets and other pot-plants in the bedrooms; and attractive quilted spreads are on some of the beds.

For dinner, Denise Dove offers a set meal which may comprise a home-made soup or prawn cocktail, a meat or vegetarian dish with fresh vegetables, a gâteau or ice cream, with cheese and coffee to follow. (Supper trays, too.) As all bedrooms have intercom, breakfast can be ordered in bed.

At the back of the house is a tiny, sun-trapping patio with a few seats among the petunias and nasturtiums. One bedroom has a tented scarlet-and-green ceiling and a mural of a crusader castle in its bathroom. Another, a four-poster with lace. Most have very good en suite showers or bathrooms.

I was greatly impressed by Denise's attention to detail and the immense trouble she takes. Not many far more costly hotels provide room service free, fresh towels and soap daily, fridges with soft drinks, and complimentary carafes of sherry in every room.

There is an enormous amount to see and do in the neighbourhood: walks among the deer and chestnut trees of Bushey Park or along the towpaths, Hampton Court – with *son-et-lumière* shows at night – and its gardens (with maze), horse-racing at Kempdown and Sandhurst, tennis at Wimbledon, rugby at Twickenham, and any number of regattas and festivals in summer. Richmond deserves at least a day to itself, to explore the byways and curio shops off the green, the stunning river view from the top of the hill, and the 3000 acres of Richmond Park. There are also Georgian or earlier mansions in fine grounds (Ham House, Orleans House, Marble Hill, Syon Park, Chiswick House, Hogarth's house and Osterley Park).

The river trips from nearby Kingston Bridge are particularly worth taking, and you can go all the way to Oxford through exceptional scenery – low hills, wooded banks, small villages, elegant country houses with gardens sloping down to the river. The Maidenhead-Marlow, Henley-Sonning and Reading-Goring stretches are the best. Or you can head towards central London. (The Doves will also take visitors on their luxury speedboat up and down the Thames.)

54

Main Street, Chideock, Dorset, DT6 6JH   Tel: 0297 89368
West of Bridport. On A35 from Axminster to Bridport.

5 Bedrooms. £13.50–£19 (less for 7 nights). Prices go up in April. Bargain breaks. Most have own shower/toilet. Tea/coffee facilities. Views of garden, country. No smoking. Washing machine on request.
Dinner. £9–£11 for 4 courses and coffee, at 7.30pm. Vegetarian or special diets if ordered. Wine can be ordered. No smoking.
1 Sitting-room. With open fire, central heating, TV, record-player. Bar. No smoking.
Large garden

This pretty thatched cottage in its old-fashioned garden is on the road between Georgian Bridport and the historic town of Lyme Regis. Built in the 17th century, the guest-house has been furnished in keeping with its age. The sitting-room and bar are beamed and with log fires in winter. Two bedrooms have four-posters, and several are beamed (the ones at the back are quiet, front ones are double-glazed).

For dinner you might get a home-made soup, pork chop in orange sauce, ice cream made with Cointreau, cheese, Rombouts coffee (and free liqueur), on a table with lace cloth, cut glass and Royal Worcester china. For breakfast, try the coddled eggs or one of many other imaginative options. Cream teas sometimes available.

Ann and Brian Hardy lend visitors Ordnance Survey maps and give advice. For example, they can tell you where to find fossils easily plucked from the Blue Lias clay, or where the best walks are on clifftops or through valleys – and if you want a lift back at the end of a walk, they are willing to come and fetch you in their car. They also show a film of Dorset.

Car washing and vacuuming facilities free.

Chideock itself is a very pretty village of thatched cottages, in a fold of the west Dorset hills designated an area of outstanding natural beauty. At nearby Morcomblake, you can visit Moores Biscuit Bakery (famous for Dorset Knobs) and its shop selling West Country products. The sea is close and much of the coastline hereabouts belongs to the National Trust. Within a short distance are Lyme Regis, Charmouth, Abbotsbury (swannery and subtropical gardens), Chesil Beach, Portland and Weymouth – all on the coast. Among the hills and vales, the farmlands and streams, are Sherborne (castle and abbey), Parnham House and Cricket St Thomas, Cerne Abbas (abbey and the giant cut in the chalk hills nearly two thousand years ago) and Beaminster (Georgian houses). There are fine gardens at Forde Abbey and Clapton Court.

Readers' comments: Beautifully appointed house, historic without detracting from 20th-century comforts, comfortable, friendly, good food. Very helpful and pleasant, well prepared food but not too exotic. Charming house and owners. A delight; meal was exceptionally good value, owners have warmth and humour. Comfortable room, excellent meals, many little extra touches.

For explanation of code letters (C, D, H, PT, S, X) see page xxxiv.

CHISWICK HOUSE

C D H PT

Meldreth, Hertfordshire, SG8 6LZ   Tel: 0763 260242
South-west of Cambridge. Nearest main road: A10 from Cambridge to
Royston.

7 Bedrooms. £16–£18. All have own bath/
shower/toilet. Tea/coffee facilities. TV on
request. Views of garden. No smoking.
Dinner £10 or £12 for 3 courses and coffee,
at 7 – 8pm. Vegetarian or special diets. Wine
can be brought in. No smoking. **Light
suppers** if ordered.
1 Sitting-room. With open fire, central
heating, TV. No smoking.
Large garden

Elbourns have lived in this house near Cambridge for a century. When the latest
generation, John and Bernice, set about renovating it, they uncovered beams with
drawings and lettering from the 15th century. It originally had no chimney or
fireplaces: these 'mod cons' came in during Tudor times. Over one fireplace is the
coat-of-arms of James I: it is believed he used the house as a hunting-lodge (he had
a palace at nearby Royston, of which fragments still remain), and the panelling in
the dining-room dates from his reign.

The house, although modernized, still has a very historic look, with old oak
beams, polished woodwork and flowers in every room. Carved chairs surround a
refectory table, there is a Knole sofa, and brass-studded leather chairs. One of the
beamy bedrooms opens onto the garden. Some others are in converted stables
(opening onto their own garden, with lily-pool).

In a glass sun-room, dinners are served – such as smoked mackerel, chicken
breasts in tarragon sauce and lemon meringue pie.

Many people stay here as a base from which to visit Cambridge, but north
Hertfordshire is itself worth exploring. Royston, a town of narrow streets and old
inns, has a strange man-made cave beneath its streets with carvings of the
Crucifixion. Baldock, with many 18th-century houses, is distinguished by a main
street lined with trees and grassy banks. Ashwell's Roman origins are shown in its
unusually spacious planning, and the traces of a Roman road can still be seen
nearby; there are fine 17th-century houses with decorative plasterwork (pargetting) and ash trees still grow around the spring which gave it its name.

From Meldreth it is no distance to the borders of three other counties –
Cambridgeshire (Cambridge itself, Newmarket of racing fame, and St Neots – its
market square flanked by the Great Ouse river and its church adorned with
wonderful carvings; Gog Magog Hills for a view of the university spires; stately
Wimpole Hall); Essex (mediaeval Saffron Walden and further south the picture-
esque Rodings – eight waterside villages, the great 17th-century house of Audley
End, much-photographed Wendens Ambo and Finchingfield, the three historic
Bardfield villages); and Bedfordshire (Bedford itself, Whipsnade Zoo park, stately
homes such as Luton Hoo, Ampthill's park, Houghton House ruins – Bunyan's
'House Beautiful', the water gardens of Wrest Park, Sandy's RSPB reserve,
historic aircraft at Biggleswade). Altogether, this is an area of great variety and yet
one which many tourists merely pass through on their way to more famous places.

Readers' comments: Unassuming, hospitable hostess; homely, comfortable rooms.
How relaxed we felt! Excellent. Very nice people.

CHITHURST FARM
Chithurst Lane, Smallfield, Horley, Surrey, RH6 9JU   Tel: 034284 2487
North of Gatwick. Nearest main road: A23 from Redhill to Crawley.

3 Bedrooms. £12–£15 (less for 7 nights).
Prices go up in June. Tea facilities. TV.
Views of garden, country. No smoking.
Light suppers if ordered.
1 Sitting-room. With open fire, TV. No
smoking.
Large garden
Closed in December and January.

Despite being so near Gatwick (and even London is only 35 minutes from the nearest rail station), this farm seems truly remote, reached by a long and winding lane. Built in the 16th century, it has tile-hung walls of mellow red brick against which the japonica flowers in spring.

Inside are low beams and a twisting staircase leading to simple but spacious bedrooms. These have double-glazing so that the sound of aircraft (numerous only during the day in summer) is not disturbing, with air-conditioners providing fresh air. In the visitors' sitting/dining-room, armchairs and a rocking-chair are grouped around a huge inglenook fireplace, its original spit-rack still in place.

Visitors are welcome to watch cows being milked, and to buy home-made jams. This is a good area for walking in the North Downs. There are several stately homes, gardens (such as Wakehurst), and bird or wildlife parks nearby. Even Brighton in one direction, and the Kentish Weald in the other, are soon reached. Nearby, several old towns like Horsham and Dorking are worth exploring. Churchill's house (Chartwell), the Bluebell steam railway, Hever Castle, Box Hill, Tunbridge Wells and Ashdown Forest are all very popular as are the many pick-your-own fruit farms. Chessington World of Adventures, a 65-acre site comprising a zoo and entertainments, is half an hour away.

Some people stay at the farm before flying from Gatwick, and if necessary Mrs Tucker will leave early breakfasts ready. A nearby garage will house your car, with free transport (24 hours a day) to and from the airport – where parking would cost you far more.

In the vicinity of Gatwick are the Victorian walled garden of Stanhill Court (a Victorian baronial pile, now a hotel) and a zoo where you can walk inside the big aviary and the butterfly garden. The monkey island is another popular feature there.

Mrs Tucker does not provide full evening meals, but has a list of recommended local restaurants etc. which do, such as the Hedgehog Inn, nearby. Chithurst Farm is remarkably good value for this area.

Readers' comments: Charming. Pleasant attention.

Prices are per person in a double room at the beginning of the year.

57

★ **CHOIR COTTAGE**   **C·D**

50 Ostlers Lane, Cheddleton, Staffordshire, ST13 7HS   Tel: 0538 360561

South of Leek. Nearest main road: A520 from Stone to Leek.

3 Bedrooms. £16–£18 (less for 2 nights). Prices go up in April. Bargain breaks. All have own shower/toilet. Tea/coffee facilities. TV. Views of garden, country. No smoking in some rooms.

Dinner. A la carte or £15 for 4 courses (with choices) and coffee, at times by arrangement. Vegetarian or special diets if ordered. Wine can be brought in. **Light suppers** if ordered.

1 Sitting-room. With central heating.

Small garden

The 300-year-old cottage once belonged to the village church and was rented out to raise funds for the choir. Before that, it had been a lodging-house on what was a principal coach route to Manchester – hard to imagine, for the lane is now just a quiet byway. It is built of reddish sandstone, made even more colourful by the tubs and hanging-baskets of flowers which the Sutcliffes have added.

Visitors who sleep in the cottage have the choice of a ground-floor room with four-poster bed draped with a pink valance (this room has its own private patio enclosed by flowering shrubs) or, up a steep stair, a small suite. Here, too, is a king-size and handsomely carved four-poster in one beamed room with tiny windows, a small, private sitting-room, a curtained alcove outside with a child's bed, and a shower room. A third bedroom (in the house) also has sliding glass doors opening onto a patio, and a view of fields.

Meals are served in the house, where there is a sitting-room and an adjoining sun-room (also opening onto the patio) with bamboo chairs from which to enjoy the hill scenery. For dinner Elaine prepares such meals as leek soup, chicken breasts in mushrooms and cream, and a flan of raisins, nuts and rum.

Readers' comments: Excellent food. Made us very welcome. Every comfort. Charm and hospitality of the owners. Excellent cook. Service and food first-class, with many personal touches. Superb; and excellent value. Beautifully decorated, price very reasonable. Meals a gourmet delight! Every attention and kindness.

On the north side of Leek, in the rural hamlet of Heaton, is 17th-century **FAIRBOROUGHS FARM** (tel: 0260 226341). From the mullioned windows of every spacious room are lovely views. In the big, beamed dining-room Elizabeth Lowe serves such typical farmhouse meals as home-made mushroom soup, roast beef and fruit pies (beside a crackling fire when evenings are cool). One of the two bedrooms has an antique Scottish pine bed. £12.

Readers' comments: A charming couple. Highly recommended.

CHURCH FARM

High Street, Roxton, Bedfordshire, MK44 3EB   Tel: 0234 870234
North-east of Bedford. Nearest main road: A428 from Bedford to Huntingdon.

2 Bedrooms. £14. Tea/coffee facilities. TV. Views of garden. Washing machine on request.
1 Sitting-room. With open fire, central heating, TV.
Large garden

It is a surprise to find such a peaceful village (a thatched church as well as thatched cottages) so close to the busy Great North Road, the A1, and in it this house – part 16th- and part 18th-century. One bedroom has a royal coat-of-arms carved in the wall, dating from Stuart times.

A beautiful breakfast-room has a Chippendale-style table and a sideboard with its original brass rails. The bedrooms are in a guest wing (one has a particularly handsome wardrobe); all rooms are furnished with an informal mixture of family antiques. There is a pleasant sitting-room in shades of cream and brown with a log fire. (For dinner, Janet Must recommends restaurants in either St Neots or Bedford, both a few miles away, or else local village inns.)

Visitors who stay here are often surprised to discover Bedfordshire's little-publicized charms, particularly its pretty villages, many of which are sited on wandering streams. Popular outings include not only Bedford (with the John Bunyan museum, the art collection in the Cecil Higgins gallery, a church with carved angels in the roof and pretty riverside lawns) and Cambridge, but the English Heritage properties of Wrest Park and Bushmead Priory, Shuttleworth's historic aircraft collection, the Swiss Garden, stately homes (such as Luton Hoo, Woburn Abbey and Hatfield House), Grafham Water and Olney (for its antique shops and boutiques). Sandy has the RSPB's headquarters and bird reserve, Huntingdon its Cromwell associations. In 15 towns or villages of Bedfordshire there are antique shops; there are also a number of pick-your-own fruit farms, first-class garden centres, and good but not strenuous walks.

Almost the whole of Bunyan's life was played out in Bedfordshire, and it is possible to follow a Bunyan trail, starting at Elstow (where he was born in 1628 and grew up to follow his father's trade – a tinker, a mender of cooking pots and suchlike). It was at Lower Samshill that he was first arrested for preaching; and at Bedford that he spent much of his life in prison. Mementoes (including his portable anvil) are in the Bunyan Museum, near the meeting-house which has scenes from *The Pilgrim's Progress* in bas-relief on its doors.

Bedroom at the Old Rectory, Standlake (see page 225)

★ CHURCH FARMHOUSE
3 Main Street, East Ayton, North Yorkshire, YO13 9HL Tel: 0723 862102
West of Scarborough. Nearest main road: A170 from Thirsk to Scarborough.

C D H PT X

5 Bedrooms. £18–£23 (less for 3 nights). Bargain breaks. Some have own bath/shower/toilet. Tea/coffee facilities. TV. Views of garden, country. No smoking. Washing machine on request.
Dinner. £12.50 for 3 courses (with some choices) and coffee, at about 7.30pm. Vegetarian or special diets if ordered. Wine can be ordered. **Light suppers** if ordered.
2 Sitting-rooms. With open fire, central heating, TV, record-player.
Small garden

Not in the countryside but in the middle of a picturesque village, this 18th-century farmhouse has rooms at the back which are quiet and all of them have character. In the thick-walled, pink sitting-room, there is a log fire on the brick hearth, pink and green velvet armchairs surround this, and 'country Chippendale' chairs are at the dining-table. A second sitting-room has an unusual ceiling of wood boards. There is a flowery courtyard at the back, with pool and fountain; and a landscaped garden. Here a stone outbuilding houses a games room with table tennis and snooker.

With the help of some young part-timers from the village, Sally Chamberlain produces excellent home-cooked dinners and sometimes bakes her own bread. Said one visitor: 'The pudding trolley fairly groans'. Cakes and tea are free on arrival. Sometimes she serves mushroom vol-au-vents as a starter or hot, spiced grapefruit as an alternative to home-made soups. The main course could be an 8-oz steak, fish straight from nearby Filey, pork in orange sauce, or lasagne accompanied by garlic bread. Popular puddings include pavlovas, Bakewell tart, strawberry mousse and a gâteau with oranges, ginger and brandy in it. Sally likes children and encourages them to join in with the cooking if they enjoy this.

East Ayton is well placed to visit both the superb Yorkshire coast, where safe sandy beaches alternate with towering cliffs, and the North Yorkshire Moors (national park). There are excellent walks by the River Derwent and in lovely Forge Valley. Within an hour's drive is a choice of beaches (at Filey, Sandsend and Whitby, for instance, as well as at nearby Scarborough); abbeys at Rosedale and Rievaulx; castles at Helmsley and Pickering; Flamingoland zoo park; and great Castle Howard. There is a steam railway right across the moors. Theatres and other entertainments are available at Scarborough which is also a good shopping centre. York is within driving distance.

Roads southward go to Flamborough, a great chalk headland the sheer cliffs of which accommodate thousands of seabirds; on the way, one passes 18th-century Sewerby Hall, and the road goes through the middle of a prehistoric promontory fort. The seaside resort of Bridlington is near here (sands, harbour and a notable priory church) and the old town of Beverley with its lovely minster.

Readers' comments: Comfortable and well furnished, excellent cooking. A splendid, comfortable bedroom. Nothing was too much trouble for Mrs Chamberlain. Delighted. Food fantastic; delicious. Cooking excellent. Charming and attentive staff.

★ **CHURCH HOUSE**   **C(12) X**
Grittleton, Wiltshire, SN14 6AP   Tel: 0249 782562
North-west of Chippenham. Nearest main road: M4 (junction 17 or 18).

4 Bedrooms. £18–£21 (less for 3 nights). Prices go up in April. Bargain breaks. All have own bath/shower/toilet. Tea/coffee facilities. TV. Views of garden, country. Washing machine on request.
Dinner. A la carte or £12 for 4 courses (with wine) and coffee, at 8pm. Non-residents not admitted. Vegetarian or special diets if ordered. No smoking. **Light suppers** if ordered.
2 Sitting-rooms. With open fire, central heating, TV, piano, record-player.
Large garden

This little-known but very beautiful village lies just off the M4 midway between London and Wales: a cluster of elegant houses, a great Tudor-style mansion and church, all built from golden Cotswold limestone.

Church House began life in 1740 as a huge rectory, which it took six servants to run. Around it are lawns with immense copper beeches (floodlit at night), an orchard, fields of sheep and a swimming-pool, well heated in summer (84°) – as well as a walled vegetable and fruit garden which provides organic produce for the kitchen, where Anna Moore produces imaginative meals if these are ordered in advance. A typical menu might comprise sorrel soup, chicken in a creamy apricot-and-curry mayonnaise, a tart of fresh peaches, English cheeses, fruit and wine (included in the price).

She and her family treat all visitors as house guests. If you want to meet Grittleton people, she will invite some to dinner, and she often escorts overseas visitors on sightseeing tours. Some she takes to the Royal Shakespeare Theatre (Stratford is 1½ hours away), with a champagne picnic supper on the banks of the Avon afterwards. The Moores are a musical family, and occasionally arrange music evenings – there is one huge room with a grand piano used for this purpose. Watching polo can be arranged. There is a croquet lawn and sun-bed.

The house has handsome and finely proportioned rooms. In the yellow sitting-room (which has an immense bay window overlooking the garden) are antique furniture, interesting paintings and a large log stove. The dining-room is equally handsome: raspberry walls, an Adam fireplace of inlaid marble and, on the long mahogany table, silver candelabra and Victorian Spode Copeland china. The most impressive architectural feature is the graceful staircase that curves its way up to the second floor, where the guest rooms are. These bedrooms are furnished with antiques.

There is an immense amount to see and do in the neighbourhood. Close by is Badminton (celebrated for the annual horse-trials, attended by the royal family); Bath is only 12 miles away; and the many historic (and prehistoric) sites of Wiltshire, such as Avebury, are all around. Both the West Country and the Cotswolds are accessible from Grittleton. Malmesbury Abbey, Castle Combe, Westonbirt Arboretum and the gardens at Bowood, Broadleas and Sheldon Manor are favourite sights.

Readers' comments: Anna Moore is an excellent cook. Bedrooms spacious and most comfortable.

Lyonshall, Herefordshire, HR5 3HR　Tel: 05448 350
West of Leominster. Nearest main road: A44 from Leominster to Kington.

3 Bedrooms. £14–£16 (less for 3 nights). Bargain breaks. Some have own bath/toilet. Tea/coffee facilities. Views of garden, country. Washing machine on request.
Dinner. £8 for 3 courses (with choices) and coffee, at 7.30pm. Non-residents not admitted. Vegetarian or special diets if ordered. Wine can be brought in. **Light suppers** if ordered.
1 Sitting-room. With open fire, central heating, TV.
Large garden

Venture into the barn here and you may be tempted to order a unique creation: a pin-tucked blouse, lace- or ribbon-trimmed in Edwardian style, each specially designed for its recipient by Eileen Dilley (formerly a London fashion designer). Now she uses the barn as a display centre for these and other crafts – all in Edwardian style: other garments (including children's), lavender bags, dolls, cushions.

The 18th-century house, too, is filled with her work and with Edwardiana she and her husband have collected. All the furnishings are from that period, with bedrooms named after celebrities of the time such as Baden-Powell, Nellie Melba and Conan Doyle (who lived near here while writing *The Hound of the Baskervilles*, using a well-known local name in its title). Every room has frilled curtain-ties or cushions she has made; fans, fashion prints or valentines she has collected. In one of the large bedrooms is a four-poster; and in the dining-room each lace-covered table has its own distinctive pattern of Edwardian bone china. Her traditional teas are served to the public (winning Eileen 'Tea Place of the Year' award in 1987); dinners are for residents only. The latter may comprise a tuna-and-sweetcorn starter, pork in mustard sauce and peach meringue, for instance. There is much emphasis on local produce and recipes.

Outside are donkeys in a paddock, many trees including a specimen copper beech in the garden, spring lambs and fine views beyond the haha.

Whichever way you drive there is plenty to see. Hereford (with cathedral and its unique treasure, the Mappa Mundi, which was saved by a whisker from sale abroad in 1989), Leominster (market town, with many antique shops), hilly mid-Wales, the Elan Valley, Llandrindod Wells (old-fashioned spa), Welsh seaside resorts, the black-and-white villages typical of Herefordshire, several stately homes (Croft Castle, Berrington Hall and Burton Court, for instance). Clee Hill is a well-known beauty-spot in the direction of historic Ludlow and the outstanding castle of Stokesay. Symonds Yat is a celebrated viewpoint above the Wye Valley. Walkers head for Offa's Dyke, bookworms for Hay-on-Wye, garden-lovers for Hergest Croft.

Readers' comments: Excellent quality. Highly recommended, excellent food; I have been four times in one year. Superior to lots of hotels.

For explanation of code letters (C, D, H, PT, S, X) see page xxxiv.

THE CITADEL   C D

Weston, Shropshire, SY4 5JY   Tel: 063084 204
North of Shrewsbury. Nearest main road: A49 from Shrewsbury to
Whitchurch.

3 Bedrooms. £18. Some have own bath/
shower/toilet. TV. Views of garden, country. Washing machine on request.
Dinner. A la carte or £12 for 4 courses (with
choices) and coffee, at 7–7.30pm. Non-
residents not admitted. Vegetarian or special
diets if ordered. Wine can be brought in. No
smoking. **Light suppers** if ordered.
1 Sitting-room. With open fire, central heating, TV, piano.
Large garden
Closed   from   November   to   March
inclusive.

The castellated turrets of this unusual red sandstone mansion have never known a
shot fired in battle. Erected in 1820 when the fashion for mock-Gothic architecture
was at its peak, it was built as the dower house for Lady Jane Hill – the Hills lived
in nearby Hawkstone Hall.

The interior is equally striking: some rooms – including one guest bedroom –
are round, windows are deep-set, and ceilings are particularly decorative. From
the cobbled terrace there are views of the Welsh hills and of Hawkstone Park (now
a golf course). Among its trees are follies (a tower and an obelisk) and caves.

One enters through a round hall with an inlaid octagonal table; the ceiling has
decorative ribs and bosses. In the huge celadon-green dining-room the coffered
ceiling is embellished with plasterwork vines. There is a sitting-room (chocolate
and cream) which houses a grand piano; as well as a billiard room with terracotta
ceiling. An unusual stone staircase leads up to the turret bedrooms; one of the
bathrooms is of Edwardian splendour and one of the bedrooms has a canopied bed.
All are immaculate.

Sylvia Griffiths serves such dinners as cheese and asparagus flan to start with,
jugged pheasant and chocolate roulade.

Apart from the scenery of one of England's loveliest and most peaceful counties,
the greatest attraction of the area is historic Shrewsbury – perched on a hill almost
islanded by a great loop of the River Severn. It deserves repeated visits to explore
twisting lanes (with such curious names as Dogpole, Shoplatch or Coffeehouse
Passage), the castle, the main square with flower-baskets hung around an open-
pillared market hall, and all the exceptionally decorative black-and-white houses
with carved figures of warriors and other characters. Wealthy wool-merchants
built impressive homes here, and helped to enrich the colourful church with
stained glass and carved angels. Among the zigzag alleys are craft and curio shops.
Ellis Peters' novels are set in the area.

The house of Clive of India is open as one of Shrewsbury's many museums (a
good china collection); and between the town walls and the river are the Quarry
Gardens. Percy Thrower designed these.

Other places of interest in north Shropshire include Georgian Ellesmere and its
surrounding lakes (seven of them); the little market town of Wem; the curiously
named Ruyton-XI-Towns; Hodnet, particularly rich in black-and-white houses
and with fine gardens around Hodnet Hall.

Readers' comments: Most interesting house. Delightful stay.

63

CLANDON MANOR FARM   C(10) **PT X**
Back Lane, East Clandon, Surrey, GU4 7SA   Tel: 0483 222357 and 222765
(Fax: 0483-223-585)
East of Guildford. Nearest main road: A246 from Leatherhead to Guildford.

3 Bedrooms. £11. Tea/coffee facilities. TV.
Views of garden, country.
1 Sitting-room. With central heating, TV.
Small garden

When financial disaster struck Sir Freddie Laker, this immaculately kept farm
was one of the properties he had to sell. Its purchaser, surprisingly, was Sally
Grahame, who hitherto had led a typically Kensington life as an interior designer.
But inside Sally the townee there was clearly a country-girl struggling to get out,
and she took to this life like one of her newly-acquired ducks to water.

On the farm are a hundred cattle; innumerable pigs, free-range chickens, geese,
Khaki Campbell ducks, rabbits and fifty horses. The horses include some pale
mink-coloured Norwegian Fiords, rare in this country, and at their superb best
when pulling the maroon Victorian landau which Sally hires out for weddings and
suchlike, complete with uniformed coachman and groom.

The black-and-white beamed cottage which contains guests' bedrooms (simply
furnished and without washbasins), one downstairs, is surrounded by lawn,
farmyard and flint barns hung with baskets of geraniums and often crammed with
hay, oats or barley. Mrs Haines, wife of Sally's farm manager, comes in to cook
breakfast. For other meals, most visitors go to the Queen's Head opposite.

East Clandon, itself a very lovely old village, is well placed for exploring the
many others hidden in the folds of the North Downs – much of the landscape
protected by the National Trust which also owns a large number of the stately
homes near here. Beauty-spots (many accessible to motorists as well as walkers)
have great variety: the spectacular summit of Box Hill, the woods of Leith Hill, the
blue Silent Pool near Albury, clock with automaton at Abinger Hammer. Bird
World near Farnham is well worth a long visit.

Readers' comments: Very good; friendly. Excellent value; and excellent food at the
Queen's Head.

Also in this area is **HAZELGROVE** at
West Horsley, a comfortable and well-
kept 'twenties house with lovely garden
and sun-room, on the road to Leatherhead. Jean Green can provide snack
meals as well as breakfast. (Tel:
048 65 4467.) Visitors watch her occasional dog-training classes and can buy
orchids from her greenhouse. No
smoking. From £15 to £16.

CLAY LANE HEAD FARMHOUSE

C

Cabus, Garstang, Lancashire, PR3 1WL   Tel: 09952 3132

North of Preston. On A6 from Preston to Lancaster.

3 Bedrooms. £11–£12 (less for 7 nights). Prices go up in April. Tea/coffee facilities. Views of garden, country.
Dinner. £8 for 4 courses and coffee, at 7pm (not on Mondays). Non-residents not admitted. Vegetarian or special diets if ordered. Wine can be brought in.
2 Sitting-rooms. With open fire, TV, piano, record-player.
Small garden
Closed in January and February.

Though hardly off the beaten track – it stand on the A6 – Clay Lane Head Farmhouse could easily be missed as one sped by, on the way to or from Scotland or the Lake District. It would be a good place to break a long journey, though it deserves more than a brief overnight visit, for both the house and the surroundings have much to offer visitors who like an easygoing atmosphere.

The stone house, which is more characterful than it appears to be from the outside, is basically 16th century, and some of the internal walls are of plastered reeds. It is a rambling, beamy old place, full of family antiques and Victoriana, with a book-lined sitting-room to sprawl in (it has a log fire); and it has not been modernized. The rooms face away from the main road.

Joan Higginson, a pharmacist, dispenses good food home-made from fresh ingredients. A typical dinner might be creamy carrot soup, steak braised with mushrooms and lemon meringue pie. There are goats too, and ponies for children to ride; and though this is no longer a working dairy-farm, there are cattle, hens and sheep. Bicycles on loan and riding available.

The immediate surroundings are not exciting, but there is good reason to investigate the hinterland – notably the Trough of Bowland, which is like a miniature Lake District without the lakes. The steep, heather-covered hills here are excellent for walking and picnicking, and there are picturesque stone villages and mansions to visit. One such is Browsholme Hall, a little-altered Jacobean house still in the possession of the family which provided the hereditary Bow-bearer of Bowland. Historic towns such as Lancaster and Clitheroe are not far, and the Lake District and the resorts of the Lancashire coast are within an easy day-trip. Other popular outings include Lancaster Castle, Cockersand Abbey, Sunderland Point, Beacon Fell country park and Brock Bottom nature trial.

Because the M6 motorway is near, it is easy to get to Lancashire's great cities which, although no great pleasure in themselves, do house a number of places of considerable interest – such as the restored Albert Dock and an outpost of London's Tate Gallery at Liverpool, and the outstanding Museum of Science and Granada Studios in Manchester. Blackpool, with its famous tower and miles of sands, is near: the latest attraction there is a huge tropical indoor swimming-pool. In this direction, too, is Fleetwood (port and fishmarket) and the pleasant resort of Lytham St Anne's.

Readers' comments: Very enjoyable. Excellent cooking and attentive service. Concerned for our every comfort, spotless rooms, excellent dinner. Interesting place, excellent food. Very satisfactory.

CLAYBATCH FARMHOUSE S

Blatchbridge, Somerset, BA11 5EF Tel: 0373 61193
South of Frome. Nearest main road: A361 from Frome to Shepton Mallet.

rear view

2 Bedrooms. £16–£18 (less for 2 nights). Prices go up in April. All have own bath/shower/toilet. Tea/coffee facilities. TV. Views of garden, country. Washing machine on request. **Dinner.** £11.50 for 4 courses, and coffee, at 7.30pm. Non-residents not admitted.

Vegetarian or special diets if ordered. **Light suppers** if ordered. **1 Sitting-room.** With open fire, central heating, TV, piano. **Large garden** Closed from mid-December to mid-January.

Jacqueline George has two outstanding talents. She is a professional cook of high calibre, and she has a flair for combining beautiful colours. Her early 18th-century home is a perfect setting for both her skills.

The big sitting-room is memorable. Duck-egg blue walls and the mellow patina of walnut furniture contrast with the brilliance of apricot chairs grouped round a stone fireplace – their colour echoed in Warners' pheasant and peony fabric on the sofas. (When I was there Jackie had put a great bowl of matching roses on a table.) Big casement doors open onto a sloping lawn, flowerbeds and water-garden. The dining-room has Chippendale-style chairs (Prince of Wales' feathers decorate their backs) with tapestry seats made by her aunt; and on the coral walls hang oil paintings. Here Jackie serves such dinners as cheese mousse in smoked trout; lamb en croûte (or game shot by Ryan) with garden vegetables; chocolate meringues; and cheeses (pre-dinner drinks and wine are included).

Bedrooms, too, are charming with little rosebuds on one bedspread, Chinese pavilions on another, for example.

Claybatch used to be part of the Longleat estate. The great Elizabethan mansion of Longleat is one of England's stateliest of homes, full of art treasures and famous for its free-ranging lions in part of the grounds landscaped by Capability Brown. Stourhead, too, is near: a Palladian mansion with fine gardens.

Somerset is a county of great beauty, its landscape punctuated by impressive church towers from the resplendent Perpendicular period of mediaeval architecture, big stone barns and little stone villages, with Bath itself just over the county boundary to the north and mysterious Glastonbury still drawing pilgrims to its holy places. Geology is what accounts for its great variety, with buildings made of stone that ranges from lilac to gold (for every quarry is different), and a landscape of hills and levels contrasting with one another. Monks drained marshes (still crisscrossed with their ancient ditches) between hills of great beauty but quite dissimilar from one another – the Mendips, the Quantocks and Exmoor. Where streams carved their way through rock there are gorges and caves.

Readers' comments: Made most welcome, delicious meals, beautiful home.

★ CLEAVERS LYNG
C D S

Church Road, Herstmonceux, East Sussex, BN27 1QJ   Tel: 0323 833131
East of Hailsham. Nearest main road: A271 from Horsebridge towards Bexhill.

8 Bedrooms. £15.25 (less for 7 nights). Prices go up in March. Tea/coffee facilities. TV. Views of garden, country. Balconies (some).

Dinner. £7.95 for 3 courses (with choices) and coffee, at 7pm. Non-residents not admitted. Vegetarian or special diets if ordered. Wine can be ordered.

1 Sitting-room. With open fire, central heating, TV. Bar.

Large garden. Children's play area.

The unusual name means a woodcutter's (cleaver's) hill by a marsh (lyng). Many centuries ago this was a yeoman's house – with a tile-hung exterior typical of Sussex, and an interior given character by beams, and an inglenook fireplace in the dining-room. Marylin Holden and her son Neil have been running it for many years as a small hotel.

The bedrooms are prettily furnished, and some have views of the garden and its apple-trees with the far distant hills beyond.

Good meals with plenty of choices – home-made soups or seafood cocktails, roasts or game pies, lemon chiffon or mincemeat tarts, are just examples. Home-made preserves are on sale. On Sundays there is always a traditional lunch with a choice of two roasts.

Herstmonceux village is the centre of Sussex trug-making (trugs are traditional garden baskets made from slats of willow), one of many pretty Downland villages around here. Many craftsmen work here and wrought iron is a local speciality. Popular sights include Michelham Priory, Batemans (Kipling's home), Battle Abbey, Pevensey Castle and picturesque Alfriston. The coast is near, with such resorts as Hastings (where there is a new show called the 'Domesday Experience', a history of smuggling in the caves, and a vast new shopping centre) and Eastbourne.

Readers' comments: Very welcoming. Excellent, have stayed many times. Beautiful position, and a comfortable stay. Good value and quiet.

In the picturesque old town area of Hastings, Dorothea and Stanley Pelling (at **105 HIGH STREET**) take bed-and-breakfast guests in their attractive little Georgian house. At the back, a tiny garden (all steps and terraces, clinging to the steep hillside) is an afternoon suntrap. No smoking. Tel: 0424 424894. £11.

Readers' comments: Charming house, cosy and well-loved, unpretentious. Gracious hosts. Great value.

67

CLEY MILL   C D
Cley-next-the-Sea, Norfolk, NR25 7NN   Tel: 0263 740209
West of Cromer. Nearest main road: A149 from Wells-next-the-Sea to Cromer.

5 Bedrooms. £18–£21 (less for 3 nights). Prices go up in March. Bargain breaks. Some have own bath/shower/toilet. Tea/coffee facilities. Views of garden, country, sea, river. Balcony (one). Washing machine on request.
Dinner. A la carte or £14 for 3 courses and coffee, at 7pm. Vegetarian or special diets if ordered. Wine can be ordered or brought in.
Light suppers if ordered.
1 Sitting-room. With open fire, central heating, TV.
Small garden
Closed from mid-January to end of February.

On the enthusiastic recommendation of a friend, I made my way to this most unusual of guest-houses – not, in fact, next to the sea (for centuries of silting up followed by land reclamation have left Cley a little way inland) but overlooking a rivulet winding its way through salt marshes where cattle graze.

Once Cley was a principal port of East Anglia, and great ships came to collect wool, and flour from the mediaeval windmill (the present structure dates from the 18th century). Milling ceased in 1921, since when generations of the Blount family have lived in it: one of the most celebrated visitors was the Duchess of Bedford who learned to fly when she was about seventy, and was lost flying at sea in 1937.

Only a few years ago, it was completely renovated. One enters through the beamy dining-room. The circular sitting-room has big armchairs around the brick fireplace, where Toby jugs are arranged, and window-seats overlooking the marshes. Upstairs, bedrooms are named according to the original purpose which they served: for instance, in the Wheat Chamber flour was sifted; in the Stone Room above it the flour was ground. Lace bedspreads and wildflower curtains contrast with brick walls, now painted white, and soft green carpet. One room has a balcony running all round the mill, with views on one side to Blakeney Harbour and on the other to the pantiled roofs and chimney-pots of Cley, its flint gables and its walls with hollyhocks peering over the top. Higher still are observation and information rooms, with telescope. (Book well ahead in summer.)

The Mill is run by Carolyn Hederman, who produces such meals as roast lamb, casseroles, or fish with hollandaise sauce; followed by lemon soufflé or mousse.

Cley is in the centre of the north Norfolk coast; a shoreline of cliffs and sands now officially protected for its beauty and its wildlife. Inland are woods, heath and pretty villages of flint walls or (eastward) red carr stone, with inns where crab salads are as common as ham sandwiches. The National Trust owns a number of stately homes which, along with castles and almost cathedral-like churches, innumerable craft studios and wildlife reserves, provide plenty of opportunities for sightseeing. Blakeney's waterfront is always lively with boats; Cromer is a family seaside resort in the old-fashioned style. Holkham Hall, Felbrigg, Blickling Hall are near and the royal gardens at Sandringham a little further.

Readers' comments: Cooking and hospitality could not be faulted. Comfortable; food very good. Excellent. Shall return. Interesting and friendly. High praise for standards and culinary expertise. Interesting situation.

★ **CLIFF HOUSE**   **C PT S X**
Devonport Hill, Kingsand, Cornwall, PL10 1NJ   Tel: 0752 823110
South-west of Plymouth (Devon). Nearest main road: A374 from Plymouth
towards Looe.

3 Bedrooms. £10–£16 (less for 5 nights). Prices go up in July. Bargain breaks. Some have own bath/toilet. Tea/coffee facilities. TV. Views of garden, country, sea. Balcony. No smoking. Washing machine on request. **Dinner.** A la carte or £10 for 4 courses (with choices) and coffee, at 7pm. Vegetarian or special diets if ordered. Wine can be brought in. No smoking. **Light suppers** if ordered. **2 Sitting-rooms.** With open fire, central heating, TV, piano, record-player. No smoking. **Small garden**

Just across the Devon/Cornwall border lies a neck of land that is almost an island, and which most tourists pass by. But if one leaves the main road to follow a woodland route along the winding banks of the River Lynher (frequented by swans), one comes to a little world of billowing green hills and high-banked lanes that plunge up and down until, right at the tip, one reaches the Mount Edgcumbe estate and the points at which ferries (car or pedestrian) arrive from Plymouth as they have done since time immemorial. This is the Rame peninsula, an area of outstanding natural beauty; and here, in a fishing village of coloured or red sandstone cottages, a maze of tortuous byways, small shops and bistros, is 17th-century Cliff House – perched high above the sea and within a few yards' of the south Cornwall coastal path.

From its hexagonal bay windows or the verandah, one can watch naval ships passing in and out of Plymouth Sound or, in the opposite direction, children playing on the sands of Cawsand Bay. To make the most of these views, the sitting-room (with sofas and log stove, the television end curtained off) is on the first floor. On the walls are theatrical posters – Ann Heasman used to organize art exhibitions at Manchester's Theatre Royal.

Some bedrooms, too, enjoy these views – the largest having armchairs in the bay window. There is one with a cupboard full of books for children.

Ann is not only a fount of information about the locality but an enthusiastic wholefood cook – of such meals as garlic mushrooms, pork Stroganoff and rhubarb fool – and she bakes her own bread.

The house is on the edge of the Mount Edgcumbe country park, at its heart a much restored Tudor mansion and fine gardens, both landscaped and formal. As well as developing the gardens, successive generations created such adornments as an orangery, shell fountain, conservatories, a fern dell, pavilions and memorials. There are also fortifications, Tudor and Napoleonic, to guard the sea approaches.

The whole peninsula is so full of interest that it would take a long holiday to explore it all. Every walk has unusual views: from the obelisk near Cremyll, one looks across to the most historic part of Devonport dockyard; at Empacombe, a path goes by an 1812 redoubt (with lake view); there are all sorts of 'finds' to be made – a mediaeval well-house, a track where thousands of glow-worms glow after dark, Tudor fish cellars where pilchards were cured, houses built into the cliffs (and with secret courtyards used by smugglers), a grotto of 1827, a headland chapel of 1397, secret coves and razor-sharp rocks which are the haunt of sea birds.

★ **COACH HOUSE** C D H S
Crookham, Northumberland, TD12 4TD Tel: 089082 293
East of Coldstream (Scotland). Nearest main road: A697 from Wooler to
Coldstream.

9 Bedrooms. £17–£26 (less for 7 nights). Bargain breaks. Some have own bath/shower/toilet. Tea/coffee facilities. TV. Views of garden, country. Washing machine on request.
Dinner. £10.50 for 4 courses (with choices) and coffee, at 7.30pm. Non-residents not admitted. Vegetarian or special diets if ordered. Wine can be ordered. No smoking.
Light suppers if ordered.
2 Sitting-rooms. With open fire, central heating, TV, record-player. Bar.
Large garden
Closed from December to March inclusive.

This is almost on the border of Scotland, and very close to the site of Flodden Field, where in 1513 Henry VIII's armies slaughtered the King of Scotland and 10,000 of his followers: the very last mediaeval battle with knights wearing armour, and swords or arrows the principal weapons. Each August there is a tremendously emotive spectacle commemorating it, with 200 horsemen bearing down at a canter after being led by the Coldstream Guards across the old bridge.

The Coach House is a group of several old farm buildings forming a square around a courtyard which traps the sun. What was the coach house itself is now a highly individual sitting-room, with lofty beamed ceiling and great arched windows where there used to be doors for the carriages. One looks onto an orchard. Colours are light and cheerful, and there is a log fire in an enormous brick fireplace. The dining-room was once a smithy and the forge still stands at one end.

An old dower house is now used for a daytime restaurant, and a billiards room. It has panelled doors of stripped pine, pointed 'gothick' windows, rare chestnut beams, an old Victorian kitchen-range, and two immensely high attic bedrooms.

In the main part, some of the ground-floor bedrooms look onto paddocks where goats graze. All are light and airy, with interesting paintings and a file of leaflets on the many local places worth visiting. They have fridges which guests find useful for a variety of purposes (baby's feeds, dog's meat, insulin or soft drinks) and toasters: there are reduced prices for people who make their own breakfast.

The owner, Lynne Anderson, used to travel a great deal when she was a singer, and so has a lot of practical ideas about what travellers need – disabled travellers in particular. She had doorways made wide, and steps eliminated.

Porridge is properly made from pinhead oatmeal, and breakfast includes bacon from an Edinburgh smokery, beef sausages from a local butcher, and free-range eggs. Dinner has a choice of starters; a roast or casserole; puddings like lemon meringue pie or almond ice cream with damson sauce; cheese and coffee.

Readers' comments: Very friendly and welcoming, exceptionally well organized; most impressed. Warm and friendly owner; professional efficiency. A great success! Wonderful. So much room, the very best breakfast, and Lynne is exceptionally good at making guests at ease with one another.

COACH HOUSE

Scotland Road, Dry Drayton, Cambridgeshire, CB3 8BX   Tel: 0954 782439
North-west of Cambridge. Nearest main road: A604 from Huntingdon to
Cambridge.

4 Bedrooms. £18–£21 (less for 3 nights). All have own bath/shower/toilet. Tea/coffee facilities. TV. Views of garden. No smoking.

1 Sitting-room. With central heating, TV. No smoking.
Large garden
Closed from December to mid-March.

Not so very long ago, what is now an immaculate reception room (with pink walls and chinoiserie curtains) contained mounds of dung, for it had been stables. The transformation wrought by Catherine Child at this lovely 18th-century coach house was total. It is now a house of considerable charm and great comfort. The extensive grounds have been landscaped with imagination: moorhens inhabit the lily-pond and can be watched while guests take breakfast. There is an air of tranquillity which can be enjoyed from the rooms, because all face south to the garden. The Victorian summerhouse is a particular delight.

The rector who, a century ago, stabled his horses here must have been a man of considerable substance, keeping several carriages and maintaining his own forge. The forge fire still burns, built into a corner of the entrance hall.

A handsome pine staircase rises to the bedrooms but offers temptations to linger on the way up, for one large window and a blocked-up doorway have been filled with shelves to display small bits of Victoriana (for sale – they are provided by antique-dealer friends of Catherine). Bedrooms are light and pretty, with excellent facilities. The best has a king-size brass four-poster, its valance beribboned and its quilt and draperies matching the pink bathroom.

Guests have the use of a large dining-room with mahogany tables for breakfast, which includes an array of home-made preserves, and of a small television room. (And there's a lovely room to hire for groups, music-making and suchlike.)

In the folders of local information provided for guests Catherine lists recommended eating-places (such as Trinity Foot or the Three Horseshoes inn at nearby Madingley or the Plough at Coton, and many in nearby Cambridge, of course). She can arrange for private guided tours round Cambridge. Go to Huntingdon for the Oliver Cromwell museum (this was his birthplace) and to St Ives; there are several stately homes within easy reach; and close by is the American Cemetery, which is well worth a visit. Grantchester and Duxford's aircraft museum are also near.

Readers' comments: Very warm welcome, such pretty bedrooms, a lovely outlook. Lovely house. Every conceivable care given to visitors' requirements. Totally impressed by it all! Has great character, most peaceful. Best breakfast ever.

71

COASTGUARDS

St Agnes, Isles of Scilly, TR22 0PL   Tel: 0720 22373

2 Bedrooms. £13. Tea/coffee facilities. Laundry done (within reason) for week-long visitors.
Dinner. £5.50 for 2 courses or £8 for 4 courses and coffee, at 6.30pm. Non-residents not admitted. Vegetarian or special diets if ordered. Wine can be brought in.
1 Sitting-room. With open fire.
Small garden
Closed from November to March or Easter.

There are very few coastguards living in the many coastguard cottages still left around the shores of England: electronic surveillance has taken over from the man with the spyglass. Needless to say, such cottages were always well sited for sea views, on coasts where high seas and jagged rocks make spectacular scenery, but are hazards for ships, and where coves and inlets were an attraction to smugglers.

One such group of cottages stands on a high point of St Agnes, a little island so unspoilt that there are no cars and no hotel – only a small shop with a good selection of drinks and books. It is a paradise for those who want nothing more than sunshine early or late in the year, wildflowers, walks, birdwatching and peace.

Wendy and Danny Hick live in one of these cottages, with a couple of rooms for guests. They have furnished the rooms simply but attractively, with interesting objects around. (No washbasins.) The sitting-room has a William Morris suite and brown tweed curtains, polished board floors, many books on the shelves and an open fire for chilly evenings. The pieces of iron-studded furniture are from Curaçao, where Danny's father was a mining engineer. The collection of old bottles (from inkwells to flasks that contained sheep-cures) are mostly local finds. Danny makes ship models sold in London's West End galleries and abroad.

The food is all of a very good, homely style: bread is home-baked, soups home-made, clotted cream is from a friendly neighbourhood cow, fish (of course) straight out of the sea, and new potatoes from the fields around.

Visitors reach St Agnes via St Mary's from which boats take them in 15 minutes to the little quay at St Agnes. (Wendy will supply all the times etc. for getting to Scilly by rail and boat or helicopter.) Luggage is conveyed for them up the steep track that leads to the few cottages; past the Turk's Head inn (for a really succulent Cornish pasty, pause here!); and past Rose Cottage and Covean which serve Cornish cream teas and light lunches. Whatever track you follow, there is a superlative view at every turn. This is a great place for birdwatchers, particularly in autumn when rare migrants arrive. But even at other times it is a pleasure to watch the red-legged oystercatchers, for instance, scuttling like busy mice among the rock-pools on the shore. Around the lighthouse (built in 1680) are fields from which daffodils and narcissi are sent early in the year to mainland florists. There are strange rock formations and islets, deserted sandy coves and pools, a simple church (built from money raised by salvaging a wreck), and – a mystery – the centuries-old Troy Town maze by a remote cliff edge.

Readers' comments: Excellent in every respect. Good food, lovely scenery, such nice people. Warmly welcomed, well looked after, delicious food, excellent value; beautiful and peaceful place. Superb food and hospitality.

COBLERS

South Creake, Norfolk, NR21 9PF   Tel: 032879 200
North-west of Fakenham. Nearest main road: A148 from Cromer to
King's Lynn.

2 Bedrooms. £18. Prices go up in April. Each has own shower/toilet. Tea/coffee facilities. Views of garden. No smoking. Washing machine on request.

1 Sitting-room. With open fire, central heating, TV. Also an upper room in adjoining barn.
Small garden

The U-shaped house encloses a particularly pretty little garden that comes as a surprise when one turns in from the main road. Arches and hanging baskets of flowers surround the lawn and a sun-trapping patio, stone hounds guard a lily-pool (lit up at night), there are tubs of marigolds, and one can open a narrow wrought-iron gate to watch trout and ducks in the clear stream flowing by.

Ian Dow was formerly a theatrical production manager – hence the many theatrical designs, photographs and posters around the house. The small sitting/dining-room is crammed with other interesting objects – from samplers and old jigsaw pictures to portraits of his Scottish ancestors. For dinner, the Dows recommend Cartwrights restaurant ('the best fillet steaks anywhere') or the Orchard inn. At breakfast there are home-made bread and marmalade, and lots of fruit.

The bedrooms are attractively furnished with, for instance, both furniture and walls painted dark billiardcloth green to contrast with the shaggy rust carpet in one room; ivy trellis paper in another which has fabrics striped in cobalt blue.

South Creake is centrally placed for enjoying many of Norfolk's contrasting areas – the scenic coast lies six miles north. Cockthorpe Hall has a toy museum, Hunstanton an underwater sea life centre.

Readers' comments: Very friendly atmosphere. The Dows spoil their guests. Absolutely delightful. Friendly and helpful. The best 'Off the Beaten Track' we've been to.

A little further west is Docking, where Margaret Robinson caters inexpensively for bed-and-breakfast guests in her immaculate 18th-century **HOLLAND HOUSE** (tel: 0485 518295). There are paintings and busts throughout, the sitting-room has an open fire and the walled garden is adorned with abstract sculptures. Most people dine at the Pilgrim's Reach. From £13 to £15.

COCKETT'S HOTEL   D X
Market Place, Hawes, North Yorkshire, DL8 3RD   Tel: 1969 667312
Nearest main road: A684 from Sedbergh to Leyburn.

8 Bedrooms. £16–£22.50 (less for 3 nights). Prices go up in March. Bargain breaks. Some have own bath/shower/toilet. Tea/coffee facilities. TV. Views of garden, country. No smoking.
Dinner. A la carte or £14 for 4 courses (with choices) and coffee, at 7pm. Vegetarian or special diets if ordered. Wine can be ordered. No smoking.
1 Sitting-room. With open fire, central heating. **Bar.**
Small garden
Closed from mid-November to 23rd December.

'God being with us Who can be against' is carved deep into the stone lintel of a door, together with the date 1668. It was the main entrance to a hostel once used by Quakers travelling to distant meeting-houses.

Things are different now. One steps from the paved forecourt into a snug little bar with leather chairs and racing-prints all over the walls – most visitors much prefer this to the larger, pine-panelled sitting-room elsewhere. Adjoining it is a dining-room where, on lace-covered tables, are served imaginative meals. There is always plenty of choice at each of the courses, with many French specialities such as lamb Argenteuil (it is cooked with asparagus and cream), or chicken Marika (cottage cheese and green peppercorns go into the sauce), or duck-breasts stuffed then braised in lettuce leaves. The cheeseboard usually has up to eight different types of Yorkshire farm cheeses.

Jacqueline Bryan's and John Oddie's hotel is something of a gallery, with over two hundred pictures on its walls. Every room has interesting furniture, too: one four-poster, with barley-sugar posts, is covered in a scarlet dragon fabric; another, of pine, has pale green chintz. One's eye is caught by interesting details everywhere: satinwood bedside cupboards, art nouveau fingerplates on the doors. For quiet, ask for a back room.

In the annexe (over an art gallery) are the two least expensive bedrooms, which would make an ideal suite for a family wanting to be self-contained.

Hawes, its buildings clustered around a stream, is near the head of Wensleydale from which the spectacular Buttertubs Pass leads to Swaledale (described elsewhere): the 'butter tubs' are curious holes in the rock. The dale's crags and waterfalls, castles and history museums, attract visitors from all over the world.

(As this edition was going to press, I heard that ownership is changing.)

Readers' comments: Food excellent, rooms comfortable, Jackie and John really made the week for us. Felt very welcome, interesting food and rooms, friendly staff. High standard. Cuisine excellent. Delightful. Excellent dinner. Friendly.

74

COLLEGE FARMHOUSE

Thompson, Norfolk, IP24 1QG   Tel: 095383 318

North of Thetford. Nearest main road A1075 from Thetford to Watton.

4 Bedrooms. £14–£15. Prices go up in   Washing machine on request.
April. TV. Views of garden, country.   **Large garden**

Over six centuries ago, colleges (meaning residential communities) of some half-dozen priests were established in various parts of East Anglia, to serve local communities. This house was built for one of them. When these colleges were (like the monasteries) disbanded by Henry VIII, it became a private house: the new owner had his coat-of-arms put above the main fireplace. Later, carved oak panelling with fluted pilasters was put into the dining-room; a second storey was added; and then all manner of Victorian or later accretions followed. These last have been gradually removed, revealing forgotten fireplaces and beams masked by hardboard. A tremendous task; and when it was begun the only running water was from leaks in the roof. The house is therefore full of curious architectural features – Gothic windows blocked up, walls (some three feet thick) with odd curves, steps up and down.

Lavender Garnier has collected together interesting pieces of furniture and some ancestral portraits (including a great-grandfather who took part in the first Oxford and Cambridge boat-race, and selected dark blue as Oxford's now famous colour). Bedrooms have pleasing fabrics – brilliant nasturtiums on the bed of one room, for instance; yellow linen bedheads in another white-panelled room – and in one the basin is set in a thick, handsome plank of polished elm. Each bedroom has armchairs and TV, as there is no sitting-room for guests' use.

Outside, a lovely old garden slopes down to eel ponds, and flint walls make a perfect background to the roses, herbaceous borders and a great beech.

Breakfast is the only meal served, but there is good inn food at the thatched Chequers, a mile away.

Thompson is in an attractive, leafy part of Norfolk, where the landscape undulates and villages are pretty. There are varied options for day-outings – from the very beautiful Norfolk coast to Cambridge, from Norwich and the Broads to Bury St Edmunds (described elsewhere in this book). Breckland is an area of heath and meres, with little population now but a considerable history (explained in Thetford's museum, in a Tudor house). Visit Brandon to see the variety of ways flints are used in building; and Grimes Graves where prehistoric man mined the chalk to find these, for use as tools and weapons. Castle Acre lies within Norman earthworks (the priory remains are impressive); near Denver is an unusual windmill, and the 15th-century Oxburgh Hall is moated.

COOMBE FARMHOUSE
Widegates, Cornwall, PL13 1QN   Tel: 05034 223
North-east of Looe. On B3253 from Looe to Widegates.

9 Bedrooms. £14.50 (less for 2 nights if dinner is taken). Prices go up in April. Bar-gain breaks. Some have own shower/toilet. Tea/coffee facilities. TV. Views of garden, country, sea. No smoking. Washing machine on request.
Dinner. £10 for 4 courses and coffee, at 7–8pm. Non-residents not admitted. Vegetarian or special diets if ordered. Wine can be ordered. No smoking. **Light meals** if ordered.
1 Sitting-room. With open fire, central heating, TV, video films. Bar. No smoking. **Large garden**
Closed from November to February inclusive.

Built on a marvellous site with a distant sea view between hills, this very spacious and comfortable 'twenties house had long been coveted by Alexander Low, who used to bring his family regularly to Looe for holidays. When at last it came up for sale, it had deteriorated into a seedy guest-house. But he and Sally have transformed it and its grounds, and every year sees still further improvements (a swimming-pool and a stone-walled games room for snooker and table tennis are the most recent).

Alex frequents salerooms to find additions to the already rich array of antiques, paintings and interesting objects with which he has filled the house.

The dining-room extends into a glassed-in verandah from which there are views of terraced lawns where peacocks roam, and of a pond (one of several) frequented by ducks and coots. Elsewhere, geese and ponies graze, there are woods with rhododendrons, camellias grow wild and there is croquet.

All rooms have an abundance of pot-plants, flowers are put on each green-clothed dining-table, and on cool nights log fires crackle on two hearths. My bedroom (like several, very big indeed) opened straight onto the garden. Others upstairs have armchairs or, in one, a big sofa from which to enjoy the view.

Alex used to travel a lot and knows what makes guests feel truly at home. They are welcome to take picnic lunches into the garden, for instance; and to help themselves to drinks, writing down in a book what they have had.

A typical dinner prepared by Sally may comprise something like home-made soup, roast duck and a fruit sponge accompanied by Cornish clotted cream.

Readers' comments: Excellent! Friendliness and warmth. A wonderful experience. Place superb, hospitality gracious. A haven of peace. Excellent food.

When Coombe Farmhouse is full, the Lows recommend the old **SLATE HOUSE** at nearby Bucklawren (tel: 05034 481), the home of Bettyan Baynes-Reid. She serves such meals as Stilton soup, pheasant, and hazelnut meringue (much produce is home-grown). £12.

Readers' comments: Beautifully appointed, delicious cooking, reasonably priced, peaceful.

CORFIELD HOUSE   D H S

Sporle, Norfolk, PE32 2EA   Tel: 0760 23636
North-east of Swaffham. Nearest main road: A47 from King's Lynn to
Norwich.

5 Bedrooms. £15–£17. All have own bath/
shower/toilet. Tea/coffee facilities. TV.
Views of garden, country.
Dinner. £9.50 for 4 courses and coffee, at
7.30pm. Vegetarian or special diets if
ordered. Wine can be ordered. No smoking.
Light suppers if ordered.
1 Sitting-room. With open fire, central heating. No smoking.
Small garden
Closed from Christmas to late March.

Turning their backs on the London rat-race, and arming themselves with Delia
Smith's cookery books plus a lot of determination, Linda and Martin Hickey
moved here with their little daughter to build a new life running their own
guest-house. Much hard work went into adapting the early Victorian farmhouse
and creating a particularly pretty garden, its path to the front door bordered with
roses and lavender and its apple-trees a froth of pink in spring.

Inside, Linda has used delicately patterned wallpapers, much pine and rattan
furniture, lace bedspreads, soft blues and pinks. There is a ground-floor room
with bathroom that would particularly suit any handicapped person.

A typical dinner might comprise crab and avocado salad, beef bourgignonne,
raspberry clafouti (a type of pancake) and some unusual English cheeses from
Swaffham's Saturday market – all served on rose-patterned Doulton china.

Linda helps in Swaffham's Tourist Information Centre and so is a mine of
information about the area. Nearby Swaffham has a huge market square with an
18th-century Ceres on top of a cupola and many other buildings of the same date
(Nelson used to stay at Montpelier House). The hammerbeam roof in the church is
impressive, and in the local history museum are everything from fossils and
stone-age tools up to Victorian artefacts.

Readers' comments: Strongly recommended. Excellent value.

At South Acre, within sight of Castle
Acre's castle, is **HALL FARM** – a
Tudor house with an ogee brick fireplace and great beams within the flint
walls in which later generations in-
serted big sash windows.

Susan Fountaine will, if this is
ordered in advance, provide dinner
which might comprise gazpacho, the
estate's own venison or pheasant and
lemon soufflé – served in a dining-room
with coral walls and pine-shuttered
casements opening onto the lawn. A
handsome staircase leads to large and
colourful bedrooms of which the green
family suite is most impressive: very

big, with dressing-rooms and spacious
bathroom; and from one of its several
windows a view of horses and ducks in
the farmyard. Tel: 0760 755406. From
£17.50 to £20.

CORNER ELM

Netton, Wiltshire, SP4 6AW   Tel: 0722 73 314

North of Salisbury. Nearest main road: A345 from Amesbury to Salisbury.

3 Bedrooms. £15 (less for 7 nights). Prices go up in April. Bargain breaks. Tea/coffee facilities. TV. Views of garden, country. No smoking. Washing machine on request.

Dinner. £10 for 4 courses and coffee, at 7.30pm. Non-residents not admitted. Vegetarian or special diets if ordered. Wine can be brought in. No smoking.

1 Sitting-room. With open fire, central heating, TV.

Small garden

Closed late November and December.

Once called the Wool House, this was a wool-collecting depot for the area; drovers going from the Marlborough Downs to Wilton Sheep Fair used to pass the door. In 1854 it became a dwelling, being converted into a rambling house and re-named for the great elm outside (now a colossal hollow trunk prettily draped with flowery Russian vine); this was one of a series of elms known as 'mile elms' that used to mark the way from Durnford to Salisbury. Diana Howard has furnished all rooms to very high standards. In the sitting-room, for instance, are velvet chairs in blue and deep rose, toning with the carpet, which look well against a deep pink marbled wallpaper; at deep-set sash windows with white shutters are pretty blinds matching the wallpaper and appliquéd with flowers from the curtain fabric, their colours echoing those of her huge velvety gloxinias. There is an open fireplace with log fire. One of the bedrooms, blue and cream, has frilled curtains and a lace bedspread.

In a low-beamed dining-room Diana serves breakfast and dinner (on some nights only). A typical meal: mackerel pâté, chicken Marengo with garden vegetables, raspberry bavarois and cheeses. The house is beautifully situated midway between Salisbury and Stonehenge in the scenic Woodford Valley. Wilton's historic carpet factory and Wilton House are just over the hill.

In the same lovely valley, at Lower
★ Woodford, are **MANOR FARM COTTAGES** (tel: 0722 73393) where each party of visitors has its own cottage – thatched and mediaeval or flint-walled and Victorian; gathering together with others in one of these for breakfasts and the light suppers Elva Randall provides on request (unless you prefer to cook your own in the fully equipped kitchen available in each cottage; or to eat at the Wheatsheaf Inn close by, which has an excellent chef). The cottages are furnished simply but

pleasantly, well carpeted, and with restful colour schemes of pink or blue. All have gardens, sitting-rooms and washing machines. From £14 to £16.

Book well ahead: many of these houses have few rooms. Do not expect dinner if you have not booked it or if you arrive late.

THE COTTAGE

Westbrook, Bromham, Wiltshire, SN15 2EE   Tel: 0380 850255
South of Chippenham. On A3102 from Calne to Melksham.

3 Bedrooms. £16–£17.50. Prices go up in May. All have own shower/toilet. Tea/coffee facilities. TV. Views of garden, country. **1 Sitting-room.** With central heating.

Large garden with 9-hole putting. **Closed from December to February inclusive.**

Converted stables, weatherboarded and pantiled, provide the accommodation here, in a quiet hamlet once the home of Thomas Moore, the Irish poet. The adjoining mediaeval cottage was originally a coaching inn.

Inside, the roof beams are still visible. The bedrooms have been furnished in keeping with the style of the building and Gloria Steed has added such decorative touches as patchwork cushions and pincushions which she made herself. Through the bedroom windows one can sometimes see deer and rabbits, with a distant landscape created by Capability Brown in the 18th century.

At breakfast (in a room with rough white walls, small William Morris armchairs and beautifully arranged flowers) there will be, in addition to the usual things, home-made muesli and some very special jams from France. For other meals, Gloria can show you menus from inns and restaurants within a few miles (I ate very well at the Lysley Arms). Occasionally she invites guests to a barbecue.

This is very lovely walking country, and with lots of sightseeing possibilities too (Lacock, Avebury and Bath are all within a few miles; and Bowood House is close – an Adam building in superb grounds, with lake and cascade). Chippenham and Devizes are historic market towns, with fine churches and other buildings of golden stone. Castle Combe is a much-photographed village in a dramatic setting – woods above it, stream through it, mellow stone cottages and fan-vaulted church. Corsham Court, and the waterside at Devizes, are well worth visits. This part of Wiltshire is very rustic but with fine limestone houses built in the centuries when wool brought wealth. Riverside pastures contrast with hills and wooded dells. Sheldon Manor and Stourhead have exceptional gardens. A good area for hunting antiques, or buying farm produce.

Readers' comments: Full of charm and character. We couldn't have asked for more.

COTTESWOLD HOUSE   C(10) **PT S X**

Market Place, Northleach, Gloucestershire, GL54 3EG   Tel: 0451 60493
Nearest main road: A40 from Oxford to Cheltenham.

4 Bedrooms. £14–£16.50 (less for 4 nights). Prices go up in June. Some have own bath/ toilet. TV. Washing machine on request.
1 Sitting-room. With central heating, TV.

This is not strictly 'off the beaten track', being in the centre of the historic little town, but now that heavy traffic has been diverted, Northleach is quite a quiet place. The house has tremendous character, after being carefully restored by Patricia Powell a few years ago. Zigzagging passages lead to roomy bedrooms with rugged stone walls and low oak beams now exposed. She has furnished all the rooms with good carpets and folkweave or similar fabrics. Guests breakfast in a dining-room with oak furniture, including a vast carved chest, and can use the sitting-room and its comfortable yellow armchairs – big and velvety. There are good places for dinner within a few yards, such as the Wheatsheaf and Wickens.

There is plenty of interest within easy motoring distance. For example, Cirencester still has a lively market (I recommend the farm cheese stall) outside its almost cathedral-like church. The Corinium Museum is one of the country's best-displayed Roman museums, and there is a flourishing craftsmen's market in a former brewery. The most picturesque villages and lanes of the Cotswolds are close – stately homes, gardens, a Roman villa, the source of the Thames, handsome Cheltenham, Gloucester's cathedral and the colleges of Oxford, too.

The principal attractions of Northleach itself are the splendid church, an old merchant's house now housing the 'World of Mechanical Music' (its owner is a restorer of clocks and musical boxes), and the collection of agricultural wagons and tools housed in a one-time 'house of correction' – an award-winning museum. There are reconstructed prison cells on show here, too.

Folly Farm has 140 breeds of waterfowl and rare poultry in natural surroundings, while at Denfurlong Farm there is an explanatory trail among the crops and animals (this is near Chedworth's fine Roman villa). But for the biggest collection of rare farm breeds go to the Cotswold Farm Park.

The area has a number of prehistoric remains such as the long barrow. This is near Bibury, to which visitors flock to see the working watermill (inside it is an exhibition about William Morris and the Arts and Crafts Movement, while outside are – still more! – rare breeds and a trout farm). Across the stream here, at Arlington Row, is a particularly pretty line of weavers' cottages now owned by the National Trust; and at Barnsley House you can visit the very lovely garden with 18th-century summerhouses and a decoratively planted 'potager' of vegetables. If you want a superb spot for a picnic lunch go to the 900-foot Kilkenny viewpoint.

Readers' comments: Eminently satisfied, thoroughly enjoyed it. Real home from home.

80

★ **COUNTRY HOUSE** C(9)
Hastings Road, Winchelsea, East Sussex, TN36 4AD Tel: 0797 226669
South of Rye. Nearest main road: A259 from Hastings to Folkestone.

3 Bedrooms. £16.50–£18 (less for 3 nights). All have own bath/shower/toilet. Tea/coffee facilities. TV. Views of garden, country.
Dinner. A la carte or £8.50 for 3 courses and coffee, at 7.30pm. Non-residents not admitted. Vegetarian or special diets if ordered. Wine can be ordered.
1 Sitting-room. With open fire, central heating, record-player. Bar.
Large garden
Closed from mid-December to mid-January.

National Trust landscape surrounds this 18th-century farmhouse, set back from the road, and in a walled garden is a variety of butterflies and birds. Flowering shrubs surround a lawn with lily-pool and brick terrace, and an adjoining brick barn is smothered in a mass of wisteria blossom every summer.

Mary Carmichael's decorative touches include festoon blinds and cane bed-heads with flowery duvets; padded blue velvet with pine bedroom furniture (this room has a sofa); in yet another room, a fabric patterned with garlands and bows. Many rooms have garden or hill views.

For pre-dinner drinks (or after-dinner coffee) there is a sitting-room with log fire; and in the candlelit dining-room are served such meals as fish chowder, lamb in sauce with asparagus and mushrooms and baked Alaska. (For SOTBT's 10th anniversary year, many proprietors will – during October 1991 – do extra-special meals for SOTBT visitors at no extra cost, if ordered in advance.)

Unlike its neighbour Rye, the town of Winchelsea is not particularly famous and I have always found it quiet when Rye was thronged with tourists. It is a delightful unspoilt little place in which to wander, near beautiful countryside and coast.

Readers' comments: Comfort surpassed my expectations. Delightful place, beautifully decorated. Welcoming and helpful. Food, service and accommodation of the highest standard, and exceptionally good value. Excellent.

Within the Edwardian-style **WIN-CHELSEA TEA ROOM** (in the town, on quiet Hiham Green) are spacious, well-equipped and stylish bedrooms. Downstairs bedrooms open onto a little garden. They have lace spreads, buttoned velvet bedheads and wildflower wallpapers. Organic produce is used for such dinners as home-made pâté, chops and fruit tart. The house is run by Shirley Wright on behalf of a charitable trust. Tel: 0797 226679. From £16.50.

Readers' comments: Excellent in every way.

COVE HOUSE

Ashton Keynes, Wiltshire, SN6 6NS Tel: 0285 861221
North-west of Swindon. Nearest main road: A419 from Swindon to Cirencester.

3 Bedrooms. £17–£20 (less for 2 nights). Discounts for repeat bookings. Some have own bath/shower/toilet. Tea/coffee facilities. TV (in one). Views of garden.
Dinner. £12 for 3 courses and coffee, at 7.30pm. Non-residents not admitted. Vegetarian or special diets if ordered. Wine can be brought in. No smoking. **Light suppers** if ordered.
2 Sitting-rooms. With open fire, central heating, TV.
Large garden

The narrow trickle running through this little village is in fact the infant Thames; you can walk right to its source from here. All around is a chain of large pools (originally gravel-diggings) now known as the Cotswold Water Park, which more or less encloses Ashton Keynes as if it were an island: birdwatchers come here to view the waterfowl.

Here Peter and Elizabeth Hartland live in one half of a 17th-century manor house (with later alterations) surrounded by a particularly lovely and secluded garden which has a succession of lawns and a paved carriage-yard with barbecue beside its lily-pool. One of its previous owners was Puritan John Richmond, who had a part in founding Taunton, Massachusetts.

Indoors is a large, friendly sitting-room; a dining-room that has interesting wallpaper, antiques and huge heirloom paintings; and Elizabeth's lovely flower arrangements everywhere. In the small library is an alcove lined with a large-scale, illuminated map of the area. Here Peter keeps a collection of packs for visitors, each full of carefully compiled information about various day-outings and his own 'good food guide' to local eating-places. Yet another sitting-room, upstairs, is for TV and viewing a video of local sights.

Bedrooms have individuality – one green-and-white sprigged; another full of clematis; a third (turquoise, with brass bedheads) has an unusual domed ceiling. Flowers are usually present.

Elizabeth uses garden produce for meals, at which the Hartlands dine with their guests. You might start with gazpacho or home-made pâté, perhaps; to be followed by a roast or salmon mayonnaise and then perhaps fruit sorbets or rhubarb-and-orange pudding.

Ashton Keynes is on the edge of the Cotswolds. Among other sightseeing possibilities the following are within an easy drive: Cheltenham, Oxford, Burford, Avebury, Bath, Stratford-upon-Avon, Marlborough, Blenheim, Cirencester, Malmesbury, Bibury village – also the gardens of Hidcote, Barnsley House and Kiftsgate. Ashton Keynes has an outstanding farm shop (meat etc.), with fruit and trout farms nearby. Antique shops are numerous.

Readers' comments: Stayed several times. Excellent in all respects. Beautiful house, relaxed and friendly hosts.

For explanation of code letters (C, D, H, PT, S, X) see page xxxiv.

COWLEIGH PARK FARMHOUSE

Cowleigh Road, Great Malvern, Worcestershire, WR13 5HJ
Tel: 0684 566750
Nearest main road: A449 from Worcester to Ross-on-Wye.

3 **Bedrooms.** £15–£17 (less for 5 nights). Bargain breaks. Some have own shower/toilet. TV. Views of garden, country. No smoking. Washing machine on request. **Dinner.** £9.50 for 3 courses (with choices) and coffee, at 7pm (Monday–Friday only).

Non-residents not admitted. Vegetarian or special diets if ordered. Wine can be ordered or brought in. No smoking. **Light suppers** if ordered.
Large garden

The half-timbered house is 350 years old, and some of its beams even older (taken from a 13th-century moated manor house which once stood in the field behind it). Approaching it from the high Malvern Hills, one passes along lanes of larches and crags, shadows alternating with sunshine, the distant landscape vanishing into a soft haze. On driving up to the door, there is a tranquil scene – snowy alyssum spreading over old stone walls, an ancient cider-press on the brick terrace. (The Worcestershire Way starts here.)

Beyond the slate-flagged hall, Sue Stringer has furnished the low-beamed rooms attractively – buttoned velvet chesterfields, a Gillow table of walnut and bevelled glass, and a grand piano in the sitting-room where logs are stacked in the large brick inglenook; and in the dining-room (which has a very pretty Victorian cast-iron grate) there are spoon-back chairs and mulberry walls. Bedrooms have deep-pile carpets, stripped pine, board-and-latch doors, and soft colours such as beige or pink. One has a particularly pretty view, of lily-pool and rock-garden.

Sue's dinners are imaginative – starting with, for instance, Stilton-and-apple soup or salade niçoise; possibly with goulash to follow and blackcurrant gâteau.

★ Nearer the town centre is **ONE-EIGHT-FOUR**, set high up in West Malvern Road (tel: 06845 66544), from which there is an uninterrupted rural view to the hills of Wales over 30 miles away. The rooms are on five floors, with sparkling colour schemes and unusual antique bedheads.

For breakfast Jan Kellett serves all the usual things, plus such imaginative options as fruits already peeled and sliced, fresh-baked scones and muffins, and vegetarian selections. Light suppers are provided. From £16 – £19.

CRAB AND LOBSTER INN

C PT S

Foreland, Isle of Wight, PO35 Tel: 098387 2244
East of Bembridge. Nearest main road: A3055 from Ryde to Shanklin.

5 Bedrooms. £13.50–£14 (less for 7 nights). Bargain breaks. Tea/coffee facilities. Some have sea views.
Dinner. A la carte, from 7pm. Vegetarian or special diets if ordered. Wine can be ordered. **Light suppers**.

1 Sitting-room. With central heating, TV. Bars.
Closed from December to February inclusive.

This old inn perched on a clifftop provides simple accommodation and spectacular views over the Channel. David Hill will tell you the inn was not named after the plentiful local shellfish but a New Zealand shrub (Puniceus) which has flowers that look like crab or lobster claws and which grows by its walls. Before he took over the inn he used to have the job of advising hotels on their wine, so naturally his are good value. Good straightforward food – big lobsters straight from the sea.

The inn started in 1810 as tea-rooms, but one day the clifftop garden fell into the sea. The dining-room, with big windows is very attractively decorated (as is the adjoining bar); its walls are white-painted boards, and there are pot-plants everywhere. In the main bar are casks of sherry, peach and apricot wine, mead and scrumpy alongside more conventional drinks. There is a second bar with darts etc.

Outside are the weatherboarded watchtower of the coastguards who keep a careful eye on the reef below, footpaths along the clifftop or down to the sands, and, out in the sea, the enormous old Nab Tower that was built in Southampton and towed to its site in the days when French invasion was feared, later to be used for suspending anti-submarine nets across the approaches to the Solent. David and the coastguards who frequent the bar are full of anecdotes about such local oddities, and about some of his past visitors ('we get prince and pauper here'), who have included the French Ambassador on one occasion, and Edward Heath with the crew of *Morning Cloud* on others. The inn is very busy in high summer.

Bembridge itself is an interesting little place with a lifeboat house open to the public, sailing harbour and a particularly good maritime museum. Coast and rolling countryside are equally lovely here. Although it is at the east end of the island where most of the resorts are, it is not difficult to get to the wilder west end. There is a lot to visit here; many stately homes, fossils around Sandown (visit the geology museum to identify your finds), a first-rate wildlife park, botanical gardens with an intriguing museum of smuggling, Queen Victoria's house outside the sailing centre of Cowes, beautiful Blackgang Chine with one lovely garden after another, a centre with dozens of craftsmen at work, Carisbrooke Castle.

Readers' comments: Food excellent; service most attentive.

84

CRIB FARM
Luddenden Foot, West Yorkshire HX2 6JJ   Tel: 0422 883 285
West of Halifax. Nearest main road: A646 from Hebden Bridge to Halifax.

4 Bedrooms. £10–£12. Some have own bath/shower/toilet. TV. Views of garden, country. No smoking.
Dinner. £6 for 3 courses (with some choices) and coffee, at 6.30pm. Vegetarian or special diets if ordered. Wine can be ordered or brought in.
1 Sitting-room. With open fire, central heating, TV, piano. Bar.
Large garden

A necessary break to change horses on the long cross-Pennine journey from Lancashire to Yorkshire brought this 17th-century moorland house into being, for originally it was a coaching inn. Centuries later it became – and still is – a dairy-farm, though its role as a haven for travellers continues too, even though they now arrive by car, by train (to Halifax) or even by air (to Leeds). The Hitchen family have been here since 1815.

The old house has a warm and hospitable atmosphere, with rooms decorated in light and cheerful colours. Comfortable and unpretentious, it has been recommended to me by friends who also praise Pauline's cooking. A typical menu: melon or home-made asparagus soup, home-reared turkey with garden vegetables, a choice of puddings from strawberries and cream to apple pie, or cheeses.

Luddenden Foot, which lies below the farm, once had a railway station, where Branwell Brontë worked as a clerk, and the village will be familiar also to viewers of Thora Hird's 'In Loving Memory'. From the farm there are sweeping views to the wild uplands of Midgley Moor, but down below Branwell found his station dank and depressing – 'hacked out of a great black rock-face', as Lynne Reid Banks describes it in *Dark Quartet*. He, the rich son of a local mill-owner, and Irish labourers together drank themselves silly at local inns; and it was at Luddenden that he first took drugs too, stealing money from the station till to pay for them.

Bank House (1650) at Luddenden is the earliest surviving example of a south Pennine laithe house – that is, house, barn and cow-byre all under one roof.

Beyond Ripponden lies the best-preserved Roman road in Britain, running across the Blackstone Edge: its big stone setts have survived nearly 2000 years of wind and weather some 1500 feet up on the desolate moors.

Not much further afield are Haworth (the Brontës' home), the Worth Valley steam railway, the villages where 'Emmerdale Farm' and 'Last of the Summer Wine' have been filmed for television, and Bingley of the five-rise locks. Bradford is well worth several day-trips for its splendid architecture, the outstanding National Photographic Museum, bargains at the many woollen mills and much else. But above all, the moor and the dales can be explored from here, with their great crags, tremendous views, waterfalls and streams. Some people come to them for the climbing, golf, riding, angling or other sports; many simply for the peace.

> Prices are per person in a double room at the beginning of the year.

CROSS LANE HOUSE

Allerford, Somerset, TA24 8HW   Tel: 0643 862112
West of Minehead. Nearest main road: A39 from Minehead to Porlock.

3 Bedrooms. £14. Tea/coffee facilities. TV. Views of garden, country. Washing machine on request.
Dinner. A la carte, from 7pm (except Sundays). In winter, book meals in advance (Thursday–Saturday). Vegetarian or special diets if ordered. Wine can be ordered.

1 Sitting-room. With open fire, TV, record-player. Bar.
Small garden
Closed in November.

At picturesque Allerford, a few miles from Minehead, is Cross Lane house, its restaurant well known to gourmets in the area (and, although on the A39, it has fairly quiet rooms, inexpensive and with country views). Lawrie Pluck's gourmet cooking began in a tent on safari when he lived in Kenya and when camping near here as a student. He and his Dutch-born wife Ida honeymooned here. Then he had a career in computers until, at 48, he at last realized his ambition to start a first-rate restaurant in the area.

Inside the old farmhouse, a small sitting-room is filled with African carvings among a host of other objects, and leather sofas. An old wig-cupboard has survived the centuries. The dining-room is furnished with spindleback chairs and gingham cloths on the tables. All rooms are simple and unpretentious.

As to the most important thing at Cross Lane, the food, the menu is extensive and contains some surprises. Some dishes are very English – such as watercress soup, salmon mousse, local venison (simmered in wine, cream and herbs) or the cider syllabub from a recipe of 1600. But, from travels, Lawrie has also collected a number of exotic recipes. He does an Indonesian rijstaffel once a week in winter. Lamb comes with a peanut sauce. And, an indication of his attention to detail, when he cooks a Kenyan curry he often offers Kenyan beer with it.

15th-century **OLD MANOR** at Dunster (tel: 0643 821216) stands on marshes that lead to the sea. There is a chapel over the front porch: its barrel-vaulted roof has carved bosses.

Gillian Hill's bedrooms differ, the most striking being a huge room with the wood pegging of the cruck-beamed roof open to view. Some other rooms are in a Victorian addition. (B & B only.) From £16.50 to £22.

Readers' comments: A most enjoyable two weeks.

CROSSWAYS FARM

C PT X

Abinger, Surrey, RH5 6PZ   Tel: 0306 730173
South-west of Dorking. Nearest main road: A25 from Guildford to Dorking.

3 Bedrooms. £13–£14 (less for 5 nights). Bargain breaks. Some have own bath/toilet. Tea/coffee facilities. Views of garden, country. No smoking. Washing machine on request.
Dinner. £8 for 3 courses and coffee, at 7pm. Non-residents not admitted. Vegetarian or special diets if ordered. Wine can be brought in. No smoking. **Light suppers** if ordered.
1 Sitting-room. With open fire, central heating, TV, piano, record-player. No smoking.
Small garden with croquet and putting.

Meredith's *Diana of the Crossways* (one of those books most people have heard of and few have read) took its title from this historic building of unusual architectural interest, which featured in a television film about the 17th-century diarist John Evelyn.

One steps through the arched door in a high wall to find a small, enclosed garden with a flagged path leading to the wide front door of the house. In its façade decorative brickwork combines with local sandstone, and Dutch-style arches curve over the small-paned windows. There is an immense chimney-stack towering above – 30 feet in circumference. But the most striking feature of all is the great oak staircase inside, its two flights leading up to large, beamed bedrooms, simply but comfortably furnished (there is a suite consisting of a double and a twin room with bathroom); the balusters and newels are handsomely carved.

The house has had many owners since it was built about 1620. For the last quarter-century, the Hughes family have farmed here, producing beef and corn. Sheila Hughes serves homely farmhouse meals (like Irish stew, fish pie, roast chicken etc.) usually with garden vegetables; or you can eat outstandingly well at, for instance, nearby Wootton Hatch. Breakfast options include, if ordered in advance, such extras as fishcakes or kidneys.

Crossways is attractive to many people: walkers, because both the Pilgrims' Way and the Greensand Way are near (and you need no car – buses can be picked up only yards away); continental visitors, because it is a good half-way stop en route to the West Country or to Wales. And for Londoners, it's an ideal weekend retreat: a drive of only half an hour or so. Leith and Box hills are near; Polesden Lacey and Clandon Park; also the RHS gardens at Wisley, and countless antique shops.

Guildford's modern cathedral has notable engraved glass, its castle ruins are surrounded by pleasant gardens, and the river trips are of great interest. Hatchlands (NT) is a house with magnificent Adam rooms, a garden designed by Gertrude Jekyll and a collection of historic pianos, while at Loseley Park (Tudor) is a dairy-farm where the celebrated ice creams are made.

Northward is Esher and grounds (with lake) landscaped by William Kent; at Claremont, the National Trust sometimes stages magnificent fêtes; and at Painshill Park, Cobham, there are lake, follies, grotto and Chinese bridge. Garden-lovers will enjoy the hilly Winkworth Arboretum near Godalming, at its best in spring or when autumn colours blaze.

Readers' comments: Warm welcome. Comfortable.

CROWN INN

C(14) PT X

Downham Market, Norfolk, PE38 9DH   Tel: 0366 382322
South of King's Lynn. Nearest main road: A10 from Ely to King's Lynn.

rear view

10 **Bedrooms.** £16–£19. Bargain breaks. Some have own bath/shower/toilet. Tea/ coffee facilities. TV. Washing machine on request.
Dinner. A la carte, at 6–10pm. Vegetarian or special diets available. Wine can be ordered.
Light suppers if ordered.
1 **Sitting-room.** With log-effect fire, TV. Bar.

The unassuming and small façade of this inn, facing the market square, gives no hint of what lies behind. The 17th-century building straggles far back, and when you pass under the high arch (built for coaches) you come first to the bar, with rooms above, and beyond them to what was once a considerable range of stables – since converted into restaurant and kitchens: black-and-white pantiled buildings, with hanging baskets of flowers. This was once a yeomanry centre. John Champion (formerly a civil engineer) keeps the bar-room more or less as it was for the last century or so – oak-panelled, jugs hanging from its beams, a brick hearth at each end. The bar is made from sherry casks, and on the walls are wartime photographs of the famous Pathfinders air squadron who, based nearby, used this bar as their 'local'.

The stable restaurant has been discreetly converted: floors and walls are of brick, solid elm tables stand in each former loose-box. A chef works in full view at one end, cooking griddled steaks or chops, for instance. Gâteaux, pâtés and everything else are made in the kitchens. Breakfasts are served elsewhere – in a low-beamed Dickensian parlour, beyond which are two very handsome Jacobean staircases leading to the bedrooms (and a residents' sitting-room). These are spacious and furnished to a much higher standard than is usual in country inns: most have beautiful bathrooms.

From Downham Market one can tour north Norfolk. Royal Sandringham is a few miles in one direction, Ely Cathedral in the other. Nearby King's Lynn certainly needs more than a flying visit because its mediaeval quarter alongside the river holds so much of interest. Just walking along the quays, through courts and alleys, into the cathedral-like church and to the immense market square is pleasure in itself. In addition, there are museums, art gallery, theatre in a historic building and snug inns to visit. Eastward lies one of East Anglia's finest coastlines (an area of outstanding natural beauty) with a string of bird reserves and natural shoreline. One can visit Houghton Hall and three older National Trust mansions from here, the Norfolk lavender fields, the fens, the Caithness glass factory (with bargains), Castle Rising, the cliffs of Hunstanton, Nelson's birthplace, and also the Peterborough area. The fens have a strange, wild beauty all their own. Peterborough's cathedral is one of the great splendours of the area, but its museum, riverside gardens and old byways are well worth visiting too. Go to Wisbech for a Dutch-style town (and Peckover House) and the surrounding tulip-fields in spring; to Spalding for the flower festival.

Readers' comments: Most welcoming. Comfortable character, friendly.

CRYER HOUSE   **C D**
Castle Street, Castleton, Derbyshire, S30 2WG   Tel: 0433 20244
West of Sheffield (West Yorkshire). Nearest main road: A625 from Sheffield to
Chapel-en-le-Frith.

2 Bedrooms. £11.50–£12.50. Prices go up
in April. Tea/coffee facilities on request.
TV. Views of garden, country.
Light suppers up to 6pm.
Small garden

Castleton's main claim to fame is its range of huge underground caves (several can
be visited), from one of which is mined a very pretty stone, unique in the world,
called Blue John – elegant trinkets made from it are lovely souvenirs to take home.
Another would be a local landscape by actor-artist Terence Skelton.

Wisteria-covered Cryer House (named after a 17th-century rector who owned
it) is where he lives with his wife Felicity, a former theatrical director, and their
children. They have furnished the house with great flair: excellent colours and well
chosen furnishings in every room. On the ground floor is a tea-room (board floor,
pine tables and benches). Breakfast and early snack suppers are served either here
or in the new conservatory adjoining it. Packed lunches are available, but for other
meals there is a choice of four inns in the village which have restaurants or provide
good bar meals; then after dinner one can relax in their little cottage garden,
brimming with flowers, and watch the world go by. On summer weekends, the
village is thronged with tourists.

To see Castleton's centuries-old garland ceremony, stay at the end of May.

The High Peak of northern Derbyshire is in complete contrast to the rest of the
county. Here the crags that rise from windswept heather moors are wild and
challenging. No towns – only stone hamlets sheltering below the towering ridges.
This is where you will see climbers and pot-holers (hang-gliders too), and where
even the less intrepid can explore winding footpaths or go down to caves of
stalactites and stalagmites, some visited by boat. Some of the loveliest hamlets are
Abney (with gorge), Baslow (mediaeval bridge), Castleton itself (and Peveril
Castle), Edale (gorges, crags and a path up Kinder Scout, over 2000 feet high),
Eyam (in wild, open country with superb views and a prehistoric circle). Eyam is
'the plague village': to prevent infection spreading, in 1666 the heroic villagers
deliberately cut themselves off to die alone. Grindleford is celebrated for sheepdog
trials on the moors and for Longshaw Park (1000 acres, NT). Axe Edge Moor and
the Goyt Valley are two areas of outstanding scenery; so is the Snake Pass; and the
chain of reservoirs starting with Lady Bower.

In the Sheffield direction are still more caves of stalactites at Bradwell (where
caving techniques are taught), the Ridgeway cottage industries centre; and a new
country park (Rother Valley) with boats and watersports. Around Chesterfield
(which has a fine church and three museums) are more landscaped reservoirs and,
as well as world-famous Chatsworth, the stately homes of Barlborough Hall
(Elizabethan) and Bolsover Castle on a wooded hilltop. Pilsley's herb garden has
panoramic views.

Readers' comments: A warm welcome; comfortable, spacious rooms, lovely conservatory.

DAIRY FARM

Cranford St Andrew, Northamptonshire, NN14 4AQ Tel: 053678 273
East of Kettering. Nearest main road: A604 from Kettering to Huntingdon.

3 Bedrooms. £16–£20 (less for 4 nights). Some have own bath/shower/toilet. Tea/coffee facilities. TV. Views of garden, country. No smoking. Washing machine on request.
Dinner. £10 for 3 courses (with choices) and coffee, at 7pm. Non-residents not admitted. Vegetarian or special diets if ordered. Wine can be brought in. No smoking. **Light suppers** sometimes.
1 Sitting-room. With open fire, central heating, TV, record-player. No smoking.
Garden with croquet.

This is not in fact a dairy-farm but arable and sheep. Its name derives from the old dairy around which the manor house was built, in 1610. It is a fine building with mullioned lattice windows in limestone walls and a thatched roof. Its noble chimney-stacks, finials on the gables, dormer windows and dignified porch give it great character. In the grounds stands a circular stone dovecote (mediaeval) with unique rotating ladder inside, used for collecting the birds from the 400 pigeonholes that line it.

Audrey and John Clarke have hung old family portraits in the sitting-room, and furnished the house with things like an oak dresser, chests and ladderback chairs that are in keeping with it. Some bedrooms overlook church and mansion nearby.

Meals consist of straightforward home cooking – soups, roasts, fruit pies – using fruit and vegetables from the garden. Mrs Clarke also does a cordon bleu menu, which costs a little more and has to be ordered ahead.

Visitors enjoy local walks (beside a willow-fringed stream, across-country, or simply to the Woolpack Inn). This is good cycling country, too. Sightseeing possibilities include Burghley House, Rockingham Castle, the mediaeval stone town of Stamford, Althorp (home of the Princess of Wales's father), Lamport and Kirby Halls, Peterborough Cathedral, Cambridge, Uppingham and Oundle. And at Kettering, Wicksteed Park is an ideal place to take children. Oundle is as attractive as many old Cotswold towns, for the local stone is the same, but much less frequented by tourists. The buildings of its famous public school are like an Oxford college. One can take boat trips on the River Nene, and visit watermills and a country park just on the outskirts, or the gardens at Coton Manor. For the equestrian-minded, there are the Burghley horse trials in September.

The farm is close to the borders of both Cambridgeshire and Bedfordshire which means that it is also easy to visit such places of interest as Elton Hall, Hinchingbrooke House (a much altered Norman nunnery) and 18th-century Island Hall; or Bromhall water mill on the banks of the Ouse, Stevingdon windmill, Stagsden bird gardens and all the Bunyan sights in and around Bedford (which has the exceptional Cecil Higgins art gallery too). Grafham Water is a big, naturalized reservoir. Huntingdon has a Cromwell museum in the school where he (and Pepys) were educated in the 17th century.

Readers' comments: Very special, will return. Delicious food; peaceful; attentive hosts. Very kind, food plentiful, peaceful. Delightful house and setting.

DAISY BROOK   C

Forest Lane, Lacock, Wiltshire, SN15 2PN   Tel: 024973 257
South of Chippenham. Nearest main road: A350 from Chippenham to
Melksham.

2 Bedrooms. £13.50 (less for 7 nights).
Prices go up in March. Bargain breaks. Tea/
coffee facilities. Views of garden, country.
Washing machine on request.
Dinner. £7 for 3 courses (with choices) and
coffee, at 7pm. Non-residents not admitted.
Vegetarian or special diets if ordered. Wine
can be ordered or brought in.
1 Sitting-room. With open fire, TV.
Small garden

It is rare for an entire village of such beauty as this to have been preserved (by the
National Trust) just as it was in the 18th century, and with many buildings much
older than that.

On the outskirts, in rural seclusion, stands this 18th-century stone cottage,
behind a low wall on which stonecrop and other sedums grow in profusion. On
sunny days, Joy Ames will welcome you with tea in the garden, beyond the
petunias and lobelias of which is a far view of Bowden Hill (also National Trust
property). The site of a Roman road goes through the garden.

Go in through the low porch and you will find small, beamed rooms with
Liberty's Iolanthe fabric (an art nouveau pattern) used on the sofa and for
curtains, a log stove and pot-plants. There's a white and green dining-room with
mahogany tables; and, up a steep stairway, fresh-looking bedrooms that are pale
and trim.

When Joy serves dinners (not in high season) you might be offered such a meal
as salad niçoise, tarragon chicken with lyonnaise potatoes and home-grown
vegetables, followed by a pavlova.

In Lacock's winding streets are grey stone houses with gothic arches, half-
timbered cottages, a lovely church, big mediaeval barn and the cloistered abbey
which, after the dissolution of the monasteries by Henry VIII, was converted into
a mansion – here, in Victorian times, lived Fox Talbot, pioneer of photography.

Just within the village is the **OLD
RECTORY** (tel: 024973 335), built for
a newly appointed rector and his bride-
to-be in 1866. But on the wedding-day
it was revealed that – shock! horror! –
he already had a wife overseas.

This less than virtuous life-style had
not inhibited him, however, from
filling the house with sanctimonious
detail. One enters through an ecclesias-
tical-style oak door within a pointed
arch; to either side are stained glass
windows. A particularly fine yew staircase leads up to very well equipped
bedrooms which Margaret Addison has
furnished with style, using chinoiserie

fabrics, pink moiré (in a four-poster
room) or Laura Ashley prints. Each has
an immaculate modern bathroom.
Breakfast only (visitors dine at, for instance, the George Inn). £15.

DAMSELLS LODGE

C D H PT

The Park, Painswick, Gloucestershire, GL6 6SR   Tel: 0452 813777
North of Stroud. Nearest main road: A46 from Stroud to Cheltenham.

3 Bedrooms. £16.50–£17.50 (less for 3 nights). Bargain breaks. One has own shower/toilet. Tea/coffee facilities. TV. Views of garden, country. Washing machine on request.
1 Sitting-room. With log stove, central heating, TV, piano, record-player.
Small garden

This very comfortable house was originally the lodge to the nearby mansion. It is in a peaceful rural lane and has truly spectacular views from every window across a small garden of lawns, stone terrace and flowering shrubs. Only breakfast is provided – guests eat dinner at the nearby Royal William or in one of Painswick's restaurants: the Royal Oak or Country Elephant, for instance.

Judy Cooke is a welcoming hostess who soon makes friends with her visitors. She has made the Lodge immaculate and very comfortable. The huge sitting-room has windows on three sides, and a big log stove. Everywhere there are thick carpets and good furniture (even the bathroom is pretty luxurious). In my view, the best bedroom is one separate from the house: it is in a one-floor garden cottage, with huge sliding windows through which to step straight onto the lawn or to view the distant hills while still in bed, and ideal for anyone who finds stairs difficult. Peter is a landscape gardener; and some shrubs and conifers are for sale.

Painswick church is famous for its 99 enormous yews, centuries-old, clipped into arches or other neat shapes, and for its fine peal of twelve bells. When the September yew-clipping takes place, children dance and sing round the church. The village has many antique shops. To the north lies the cathedral city of Gloucester (it houses the outstanding National Waterways Museum, among many other sights), and to the south the wooded Cotswold Hills, with particularly spectacular views from Minchinhampton and Rodborough commons (National Trust land). Go west for the Severn estuary with its throngs of seabirds and geese.

The steep ups and downs of this hilly area mean there are many scenic car rides – for instance, in the direction of Prinknash Abbey (part mediaeval, part modern – with a viewing gallery above the monks' pottery and a collection of exotic birds) from which there are views to the River Severn – or go to the observation point high above the beech woods of Cooper's Hill, topped by a maypole. Further on is Crickley Hill (with three trails to choose from – geological, archaeological or ecological – and more superb views). You could return via Birdlip and Sheepscombe; or take the Ermine Way (a Roman road, straight as a spear) to Cirencester (described elsewhere), perhaps returning via Sapperton, sited on a steep ridge which overlooks the 'Golden Valley' of the River Frome – truly golden in the autumn, when the beech woods turn colour. (The church at Sapperton has splendid carvings and several houses were designed by Gimson and his associates who lived here.)

Readers' comments: Excellent accommodation; the place and the owners delightful. Immaculate; lovely setting, gorgeous view; helpful.

DEERFELL

Blackdown Park, West Sussex, GU27 3LA   Tel: 0428 653409
South of Haslemere. Nearest main road: A286 from Haslemere to Midhurst.

2 Bedrooms. £14 (less for 4 nights). Bargain breaks. All have own bath/shower/toilet.

Tea/coffee facilities. TV in one. Views of garden. No smoking. Washing machine on request.
Dinner. £8.50 for 3 courses (with choices) and coffee, at 7.30pm. Non-residents not admitted. Vegetarian or special diets if ordered. Wine can be brought in. No smoking. **Light suppers** if ordered.
1 Sitting-room. With open fire, central heating, TV, piano, record-player. No smoking. **Large garden**
Closed from 20 December to 7 January inclusive.

The Black Down, a Stone Age stronghold 8000 years ago, rises to nearly 1000 feet. The ferny lane that winds up it, beech trees arching overhead, gives way to sandy heathland where, in Tudor times, iron nodules were grubbed up to be forged into guns, pots and the decorative firebacks that are to be seen in old houses for miles around. To provide power for their forges, the ironworkers dammed streams – hence the chain of 'furnace ponds' which one passes on the way up.

One of the wealthiest ironmasters built himself in 1607 a mansion that is still here (and Deerfell was originally its coach house, erected three centuries later). Cromwell occupied it during the Civil Wars, and Tennyson was a frequent visitor; you can see the home he built and where he died, at the National Trust carpark.

As to Deerfell, its conversion from coach house to home was well done, retaining such features as stone-mullioned windows and latched board doors, but with such modern additions as a glass sun-room and a fireplace of green marble. Elizabeth Carmichael has furnished it with antiques, old rugs and colour schemes which are predominantly soft brown and cream. Bedrooms are comfortable and spacious; her meals well-cooked, ample and unpretentious – for instance, leek soup, cottage pie and a tart of wild blackberries.

In the middle of Haslemere itself is **TOWN HOUSE** (tel: 0428 3310), an outstanding building of 1635 which has a remarkable inlaid oak staircase, with panelled and pilastered walls adorned by carved pears and pomegranates – as well as a pink-and-white sitting-room overlooking the walled garden. Anthea Smyrk has furnished the rooms – which include a family suite – with antiques and Laura Ashley fabrics. The breakfast-room is also panelled. (For dinner, most visitors stroll to the White Horse coaching inn nearby –

gourmets, to Morels.) Previous inhabitants of the house include General Oglethorpe, who founded Georgia. From £16 to £18.

DORNDEN

C D

Church Lane, Old Sodbury, Avon, BS17 6NB Tel: 0454 313325
North-east of Bristol. Nearest main road: A432 from Bristol to Old Sodbury.

9 Bedrooms. £20 (much less for 4 nights, or at weekends too). Prices go up in February. Bargain breaks. Some have own bath/shower/toilet. TV. Views of garden, country. Washing machine on request.
Dinner. £7 for 3 courses (with choices of sweet) and coffee, at 6.45pm. Non-residents not admitted. Vegetarian or special diets if ordered. Wine can be brought in.
1 Sitting-room. With central heating, TV, piano.
Large garden

An immaculate garden surrounds the big guest-house – flowerbeds and box-hedges in trim and neat array, with a large vegetable and fruit garden to supply the kitchen. From its lawns and grass tennis court, set high up, there are splendid views.

This is the place for a quiet stay, well placed for exploring the scenic counties of Avon, Somerset, Wiltshire and Gloucestershire around it. All the rooms are sedate and comfortable in a style appropriate to what was, in mid-Victorian days, a vicarage and with features of the period still retained – from the beautifully polished tiles of the hall to the terrace onto which the sitting-room opens.

Daphne Paz serves traditional favourites at dinner – such as pork chops or trout with almonds, followed by a choice of two puddings (rice, trifle, plum-and-almond tart or cheesecake, for instance) and then cheeses: very moderately priced.

Old Sodbury is conveniently near a motorway yet is a quiet retreat at the south end of the Cotswolds. In its immediate vicinity are 17th-century Dyrham Park (which the National Trust regards as one of its most spectacular properties – its tapestries and its gardens are outstanding), Tudor Thornbury Castle and other stately homes as well as Westonbirt Arboretum.

Quickly reached from, for instance, London, it is also well placed as a centre from which to go sightseeing. Bath and Bristol are near, and Wales only a short hop across the Severn estuary; while, using the M5, one can quickly arrive in Somerset, Devon and the rest of the West Country. But there is no need to go far.

Close by is Castle Combe – a most picturesque village, nestling in a valley around which wooded hills climb high (it's a place of mellow stone houses, a turreted church with lovely fan-vaulting, canopied market cross, and a twisting brook that flows under its ancient bridge). And other lovely villages (Biddestone and Badminton in particular). Two things contributed to the beauty of north-west Wiltshire: the fact that wealth (from wool weaving) was amassed during a period of fine architectural style, and the availability of lovely gold or creamy stone with which to build. Rivers watered fertile pastures and carved out valleys where woodlands flourish.

The Romans left remains in Bath and elsewhere; in mediaeval times, great churches were built throughout the region.

Readers' comments: Strongly recommended. Cooking of high standard. Excellent value. Very friendly.

94

★ DOWN COURT   D PT S

Slad, Gloucestershire, GL6 7QE   Tel: 0452 812427
North of Stroud. Nearest main road: A46 from Stroud to Cheltenham.

2 Bedrooms. £13.50–£15 (less for 7 nights). Prices go up in April. Bargain breaks. Tea/coffee facilities. Views of garden, country. No smoking. Washing machine on request. **Dinner.** £9.50 for 4 courses and coffee, from 7.30pm. Non-residents not admitted. Vegetarian or special diets if ordered. Wine can be ordered or brought in. **Light suppers** if ordered. **2 Sitting-rooms.** With open fire, central heating, TV, piano, record-player. **Large garden. Closed from November to February inclusive.**

Slad is the hamlet where Laurie Lee grew up (he still lives near the inn), and on your way to Down Court you may pass many of the scenes in his *Cider with Rosie* – the school, the squire's house – Steanbridge (once a cloth mill, one of many in the Frome Valley), the Lees' childhood home, the workhouse, and the pool where Miss Flynn drowned herself.

When the BBC filmed *Cider with Rosie* (1971), they used Down Court for the interior shots and its paddock for the final haymaking scene with the memorable cider; and on the video which the Mills show interested guests you may recognize details like the big cheval mirror in your bedroom. Village children acted the part of the Lee children. Anne Mills assisted with props and other help during the year-long filming, and has many behind-scene stories to tell. There are auto-graphed copies of *Cider with Rosie* which visitors can buy.

As to Down Court, despite its rather grand name it began life in 1620 as five one-roomed cottages in a courtyard for farm workers' families, with a communal well outside. Walls are two-feet thick, windows stone-mullioned, ceilings low and beamed, fires set in huge stone inglenooks. Now there are fine antiques (unusual French chairs, for instance, and a single-handed clock that dates back to the 17th century), and a high standard of comfort. Anne has made many of the furnishings herself, particularly patchwork cushions and window-seats in the attractive bedrooms from which there are tranquil hill views. In the larger of the two sitting-rooms is an Erard grand piano (1820).

After qualifying at Bath Catering College, Anne was at the Dorchester Hotel for a while, later doing private catering of a high order. For five years she worked for Prince and Princess Michael of Kent who – like other royals – live near here. Today visitors to her home enjoy the same high standard of cooking.

I selected courgette soup, chicken in a creamy lemon sauce and a deliciously light summer pudding. Most vegetables and fruit come from the garden.

Readers' comments: Excellent hospitality, faultless service. We altered our itinerary in order to return again! Excellent food, environment peaceful. Idyllic; glorious views. A perfect stay; wonderfully comfortable rooms.

DRAKESTONE HOUSE   C D

Stinchcombe, Gloucestershire, GL11 6AS   Tel: 0453 542140
South-west of Stroud. Nearest main road: A38 from Bristol to Gloucester.

rear view

Tea/coffee facilities and TV on request.
Views of garden, country. No smoking.
Washing machine on request.
Dinner. £12.50 for 4 courses (with choices of pudding) and coffee, at 7.15pm. Non-residents not admitted. Vegetarian or special diets if ordered. Wine can be brought in. No smoking.
1 Sitting-room. With open fire, central heating, piano, record-player.
Large garden

3 Bedrooms. £17. Prices usually go up in April. Some have own bath/shower/toilet.

Closed from mid-October to March inclusive.

How many centuries does it take for a house to mellow until it and its landscape seem one? Drakestone House was built in 1911, yet it looks as if it grew out of the Cotswold hills long, long ago. It was based on a design by the celebrated Cotswolds designer Ernest Gimson – a disciple of William Morris. Into its construction went details salvaged from older buildings – a scalloped alcove rescued when an 18th-century cottage was demolished, and even older painted tiles from Delft for several hearths. Windows have small casements and some have window-seats; there is white-painted panelling in the sitting-room, and beams across the decoratively plastered ceiling. Outside is a typically formal Edwardian garden, with grassy terraces bordered by clipped yews and great copper beeches, from which there are views right across the Vale of Berkeley to the hills of Wales.

This fine house was built for Hugh St John-Mildmay's grandparents, but by the time he inherited it, it was rather run down (and devoid of furniture). He and Crystal not only restored it but filled it with appropriate furnishings which include such things as buttoned velvet chesterfields, an inlaid chest, 18th-century prints, a Chippendale high-chair for a baby, and a very early tabletop piano (1790 – before foot-pedals were invented). In curious harmony with these are carvings they collected during 10 years in west and north Africa: dance masks, fertility dolls, intricately shaped shutters and much else. Bedrooms, too, are full of such treasures – even the principal bathroom is very pretty.

When Crystal provides dinner it is likely to be such a meal as: spinach soup; chicken in a sauce of mustard, cream and mushrooms; cheese with salad; and then a choice of puddings such as hot pears in syrup or cold chocolate pudding.

Apart from the scenic splendours of the immediate neighbourhood, there is easily a week or more of varied and interesting excursions one could make each day. For example, Painswick village and church are not only exceptionally beautiful but there is also a unique rococo garden there – the only early 18th-century garden to have survived in its entirety. It was recently discovered, hidden in a Cotswold valley, and its vistas, woodland walks and picturesque buildings are still being restored. Then there is Slimbridge, 800-acre home to thousands of swans, geese, ducks and flamingos: in winter they are floodlit in the evening. There are observatories from which to watch these and other water-birds; a tropical house with humming-birds; and exhibitions. Paintings by Sir Peter Scott (who lived at Slimbridge) are on sale. There is also a bird park at Prinknash Abbey, where the monks make distinctive pottery for sale on a hill south of Cheltenham, itself needing a whole day to explore.

DUDDON LODGE   S
Tarporley, Cheshire, CW6 0EP   Tel: 0829 781372
East of Chester. Nearest main road: A51 from Chester to Tarporley.

4 Bedrooms. £16–£19. Prices go up in April. Some have own bath/shower/toilet. Tea/coffee facilities. TV. Views of garden, country. Washing machine on request.
Light suppers if ordered. Vegetarian or special diets if ordered. Wine can be brought in.
1 Sitting-room. With open fire, central heating, piano. No smoking.
Large garden
Closed from December to February inclusive.

Dickory Joynson has furnished every room beautifully in this 18th-century house. It would particularly appeal to anyone interested in the arts, not only for its contents (grand piano, countless paintings, antiques and fine old linens for which Dickory scours local markets) but because she is so well informed about arts festivals, opera and similar events in the region.

In the dining-room (with pheasant wallpaper and table laid with antique silver) hangs a poignant group portrait of the five Becher sisters with an empty space for the sixth, who died in the Black Hole of Calcutta. The sitting-room has two alcoves filled with porcelain and a bay window framed in jasmine which opens onto a short rose-walk.

A graceful stair with striking sea-green wallpaper leads to attractive bedrooms. There is a suite (with dressing-room, oval bath in bathroom, separate toilet) which has a splendid 'twenties set of furniture in figured walnut. In another room is a collection of blue glass and of sculpture by the Joynsons' son. The 'bird room' contains a Heals' 'half-acre' bed of cane and mahogany, made in the 'thirties. Finally, for the nimble, there is an attic room reached by a winding stair. Through the bedrooms' sash windows or 'Norfolk lights' are views of the garden, croquet lawn or grass tennis court.

Beyond the winding lawns and beds of flowering shrubs and hidden by cypress hedges is a large, warm swimming-pool enclosed by a blue 'bubble'.

B & b only, but if ordered in advance Dickory will prepare such 'light' suppers as salmon or mackerel pâté, steak and kidney pie and raspberries and cream.

The nearest small town, Tarporley, is surrounded by golf courses and rich farmland, its ancient churchyard filled with roses in summer. There are plenty of pleasurable strolls to be found around here, beginning with Tarporley's secretive alleyways behind its handsome buildings; and the lane between the watermill and its pool at Little Budworth (there is also a country park near here). Northwards is Delamere Forest, 4000 acres of dense woodland concealing bright gleaming meres and threaded with well-marked footpaths.

Still further, in the direction of the Mersey estuary, are Daresbury (in the church of which Alice and the Mad Hatter are depicted in stained glass, for this was the birthplace of Lewis Carroll), and Helsby Hill from which there are fine views across marshes to the estuary – and of climbers practising on its rocks. Liverpool is soon reached from here, via the Mersey tunnel – well deserving of a visit to see its waterside maritime museum, two modern cathedrals, outstanding art gallery and concert hall among much else.

EASTON HOUSE

Chidham, West Sussex, PO18 8TF   Tel: 0243 572514
West of Chichester. Nearest main road: A259 from Chichester towards
Portsmouth.

2 Bedrooms. £13–£15. Prices go up in
April. Bargain breaks. One has own bath/
toilet. Tea/coffee facilities. Views of garden,
country, sea. No smoking. Washing
machine on request.
Light suppers if ordered. Vegetarian or
special diets.
1 Sitting-room. With log stove, central
heating, TV, piano, record-player.
Small garden

Every corner of this Tudor house has been filled by Mary Hartley with unusual
furniture and trifles. A modern white-and-red poppy wallpaper contrasts with old
beams, oriental rugs with stone-flagged floor, scarlet folkweave curtains with
antique chandeliers. Jim Hartley collects mirrors (Spanish, art deco, rococo –
every conceivable kind) and pictures of cats; Mary makes patchwork; guests play
on the Bechstein if so inclined. It's a free-and-easy atmosphere, a house full of
character and cats. Even the bathrooms are pretty, with sprigged wallpapers.

Although only breakfast is served (one can dine well in Chichester, particularly
at Thompson's, at the Old House at Home in Chidham, or in nearby waterfront
inns), visitors are welcome to linger in the comfortable lime-green sitting-room
with its log stove (where tea is served on arrival); or in the garden, under the shade
of magnolia and walnut trees.

Peaceful Chidham looks across an inlet to ancient Bosham, one of the most
picturesque sailing villages on the winding shores of Chichester's lovely natural
harbour (with boat trips): very popular and crowded in summer. Chichester
itself is near. It has a mediaeval cathedral, Georgian houses and a theatre.

Wherever you drive or walk there is fine scenery; and plenty of interesting sights
within a few miles – such as the Weald and Downland Open-Air Museum (acres of
ancient buildings reconstructed), the huge Roman palace of Fishbourne, a
brass-rubbing centre in Chichester and crafts complex in Bosham (which also has
an open-air theatre), fine gardens at West Dean, a fascinating 'live' museum of
mechanical music (organs, pianolas etc.), military aircraft at Tangmere, rose
nursery at Apuldram, Kingley Vale nature reserve and Goodwood House.

Readers' comments: Peaceful house with great character, very reasonably priced. A
marvellous place. Mrs Hartley anticipates her guests' every need. Excellent.

Further down the lane is the **OLD
RECTORY** (tel: 0243 572088), built
in 1830 and now well-furnished by
Anna Blencowe in traditional country-
house style. The large garden has a
swimming-pool (unheated) and the sitting-room a grand piano. Bed-and-
breakfast only. From £13 to £17.
Readers' comments: Wonderful garden
and furniture.

EDENBRECK HOUSE   D PT

Sunnyside Lane, Lancaster, LA1 5ED   Tel: 0524 32464
Nearest main road: A6 from Preston to Kendal.

5 **Bedrooms.** £15–£20. All have own bath/shower/toilet. Tea/coffee facilities. TV. Views of garden, country.
1 **Sitting-room.** With open fire, central heating, record-player.
Large garden

To find this secluded house, with views of fields and hills, actually *in* the city of Lancaster is one surprise. Another is that, though it presents all the detail and dignity of an 1860s mansion, it was built only a few years ago. Margaret Houghton and her husband wanted to recreate the style of a 'gentleman's residence' of that era – with all that implies in terms of quality, comfort and spaciousness – and the thought and care they put into it are impressive. They sought out furniture of the period too; but into old marble washstands modern basins have been fitted, and in the largest suite, running from front to back of the house, is an outsize Jacuzzi bath and a bidet. The pink double bed is on a pink-carpeted dais. One room has a four-poster. As the house is hard to find, the Houghtons will escort your car (from the station), or give you a lift.

Only bed-and-breakfast is served but Lancaster has many eating-places: Elliot's restaurant is very popular with visitors. Within easy reach are Blackpool and the Lake District. At Barton Grange is a good garden centre. Lancaster itself is a historic city, often overlooked by tourists. Even its name is historic, describing its role as a Roman fort (*castra*) on the River Lune. It is well worth visiting the quay, no longer busy and with its handsome Custom House (portico and pillars) now turned into a maritime museum. The wealth of trade conducted via the river in the 18th century accounts for the multitude of fine houses from that period which still make Lancaster an attractive city.

Readers' comments: Beautiful house and setting; luxurious; unsurpassed hospitality. Beautifully decorated, outstanding value. Excellent in every way. Well kept, pleasant, outstanding value. Very comfortable. Quality of bedrooms outstanding. Enormous breakfast choice. Value for money.

Economical bed-and-breakfast is to be ★ had at **THIE-NE-SHEE**, Over Kellett (tel: 0524 735882). Both the neat bedrooms in this bungalow, built in 1952 as a farmhouse, are on the ground floor, and they have fine views across a luxuriant garden. Beyond Morecambe Bay, one can see on the horizon Black Combe at the south-west corner of the Lake District. Owners are Margaret and Malcolm Cobb (he, being a railway

enthusiast, was attracted to this area by Steam Town at Carnforth, as well as by the pleasant countryside that surrounds the house). From £9.50 to £11.

★ **EDGCOTT HOUSE** C D S X

Exford, Somerset, TA24 7QG Tel: 064383 495

South-west of Minehead. Nearest main road: A396 from Tiverton to Dunster.

4 Bedrooms. £13 (less for 7 nights). Prices go up in April. Bargain breaks. One has own bath/shower/toilet. Views of garden, country. Washing machine on request.
Dinner. £8 for 4 courses (with choices) and coffee, at 7.30pm. Non-residents not admitted. Vegetarian or special diets if ordered. Wine can be brought in.
1 Sitting-room. With open fire, central heating, TV, piano.
Large garden

Trompe l'oeil murals, in 'Strawberry Hill gothick' style, cover the walls of the long dining/sitting-room. They were painted in the 1940s by George Oakes, who is now a director of the distinguished interior decorating firm of Colefax & Fowler. The tall bay windows of this room open onto a tiled terrace from which there is a fine hill view beyond the old, rambling garden where yellow Welsh poppies grow in profusion, and wisteria clambers over the pink walls of the house. In the long entrance hall (red quarry-tiled floor contrasting with whitewashed stone walls) are Persian rugs and unusual clocks. Bedrooms are homely; throughout there is a mix of antique and merely old furniture, with more *trompe l'oeil* alcoves or doors.

Gillian Lamble's style of cooking is traditionally English and she serves such meals as mackerel pâté, roast lamb, lemon meringue pie and cheeses.

Exford is right in the middle of Exmoor, a national park that was once, a thousand years ago, a royal hunting forest. It is a region of varied scenery – part of the moor is green and pastoral, part wild heath, and to the north it goes to the sea.

Readers' comments: Mrs Lamble is kindness itself. A house of character. She went out of her way to be helpful.

Outside nearby Luckwell Bridge is an 18th-century farm with apricot walls: ★ **CUTTHORNE** (tel: 064383 255), where Ann Durbin – who once ran a restaurant – can produce anything from simple to gourmet candlelit dinners. Bedrooms in the house vary, some homely but one with a carved and tapestry-hung four-poster. In the sitting- and dining-rooms are antique rugs, log fires and brass-rubbings.

There is also a courtyard where chickens roam, a pond with exotic species of ducks and geese, and swings in a children's play area. From £13.50 to £18.50.

★ **EDGEHILL HOTEL**   **C D PT**
2 High Street, Hadleigh, Suffolk, IP7 5AP   Tel: 0473 822458
Nearest main road: A1071 from Ipswich towards Sudbury.

12 Bedrooms. £15–£32 (four-poster room). (Less for 7 nights.) Bargain breaks. Some have own bath/shower/toilet. Tea/coffee facilities. TV. Views of garden, country. No smoking in one room. Washing machine on request.
Dinner. £11 for 3 courses (with choices) and coffee, at 7pm. Vegetarian or special diets if ordered. Wine can be ordered. No smoking.
Light suppers if ordered.
1 Sitting-room. With central heating, TV.
Large garden

Hadleigh, once a rich wool town, went through bad times but is now prospering again. As a result, its very lengthy High Street is full of shops enjoying a new life as wine bars, antique shops and so forth. It is a street of colourful façades, gables, pargetting (decorative plasterwork), overhanging bay windows, carved wood details, ornamental porches and fanlights over the doors. Behind lie meadows and a river.

One of the High Street's many fine historic buildings to have been rejuvenated is a Tudor house with Georgian façade which is now this private hotel. Rodney Rolfe, formerly the manager of a motor dealer's, took over Edgehill Hotel in 1976 and began to convert it. The well-proportioned rooms have been furnished in good taste, and attractive wallpapers chosen for each one. In all the spacious bedrooms there are thick-pile carpets and good furniture. The large sitting-room has glass doors opening onto the walled garden where there is an annexe with some bedrooms (in which continental breakfasts are served).

Angela Rolfe, previously a teacher, and her mother do all the cooking and use home-grown raspberries, strawberries, vegetables and other produce from the kitchen garden. She serves soup, roasts, organic vegetables and desserts such as raspberry pavlova, ginger meringues, rhubarb and ginger fool (not on Sunday; and always ordering ahead is necessary). She is not only a good cook, but also makes and sells crafts.

This is a good base from which to explore the very pretty countryside and villages nearby, and such well-known beauty-spots as mediaeval Lavenham, Dedham, Woodbridge on the Deben estuary, Kersey and Long Melford.

In addition, Suffolk has a tremendous variety of interest for garden-lovers. For instance, there are in the vicinity of Hadleigh and Ipswich a council-house garden shown on 'Gardener's World' (at Charsfield), colourful woodland gardens at Little Blakenham with a number of rarities, the seed-trial fields of Thompson and Morgan and formal riverside gardens around Letheringsett's watermill.

Wind and watermills are a particular feature of the Suffolk countryside. Some notable ones are Bardwell windmill where you can buy stone-ground flour (occasionally, the mill is operated by steam); Buttrums 6-storey windmill at Woodbridge – where there is also the famous watermill operated by the movement of the tides; the marsh drainage mill at Herringfleet on the edge of the Broads; a superb 18th-century windmill at Saxtead and others at Thelnetham and Thorpeness (the latter with milling museum).

Readers' comments: Absolutely excellent. High standard.

★ ELDOCHAN HALL   C D PT S
Willimoteswyke, Bardon Mill, Northumberland, NE47 7DB
Tel: 0434 344465
West of Hexham. Nearest main road: A69 from Haltwhistle to Haydon Bridge.

2 Bedrooms. £12.50–£13.50 (less for 3 nights). Prices go up at Easter. Bargain breaks. Both have own toilet. Tea/coffee facilities. Views of garden, country, river. No smoking. Washing machine on request. **Dinner.** £8 for 3 courses and coffee; times by arrangement. Non-residents not admitted. Vegetarian or special diets if ordered. Wine can be brought in.
1 Sitting-room. With open fire, central heating, TV, piano, record-player.
Large garden

No stranger would guess that an extraordinary enclave lies just to one side of the busy Newcastle–Carlisle road, reached only by an inconspicuous turning or, from the east, by a network of narrow roads which lead to nowhere. It is where the rushing River Allen slows down to meet the South Tyne in its valley bottom. To reach Eldochan Hall, you will drive through old mixed woodland, pass a bastle house (an old fortified farmhouse – bastle is the same as *bastille*) and a miniature hamlet with a picture-postcard church and graveyard, and at the end of this winding road, probably having taken a wrong turning or two, you will see a half-ruined castle built into a farmstead. Eldochan Hall, which lies below the castle, is perhaps two centuries old, probably built on the site of another bastle.

The stone-slated porch leads into a dining-room with an old kitchen range, now with a wood stove incorporated. Here, teacher's wife Elaine MacDonald serves meals (such as melon, pork casserole, and chocolate pudding) when the house is full. When guests are few, they eat in what amounts to a private sitting-room, off which opens the best bedroom. This, like the upstairs rooms, has a pleasant mixture of antique and modern furniture. Much of the neat modernization of the house was the MacDonalds' own work. A stream rushes past the garden.

For walkers, there are footpaths and the wooded Allen Banks estate; for the carless, a railway station is only half a mile away over a footbridge. Photographers and naturalists will make the most of the nearby nature reserve, the tree-lined river banks, and the picturesque buildings at Beltingham and along little-used lanes.

A few miles away, Isabel and John Wentzel offer b & b plus imaginative cooking (for vegetarians especially) at
★ **CROWBERRY HALL** (tel: 0434 683392), a one-time farmhouse set in a very secluded spot overlooking the valley of the East Allen. Mrs Wentzel, who makes preserves for sale, also organizes craft courses in, for example, lacemaking and needlepoint. Apart from the peace and quiet, the big attraction of this area is the opportunity for walking. From £9.50 to £10.

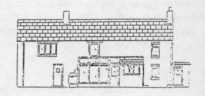

Readers' comments: Enjoyed the cooking, home-made wine and magnificent walks.

ELM FARMHOUSE

C(10)

Fulbrook, Oxfordshire, OX8 4BW   Tel: 099382 3611
North of Burford. Nearest main road: A361 from Burford to Chipping Norton.

7 Bedrooms. £17.50–£25 (less for 3 nights). Bargain breaks. Some have own bath/shower/toilet. Tea/coffee facilities. TV. Views of garden, country. No smoking.
Dinner. £14 for 4 courses (with choices) and coffee, at 7.30pm. Non-residents not admitted. Vegetarian or special diets if ordered. Wine can be ordered.
2 Sitting-rooms. With open fire, central heating, TV, record-player. No smoking in one. **Bar.**
Garden
Closed from mid-December to end of January.

Although built only in 1897, this handsome house is in traditional Cotswold style – constructed of golden limestone, with gables, two-foot thick walls, mullioned windows that have shapely dripstones above them, and a roof of stone slates. Sue and David Catlin have furnished its large rooms handsomely. The south-facing sitting-room has damask wallpaper, chrysanthemum-patterned sofas and a brass-legged coffee table drawn up by the Minster stone fireplace; and in the dining-room Royal Worcester china on pink tablecloths. Bay windows overlook a croquet lawn, herbaceous borders sheltered by stone walls, and a paved terrace from which there are views of fields, stream and some fine specimen trees. Off the hall, a bar leads to a television room.

A great Jacobean staircase sweeps up to well-equipped and agreeably furnished bedrooms – the blue room has a particularly attractive garden view.

Dinners here have imaginative touches (and choices at several courses). One example: courgette and fennel soup, lamb with such vegetables as cucumber in herbs or baked aubergines, black cherry jelly with Kirsch cream, cheeses.

The northward part of the Cotswolds, not greatly frequented by tourists, has very fine views across the Evenlode Valley. All the famous beauty-spots like Bourton-on-the-Water and the Tews are within easy motoring distance.

Readers' comments: Beautiful house. Most friendly and helpful. Will go there again. Pleasant, comfortable rooms and good food.

At Westhall Hill, Fulbrook, is the **DOWER HOUSE** (tel: 099382 2596), another handsome house of golden stone, which Diana Westall has furnished with flair. You might sleep in a four-poster, or a brass bed with porcelain panels in a room with panoramic views on two sides and a bathroom which, like other rooms, has William Morris wallpaper. (B & b only: plenty of restaurants in Burford.) Parked outside is likely to be the Westalls' 1938 Alvis tourer. From £14 to £15.

ELM HOUSE   **C D PT S**
Upper Holt Street, Earls Colne, Essex, CO6 2PG   Tel: 0787 222197
North-west of Braintree. Nearest main road: A604 from Colchester to Halstead.

4 Bedrooms. £16.50 – £24 (less for 5 nights). Prices go up in April. Some have own bath/ toilet. Tea/coffee facilities. TV. Views of garden. Washing machine on request.
Dinner. From £10 for 4 courses (with choice of puddings) and coffee, at about 7.30pm. Vegetarian or special diets if ordered. Wine can be brought in. **Light suppers** if ordered.
2 Sitting-rooms. With open fire, central heating, TV.
Garden
Closed from mid-December to February inclusive.

This gracious 18th-century house has been furnished with suitable elegance. The moss-green and pale gold sitting-room is furnished with antiques (its high French doors open onto a terrace and large garden where meals are occasionally served). In the dining-room, which is sage-green, the mahogany table is laid with white-and-gold Spode and silver candelabra at dinner time. There is also a reading/ writing-room for guests who want complete quiet.

Although on a main road, the house provides quiet bedrooms at the back, overlooking the walled garden (windows are double-glazed). I liked the coffee-and-white room with William Morris curtains; another is huge, with windows on three sides. There are pretty antique iron beds (painted white or black, with bright brass knobs) coupled with the modern comfort of warm duvets. Details like brass curtain-poles and decorative fanlights catch one's eye.

Lady Larcom so much enjoyed entertaining that she started to run a private catering service and to take guests in Elm House. Dinners here are therefore rather special. They may begin with bouillabaisse or smoked haddock soup, for example, followed perhaps by beef bourguignonne or stuffed peppers (baked in tomato and mushroom sauce, topped with sour cream, and served with wild rice and salad), then may come iced coffee soufflé or gooseberry mousse and cheeses.

Earls Colne is in one of the best parts of Essex – the north-east. This is a region of peaceful water-meadows with willows, outstanding churches and great historic interest. Colchester is an exceptional Roman/Norman city, described elsewhere. All down the coast are winding creeks and wildernesses that attract migrant waterfowl. Where once the Vikings sailed in to plunder, boat enthusiasts now go yachting. There is very varied scenery to explore inland: heaths, woods and villages that once prospered from weaving wool and are still beautiful today.

The area has, too, plenty of sightseeing possibilities. For instance: Gosfield Hall (Tudor), the historic walled and water gardens of Saling Hall, the world's oldest timber-framed barn at Coggeshall which the National Trust only recently restored (it was built in Norman times), the working silk mill at Braintree, boat trips on Gosfield Lake, walks in ancient Chalkney Wood, and a variety of local museums or galleries – from Braintree's heritage centre to the art exhibitions in Finchingfield's Guildhall, and bygones in Great Bardfield's charity cottage.

Readers' comments: Lady Larcom was most hospitable, her home is very comfortable, and every meal was a delight.

ENFORD HOUSE

C D PT

Enford, Wiltshire, SN9 6DJ Tel: 0980 70414
South-east of Devizes. Nearest main road: A345 from Marlborough to Salisbury.

3 Bedrooms. £13–£15. Prices go up in April. Tea/coffee facilities. Views of garden. No smoking. Washing machine on request. **Dinner** (when available). £11 for 4 courses (with choices) and coffee, at 7–8pm (must be ordered by lunchtime). Wine can be brought in. **Light suppers** if ordered.
1 Sitting-room. With open fire, central heating, TV.
Small garden

The latest in telecommunications and 4000-year-old mysteries oddly combine in the telephone number of this house – Stonehenge 70414: this world-famous monument is only a few miles away. In fact, Enford (being in Salisbury Plain) is surrounded by prehistoric remains of many kinds.

The 18th-century house (once a rectory) and its garden are enclosed by thatch-topped walls – a feature one often finds in those parts of Wiltshire where, stone being non-existent, a mix of earth and dung with horsehair or else chalk blocks were used to build walls (which then needed protection from rain). The house has pointed 'Gothick' windows on one side, doors to the garden on another. Antiques furnish the panelled sitting-room, which has a crackling fire on chilly nights. Bedrooms are simple, fresh and conventionally furnished.

Sarah Campbell serves, on pretty Watteau china, soups that she makes from garden vegetables, roasts, puddings such as gooseberry fool or lemon soufflé, then cheeses. The Campbells tell their guests a great deal about the area – not just its historic sights for they are knowledgeable about its wildlife (Salisbury Plain has a tremendous variety of wildflowers as well as larks and lapwings), where to go for the finest views from the surrounding downs, the best walks (paths beside the historic Kennet & Avon Canal are level and the scene very pretty) and the best inns. The Avon rises in the downs north of here, flows through an exceptionally lovely valley all the way into Salisbury and thence through Hampshire to the sea at historic Christchurch – it would be possible to follow its course by car, passing through many pretty villages along the way. In Enford itself, Chisenbury Priory Gardens attracts a lot of visitors (Wednesday afternoons, summer only).

The vast green undulations of Salisbury Plain have changed little over the centuries; its grandeur is as imposing as ever, its fields of grain sweeping to the horizon like a prairie.

Near Enford is the lovely Vale of Pewsey: Pewsey itself (under an hour from London by train) is a small town of thatched cottages and 18th-century houses with a statue of Alfred the Great near the river. At the other end of the Vale is the market town of Devizes (its museum holds many of the prehistoric remains found in the Plain) and beyond it Trowbridge, the handsome stone buildings of which were built by rich cloth-merchants descended from Flemish weavers who fled here during periods of religious persecution. Another weavers' town is Westbury, near which is one of Wiltshire's many famous white horses, cut through the turf.

Readers' comments: Everything quite delightful. A charming hostess and excellent food.

105

ESHTON GRANGE

C(8) S X

Gargrave, North Yorkshire, BD23 3QE   Tel: 0756 749 383

North-west of Skipton. Nearest main road: A65 from Skipton to Settle.

4 Bedrooms. £17 – £20. Bargain breaks. All have own bath/shower/toilet. Tea/coffee facilities. TV. Views of garden, country, river. No smoking. Washing machine on request.

Dinner. £8–£10 for 3–4 courses (with choices) and coffee, at 6.30–8pm. Non-residents not admitted. Vegetarian or special diets if ordered. Wine can be brought in.

1 Sitting-room. With open fire, central heating, TV.

Inquisitive brown eyes watched my arrival: two of the Eshton Grange stud of tiny Shetland ponies were in a paddock overlooking the courtyard.

Judy and Terry Shelmerdine have created a comfortable, informal atmosphere in their home even though it is furnished with fine antiques and good paintings, many by Judy. It has stone inglenooks, chintz or tapestry chairs and deep-set windows.

The beamed bedrooms are on two floors – at the top is a big attic room ideal for a family, for children shin up a ladder to their beds in the apex of the roof, tucked away above the king-post which supports it. It's a higgledy-piggledy room, with pretty trellis wallpaper, a circular window, and in one corner a cooker useful for preparing the children's supper.

Dinners are traditionally English – home-made soup, roast chicken with all the accompaniments, sherry trifle, and cheese, for example. You help yourself to as much as you want. (Must be ordered in advance.)

Eshton is surrounded by beautiful views. It is near Malham (in Airedale) famous for its massive crags, tarn (lake) belonging to the National Trust, and cove – a huge circular cliff. Go to Gordale Scar for the sight of twin waterfalls in a 300-foot gorge. There is a moorland road through wooded Littondale to Arncliffe and Litton, villages with quaint houses, ancient churches, swirling rivers – and few tourists.

Readers' comments: Owners, room, food and views fantastic! A good place, very reasonably priced. Bang on! – have stayed twice. A charming couple, dinner was excellent, and very good value for money. Most comfortable. Beautiful setting.

Shetland ponies at Eshton Grange

FAIRFIELD HOUSE

44 High Street, Corsham, Wiltshire, SN13 0HT   Tel: 0249 712992
South-west of Chippenham. On A4 from Bath to Chippenham.

4 Bedrooms. £12.50–£13.50. Prices go up in April. All have tea/coffee facilities. TV. Washing machine on request.
Small garden

Within a peacock's cry of Corsham Court (a palatial Elizabethan mansion with a famous collection of paintings and other treasures) is a quiet and picturesque street which, in the 17th century, was lined with the cottages and workrooms of Flemish weavers. Fairfield House is one of few to have survived from then, for an explosion of gunpowder stored nearby (during the building of Brunel's Box Hill railway tunnel, one of his greatest feats) devastated much of the street.

During the building of the two-mile tunnel (1836–41), every spare bed in Corsham was occupied by railway navvies working on the 'monstrous and extraordinary, most dangerous and impracticable tunnel'. Men and horses were the only power available to get through the rock (solid Bath stone for much of the way), working by candlelight; every week, a ton of candles and a ton of gunpowder were used; and, in all, 30 million bricks to line the tunnel which the sceptics said Brunel could never complete. Today's high-speed travellers whisk through it with little thought of how it was built.

At Fairfield House, one steps straight into a low, white breakfast-room with jade paintwork and curtains, beyond which lie two bedrooms and bathroom, with more upstairs. Christine Reid has furnished all of these with exceptional grace – using either silky cream duvets or pretty patchwork (made by her mother) on the beds, wallpapers patterned with small roses or with Chinese-style pheasants. White-shuttered windows are set in deep embrasures; fresh or dried flower arrangements are everywhere. This is altogether an exceptionally attractive small house, and very good value. (Breakfast only; for dinner, visitors go to the Weaver's Loft, Methuen Arms or other restaurants in the little High Street.)

Wiltshire is, I feel, an undervalued county, for in addition to its rolling countryside there is so much to see – outstandingly, its 4500 prehistoric sites (of which Stonehenge may be the most famous but is less impressive than Avebury). Great houses include Wilton, Stourhead, Mompesson House (within the precincts of Salisbury Cathedral); even nearer, Bowood, Lacock Abbey and Longleat. In fact, the county has more listed buildings than any other, and many of its villages are little beauties. Corsham has the unusual Bath Stone Quarry Museum.

Readers' comments: Delightful; great food; very welcoming.

When writing to me, if you want a reply please enclose a stamped addressed envelope.

★ **FITZ MANOR** C D S

Fitz, Bomere Heath, Shropshire, SY4 3AS Tel: 0743 850295
North-west of Shrewsbury. Nearest main road: A5 from Shrewsbury to
Llangollen.

3 Bedrooms. £15 (less for 7 nights). Bargain breaks. Some have own bath/shower/toilet. Tea/coffee facilities. Views of garden, country. Washing machine on request.
Dinner. £10 for 4 courses and coffee, at times to suit guests. Non-residents not admitted. Vegetarian or special diets if ordered. Wine can be brought in. **Light suppers** if ordered.
2 Sitting-rooms. With open fire, central heating, TV, record-player.
Large garden

This outstanding manor house was built about 1450 in traditional Shropshire style – black timbers and white walls. It is at the heart of a large farm where vegetables and grain are grown.

The interior is one of the most impressive in this book. A vast dining-room with parquet floor and Persian carpet overlooks rosebeds, pergolas and yew hedges. It is furnished with antiques, paintings by John Piper and a collection of Crown Derby. In the oak-panelled sitting-room there are damask and pink velvet armchairs around the log fire (or guests can use the glass sun-room). Between these two rooms are the arched hall and a winding oak staircase; one door here is carved with strapwork and vines, on the walls are ancestral portraits, and on the tiled floor Persian rugs and oak chests.

Bedrooms differ in size. For instance, adjoining one huge room with armchairs from which to enjoy views of the Severn Valley and Welsh Hills is a white cottage-style bedroom – a useful combination for a family (and Fitz Manor has a playroom with toys for children).

Dawn Baly's candlelit dinners often start with home-made pâté or soup; casseroled pheasant or wild duck sometimes appear as the main course, with home-grown vegetables; puddings may be fruit pies, meringues or chocolate mousse; and then there are cheeses – unless visitors want only a salad or shepherd's pie supper.

The garden is still much as it was when laid out in Tudor times, although now there is a heated swimming-pool and croquet lawn. Guests are encouraged to use the land – for barbecues, picnics, swimming or fishing in the river. Though Fitz Manor is a stately home in miniature, the atmosphere is very friendly and easygoing.

Although the historic town of Shrewsbury is the main attraction, there is plenty more to see in the lovely countryside around here – as varied as rural crafts in the Old Rectory at Melverley (where there is one of the country's oldest timber-framed churches, too); Adcote, a house built by Norman Shaw (now a school but open to the public for part of the year); and, a little further north, Whittington Castle and Oswestry which has a museum of vintage bicycles and canalside walks in the vicinity.

For those interested in England's industrial heritage, the Ironbridge Gorge Museum at Telford (within easy motoring distance) has a fascinating series of displays, exhibits and reconstructions, as well as access to the world's first iron bridge.

FLEARDON FARM   S
Lezant, Cornwall, PL15 9NW   Tel: 0579 70364
South of Launceston. Nearest main road: A388 from Launceston to Plymouth.

2 Bedrooms. £15–£17. Prices go up in July. Both have own bath/shower/toilet. Views of garden, country. No smoking. Washing machine on request.
1 Sitting-room. With open fire, central heating, TV. No smoking.
Large garden

Tolkien devotees should head for Lezant because here, in the newly modernized barns of Fleardon Farm, is an art gallery displaying the work of Roger Garland, illustrator of all those brilliant and intricate covers to the Hobbit books.

The farmhouse itself belongs to his parents and here Doreen Garland welcomes bed-and-breakfast guests (for dinner, they usually go to the Sportsmans Inn, Penpill Farm restaurant or the White Hart in Launceston). The 250-year-old house has a surprising interior after one enters through a conventional porch (filled with geraniums), for there is a big open-plan kitchen/dining area with mahogany staircase to the floor above. The large sitting-room with windows on three sides has a log stove, sofas and a profusion of pot-plants. A handsome feature is the polished hardwood floors throughout. The bedrooms have pleasant views (and excellent bathrooms): one overlooks the cobbled courtyard, another a waterfall and stream.

The grounds are full of interest. In addition to a lawn with flowerbeds and shrubs, there is a decorative folly with weathervane, a great monkey-puzzle tree, and a lake frequented by Canada geese.

Readers' comments: All in superb order. Unobtrusive help and friendliness.

A few miles north of Launceston is the remote village of North Petherwin and 17th-century **WINNACOTT FARM** (tel: 056685 366) with the pleasant, homely accommodation typical of most working farms. In the oak-furnished dining-room with Royal Worcester china, Greta Bird serves such meals as courgette soup with rolls (both home-made), roast lamb and up to five home-grown vegetables, a spicy fruit and almond crumble (the custard is made with eggs from her ducks), unusual cheeses and fruit. At breakfast there are a dozen honeys to choose from. Bedrooms are well-equipped (TV etc.) and very moderately priced. Outside are a small arboretum above a pool with ducks; an aviary of finches; and rare

breeds of chickens. From £10.50 to £15.

Readers' comments: Well decorated, lovely meals, friendly atmosphere. Charming, quiet. Real personal hospitality, excellent meal imaginatively prepared.

FLEUR-DE-LYS INN

C D S

Cranborne, Dorset, BH21 5PP   Tel: 07254 282

South-west of Salisbury (Wiltshire). Nearest main road: A354 from Salisbury to Blandford Forum.

8 Bedrooms. £17–£21 (less for 7 nights). Bargain breaks. Some have own bath/shower/toilet. Tea/coffee facilities. TV. Views of country. Washing machine on request.
Dinner. A la carte or £17 for 3 courses (with choices) and coffee, at 7.30–9.30pm. Vegetarian or special diets if ordered. Wine can be ordered. **Light suppers** if ordered. **1 Sitting-room.** With open fire, central heating, TV. **Bar.** **Small garden**

> 'Where is the food, in toil's despite?
> The golden eggs? The toast? The tea?
> The maid so pretty and polite?
> These things are at the Fleur-de-Lys.'

Rupert Brooke (he of the 'honey still for tea') was also inspired to write a long poem about quiet pleasures and good food when he visited Cranborne's Fleur-de-Lys inn (in 1914 he was stationed at the barracks of nearby Blandford Forum).

The inn's history goes far back – to the 11th century – and mediaeval stones uncovered during building work may have come from a monastery that once stood where the church is now. Other finds included 17th-century documents, copies of which are on show. Infamous Judge Jeffreys (notorious for sending to the gallows hundreds of rebels in the revolt against James II led by the Duke of Monmouth) stayed here, and so did Hardy. In *Tess of the d'Urbervilles* Hardy describes a dance in the inn's barn; how one haymaker said 'the maids don't think it respectable to dance at the Flower-de-Luce'; and how Alec d'Urberville accosted Tess there.

Today, Charles Hancock provides comfortable bedrooms for travellers; and good food (including vegetarian choices) is served in the inn's very traditional, panelled bar, on tables covered with green cloths. You can either have substantial bar snacks or choose from a full à la carte menu featuring traditional English dishes such as whitebait, venison and meringues.

Cranborne is in the middle of Dorset's lovely countryside, with the ancient wooded hills close by. Trout streams wander through the landscape, there are historic houses in plenty and countless gardens (and Lady Salisbury's garden centre, which specialises in old roses). Within easy motoring distance are the cathedral city of Salisbury, the big seaside resort of Bournemouth, the New Forest, impressive Wimborne Minster, and picturesque Fordingbridge.

For a good day-drive, explore Cranborne Chase, one of England's most scenic but little frequented areas, on the steep and winding road from Tollard Royal.

Readers' comments: Most enjoyable. Excellent meals.

★ **FOLDGATE FARM**   **C S**
Corney, Cumbria, LA19 5TN   Tel: 06578 660
North-west of Millom. Nearest main road: A595 from Whitehaven towards
Millom.

3 Bedrooms. £11–£11.50 (less for 3 nights).
Views of country, sea, river. No smoking.
Washing machine on request.
Dinner. £6.50 for 3 courses and coffee, at
6pm. Non-residents not admitted. Vegetarian or special diets if ordered. Wine can
be brought in. No smoking. **Light suppers** if
ordered.
1 Sitting-room. With open fire, central heating, TV. No smoking.
Small garden
Closed in December.

A real Cumbrian farm, and well outside the main tourist areas, it covers 100 acres
on which are kept Swaledale and Herdwick sheep as well as some cattle. The
approach to the farm is through a cobbled courtyard, with a great stone byre and
stables at one side, Muscovy ducks perching on a dry-stone wall, and sundry old
iron pots and kettles filled with stonecrop, London pride or primroses. A stream
slips quietly by. Pat, the sheepdog, comes bounding out to greet visitors.

The rooms have old furniture. Guests sometimes eat with the family, by a
dresser where mugs hang, the clothes airer suspended overhead and a grandfather
clock ticking in one corner. There are bacon-hooks in the ceiling, old horn-
handled shepherds' crooks stacked in the hall, and a bright coal fire in the
evenings.

Mary Hogg does most of the talking as she serves guests a proper farmhouse
meal, and her husband is glad to tell visitors about his sheep and all the local
goings-on – guests are welcome to watch the life of the farm, and to join in at
haymaking time in July or August.

You'll get real country fare here: Cumberland sausage, 'tatie pot', plum
pudding with rum sauce, farm duckling, Herdwick lamb or mutton, rum butter
on bread, currant cake with tea on arrival and at bedtime, and jams made from
local bilberries, pears, or marrow and ginger. There are free-range eggs for
breakfast. This is a thoroughly unpretentious, homely and friendly place to stay –
but not for those who want everything shiny as a new pin.

As to the countryside around, there are the moors of Corney Fell close by and
roads winding up and down, with sea views. An unusual attraction is a smokery
(for meats) where visitors are welcome.

Up the coast from Corney is Ravenglass, a port from Roman times but long since
silted up. It is the terminus of a narrow-gauge railway, built to transport iron ore
but now a very popular tourist ride. Take it to Boot for a drink at the pub and a
look round the craft gallery and the corn mill (not working), then return to the mill
at Muncaster (which is working during the summer). At Muncaster Castle, they
breed and release owls, which you can see. Transport enthusiasts will want to visit
the railway museum at Ravenglass, the motorcycle collection at Broughton in
Furness, and the motor museum at Holker Hall. At Sellafield, the visitor centre of
the nuclear industry has become a popular tourist attraction.

Readers' comments: Excellent food, good company. Good food. Lovely welcome. A
great success. Never a dull moment. Food, atmosphere and welcome couldn't be
faulted.

FORD FARMHOUSE

C(10) D S X

Harberton, Devon, TQ9 7SJ   Tel: 0803 863539
South of Totnes. Nearest main road: A381 from Totnes to Kingsbridge.

3 Bedrooms. £15 (less for 7 nights). Prices go up in May. Bargain breaks. Some have own shower/toilet. Tea/coffee facilities. TV. Views of garden, country, sea, river. Washing machine on request.
1 Sitting-room. With central heating, TV.
Small garden

In this little village are two houses of outstanding excellence. For years, **Preston Farm** has been one of the most popular places in this book (see elsewhere); now I am glad to include another, at the other end of the village, which will be of particular appeal to gourmets.

Within the white walls are a low-beamed dining-room with stone fireplace (furnished with country Chippendale chairs and a dresser with pretty plates), an upstairs sitting-room, and delightful little bedrooms, one with patchwork spread, some with flowery views of the small, wandering garden and its stream.

For evening meals, Sheila Edwards recommends the Church House Inn. It is only two minutes' walk away.

Each day's breakfast is different, with options such as particularly tasty sausages, kidneys or liver, teacakes or croissants.

The dilemma is to choose which of Harberton's houses to stay at!

Within a short drive one can reach Exeter, all the resorts and beaches of Torbay, Plymouth and innumerable beauty-spots in the countryside and along the coast. Dartmoor has a wild beauty all its own – a vast expanse of open country (one of the National Parks) with market towns and villages here and there, streams in the valleys and rocks high on the hills where sometimes mist or rain are dense. Nature trails, prehistoric remains, Buckfast and Buckland abbeys, steam railway, butterfly farm, Shire Horse Centre, Dartington Hall, great gardens, six garden centres, museums and historic buildings are among the sightseeing possibilities.

There is always something new to be enjoyed in South Devon. Among the more recent additions to the scene, some of the most popular include the English Riviera Centre at Torquay (a leisure centre with flume wave pool, whirlpool baths and so on), and Plymouth's Dome – an interpretation centre covering history from the Stone Age to satellite technology. For a scenic railway journey, take the Tamar line (Plymouth to Gunnislake).

Readers' comments: Excellent. Superb breakfast. Nothing too much trouble – couldn't fault a thing. Delightful house and garden.

Prices are per person in a double room at the beginning of the year.

Book well ahead: many of these houses have few rooms. Do not expect dinner if you have not booked it or if you arrive late.

FORTITUDE COTTAGE

C D PT

51 Broad Street, Old Portsmouth, Hampshire, PO1 2JD   Tel: 0705 823748

Nearest main road: A3 from London to Portsmouth.

3 Bedrooms. £14–£15 (less for 3 nights). Prices go up at Easter. Some have own bath/shower/toilet. Tea/coffee facilities. TV. Views of sea. No smoking.

Carol Harbeck's little cottage – one room piled on top of another – backs onto her mother's (also a guest-house), with a flowery little courtyard and fountain between the two. Hers is named for the Fortitude Inn, which was once next door; itself named for HMS *Fortitude*, a ship-of-war which ended its days as a prison hulk in the harbour – overlooked by the big bay window of Carol's first-floor sitting-room. This is Portsmouth's most historic area. From here, Richard Lionheart embarked for the Crusades, Henry V for Agincourt, and the first settlers for Australia. It's a place of ramparts and bastions, quaint buildings and byways, much coming-and-going of ships and little boats. Now the waterbus leaves from the quay just outside.

All the rooms in the cottage are prettily furnished – even the bathroom; and Carol (who provides only bed-and-breakfast) can recommend a dozen good eating-places nearby. Handy as a stopover for people using Portsmouth's port, Fortitude Cottage deserves a longer stay. For Portsmouth (and its adjoining Victorian resort, Southsea) have so much to offer: HMS *Victory*, the *Mary Rose*, HMS *Warrior*, the Royal Navy's museum and that of the Marines, cathedral and historic garrison church, Henry VIII's Southsea Castle, the D-Day museum, Hayling Island and the wild places of Chichester Harbour, clifftop Victorian forts, Roman/Norman Portchester Castle, submarine museum at Gosport, a big new leisure centre, other museums (including Dickens's birthplace), the Searchlight Tattoo every September, trips to the Isle of Wight, and a fine downland countryside to explore inland. Southsea has outstanding seafront gardens. There are boat trips to Spitbank Fort and Southsea is an antique-hunter's paradise.

Readers' comments: Excellent accommodation, spotless. Absolutely excellent, high standard. Delightfully unusual.

Near the city is Denmead and **FOREST GATE** (tel: 0705 255901), the graceful 18th-century house of Torfrida Cox and her husband, with a large garden. It is on the 70-mile Wayfarers' Walk. This is an informal home furnished with antiques. Meals (which have to be ordered in advance) include such dishes as Armenian lamb pilaff or mousssaka, mousses or lemon meringue pie. From £14 to £16.

FOX INN   C D S X

Ansty, Dorset, DT2 7PN   Tel: 0258 880 328

West of Blandford Forum. Nearest main road: A354 from Salisbury to
Dorchester.

14 Bedrooms. £19–£23 (less for 2 nights).
Prices go up in October. Bargain breaks. All
have own bath/shower/toilet. Tea/coffee
facilities. TV. Views of garden, country. No
smoking. Washing machine on request.
Dinner. A la carte or £9 for 3 courses (with
choices) and coffee, at 7–10pm. Vegetarian
or special diets if ordered. Wine can be
ordered. No smoking. **Light suppers** if
ordered.
1 Sitting-room. With open fire, central heating, record-player. No smoking. **Bars.**
Large garden

Although not particularly old (it started its flint-and-brick life as a Victorian
home), the Fox is full of character and has a great reputation for food – from its
cold carvery to its charcoal grill. Thirty salads; fourteen meats which include
pheasants and ham on the bone; jacket potatoes with unusual fillings; pies, granary
bread and home-made soups: this is exactly what authentic pub food should be but
so rarely is. And, on top of this, the Fox is in one of the most rural parts of Dorset,
surrounded by exceptionally fine scenery.

There is a succession of bars, used by locals at least as much as tourists. One has
a huge collection of Toby jugs (800 at the last count), and another hundreds of
plates. A new bar area has been opened up for family eating. Among the inn's
nooks and crannies are a children's games room, complete with giant ludo board
and cartoon videos, and a skittle alley. Outside there is a swimming-pool, two
slides and a garden with Wendy house. A busy convivial pub.

Kathryn Witheyman has made the bedrooms very comfortable – some have
sofas which is a thoughtful touch.

Ansty is well placed for visiting Dorchester and the Dorset County Museum,
Athelhampton House, Chard and Forde Abbey, Corfe Castle, the swannery at
Abbotsbury, the old market town of Blandford Forum, picturesque Milton Abbas
and its great abbey church, the giant of Cerne Abbas, Shaftesbury and Sherborne –
a particular jewel, often passed by. The Blackmoor Vale is undulating country
threaded by streams, spreading northward into Wiltshire. Eastward is Cranborne
Chase, less well known than some of Dorset's beauty-spots yet well worth
exploring because there are exceptionally fine views from its hills with pretty
valleys and villages in between. To the south lies Dorset's heritage coast, and the
old-fashioned resorts of Weymouth and Swanage.

Hardy enthusiasts enjoy identifying Dorset villages with places in his books,
such as Puddletown (which he renamed Weatherbury), in the church of which is
just such a gallery as accommodated the church band in *Under the Greenwood Tree*
('Their strings, from recent long exposure to night air, rose whole semitones, and
snapped with a loud twang at the most silent moment . . . The vicar looked
cross.'). It is worth looking at the tombs, brasses and oak roof too. Hardy's
birthplace at nearby Higher Bockhampton is a woodland thatched cottage along a
footpath (much photographed but rarely open to the public); and at the church
of Stinsford ('Mellstock' in his books) is buried his heart – his ashes are in
Westminster Abbey – and also the body of C. Day Lewis.

114

FOXHILL

Kingsey, Buckinghamshire, HP17 8LZ Tel: 0844 291650
South-west of Aylesbury. Nearest main road: A4129 from Princes Risborough
to Thame.

3 Bedrooms. £15–£16. Prices go up in
February. Some have own shower. Tea/
coffee facilities. TV. Views of garden,
country. No smoking.
2 Sitting-rooms. With central heating, TV.
No smoking.
Large garden
Closed in December and January.

The instant impression is delightful: sparkling white house beyond green lawns
where Muscovy ducks waddle with their young towards a pool crossed by an
arching stone bridge. The gnarled remains of an immense 500-year-old elm tree
stand beside the drive. At the back of the house is a garden with heated
swimming-pool, against a distant view of the Chiltern Hills.

The interior is just as attractive. The house having been the home of architect
Nick Hooper and his family for many years, it is not surprising that its modernization was done with imagination and with care to respect its 17th-century origins.
In the hall, floored with polished red quarry-tiles, a wrought-iron staircase leads
up to bedrooms with beamed ceilings, attractive wallpapers and rugs, and restful
colour schemes. Board doors have the original iron latches. The breakfast-room
(which also serves as a sitting-room) has brown gingham tablecloths and rush-
seated chairs. Here Mary-Joyce – a warm, gentle hostess – serves only breakfast,
recommending for other meals restaurants in the ancient market town of Thame,
only a few minutes away.

Thame is a lively place in autumn when the mile-long market place at its heart is
filled with stalls for the annual fair, and is a mecca for gourmets; beyond lie all the
attractions of Oxfordshire described elsewhere in this book. In west Buckinghamshire, too, there is plenty – from the wooded hills of the Chilterns down into the
fertile Vale of Aylesbury. Early in the year there are bluebells and cherry blossom;
in autumn the beech woods blaze with colour.

The centre of Aylesbury is picturesque, threaded with pathways and courtyards
to explore on foot (one of the many inns, the King's Head, belongs to the National
Trust). Of many villages worth visiting, go to Long Crendon not only for the
nearby lovely bridge and rose-covered cottages but for two 15th-century houses
(one belonged to Catherine of Aragon and is now owned by the National Trust). At
Waddesdon is the Rothschild mansion, looking like a French château (also
National Trust property); at Upper Wichendon, high up, a dramatic view of the
Thames; Cuxham, in good walking country, has a stream through the middle.
Hughenden Manor was Disraeli's house. Waterperry's gardens are outstanding.

All these are very near. Visitors staying for some time can also from here explore
Oxford, West Wycombe, old Amersham, Henley and other Thames-side towns
(even Windsor), and any number of castles, stately homes, museums, antique
shops etc. London is only an hour away.

Readers' comments: Wonderfully kind hosts, lovely home, top of our list! Beautiful
house, meticulously kept; charming, friendly and helpful. The Hoopers and their
home are charming.

Caldbeck, Cumbria, CA7 8DS   Tel: 06998 633
South of Wigton. Nearest main road: A595 from Carlisle to Cockermouth.

3 Bedrooms. £12–£12.50 (less for 5 nights). Prices go up in March. Views of garden, country, river. No smoking. Washing machine on request.
1 Sitting-room. With open fire, central heating, TV.
Small garden
Closed from December to February inclusive.

As the name suggests, this farmhouse has a long history. The Prior of Carlisle built a hospital here, which was dissolved in the reign of King John. The 12th-century part of the house was once the monks' refectory (hence the name 'hall'), with the hospital proper next door.

Today it is the centre of a 140-acre sheep- and dairy-farm. Caldbeck Fells rise up above the village where John Peel was born and is buried (the little churchyard is right opposite Friar Hall, across a tiny humpback stone bridge spanning a tumbling stream with a weir). The Blencathra foot-hounds still roam these fells in winter, just as they once did with John Peel – but now hang-gliders go up there too.

Guests use a snug sitting/dining-room with big leather armchairs, crimson velvet curtains and, on wintry evenings, logs blazing in a fireplace made of greenish Buttermere slate, casting a flicker on the gleaming brass fire-irons. The ceiling is beamed, the walls are thick.

All the bedrooms look across the tiny garden and the stream to the far hills beyond, and to a sky of scudding clouds when the wind blows. Fresh paint and light colours make them attractive; carpets are good; colour schemes simple.

For dinner most visitors go to the village inn, the Oddfellows Arms, or else to Monoley's restaurant. Only a few miles away is Park End restaurant.

Caldbeck is one of the Lake District's prettiest villages, with a pond (used by Muscovy ducks), an old inn, and a Wesleyan chapel carved with the reminder, 'Remember NOW thy creator'. The approach from the north is particularly lovely, driving across a heath with gorse towards a view of a green valley, with bracken-coloured hills beyond.

In the graveyard of the pleasant church of St Kentigern (a.k.a. St Mungo) lie not only John Peel but the real-life original of the heroine of Melvyn Bragg's novel *The Maid of Buttermere*. To the south of the village, Carrock Fell is known for the variety of minerals which can be found.

Apart from all the obvious attractions of the area, visitors often enjoy going to the October auctions (in Wigton) of horses and Shetland ponies, although the spectacle of foals being separated from the mares can be distressing. Bassenthwaite Lake, Carlisle Castle and Cockermouth are other attractions.

Readers' comments: Beautiful view; comfortable bedroom. Good home cooking; made very welcome; pretty view of the beck. Thoroughly enjoyed our visit, well looked after. Food excellent, house delightful, shall return. Most enjoyable, excellent food, will return. Superb.

★ FRITH FARMHOUSE

Otterden, Kent, ME13 0DD Tel: 0795 89701

South-west of Faversham. Nearest main road: A20 from Maidstone to Charing.

3 Bedrooms. £17.50–£20 (less for 4 nights). All have own shower/toilet. Tea/coffee facilities. TV. Views of garden, country. No smoking. Washing machine on request.

Dinner. £13.50 for 4 courses (with choices), wine and coffee, at 7.30pm. Non-residents not admitted. Vegetarian or special diets if ordered. Wine can be brought in. **Light suppers** if ordered.

1 Sitting-room. With open fire, central heating, piano, record-player.

Large garden

Once, there were cherry orchards as far as the eye could see: now Frith has only six acres. (From their fruit – 'If I can grab it before the birds do!' – Susan Chesterfield makes sorbets for her gourmet dinners.)

They say money doesn't grow on trees. Not true, for those cherry trees financed the building in 1820 of this very fine house where a fountain plays outside the pillared front door, and alcoves of bookshelves flank the pine fireplace. Maroon damask wallpapers and sofas are in keeping with its style.

In a very lovely dining-room, fiddleback chairs and a collection of antique plates contrast with a bold geometrical 'Kazak' print (Liberty's) used for the curtains, and with the octagonal white dishes of German bone china on which Susan serves such meals as avocado with taramosalata, sorbet, lamb steaks with capers, meringues glacés and cheeses (wine included).

A recent addition is a polygonal conservatory, decorated and furnished entirely in white, where Susan provides not only breakfast but dinner parties for local people. It overlooks a court with another fountain.

The house is so high up on the North Downs (an area of outstanding natural beauty) that its views across orchards and woods extend – in the case of one of the pretty bedrooms – as far as the Isle of Sheppey, which is a distant twinkle of bright lights after darkness falls. The Downs can be explored at the pace of bygone days in the Chesterfields' own landau: details on request.

Canterbury is, of course, the magnet which draws most visitors here but there is a great deal more to east Kent than this. For a scenic drive, go across the North Downs to the valley of the River Stour, the Tudor village of Chilham (with castle, grounds and Battle of Britain museum) and then to another secluded village, Hastingleigh, with a nearby wildlife reserve.

There is a particularly pretty little cottage at Eastling, in the Faversham direction: **PLANTATION HOUSE** (tel: 079589 315), where Dany Fraser takes visitors for bed-and-breakfast and will provide light suppers if ordered in advance. Half-timbered and with low beams, a Tudor brick hearth and French provincial furniture, it has an unusually large and wandering garden concealed behind it. From £10 to £12.

GEORGIAN TOWNHOUSE

11 Crossgate, Durham, DH1 4PS   Tel: 091 3868070

Nearest main road: A690 from Crook to Durham.

rear view

6 Bedrooms. £17.50–£20. Prices go up in April. Bargain breaks. All have own bath/shower/toilet. Tea/coffee facilities. TV (some). Views of garden, cathedral. Balcony.
1 Sitting-room. With open fire, central heating.
Closed from 21 December to 1 February inclusive.

Minutes by foot from the centre of the city, Crossgate is a fairly quiet street of mainly Georgian-fronted houses. This is one (or rather two) of such.

Architect's wife Jane Weil has decorated her six bedrooms with great flair, from the simple beamed attic to the more elaborate rooms below, with swags of fabric over windows and bedheads. All have their own bathrooms. Downstairs, the sitting-cum-breakfast room has dark green walls, leaf green carpet, and soft furnishings in red, green and cream – a bold and agreeable colour scheme. A polygonal sun-room with white cast-iron furniture (sometimes used for breakfast) leads to a tiny garden, where a floodlit statue stands in a pool. Ingenious decorative arrangements abound in the house.

Two pubs are close (for which reason the back bedrooms might be preferable, at least on Fridays and Saturdays). Downhill is the 12th-century church of St Margaret of Antioch and the river. Durham is surprisingly badly off for good restaurants, but Mrs Weil can direct visitors to the best there are.

The city is best known for its Norman cathedral (one of the gems of European architecture) and castle, which surmount what is almost an island in a loop of the River Wear. The riverside walk is very attractive, or one can hire a boat. There are some good museums too, such as the Gulbenkian collection of oriental art, which is attached to the university; a visit here also gives an opportunity of seeing some interesting modern architecture.

The city centre has many pleasant old streets. Go to the covered market for bric-à-brac and very fresh fish from the east coast.

A little further up Crossgate is **COLEBRICK** (No. 21), which possesses the considerable advantages for this area of having private parking space and of being set back from the road behind a front garden. The cream-and-pink bedrooms and the bathroom are on the ground floor. There are splendid views from the family's large, first-floor sitting-room (with balcony) of the cathedral and castle. Evening meals will be cooked (by special

arrangement) by Freda Mellanby. (Tel: 091 3849585.) No smoking. £17.50.

For explanation of code letters (**C, D, H, PT, S, X**) see page xxxiv.

GOLDEN CROSS FARM
Siddington, Cheshire, SK11 9JP Tel: 0260224 358
South-west of Macclesfield. Nearest main road: A34 from Manchester to
Congleton.

4 Bedrooms. £12. Tea/coffee facilities.
Views of garden, country. No smoking.
Washing machine on request.
1 Sitting-room. With open fire, central heat-
ing, TV, piano. No smoking.
Large garden

Centuries ago it was believed that a spirit of fertility resided in the last stalks of
wheat harvested in each field. So the reapers carefully preserved these, twisting
them into the shapes of little idols, 'corn dollies', to be preserved in the homestead
until next spring when they were returned to the fields.

Such superstitions have died out now, but not the skill of making corn dollies. A
leading craftsman in this field is Raymond Rush, engineer turned dairy-farmer (he
has a herd of pedigree Guernseys at Golden Cross). He not only demonstrates
dolly-making but every year places hundreds of straw decorations for the harvest
festival in Siddington's 14th-century church. Visitors who stay at his farm are
welcome to watch him at work in one of the outbuildings – and to pick up useful
country lore about, for instance, how to get rid of slugs (saucers of beer) or greenfly
(water laced with cigarette ends).

Golden Cross was an inn before it became a farmhouse a century ago. The
Rushes have given it yet another role as a guest-house (comfortable and spotless),
boldly decorating its low-ceilinged dining-room with a gold tile wallpaper, and
installing a spectacular bathroom with bidet, plum-coloured wallpaper and carpet
to match. Outside is a pretty garden, and among the ivy growing up the walls are
the nests of spotted flycatchers, blackbirds and tree-creepers. Altogether a place
made for holiday memories.

Most visitors dine at the Davenport Arms, Marton.

Siddington is in a scenic area. One can walk in a bluebell valley, a daffodil dell,
around a mere or along an ancient 'salt trail'; or visit such stately homes as Little
Moreton Hall (NT), Capesthorne Hall and Tatton Park. Other diversions are the
watermill at Nether Alderley (NT) and Joddrell Bank's radio telescope.

Apart from its famous city, Chester, Cheshire is not widely appreciated as a
good place for a holiday. True, there are industrial parts, but most of the county is
very peaceful. In the big central plain, cows graze in lush green pastures spangled
with buttercups (Cheshire cheese in the making!). There are ancient woodlands
dotted with secret meres, and villages or towns distinguished by the county's
famous mediaeval 'magpie' houses: white walls with box frames of black-painted
timbers. The slow-running River Dee has, over countless millennia, created the
wide and sandy estuary which divides the flowery Wirral peninsula from the
mountains of North Wales.

It is worth going to the tops of any of the numerous wooded peaks to enjoy the
panoramic views: from Beeston Castle you can see eight counties.

Nearby north Staffordshire, too, is worth discovering (another underrated area
of great beauty – part of it falls within the Peak District National Park). For
instance, past the market town of Leek is Waterhouses, with the county's arts
centre, and there are fine gardens at Biddulph Grange.

119

Main Street, Clanfield, Oxfordshire, OX8 2SH   Tel: 036781 266
South-west of Witney. Nearest main road: A4095 from Witney to Faringdon.

3 Bedrooms. £13–£15. Prices go up in April. Bargain breaks. Some have own bath/toilet. Tea/coffee facilities. Views of garden, country, river. No smoking. Washing machine on request.
1 Sitting-room. With central heating, TV.
Small garden

A willow-fringed stream runs alongside the village road as it pursues its course to the Thames. On the other side are an 18th-century cottage, Victorian shop and old granary that have been turned into a guest-house – the former shop provides a particularly spacious sitting-room with windows on both sides and a door to the garden at the back. The best and quietest bedroom is on the ground floor (with its own bathroom); the others are above. Throughout, the house is spotless, airy and decorated in light and pretty colours. Rosina Payne serves only breakfast, recommending the Tavern (just up the road) for other meals.

This part of the Cotswolds is full of interest. One drives through a landscape threaded with streams, among fields where cows or sheep doze in the sun. In late spring, Queen Anne's Lace billows along every verge, and apple-blossom dances in sugar-pink against bright blue skies. The lanes lead one to such famous sights as Bourton-on-the-Water, Stow-on-the-Wold, Bibury watermill, Lechlade, Burford (and its wildlife park), Witney's farm museum or old Minster Lovell Hall. Further afield are Cirencester, Cheltenham, Oxford and Woodstock (with Blenheim Palace). But there is no need to go far for interesting things to do. Just along the road is Radcot and the oldest bridge over the Thames, from which (in summer) narrow-boat trips set out for 18th-century Lechlade where four counties meet near Halfpenny Bridge – so-named for the toll which once had to be paid – and the ruins of St John's priory. (The boat can take wheelchairs, incidentally.) And at Friars Court on the edge of the village is a leisurely farm trail along which you will see cricket-bat willows by the Thames, wildflowers, a lake frequented by wildfowl and cormorants, pretty copses and the 800-year-old moat around Friar Court, full of big fish. Some of the woodlands are hundreds of years old, others recently planted by conservationist-farmer John Willmer. William Morris's Kelmscott Manor is near, and Buscot House which stands in a park with three lakes. The large and attractive old village of Bampton is famous for Morris-dancing, and beyond it is Stanton Harcourt with Wesley's cottage and Pope's tower (both men visited here).

Southward lies the pleasant market town of Faringdon (described elsewhere) and the Berkshire Downs on which is the prehistoric figure of a horse cut through the turf to the white chalk below: scenery in marked contrast to the water-meadows around the Thames and the rich farmlands of the Vale of the White Horse. One can walk the ancient Ridgeway high up, or meander along paths beside the Thames in its valley – with waterside inns at which to linger; or follow scenic drives through such pretty villages as Little Faringdon (with mill).

THE GRANARY
Fenny Compton Wharf, Warwickshire, CV33 0XE   Tel: 029577 214
South-east of Leamington Spa. Nearest main road: A423 from Coventry to
Banbury.

3 Bedrooms. £15. All have own shower/
toilet. Tea/coffee facilities. Views of garden,
country. No smoking.
1 Sitting/dining-room. With fire, central
heating, TV.
Large garden
Closed in December.

On the banks of the Oxford Canal, where colourful narrowboats pass by, the
Cotterills – local farming people – inherited a derelict 18th-century warehouse,
and completely rebuilt it to make a new home for themselves (upstairs) and rooms
for guests (on the ground floor).

Everything indoors has been very neatly done, with pale colours predominating, while the garden outside is (though only a few years old) beautifully
landscaped, rock plants and flowering shrubs grouped round a smooth lawn where
one may sit to watch the boats glide by. All around are fields.

Dinner can be had at the waterside George & Dragon near the house, or at other
restaurants (June Cotterill gives guests a list of eating-places which she recommends).

The hamlet is close to where three counties meet: Warwickshire, Oxfordshire
and Northamptonshire. Favourite day trips for visitors include Coventry
Cathedral, Northampton, the colleges of Oxford, the Cotswolds and the fruitful
Vale of Evesham as well as the gardens of Hidcote and Kiftsgate.

A 'hostess of the year' award was once
won by Deborah Lea – the most unassuming of people – who with her
★ brother runs **CRANDON HOUSE** at
Avon Dassett (tel: 029577 652) as a
guesthouse on a smallholding where a
few Jersey cows, sheep and poultry
roam free. One can sit in the glass
sun-room to watch the geese and ducks
enjoying life, with a view of hills
beyond. There is a separate television
room with log stove, and terrace outside; in another direction, the small
disused quarry (now overgrown) from
which Crandon stone was hewn is a
picturesque feature. Everything about
this house, built in the 1950s, is solidly
comfortable. The pink or blue bedrooms have nice pieces of furniture (a
walnut suite, for instance, and a shell-

back brocade chair) and large windows. Deborah produces, as she says,
'plain old-fashioned food' which her
visitors love – a variety of soups, roasts
and casseroles, bread-and-butter pudding, for example. From £13 to £17.

Readers' comments: We felt extremely
welcome, no detail was overlooked.

121

THE GRANGE

C(5) **D S X**

Sunderland Hill, Ravensden, Bedfordshire, MK44 2SH Tel: 0234 771771
North of Bedford. Nearest main road: A428 from Bedford towards St Neots.

3 Bedrooms. £15 (less for 3 nights). Some have own bath/shower/toilet. Tea/coffee facilities. TV. Views of garden, country. No smoking. Washing machine on request.
Dinner. £11 for 3 courses (with choices), sherry and coffee, from 6pm. Vegetarian or special diets if ordered. Wine can be ordered or brought in. No smoking. **Light suppers** if ordered.
2 Sitting-rooms. With log stoves, central heating, TV, record-player.
Large garden

This large manor house has been divided into three dwellings, of which No. 1 is the handsome home of Patricia Roberts, with views downhill of terraced lawns and great cedars, flowering shrubs and a copper beech. Patricia has furnished the rooms in keeping with the architectural style. Good paintings (some by her daughter) hang on silky coral walls; silver, big velvet armchairs and Chippendale furniture are in one room; in another the tulips and pinks of curtain and sofa fabric have inspired the colour scheme for the whole room. Even the bathrooms are carpeted and have flowery wallpaper. The snug little dining-room is in fact a book-lined alcove behind a blue satin curatin (sometimes another is brought into use when there are two families being accommodated).

Meals are very attractively presented. Salmon and pheasant often appear on the menu but guests can have whatever they like if it is ordered in advance. Beans, asparagus, strawberries and spinach are among the produce grown in the garden; honey comes from the Grange's own hives.

Patricia has much information to share about sightseeing in Bedfordshire, and about the best places in which to hunt for antiques. The 36 Squadron of the US Air Force was based at The Grange.

It is still possible to identify, in and around Bedford, places which inspired passages in Bunyan's *The Pilgrim's Progress*. Bedford has, in addition to its Bunyan Museum and a notable church, a good traffic-free shopping centre, twice-weekly market and fast trains to London. There are long garden walks beside the lovely River Ouse (boat trips, too). All around the town are pretty villages. At Cardington one can see ballooning and the giant sheds which once housed airships. Elstow (Bunyan's birthplace) has an old moot hall with museum, and half-timbered houses; Felmersham is a boating centre; Harrold has an ancient bridge and country park, Odell castle grounds, Podington old cottages and Hinwick Hall. A nature reserve in gravel-pits is at Sharnbrook, bird gardens at Stagsden, a windmill at Stevington, an extraordinary Tudor dovecote (for 1500 birds) at Willington, and plenty of fine mediaeval churches throughout the area. A little further afield, Woburn Abbey (and safari park), Whipsnade Zoo, Dunstable Downs (to watch gliders), Wrest Park Gardens, Luton Hoo (art treasures), Castle Ashby and Chicheley Hall are other sights well worth half a day each. With so much of interest it is surprising that Bedfordshire is rarely thought of as a holiday destination – particularly by Londoners (only ¾ hour away).

Readers' comments: Nothing too much trouble. Food delicious.

122

★ THE GRANGE

C(7) S

Torrington Lane, East Barkwith, Lincolnshire, LN3 5RY   Tel: 0673 858249
North-east of Lincoln. Nearest main road: A157 from Wragby to Louth.

3 Bedrooms. £15–£17. Prices go up in March. Bargain breaks. All have own bath/ shower/toilet. Tea/coffee facilities. **TV.** Views of garden, country. No smoking. Washing machine on request.
Dinner. £8 for 3–4 courses (with choices) and coffee, at 7pm. Vegetarian or special diets if ordered. Wine can be brought in. No smoking. **Light suppers** if ordered.
1 Sitting-room. With open fire, central heating, piano. No smoking – another room is kept for smokers.
Large garden

Anne Stamp frequents salerooms for the 'unconsidered trifles' which give so much character to her home – such things as the looking-glass painted with flowers, the Victoriana in the sitting-room, the old baskets which, along with dried flowers, hang from kitchen beams, china in the alcoves, and chairs with heraldic lions.

The house deserves all the thought she puts into it. Built in 1820, it has a pink-walled hall with stained-glass door, black-and-white floor tiles and a graceful staircase. Sash windows are deep-set in shuttered embrasures. Anne has furnished the sitting-room with pink and blue flowery sofas and prettily draped curtains. A second (family) sitting-room, with television, leads to a conservatory full of flowery pot-plants and a lawn with swing-settee, croquet and tennis.

Along a Turkey-carpeted corridor are equally attractive bedrooms – for instance, one has William Morris tiger-lilies on blinds, wallpaper and bedspread (and a sparkling, all-white shower room); another, delicate lace and roses; a third, cream satin (its gold-tapped bath is oval).

Anne (who writes short stories for women's magazines when not looking after her guests) serves such well chosen menus as cucumber soup, pheasant, and half-melons filled with raspberries (there are choices of starters and puddings). And when a long-stay visitor suggested she might want a night off, she declined – saying she preferred to stay in and enjoy her guests.

Lincolnshire is the county to choose if you want to unwind in the peace of a remote and solitary countryside, where the skies are open wide and the pace is slow-changing. One can motor at leisure untroubled by other traffic.

Caistor is high enough up in the Wolds to have views of distant Lincoln Cathedral. It developed from a Roman camp (some walls and a well remain) to a peaceful market town. In its part-Saxon church is a fine Crusader tomb. Kingerby, too, has outstanding church monuments and woodlands full of wildflowers in spring. Tealby is a particularly beautiful Wolds village by the River Rase where Tennyson often walked to Hainton where there is a park that was landscaped by Capability Brown. Redbourne is famous for a great hall (once owned by the descendants of Charles II and Nell Gwynn), surrounded by 300 acres of park – and it has another church well worth visiting. Gainsborough (where Canute was married, in 868; where several Civil War battles were fought; and on which George Eliot based her *Mill on the Floss* because the river's spring tides rise so dramatically) has old warehouses and a hall where Henry VIII met Katharine Parr. But of course it is Lincoln itself which is the principal magnet.

Readers' comments: Most enjoyable, strongly recommended.

123

GRASSFIELDS

Pateley Bridge, North Yorkshire, HG3 5HL   Tel: 0423 711412
North of Harrogate. Nearest main road: A59 from Harrogate to Skipton.

9 Bedrooms. £18–£19 (less for 3 nights). Prices go up in April. Bargain breaks. All have own bath/shower/toilet. Tea/coffee facilities. Views of garden, country. Washing machine on request.
Dinner. £9.50 for 3 courses and coffee, at 8pm. Non-residents not admitted. Vegetarian or special diets if ordered. Wine can be ordered.
2 Sitting-rooms. With open fire, central heating, TV. Bar.
Large garden
Closed from November to February inclusive.

This country house is set back from the road, in its own gardens: it is a handsome Georgian building surrounded by lawns and trees. All the rooms are spacious, well maintained and comfortably furnished. Barbara Garforth studies her visitors' interests and provides helpful information on local areas of interest, including many local walks. There is a tranquil and informal atmosphere.

Meals are prepared from local vegetables and produce wherever possible, including free-range eggs and Nidderdale lamb. A typical menu: grilled grapefruit, braised steak and fresh fruit salad in generous quantities. There is a wide selection of wines.

Pateley Bridge is an interesting small town (in 1982 it won the award for Europe's best floral village), with a number of good shops, set on a junction of several roads, which makes it a fine centre from which to go sightseeing. Grassfields is in the heart of Nidderdale, where there are crags, glens, lakes and How Stean gorge.

A number of Yorkshire's most historic towns are within easy reach and there are many pretty villages, particularly in nearby Wharfedale. Fountains Abbey is probably the most spectacular sight in the neighbourhood but there are many other abbeys and castles too, caverns like Stump Cross and strange rock formations like Brimham, rivers and lakes, interesting shops, old inns, nature trails and much else.

To understand the area it is a good idea to visit the Daleslife Centre in Kilnsey Park near Skipton where a shepherd's year, dry stone walling and so forth are explained. In that direction too are the terraced gardens of Parcevall Hall with splendid views.

Near Boroughbridge you can see the remains of a Roman town, now called Aldborough; Markenfield Hall is an early moated house (interior of little interest, however); Norton Coyers near Ripon is more interesting as its contents include Brontë memorabilia, and Ripley Castle has a good display of armour.

At Ripon is an unusual museum in an old gaol, with displays about policing from the 17th century onwards, while Grassington's cottage museum features rural history.

Readers' comments: Stayed twice: excellent. Most comfortable and quiet. Most helpful. Very fine food. Well furnished. Good food and plenty of it. Thoroughly enjoyed our stay, and every mouthful.

9 Gratwicke Road, Worthing, West Sussex, BN11 4BH Tel: 0903 213000
Nearest main road: A24 from Dorking to Worthing.

4 Bedrooms. £15–£17 (less for 7 nights).
Tea/coffee facilities. TV. No smoking.
Washing machine on request.
Snacks if ordered.
1 Sitting-room. With open fire, central heating, TV, piano, record-player. No smoking.
Patio
Closed in December and January.

Royalty put Worthing on the map nearly 200 years ago, when Princess Amelia (youngest daughter of George III) visited what was then merely a fishing village. This patronage immediately made Worthing fashionable as a seaside resort, but not many buildings survive from that period, except in watercolours displayed in the town's museum. However, there is still an old quarter, and it is here that Gratwicke House (1878) is found, in a sidestreet only a minute from the sea.

From the outside it looks just like many another. But Barbara and Rupert Webb, an actress and a former county cricketer, have decorated the interior with great flair – Rupert did all the work himself. There is a shell-pink sitting-room with gilded mirrors, grand piano, Victoriana, leafy plants and open fire – rather as it may have looked when the house was first built. In total contrast is the pine dining-room where swags of dried flowers and a trellis ceiling give a country air to the room. Photos from Barbara's theatrical past and Rupert's cricketing high days hang on the walls here. The window, with festoon blinds, overlooks a tiny courtyard garden. Breakfast is served on Royal Worcester china (no dinners, but this part of Worthing is an enclave of restaurants, such as La Difference).

Every room is a pleasure to look at, with inspired combinations such as a pheasant wallpaper with a watermelon carpet; poppy pictures and poppy cushions contrasting with a cool colour scheme of moss green and white; pink and white lacy fabrics in a bedroom with stripped pine. One very charming single room has flowers and butterflies painted on the built-in cupboard and bedhead. All bedrooms have very good armchairs.

Readers' comments: Charm itself, warmly welcoming, and a sense of freedom.

Just outside Worthing is the old village of Sompting, with a Rhenish-style Saxon church and **UPTON FARMHOUSE** (tel: 0903 33706), behind the handsome 18th-century façade of which are parts built in the 15th century. The rooms – which have soft colours and deep, velvety carpets – are exceptionally spacious, immaculate and well-equipped; and Penny Hall is a particularly caring hostess. B & b only. (In high summer, bookings at

weekends usually have to be for at least 2 nights.) £15.

GREY GABLES
C D

Norwich Road, near Cawston, Norfolk, NR10 4EY   Tel: 0603 871259

North-west of Norwich. Nearest main road: A140 from Cromer to Norwich.

6 Bedrooms. £17–£22 (less for 7 nights). Prices go up in March. Bargain breaks. All have own bath/shower/toilet. Tea/coffee facilities. TV. Views of garden, country.
Dinner. £14 for 3 courses (with choices) and coffee, at 7pm. Vegetarian or special diets if ordered. Wine can be ordered. No smoking. **Light suppers** if ordered.
2 Sitting-rooms. With open fire, central heating. **Bar.**
Large garden

Every year James and Rosalind Snaith travel in Europe looking for interesting new wines and recipes to add to their repertoire, for this former rectory is no ordinary guest-house. There is a choice of a three-course dinner or five-course feast that may include, after an hors d'oeuvres, creamed salmon or Italian bean soup, chicken Wellington with apricots in puff pastry, or fillet steak with Marsala sauce, choux filled with lemon curd and cream, and then cheeses.

They have rung the changes on blue-and-beige colour schemes in nearly every room from the Victorian-style sitting-room and up the elegant mahogany staircase to the bedrooms. Dinner is eaten at mahogany tables with velvet-upholstered chairs; silver, rosy Royal Albert china and candles make it an elegant occasion. I was looking at a needlework sampler made by Rosalind's great-aunt in the 'twenties when her mother told me embroidery had been a family tradition through at least four generations of craftswomen ('We never buy anything if we can embroider it ourselves!'): Rosalind herself continues it.

My favourite bedroom is no. 1: pretty fireplace, big bay windows.

Readers' comments: Excellent; marvellous food. Very friendly, good food.

The large landscaped garden is a big attraction at **GLAVENSIDE**, Letheringsett (tel: 0263 713181), restored by John Cozens-Hardy. There are lawns and rosebeds, streams with ponds and waterfalls, a rock garden and an area of heathers. He has got the old hydraulic ram to raise water; and the waterwheel (1802) of the mill turns again (you can buy stone-ground flour there). It is safe for children to paddle in the River Glaven, or to take out a boat on the millpond; visitors can also play croquet or deck tennis on the lawns, or walk by the river. The house is handsome; the furnishings homely. (Bed-and-breakfast only.) £12.

Readers' comments: Comfy beds, a relaxed holiday.

GREYS

Margaret Roding, Essex, CM6 1QR   Tel: 024531 509

North-west of Chelmsford. Nearest main road: A1060 from Bishops Stortford to Chelmsford.

3 Bedrooms. £13. Prices go up in October. Tea/coffee facilities. TV. Views of garden, country. No smoking.
Light suppers if ordered.
1 Sitting-room. With central heating, TV. No smoking.
Large garden

Once a pair of farmworkers' cottages, Greys became the Matthews' home when they moved out of their large farmhouse to let their son take over management of the farm. They painted the exterior apricot – in typical East Anglian style – and furnished the rooms simply (a mixture of Habitat and antiques) and with light, clear colours. The beamed breakfast-room has pine furniture and clematis-patterned curtains; from the sitting-room, glass doors open onto the large garden.

'It's lovely when guests book in for one night and then stay for several,' says Joyce. This often happens because so many people think Essex consists of Dagenham's motorworks, Southend's trippers and little else – then, when they come here, find a revelation.

The eight Roding villages include some of England's prettiest, in an area of winding streams and lanes, flowery inns, colour-washed houses with pargetted walls (decorative plasterwork) under thatched roofs. Many visitors arrive at Harwich or at Stansted airport, then base themselves here to visit London (¾-hour by train from Epping), Cambridge, Roman Colchester and the rest of East Anglia. But there is much to enjoy close by including picturesque Thaxted (which has music festivals and a church of cathedral-like splendour), old Dunmow which still has the four-yearly award of the Dunmow Flitch (bacon) to happily married couples – the next ceremony, complete with bewigged judge, will be in 1992, Greenstead (unique Saxon church made of wood), and the attractive towns of Saffron Walden and Bishops Stortford. Audley End is one of England's most splendid Jacobean mansions.

These are only a beginning. Go to Waltham Abbey for the enormous church where King Harold was buried after defeat by William the Conqueror. To Maldon to see great russet-sailed sailing-barges along the picturesque waterfront. To Mersea for the oysterage. To Clacton for the pleasures of an old-fashioned seaside resort. At Mountfichet Castle you might find a wildflower festival in full swing or a herbal weekend; in one of many fine manor gardens, a typical country fête; on village greens, Morris dancers; windmills in full sail; great shire horses on show at Toppesfield; displays of sheep-shearing; exhibitions by the many local craftsmen and artists; guided walks. The area also has the Imperial War Museum's collection of historic aircraft, etc. (at Duxford), two wildlife parks and numerous National Trust properties within easy reach. Saffron Walden has a museum internationally renowned for its 'worlds of man' gallery, particularly the Aborigine exhibits.

Every night you could dine at a different, excellent local inn: the Black Bull at Fyfield, the Cock & Bell at High Easter, and many others. This is a fruit-growing area with plenty of pick-your-own opportunities for the last day of one's visit, too.

GROVE HOUSE

Hamsterley Forest, County Durham, DL13 3NL   Tel: 0388 88203
West of Bishop Auckland. Nearest main road: A68 from Darlington to Consett.

4 Bedrooms. £17–£17.50 (less for 7 nights). Bargain breaks. Tea/coffee facilities. Views of garden, country. No smoking. Washing machine on request.
Dinner. £9 for 4 courses and coffee, at 7.30pm. Vegetarian or special diets if ordered. Wine can be brought in. No smoking. **Light suppers** if ordered.
2 Sitting-rooms. With open fire, central heating, TV, record-player. No smoking. **Large garden** with croquet.

Hamsterley Forest is a 5000-acre Forestry Commission holding in the hills of County Durham. Much of it consists of commercial conifers, but down one side lie 1000 acres of old mixed woodland, which the Forestry Commission manages for recreational purposes, with drives, waymarked walks, two rivers, a visitor centre, and so on. A few houses are buried in this beautiful forest, among them Grove House, which was once an aristocrat's shooting box. (Another is the home of David Bellamy, the television naturalist.)

Grove House is now the home of businessman Russell Close, his wife Helene, and their three children. It is a peaceful place, surrounded by its own big gardens and reached only by a forest road (private but metalled). The windows of the prettily furnished guest rooms look across the lawn into the forest, where you can see woodpeckers at work. Birdsong is the loudest sound you will hear.

The downstairs rooms have a touch of aristocratic grandeur, with the addition of some unusual fittings brought from Germany by Helene's grandparents, from whom she inherited them (notice the art deco doorhandles). Settees and armchairs in the enormous sitting-room are covered in William Morris fabrics.

Helene prepares all the food from fresh ingredients. Meals usually consist of a first course such as a fish gratin; home-made soup; followed by a main course which is often game from the forest; and then a cold sweet such as meringues with ice cream and hot chocolate sauce. She discusses guests' preferences beforehand.

Should you tire of walking, driving, cycling, or simply sitting in the forest, there is a huge expanse of deserted heather moorland a few miles away. The other attractions of this little-known county include High Force waterfall, Raby Castle, the magnificent Bowes Museum (château-style), Beamish open-air museum and of course Durham Cathedral. (Bicycles on loan.)

Readers' comments: Delicious, imaginative food. Fairytale house in beautiful setting. Good value. Greeted as old friends. A wonderful 'find'; it was perfect. Idyllic. Exceptionally varied menus, beautifully cooked.

★ **GUITING GUEST-HOUSE**   **C D PT S**
Post Office Lane, Guiting Power, Gloucestershire, GL54 5TZ
Tel: 04515 470
East of Cheltenham. Nearest main road: A436 from Andoversford towards
Stow-on-the-Wold.

4 Bedrooms. £14 (less for 3 nights). Prices
go up in April. Some have own shower/bath.
Tea/coffee facilities. TV. Views of garden,
country. Washing machine on request.
Dinner. A la carte or £9 for 3 courses (with
choices) and coffee, at 7pm. Non-residents
not admitted. Vegetarian or special diets if
ordered. Wine can be brought in. No smoking. **Light suppers** if ordered.
2 Sitting-rooms. With open fire, central
heating, TV, record-player.
Small garden

This is a quintessential Cotswold village with stone cross on a green, mossy roofs,
roses and wisteria clambering up mellow, sun-soaked walls – much of it just the
same as four centuries ago. The name refers to the River Windrush which flows by
('gyting' is Saxon for a rushing brook) and to a 13th-century magnate, le Poer, who
owned the village at the time when wool-weaving was beginning to make it a
prosperous little community, soon to have its own market. But even in prehistoric
and Roman times, there was a settlement here.

The village once had five inns – of which this house, then known as The Bell,
was one – thronged with beer-drinkers during the Whitsuntide Fair. It still has its
celebratory occasions but of a quite different kind: an annual music festival every
July. And there are still hill sheep with particularly fine, white fleece – though
preserved as a rare breed now, at the nearby farm park (see below). All around are
lanes or footpaths with a great variety of wildflowers.

Changes to the 450-year-old guest-house have been done with sensitivity. New
pine doors have wood latches; the dining-room floor is made of solid elm planks
from Wychwood Forest; logs blaze in a stone fireplace with ogee arch; and in the
snug sitting-room are flagstones with oriental rugs (elsewhere in the house are rag
rugs which Yvonne Sylvester made herself). Yvonne has filled a bay window with
begonias and shelves with china that she collects; her meals are served on
wildflower-patterned bone china. Bedrooms are pleasantly decorated, with such
touches as beribboned cushions or an old cane-backed rocking chair, and four-
posters. I particularly liked no. 2: through its stone-mullioned window is a view of
another cottage made colourful by hanging flower baskets.

As to dinner, Yvonne will cook whatever you want but a favourite menu is
smoked trout from a nearby fish farm, chicken in a lemon and grape sauce,
strawberry mousse and cheeses.

The Cotswold Farm Park just north of the village is home to the Rare Breeds
Survival Trust which exists to preserve historic breeds of farm animals that might
otherwise die out, and here you can spend a day among, for instance, little Soay
sheep first domesticated by Stone Age man and striped piglets of a prehistoric
strain. Children can stroke baby animals in Pets Corner, adults can follow farm
trails or watch various husbandry demonstrations. Also in the area is Folly Farm
with hundreds of waterfowl in natural surroundings, which children can feed.

Readers' comments: Extremely welcoming, nothing was too much trouble. Went
out of their way to look after children.

★ **GUY WELLS**
Eastgate (road), Whaplode, Lincolnshire, PE12 6TZ   Tel: 0406 22239
East of Spalding. Nearest main road: A151 from Spalding to King's Lynn.

3 Bedrooms. £13–£14 (less for 5 nights). Prices go up at Easter. Tea/coffee facilities. TV. Views of garden, country. No smoking.
Dinner. £8 for 3 courses (with choices) and coffee, at 7pm. Vegetarian or special diets if ordered. Wine can be brought in. No smoking. **Light suppers** if ordered.
1 Sitting-room. With open fire, central heating, TV, piano. No smoking.
Large garden

Springs in the land around this Queen Anne house are what gave it its name. It is in a lovely and secluded position, surrounded by a traditional garden, trees, and beyond that the fens. The Thompsons have daffodil and tulip fields as well as glasshouses where they cultivate spring flowers and lilies.

The interior of the house is full of imaginative touches – like the addition of an alcove with domed top and scallop-edged shelves to one side of the brick hearth where a log stove stands. Raspberry velvet tub chairs contrast with homely stripped-pine doors. And there is no sound louder than a slow-ticking clock.

Hall and staircase are pretty (with sprigged wallpaper, prints and bouquets of flowerheads dried by Anne), leading to the bedrooms – one of which is huge, with antique bedhead and an old cedar chest. The best one of all has a spread with tucks and pink ribbons, and windows on two sides. One has a half-tester bed.

Visitors who choose Guy Wells do so in order to explore the superb churches of the county, to enjoy its bird life or the spring flowers, for the easy cycling (it's a level area) or just for the peace.

And for Anne's wholefood cooking (using their own vegetables and eggs). She makes all her own pâtés, soups, quiches or ratatouille for starters; a traditional roast or casserole may follow; and puddings like raspberry pavlova, cheesecake or (a speciality I found delectable) a crème brûlée in which yogurt combines with cream as a topping to brandied grapes.

From Whaplode, one can easily explore most of Lincolnshire and much of Cambridgeshire, too – Peterborough, in particular, is worth a day for its cathedral, river trips, local museums and shopping centre, all described elsewhere. There is a butterfly park nearby. Great churches, Springfield bulb gardens, windmills, and many garden centres add to the interest of the area. Also easily accessible are King's Lynn, and royal Sandringham House which is now open to the public during the summer.

Go to Boston for its great church and the Guildhall (museum, and the cells where the Pilgrim Fathers were imprisoned). Great houses in the vicinity include magnificent Belton and Burghley. Harlaxton Manor (its huge conservatory stocked by Kew Gardens), mediaeval Grantham House, and Woolsthorpe Manor (birthplace of Isaac Newton) are all in or near Grantham.

Readers' comments: Lovely people. Enjoyed the cooking so much. Delightful lady, friendly, excellent cook, very pleasant house. Lovely place, superb food, nice lady. Very warm welcome, happy atmosphere, glorious food. Interesting part of the country, have visited twice. Welcoming couple, pleasant place.

★ **THE HALL**   **C(5) D PT S**

Great Hucklow, Tideswell, Derbyshire, SK17 8RG   Tel: 0298 871175
East of Buxton. Nearest main road: A623 from Chapel-en-le-Frith towards
Chesterfield.

3 Bedrooms. £15–£16. Prices go up in May.
Views of garden, country.
Dinner. £10 for 3 courses and coffee, at
7pm. Vegetarian or special diets if ordered.
Wine can be brought in. **Light suppers** if
ordered.
1 Sitting-room. With open fire. No
smoking.
Large garden
**Closed from December to February
inclusive.**

This, like many Derbyshire villages, is famous for summer 'well-dressings': huge
mosaics of flower-petals depicting religious themes, each ushered in by a blessing
of the well. To enjoy this floral event, stay at The Hall, where you can also see the
Whatleys' south-facing garden when it is at its most colourful (Angela grows
the vegetables, her mother-in-law – who lives in the Hall's converted barn – the
flowers).

The sandstone Hall was built – on mediaeval foundations – soon after Charles I
became King. Like **Highlow Hall** (see elsewhere), it was one of several in similar
style which a Derbyshire farmer (Bagshaw, in this case) provided for each of his
sons. Rows of small, mullioned windows give it particular charm, and in the
former kitchen (now a sitting-room) the original fireplace, which would have
housed a great spit, has been exposed. Walls three feet thick, which keep the house
warm in winter and cool in summer, have here been painted cream, a good foil to
the handsome furniture and unusual mirrors (some for sale) which John makes in
his spare time. He has restored an unusual, very narrow, cellar-to-attic window
(diamond-paned) which lights the staircase.

His craftsmanship is evident in the bedrooms too. For instance, in one of the
very big family rooms there is a huge cockerel he carved, as well as stools and
bedside tables made by him. The bath- and shower-rooms (cork, pitch-pine and
unusual tiles) have more of his decorative mirrors. (No washbasins in bedrooms.)

Angela is a discriminating cook, using fresh garden produce, local game, and
imaginative recipes. A typical dinner might comprise her own liver-and bacon pâté
(with watercress and toast); chicken pie accompanied by ratatouille, boulangère
potatoes and other vegetables; then unusual water-ices (such as gooseberry and
elderflower, or blackcurrant-leaf) accompanied by home-made biscuits.

All around are the hills and lovely valleys of the Peak District and such sights as
Chatsworth (and its garden centre), Haddon Hall, and Monsal Dale. Lea Gardens
are noted for rhododendrons. Buxton, over 1000 feet up in the hills, is a spa that
was laid out in the 18th century to rival Bath. You can drink the waters (palatable –
unlike many!) which well up. hot, from underground springs; attend the opera;
peer at insects in the unique micrarium; or walk in the fine gardens and shopping
streets.

Readers' comments: More than satisfied. Dinner one of the most superb meals I
have ever had, quite perfect. Most friendly welcome. Most enjoyable. Very
comfortable. Excellent food.

HALL BANK HOTEL

Beck Lane, Bingley, West Yorkshire, BD16 4DD   Tel: 0274 565296
Nearest main road: A650 from Bradford to Keighley.

9 Bedrooms. £18. Prices go up in March. Bargain breaks. All have own bath/shower/toilet. Tea/coffee facilities. TV. Views of garden, country. Washing machine on request.
Dinner. A la carte or £8.50 for 3 courses (with choices) and coffee, at 6.30–7.30pm. Non-residents not admitted. Vegetarian or special diets if ordered. Wine can be ordered. No smoking. **Light suppers** if ordered.
1 Sitting-room. With central heating, TV. Conservatory.
Small garden

The peaceful country surroundings come as a surprise to many. This Victorian house of brown stone (millstone grit), once the residence of an American consul, is perched high in its own grounds overlooking the Aire Valley, woods and moors: from its sun-parlour or its paved terrace visitors often enjoy spectacular sunsets. The hotel is now run by Emmie and Jack Wright; with meals cooked by their son-in-law, a professional chef. All rooms have been refurnished to a high standard of comfort if not elegance.

A typical dinner might (from several choices) comprise turnip soup, duck or trout, and a gâteau.

There's plenty to see and do in this part of Yorkshire: moorland walks, a nature trail, the spectacular five-rise and three-rise locks on the canal which descends steeply near the hotel: hang-gliding, golf, riding, boating; Shipley Glen (ravine and stream); Saltaire model village – a very early little garden city (the woollen mill has a shop with sweaters and tweeds at half price, and canal cruises start here); stately homes like Harewood and the National Trusts's Jacobean mansion, East Riddlesden Hall; Haworth (the Brontës' home); the Worth Valley steam train; Skipton (castle); ruins like Bolton Abbey and Kirkstall. York, Harrogate and the Dales are within reach. (Escorted car tours by arrangement.)

A cultural explosion is taking place in West Yorkshire: a new £13-million theatre in Leeds, as well as Opera North and the Northern Philharmonia; in Halifax, a sculpture park, the Compass Theatre and the Northern Ballet; in Huddersfield, an international festival of modern music every year. Outstanding modern buildings and inspired conversions of former woollen mills house these enterprises. A fine but disused rail station of 1855 is to house the National Children's Museum, everything touchable or do-able; Victorian quarters and canal frontages are being restored; everywhere, transformation is racing ahead.

The city of Bradford (J. B. Priestley's 'Bruddersford') has some unusual museums. Of national importance is that of photography, film and television, which has done much to help the city's recent and rather unlikely growth as a tourist centre. There is also a museum of colour, an industrial one devoted to the city's past greatness as a textile centre, and one of rocks and gems, which also includes a walking-stick hall. Cartwright Hall is an art gallery with works by Reynolds and local lad David Hockney.

★ HARDINGLAND FARMHOUSE   S

Macclesfield Forest, Cheshire, SK11 0ND   Tel: 0625 425759
East of Macclesfield. Nearest main road: A537 from Macclesfield towards
Buxton.

3 Bedrooms. £12.50–£17.50. Some have own bath. Tea/coffee facilities. TV. Views of garden, country. Washing machine on request.
Dinner. £9 for 3 courses and coffee, at 7pm. Non-residents not admitted. Vegetarian or special diets if ordered. Wine can be brought in. Light suppers if ordered.
1 Sitting-room. With open fire, central heating, TV.
Large garden
Closed from December to February inclusive.

It is exceptional to find at one house outstanding surroundings, food and furnishings: Hardingland is just such a place.

The secluded house is perched high up on the fringe of the Peak District, on a hillside with stupendous panoramic views below. Ann Read's reputation is so high that she has cooked for such demanding clients as the Manchester Stock Exchange. And her 18th-century house has been furnished with style.

Before her marriage, Anne was a professional caterer, winning an award at Buxton's Salon Culinaire in 1989. She uses a great many of John Tovey's Miller Howe recipes when she prepares for her visitors such meals as: tarragon apples with Boursin cheese; lamb cutlets in ginger and orange sauce; an array of imaginative vegetables like French beans with almonds, caramelized carrots, herbed potatoes and orange and sunflower-seed salad; chocolate pots. The Reads' own smallholding provides beef and lamb; venison comes from forest deer.

The large sitting-room has comfortable sofas covered in a William Morris satin. Between the deep-set windows watercolours hang on the walls. The beamed dining-room is furnished in Regency-style, and one of the bedrooms has an attractive apricot and pale turquoise colour scheme. Bathrooms are excellent: carpeted, with pretty tiles.

Outside, wide stone steps beside a lily-pool lead to a paved garden and lawn sheltered by a stone-walled herbaceous bed. The garden is high above a deep valley across which are hills, the pine plantations of Macclesfield Forest, three reservoirs which provide havens for wildlife, and the headland of Tegg's Nose – now a country park open to visitors. Beyond the Cheshire plain are the hills of Shropshire, while in the other direction the peaks of Derbyshire are only a few miles away: one of the most scenic drives in the area is from Congleton to the spa town of Buxton, steeply up and down, crossing rocky streams, with rhododendrons and larches lining the winding road. At Buxton there is all the elegance you would expect of a spa town, a micrarium (for viewing insect life in close-up) and a steam centre.

In characterful Macclesfield, once a silk-weaving town, is an interesting museum of textile history; nearby are stately homes such as Adlington, Gawsworth and Capesthorne halls. Another historic town, Knutsford, was the inspiration of Mrs Gaskell's *Cranford*; and near a third, Nantwich, is Bridgemere Wildlife Park as well as Stapeley water gardens. Chester itself is within an easy drive – its historic streets and cathedral are famous, and it has an exceptionally good zoo too, with gardens.

HARE AND HOUNDS INN

C P T S X

Talkin, Cumbria, CA8 1LE Tel: 06977 3456/7
South of Brampton. Nearest main road: A69 from Carlisle to Brampton.

4 Bedrooms. £14 (less for 4 nights). Prices go up in April. Bargain breaks. Some have own bath/shower/toilet. Tea/coffee facilities. TV. Views of garden, country.
Dinner. A la carte or £8 for 3 courses (with choices) and coffee, at 7–9.30pm. Vegetarian or special diets if ordered. Wine can be ordered.
1 Sitting-room. With open fire, central heating, TV. **2 bars.**
Small garden

You could easily pass by this unassuming little inn in the middle of a quiet village – but there is more to it than meets the eye. Even the public bar is a bit different from the average, with heavy elm tables, logs in stone fireplaces at each end, and over the bar itself heraldic panels of stained glass. There is a separate family room, still with the old black-leaded kitchen range and brass fender, where children's menus are served.

Tucked away behind all this are peaceful, beamed bedrooms, and a farm-cottage annexe, quite attractively furnished and with pretty duvets on the beds. One has a four-poster.

The inn is run by a friendly young couple, Pauline and John Goddard, who maintain its reputation for good, simple food at modest prices and for interesting breakfasts (a variety of waffles, for example).

Talkin itself is situated in an interesting part of the country, surrounded by fells that are popular with walkers and near a large, unspoilt tarn with various water-sports. Hadrian's Wall is quite near: the most interesting parts at this end of it are the Banks Burn stretch and the fort at Birdoswald. The Scottish border-country and the Lake District are easily reached too, and the beautiful Eden Valley lies to the south. Brampton is an old market town; Alston and the city of Carlisle are not far. Talkin used to be a stopping-place for monks making their way to Lanercost Priory: part of this is in ruins, but the lovely nave is still used as a church and what was the guests' solar is a village hall.

★ For farmhouse accommodation at its most comfortable, **HULLERBANK** (tel: 06976 668) is only half a mile from Talkin. Prices in this neat 17th-century house are moderate, especially since all rooms have their own bath or shower. The setting is sheltered and peaceful, and the food, which includes lamb produced on the smallholding, fruit and vegetables from the garden, and trout from a local fish farm, is all home cooked by Sheila Stobbart. From £14.50 to £15.

Readers' comments: Comfortable facili-ties, friendly hosts, a lovely part of the country, and a reasonable price. We are definitely planning a return visit . . . Very friendly. I can definitely recommend Hullerbank. Enjoyable.

HATTON HALL
Hatton Heath, Cheshire CH3 9AP   Tel: 0829 70601
South-east of Chester. Nearest main road: A41 from Chester to Whitchurch.

4 Bedrooms. £16–£18 (less for 3 nights). Some have own bath/shower/toilet. Tea/coffee facilities. TV. Views of garden, country, moat. Washing machine on request.
Light suppers if ordered.
Large garden.

A moat dug by Normans surrounds this large 18th-century house, at the heart of a big dairy-farm. Once there was even a drawbridge.

The bedrooms are beautifully decorated and particularly well equipped (bathrooms quite luxurious). Australian-born Shirley Woolley likes, for instance, traditionally rosy cretonnes, countrified Chippendale chairs, an abundance of dried flowers, antique bedspreads of white crochet. One room has a chair from the Prince of Wales' investiture at Caernarfon Castle at which Shirley's father-in-law (Lord Woolley, former president of the NFU) was a guest.

Visitors dine in Chester or at the Pheasant Inn, Burwardesley, as Shirley serves only breakfast (though for women travelling alone, she will do dinners), which includes unusual home-made jams (such as sloe-and-ginger or strawberry-and-loganberry) as well as honey 'which I steal from my bees at great risk to my person!' On the table will be flowers and fine china.

Beyond the garden and the rose-bordered moat are stables with a dozen horses (trained to compete at horse shows) as well as geese and free-ranging chickens ('I would use my own eggs if only I could find them!').

Chester, described elsewhere, is only a few miles away as is (in the opposite direction) little Malpas where old houses overhang steep streets; in its mediaeval church of red sandstone are carvings, stained glass and a superb parish chest.

At nearby Tattenhall is a big dairy-farm and a 300-year-old house, **NEWTON HALL** (tel: 0829 70153), surrounded by gardens and fine views of both Beeston and Peckforton castles. Anne Arden's rooms have an air of solid comfort (the blue bedroom is particularly beautiful, with handsome Victorian mahogany furniture). In the breakfast room are wheelback chairs, oak table and dresser, the original quarry tiles, a brick fireplace, huge beams and oak doors with great iron hinges. Like those in the sitting-room, its casements open onto sweeping lawns. (Snack suppers if ordered.) £15.

★ **THE HAVEN**   C D H PT S
Hardwicke, Herefordshire, HR3 5TA   Tel: 04973 254
West of Hereford. Nearest main road: A438 from Hereford to Brecon.

6 Bedrooms. £15.75–£19.75 (less for 2 nights). Prices go up in April. Some have own bath/shower/toilet. Tea/coffee facilities. TV. Views of garden, country. No smoking. Washing machine on request.
Dinner. £8.25 for 3 courses (with choices) and coffee, at 7.30pm. Non-residents not admitted. Vegetarian or special diets if ordered. Wine can be ordered. No smoking.
Light suppers if ordered.
2 Sitting-rooms. With open fire, central heating, piano. Bar. No smoking in one.
Large garden
Closed in December and January.

'The long-talked-of Hardwick Bazaar for the Home Missions . . . Mary Bevan was radiant with her beautiful eyes and brow. Everybody was buying everything at once. The Volunteer Band banged and blasted away. Persons ran about in all directions with large pictures and other articles, bags, rugs, cushions, smoking caps, asking everyone they met to join in raffling for them.'

Thus Kilvert (a frequent visitor when this house was a vicarage and its garden much used for charity fêtes) wrote in his now famous diary, on 29 August 1870 – with an eye, as usual, for a pretty girl. Kilvert says that paintings done by the vicar's wife were auctioned – but her flowers and birds still adorn the door to one of the sitting-rooms. Here, through shuttered windows, are views of the Radnor Hills, and alcoves are filled with china. In the other sitting-room, books and old local maps line the walls; and there is a cabinet of fifty little drawers which Mark Robinson has filled with information for visitors.

There is a ground-floor bedroom (with bathroom) equipped to suit disabled people – even a wheelchair for use under the shower – and with a view of the unheated swimming-pool in the garden. Janet Robinson has stencilled the walls with a waterlily pattern to match the Liberty fabrics used in the furnishings.

In the dining-room she has stencilled cornflowers to match the festoon blinds of the bay windows; a collection of childhood birthday cards from the 'thirties is a feature elsewhere; and in every room her flair for decoration is evident – a pretty chinoiserie wallpaper here, a sweet-pea paper there, cane bedhead in one room and a huge four-poster in another. One bathroom (raspberry and gold, with sunken bath, bidet and two basins) is not so much a bathroom as an event.

Because Janet enjoys cooking (and studied traditional country recipes at Hereford Technical College), meals are unusually imaginative. A nut-and herb roulade might be followed by beef casseroled with ginger and then a creamy fool.

The Robinsons occasionally run special activity weekends on such subjects as Kilvert's diary, book-collecting (Hay-on-Wye is near) or 'hidden treasures' (visits to little-known or private houses of historic interest).

Beyond the large garden are paddocks brilliant in spring with snowdrops, miniature daffodils, frittillaries, cowslips and bluebells growing wild.

Readers' comments: Exceptional, have booked to go again. Kind and genuine hospitality. Very comfortable; food lovely. Very thoughtful, cooking outstanding.

HAZEL TREE FARMHOUSE   C H S

Hassell Street, Hastingleigh, Kent, TN25 5JE   Tel: 023375 324
East of Ashford. Nearest main road: A20 from Folkestone to Ashford.

5 Bedrooms. £14.50–£15.50 (less for 3 nights). Prices go up in July. Bargain breaks. One has own washbasin/toilet. Tea/coffee facilities. TV. Views of garden, country. Washing machine on request.
Dinner. £7 for 3 courses (with choices) and coffee, at 7.30pm. Non-residents not admitted. Vegetarian or special diets if ordered. Wine can be brought in. **Light suppers** if ordered.
1 Sitting-room. With open fire, central heating, TV, piano.
Large garden
Closed from November to February inclusive.

Small though this is, it is a true hall house: that is to say, an early mediaeval structure in which the ground floor consisted of one high communal room originally rising to the roof, with only a screen wall separating it from the dairy, now used as the kitchen.

Christine Gorell Barnes and her artistic family have contributed greatly to the character of the old house, filling it with their paintings, tapestries and the results of a lifetime of collecting. There are old chests in a corridor, patchwork curtains and spreads on old brass beds, bunches of dried flowers and hop bines over a brick inglenook, books everywhere, and on the landing many generations of dolls, dolls' house and toys which young visitors are allowed to play with. One unusual treasure is an old dulcitone – a keyboard instrument in which the hammers strike a graduated row of steel tuning-forks, with bell-like sounds. Bedrooms are furnished in simple cottage style: I particularly liked a ground-floor one with pine walls. Outside is a willow-fringed pool and a field with Christine's 14 sheep.

Meals are, like the old house itself, out of the ordinary. When I called, Christine was preparing borscht (beetroot soup), chicken baked with courgettes and accompanied by dauphinoise potatoes, and a spicy pumpkin pie.

WALNUT TREE FARMHOUSE at Lynsore Bottom has one of the prettiest exteriors in Kent. Inside, too, it is full of charm. Gerald Wilton makes furniture, very decorative carved signboards, colourful decoy ducks and much else in the house – including the long oak table which looks as if it, like the house itself, dates from the 14th century; and the painted clock with a picture of the farm on its face.

Guests' bedrooms (some in the house and others in a former apple-loft) are reached by broad step-ladders. Every wall and floor slopes a little. Crisp white fabrics, flower-sprigged, and pine fitments combine to give rooms an airy, cottagey feel. An attic one with low windows has the ancient king-post that supports the whole structure. (B & b only.) Tel: 022787 375. £16.

Readers' comments: Have returned many times, most exceptional. A lot of thought and care; made most welcome. Beautifully furnished. Made to feel like guests of the family.

137

Ryarsh, West Malling, Kent, ME19 5JU   Tel: 0732 842074
West of Maidstone. Nearest main road: A228 from Tonbridge to Rochester.

3 Bedrooms. £15–£18 (less for 2 nights). Prices go up in July. Bargain breaks. Tea/coffee facilities. TV. Views of garden, country. No smoking. Washing machine on request.
Dinner (must be ordered in advance). £10 for 4 courses (with choices) and coffee, at 7.30pm. Non-residents not admitted. Vegetarian or special diets if ordered. Wine can be brought in. No smoking. **Light suppers** if ordered.
1 Sitting-room. With open fire, central heating, TV, piano, record-player. No smoking.
Large garden

Perched on a hilltop, this red brick farmhouse with dormer windows in the roof and clematis around the porch is at the heart of a smallholding which provides much of the produce that Jean Edwards (once a health visitor) enjoys cooking for her guests. Until a few decades ago, the old house was occupied by generations of the same farming family which built it in the 17th century. All around are country lanes, fields, woodlands and two long-distance footpaths.

The little sitting-room has very comfortable armchairs grouped around the brick hearth (stacked with logs), which still has the old bread oven alongside. It's a cosy room, with the soothing sound of clocks ticking, Gem (the Edwards' Jack Russell terrier) snoozing on the hearth, a collection of china pigs and good books.

Jean enjoys cooking a wide repertoire of dishes (whenever she and her husband travel in the wine regions of France, she always returns with new recipes). She bakes her own bread; honey, eggs, geese and lamb are home-produced.

Beamed bedrooms with white-boarded, latched doors are prettily furnished with Laura Ashley fabrics and attractive colour schemes (pink- or blue-and-white, or moss-green with red-and-white). The Edwards have collected stuffed birds and maps for the walls, and pot-plants for every window-sill. Through the windows are views of the Downs or of the garden which, even in winter, is colourful with witch hazel, holly berries and winter-flowering cherry trees. There's an old pump in it, a swing-seat on the brick patio, and a children's swing. Rooms are small.

Although only an hour from South London (Heathrow and Gatwick airports are even closer), this is a good centre from which to explore rural Kent, the mediaeval bridges of the upper Medway, and any number of castles – Allington, Leeds, Hever, Rochester – and historic buildings – Boughton Monchelsea house, the friary at Aylesford, Sissinghurst with its famous gardens, the Archbishop's Palace at Maidstone, Chartwell (Churchill's home) and Ightham Mote. There's county cricket, boating and sailing, and a famous collection of carriages at Maidstone. But the scenery is the main thing: hills, orchards, streams, hop gardens with their conical oast houses (you can visit Whitbread's hop farm), half-timbered cottages, picturesque villages like Loose (a stream threads its way among the houses). West Malling is largely Georgian, with Norman remains.

Readers' comments: Very good indeed. As charming as could be; convivial hosts; mouth-watering and plentiful food. Charming house, food delicious.

HERMITAGE MANOR

Canon Pyon, Herefordshire, HR4 8NR   Tel: 0432 760317

North-west of Hereford. Nearest main road: A4110 from Hereford to
Knighton.

3 Bedrooms. £17.50. Bargain breaks. All
have own bath/shower/toilet. Tea/coffee
facilities. Views of garden, country.
Washing machine on request.
3 Sitting-rooms. With open fire, central
heating, TV, piano. No smoking in music
room.
Large garden
**Closed from December to February
inclusive.**

An *escalier d'honneur* sweeps grandly up to the front door which opens into a room
of baronial splendour, its ceiling decorated with Tudor roses and strapwork,
motifs which are repeated on the oak-panelled walls. Through stone-mullioned
bay windows are some of the finest views from any house in this book. There is also
a very lovely music room (damask walls and velvet chairs are in soft blue; the
limewood fireplace has carved garlands). Throughout, carpets and other
furnishings are of equal quality to the architecture.

The recently converted bedrooms, and their bathrooms, are of the highest
standard and very large. No. 6 has a view of a hillside spring flowing through
stepped pools of pinkish limestone (from a quarry in the area) which Shirley
Hickling created when she was converting this exceptional house. She serves
bed-and-breakfast only – but there are good inns nearby, and Hereford is only ten
minutes away.

Walking and watching the deer or birds are main attractions in this scenic area –
the Wye Valley (with Symonds Yat viewpoint), Malvern Hills, Welsh border,
Offa's Dyke path, Brecon Beacons and Black Mountains are all accessible. This is
a county of woods and streams. In addition there are historic houses such as
Berrington Hall to visit, rural museums, Croft and other castles and abbeys.

Readers' comments: Magnificent view, magnificent bedrooms.

Judy Seaborne's very good home cooking is the main attraction of **STONE
HOUSE FARM**, Tillington (tel:
0432 760631). The setting is very
peaceful, with fine views, and children
in particular enjoy spring visits when
there are lambs, calves and foals to be
seen. A typical meal: home-made soup,
a roast (the farm's own meat), fruit pie
– served from Royal Worcester dishes,
in a dining-room with open fire. (Milk,
butter and cream are also usually from
the farm.) Made of solid stone, the
house is well away from any road, and
has fine greenery beyond its small

orchard. There is an old pump in the
front garden. £16.

Readers' comments: Well fed and received with great friendliness. Food of
high quality and ample. Most welcoming; excellent cook.

139

★ HIGH GREEN HOUSE   C D H S X

Nowton, Suffolk, IP29 2LZ   Tel: 0284 86293
South of Bury St Edmunds. Nearest main road: A134 from Bury St Edmunds to Sudbury.

5 Bedrooms. £15–£16. Prices go up in April. Bargain breaks. All have own shower/toilet. Tea/coffee facilities. TV. Views of garden, country. No smoking. Washing machine on request.
Dinner. £8 for 4 courses (with choices) and coffee, at 7.30pm. Non-residents not admitted. Vegetarian or special diets if ordered. Wine can be ordered. No smoking. **Light suppers** if ordered.
1 Sitting-room. With open fire, central heating, TV. Bar. No smoking.
Large garden

Part Tudor and part Victorian, this delightful house is truly secluded – surrounded by brimming herbaceous borders, a paddock of geese and an old well, with wheat fields beyond. There are a lily-pool (it is all that remains of a moat), troughs of begonias and fuchsias, and, where only the great frame of a mediaeval barn survives, Rosemary Thew has created a suntrap in which to sit, training scented roses and wisteria over the timbers and placing seats to face the view.

The interior of the house is full of nooks and crannies, cabinets of old china and glass, antique furniture and low beams. There are oriel and mullioned windows, a brick fireplace, and wrought-iron hinges on bedroom doors. Some bedrooms are small and simple; but one has a four-poster, windows on three sides, a carved chest and a cheval mirror with painted flowers. Rosemary (who worked with physically handicapped people until her retirement) has also provided a downstairs bedroom ideal for a disabled person.

Dinner can comprise a chicken vol-au-vent as a starter, then a good roast joint, profiteroles and cheese. She is a genial, informal lady with whom one immediately feels at home; and, because she was formerly clerk to the local council, she is a mine of information about the area (and its people).

Bury and its environs are described elsewhere. Also within easy reach are the great houses of Ickworth and Melford; pretty villages like Clare and Cavendish; the gardens at Bressingham – and antique shops everywhere.

Readers' comments: Warm welcome and excellent food. Most tranquil house. Miss Thew is delightful. Charming building; a bargain; Miss Thew is a character. Peaceful and friendly, nothing too much trouble. Warm welcome and personal attention. Took a lot of trouble; fed us royally. Lovely garden. Good food. Very good; charming lady.

Book well ahead: many of these houses have few rooms. Do not expect dinner if you have not booked it or if you arrive late.

HIGH GREENRIGG HOUSE

C(5) **D H S**

Caldbeck, Cumbria, CA7 8HD   Tel: 06998 430

South-east of Wigton. Nearest main road: A595 from Carlisle to Cockermouth.

8 Bedrooms. £18 (less for 7 nights). Prices go up at Easter. Some have own bath/shower/toilet. Tea/coffee facilities. TV. Views of garden, counrty. No smoking. Washing machine on request.
Dinner. £10 for 4 courses (with choices) and coffee, at 7pm. Vegetarian or special diets if ordered. Wine can be ordered. No smoking.
3 Sitting-rooms. With open fire, central heating, TV, record-player. **Bar.**
Large garden
Closed from November to February inclusive.

Hidden in the moors above the village, this 17th-century house has great character, with low doorways and stone lintels. Inside, modern furnishings have been well chosen to suit the beamed interior with no attempt at a 'ye-olde' effect. Pine and cane predominate in the dining-room; in the sitting-room, once a cow byre, ceilings and floor are cork-covered, and there is a self-service alcove where visitors can make unlimited tea and coffee. The bedrooms (which include some on the ground floor) have pine fittings and bedheads, and they give fine views of the surrounding fells. Good food is a speciality of Robin and Fran Jacobs (who used to be an engineer and a social worker respectively). They share the cooking and make their own bread and marmalade. A typical dinner might comprise marinated mushrooms, beef goulash, Lancaster lemon tart, and Stilton.

There is plenty of room for quiet relaxation in the evening; or one can go to a games room with a mezzanine bar, where plate glass has replaced the barn doors. This being an outstanding area for walkers, well away from the crowded part of the Lake District, the Jacobs, with the help of a National Park ranger, have prepared a well-produced booklet of recommended routes.

The Caldbeck area has attracted a number of celebrities to live (Chris Bonington the mountaineer and Sir Fred Hoyle the astronomer, for example) and a lot of craftspeople. Margaret Forster, who has a home nearby, set her novel *The Bride of Lowther* in the area: it conveys the nature of Cumbrian life very well. Apart from Carlisle (cathedral, castle and museums), the nearest place of any size is Wigton. This is the home town of Melvyn Bragg, and he based his book *Speak for England* on interviews with the townspeople.

A fairly recent addition to what was always a pretty and interesting village is, in the converted Priest's Mill, a group of shops for books, antiques and various crafts, and a wholefood restaurant. Caldbeck is just inside the National Park, but is still quiet when other parts of the Lake District are over-full of holiday-makers.

Readers' comments: Most enjoyable. Food superb. Will stay again.

★ **HIGH POPLARS** C D S X
Hinton, Saxmundham, Suffolk, IP17 3RJ   Tel: 050270 528
North-west of Aldeburgh. Nearest main road: A12 from Ipswich to Lowestoft.

4 Bedrooms. £18–£22 (less for 7 nights). Bargain breaks. Some have own bath/ shower/toilet. No smoking. Washing machine on request.
Dinner. £12.50 for 3 courses (with choices) wine and coffee, at 8pm. Non-residents not admitted. Vegetarian or special diets if ordered. Wine can be brought in. No smoking. **Light suppers** if ordered.
1 Sitting-room. With open fire, central heating, TV.
Small garden

For four centuries, right up to 1976, the same family, Blois, farmed here: there are memorials to them in Blythburgh Church. The earliest of the Blois were related to the Norman King Stephen; the latest still live nearby, at Cockfield Hall.

Now the half-timbered house is Mary Montague's home and on its old brick walls hang pictures, some of which are even older than they. She has furnished the house with unusual antiques such as a Spanish dresser, a collector's cabinet from the 18th century, country dining-chairs and sofas upholstered in an art nouveau Liberty fabric. On the dining-room floor are heavy tiles of local clay; and up winding stairs are big bedrooms (one of which has exposed joists separating two single beds) with, for instance, pink patchwork spreads and cushions, and particularly good bathrooms.

For dinner, Mary prepares such meals as mushrooms in garlic or Cromer crabs to start with; roast beef or sole stuffed with mushrooms and prawns; then Belvoir pudding (a steamed lemon pudding with meringue and apple surrounding it) or crème caramel: wine is included.

Hinton is in P. D. James' country (the story of *The Black Tower* is sited nearby), an area where wildlife still flourishes – barn owls nest in the lane, you may hear nightingales, and there are masses of such wildflowers as cowslips, scabious and primroses. Mary's own pond is frequented by herons, kingfishers and ducks.

The hamlet lies a little way inland from Suffolk's 'heritage coast', now carefully conserved as an area of outstanding natural beauty: stretching from the fishing port and sandy resort of Lowestoft in the north, via the old-fashioned seaside towns of Southwold (a flowery place, with a series of village greens) and Aldeburgh, to the big Victorian resort of Felixstowe in the south. Because the sea constantly erodes this coast (go to nearby Dunwich to see this most dramatically – the whole of the mediaeval port has been lost to the tides), the principal road along it, the A12, is inland, crossing innumerable creeks and streams.

Among the crops are villages of great variety, some houses with walls of flint, others of brick – with pantiled roofs and shapely gables as in Holland, just across the sea from here – and still others of colourwashed plaster, often with thatched roofs. Barns are typically black with red roofs; surviving windmills, sparkling white. At Blythburgh is a great church with huge clerestorey through which you can see the sky on the other side, rearing up above a sandy heath of dunes and gorse. Further on, the landscape changes to marsh and moor, then bracken, roadsides brilliant with wildflowers, butterflies and birds thronging the Gwatkin Nature Reserve. The lanes beyond pretty Southwold pass oak woods, cottage-gardens and rivers with yellow waterlilies.

142

HIGH WINSLEY COTTAGE   S X

Burnt Yates, North Yorkshire, HG3 3EP   Tel: 0423 770 662
North-west of Harrogate. Nearest main road: A61 from Harrogate to Ripon.

5 Bedrooms. £16–£19 (less for 7 nights). Prices go up in April. All have own bath/shower/toilet. Tea/coffee facilities. TV. Views of garden, country. No smoking. **Dinner.** £7 for 3 courses and coffee, at 7pm. Non-residents not admitted. Vegetarian or special diets if ordered. Wine can be ordered. No smoking.
2 Sitting-rooms. With open fire, central heating, TV.
Large garden

Weird shapes loom above the moors – a 50-acre outcrop of stone which wind and rain have carved into surreal forms: Brimham Rocks.

Off the road leading to these is a one-time farm cottage now much extended, which has been modernized with care by Clive and Gill King. From the parquet-floored dining-room one steps down to a sitting-room where rosy sofas face a log fire and sliding glass doors open onto a terrace with views to the far hills. Lawn, flowers, orchard and a population of bantams and guinea-fowl add to the charm.

Colour schemes have been well chosen, here and upstairs. A blue-and-white bedroom with matching bathroom has bedspreads of pin-tucked satin; Laura Ashley briar-roses predominate in another, furnished with antiques; and I particularly liked a large room with windows on two sides and comfortable armchairs from which to enjoy the views.

Gill was once one of 'Miss Gray's young ladies' at the Bay Tree, Burford: those readers who knew the cooking standards there will rightly guess that High Winsley Cottage, too, can be depended upon for good and imaginative food. Gill also lived, and cooked, in Paris for a while.

She puts as much care into making shepherd's pie, for instance, as into a dinner such as lemons with a stuffing of smoked fish, pork in a spiced orange sauce and apple jalousie. Her own or local produce is used; bread is home-baked.

Burnt Yates is not only in the middle of a very scenic area (Nidderdale is among the loveliest yet least frequented of the Yorkshire Dales, and popular Wharfedale is not far away) but is also close to several traditional spa towns – Harrogate (described elsewhere), Ripon (with cathedral), and, one of my favourites, Ilkley, a delightful little town in the valley of the River Wharfe. It is particularly pretty in spring when the cherry-blossom is out on the trees that line its shopping streets, and the riverside gardens are coming into flower. The town has excellent restaurants, tea-rooms and bakers; a grocer specializing in cheeses and ham on the bone for picnics; plenty of bookshops, antique and craft shops; and historical interest, from ancient Saxon monuments to Tudor and 18th-century buildings. The invaluable local guide (free from the Tourist Information Centre in the library) gives maps for walks, short and long; tells you where to watch fell-racing, hang-gliding or international tennis. It lists other places for outings: caverns, ruins, picturesque villages and much else. North Yorkshire is a county that offers great variety to the visitor.

Readers' comments: Excellent in every respect. Hospitality and food superlative. Excellent, considerate hosts.

143

★ **HIGHFIELD**   C PT S X
Ivington Road, Leominster, Herefordshire, HR6 8QD   Tel: 0568 3216 (or
613216 from spring)
Nearest main road: A44 from Worcester to Leominster.

3 Bedrooms. £14.50–£16 (less for 7 nights). Prices go up in April. Bargain breaks. All have own bath/shower/toilet. Tea/coffee facilities. Views of garden, country. No smoking. Washing machine on request.
Dinner. A la carte or £7.50 for 3 courses (with choices) and coffee, at 7–7.30pm or when requested. Vegetarian or special diets if ordered. Wine can be ordered. **Light suppers** if ordered.
2 Sitting-rooms. With open fire, central heating, TV, record-player. No smoking in one.
Large garden

Twin sisters Catherine and Marguerite Fothergill so loved cooking and entertaining that they gave up London careers (both were science teachers) to come here and make a full-time occupation of these pursuits. They had learnt their cooking skills first from their mother and later by attending different courses run by Robert Carrier and Prue Leith. They chose Herefordshire partly because it provides superb produce – beef, lamb, salmon, fruit – to which can now be added their own garden vegetables.

The big comfortable house, built in Edwardian times, stands among fields just outside the old market town of Leominster. The sisters have furnished it handsomely – Chippendale-style chairs in the dining-room, for instance, scalloped pink tablemats and napkins (with flowers and candles to match), Eternal Beau china, William Morris armchairs. Outside are sunny rosebeds, neat borders of lobelia and snapdragons, the remains of an old orchard and, on a paved terrace, white cast-iron chairs and tables from which to enjoy the scene, drink in hand. And every bedroom, too, has a scenic view.

Not only are dinners very special but breakfasts too can be memorable – with such options as home-made brioches, fishcakes, kedgeree, home-cooked ham.

As to other meals, residents can choose from the house menu or a gourmet one (or just have a snack). On the gourmet menu are such choices as avocado with curried egg sauce or watercress custard to start the meal; chicken-and-Stilton roulades or pheasant casseroled with chestnuts; raspberry bombe or sorbets in ginger baskets; and a savoury such as 'devils on horseback' or walnut cheese tarts.

Leominster was originally named 'church in the marshes' for here was a Celtic church long before it became a Saxon town, growing wealthy from the sheep that became known as 'Lempster's ore'. It is worth exploring on foot to discover its decoratively timbered mediaeval buildings which overhang narrow streets, old inns (particularly the ancient Chequers), the priory church with Norman and later features – also a ducking-stool – and the priory hospital, Grange Court (superb carvings by Charles I's carpenter) and decorative 18th-century almshouses.

All around the town are cider orchards (and cider mills where there are tastings), fields of the famous Herefordshire cattle, and picturesque black-and-white villages. Places to visit include Berrington Hall (gardens by Capability Brown) and 14th-century Croft Castle (paintings and fine furniture).

Readers' comments: Nothing was too much trouble. Cooking, service and friendliness made my stay seem like a house party. Excellent food and attention.

HIGHLOW HALL

near Hathersage, Derbyshire, S30 1AX   Tel: 0433 50393

West of Sheffield (West Yorkshire). Nearest main road: A625 from Sheffield to Chapel-en-le-Frith.

CDS

6 Bedrooms. £15 (less for 7 nights). Tea/coffee facilities. Views of garden, country. Washing machine on request.
1 Sitting-room. With open fire, TV.
Large garden
Closed from mid-November to mid-March.

At the heart of this huge farm (raising sheep and cattle) is a castellated, stone manor house of considerable historic interest – complete with not one but four ghost stories. It is one of several similar ones in the Peak District built by a 16th-century farmer for each of his sons: his name, Eyre, is now famous because Charlotte Brontë, who stayed at Hathersage vicarage, took it for her heroine Jane Eyre. (And in the locality was a house which had burned down with, reputedly, a mad woman in it – inspiration for Thornfield Hall.) In the square porch is a massive front door with old iron studs and hinges; the windows have stone mullions and small panes; and above the rugged walls of gritstone is a roof of dark stone slates. It is as if the house grew out of the land itself, for this is the northern (or 'dark') part of the Peak District, in contrast to 'white' limestone peaks further south.

The sitting-room was added in Georgian times, so it has large sash windows with views of the far moors, where the Wains' sheep graze, rising to slopes brilliant with heather in September and rusty bracken in October. Deep, velvety chairs are grouped round a blazing fire on cold days. Adjoining is the dining-room, with comfortably upholstered chairs around each table. Bed-and-breakfast only; most visitors dine at the Poacher's Arms or Hathersage Inn.

Bedrooms are roomy and comfortable, some with ancient stonework and all with fine views – not another building is in sight. The house is 800 feet above sea level (its name derives from 'high hlaw', meaning 'high hill'). One may wake in autumn to frost-sugared grass and grazing sheep; and, beyond, a line of graceful pines.

Margaret Wain will show you the most ancient part of the house: the huge stone-flagged hall with great oak staircase. This was once the kitchen, and it still has an old stone sink, stone cheese-press, and ancient chest. It is now used for dinner parties (minimum booking, 12 people).

Many visitors come here simply for the scenery and the peace; but there are plenty of places worth visiting (and, of course, glorious walks – the Pennine Way starts in the Peak District). There are the Blue John caverns, the summer 'well-dressing' ceremonies in the many historic villages, interesting old towns such as Buxton and Bakewell, and the city of Sheffield – a great deal more than just an industrial centre (its art gallery, cathedral and theatre are all good).

Readers' comments: Quite delightful; beautifully furnished; friendly and obliging; very impressed – made most welcome. Very hospitable; comfortable, quiet and in beautiful countryside. A wonderful experience; a beautiful setting.

145

★ HILL FARMHOUSE   C D S
Hitcham, Suffolk, IP7 7PT   Tel: 0449 740 651
North-west of Ipswich. Nearest main road: A45 from Bury St Edmunds to
Ipswich.

4 Bedrooms. £12–£14 (less for 5 nights).
Some have own bath. Tea/coffee facilities.
Views of garden, country.
Dinner. £7.50 for 3 courses (with choices)
and coffee, at times to suit guests. Non-
residents not admitted. Vegetarian or special
diets if ordered. Wine can be brought in. No
smoking. **Light suppers** sometimes.
2 Sitting-rooms. With open fire, central
heating, TV. No smoking.
Large garden
Closed from November to March
inclusive.

Part Tudor, part early Victorian, this handsome house provides a choice between
the spacious, traditional bedrooms at the front of the house (with cornfield views);
or the snug low-beamed ones at the back, with little oak-mullioned windows and
rugs on brick floors. The latter share a kitchenette for guests' use, while the brick
oven and hearth of Tudor times are now a decorative feature, which Pippa
McLardy fills with arrangements of dried flowers.

One enters the main house through a hall of powder-blue and white, with
cherry-carpeted staircase. Pale pink sitting- and dining-rooms have mahogany
antiques, a carved pine fireplace and views of countryside or garden (there are
duckponds, a freestanding swimming-pool and slides etc. for children). Pippa is
an imaginative cook: for dinner one might choose between fennel Mornay or
stuffed vineleaves; pork normande or Scotch salmon; raspberry-and-cream choux
or lemon sorbet. Eggs and vegetables are mostly home-produced.

Hitcham is centrally placed within a triangle of historic towns (Bury St
Edmunds, Sudbury – Gainsborough's birthplace – and Ipswich) and surrounded
by very lovely countryside, ideal for walking as well as touring. The great
mediaeval 'wool' churches of the area are justly famous.

This unspoilt region is a patchwork of farmland and fens, low hills and a varying
shoreline (much favoured by birdwatchers), secretive valleys and wild heaths.
Sunny and dry, though sometimes windy, it is nevertheless relatively free of traffic
and tourists – by comparison with, say, the West Country – and over all is that
wonderful sky, the light of which inspired so many famous landscape paintings.

On the other side of Hitcham is **MILL**
HOUSE (tel: 0449 740 315) where
once lived the miller whose windmill –
long gone – is depicted on the front of
the house. Judith White has furnished
the bedrooms with rose-sprigged
fabrics and velvet bedheads, the
stone-walled dining-room with maple
furniture (there is no sitting-room).
Outside is a large landscaped garden,
tennis court, and peacocks as well as

ducks. A typical dinner: pâté, chicken
chasseur and trifle. From £11 to £12.

★ **HOE HILL**   C(5) **S X**
Swinhope, Lincolnshire, LN3 6HX   Tel: 047283 206
North-west of Louth. Nearest main road: A16 from Louth to Grimsby.

facilities. Views of garden, country. No smoking. Washing machine on request. **Dinner.** £8.50 for 3 courses (with choices) and coffee, at 7–7.30pm. Vegetarian or special diets if ordered. Wine can be brought in. No smoking. **Light suppers** if ordered. **1 Sitting-room.** With open fire, central heating, TV.

3 Bedrooms. £11.50–£12.50 (less for 2 nights). Prices go up in March. Tea/coffee

Large garden
Closed in January.

'You're lucky to be going there!' said the garage proprietor from whom I asked the way. So good is Erica Curd's cooking that she often gives demonstrations to groups of six in her impressive kitchen which has a U-shaped counter.

One enters the white house, built in 1780, through a porch filled with geraniums. Off a poppy-papered hall is the large and attractive sitting-room, its light pink and clear blue scheme picking up the colours from a Raoul Dufy print of Nice. Antiques and a marble fireplace contrast with modern furniture (and bar) of bamboo. Glass doors open onto a terrace and croquet lawn shaded by a big chestnut tree. One of the pretty bedrooms, convenient for any handicapped person (with wash-basin and toilet next door), is on the ground floor.

As to the meals which have won Erica so much local renown, you might be offered a choice of cheese-stuffed mushrooms or watercress soup with home-baked rolls before, for instance, roast duck (or fish straight from Grimsby, or local game perhaps), served on lily-of-the-valley plates. The choice of puddings might be a home-made sorbet accompanying melon and crème de menthe or a traditional favourite such as bread-and-butter pudding. With the coffee come chocolates. Breakfasts, too, are impressive with such options as Lincolnshire sausages, kippers and occasionally, Arbroath smokies.

For those who like to seek out lovely but little frequented parts of England, the Wolds – where Swinhope lies – will come as a pleasant surprise.

The vast county of Lincolnshire could easily be three, each with its own character. The northern part, Lindsey, has forty miles of chalk hills, once wooded but now farmed (totally different from the huge expanse of flat fens to the south, drained long ago to provide the richest agricultural soil in Britain).

The northern Wolds rise high and have extensive views, but the southern part is 'Tennyson country' (he used to play skittles in the White Hart at Tetford). To either side of the Wolds are attractive old market towns: 18th-century Louth (which not only has a fine market hall but a 16th-century church with the tallest spire in England), and Market Rasen, originally a Roman settlement. Somersby has Tennyson's birthplace and Harrington Hall the garden that inspired him to write 'Come into the garden, Maud'. The area is one of woods and streams.

There is a particularly fine drive to the coast, 'the bluestone route', along which you may motor for an hour without encountering another car. Such old-fashioned resorts as Sandilands and Sutton-on-Sea are worth seeking out.

Readers' comments: Absolutely first-rate, the best I have found. Meals excellent, greeting warm and sincere. We have made this a regular venue for family get-togethers.

147

HOLEBROOK FARM

C H X

Lydlinch, Sturminster Newton, Dorset, DT10 2JB   Tel: 0258 817348

South-west of Shaftesbury. Nearest main road: A357 from Sturminster Newton to Stalbridge.

6 Bedrooms. £14–£17 (less for 4 nights). Bargain breaks. Some have own shower/toilet. Tea/coffee facilities. TV. Views of garden, country. Washing machine on request.
Dinner. £9 for 3 courses and coffee, at 7pm. Non-residents not admitted. Wine can be brought in.
4 Sitting-rooms. With open fire, central heating, TV.
Small garden

A long track brings one into the yard of this large farm; on one side are stables handsomely converted into bedrooms, and on the other the back of the stone house itself where there are more bedrooms. You are likely to enter via the big old kitchen, with its original flagged floor and stone ovens carefully preserved – it is here that Sally Wingate-Saul serves dinner. (The main course may be anything from lasagne to – once a week – pheasant; puddings include such calorific treats as chocolate roulade or treacle tart with sultanas and lemon; and there are always prize-winning local cheeses too.)

From a gracious sitting-room (shell-pink walls, pale blue damask chairs, log fire) deep-set, pine-shuttered windows overlook the lawn at the front of the house beyond which are apple trees and a kitchen garden. Clematis and a grape-vine clamber up the walls. The house is full of interesting objects which the Wingate-Sauls acquired on travels to the Seychelles, the Pitcairns and Australia; and in a huge attic bathroom is a varied collection of hats (to which visitors have contributed).

The stable rooms include some that are enormous, each with sitting-room and bathroom. Stripped pine has been used a lot, and old horse-stalls retained as room dividers. Small concealed kitchens are useful for visitors who want to prepare any meals themselves, and there are plenty of armchairs.

At Shaftesbury, King Canute died; and the remains of King Edward (martyred at Corfe Castle) were brought here. This ancient town is perched high on a hilltop overlooking the lovely Blackmoor Vale, and from its centre the picturesque cobbled street of Gold Hill makes a steep descent. Church, museum of curiosities and the Grosvenor Hotel are all well worth a visit – the last because it houses (upstairs) an incredible sideboard depicting the Battle of Otterburn carved from one massive piece of wood.

All around Sturminster Newton are other places of scenic or historic interest – Blandford Forum, Milton Abbas, Dorchester, Cerne Abbas and the villages in between.

North Dorset is not so much frequented by tourists as the coastal area even though its landscape is very fine, and there is much to see. Sherborne, for instance, is one of my favourite towns: it has an abbey church of quite exceptional beauty – its fan-vaulting alone would make it worth a detour.

Readers' comments: Made so welcome and had a lot of fun. Very good, organized hosts. Relaxed and helpful. Excellent accommodation, helpfully equipped. Meal delicious and outdoor pool a boon. Very good value.

★ **HOLLY TREE** C(10) **S X**
East Witton, North Yorkshire, DL8 4LS Tel: 0969 22383
South-east of Leyburn. Nearest main road: A6108 from Masham to Leyburn.

4 Bedrooms. £15–£17 (less for 7 nights). Prices go up in April. All have own bath/shower/toilet. Views of garden, country. No smoking. Washing machine on request. **Dinner.** £10 for 5 courses (with choices) and coffee, at 7.30pm. Non-residents not admitted. Vegetarian or special diets if ordered. Wine can be ordered. No smoking. **Light suppers** if ordered.
2 Sitting-rooms. With open fire, central heating, TV. No smoking.
Small garden
Closed in January.

This is in one of Wensleydale's more peaceful villages, a pretty group of cottages around a green, where sometimes strings of racehorses trot by on their way to exercising on the moors. All around is some of England's most magnificent scenery – the Yorkshire Dales – and towns which are honeypots for antique collectors. In the 12th century, part of the house provided stabling for the horses of monks travelling between the great Cistercian abbeys which are a feature of this area. A curiously shaped breakfast-room, with built-in settle and window-seat, was the 'snug' when the house used to be an inn.

Beyond the sitting-room, which has a crackling fire and huge grandfather clock, are two small garden-rooms with glass doors opening onto terrace and lawn with seats from which to enjoy the far view. The formal dining-room has scarlet walls and curtains contrasting with white shutters, green alcoves filled with flowers, antique furniture. Everywhere there are steps and odd angles.

Bedrooms are particularly pretty. One, for instance, has a brass bed with white and apricot draperies; in its bathroom (blue poppy wallpaper, pale blue curtains) are two basins and a bidet. Another has a rose-swagged frieze, pink-and-white beds, and a green chaise longue skilfully upholstered by Andrea Robson herself. There is also a garden bedroom with its own shower, basin, toilet and foyer.

But Andrea Robson's greatest skill is cookery (she won the Gas Boards' 'Cook of the Year' award in 1981). Typically, one of her dinners (preceded by free sherry) might comprise salmon mousse and then her own recipe for chicken breast en croûte (it has a mushroom stuffing and a coat of pâté and ham, inside a flaky-pastry crust). The pudding might then be pears – stuffed with walnuts and cherries, coated with chocolate and brandy, and served with cream.

Altogether, this is a house that has everything – memorable food, attractive rooms, and lovely surroundings. (Horse riding can be arranged.)

Wensleydale is described more fully elsewhere. The nearest small town is Middleham: 18th-century houses cluster around the market place, there's a ruined castle, and racehorses can be seen exercising on the surrounding moors. Well worth a visit are Wensley's riverside church, Ushaw bridge, Jervaulx Abbey and an inn (at Carlton, in Coverdale) with a Saxon burial-mound in its yard. Richmond (with castle), Ripon (cathedral) and Newby Hall are all near – the last with fine gardens. A good area for antiques.

Readers' comments: More than comfortable. Food truly excellent. Rooms delightful. A lovely home. Very warm welcome. Wonderful food and accommodation. Very comfortable, superb cuisine, delightful house. Cannot be faulted.

149

★ **HOLMHEAD**   **C PT**
Greenhead, Northumberland, CA6 7HY   Tel: 06972 402 or 0697747 402
West of Haltwhistle. Nearest main road: A69 from Brampton to Haltwhistle.

4 Bedrooms. £16.50–£17.50 (less for 4 nights). Prices go up in April. Bargain breaks. All have own shower/toilet. Tea/coffee facilities. Views of garden, country, river. No smoking. Washing machine on request.
Dinner. £10 for 3 courses and coffee, at 7.30pm. Non-residents not admitted. Vegetarian or special diets if ordered. Wine can be ordered. No smoking.
2 Sitting-rooms. With central heating, TV, record-player. Bar. No smoking in one.
Large garden with games.

Beside a salmon river, just where the walkers' Pennine Way crosses the Roman Wall, this remote house has the ruins of Thirlwall Castle looming overhead (Edward I once stayed there). Just outside are the remains of a Roman turret, somewhere under the lawn or sunken garden, awaiting excavation; and some Roman stones were re-used when the house was built. All this, with the distant moors, is within view through the windows of the guests' large and comfortable sitting-room upstairs – copiously equipped with games, toys and facilities to make unlimited hot drinks. Pauline Staff used to be a tour guide, and so is immensely helpful with advice on sightseeing. She occasionally gives visitors talks with slides, or may even show them around. Pre-Christmas party weekends are run; and discounts on tickets to museums are available.

There is now a bridge over the river which used almost to isolate the house; there are farm gates to open as one crosses the fields.

Although some of the bedrooms are on the small side, there are all kinds of unexpected 'extras' in this out-of-the-way house: a solarium; foot-massager for weary walkers; pure spring water; table tennis; snooker; snacks at any hour; the freedom of the kitchen – and the company of Rex, a Hungarian visla hound. Pauline likes to cook local dishes and has even experimented with Roman recipes cooked in the area around AD 300 (one favourite is honey-roast ham in pastry). She makes all the preserves, chutneys, cakes and scones. A typical dinner might comprise: melon with kiwi fruit; trout in hollandaise sauce; almond meringue with wild raspberries in whipped cream.

Breakfast choices include haggis, black pudding, kedgeree, muffins, crumpets and occasionally a Scandinavian buffet.

This is a splendid area for walks (with or without a National Park guide). The Northumberland National Park starts here; there are associations with Walter Scott and Catherine Cookson. You can look at working shire horses, Roman forts or prehistoric remains (including rock carvings), four castles, Hexham Abbey, Lanercost Priory, Beamish's celebrated open-air museum, stately homes. Some of the most popular sights include the Roman Army Museum, Naworth Castle and Talkin Tarn. But it is, of course, Hadrian's Wall that is the biggest attraction of all.

Readers' comments: Food very good, Mrs Staff a marvellous help. Enjoyable. Well cared for and well fed. Fell for it completely. Orderly and civilized.

150

★ **HOME FARM** C D PT

Church Lane, Old Dalby, Leicestershire, LE14 3LB Tel: 0664 822622
North-west of Melton Mowbray. Nearest main road: A46 from Leicester to
Newark-on-Trent.

3 Bedrooms. £12–£14 (less for 5 nights).
Prices go up in April. Tea/coffee facilities.
TV. Views of garden, country. No smoking.
Washing machine on request.
Light suppers if ordered. Vegetarian or
special diets. Wine can be brought in. No
smoking.
1 Sitting-room. With open fire, central
heating, TV, piano. No smoking.
Small garden

Set in an idyllic garden and facing the church, this 18th-century house (extended
in 1835) has great charm and an atmosphere of peace. Clematis and quinces grow
up its walls. Beyond espaliered apples and herbaceous beds are lawns and a kitchen
garden. (It is no longer a farm.) Some plants are for sale.

Indoors, every room has old furniture, pot-plants and white walls. Country-
style dining-chairs surround the long table where breakfast is served, a fire
crackling on chilly mornings. Val Anderson's collection of 'twenties and 'thirties
photographs of local hunting personalities hangs here (including one of the then
Prince of Wales, who first met Mrs Simpson at nearby Burrough Court).

Normally, Val serves only breakfast as the snug little Crown Inn nearby is
popular for other meals: 'the best food in the Vale of Belvoir', Val says. However,
she is prepared to offer guests snack-type meals (soup, quiche, salad, cheese or
pâté) if booked in advance. Home-grown fruit is served at breakfast.

Guests at Home Farm find plenty to do in the area, visiting Belton and Burghley
houses, Belvoir Castle, Newstead Abbey (Byron's house), Wollaton Hall,
Whatton Gardens and the Donington Motor Museum. Calke Abbey, with a
famous state bed, has fine grounds laid out in 1772. The National Watersports
Centre, Trent Bridge and Rutland Water are other attractions. (The Andersons
can also arrange for visitors to be guided around the more remote and interesting
parts of Leicestershire provided advance notice is given.)

Loughborough is worth a visit to see round the bell-foundry and its museum;
also the steam railway, and, in the vicinity, one of the county's several farm trails
or farm parks (Broomriggs Farm). Beyond Loughborough lie Desford's tropical
bird gardens, Ashby-de-la-Zouche castle, and Staunton Harold's extensive crafts
centre (there is an unusual Cromwellian church here, too). The county has an
industrial heritage trail of which the Moira blast furnace near Ashby is an
outstanding feature. Ancient Charnwood Forest, too, is in this direction; and
Breedon-on-the-Hill, the church of which was once a Saxon abbey.

Leicester itself is an unlovely city with little left from the past except its
mediaeval guildhall and much altered cathedral but it has about a dozen museums,
some with a technological emphasis – there is even one devoted to the history of
gas! – and botanical gardens run by the university. In this direction are Belgrave
Hall (Queen Anne), the ruins of Bradgate Hall – associated with Lady Jane Grey,
Kirby Muxloe castle and, as a complete contrast, the carefully preserved cottage of
a framework-knitter's cottage shop (at Wigston) and, in the city, a Victorian
brewery. The site of the Battle of Bosworth is now an excellent heritage centre,
with the battle sometimes re-enacted.

HOOK GREEN POTTERY

Hook Green, Lamberhurst, Kent, TN3 8LR   Tel: 0892 890504
East of Tunbridge Wells. Nearest main road: A21 from Tonbridge to Hastings.

2 or 3 Bedrooms. £10–£15. Prices go up in April. Tea/coffee facilities. Views of garden, country. Non-smokers preferred. Washing machine on request.
Dinner (if ordered). £6 for 3 courses and coffee, from 7pm. Non-residents not admitted. Vegetarian or special diets if ordered. Wine can be brought in. **Light suppers** if ordered.
1 Sitting-room. With open fire, central heating. Non-smokers preferred.
Large garden

Don Morgan threw up a career as a London art director, trained as a potter at Dartington in Devon for 2 years and then returned to this house – tile-hung in typical Kent style – as both home and studio. You can buy his wares here.

Outside are geese and a croquet lawn; jasmine, fuchsias and climbing geraniums. One enters through Don's brick-floored showroom, via the kitchen, to a sitting/dining-room which has a large table at the window and a log stove on the great hearth of nooks and crannies; a poppy and iris wallpaper (an old American design) decorates the walls. Upstairs is an old four-poster, broderie anglaise draping the top, in a room with French flowery blue wallpaper and an old Victorian fireplace complete with trivet. There's a view of the local inn, a picturesque half-timbered building. Sometimes the Morgans let the rooms of their two art-student sons; and are hoping to convert an outbuilding to provide more.

As to dinner (served on – what else! – Don's pottery), Ruth produces such meals as a help-yourself chicken casserole or moussaka with garlic bread; blackcurrant crumble or local raspberries and cream, then cheeses. Organically grown vegetables come from the garden, and Ruth has a good repertoire of vegetarian dishes.

This is a part of Kent which I love. I once spent a day visiting churches in chronological sequence of their architectural styles, encircling Tunbridge Wells. I started with the Norman ones at little Capel (wall-paintings) and Pembury; then Goudhurst, Early English (painted roof, colourful monuments); into Tunbridge Wells itself for the 17th-century church of Charles the Martyr (one of Wren's plasterers created the ornate ceiling of cherubs and garlands); northward to Speldhurst for its Burne-Jones windows, some of his finest work; and finally a 20th-century touch: stained glass by Chagall in Tudeley's Norman church.

Just down the road, on the outskirts of Lamberhurst, is **FURNACE FARM**, surrounded by acres of strawberry fields. One beamed bedroom (with shower) is on the ground floor, adjoining a sitting-room with brick fireplace and an iron fireback with lion and fleur-de-lys dated 1641. Mary Barnes serves such dinners as melon with Parma ham, beef in wine (with garden vegetables) and, of course, strawberries often appear in mousses or other

puddings. (Tel: 0892 890788.) Guided car tours available. From £15 to £17.50.

★ HURDON FARM

CHS

Hurdon, Cornwall, PL15 9LS   Tel: 0566 772955
South of Launceston. Nearest main road: A30 from Launceston to Bodmin.

6 Bedrooms. £12–£14 (less for 3 nights). Prices go up in April. Bargain breaks. Some have own bath/toilet. TV. Views of garden, country.
Dinner. £7.50 for 4 courses and coffee, at 6.30pm (on 6 nights a week). Non-residents not admitted. Vegetarian or special diets if ordered. Wine can be brought in. No smoking. **Light suppers** if ordered.
1 Sitting-room. With open fire, TV.
Large garden
Closed from November to mid-April.

The 18th-century stone house is in a picturesque area, not far from Dartmoor and Bodmin Moor (both the north and south coasts are within reach, too). It has large sash windows with the original panelled shutters and built-in dressers in the dining-room. The sitting-room has large and comfortable chairs and a great log stove. The most interesting room is, however, the big kitchen-scullery where an old slate sink and pump stand alongside the modern washing machine, and in the granite fireplace is an array of old jacks, trivets, and a built-in Dutch oven.

Upstairs, all is spick-and-span with fresh paintwork and light, bright colour schemes in the bedrooms. There is also a family suite (made pretty by an old-fashioned rosebud wallpaper) on the ground floor, where the dairy used to be.

Meals, prepared by Margaret Smith and her daughter, are above average 'farmhouse fare', with imaginative starters, in particular. Her soups are accompanied by home-made rolls; lamb or coq au vin by such vegetables as courgettes au gratin, cabbage cooked with onion and bacon, potatoes lyonnaise (with milk and cheese) or creamed turnips; her puddings include raspberry pavlovas, chocolate rouleau and home-made ice creams – always followed by cheeses. She uses the farm's own produce and clotted cream.

Visitors can join in farming activities. Some even rise at 6am to give J.R. his bottle; *this* J.R., too, is a black sheep but the bottle contains milk not whisky!

From Launceston you can visit the majestic and romantic north Cornish coast, described elsewhere in this book, or head inland to wild Bodmin Moor to discover hidden, unspoilt villages. The coast has stark cliffs, waterfalls and wide sands; the moor, high tors that can be reached only on foot or horseback. Don't miss the elaborately carved church (St Mary's) in Launceston itself, an old-world market town. The area is full of Arthurian legends; and Daphne du Maurier's Jamaica Inn is on the moor. An otter park, a steam railway, Lydford Gorge and Launceston Castle add to the interest of the region.

Children would enjoy visiting the resort of Newquay for its aquarium, zoo, cottage museum of curios, 'Tunnels through Time' (life-size figures portray Cornish legends), the farm park (at Summercourt), and 'World in Miniature' (replicas of famous buildings in landscaped gardens).

Readers' comments: Charming lady. Recommended for value, friendliness and atmosphere. Fantastic, very good value. Lovely room. Superb atmosphere. Idyllic – we were spoilt! Excellent meals, very comfortable, very reasonable. Enjoyable and relaxing. We return year after year. Well above average farm cooking. Food of the highest standard. Everything immaculate.

★ HUXTABLE FARM   C D H

West Buckland, Devon, EX32 OSR   Tel: 05986 254
East of Barnstaple. Nearest main road: A361 from South Molton to Barnstaple.

6 Bedrooms. £15–£17. Bargain breaks. All have own bath/shower/toilet. Tea/coffee facilities. TV. Views of garden, country. Washing machine on request.
Dinner. £10 for 4 courses (with choices) and coffee, at 7.30pm. Non-residents not admitted. Vegetarian or special diets if ordered. Wine can be brought in. No smoking.
2 Sitting-rooms. With open fire, central heating, TV.
Small garden and farmland.

Oak beams and screen panelling, bricks for open fireplaces and bread-ovens, flagstones for the floors – all are still to be seen in this house built in 1520, and capable of lasting another four centuries.

The main room of Huxtable Farm was originally a hall house before being converted into a long-house (that is to say, rooms at one end, cattle byre at the other, all in one long row), and around it were added outbuildings that include a barn and roundhouse (now providing extra accommodation). Today it is the very comfortable home of Freddie and Barbara Payne, a doctor and a teacher, both much-travelled – which accounts for the presence of such touches as carved window-frets from the Yemen (now used as cupboard doors) and a collection of Mediterranean plates. These exotic additions combine happily with such very English furnishings as an oak chest and sideboard, country Chippendale chairs and pewter plates. Their son, Anthony, farms the land, and his wife, Jackie, manages the accommodation.

On the farm are sheep (in April, lambs), pygmy goats, and a kitchen garden with vegetables, fruit and herbs. Children are encouraged to feed the animals, pick wild strawberries from the banks of a private lane, and get up early to spot deer which stray in from the adjoining woods. There is a stream to paddle in – and a particularly well-equipped games room, a sauna, and 6-hole practice golf course.

The Paynes really do welcome even the smallest children, not just tolerate them; and provide not only cot and high chair but even a baby alarm and nightlight in the big family room; and kitchen high-teas and breakfasts specially for children. Teenagers can sleep in a caravan, if preferred, either close to or distant from the house.

Bedrooms in the farmhouse are cottagey in style (those in the barn have modern louvred pine cupboards and a light, airy look: pink and white, with bamboo furniture; bathrooms are as beautiful as the bedrooms).

Barbara won a 'Taste of Exmoor' award for her cooking (both Exmoor and Dartmoor are within view of the farm). A typical 4-course candlelit dinner starts with, perhaps, a choice of artichoke soup or mackerel pâté made with the farm's own cottage cheese; then there might be roast lamb and vegetables (both from the farm) with an interesting sauce; followed by the choice of a creamy dessert, possibly using whortleberries picked on the moors, or a hot fruit pudding – you help yourself from a sidetable – and cheeses. With coffee there may be home-made fudge. Bread is home-baked, and with your meal is offered a complimentary glass of Freddie's home-made wine (elderberry, rhubarb or raspberry). Altogether, this is a very special place of great individuality.

154

Wargrave, Berkshire, RG10 8ET   Tel: 0734 402230
West of Maidenhead. Nearest main road: A4 from Maidenhead to Reading.

2 Bedrooms. £16. Bargain breaks. One has own bath/shower/toilet. Views of garden, country, river. Washing machine on request.
1 Sitting-room. With open fire, central heating, TV, piano, record-player.
Large garden

This 18th-century house is a combination of two flint cottages, one of which started life as a beer-house for passengers awaiting the ferry across the Thames. The ferry is no more, but the Hermons keep a dinghy in which one can explore this lovely reach of the river – frequented by herons as well as ducks and swans.

Past the hall with its array of Toby jugs on an inlaid dresser is a sitting-room with old-fashioned sofas (big and comfortable), oriental rugs on a wood block floor, mementoes of Eton (hatbands and the House Rules of the 1920s), and an open fire. The dining-room has unusual chairs, each carved with an English monarch, around a large oval table. Other unusual antiques include a cockfighting chair in one bedroom that is attractively furnished with waterlily bedspread and curtains (the large, well-equipped bathroom has swan towels, and there are swans on doorknobs and fingerplates too). In a charming little single room even the cupboard doors are decoratively wallpapered. There are views of rosebeds, a summerhouse and the river. (The summerhouse is used for teas.)

There are good places in the village at which to dine, such as the Bull Inn.

Wargrave is surrounded by the Chiltern Hills (famous for their beech woods), close to Windsor, Henley (for its regatta), Oxford, Blenheim and many pretty villages. The Royal County of Berkshire is a historic area, and one of great beauty. Windsor Castle is the largest inhabited castle in the world, with Eton just across the river and Tudor Dorney Court nearby. Walkers enjoy the Great Park and the Savill Garden, children Thorpe water park and the Windsor safari park.

Events of national importance include polo at Smith's Lawn, racing at Ascot, horse and rose shows, and carriage-driving championships. Go to Maidenhead for shopping, picturesque river locks, and the shire horse centre, Cliveden for landscape and the Astor mansion (now a hotel), picturesque Cookham (Stanley Spencer gallery). Marlow and Hurley are other riverside spots worth visiting. Plenty of entertainments, too – the Wilde Theatre is an outstanding arts centre, for instance. Stately homes are numerous, and scenic drives into the hills lead to some fine viewpoints.

It is also an area of countless good restaurants, antique shops and crafts – with all the riches of Oxfordshire and Buckinghamshire only a few miles further. (Bicycles on loan.) This winding stretch of the Thames (Sonning to Maidenhead) is the finest – in summer, made lively by the launches, punts and canoes that pass by the riverside inns and houses with trim gardens, and throng the locks.

The M4 motorway to London and Heathrow is near; good trains and coaches, too, to London.

KARSLAKE HOUSE HOTEL   C D S

Winsford, Somerset, TA24 7JE   Tel: 064 385 242
South of Minehead. Nearest main road: A396 from Minehead to Exeter.

7 Bedrooms. £17–£26 (less for 7 nights). Bargain breaks. Some have own bath/shower/toilet. Tea/coffee facilities. TV. Views of garden, country. No smoking. Washing machine on request.
Dinner. £12 for 4 courses (with choices) and coffee, at 7.30pm. Vegetarian or special diets if ordered. Wine can be ordered. No smoking. **Light suppers** if ordered.
1 Sitting-room. With open fire, central heating. **Bar.**
Small garden
Closed from November to week before Easter.

This one-time malthouse (parts of it date from the 15th century) is now run very professionally by Fred Alderton and Jane Young. July is an ideal time to visit, when high Exmoor, unlike some places, has few visitors.

Beyond the large, light dining-room is a small bar; and, for residents, there is a sitting-room. Narrow, scarlet-carpeted passages twist and turn. Upstairs are pleasant bedrooms – two of the nicest have views of the garden lawn and herbaceous borders. The bathrooms are attractive. There is one ground-floor bedroom.

There are always choices on the 4-course menu: I chose a delectable carrot and coriander soup, tender Exmoor lamb (garden vegetables included snapper peas), farmhouse Stilton, then raspberry and almond tart – all cooked to perfection.

Winsford, an ancient village (and birthplace of Ernest Bevin), has eight bridges over the several streams which converge here, thatched cottages, a crafts centre in an 18th-century chapel, and the Royal Oak inn (12th century) which provided material for Blackmore's book *Lorna Doone*. It is a good centre from which to explore Exmoor: quite near are the Caractacus Stone, a 5th-century memorial to a nephew of Caradoc, one of the most valiant defenders of Britain against the Romans; prehistoric burial mounds; and Tarr Steps, a prehistoric bridge.

Towards the Devon border is 'Lorna Doone country' (Oare church, in lovely woods, was the scene of her wedding). In this direction too is Hay Culbone church, said to be the smallest in England; and also Dunster Castle with its working watermill (18th-century). The West Somerset Rural Museum at Allerford is in a thatched house with riverside garden.

Minehead is a popular seaside resort with attractions like a steam railway and an animated show of the Merlin legends, as well as the enormous leisure park called Somerwest World. If you want to see a traditional industry at work go to John Wood's sheepskin tannery near here.

Among many stately homes in the area are the Elizabethan halls of Combe Sydenham (in a deerpark), Gaulden Manor and Dodington Hall (near the last is an unusual sight, the Sheep Milking Centre). Spinning and weaving is on show at the Quantock Weavers, Over Stowey.

Readers' comments: High standards, we were delighted. Charming and hospitable, food excellent, rooms spotless and comfortable. Excellent food, lovely rooms.

KIMBERLEY HOME FARM   C(5) S
Wymondham, Norfolk, NR18 0RW   Tel: 0953 603137
South-west of Norwich. Nearest main road: All from Norwich to Thetford.

4 Bedrooms. £27.50 including dinner. Some have own bath/shower/toilet. Tea/coffee facilities. TV. Views of garden, country. Washing machine on request.
Dinner. 3 courses and coffee, at guests' convenience. Wine can be brought in. **Light suppers** if ordered.
1 Sitting-room. With open fire, central heating, TV, record-player.
Large garden with hard tennis court.
Closed from December to March inclusive.

This is a beautifully furnished farmhouse with stables at the front and a large garden at the back, onto which the glass doors of the large sitting-room open. There is a pond with ducks. Apart from the hundreds of acres of crops, the main activity at Kimberley is training and racing horses.

The bedrooms are particularly pretty, the bathroom excellent, and the dining-room has a long Regency table. Jenny Bloom is not only an excellent cook but a generous one, leaving pheasants or joints of meat on a hot-tray from which guests may help themselves, and apt to whisk away a half-demolished chicken merely in order to replace it with a fresh one. Starters are imaginative (avocado mousse, for instance), and puddings delicious.

You can have the exclusive use of rooms if you wish, or get more involved with the family and the activities of the farm. Jenny is a charming hostess.

Norwich is one of the most beautiful of mediaeval cities, complete with castle and cathedral, full of craft and antique shops in cobbled byways. The county has a great many stately homes and even statelier churches, wonderful landscapes and seascapes, and, of course, the Broads. The Sainsbury Art Centre outside Norwich is exceptional. The Norfolk coast, King's Lynn and Cambridge are all about one hour away.

This is an excellent spot from which to explore in all directions. Bressingham Hall has fine gardens and steam engines. Beyond Diss (market on Fridays) are the very colourful villages of Burston and Shelfanger. East Dereham has an unusual town sign (two legendary does), an interesting church, an archaeological museum in cottages with decorative plasterwork. Go to the Norfolk Wildlife Park to see bears and otters, to Harleston for spring blossom or summer roses and the River Waveney. Further afield, in Suffolk, there are historic Bungay and Earl Soham, riverside Debenham, Framlingham Castle, Heveningham Hall and a museum of rural life at Stowmarket. Yoxford village is famous for its cottage gardens. Farming is done on a prairie-size scale, but villages with their little greens, and occasional windmills, are a pretty sight.

The Broads are near (a new feature is the steam train between Wroxham and Aylsham). At Tasburgh are the gardens of Elizabethan Rainthorpe Hall, with trees of botanical interest; at Badley Moor, a butterfly centre; in the direction of Diss, a monkey sanctuary; and near Fakenham one of the world's largest waterfowl collections.

Readers' comments: Total peace, comfortable rooms, delicious food. Comfortable, and very good food.

KING'S LODGE   **C D S X**
Andover Road, Whitchurch, Hampshire, RG28 7AS   Tel: 025689 3644
East of Andover. Nearest main road: A34 from Newbury to Winchester.

rear view

2 Bedrooms. £16. Bargain breaks. Both have own bath/shower/toilet. Tea/coffee facilities. Views of garden, country, river. Washing machine on request.
Dinner. £12 for 4 courses (with choices) and coffee, at times to suit visitors. Non-residents not admitted. Vegetarian or special diets if ordered. Wine can be ordered or brought in. **Light suppers** if ordered.
2 Sitting-rooms. With open fire, central heating, TV, piano.
Large garden with croquet and parkland.

On 20 October 1644, King Charles I wrote to his nephew urging him to bring more troops here quickly: it was at this house that he penned his desperate letter and visitors can go up the great oak staircase to sleep in the 'King's room'. (A week later the King successfully resisted Cromwell's advance at the second Battle of Newbury.)

Some may prefer the big blue room, however, for its windows on two sides and view of the famous River Test.

Downstairs is a large and handsome sitting-room and the dining-room, with an 'upright grand' piano, country Hepplewhite chairs at a table in a big bay window, comfortable old armchairs around a log stove and innumerable family mementoes – some from China where Hermione Goulding's father was stationed, and others from Hong Kong and Singapore where her husband served.

Outside are lawns, fruit trees, flint walls, herbaceous flowerbeds and a riverside walk. Also a kitchen garden from which come peas and beans for soups, vegetables to accompany such main courses as steak-and-kidney pie, and fruit for raspberry fool and to serve with the cheeses.

Whitchurch is the home of Lord Denning (who lives next door) and of Richard Adams ('Watership Down' is nearby). Its other claim to fame is the riverside silk-mill which wove the fabric for the Princess of Wales' wedding-dress.

Also in the vicinity are war paintings by Stanley Spencer (at Sandham Memorial Chapel), Winchester Cathedral, Hilliers' aboretum (the world's largest collection of temperate trees and shrubs), Mottisfont Abbey (rose gardens), Exbury (rhododendrons), Windsor and the Savill Gardens. Many visitors go to such stately homes as Stratfield Saye (Duke of Wellington's home), Littlecote, Broadlands (Lord Mountbatten's home), Wilton and the Vyne, as well as Jane Austen's home at Chawton. Whitchurch is also on the edge of the Wiltshire Downs with their many prehistoric remains, including Stonehenge.

The scenery around here is high and open; big fields with white flints are covered with golden grain in summer. By contrast, paths lead to a riverside where rushes and other waterplants grow green, and on the banks purple loosestrife and willow-herb flourish.

Readers' comments: Wonderful food, so welcoming, made us feel like family friends. Charming hostess. Very good indeed.

★ **KING'S LODGE**   **C D S**

Long Marston, Warwickshire, CV37 8RL   Tel: 0789 720705
South-west of Stratford-upon-Avon. Nearest main road: A439 from Stratford
towards Evesham.

4 Bedrooms. £15.50–£22 (less for 3 nights).
Some have own bath/toilet. Views of garden.
Dinner. £8.50 for 3 courses (with choices)
and coffee, at 7pm. Non-residents not
admitted. Vegetarian or special diets if
ordered. Wine can be ordered. No smoking.
Light suppers if ordered.
1 Sitting-room. With open fire, central heating, TV. Bar.
Large garden
Closed in December and January.

With his father beheaded and Cromwell ruling England, young Charles II (only
twenty-one) made a desperate attempt in 1651 to regain the throne. Badly defeated
at Worcester, however, he became a fugitive on the run – for weeks eluding escape
by means of disguises and hiding-places, as he made his way to the coast and
France.

To get through Stratford-upon-Avon, swarming with Cromwellian troops, he
dressed himself as the manservant of Miss Jane Lane (sister of one of his colonels),
and together they rode to Long Marston and the house of her kinsman, John
Tomes. This was on 10 September; and I stayed there on almost the same date,
dining in the hall with great inglenook fireplace where he had a narrow escape: on
being asked by the cook to wind up the jack that operated the roasting-spit, his
ignorance of this homely task nearly gave the game away. Although other parts of
the Tudor house have changed, this room is much as it was when he stayed here –
and outside, too, the scene has altered very little. Probably, the willow-fringed
duck-pond and the mulberry and pear trees are very like what he saw.

When the house came up for sale many years ago, George and Angela Jenkins
(who lived locally) could not resist buying it, even though it was very neglected and
rather too large for their family. To pay for its restoration and upkeep, they
decided to take paying guests.

After dinner (plain home cooking, often with produce from the garden) at a big
refectory table by the famous fireplace, visitors can sit in a sitting-room or out in
the large garden. One bedroom has a four-poster made from elms felled in the
grounds and a fine stone fireplace on which the Tomes children inscribed their
initials over three centuries ago. The house is full of old pictures and trifles which
the Jenkins have collected, many relating to Charles II or the Tomes family who
sheltered him.

The house is ideally placed for visiting the beauty-spots, gardens and historic
sights of three counties – Warwickshire, Gloucestershire (the Cotswolds), and
Oxfordshire. Head for Evesham if you want pick-your-own fruit and to Stratford
for its Shakespeare sights. Close to King's Lodge is an antiques warehouse.

Readers' comments: Delighted with situation, food and hospitality. Enjoyable and
interesting. Very good value. Have returned because of friendly, unassuming
service. Lovely house, good accommodation and food. Very nice people.

Great Rissington, Gloucestershire, GL54 2LP   Tel: 0451 20388
North-west of Burford (Oxfordshire). Nearest main road: A424 from Burford to
Stow-on-the-Wold.

10 Bedrooms. £17–£24 (less for 7 nights). Bargain breaks. All have own bath/shower/toilet. Views of garden, country. Washing machine on request.
Dinner. A la carte, at 7pm. Vegetarian or special diets if ordered. Wine can be ordered. **Light suppers** if ordered.
1 Sitting-room. With open fire, central heating, TV. **Bar.**
Large garden

This is exactly what one asks of a typical old Cotswold inn! The interior is a place of little windows, zigzag corridors, quaint oak doors and thick stone walls; outside, magnificent views of the countryside, looking across to some of the highest Cotswolds. Kate and Richard Cleverly have furnished the bedrooms with care – restful colours, everything neat, a pretty tulip wallpaper in one room, and in the dining-room pine chairs at lace-covered tables with candle-lamps lit at night. The menu is à la carte, with such dishes as Stilton-topped fillet steaks, veal-and-sweetcorn pies, salmon-and-prawn mousse, lamb with apricots. Outside is a landscaped garden from which to enjoy the summer view with a glass of 'real ale' in hand; a covered swimming-pool (heated to 80°) and a summerhouse-cum-aviary. In cold weather, there is a log fire in the bar, and in the attractive residents' sitting-room. The restaurant extension was created from an old barn and is furnished with Laura Ashley fabrics.

Richard is an imaginative as well as skilled craftsman: the carving of a lamb over the sitting-room fire is his, and so are the conversions of old doors, pews and school desks to new uses. He has even made a four-poster with carved decorations. A recent addition is the conversion of the stables into two double bedrooms, with en suite showers. Both have exposed stone walls and beams, chintz curtains and bedspreads.

The Lamb is midway between two famous Cotswold villages (Bourton-on-the-Water and Burford, described elsewhere in this book). Most people come here simply for the scenery, but also in the vicinity are the Cotswold Wildlife Park, a rare breeds farm, and – only a little further – Oxford, Stratford-upon-Avon, Warwick and Woodstock (with Blenheim Palace). Moreton-in-Marsh and Broadway are picturesque villages. For gardens, go to Sezincote and Hidcote (and to Burford's garden centre) and nearly every village has antique shops. In spring, the Badminton horse trials are very popular with visitors. This is a good area too for pick-your-own fruit.

Readers' comments: Excellent.

LANGLEY WOOD

D

Redlynch, Wiltshire, SP5 2PB Tel: 0794 390348
South-east of Salisbury. Nearest main road: A36 from Southampton to
Salisbury.

3 Bedrooms. £16.50. Views of garden.	**2 Sitting-rooms.** With open fire. **Bar.**
Dinner. A la carte. Wine can be ordered.	**Large garden**

A restaurant of distinction is the principal *raison d'être* of Langley Wood, but it has
comfortable bedrooms too – overlooking the surrounding lawns and woods. The
house began life as three 17th-century cottages, but was transformed at the turn of
the century. Panelling, Georgian doors and other handsome details were added. It
still retains the sedate, old-fashioned style of that period, with dinners enjoyed by
candlelight and, on chilly evenings, a log fire blazing. There are spacious (but not
elegant) bedrooms.

David and Sylvia Rosen used to run a bistro near London's Camden Town, an
area much populated by connoisseurs of good food; and many of the favourite
dishes from those days are now enjoyed at Langley Wood – things like baked
carrot and Gruyère with fresh tomato sauce, roast stuffed fillet of beef, hazelnut
meringue with strawberries; and vegetarian dishes. (Gourmet food, priced accordingly.

Visitors who stay here can quickly reach Salisbury in one direction or the New
Forest in the other: Redlynch is close to the border of Hampshire, and of Dorset.

Wiltshire, despite its low population (which makes it a quiet and attractive place
in which to travel), has a number of great houses such as Wilton and Stourhead,
and great prehistoric remains too (Stonehenge and Avebury in particular). There
is magnificent scenery on its chalk hills and by its many rivers and streams, where
undisturbed villages are to be found.

In addition to Salisbury's ancient streets and cathedral, and the historic site of
Old Sarum, there are such outstanding places of interest as Salisbury Plain (wide
open spaces, changing skies and mossy villages), Marlborough and its downs,
innumerable prehistoric sites, old Amesbury (where Queen Guinevere is said to
have been buried), Devizes with its noble market square and Norman church,
Shaftesbury (abbey and cobbled lanes) and, of course, the coast with Bournemouth and its sandy beaches. Weyhill Hawk Conservancy and Broadlands
(Mountbatten's house) are very popular and there are at least eight fine gardens to
visit. Breamore is a Tudor mansion; a Roman villa at Rockbourne and picturesque
villages are not far away.

For explanation of code letters (C, D, H, PT, S, X) see page xxxiv.

LANNARDS

Okehurst Lane, Billingshurst, West Sussex, RH14 9HR   Tel: 040 3782692
South-west of Horsham. Nearest main road: A29 from London to Chichester.

3 Bedrooms. £14–£15. Prices go up in April. Bargain breaks. Tea/coffee facilities. TV. Views of garden, country. No smoking. Washing machine on request.
1 Sitting-room. With central heating. No smoking.
Small garden

This is one for collectors of modern art – paintings, ceramics or silver; for adjoining the house of cedar shingles where guests are accommodated is an octagonal gallery of pine and glass where a discriminating display of fine arts is exhibited for sale. It is the brainchild of Betty Sims, herself an accomplished potter, on whose husband's farm is this unusual gallery-cum-guest-house.

Lannards is also an ideal place at which to stay if antiques interest you, for within yards is an outpost of Sothebys (a Tudor mansion where auctions are held).

All bedrooms are on the ground floor – neat modern rooms with pale colours and built-in cupboards. There is a comfortable sitting-room, lawn with tables and rural views all round. (Bed-and-breakfast only. For dinner Sheila recommends a local Italian restaurant.)

Nearby Billingshurst is one of many pretty Sussex villages, sited on the road the Romans called Stane Street (it ran from London to Chichester). It is well placed to visit – to the south – Brighton (Pavilion, etc.) and other coastal resorts beyond the South Downs. Arundel (castle, wildfowl reserve) and also innumerable stately homes such as Petworth, Parham and Hever Castle are near.

In pretty Billingshurst itself, right by the mediaeval church, is a beamy 17th-
★ century house, **CHURCHGATE** (tel: 0403 782 733) which Sheila Butcher has furnished in traditional country-house style. Views from its windows (double-glazed in case light sleepers are disturbed by bell-ringing or passing cars) are of a flowery little garden and the church. Dinner (to be ordered in advance) might typically be pâté, coq au vin, home-made ice cream and cheeses (choices are offered). In the sitting-room is a piano which guests are

welcome to play, television and a good selection of books. £15.

Readers' comments: Excellent, personal service.

Prices are per person in a double room at the beginning of the year.

★ LANSDOWNE HOUSE   C(5) **H PT S X**

Clarendon Street, Leamington Spa, Warwickshire, CV32 4PF
Tel: 0926 450505 or 421313
Nearest main road: A425 from Warwick to Southam.

15 Bedrooms. £16.50–£18.90 (less for 5 nights). **If included in a 3-night half-board stay, Sunday's accommodation is free to readers of this book except at peak periods.** Prices go up in September. Bargain breaks. Some have own bath/shower/toilet. Tea/coffee facilities. TV. Laundry and dry-cleaning: 8-hour service.
Dinner. £13 for 3 courses (with choices) and coffee, at 6.30–8.30pm. Vegetarian or special diets if ordered. Wine can be ordered. No smoking. **Light suppers** if ordered.
2 Sitting-rooms. With open fire, central heating, TV. **Bar.**

A pretty creeper-covered house built in the 18th century, this small hotel cannot be described as truly 'off the beaten track' for it stands at a crossroads not far from the centre of Leamington. But bedroom windows are double-glazed to reduce any sound from traffic – and the hotel is of such excellence that I wanted to include it.

When David and Gillian Allen took it over they decided to furnish it to a very high standard and in keeping with its architecture. There is a particularly pretty sitting-room with sea-green and strawberry Victorian sofas, for example; in the small dining-room, meals are served on fluted Rosenthal china and wine in elegant glasses; the bar has cherry buttoned seats; and every bedroom is attractively decorated in soft colours with well chosen fabrics, stripped-pine furniture and thick, moss-green carpet. (No. 2 is the quietest, with roof-light not windows.)

The same care goes into the food. David, who trained as a chef in Switzerland, is a perfectionist. He sends to Scotland for his steaks, to the Cotswolds for his trout, has coffee specially blended to his taste, and damson and other sorbets made for him on a fruit farm nearby. Connoisseurs will appreciate some little-known wines among his very good selection, and the range of malt whiskies.

There are always several choices of good English dishes at dinner. Starters include particularly imaginative soups (such as celery-and-walnut or cream of parsnip), while main courses are likely to be such things as roast pork with freshly chopped rosemary or liver-and-bacon with fresh sage. Puddings might include walnut and chocolate fudge pudding or fruit cobbler.

Royal Leamington Spa is a health resort with a saline spring. It has fine Georgian terraces and lovely riverside gardens. A good base from which to visit not only Warwick and Kenilworth castles, described elsewhere, but also Coventry (modern cathedral, some historic buildings), Southam (old market town), Stoneleigh (mediaeval village and the great National Agricultural Centre) and fine country-side towards Stratford-upon-Avon. The Mill gardens in Warwick and Jephson gardens in Leamington are worth seeking out.

For residents there are discounts at Warwick Castle (where Tussaud's 'royal house party' is a superb show) and many other sights. Free guided local walks.

Readers' comments: Excellent. Charming features, food excellent.

★ **LASKILL HOUSE FARM**　　　　　　　　　　　　**C D H PT S**
Hawnby, North Yorkshire, YO6 5NB　Tel: 04396 268
North of Helmsley. Nearest main road: A170 from Thirsk to Helmsley.

6 Bedrooms. £14.50–£17. Bargain breaks. Some have own bath/shower/toilet. Tea/coffee facilities. TV. Views of garden, country, river. No smoking. Washing machine on request.
Dinner. £9 for 4 courses and coffee, at 7pm. Non-residents not admitted. Vegetarian or special diets if ordered. Wine can be ordered. No smoking.
1 Sitting-room. With open fire, central heating, TV. No smoking.
Large garden

This stone farmhouse lies in a hilly, wooded area of great scenic splendour ('Herriot country'), and close to famous Rievaulx Abbey. Its courtyard is made pretty with stone troughs, flowers and rocks; and around lie 600 acres with cattle and sheep or wheat. There are white iron chairs for guests in the garden and a duck-pond. Children are welcome to help feed the calves and to hold the lambs.

In the sitting/dining-room is oak furniture hand-carved by local craftsmen, each of whom 'signs' his work with his own particular symbol – an acorn, a beaver or a stag's head. Here Sue Smith serves home-made soup or pâté before a main course which is likely to comprise meat and vegetables from the farm, followed by (for instance) lemon meringue pie or a fruit fool, and then an interesting selection of cheeses. Often there is a chance to see James Herriot himself, as he sometimes opens fêtes or gives talks.

The bedrooms vary in style: I particularly liked 'the blue room' with its sprigged wallpaper, thick carpet and cretonne fabrics. Two, with bathrooms, are in a beamy outbuilding and open onto the lawn. There is a games room.

The North York Moors are one of England's finest national parks: whether you walk or drive, the views are spectacular, particularly when the heather blooms.

Readers' comments: Comfortable, welcoming, and good food. Excellent meals, complete relaxation. Charming and considerate hostess. Delightful; everything perfect. Mrs Smith was so welcoming and easy to get on with. Food excellent. Beautiful location. Comfort, good food and congenial company. Delightful room.

★ A little further south is **NEWTON GRANGE FARM** (tel: 04393 262) where Sue Ward's immaculate rooms have exceptionally fine views – and a few miles away is one that James Herriot described as the finest in England. Sue serves simple, generous meals (home-made soup, roast beef and apple pie, for example), or there are good pub restaurants nearby for a change. The house is a good choice for those who want a genuine and unpretentious farm holiday. From £12 to £13.

Readers' comments: Careful attention to detail, like clean towels daily and excellent breakfast. Excellent value.

LEIGH COURT **C D**

Leigh, Worcestershire, WR6 5LB   Tel: 0886 32275

West of Worcester. Nearest main road: A4103 from Worcester to Hereford.

3 Bedrooms. £15–£16.50 (less for 3 nights). Bargain breaks. Some have own shower/toilet. Tea/coffee facilities. Views of garden, country.
Dinner. £10.50 for 4 courses and coffee, at 7pm. (Not on Wednesdays and Thursdays.) Non-residents not admitted. Vegetarian or special diets if ordered. Wine can be brought in. No smoking.
2 Sitting-rooms. With open fire, central heating, TV, record-player, snooker.
Large garden
Closed from mid-October to mid-March.

Passers-by often pause here, just to look – not only at the 16th-century manor house of mellow brick, with gables in both Dutch and Flemish style, but also at the 14th-century cruck barn, the biggest of its kind in the world.

Sally Stewart's ancestors were bailiffs here when, before Henry VIII dissolved the monasteries, the abbots of Pershore were lords of the manor.

She and her civil engineer husband modernized the comforts of the house when they inherited it in 1960, but have carefully preserved all the fine architectural detail. The entrance hall is particularly striking, a tiled floor and traditional acanthus-patterned wallpaper (blue-and-white) setting off the white staircase, handsome sash windows and fanlight over the door. The sitting-room has a pretty fireplace, all curlicues and swags, round which velvet or cretonne chairs are drawn up, while portraits of ancestral aunts adorn the walls. In the dining-room (in fact, in all rooms) there are family antiques; sprigged blue cloths cover the tables; and from the bay window there is a fine view of a weeping ash, the nearby 13th-century church and a huge copper beech. Throughout the house, there are good wallpapers, homely old-fashioned furniture and (from room 3 in particular) fine views.

This is a good place for anyone who enjoys dogs and other animals for Sally breeds pedigree pugs, Cavalier King Charles spaniels and golden retrievers. (If you want to bring your own dog, it must have been vaccinated.) In the grounds, where hens range free, you will find a variety of rare farm breeds.

Sally serves such dishes as fish mousse, pot-roast pheasant and apple Charlotte.

In the grounds, a riverside walk appeals to many visitors (there is another good, level walk along the track where once a railway ran). In autumn, you can see the farm's cider mill in action, and taste the results. Coarse fishing available.

People touring by car use Leigh Court as a base to visit Malvern, Worcester (with china factory, cathedral etc.), Upton-on-Severn, Ledbury, Stourport-on-Severn and Evesham.

Readers' comments: Very comfortable; food delicious. Most enjoyable. A delightful week. Excellent food; peaceful. Enjoyed it so much I returned for a further eight days. Friendliness, hospitality and food delightful. A splendid stay.

165

LEWORTHY FARMHOUSE   CHX

Leworthy, Devon, EX22 65S   Tel: 0409 253488

East of Bude (Cornwall). Nearest main road: A388 from Holsworthy to Launceston.

12 Bedrooms. £14–£16 (less for 7 nights). Prices go up in July. Bargain breaks. Some have own shower/toilet. Tea/coffee facilities. TV. Views of garden, country. Washing machine on request.

Dinner. £8 for 4 courses (with choices) and coffee, at any time. Non-residents not admitted. Vegetarian or special diets if ordered. Wine can be ordered. No smoking. **Light suppers** if ordered.

2 Sitting-rooms. With open fire, central heating, TV, piano, record-player. Bar.

Small garden

Genial Eric Cornish deservedly won the AA's 'Farmhouse of the Year' award in 1981. His guests are greatly appreciated by him, and he goes to considerable lengths to give them a good time – young children in particular. Dozens of their drawings and letters to him are pinned up around the bar.

He has added to the rooms in the farmhouse to provide more accommodation in a bungalow close by, and sometimes has as many as forty people staying – laying on for this huge house-party all kinds of evening entertainments (games, dancing, conjuror, film) for which there is no extra charge. This is obviously appreciated by families tired of the spend-spend-spend involved in keeping the youngsters entertained in most resorts. Eric also takes visitors on tractor-drawn hay-rides (dogs following) to see the crops, sheep, beef-cattle, lake, river and woods, while explaining to them what work is going on. It's a place where parents can leave their older children to go their own way – they find plenty to do, like organizing table tennis, or badminton competitions. There are deer, herons and even otters to be spotted; abundant wildflowers; and lots of good picnic spots within the farm estate. In low season, crafts including patchwork and farm activity courses are run; the latter include wine-making, clay pigeon shooting, fishing and pub skittle matches. And there is a wheelchair.

Something new is always afoot, so Eric and Marion keep in touch with past guests by means of a circular letter with news of what has been happening to the various pets and the family. Cormorants steal the trout, son Paul returns from Australia, 'Willigrub' gets booked for next season – it's all reported in these letters. Many guests become lifelong friends, and most get involved in one way or another (the gumboot rack was made by a group of dads).

The bedrooms, like all the other rooms, are comfortable, but Leworthy makes no attempt to be elegant. The best rooms are in a converted farm building called Leeside. Marion produces typical farmhouse meals such as soup, roast beef, fruit pie and cream, cheese, coffee.

There is so much going on that many people hardly stir. However, within a short drive are the beaches of Bude and superb clifftop views, Hartland's dramatic reefs and lighthouse and quaint Clovelly. Holsworthy is only three miles away.

Readers' comments: Very much enjoyed the Cornishes' company; they make you feel welcome. A delightful couple who spared nothing to see that everyone had a good time. We had a high time! So genial and helpful; constant laughter.

166

LINDISFARNE HOTEL

Holy Island, Northumberland, TD15 2SQ   Tel: 0289 89273
South of Berwick-upon-Tweed. Nearest main road: A1 from Alnwick to
Berwick.

7 Bedrooms. £13–£16 (less for 7 nights).
Prices go up in March. Some have own
bath/shower/toilet.   Tea/coffee facilities.
TV. Views of garden. Washing machine on
request.
Dinner. A la carte or £10 for 3 courses (with
choices) and coffee, at 7–8pm. Vegetarian or
special diets if ordered. Wine can be
ordered. **Light suppers** if ordered.
2 Sitting-rooms. With central heating. **Bar.**
Large garden
Closed from December to February
inclusive.

It is a great pity that this island, so beautiful and so full of history, is ill-provided
with good accommodation.

One drives across a causeway (impassable at high tides, so check before
arriving). Sir Walter Scott described it:

> 'Dry shod, o'er sands, twice every day,
> The pilgrims to the shrine find way.
> Twice every day the waves efface
> Of staves and sandalled feet the trace.'

It was at this holy place that monks illuminated the Lindisfarne Gospels over
twelve centuries ago, made mead from honey (you can still buy this on the island)
and built a priory the ruins of which to this day soar majestically. It is – except
when coachloads of summer trippers ruin it – a place of beauty and mystery. Over
all presides Lindisfarne Castle, topping a steep rock. This was built in Tudor
times, a rather cosy little castle. Well modernized in 1903 by Sir Edwin Lutyens, it
is filled with furniture and textiles chosen to harmonize with their surroundings.
There is now an outstanding museum of Saxon history, too.

The Lindisfarne Hotel is unpretentious, well kept, and furnished in conventional style. From the choices on Susan Massey's 3-course dinner menu, one might
perhaps choose, for instance, grapefruit with crème de menthe, seafood casserole,
roast lamb or Holy Island crab, and a creamy dessert. In the bar are 113 different
whiskies. Based here one could enjoy not only the tranquillity of the island and its
wildlife after the coachloads have gone home, but also explore much of mainland
Northumberland by day.

For instance, the border town of Berwick-upon-Tweed is only a little way
further north. Its three bridges bestride the estuary, there are fine walks along the
Tudor fortifications encircling it – some of Europe's best mediaeval walls and
bastions, and the busy market is frequented by Scots as well as the English. Other
attractions in the region are Norham Castle, quaint little Ford – a model village of
the Victorian era, still with smithy and a village hall lined with murals painted by
the Marchioness of Waterford. The Heatherslaw Light Railway runs from here.
Near Wooler, centre of good walking country, is the site of the Battle of Flodden;
and round Chillingham Castle roam the famous white cattle, sole survivors of a
wild breed once common in Britain. Along the coast to the south is a succession of
spectacular castles, Craster (for kipper teas) and the little harbour of Seahouses –
boats go from here to the Farne Islands where seals and puffins are to be seen.

LINK HOUSE

C(8) **PT S**

Bassenthwaite Lake, Cumbria, CA13 9YD   Tel: 059681 291
East of Cockermouth. Nearest main road: A66 from Keswick to Cockermouth.

8 Bedrooms. £18–£21. Prices go up in May.
Bargain breaks. All have own shower/toilet.
Tea/coffee facilities. TV. Views of garden,
country.
Dinner. £10 for 5 courses (with choices) and
coffee, at 7pm. Vegetarian or special diets if
ordered. Wine can be ordered.
2 Sitting-rooms. With open fire, central
heating. **Bar.**
Small garden
Closed in December and January.

Teacher May Smith so much enjoyed cookery as a hobby that eventually she gave
up her career to start a new one, running a guest-house. That is why Link House,
outwardly similar to many others in the Lake District, is in fact very different in
the kind of meals that are served.

The small Victorian house stands in a garden near the north end of the lake.
Everything inside is spick-and-span. One bay-windowed sitting-room has a log
fire and comfortable chairs; the other, a conservatory bar, is attractively furnished,
with cane seats and tiled floor. Beyond this is the dining-room where tables are laid
with pink linen napkins, Wedgwood china, decorative silver and Cumbria crystal
goblets; it is a light room with windows on two sides. The bedrooms are equally
pleasant: pine woodwork and pale shades in one, modern furniture and cheerful
colours in another, and so on. All around are fells and forests.

Dinner is a five-course meal with coffee. Prawn, celery and apple cocktail might
be followed by a herby tomato soup (home-made), lamb roasted with rosemary,
strawberry meringues, and then cheeses (with choices at most courses). Bread is
home-made.

Bassenthwaite Lake is the most northerly of the lakes and the only one with the
word 'lake' in its name, the rest being 'meres' or 'waters'. On one side is the great
peak of Skiddaw and on the other Thornthwaite Forest, with a visitor centre
provided by the Forestry Commission. By it is Mirehouse, one of the least
intimidating of mansions: children have been known to be led to find a sweet in a
secret drawer in a bureau, and the sound of the grand piano is heard on occasion. It
is still in the possession of the family whose ancestors entertained Tennyson and
Carlyle there. As well as maintaining a domestic atmosphere in the house itself,
they have provided an adventure playground in the grounds.

Westward is Cockermouth, Wordsworth's birthplace. Less crowded than other
Lake District towns, it has plenty of antique shops. On the way there, Wythop
Mill, with a display of old woodworking and wheelwrighting tools, is a good stop
for tea or coffee, as is Thornthwaite Gallery off the same road, where there is an
outstanding choice of crafts and pictures. Near Keswick, pleasant but often
crowded during the tourist season, are a stone circle and the famous Manesty
Gardens. Beautiful Derwent Water is to the south.

Readers' comments: Could not have been more helpful; food ample and delicious.
Food, service and friendly atmosphere truly excellent. Lovely setting.

LISLE COMBE   C PT S
St Lawrence, Isle of Wight, PO38 1UW   Tel: 0983 852 582
West of Ventnor. Nearest main road: A3055 from Ventnor to Niton.

4 Bedrooms. £12.50–£14. Prices go up in   **1 Sitting-room.** With open fire, TV.
July. Tea/coffee facilities. Views of garden,   **Large garden**
country, sea. No smoking.

> 'East of the garden, a wild glen glimmers with foxgloves,
> And there, through the heat of the day,
> In a fern-shadowed elf-ring of sand, with pine logs round it,
> Three bird-voiced children play,
> With a palm to shelter their golden heads from the sun,
> When the noon-sun grows too strong . . .'

One of Alfred Noyes' 'bird-voiced children' about whom he wrote this poem in
1936 now owns that garden, glen and the family home. Hugh Noyes grew up to
become *The Times* parliamentary correspondent until 1982, but is now occupied in
dairy-farming and breeding rare species of waterfowl. Surrounding the house is a
rare breeds and waterfowl park (in 30 acres of outstanding natural beauty) to
which guests have free access.

Visitors staying at Lisle Combe see not only the scenes which inspired so many
poems but many of the poet's possessions, such as a series of watercolours by
Frederick Weld (who became New Zealand's first Prime Minister); and all his
papers are preserved in his still intact library.

The house itself is exceptional. It was built in the early 19th century – but in
Elizabethan style, by the same Lord Yarborough whose monument dominates one
of the island's hills (he was a considerable landowner on the island – Pelham
Woods, opposite the house, carries his family's name).

It has barley-sugar chimneys and lozenge-paned bay windows, many overlooking the English Channel; and a paved verandah with grapevine where breakfast is
sometimes served. Hugh's mother brought to the house some very exceptional
furniture and paintings that were salvaged when, in the 'thirties, her former home
– Lulworth Castle (in Dorset) – was burnt down. One of the most attractive rooms
is a small, pale-blue sitting-room with sea views. Through the garden and among
palm trees, pools and streams a path leads down to the sandy beach: an idyllic spot.

(No dinners: Judy recommends such nearby inns as the Crown at Shorwell or
the New Inn at Shalfleet, or the Seaview Hotel.)

Lisle Combe is close to Ventnor's botanical gardens, full of subtropical flowers,
and with an excellent museum of smuggling through the centuries. This south-
facing part of the coast is the warmest, and Ventnor itself looks rather Mediterranean because the houses are built on terraces zigzagging steeply down to the sea.

169

LITTLE LODGE FARMHOUSE

C(6)

Broughton Green, Hanbury, Worcestershire, WR9 7EE   Tel: 0527 821305

East of Droitwich. Nearest main road: A38 from Birmingham to Worcester.

3 Bedrooms. £17–£19 (less for 3 nights). Prices go up in June. All have own bath/shower/toilet. Tea/coffee facilities. Views of garden, country. No smoking. Washing machine on request.

Dinner. £14 for 3 courses and coffee, at 7pm. (Tuesdays and Thursdays only.) Non-residents not admitted. Wine can be brought in.

1 Sitting-room. With open fire, central heating, TV.

Large garden

Closed from November to mid-April.

Once there was a great deer forest all around a mere woodland clearing where this secluded house, originally a hunting lodge, was built about 1650. Now, nearly all the oaks gone, its surroundings are a patchwork of farmlands and fields for the thoroughbred horses which the Chuggs breed (Robert used to be a jockey), with a distant view of the Clent Hills. In the grounds is a tiny building that was once a schoolroom for local children.

The beamed sitting-room with inglenook fireplace is on two levels and, like all rooms here, has very lovely fabrics to complement the antique furniture. There are hedgerow fruits in the dining-room fabrics, Warner peonies in the coral and green sitting-room, Colefax roses in one bedroom and Jane Churchill garlands in another.

In a very pretty attic room, Jackie herself stencilled the ribbons that decorate the walls. Everywhere she has placed decorative arrangements of dried flowers.

Another of her talents is cookery (she trained at the celebrated Tante Marie School), and at each meal she offers – if it is arranged in advance – a choice of such dishes as egg-and-prawn mousse, duck with Morello cherry sauce and gâteau Diane (which is chocolate-filled meringue). Even breakfasts are rather special, with such options as *fromage frais* to accompany fruits, granary bread, black pudding from Stornoway, etc.

Worcestershire is one of England's loveliest counties (particularly to the south). The highest point is in the Clent Hills, rising to 1000 feet, among which you can drive or walk to explore their woodlands and pools; and there are hills to the west, too. The Severn is a lovely river to follow down from Stourport to where, beyond the cathedral city of Worcester, it joins the pretty River Teme in an area well-known for its orchards, hops, dairy-cattle and lush meadows. At Droitwich, water saltier than the Dead Sea is pumped up from subterranean sources 200 feet down – so buoyant that visitors bathing in it float unsinkably. It was these baths that turned the market town into an elegant little spa, still functioning.

Readers' comments: A marvellous place. I could not find fault anywhere.

170

LITTLE PARMOOR
C(5) **X**

Frieth, Oxfordshire, RG9 6NL   Tel: 0494 881447

North-east of Henley-on-Thames. Nearest main road: A40 from Oxford to
High Wycombe.

3 Bedrooms. £16.50 (less for 4 nights). Tea/
coffee facilities. TV. Views of garden, country. No smoking. Washing machine on request.

Dinner. £10 for 3 courses (with choices) and
coffee, at 7.30pm (if booked in advance).
Non-residents not admitted. Vegetarian or
special diets if ordered. Wine can be brought
in. No smoking.

1 Sitting-room. With open fire, central heating, record-player. No smoking.

Large garden

Within a mere half-hour of Heathrow (and little further to London) is a peaceful
spot among the lovely Chiltern Hills, and in it this attractive house built in 1724.
(It used to be the house of the estate manager who looked after the lands of Sir
Stafford Cripps' father, Lord Parmoor, when he occupied the nearby great house.)

Inside are pale green and white panelling, log fires and watercolours painted by
Wynyard Wallace's grandfather. An elegant pine staircase leads to one pretty
white-panelled bedroom and another, single, that is very good – unlike so many
single bedrooms. Children particularly like the attic rooms above, with circular
windows and sloping ceilings. Julia provides breakfast (sometimes taken under
the vine outside) and dinners which may include such dishes as home-made
vegetable or fish soup, Chiltern game pie with locally grown vegetables, and lemon
meringue pie. Also, within five miles are ten inns all of which serve good food.

Although so many busy roads skirt this area, it is very secluded and few
motorists explore its narrow lanes where boughs reach overhead, pheasants dart
from hedges or vanish into the glades, beech woods turn to fiery colours in
autumn, and one finds unknown villages tucked away, built in the mixture of flint
and brick which is traditional in these parts.

Southward is one of the finest and most winding stretches of the River Thames –
from Sonning through Henley (of regatta fame) and Maidenhead to Windsor, best
explored by boat – arguably at its best in uncrowded autumn when the hills
descend to the river in a blaze of colour. The scene constantly changes: weirs,
bridges, locks and islands along the way; meadow banks dotted with historic
mansions, abbeys, boat-houses and inns. From summits of hills there are superb
views of it all. Along the river itself, visit Sonning and Shiplake, Cookham for
Stanley Spencer's paintings and for its backwaters, Hurley, Marlow, the beech
woods of Cliveden, picturesque Boulter's Lock (well-described in Jerome K.
Jerome's *Three Men in a Boat*), busy Maidenhead with two fine bridges, and Bray
(the village of the turncoat Vicar of Bray). Then come the splendours of Windsor
Castle and Eton College. Edwardian houses and well-kept gardens line the banks,
and here are the willows of Kenneth Grahame's *Wind in the Willows*, together with
the summer wildflowers he described – 'purple loosestrife shaking luxuriant
tangled locks; willowherbs, tender and wistful like a pink sunset cloud; comfrey,
the purple hand-in-hand with the white; and the diffident dog-rose . . . June at last
was here.'

Readers' comments: Made us feel part of the family.

LODGE FARM

near Fersfield, Bressingham, Norfolk, IP22 2BQ   Tel: 037988 629
West of Diss. Nearest main road: A1066 from Thetford to Diss.

3 Bedrooms. £14 – £16. Tea/coffee facilities. Views of garden, country. Washing machine on request.
Light suppers if ordered. Wine can be brought in.

2 Sitting-rooms. With open fire, central heating, TV, record-player.
Large garden

Henry VIII had a 'palace' for hunting near here (Kenninghall, of which only one wing survives), and at the boundaries of this great estate were lodges, of which this was one. Its windows and pink walls, at the top of which house-martins build their mud nests, give little hint that the house goes back so far, for each subsequent century saw additions and alterations. But inside are chamfered beams, low ceilings, odd steps and angles – this is definitely not a house for less agile visitors!

David and Pat Bateson have furniture that is very much in keeping – for instance, a wedding-chest dated 1682 and with the initials of an earlier Bateson and his bride; several Portuguese chests, iron-bound and velvet-covered; a great refectory table; and an iron fireback of 1582 which – with bellows, spit and so forth – furnishes the great inglenook where logs blaze on chilly nights.

Bedrooms are cottagey in style, one lime-and-white, one (with brass bed) pink-and-white – both with interesting pictures and trifles to enjoy. Another is connected by a very low passage to its own sitting-room and a winding stair up to two attic rooms: an ideal suite for a family (with bathroom and even a kitchen below). Indeed, this is a marvellous place altogether for a family holiday (with plenty of sightseeing outings likely to appeal to older children). Outside is a garden where chickens wander among winding beds of roses and comfrey, and the Batesons' smallholding (they keep sheep – including rare Wensleydales – ducks and horses).

Breakfast and light supper only; for a more substantial dinner, most visitors walk or drive (one mile) to the Garden House Inn.

Bressingham is famous for its live steam museum, where you can spend a day riding on the footplate of a locomotive; *and* on a narrow-gauge train through woods and acres of very lovely gardens *and* on a Victorian merry-go-round. Among the hundreds of other exhibits is the 'Royal Scot'.

It also has a notable church (one of many in Norfolk) with elaborately carved pew ends. Fersfield's church has a well known memorial of a knight with a dog.

The centre of historic Diss hums with life on market day (Friday) but the narrow, twisting lanes and the nearby meres remain peaceful.

★ **LOW GREEN HOUSE**   **C**
Thoralby, Bishopdale, North Yorkshire, DL8 3SZ   Tel: 0969 663623
East of Hawes. Nearest main road: A684 from Leyburn to Hawes.

3 Bedrooms. £14–£16. Prices go up in March. All have own shower/toilet. Tea/coffee facilities. TV. Views of garden, country. No smoking.
Dinner. £9 for 4 courses and coffee, at 6.45pm. Non-residents not admitted. Vegetarian or special diets if ordered. Wine can be brought in.
1 Sitting-room. With open fire, central heating.
Small garden

This stone house in a tiny hamlet is the home of Tony and Marilyn Philpott, who are founts of information on where to walk and what to see.

Within rugged walls are particularly comfortable and pretty rooms. (There is also a bedroom in a cottage annexe.) I had a pink-and-white bedroom with deep brown carpet; the bathroom was excellent; and in the sitting/dining-room (which runs from front to back of the house, with a picture-window looking towards Wensleydale) soft colours, deep armchairs around a log fire and plentiful books provide a relaxed atmosphere. For dinner Marilyn served – with decorative flourishes – local smoked trout, pork cooked with cream and mushrooms, blue Wensleydale cheese, and raspberry torte. With the coffee came a dish of chocolates. (All carefully prepared, and remarkably good value.)

The Yorkshire Dales have many peaks over 2000 feet high: wild and windy, with lonely farms on their foothills, sheep on the moors and waterfalls rushing down the valleys. Wensleydale is only five minutes away. Bishopdale itself follows a stream south, the road rising high up at Kidstones Pass, to join Langstrothdale and much more tourist-ridden Wharfedale. Sights worth seeing include Aysgarth Falls, Malham Cove, Hardraw Falls, Jervaulx Abbey, Fountains Abbey (and gardens), the Settle-Carlisle scenic railway, Newby Hall gardens, Thorpe Perrow arboretum, Bolton Castle. (Bicycles, including mountain bicycles, for hire locally.)

This would be a good place for a touring bibliophile. The first stop would be nearby Hawes, where there is a small and crowded secondhand bookshop specialising in fine bindings (not always open). The ropeworks in Hawes is also well worth a visit, both to see ropes being made and to buy anything from a bellrope to a lead for the dog: once in danger of closing, it is now flourishing thanks to a combination of traditional craft methods and modern technology. From Hawes, a drive over the bleak spine of the Pennines takes one to Sedbergh, where there is a bookshop specializing in valuable collectors' items and works of local interest. Kendal has a multi-storey antiquarian bookshop.

Readers' comments: Comfort, hospitality and value cannot be bettered. Lovely hosts.

When writing to me, if you want a reply please enclose a stamped addressed envelope.

★ **LOW HALL**
Brandlingill, Cumbria, CA13 0RE   Tel: 0900 826654
South of Cockermouth. Nearest main road: A66 from Keswick to
Cockermouth.

6 Bedrooms. £17–£20 (less for 3 nights).
Prices go up at Easter. Bargain breaks. All
have own bath/shower/toilet. Tea/coffee
facilities. TV. Views of garden, country,
river. No smoking.
Dinner. A la carte or £11 for 4 courses (with
choices) and coffee, at 7–7.30pm. Non-
residents not admitted. Vegetarian dishes.
Wine can be ordered. No smoking.
2 Sitting-rooms. With open fire, central
heating, TV, piano. Bar. No smoking.
Large garden
**Closed from December to March
inclusive.**

David and Dani Edwards gave up other careers to renovate this farmhouse, which
is mostly of 17th-century origin but was enlarged to accommodate a big Victorian
family. In carrying out this task, they uncovered a huge fireplace in what was the
dairy and is now the dining-room where candlelit dinners are accompanied by
classical music. They have decorated it with sprigged wallpapers and some
attractive old furniture.

There is one big sitting-room with log fire and a second, smaller one for
television addicts.

The bedrooms, most of which are spacious, give views of the Lorton fells on the
north-western corner of the Lake District or of the grounds of the house, through
which a stream runs. This is an area of great beauty, wooded rather than rugged,
where the Cumbrian mountains start their descent to sea level. It is never overrun
by tourists, yet the well known parts of the Lake District are only a short drive
away.

Dani's menus always include a vegetarian alternative to the meat course. A
typical menu: potted broccoli; soup; roast loin of pork with fig, apple and cheese
stuffing, or sweet-and-sour almonds; and either cheese or a choice of puddings –
one light, one richer, and one hot. Breakfasts are much more interesting than the
usual egg-and-bacon routine. Preserves, rolls and ice cream are home-made.
There are occasional gastronomic weekends.

Readers' comments: My favourite guest-house . . . fulfils all your criteria and more.
Extremely comfortable.

A few miles away, on the edge of the
village of High Lorton, Mrs Roberts
provides bed-and-breakfast at **OWL
BROOK** (tel: 090085 333). This
architect-designed and attractive bungalow of green lakeland slate with pine
ceilings was built a few years ago, and
all the airy bedrooms have fine views. It
lies at the end of Whinlatter Pass, the
least alarming of the Lake District
passes. From £13 to £15.

Readers' comments: Beautiful views and
utter tranquillity. Breakfasts were superb. Very friendly family atmosphere.

LOXLEY FARMHOUSE

C D

Loxley, Warwickshire, CV35 9JN   Tel: 0789 840265
South-east of Stratford-upon-Avon. Nearest main road: A422 from Stratford to
Banbury.

2–3 Bedrooms. £16–£17.50 (less for 3 nights). Prices go up at Easter. Bargain breaks. All have own bath/shower/toilet. Tea/coffee facilities. TV. Views of garden, country.
Light suppers if ordered. Vegetarian or special diets. Wine can be brought in.
2 Sitting-rooms. With open fire, central heating, TV.
Large garden. Paddock with Shetland ponies.

Loxley is a hilltop village with diminutive church. From a seat on its sloping green, where crab-apple trees are bright in autumn, there are far views across woodland and fields of red earth. Just downhill from here Loxley Farm is tucked away: a picture-postcard house of half-timbering and thatch, parts dating back to the 13th century. Perhaps Robin Hood ('Robin of Loxley') knew the house; there's a worn stone in the churchyard on which, tradition has it, he and his companions used to sharpen their arrow-tips. And certainly Charles I stayed here after the nearby Battle of Edgehill.

Inside, everything is in keeping with the style of the ancient house: low ceilings with pewter pots hanging from the beams, flagged floors, small-paned windows, log fires, oak doors. You can see the cruck construction of the house – at its heart, the unhewn trunks of two trees support the roof timbers. There is not a single straight wall or floor. Anne Horton has furnished the rooms in appropriate style. In the dining-room, leather chairs surround a large oak table; in the sitting-room are a grandfather clock and wing armchairs, with Staffordshire figures and old silver on the shelves, lavender and dried flowers.

Two of the bedrooms are in a separate, half-timbered, thatched barn conversion, together with a sitting-room and kitchen. Both have en suite bathrooms. In the main house, where breakfast is served, an additional bedroom is sometimes available for guests.

Breakfast only – with home-made buns – and early supper trays (such as smoked salmon soup, lamb hotpot, and a National Trust recipe, lemon pudding).

The broad River Avon gives character to the peaceful countryside: cattle grazing in green meadows where once Shakespeare's Forest of Arden spread for miles around. It is easy to visit Stratford-upon-Avon from here, the Cotswolds, and Oxford. It is also worth travelling to Dudley to see the excellent new Black Country Museum. Warwick Castle, Blenheim Palace, Charlecote, Hidcote (and many other great gardens) make this area a tourist honeypot.

Readers' comments: Idyllic surroundings. Much care and attention. Generous, flavoursome fare. Most welcoming and comfortable. Not a jarring note.

THE MALTINGS
Aldwincle, Northamptonshire, NN14 3EP   Tel: 08015 233
South of Oundle. Nearest main road: A605 from Thrapston to Oundle.

3 Bedrooms. £18–£19 (less for 3 nights). Bargain breaks. All have own bath/shower/ toilet. Tea/coffee facilities. Views of garden, country. No smoking. Washing machine on request.
1 Sitting-room. With open fire, central heating. TV.
Large garden

As soon as you enter the courtyard to park, you get an enticing glimpse through a stone arch (framed in honeysuckle and jasmine) of a particularly lovely walled garden. Pebble and flagstone paths pass between stone troughs of flowers, and baskets of begonias hang overhead. Beyond is an alpine bed. The garden is open to the public twice a year under the National Gardens Scheme.

This is a long, low, 16th-century house with very thick stone walls. Its barn used to provide the warmth needed to make heaps of barley sprout – the malting process which is at the heart of brewing.

Its dining-room has a Persian carpet on the wood-block floor, and antique furniture, as does the sitting-room where, from a pale green sofa, you can enjoy logs blazing in the stone fireplace or a garden view through French doors. The walls of the house are lined with portraits or animal paintings which Margaret Faulkner collects (she used to work for an art dealer).

Upstairs, a long and wavering passage leads to bedrooms that have rose chintzes or pink patchwork, for instance, and to equally attractive bathrooms. Their 17th-century doors are of stripped pine; and, like all the rooms in the house, they are very light.

As only breakfast is served, most visitors go for other meals to the Falcon Inn at Fotheringhay; the Snooty Fox at Lowick; or the Pheasant at Keyston.

There are 14 stately homes in the vicinity including Burghley and Boughton (gardens too), as well as Rockingham Castle, historic Stamford, Huntingdon for its associations with Oliver Cromwell, bird reserves, Notcutt's garden centre, and steam railways. London is less than an hour by train.

Among the other stately homes are Deene Park, 1514, which has large gardens, as does part-Norman Delapre Abbey. Elton Hall is another very ancient home (near Peterborough), built in 1475. Kelmarsh Hall is Palladian, its gardens at their colourful best in spring; handsomely furnished Lamport Hall, 1560, has in its grounds one of the first rockeries in Britain. Lyveden New Bield is the most unusual building of all, built (about 1600) in the shape of a cross, although the triangular lodge at Rushton is a close runner-up. Mediaeval Southwick Hall houses a costume museum.

This area played an important part in the Civil War and at Purlieu Farm is an exhibition about the crucial Battle of Naseby which took place near there. Kettering and Northampton have a number of museums, one devoted to leathercraft; Wellingborough has a heritage centre. There is a watermill near Oundle, and another heritage centre – devoted to steel-making – near Corby, with craft workshops and forge. Guilsborough has a wildlife park, and Lilford Park is home to a variety of farm animals and birds, with such events as sheepdog trials.

★ **MANOR FARM**　　　　　　　　　　　　　　　　　　**C D X**
Kelmscott, Gloucestershire, GL7 3HJ　Tel: 0367 52620
North-west of Faringdon (Oxfordshire). Nearest main road: A417 from
Faringdon to Lechlade.

2 Bedrooms. £13. Prices go up in April.
Bargain breaks. Tea/coffee facilities. TV.
Views of garden, country. No smoking.
Washing machine on request.
Dinner. £8 for 2 or £12 for 4 courses and
coffee, at 7pm. Non-residents not admitted.
Vegetarian or special diets if ordered. Wine
can be brought in. No smoking. **Light
suppers** if ordered.
1 Sitting-room. With open fire, central heating, TV. No smoking.
Large garden

This Cotswold stone house (at the centre of a dairy-farm belonging to the National
Trust) stands on the outskirts of a carefully conserved village – utterly peaceful,
for it is not on the route to anywhere else. Outside is a pigeon-house as old as the
rest of the buildings; paddocks with a pony, pet lambs and calves; pollarded
willows and cherry-trees that flower prettily in spring.

The 17th-century windows, stone-mullioned and with panelled shutters, are a
handsome feature of rooms which Anne Amor keeps immaculate as well as
comfortable; with, in winter, a crackling fire framed by the Adam mantelpiece
and, in summer, chairs on the lawn. For dinner, Anne serves such options as
prawn cocktail or melon for starters, roast lamb (home-produced), or chicken in a
white wine sauce, followed by a choice of desserts such as mint mousse, yogurt
cheesecake and crumbles. (On Fridays, cold snacks only.) Anne also offers packed
lunches and in each bedroom she puts home-made shortbread and fruit squashes.
You can buy her cakes and preserves to take home.

Visitors enjoy handling home-reared lambs in the spring, and looking at the
calves.

Kelmscott's greatest claim to fame is William Morris's big manor house, still
with tapestries and embroideries made by him and his wife; paintings by Rosetti;
wallpapers, tiles and textiles which Morris designed. Occasionally, one-day
embroidery courses are held here; and you can buy things made from William
Morris fabrics when the house is – infrequently – open.

The Thames (merely a stream here) is 5 minutes' walk away. In addition to
lovely countryside, visitors enjoy days spent at the Cotswold Wildlife Park,
Cogges living farm 'museum', the steam railway centre at Didcot; touring
Cotswold villages like Moreton-in-Marsh and Burford; and visiting Filkins (woollen weavers) or stately homes (Coleshill, Buscot, Littlecote, Bowood, Pusey
House and gardens, and Blenheim Palace). Oxford and Cheltenham are not far
away.

A number of circular walks can be made from Kelmscott. Other places of
interest include the market town of Wantage, prehistoric sites near Uffington, and
the trout farm at picturesque Bibury.

Readers' comments: Very comfortable and welcoming. A lovely time; highly
recommended.

Crackington Haven, Cornwall, EX23 0JW   Tel: 084 03 304
South-west of Bude. Nearest main road: A39 from Bude to Camelford.

5 Bedrooms. £18–£20 (less for 5 nights). Prices go up in June. All have own bath/shower/toilet. Views of garden, country. No smoking. Washing machine on request.
Dinner. £12 for 4 courses and coffee, at 7pm. Non-residents not admitted. Vegetarian or special diets if ordered. Wine can be ordered. No smoking.
3 Sitting-rooms. With open fire, central heating, TV. Bar. No smoking.
Large garden

Muriel Knight so much enjoys cooking and looking after guests that she gave up her job as a teacher in order to concentrate on this, in her outstandingly beautiful home near the sea (the garden of which provides fruit and vegetables).

It is a historic manor house (named in Domesday Book), much of the present building three centuries old, and furnished with taste. Past a stone-flagged hall is a beamed breakfast-room. In the cosy winter lounge is a stone pillar and wrought-iron screen concealing a log stove; leading from it is a help-yourself bar. Past the television room, there is a summer lounge which has beautiful mullioned windows and lovely views of garden, farmland and hills. In the dining-room lyre-backed chairs with yellow seats surround the mahogany table which Muriel lays with silver, cut glass and starched napkins. Equal care has gone into bedrooms that have such things as 17th-century antiques, Berlin-work window-seats, lattice windows, elegant bathrooms. (One has a Sitz bath which some elderly people appreciate.) I particularly liked the rose room.

In the grounds are a sloping lawn with herb border and, beside an old waterwheel, a games room with full-size billiards and table tennis.

Muriel's pleasure in cooking shows itself in the dinners she provides. Here is just one example. Choux-pastry swans with a filling of avocado and cream; Coronation chicken (that is, in an apricot and curry sauce) accompanied by jacket potatoes stuffed with cheese and basil, *and* cauliflower and date salad *and* rice, prawns and eggs in prawn sauce; a lemon and orange pavlova. It hardly needs saying that Manor Farmhouse is a good choice for gourmets.

In such an idyllic spot, there is little temptation to go elsewhere. However, the resort of Bude is very near and the border of Devon. Bude is more sedate than many West Country resorts, in a setting of grassy downs and golden sandy beaches on which the Atlantic thunders in.

Readers' comments: Gracious and warm, a beautiful ambience. Delightful place. We were looked after superbly. Super place, nice hosts. Peace, quiet, good food, comfort. Best holiday in 32 years. Lovely welcome. Glorious views. Food marvellous, elegantly served. Lovely relaxing atmosphere.

For explanation of code letters (C, D, H, PT, S, X) see page xxxiv.

MANOR FARMHOUSE

Wormington, Worcestershire, WR12 7NL   Tel: 038673 302
South-west of Broadway. Nearest main road: A46 from Broadway to
Cheltenham.

3 **Bedrooms.** £13.50–£16.50. Prices go up
at Easter. Bargain breaks. Some have own
shower. Views of garden, country. No
smoking. Washing machine on request.
1 Sitting-room. With open fire, central heating, TV.
Small garden

Once this house was known as Charity Farm because 'dole' was dispensed to
wayfarers. The farm was connected with Hailes Abbey (in the 13th century, its
phial of Christ's blood made it a centre of pilgrimage; now there are only ruins),
hence some ecclesiastical touches like the pointed arch beside the log fire – possibly
it was a leper window. There are leaded casements in the comfortable sitting-
room, a stone inglenook in the hall, slabs of Welsh slate on the floor, steps and
turns everywhere on one's way up to beamy all-white bedrooms well furnished
with mahogany pieces. There's still a cheese room dating from the time when this
was a dairy-farm.

What was once a cattle-yard is now a very attractive court with lawn, fountain
and stone sinks planted with flowers. To one side is an old granary of brick and
timber which dates, like the house itself, from the 15th century. From his stable
door Monty, a big hunter, watches visitors' comings and goings.

Pauline Russell serves only breakfast, recommending for other meals Goblets
wine bar in Broadway – that world-famous showplace, best known of all the
picturesque villages hereabouts and once called 'the painted lady of the Cotswolds'
because the colour of the golden stone glows so vividly here. Flower-filled,
perfectly groomed gardens do their bit too.

From here one can drive to the fruitful Vale of Evesham (loveliest in spring),
high Bredon Hill ringed by pretty villages, Tewkesbury to see the abbey, historic
Evesham for boat trips on the Avon, Pershore (abbey church and 18th-century
houses), or little Ripple with old houses around its green and quaint carvings on
the misericord seats in the church.

Through the region runs the River Avon, watering the rich fields and orchards
around it.

The area is a source of endless pleasure to anyone who enjoys discovering
little-known villages and their individual treasures. Examples are Bosbury,
surrounded by hop fields and dominated by a detached church tower fortified as a
refuge from the Welsh raiders of the 12th century; Bredon, full of black-and-white
houses and, in its church, a treasure-house of carved tombs and monuments – it
also has an immense mediaeval tithe barn; Bretforton, where the ancient and
picturesque inn – just one of many fine buildings here – is owned by the National
Trust (look for the 'witch marks' on the floor and the splendid collection of
17th-century pewter); Colwall which has a huge stone said to have been hurled
there by a giant in pursuit of his faithless wife (the scenic Jubilee Drive high up in
the hills starts here); and the two Combertons, Great and Little (the latter is in fact
the bigger one, but both are beautiful) at the foot of Bredon Hill.

MANOR HOUSE   C S
Potterhanworth, Lincolnshire, LN4 2DN   Tel: 0522 791288
South of Lincoln. Nearest main road: A15 from Lincoln to Sleaford.

4 Bedrooms. £16–£17.50 (less for 3 nights). Prices go up in April. Bargain breaks. Some have own bath/shower/toilet. Tea/coffee facilities. TV. Views of garden, country. No smoking. Washing machine on request.
2 Sitting-rooms. With open fire, central heating, TV, piano, record-player. No smoking in one.
Large garden
Closed from late December to late January.

Built at a fine period for domestic architecture (1840), the house has impressive rooms – beginning with the big entrance hall which has panelled doors and a stone-paved floor from which a white and mahogany staircase winds up, its balusters elegantly turned. A red damask wallpaper and big gilt mirror are in keeping with this setting. Off the hall is a double sitting-room, high ceilinged, with a marble fireplace and, on three sides, deep-set French windows that open onto lawns. Pink brocade curtains, Chinese carpets, chandeliers hanging from the pink ceiling, a great copper vat of logs: all combine to create a handsome effect. There is also an oak-panelled television room, its alcoves filled with books.

From the windows are views of the almost park-like garden where ponies and sheep wander. Beyond rose beds is an outsize summer-house, glass-walled and with a changing-room (for the swimming-pool), table tennis, darts, etc. One can walk from here to a pond, brook and weir frequented by waterfowl.

Bedrooms and bathrooms are excellent, and varied. One, for instance, is in a modern grey and scarlet colour scheme. Another – light and airy – has pale, flowery fabrics, polished board floors and exposed rafters overhead. Families like to book the combination of a small room (with bunks) adjoining the bedroom for parents. Some rooms are in a stable annexe, converted with much use of pine to provide not only bedrooms and family suites but also a kitchen where children's meals can be prepared.

. Visitors dine at local restaurants and inns (Washingborough Hall, the Ferry Boat at Washingborough, or the Chequers in the village).

Readers' comments: Superb house and charming hostess. Delightful house, beautiful grounds, a memorable stay.

A few miles south, at Timberland, is the 18th-century **PENNY FARTHING INN** (tel: 05267 359), a suitable choice for anyone who likes the convivial atmosphere of a village pub combined with very good food. Behind the unassuming exterior are beamy, stone-walled bars with tapestry chairs, and a separate TV room for residents. To avoid kitchen noise, ask for a bedroom at the back. Tony Daniel's cooking includes such dishes as casseroled

pheasant, guinea-fowl with port-wine sauce and carpetbag steaks. £18 (b & b).

Readers' comments: Superb cooking, enormous breakfasts, truly welcoming.

180

MAPLEHURST MILL

C(12) H

Mill Lane, Frittenden, Kent, TN17 2DT   Tel: 058080 203
South-east of Maidstone. Nearest main road: A229 from Maidstone towards
Hastings.

3 Bedrooms. £18.50 – £25 (less for 6 nights).
Prices go up in March. All have own bath/
shower/toilet. Tea/coffee facilities. TV.
Views of garden, country, river. No
smoking.
Dinner. £15 for 4 courses (with choices) and
coffee, at times to suit guests. Non-residents
not admitted. Vegetarian or special diets if
ordered. Wine can be ordered. No smoking.
Light suppers sometimes.
1 Sitting-room. With open fire, central heating, piano. No smoking.
Large garden

'It was like the Marie Celeste,' said Kenneth Parker, describing this 18th-century
mill when they took it over. It had hardly been touched since the day it ceased to
grind, and the tools of the miller's trade lay where he had left them: the governor
for the millstones, the key to open the sluices, the sack-hoist, the flour chest
beneath the chute, smutters and scourers, floury hoppers . . . On the grinding
floor, the Parkers are now creating with the help of these finds a little museum of
milling, and are researching the history of the mill, which dates back to AD 1309.
(One grisly item: they discovered that in the religious persecutions of 1557, the
miller and his wife were burnt at the stake.)

Their conversion of the mill has been faultless. It now has every up-to-date
comfort, yet the ambience of the past has been vividly preserved. Through the
entrance hall, which has baskets of dried flowers, one comes to my favourite
bedroom (being on the ground floor, it would suit anyone who finds stairs
difficult). It not only has a wide door onto a paved terrace of its own but also a
window right by the waterwheel. The mill-race flows under its floor – one can fall
asleep to the soothing gurgle of the water. Lean out of the window and you may see
trout, or a kingfisher on his favourite perch, waiting to pounce on sticklebacks.

Upstairs are dining- and sitting-rooms with exposed wall beams, low doorways,
white or pine-boarded walls, a tree-trunk that forms part of the structure, iron
pillars or mechanisms and brick or cast-iron fireplaces. Each bedroom is different
– one with lacey duvet covers and festoon blinds, for instance; another with a pine
four-poster draped with a pink and blue honeysuckle fabric; a third with flowery
Habitat linens. From some windows are views of yellow waterlilies and dabchicks
on the stream, or of cows and hayfields. You may even glimpse foxes or a heron. In
the grounds is a small vineyard.

The mill would be worth going out of one's way to visit not only for all this but
because Heather's meals are so imaginative. Here is an example: Sussex smokies
(haddock) in a cheese and wine sauce followed by chicken breasts with a sauce
made from avocados, sherry and cream (the accompanying vegetables are organically grown) and then a home-made chocolate, coffee and almond ice cream.
Afterwards, one can relax either on the waterside terrace or in the huge sitting-
room where Heather has both a clavichord and a rare grand piano, perfectly
semicircular. It is a gracious room in which the sofas are covered with cottage-
garden fabrics and aquamarine curtains hang at the casements on opposite walls.
Beauty, character, good food and peace: what more could one want?

Frittenden is a typical village of the Weald, a wooded, undulating region.

MARINA HOTEL   C D PT
The Esplanade, Fowey, Cornwall, PL23 1HY   Tel: 072683 3315
East of St Austell. Nearest main road: A390 from Lostwithiel to St Austell.

rear view

11 Bedrooms. £22–£30 **with one at £20 for SOTBT readers only.** (Less for 2 nights.) Prices go up in July. Bargain breaks. **Exclusive to SOTBT readers: £62 for 2 days' dinner, bed and breakfast, except in July and August.** All have own bath/shower/ toilet. Tea/coffee facilities. TV. Sea views, balcony (some). Washing machine on request.
Dinner. A la carte or £14 for 4 courses (with choices) and coffee, at 7–8.30pm. Vegetarian or special diets if ordered. Wine can be ordered. No smoking.
3 Sitting-rooms. With central heating. **Bar. Small garden**
Closed from November to February inclusive.

Built in 1830 as a seaside retreat for the Bishop of Truro, this fine house has been furnished with the elegance it deserves. The handsome mouldings, arches and panelling of the hall and octagonal landing are now decorated in brown and cream; and each bedroom is different – a pale colour scheme in one; sprigged covers and pine in another (its rounded window overlooking the sea); four with covered verandahs of lacy ironwork facing the tiny walled garden and waterfront beyond it. The dining-room has Indian Tree china on peach tablecloths, with spectacular views from the big picture-windows; the bar, rosy armchairs and a thick pale carpet. Recently, 8-foot marble pillars were uncovered in one bedroom.

David Johns gives equal attention to the standard of the food. Dinner is priced according to your choice of main dish, from a selection that includes (for instance) boned chicken in a sauce of mushrooms and cider, escallopes of veal with mushrooms and cream flamed in Madeira, and local fish in a variety of ways.

Fowey (pronounced Foy) is on that mild stretch of the coast known as the Cornish Riviera. It is an old and picturesque harbour of steep, narrow byways (parking is difficult; a hotel car goes to and from the town carpark), its waters busy with yachts and fishing boats. Some people arrive by car ferry. It is easy to find secluded coves and beaches nearby, or scenic walks along clifftops. The little town is full of antique, book and craft shops; historic buildings; restaurants and good food shops. Easily reached from here are Lanhydrock House and gardens, Restormel Castle, Charlestown and Wheal Martin China Clay Museum. Cornwall has a spring gardens festival – ask the Marina for a leaflet about the 55 gardens that participate. One very near here, famous for camellias in an 18th-century setting, is Trewithen; another, with superb sea views, is Trelissick; and at Probus is a series of 56 demonstration gardens.

Go to Falmouth to visit Pendennis Castle, built by Henry VIII to guard the estuary, and for the maritime museum. There are rare breeds to be seen in the country park at Kea and, near the cathedral city of Truro (which also has Cornwall's county museum), is a cider farm with activities to view.

Readers' comments: Excellent; super room. Extremely helpful. Have never experienced such professional yet personal attention.

MARSHGATE COTTAGE

C(5) **H PT**

Marshgate, Berkshire, RG17 0QX Tel: 0488 682307
West of Hungerford. Nearest main road: A4 from Marlborough to Newbury.

9 Bedrooms. £16.50–£23.75 (less for 7 nights). Most have own shower/toilet. Tea/coffee facilities. TV. Views of garden, country, canal. Some no-smoking rooms.
Light suppers if ordered. Vegetarian or special diets. Wine can be ordered.

1 Sitting-room. With fire, central heating. Bar.
Small garden

The marshes which give this cottage its name stretch down to the 18th-century Kennet & Avon Canal, a haven for birds and wildflowers. The cottage (used as a pest-house during the plague of 1640) is even older than the canal, its thatched roof descending almost to ground level; and although it has been skilfully modernized and extended everything is in keeping with its original character. Most rooms overlook the marshes, which are a sheet of yellow in buttercup-time. Wild orchids grow there, frogs croak in spring, and among the network of little streams kingfishers can be spotted hunting, or redshanks on their nests.

Mike Walker, once a journalist, did most of the conversion himself, re-using old handmade bricks and wrought-iron locks; laying floors of beautiful chestnut boards. His Danish wife Elsebeth, a biochemist, has furnished the rooms with Scandinavian taste, hunting for finds such as mirrors or stained glass in the area's many antique shops. The breakfast-room is in white and pine; dried flowers are strung along the beams; hand-thrown pots contrast with curios such as an old mangle. From a quarry-tiled hall an open-tread staircase goes up to some bedrooms (most are on the ground floor), furnished with a pleasing simplicity.

In the grounds are goats and ducks – also a 'dipping hole' (that is, the point where an underground stream pops up – watercress grows in it).

Only breakfast is provided (a chance to sample fresh duck eggs and goat's milk if you wish) because Hungerford has excellent restaurants such as the Bear.

Around Hungerford there is scenic downland in every direction, and a great many stately homes or other sights described elsewhere in this book. Nearby Newbury's Watermill Theatre is one of many interesting spots (the wheel is still to be seen). Thatcham Moors are relatively unknown even though they have an almost unique feature, a huge inland reed-bed. Walkers make for the high Ridgeway Path which is of prehistoric origin. Donnington has castle ruins.

Readers' comments: Agreeably cosy. Delightful river setting.

MELLINGTON HOUSE C PT S

Broad Street, Weobley, Herefordshire, HR4 8SA Tel: 0544 318537
North-west of Hereford. Nearest main road: A4112 from Leominster to
Brecon.

3 Bedrooms. £13.50–£16.50. Prices go up
in April. Bargain breaks. Some have own
bath/shower/toilet. Tea/coffee facilities.
TV. No smoking. Washing machine on
request.
Dinner. £7.50 for 3 courses (with choices)
and coffee, at 7.30pm. Non-residents not
admitted. Vegetarian or special diets if
ordered. Wine can be brought in. **Light
suppers** if ordered.
1 Sitting-room. With open fire, central heating, TV, piano, record-player. No smoking.
Large garden

Once, mediaeval houses were considered old-fashioned and so many householders
had new façades put on them. That is why Mellington House has a front in Queen
Anne style, but its real age is revealed at the back where the original half-timbering
is still exposed – typical of most buildings in Weobley, which is a particularly fine
mediaeval village set in the lovely Herefordshire countryside. Although the house
is in the centre of the village, it is quiet because its walls are thick and the big sash
windows double-glazed (not that Weobley gets heavy traffic).

Ann Saunders has furnished the house very pleasantly (for instance, brass beds
and wildflower duvets), the sitting-room is large and comfortable, and there is a
downstairs bedroom which Ann (a physiotherapist) provides for people who have
mobility problems. The dining-room opens onto a large, old, walled garden
where, on sunny mornings, she serves breakfast.

Although there are good restaurants in Weobley (also a craft centre, shops and
art gallery) Ann will prepare such meals as: melon, roast beef with garden
vegetables, home-made cheesecake, and cheeses.

From Weobley, there are plenty of sightseeing options. The picturesque
black-and-white village of Eardisland is close. There are a dozen bookshops (most
belonging to Richard Booth) in Hay-on-Wye, now nicknamed 'Book City'.
Brecon, Offa's Dyke and numerous stately homes provide other destinations for a
day out; and, as this is an area of orchards and nursery gardens, many people
return home laden with pot-plants and pick-your-own soft fruits. The Malvern
Hills and the Black Mountains are close, and several market towns are nearby.
Add to these the Brecon Beacons, Radnor Forest, the 'Golden Valley', Welsh and
Shropshire market towns, a motor museum, a lovely drive along Wenlock Edge,
Ironbridge Industrial Museum, the Wye Valley and innumerable garden centres.

Travel northward for Worcestershire, which has a tremendous amount to see.
Fine scenery, historic buildings (including churches), hill walks, waterside dairy-
farms, a magnificent cathedral in Worcester itself, hop fields and orchards, woods,
and sights which include Elgar's birthplace (Broadheath), an outdoor museum of
salvaged ancient buildings (at Avoncroft), the Royal Worcester porcelain museum
and factory (bargains to be had!) and a variety of stately homes. River trips, the
Three Choirs festival, delightful villages and gardens add to the area's interest.

Readers' comments: Could not praise more. Made most welcome. Extremely
comfortable. Beautiful surroundings. I will return.

Vicarage Hill, Mevagissey, Cornwall, PL26 6SZ Tel: 0726 842427
South of St Austell. Nearest main road: A390 from St Austell to Truro.

rear view

6 Bedrooms. £16–£20 (less for 7 nights half-board). Prices go up in March. Bargain breaks. Some have own bath/shower/toilet. Tea/coffee facilities. TV. Views of garden, country, sea. No smoking. Washing machine on request.
Dinner. A la carte or £11 for 4 courses (with choices) and coffee, at 7 or 7.30pm. Non-residents not admitted. Vegetarian or special diets if ordered. Wine can be ordered. No smoking. **Light suppers** sometimes.
1 Sitting-room. With open fire, central heating, record-player. Bar. No smoking. Heated sun-room.
Large garden
Closed from November to February inclusive.

Perched on a hillside above this very popular resort is a handsome 18th-century house (once a vicarage), looking south across garden and countryside towards the sea. A great picture-window in the large sitting-room makes the most of this view.

In the dining-room, dinner is served by candlelight, with Doulton daisy plates on green cloths that match the green carpet. Diana Owen's dinners are based on the best of traditional English cookery – mackerel pâté or chicken-and-leek soup might be followed by steak pie or sole stuffed with prawns. After a pudding such as chocolate fudge cake, petits fours will be served with the coffee.

I particularly liked the king-sized brass bed with crochet cover in one of the bedrooms, and the huge size of the carpeted bathroom.

At the end of June, the annual 'Mevagissey feast' week takes place here, with the Cornish floral dance through the streets. Mevagissey is still a fishing harbour though tourist shops predominate. There are a small museum of model railways, an aquarium, and shark-fishing trips. The nearest sandy beach is at Porthpean.

Readers' comments: Charming hosts who do everything possible to make your holiday a time to remember. Delighted; have booked again. Excellent value. Very friendly. Excellent food.

In Mevagissey itself, up a steep lane is
★ **ANCHOR COTTAGE,** Cliff Street (tel: 0726 842089). A 200-year-old fisherman's cottage, it is only a minute from the harbour which tends to be packed with tourists on summer days and therefore best enjoyed in the evening (Cliff Street itself is peaceful). Chrissie Stephenson's William Morris fabrics contrast with the slate walls and floor; the little dining-room overlooks a flowery courtyard. (Light suppers if ordered.) From £11 to £12.

Readers' comments: Very comfortable, well furnished and as good as any place we have found.

1 Bedroom. £13.50. Tea/coffee facilities. TV. View of garden. No smoking. Washing machine on request.
Dinner. £7.50 for 2 courses, wine and coffee, at 7pm. Non-residents not admitted. No smoking.
2 Sitting-rooms. With open fire, central heating, TV, piano, record-player. No smoking.
Small garden

'To vie with all the beaux and belles,
Away they whip to Hornsey Wells.'

So ran a jingle written in 1814 when there was a fashionable spa on the heights here, previously a holy well to which pilgrims came. It gave its name, 'moss well', to Muswell Hill, on the summit of which is now a 500-acre park with stupendous views: a site which has no equal around London. Here, in 1873, was built the great 'people's palace' (from which the first television broadcasts went out, in 1936): Alexandra Palace. Twice burnt down and rebuilt, it is still well worth a visit even when there are no special exhibitions, antiques fairs or concerts; or, perhaps for a drink in the Egyptian palm court where cool fountains play under the soaring glass roof, and to enjoy the grounds.

At the foot of the hill – now far from fashionable – are streets of terraced houses that grew up in the 1890s; among them the home of Patrick and Susie Power, who have transformed their rooms, retaining pretty iron fireplaces, decorative plasterwork and brass door-fittings, but stripping the panelled pine and creating light colour schemes (pale apricot walls and soft blue armchairs, for instance).

Meals are served in a dining-kitchen on Spode bluebird china at a round table surrounded by rush chairs: the old floor-tiles of terracotta and buff were salvaged in Norfolk, curtains and wall-frieze are of a stencilled flowery pattern. French doors open onto a narrow but secluded garden (where dinner is sometimes taken – typically, chicken in cream-and-tarragon sauce followed by lemon syllabub; wine included).

The simply furnished bedroom overlooks the garden; there is a fine lemon-yellow sitting-room with antiques on the same floor, and a very pretty bathroom.

By bus and Underground, central London is 40 minutes away.

When Middle House has no vacancy, visitors can be accommodated at the next house but one, which is very attractively furnished with antiques; the spacious bedroom here has a polished floor and Chinese rugs and the bathroom includes a Jacuzzi as well as bidet. Meals may be taken at Middle House.

Susie also runs a booking service for a few other houses elsewhere in London **(exclusively for SOTBT readers).**

THE MILL

CDH

Mungrisdale, Cumbria CA11 0XR   Tel: 07687 79659
West of Penrith. Nearest main road: A66 from Keswick to Penrith.

9 Bedrooms. £30 including dinner (less for 5 nights). Prices go up in March. Most have own bath/shower/toilet. Tea/coffee facilities. TV. Views of garden, country, river. Washing machine on request.
Dinner. 5 courses (with choices) and coffee, at 7pm. Vegetarian or special diets if ordered. Wine can be ordered. No smoking.
Light suppers sometimes, if ordered.
2 Sitting-rooms. With open fire, central heating, TV. Snooker. Table tennis.
Large garden
Closed from November to January inclusive.

It is little more than 20 years since the watermill in this Lake District valley stopped working. By the old stone building which used to house the saw which it powered is the sawyer's cottage, now a private hotel. It is a peaceful spot, with little more than the sound of the River Glenderamackin rushing down its rocky bed.

The Mill (which is next to, but not connected with, the Mill Inn) is a simple white house with moss on the slate roof and a small conservatory, facing a stone terrace and a lawn with seats by the water's edge. Eleanor and Richard Quinlan came here after years in big hotel management, having fallen for the place when they stayed as guests. Their aim is to give the polished attention to detail expected in a big establishment, combined with a less impersonal atmosphere. So Richard looks after the 'front-of-house' and the wines (on which he is an expert), while Eleanor exercises her talent for cooking. She has found sources of ingredients not usually associated with the Lake District, which explains the presence on the menu of such things as stuffed vine leaves, as well as excellent home-made soups accompanied by fresh soda bread (the last a fixture by popular demand). The main course might be quail with orange, brandy and thyme; or roast beef with mustard puddings and claret gravy. There are four or five sweets on the trolley, and cheese.

The main sitting-room is pretty (the stone surround to the log fire bears the date 1651), and there is a small TV room with well filled bookshelves. In the dining-room each small oak table has blue linen napkins, willow-pattern china, candles and a nosegay. Bedrooms are trim and simple, with restful colours.

Mungrisdale itself is a tiny village sheltered within a setting of blue-grey crags and slopes, and well placed for excursions to all parts of Cumbria. Close by are plenty of good walks (and even six-year-olds can take the fells in their stride for an hour or two, when not paddling in the stream). Castlerigg prehistoric stone circle is also nearby.

A great variety of places can be reached from here. Some people go trout-fishing, some watch the hang-gliders, some explore the strange rock formations.

Readers' comments: Beautiful, quiet, excellent food. Service attentive and friendly.

MILL HAY HOUSE

C PT X

Snowshill Road, Broadway, Worcestershire, WR12 7JS   Tel: 0386 852498
Nearest main road: A44 from Worcester towards Oxford.

4 Bedrooms. £17.50–£30 (less for 3 nights). Some have own bath/shower. Tea/coffee facilities. Views of garden, country. Balcony. No smoking. Washing machine on request.

2 Sitting-rooms. With open fire, central heating, TV.
Large garden
Closed in January and February.

Picturesque Broadway, now world-famous, can get unpleasantly crowded with tourists – but Mill Hay House, in the oldest part, lies well away from all that, a very lovely house of Cotswold stone with a mossy roof and leaded windows. At the front is a formal garden of rosebeds and clipped yews; at the back, terraced lawns are surrounded by flowering shrubs, more roses and yew hedges, and a rock garden through which a tiny rivulet trickles down to where an old watermill still stands, its great wheel spotlit at night. From some of the yews a bower has been created, sheltering a seat.

Not only is the garden, with its millpond, quite exceptional but the building too is very special. To the stone part, brick additions were made in Queen Anne's reign; there are stone-mullioned windows, and curious carved heads built in here and there.

The furnishings are of the same high order – I was very pleased to find that there is a *single* four-poster (18th-century) in one of the rooms, since singles often get the most meagre rooms. One bedroom (with king-size bed) has a view of the mill and garden. Others (one with four-poster and balcony) overlook the rose garden and pond. There is a separate family suite with two rooms and its own bathroom. Room prices vary a good deal.

Bed-and-breakfast only (served by a housekeeper); for dinner, the Snowshill Arms is recommended.

The owner, Hans Will, also owns nearby Broadway Tower and its surrounding country park. From the top of this 18th-century folly there are fine views and inside is a museum, including displays about William Morris who once lived in the tower. In the park (famous for spring wildflowers and autumn colours) are a barbecue, with meat on sale, wildlife trails, and animals for the children as well as an imaginative play centre. It's worth a whole day for the family.

Not only is there the whole of the Cotswold area to explore, but three of England's most popular tourist cities or towns are equidistant – Stratford-upon-Avon, Oxford and Cheltenham, their environs all described elsewhere.

Readers' comments: Beautiful building, exquisite garden. A real find, most comfortable.

188

MILLSIDE COTTAGE   **C D PT X**
9 Mill Street, Houghton, Cambridgeshire, PE17 2AZ   Tel: 0480 64456
South-east of Huntingdon. Nearest main road: A1123 from Huntingdon to
St Ives.

7 Bedrooms. £14–£15 (less for 7 nights). Prices go up in April. Bargain breaks. Some have own bath/shower/toilet. Tea/coffee facilities. TV. Washing machine on request. **Dinner.** £6 for 2 courses and coffee, at 6.30pm. Vegetarian or special diets if ordered. Wine can be ordered or brought in. No smoking. **Light suppers** if ordered.
1 Sitting-room. With open fire, central heating, TV, piano, record-player.
Small garden

Unlike much of the county, this area has hills (the Huntingdonshire Wolds) through which the River Ouse has cut its way, creating quite dramatic scenery: in fact, Houghton (=Hoh Ton) is Saxon for hillfoot farm. It is a pretty village which attracts numbers of visitors in midsummer, particularly when the massive 17th-century watermill (National Trust) is grinding wheat into flour (there has been a mill on the Ouse here for over a thousand years). One can cross the river by a footbridge, lingering to watch cabin-cruisers make their way through the lock below, or stroll along the riverside path, or hire a boat. And the village itself is worth exploring for it has a number of old and picturesque houses, some half-timbered and thatched. From Hartford Marina people can cruise to Bedford in one direction and Ely in the other, or even Cambridge.

Millside Cottage was a Victorian public house (once named the Brown Teapot) before conversion to a guest-house: unassuming in style, but spick and span. Bedrooms are neat, furnished in pale colours, with sprigged or flowery duvets. You can have a separate but spacious ground-floor room opening onto the garden (which has tables for teas), or stay in the house. There is a games room in addition to the sitting-room, and a dining-room where Pam Hadley serves homely (and inexpensive) meals such as roasts and fruit pies.

The former county of Huntingdonshire prospered when the River Ouse was a busy thoroughfare through it. On it stands St Neots, with a number of old inns to serve travellers by river or road. Buckden has the remains of an episcopal palace where once Henry VIII imprisoned Catherine of Aragon. On the other side of Grafham Water (a landscaped reservoir with water sports and nature trail) is Kimbolton which has handsome 18th-century houses along its broad main street and (another prison for Catherine, until her death) a Tudor castle.

All around are the winding waterways of the River Ouse and its tributaries, and the ruler-straight ditches which drain the fens. Seek out the Chinese Bridge at Godmanchester, the thatched houses of Hemingford Abbots, a moated Norman manor house on the river at Hemingford Grey, and the small town of St Ives with lovely views from the quay or from the riverside terrace of the Dolphin Hotel.

It is also worth finding Little Gidding, a remote 17th-century settlement where a London financier started a community devoted to meditation; T. S. Eliot wrote a poem about it and it continues to this day. The tiny church has a particularly tranquil ambience. Eastward lies Ramsey, with abbey ruins (NT) that include a museum of rural life.

189

MILNE HOUSE
C(5) **PT S X**

Millers Dale, Derbyshire, SK17 8SN   Tel: 0298 871832
East of Buxton. Nearest main road: A6 from Bakewell to Buxton.

6 Bedrooms. £10–£14. Tea/coffee facilities. TV. Views of garden, country, river. No smoking.
Dinner. £8.50 for 3 courses and coffee, at 7pm. Vegetarian or special diets if ordered. Wine can be ordered. No smoking. **Light suppers** if ordered.
1 Sitting-room. With open fire, central heating, TV. Bar.
Small garden

Soon after the watermill here ceased to function, Nick and Fran Davidson moved in, converting it into a home for themselves and for their business: from this out-of-the-way corner of England they run the world's largest supplier of specialist tools and materials for hand craftsmen in wood. Just across the little road is this pale stone house, clematis rambling up its walls, where the mill-owner once lived – now providing separate accommodation for visitors. (Some of these come to attend the two-day courses in wood-turning run at Milne House for beginners who go home with at least five small items completed in that period. There are other courses for experts.)

The visitors' rooms are white-walled and simply but pleasantly furnished. A family room is conveniently situated on the ground floor, and outside is a small paved terrace (racks of timber from all over the world behind it) on which to sit and enjoy the view of wooded hills opposite and the sound of water.

A local lady comes in to cook dinner (typically, this might consist of home-made soup, beef bourguignonne and trifle). Otherwise, visitors go to any of several good eating-places nearby.

They are welcome to go through the mill (its former wheelroom now displays woodware and woodworking supplies) to the very pretty garden beside the river, great crags rising up on the opposite bank.

Mid-Derbyshire is famous for its dales (river valleys) among wooded peaks: those of the rivers Dove, Noe and Derwent in particular. Wildlife, historic buildings, archaeological remains and old customs survive the years largely unchanged.

This is a limestone area, dotted with pure springs around which small spas were built (Matlock and Buxton, for instance – the latter with some crescents like Bath) and caves (Matlock and Castleton). Places to visit include Ashbourne (markets, and a very fine 13th-century church with striking monuments); old Bakewell, of Bakewell pudding fame; Birchover village, surrounded by unusual rock formations; Crich – a collection of vintage trams (you can ride in a horse-drawn one); the gorge known as 'little Switzerland', through which the Dove flows – Izaak Walton fished here; Matlock, with dramatic crags – a cable-car will take you to the Heights of Abraham.

Haddon Hall is near Rowsley, a moorland walking centre. Historic stone towns include Wirksworth (of *Adam Bede* fame) and hilly Youlgreave.

Readers' comments: Warm welcome. Good value.

190

★ MILTON FARM

C S

East Knoyle, Wiltshire, SP3 6BG   Tel: 074783 247
North of Shaftesbury (Dorset). Nearest main road: A350 from Shaftesbury to
Warminster.

2 Bedrooms. £16.50–£18 (less for 2 nights).
Prices go up in July. Bargain breaks. Both
have own bath/shower. Tea/coffee facilities.
TV. Views of garden, country. Washing
machine on request.
Dinner. £11.50 for 3 courses (with choices)
and coffee, at 7pm. Vegetarian or special
diets if ordered. Wine can be ordered or
brought in. **Light suppers** sometimes.
1 Sitting/dining-room. With open fire,
central heating.
Large garden. Heated swimming-pool.

This is a truly picturebook farmhouse – a stone-flagged floor in the entrance hall,
glimpse of a kitchen with pine table and a gun-case beside the gleaming Aga,
narrow oak staircase. In the sitting-room, which has a boarded ceiling, logs hiss
gently on the stone hearth. There are old oak furniture, deep chairs, silver and
flowers everywhere (including the bedrooms).

The Hydes removed a lot of later accretions to reveal the original beams in this
mainly Queen Anne house, and then added comfortable furniture and elegant
fabrics (such as Sanderson's 'Country Trail'). Janice Hyde serves candlelit dinners
– she is a superb cook – which consist of interesting dishes using local produce.
One example: onion quiche, followed by a huge trout from the River Nadder
(stuffed with almonds, mushrooms, lemon and I-know-not-what) and then the
lightest of mousses. Clotted cream, milk and butter are from the farm's cows;
pheasant, hare and rabbits are local. Her breakfasts are equally excellent.

Outside is a paved area with chairs facing a view of the hills, and total silence.

East Knoyle is a tiny old village with just one claim to fame: Christopher Wren
was born there (his father was rector). So was Edward Strong, who became Wren's
master mason and worked on St Paul's. In 1674, Strong built the cottage opposite,
and possibly parts of Milton Farm too. Janice Hyde can sometimes show visitors a
fascinating scrapbook of village history compiled by the local Women's Institute,
including the memories of the local blacksmith and of the postman who used to
deliver the letters on horseback. Every summer, there is a music festival in two
local castles. Just wandering around here is a pleasure in itself, enjoying willows or
magnolias or buttercups, and details like the old stone troughs or a well, and
looking for the Victorian 'bun' penny set in the wall of Penny Cottage or the
fire-bell on Bell Cottage.

There are views over the Blackmoor Vale, a windmill, bluebell woods, and the
Seymour Arms where Jane Seymour once lived.

Salisbury and Wilton House lie in one direction and in the other the ancient,
cobbled, hilltop town of Shaftesbury, followed by Sherborne – one of England's
jewels, and much underrated. It has two castles, a golden abbey, a quaint
museum, and a nearby butterfly and silkworm centre in a historic house.

Readers' comments: Janice Hyde is a delight; countryside and house are beautiful.
Delicious cooking. Very welcoming; delicious dinner; very comfortable. Welcoming and comfortable. Excellent service. Welcoming; superb cooking. Splendid
bedroom, most enjoyable dinners.

191

★ **MONAUGHTY POETH**   C(7) **D PT**
Llanfair-Waterdine, Shropshire, LD7 1TT   Tel: 0547 528348
North-west of Knighton (Powys, Wales). Nearest main road: A488 from
Knighton to Shrewsbury.

2 Bedrooms. £11.50–£13 (less for 3 nights).
Prices go up in April. One has own toilet.
Tea/coffee facilities. TV. Views of garden,
country, river. Washing machine on
request.
Light suppers if ordered. Vegetarian or
special diets. Wine can be brought in.

1 Sitting-room. With open fire, central heating, TV, piano.
Small garden
Closed from mid-December to mid-January.

Here, where the border between Wales and Shropshire runs, two sisters grew up
in the 1940s: Brenda and Jocelyn. Recently they wrote a nostalgic history of their
parish; and tiny though the village is (only nine houses, inn, church and post
office), it has a 'past' which runs to 52 pages.

The girls' great-grandfather built many of the farmhouses in the area and
worked on the huge Knucklas viaduct nearby, the stones of which came from a
demolished castle where Queen Guinevere is said to have lived. Now a scenic
railway takes tourists over its 13 arches. In the church are two unique features:
farm names on each pew (recognition that each had paid its tithe to the church),
and a barrel organ which plays hymns. Outside is 'the gypsy's grave' with an
inscription in Romany.

There are legends of the devil, memories of dancing in the village barn to the
music of gypsy fiddlers and of the tailor sitting cross-legged on his bench as he
stitched, wartime evacuees arriving (and prisoners-of-war too), and of 60,000
sheep annually thronging the lanes on their way to be auctioned at Knighton.

Monaughty Poeth itself has an 800-year-old history, for it once belonged to the
Cistercians of Abbey Cwmhir: Monaughty means 'monastery grange' and Poeth
'burnt' – the house burned down and was rebuilt in the 19th century. This is where
Jocelyn, now married to farmer Jim Williams, lives and welcomes visitors – while
her sister Brenda does likewise at **Bucknell House** (described elsewhere).

As to the accommodation at Monaughty, this is in very traditional farmhouse
style, with comfort the keynote, and in every room Jocelyn's pretty flower
arrangements. She serves only snack suppers (excellent salads and fruit pies), so
some visitors go to the picturesque old Red Lion for steaks, duck, etc.

Sitting in the garden afterwards, one looks across to the Williams' sheep hills
through which Offa's Dyke runs, and the only sound is the baaing of sheep.

Readers' comments (I have received an exceptional number): Treated like royalty!
Enjoyed every comfort. Warmest of welcomes. Large, pretty bedroom and lovely
view. Wonderful concern for her guests. Attractive accommodation. Extremely
friendly. Idyllic location. Charming and unassuming people.

MOORLANDS

Levisham, North Yorkshire, YO18 7NL   Tel: 0751 60229
North-east of Pickering. Nearest main road: A169 from Pickering to Whitby.

rear view

5 Bedrooms. £17. Bargain breaks. All have own bath/shower/toilet. Tea/coffee facilities. TV. Views of garden, country. No smoking. Washing machine on request.
Dinner. A la carte or £7.50 for 4 courses and coffee, at 6.30pm. Non-residents not admitted. Vegetarian or special diets if ordered. Wine can be ordered. No smoking.
2 Sitting-rooms. With open fire, central heating, TV. No smoking.
Large garden
Closed from November to March inclusive.

Once a vicarage, this is now a comfortable guest-house run by John and Rita Bean. Built in 1906 (the year when Galsworthy's *Man of Property* was published) the house is redolent of the secure and prosperous Edwardian era, with such handsome details as the mahogany staircase and galleried landing above. I particularly liked bedroom no. 3 which has windows on two sides to make the most of the fine views (the house is perched high up above a valley).

Outside are terraced gardens with rhododendrons and a putting green: they were laid out by Italian landscape gardeners brought here specially when the house was built. In a part that has deliberately been left natural, foxes and badgers can sometimes be spotted; and from the terrace one can see right across to the Yorkshire Wolds.

Rita's cooking is traditionally English – joints, pies, etc. She uses vegetables from the garden, fish fresh from Whitby and Lockton-reared meats. Afterwards, if the evening is chilly, guests relax by a crackling log fire in the sitting-room, or, if sunny, take their coffee in the garden.

Levisham is a particularly peaceful moorland village, hardly altered by time and right within the North Yorkshire Moors National Park. It has a station on the celebrated Moors Steam Railway; and from Moorlands' gate escorted horse-riders set off into the wilds. It is easy to get from here to the 'heritage' coast in one direction and the historic city of York in the other.

Well worth visiting in the vicinity are such sights as the Beck Isle Museum of Rural Life, in one of Pickering's fine 18th-century houses (in its seventeen rooms are old village shops reconstructed, a Victorian photography room, and agricultural exhibits); Eden Farm (a working farm with walks around it, a display explaining farm work, animals and a barn tea-room); the Ryedale Folk Museum; many abbey and castle ruins; the Yorkshire Museum of Farming; palatial Castle Howard and its art treasures; and many other activities and places described in a holiday information pack obtainable from Ryedale House (in Malton).

The limestone hills of the moors (where Swaledale and Blackface sheep wander) sweep down to the fertile Vale of Pickering and Vale of York throughout which fields of cereals or livestock predominate. Villages become colourful with flowers in spring (Farndale is famous for its wild daffodils), and the fields in summer when rapeseed is in bright yellow flower and wheat or oats are ripening to shades of gold.

Readers' comments: Very comfortable and welcoming.

193

MORAR FARM
C(6) PT

Weald Street, Bampton, Oxfordshire, OX8 2HL   Tel: 0993 850162
(Telex: 93343, Morar)
West of Oxford. Nearest main road: A4095 from Witney to Faringdon.

3 Bedrooms. £14.20–£15.30 (less for 7 nights). Bargain breaks. Tea/coffee facilities. TV. Views of garden, country. No smoking. Washing machine on request.
Dinner. £11.50 for 4 courses and coffee, at 6.30pm. Non-residents not admitted. Vegetarian or special diets if ordered. Wine can be ordered. No smoking.
1 Sitting-room. With open fire, central heating, TV, piano. No smoking.
Large garden
Closed in November.

This modern stone house, comfortable and trim, stands in an attractive garden; but what makes it a particularly nice place at which to stay is the personality of its owners. Janet and Terry Rouse are a lively couple, numbering among their accomplishments Morris-dancing, bell-ringing, barn-dancing and spinning (their pet sheep provide the fleece); and they gladly involve their guests too. One reader described Morar as the best place he had ever stayed at, because of the helpful hospitality and excellent food.

Janet takes quite exceptional care of her visitors, with much attention to detail – for instance, two fresh towels are provided every day; there are unlimited fruit juices at breakfast and a wide range of home-made preserves, as well as help-yourself strawberries and raspberries or figs, stewed fruits etc.; she does washing free for visitors who stay two weeks; and has plenty of maps on loan, fills vacuum flasks free, and gives refrigerator space to chill drinks visitors bring in.

For dinner Janet may, during winter, serve a menu such as soup made from home-grown vegetables; their own beef with Yorkshire pudding and six vegetables including red cabbage cooked with honey and juniper berries; Bakewell pudding and cream; a wide choice of cheeses and fruit. (In summer most visitors eat at the Clanfield Tavern.) Winter breaks here are 4 nights for the price of 3.

Bampton, a pretty village, is famous for its spring festival of Morris dancers when the village children all make wildflower garlands. It is well placed to visit Oxford, the Cotswold villages, Cheltenham, Blenheim Palace and gardens, Bladon (Churchill's grave), Cirencester (Roman museum), Avebury stone circle, and the Berkshire Downs. There's a wildlife park, rare farm breeds centre, arboretum, trout farm, restored watermill and farm museum all within easy reach. For garden-lovers, Pusey, Waterperry and the botanic gardens in Oxford are of particular interest.

To the attractions of Oxford's colleges, churches, Ashmolean and other museums, is now added 'The Oxford Story' which recreates the city's history with audio-visual effects.

Historic Abingdon is well worth visiting (you can take a boat from here to Oxford) and so is ancient Dorchester – both have abbey churches. Didcot has a celebrated railway centre, Wallington a castle, and Steventon a great house designed by Inigo Jones, Milton Manor: there is a lake in its grounds. Venn watermill at Garford is occasionally open on Sundays.

Readers' comments: Excellent!

194

MULBERRY HALL

Burstall, Suffolk, IP8 3DP   Tel: 047387 348
West of Ipswich. Nearest main road: A1071 from Ipswich towards Sudbury.

3 Bedrooms. £15 (less for 2 nights). Bargain breaks. Views of garden, country. No smoking. Washing machine on request.
Dinner. £11 for 3 courses (with choices) and coffee, at 7.45pm. Non-residents not admitted. Vegetarian or special diets if ordered. Wine can be brought in. **Light suppers** if ordered.
1 Sitting-room. With open fire, central heating, TV, piano, record-player.
Large garden

Cardinal Wolsey owned this house in 1523. Son of an Ipswich butcher, he had had a meteoric rise under Henry VIII (a cardinal and Lord Chancellor of England while still in his thirties) and he used his consequent wealth to commission fine properties and works of art. But in 1529, having failed Henry in the matter of divorcing Catherine of Aragon, he was stripped of nearly all his honours.

It is Henry VIII's colourful coat-of-arms which embellishes the inglenook fireplace in the big sitting-room – pink, beamed and with a grand piano. From this a winding stair leads up to well-equipped bedrooms. There is a small dining-room (green curtains and wallpaper in a sprigged Laura Ashley pattern, wheelback chairs round an oak table) where Penny Debenham serves such meals – to be ordered in advance – as trout mousse with a watercress purée; pork au poivre accompanied by dauphinoise potatoes, broccoli, courgettes and salad; fruit tartlets with elderflower cream; and cheeses. Breakfasts, too, are good, with such pleasant options as local apple-juice, chilled melon, home-baked bread and smoked haddock in addition to the usual bacon and eggs.

Outside is an exceptional garden – or series of gardens, enclosed within walls of yew or beech. Beyond a brick-paved terrace is a lawn with long lavender border, and a pergola leads past a rose garden to the tennis court with old hay-wain alongside.

Nearby Ipswich, a port even in Saxon times, has a plethora of mediaeval churches with fine monuments. The traffic in the town is heavy, so exploring is best done on foot. Wolsey made it a twin to Oxford, such was its reputation for learning – but only the gateway of his uncompleted college remains, near the quays where old inns and a classical Custom House survive. The town museum includes replicas of two local Saxon treasures now in the British Museum, the Sutton Hoo and Mildenhall finds; Christchurch Mansion (in a park) is a Tudor house with a collection of furniture and toys, as well as paintings by Constable and Gainsborough. Stroll down the Buttermarket to find the Ancient House, its façade covered in elaborate 17th-century plasterwork representing the (then) four continents: it is now a bookshop.

The surrounding scenery is of open farmland, dotted with particularly pretty villages.

Readers' comments: Beautiful house, outstanding food and service; will visit again. A lot of loving care. Bedrooms light and airy, extremely comfortable; excellent food, breakfast a highlight.

MUNK'S FARMHOUSE
Smarden, Kent, TN27 8PN   Tel: 023377 265
West of Ashford. Nearest main road: A274 from Maidstone to Tenterden.

3 Bedrooms. £15–£17 (less for 4 nights). Prices go up in March. Bargain breaks. Some have own bath/shower/toilet. Views of garden, country. No smoking.
Dinner. £12 for 3 courses and coffee, at 7.15pm. Non-residents not admitted. Vegetarian or special diets if ordered. Wine can be brought in. No smoking. **Light suppers** if ordered.
1 Sitting-room. With open fire, central heating.
Large garden

You had better behave yourself if you stay here for in the garden is a prison-cell. The old wood lock-up (double-walled and with tiny barred window), now a 'listed building', was moved here in 1850 from the village for, once the railway had been built, there was no longer a stream of drunk and brawling railway navvies needing to cool their heels in it.

The house itself has an even longer history. Weatherboarded in typically Kentish style, it was built nearly three centuries ago. Inside are beams, inglenook fireplaces, iron-latched doors, the original built-in cupboard and a very wide oak staircase: clearly the yeoman-farmer who originally lived here was a man of substance. Even the quarry tiles he laid were so large and thick that they are still as good as new. These are in the dining-room (formerly the kitchen) where guests now eat at a big refectory table. Josephine Scott serves such dinners (if these are ordered in advance) as corn-on-the-cob or melon, roast duck or whole plaice from Rye (in a creamy sauce), and gooseberry fool or raspberries with meringues.

There is a sitting-room with log fire and William Morris sofa, and pretty bedrooms with attractive 'Vanitory' units and sloping ceilings; the attic room has exposed rafters and good views.

In the garden is a large swimming-pool (a solar blanket keeps its temperature up to 70° or 80° in midsummer) where ducks gather to watch you swim.

Readers' comments: Really attractive and comfortable place, pretty garden, amiable hostess, excellent dinners.

The 15th-century **BELL INN** at Smarden (tel: 023377 283) has a façade of chequered brickwork overhung with scalloped tiles. Inside are Ian Turner's bars, two with inglenooks and all paved or brick-floored. Here one can eat very well, seated on oak settles under beams strung with hop-bines. Outdoors an iron spiral staircase, wreathed in honeysuckle, leads up to the bedrooms, still with the original board ceilings and white brick walls but immaculately furnished in soft colours. (No wash

basins.) Visitors are provided with the wherewithal to make their own continental breakfast. From £14 to £15.

NEW MOOR HOUSE   C D S

near Edlingham, Northumberland, NE66 2BT   Tel: 066574 638
South-west of Alnwick. On A697 from Morpeth to Wooler.

5 Bedrooms. £13.50–£14 (less for 7 nights). Prices go up in June. Bargain breaks.

One has own bath/shower/toilet. All have tea/coffee facilities. Views of country. No smoking.
Dinner. £7.50 for 3 courses (with choices) and coffee, at 7pm. Non-residents not admitted. Vegetarian or special diets if ordered. Wine can be brought in. No smoking. **Light suppers** only if ordered.
1 Sitting-room. With open fire, central heating, TV. No smoking.
Large garden
Closed from October to February inclusive.

Travelling north, one rounds a curve in the road and comes to a view of New Moor House, once a coaching inn. In dramatic scenery of moorland and forests, the house is set against a backdrop of the Cheviot Hills. It is bounded by Rimside Moor, once notorious for its highwaymen and subject of many songs and poems, notably the ballad of the 'Black Sow of Rimside and the Monk of Holy Island'.

When Hilary and Peter Harcourt-Brown took the house over, they refurbished it to its present comfortable standard, with antiques in keeping with the age of the house. One steps into a dining-room furnished with high-backed pews salvaged from a disused church. The beamed sitting-room, with cretonne armchairs and an open fire, is upstairs.

Hilary prepares the home-cooked meals in generous portions. A typical meal might be home-made soup, a roast with fresh vegetables, then apple pie with cream. The house has its own soft, filtered, spring water which makes a very good cup of tea. Hilary gives herself one evening off a week (Wednesday) but can recommend good restaurants in the area for dinner then.

Peter and Hilary, who breed prize-winning collies and Afghan hounds, are keen on accommodating visitors with dogs, if inoculated. (Their own dogs do not frequent the house.)

People who pause here for a night on the way to Scotland have sometimes got no further, for the area is so full of interest that one could easily spend a fortnight exploring it all. The best part of the Northumbrian coast is nearby, with its castles (Bamburgh, Dunstanburgh, Warkworth); its islands – the Farnes for seabirds, Lindisfarne for its ancient history, priory ruins and castle; and Craster where the kipper teas are so luscious that they stand comparison with treats like smoked salmon. You can find beaches with firm 'sugar' sand and rock-pools, or go on walks – strenuous or gentle – in, for instance, Coquetdale, the Ingram Valley and Langleeford or along clifftops. National Trust properties include Cragside (best at rhododendron time, early summer) and Wallington Hall (tapestries, dolls' houses and a lovely garden). Alnwick Castle, Brinkburn Priory, Chillingham's wild cattle or hang-gliders: take your pick!

At Cambo is a garden centre specializing in cottage-garden and windy-site plants.

Readers' comments: Most comfortable, delicious food. Warm welcome, comfortably furnished. Well ordered; they take pains to accommodate the varying whims of guests. Substantial servings.

★ **NEWBARN**   **C D S X**
Wards Lane, Wadhurst, East Sussex, TN5 6HP   Tel: 089288 2042
South-east of Tunbridge Wells (Kent). Nearest main road: A267 from
Tunbridge Wells to Heathfield.

5 Bedrooms. £17. Prices go up in April. Some have own bath/shower/toilet. Tea/coffee facilities. TV. Views of garden, country, lake. No smoking. Washing machine on request.
2 Sitting-rooms. With open fire, central heating, TV, piano, record-player. No smoking.
Large garden

Sitting on the brick terrace with the blue lake view below and hills beyond, I could have imagined I was in the Lake District – but this was Sussex, and London only an hour away. There was a solitary angler in a boat, rabbits and wagtails on the lawn – perfect peace!

In the 18th century this was a farmhouse, lattice-paned and tile-hung in traditional Sussex style. Indoors, knotty pine floorboards gleam with polish, there are low beams, and the wood-latched doors were specially made by a local joiner for Christopher and Pauline Willis, who took great care, when renovating the house, to ensure that every detail was in harmony.

Bedrooms are light and flowery, yellow and green, or pink and blue predominating. The sitting-room, which has an inglenook, is decorated in apricot and cream. There is a games room in one of the barns.

Only breakfast is served (with Pauline's preserves to follow – marmalade made with treacle, gooseberry jam with elderflowers, for instance) because the area is well supplied with good restaurants. Visitors are welcome, however, to bring in their own food and to use the Aga cooker.

The landscaped garden descends right to the edge of the lake, which is in fact man-made: Bewl Water reservoir. Around its perimeter and many inlets is a 15-mile footpath: there are boat cruises, a visitor centre, watersports, a wooden ark for children and picnic spots. Sometimes Morris dancing or crafts shows are to be seen. Birds from the nature reserve can be spotted. Bicycles for hire.

Bewl Water is on the Kent/Sussex border and there is so much of interest in this historic area that one could happily spend a week or two without going far afield. Beyond the reservoir is a cluster of interesting mansions. At Finchcocks, a Queen Anne house, is a collection of early pianos and other instruments which visitors can hear played. Scotney is a decorative, turreted castle with particularly lovely waterside gardens. Bayham Abbey's ruins are beautifully sited by a river. Sissinghurst has not only the Court but also Vita Sackville-West's gardens around its castle. There's a pinetum at Bedgebury, a great windmill at Cranbrook. Crittenden House is a mansion with outstanding gardens – Great Dixter, too.

Tunbridge Wells is the nearest major town, with true spa elegance, tempting shops in the Pantiles and elsewhere, curious 'twittens' (footpaths) twisting behind the backs of elegant houses; and, on its large common, strange rock formations that challenge the skills of even experienced climbers. Antique shops abound.

Readers' comments: Views and peace superb. A pleasure to stay in. Warm, comfortable and excellent decoration. Friendly and helpful. Outstanding.

NEWLANDS FARMHOUSE

Aston Magna, Gloucestershire, GL56 9QQ   Tel: 0608 50964
North of Moreton-in-Marsh. Nearest main road: A429 from Warwick to
Stow-on-the-Wold.

rear view

3 Bedrooms. £14–£15 (less for 2 nights). Prices go up in April. TV. Views of garden, country. No smoking. Washing machine on request.

1 Sitting-room. With central heating, TV. No smoking.
Large garden

The spacious and well kept rooms inside this Tudor house do justice to its handsome stone exterior, a feature of which is the big archway through which wagons entered when this was a farm.

The white hall has polished flagstones on the floor and a big dough-chest as old as the house; and off it is a very comfortable sitting-room (hung with rugby photos – Jim Hessel was president of the local club). Beamed bedrooms are roomy and the bathroom is huge, with handsome basin units. From stone-mullioned windows one can see the village and hills beyond. Everywhere are pot-plants and flowers.

Pat Hessel serves only breakfast, but collects menus of local eating-places for dinner – from the popular Bakers' Arms at Broad Campden, and the Crown Inn at Blockley, to Annie's Restaurant at Moreton-in-Marsh.

Moreton-in-Marsh is one of the Cotswolds' show towns: a wide street of handsome and historic houses, with many antique shops. All around are gently rounded hills and wooded valleys with bright streams, quiet villages of the famous Cotswold stone (don't miss Bourton-on-the-Water), the two Slaughters, Broadway, Bibury, Chipping Campden and Stow-on-the-Wold), rich farms with sheep grazing, and superlative churches and manor houses built on wealth created by the mediaeval wool trade and richly embellished. Garden-lovers enjoy Hidcote Manor and Kiftsgate in particular. Batsford is more than just a garden – it has one of the country's biggest collections of rare trees in its arboretum, oriental bronzes, and high views over the Evenlode Valley. There are displays of falconry, and 70 birds of prey on view in the 'hawk walk'. One of my favourite stately homes is near here – Jacobean Chastleton House, not too grand and with 17th-century topiary outside; and also a most unusual water garden in eastern style at Sezincote, a house designed like an Indian pavilion. The Wellington Gallery specializes in paintings and sculptures of aircraft. Pick-your-own fruit abounds in the Vale of Evesham, antique shops in the Cotswolds.

Readers' comments: Exceptionally friendly and welcoming. Very peaceful. Attractive and comfortable rooms. Most hospitable and helpful. Superb breakfasts. The house itself is a treasure. Everything was just super.

Montpellier Terrace, Cheltenham, Gloucestershire, GL50 1XA
Tel: 0242 579441
Nearest main road: A40 from Oxford to Gloucester.

8 **Bedrooms.** £17.50. Prices go up in April.
Some have own bath/shower/toilet. Tea/
coffee facilities. TV. Washing machine on
request.

In 1872, Edward Wilson was born here ('the brightest and jolliest of all our babies', his mother wrote), later to achieve fame after his death in the Antarctic on Scott's last expedition (1910). The town's museum has a whole room devoted to him, and on the Promenade is a statue of him sculpted by Scott's widow.

It is a town-centre house typical of Cheltenham's fine architecture. Built in 1830, it has the detailing which distinguishes that period: steps up to a handsome front door with pretty fanlight and columns at each side, decorative plasterwork on ceilings. Sally Rice-Evans' choice of furnishings and her colour schemes admirably complement all this. For instance, in the breakfast-room are Regency and country Chippendale chairs, and she uses shell pink and soft greens in many rooms – although one of the prettiest (and quietest, being at the back) has Jane Churchill bordered fabrics in powder-blue and white. Two bedrooms have sofas with elegant cushions: a useful feature because there is no sitting-room. One of these rooms is the best of all, a very spacious family suite in the basement. And the single room is just as attractive as the doubles. Among other thoughtful touches are bottles of spring water in each bedroom and freshly squeezed orange juice at breakfast. No dinners; but very close are a good wine bar (The Retreat), Morans and other restaurants.

At Cheltenham, Handel and Dr Johnson 'took the waters' in its early days as a spa. You can go to the grand Town Hall and there do likewise (ugh!) or else simply enjoy the architecture, mild climate, festivals of music and of literature, race course and shops. The parks, arcades and parades are made for leisurely strolling. And there are so many other things to see – such as the Dutch masters in the art gallery, Gustav Holst's birthplace (now a museum), the elegant Montpellier quarter where great caryatids – scantily draped ladies – adorn the façades, the 700-year-old rose window and the monuments in the old church, an excellent museum of local history and ecology (its Arts and Crafts Movement collection is of national importance), the Neptune fountain (surrounded by willows grown from cuttings of those that shade Napoleon's tomb on St Helena), a museum of costume and jewellery in the elegant Pittville Pump Rooms and a statue of Edward VII in plus-fours!

There is always something going on, from county cricket to vintage car rallies.

Readers' comments: Warm greeting. Beautifully furnished. The epitome of a good guest-house. Very comfortable rooms, a most fantastic breakfast. High quality and good value for money.

★ **THE NODES** C D H S

Alum Bay Old Road, Old Totland, Isle of Wight, PO39 0HZ
Tel: 0983 752859
South-west of Yarmouth. Nearest main road: A3054 from Yarmouth to
Freshwater.

11 Bedrooms. £14–£16. Prices go up in
July. Bargain breaks. Some have own bath/
shower/toilet. Tea/coffee facilities. TV.
Views of garden, country, sea. No smoking.
Washing machine on request.
Dinner. A la carte or £7.50 for 4 courses
(with choices) and coffee, at 6.30–7pm.
Vegetarian or special diets if ordered. Wine
can be ordered. No smoking. **Light suppers**
if ordered.
1 Sitting-room. With open fire, central heating, TV. No smoking. **Bar.**
Large garden

At the far west end of the island (with spectacular marine sunsets to enjoy after
dinner) is a handsome mid-Victorian mansion standing in its own grounds: it is
now a small hotel run by Kevin Harris, very suitable for family holidays.

Some of the bedrooms are in the original part of the house; while others (more
modern and compact; each with its own front door) line a courtyard at the back.
The one in the house that particularly appealed to me was the blue room, which
has a magnificent sea-captain's bed and a view of the Solent. The dining-room is
rustic in style: Italian pine and rush chairs, pink candles on chocolate or pink
tablecloths. In the courtyard bar, local real ale is served.

There are a number of choices at dinner – one might select, for example,
avocado with prawns, roast beef and hazelnut meringue. There is a long wine list.

The foothills of Tennyson Downs extend into the grounds (which include
lawns, a play area for children and a golf practice-net). Table tennis, badminton,
etc. available.

This end of the island and its superb coastline are unspoilt (much of it is
controlled by the National Trust): an area of pretty little villages, lanes and
country inns; with sandy beaches ideal for children. Visitors particularly enjoy the
Tennyson trail, Alum Bay, the Needles, Blackgang Chine and (further east)
Osborne House and Carisbrooke Castle.

Between the island and the mainland is the Solent, thronged with boats.

Readers' comments: Thoroughly enjoyed our stay; staff always smiling; Kevin
made us all feel like one big happy family. Peace and tranquillity. Thoroughly
enjoyed it; food excellent; staff could not do enough for us.

Also at this end of the island, and within two minutes of sand and sea, is
ROCKSTONE COTTAGE, Colwell
Bay, which Sheila Reason runs as an
immaculate and comfortable guest-
house with good home cooking. (Tel:
0983 753723.) From £16 to £18.

NORTH COURT

C D PT

Shorwell, Isle of Wight, PO30 3JG   Tel: 0983 740415
South-west of Newport. Nearest main road: A3055 from Totland to Ventnor.

3 Bedrooms. £13–£15.50 (less for 3 nights). All have own bath/toilet. Tea/coffee facilities. TV. Views of garden, country. Washing machine on request.
1 Sitting-room. With open fire, central heating, TV, piano.
Large garden
Closed in December and January.

Swinburne and his girl cousin used to play the organ that stands in the hall of this great 17th-century manor house – a big stone-flagged room with pale blue walls, logs piled high around the stove.

The house is now the home of John and Christine Harrison, portraits of whose ancestors hang on the walls of the large dining-room with mahogany tables and marble fireplace. The great staircase was reputedly designed by Grinling Gibbons, and nearly every room has handsome detailing from that period – arched or scallop-framed doorways, egg-and-dart mouldings, shuttered windows in thick stone walls. At the top of the house is an attic suite (and games room), very suitable for family use; but the prettiest bedroom is perhaps the blue-and-white one with bay window overlooking the tennis court.

Impressive though the house is, the really outstanding feature is the large and undulating garden with many plants of botanical interest. You can wander through woodlands or down terraces to a stream with water-plants, try to tell the time from a sundial in the knot garden, look down into the ancient bath-house, wander through arches of wisteria or lilac . . . As only breakfast is served, dinner for most people always involves a stroll through this lovely garden (opened to the public occasionally) to reach the nearby Crown Inn.

The island's coastline, its inland scenery and pretty villages appealed to the Victorians' love of the picturesque, and it was they who established it as an ideal holiday destination. Some feel that this has now ruined parts of the coast but, in a village such as this, one is well away from the summer crowds and yet so central that every part is within easy reach. Small though the island is, the scenery is extraordinarily varied – and at its best in spring or autumn, when visitors are few. You could stay a month and every day find a different 'sight' to visit, as varied as Carisbrooke Castle or Osborne House on the one hand and the ferny chines (ravines) or wildlife reserves, a working smithy or a museum of clocks on the other. Some of the least famous places are the most attractive – unspoilt villages such as Calbourne, Mottistone, Yaverland and Kingston, for instance. One of the nicest, old-fashioned resorts on the south coast is Ventnor and to the east of it lies picturesque little Bonchurch, complete with duck-pond; while on the St Lawrence side there stretches a 6-mile walk or drive among myrtles and ilex – the Undercliff, created when towering cliffs broke and slid down to the sea, a disastrous spectacle until nature moved in abundantly with self-seeded plants and trees. At the end of the Undercliff is a headland, St Catherine's Point, with lighthouse and far sea views.

202

NORTHLEIGH HOUSE

Fiveways Road, Hatton, Warwickshire, CV35 7HZ Tel: 0926 484203
North-west of Warwick. Nearest main road: A41 from Warwick to Solihull.

6 Bedrooms. £18–£20. All have own bath/shower/toilet. Tea/coffee facilities. Refrigerators and remote-control TV. Views of garden, country. No smoking. Washing machine on request.
Dinner. £13.50 for 3 courses (with choices) and coffee, at times to suit guests. Non-residents not admitted. Vegetarian or special diets if ordered. Wine can be brought in. No smoking. **Light suppers** if ordered.
1 Sitting-room. With central heating, TV. No smoking.
Small garden

A former dress designer, Sylvia Fenwick – a vivacious personality – has turned her creative talents to decorating every bedroom with elegance – each is different, each memorable, and many verge on the luxurious (for instance, double rooms have two washbasins). They are all very well equipped and heated.

The L-shaped blue suite (with kitchenette in cupboard) has a sofa, bamboo tables and a carved bed in a silk-curtained alcove. There's a huge poppy room, with white furniture, in which the pale green leafy wallpaper is matched by the carpet. Another room, Victorian and frilly in style, has a cocoa-and-white colour scheme; while yet another (the least expensive) is in Chinese style. On two sides of the big sitting-room are garden views; the room has comfortable furniture, pleasant colours and an ornate little wood-burner.

Sylvia serves supper trays, or dinners (by arrangement) at which you might get something like avocado salad, pork chops in a sauce of mustard, sugar and almonds – served with five vegetables; and a rich strawberry trifle ('I go mad with the cream!'). But she also provides guests with a map showing a dozen local inns that do good food. Because she keeps rare breeds of sheep and poultry, her own produce sometimes features in these meals.

Rural quiet surrounds the house – and yet it is only a few miles from Birmingham's National Exhibition Centre and international airport; the National Agricultural Centre; and the bustling towns of Warwick and Coventry.

Readers of Edith Holden's *Country Diary of an Edwardian Lady* will be familiar with a number of place-names around here. Knowle, a historic village on a hill, with half-timbered houses. Packwood House (NT) which has a lovely garden, conical yews representing Christ and the disciples (and fine furniture inside): Edith did many sketches here. Mediaeval Baddesley Clinton is moated.

Readers' comments: Very superior, one of the best I have found, bedrooms spacious and breakfasts excellent. First class!

NORWOOD FARM

Hiscott, Devon, EX31 3JS   Tel: 027185 260

South of Barnstaple. Nearest main road: A377 from Barnstaple to Exeter.

3 Bedrooms. £17. All have own shower/toilet. Tea/coffee facilities. Views of garden, country. No smoking. Washing machine on request.
Dinner. £10 for 4 courses (with choices) and coffee, at 7pm. Wine can be brought in. No smoking.

2 Sitting-rooms. With open fire, central heating. No smoking.
Large garden
Closed from November to January inclusive.

This is a model of what a farm holiday should be. At the heart of a hundred acres of pasture for cows (horses and other animals are kept too) is a 17th-century house with beams, inglenook and log stove on a slate hearth, panelled doors of pine, and furnishings chosen well for this setting. There are sofas of buttoned brocade in the sitting-room, a brass bed prettily draped, Laura Ashley and other good fabrics, dried-flower arrangements and on the walls Linda Richard's own accomplished paintings of local scenes. Her husband was born in this house, where three generations of Richards have farmed.

For dinner, Linda serves such meals as avocado pear, pork and apples cooked in Devon cider, fruit pie with clotted cream, and cheeses – after which (in what was once the dairy) guests relax in front of television (with video), with a book by the fire, in a Victorian conservatory, in chairs on the south-facing terrace, or strolling in Norwood's own woodlands.

Norwood is only a few miles from ancient Barnstaple which, in addition to the centuries-old attractions of its Pannier Market on Tuesdays and Fridays, has plenty of modern shops, an antiques bazaar, and a very big swimming-pool in its leisure centre. Many 18th-century buildings and a colonnaded walk survive in the centre; there is a museum of local history in a 14th-century chapel; and the bridge of 16 arches dates from the 13th century. Recent tourist attractions include Jungleland (exotic plants), a farm park at Landkey, a sheepskin tannery with workshop tours at Pilton Causeway, and the Cobbaton collection of vehicles and other relics from the Second World War.

Good beaches lie beyond Barnstaple, at Woolacombe, Saunton and Croyde which overlook Barnstaple Bay and have National Trust landscape behind them. In this direction, too, are the wildflowers of Braunton Burrows, a nature reserve with sand dunes; and one of Devon's few very fine churches, at Braunton (which also has an excellent gallery of crafts and paintings with wholefood restaurant). Along this coast are dramatic cliffs and waterfalls. Eastward lies Exmoor.

Readers' comments: Comfortably furnished; attractive dinner – generous and healthy food.

OLD BAKEHOUSE

33–35 High Street, Little Walsingham, Norfolk, NR22 6BZ
Tel: 0328 820454
North of Fakenham. Nearest main road: A148 from Cromer to King's Lynn.

3 Bedrooms. £15–£17.50. Some have own shower/toilet. Tea/coffee facilities. Views of garden, country.
Dinner. A la carte (Tuesdays to Sundays); or £10.50 for 3 courses (with choices) and coffee, at 7pm if pre-booked (Tuesdays to Fridays). Vegetarian or special diets if ordered. Wine can be ordered. Bar.

Above a restaurant renowned for good food are excellent bedrooms, some very secluded at the back (with views of a paved garden and ancient cottages that have higgledy-piggledy pantiled roofs and flint walls).

From 1550 until recent times, part of this house was a bakery and the old ovens are still to be seen. Above an ancient cellar bar is a large, lofty dining-room – in the 18th century it was a corn exchange. There is a great brick fireplace at one end, and huge iron-hinged doors. When Chris and Helen Padley took over, they painted the walls pale pink and furnished the room with pine and rush furniture. Here they serve such delectable table d'hôte meals as fresh peaches baked with cheese and herbs (for a starter), banana-stuffed chicken with a mild curry-and-almond sauce, and ice-cream coffee-cake; with a wider à la carte choice too.

The bedrooms are very pleasantly furnished in pale colours such as mushroom and beige, with pine furniture, pot-plants and bowls of pot-pourri; excellent shower rooms.

Little Walsingham is full of mediaeval charm: few villages are so well preserved. It was a pilgrims' shrine before the Norman Conquest – and still is (both Catholics and Protestants come here). Really big pilgrimages fill the village three times a year, but at other times it is peaceful. Walsingham Abbey's riverside grounds are open at certain times, there is an ancient Francisan friary, a museum of bygones, and a light railway which children enjoy. The sea shore is near, and also a great many stately homes and impressive churches for which Norfolk is famous. Chris Padley is an enthusiastic birdwatcher and this is an area of outstanding interest for its birds.

If these activities are not enough, there is plenty more to see and do in north Norfolk – such as the Sea Life Centre at Hunstanton which takes you through an underwater tunnel (there's another such at Great Yarmouth), or the orchid centre at Terrington St Clement. Fine gardens are numerous – and varied: Alby Gardens, Erpingham, has a bee garden with observation hive; Congham Hall, Grimston – herbs; Gooderstone – water gardens; Kelly's at Holt – wild fowl and other birds too; Mannington Hall, for roses, moat and lake; The Pleasaunce near Cromer, designed by Gertrude Jekyll; and Wolterton Hall's grounds.

Readers' comments: Gourmet food; friendly and efficient.

OLD BAKERY

Milton Abbas, Dorset, DT11 0BW   Tel: 0258 880327
South-west of Blandford Forum. Nearest main road: A354 from Blandford to
Dorchester.

C(12) **D S**

5 Bedrooms. £12–£17 (less for 7 nights).
Prices go up in April. Bargain breaks. Some
have own bath/shower/toilet. Tea/coffee
facilities. Views of garden, country.
2 Sitting-rooms. With open fire, central
heating, TV, piano, record-player.
Large garden and grounds

Milton Abbas looks almost too good to be true, as if it had been created specially
for a picture on a chocolate-box. Indeed, it is a special creation; for in the 18th
century it was laid out as a 'model village' when the Earl of Dorchester razed a
nearby mediaeval settlement to build himself a mansion (Milton Abbey) and
resited its inhabitants here. The broad village street, grass-verged, slopes steeply
down, lined all the way with trim white-and-thatch cottages.

One of these is the Old Bakery: the huge ovens are still there, in a vast
sitting-room where guests now relax. Margaret Penny has a decorative touch, so all
the bedrooms (and even the toilet) are attractive. There are small but pretty single
rooms – pink and lacy. She has found interesting wallpapers – poppies for one
room, wildflowers in another, navy-and-white for a third – to complement twirly
cane bedheads, board doors, neat pine cupboards within which basin and shower
are concealed in one room, and the antiques that feature in every room. (A suite
with its own sitting-room also has its own entrance.) Behind the house are woods,
pasture and stables for visitors who bring horses – this is a great area for riding and
walking. There is an inn nearby for evening meals or visitors can use the kitchen to
prepare snack suppers.

Some of Milton Abbey (now a school) can be visited, notably the huge chapel
and its striking monuments: part of a 15th-century church of cathedral-like
proportions which the Earl retained when he demolished most of the original
monastery to make his great house. The Abbey is celebrated for its music weeks.
The countryside all round is wholly unspoilt and tranquil, part of Hardy's Wessex.

Across the pretty Piddle Valley, is
Cerne Abbas and, in Duck Street,
SOUND O' WATER (tel: 030 03435),
a former inn which Jean and Doug
Simmonds have modernized to provide
a comfortable guest-house. Some
rooms are in an annexe opening onto a
pretty garden that wanders down to the
winding River Cerne. B & b only; all
Cerne's inns do good food. Cerne is a
lovely village with the famous giant on
its hillside. From £14 to £16.

OLD BOROUGH HOUSE

Bossiney, Cornwall, PL34 0AY Tel: 0840 770475
South of Bude. Nearest main road: A39 from Bude to Wadebridge.

5 Bedrooms. £11.50–£17 (less for 2 nights). Bargain breaks. Some have own bath/shower/toilet. Tea/coffee facilities. TV. Views of garden, country, sea.
Dinner. £8.50 for 4 courses and coffee, at 7pm. Non-residents not admitted. Vegetarian or special diets if ordered. Wine can be ordered. No smoking.
1 Sitting-room. With open fire, TV, record-player. Bar.
Small garden

1683 is carved on one wall of slate that came from England's largest quarry (at Delabole, near Camelford), a spectacular sight, which has been getting bigger and bigger since Tudor times. You are unlikely ever to see a bigger hole!

Once the house was the residence of mayors of Bossiney (later, of J. B. Priestley) and it is full of character. Small windows are set into the thick walls and there are low beams, steps up and down twisting corridors, a log stove in the sitting-room which has crimson velvet armchairs and chaise longue, and a bar in the roomy entrance hall. From the garden there is a sea-view, and at the front is the North Cornwall coastal road running through an area of outstanding natural beauty.

Christina Rayner serves such meals as tomato soup with cream, carbonnade of beef, crème brûlée and cheeses in a neat little dining-room overlooking the garden.

Just outside are reminders of Bossiney's past: an anvil from the former smithy, mounting-block for getting onto a horse, remains of the old prison and – just across the road – a mound on which a prehistoric fort once stood and from which Francis Drake used to make announcements when he was the town's MP. Legend has it that King Arthur's Round Table was buried under this mound – just one of the many Arthurian legends that abound in this area (Camelford was, some believe, Camelot). More realistic are accounts of how pilchards used to be laid out here to be salted and dried, and how slaves used to be auctioned. Probably there was smuggling too: there are caves at Bossiney Cove (today a safe spot for swimming).

Nearby Tintagel is a tourist honeypot. Visitors come mainly to see the ruined Norman castle high on a rocky promontory which juts out into the sea (reputedly where Arthur was born and had an earlier castle, but more certainly where there was once a Celtic monastery). From this romantic spot, a path leads down to a tunnel called 'Merlin's cave' where Arthur was supposed to have appeared.

Also in the village is 18th-century **ROSEBUD COTTAGE** (tel: 0840 770861), tucked into a quiet drive with a small, flowery garden around it. There are neat bedrooms, good bathroom and a small but comfortable sitting-room. In either the tiled hall or the little conservatory, Gill Walkley serves such meals as: home-made soup or quiche, a roast or casserole, French apple tart or lemon meringue pie, and

cheeses. Very good value. From £10.50 to £11.

OLD CUDWELLS BARN C

Lewes Road, Scaynes Hill, West Sussex, RH17 7NA   Tel: 044486 406
East of Haywards Heath. Nearest main road: A272 from Haywards Heath to
Uckfield.

rear view

2 Bedrooms. £17.50. One has own bath/
shower/toilet. Tea/coffee facilities. TV.
Views of garden, country. Washing machine
on request.
Dinner. £16 for 4 courses (including wine)

and coffee, at 7.30pm. Vegetarian or special
diets if ordered. **Light suppers.**
1 Sitting-room. With open fire, central
heating, TV.
Small garden

Cudwells was once a big farmhouse with adjacent cottages and other outbuildings
around a courtyard entered through an arch big enough for lumbering haywains.
The buildings are all still there, but now divided up and converted to make a
hidden enclave of private homes – of which the barn is one, handsomely built of
sandstone and weatherboards. It is a surprise to learn that, only a dozen or so years
ago, it still housed animals – for Roy Pontifex (an environmental consultant) has
done a superb job, almost entirely with his own hands, of transforming it into a
handsome and very comfortable house.

Traditional features that give it character include floors of brick or herringbone
woodblocks, exposed timbers in the walls, hefty rafters overhead, and a big
inglenook fireplace made of immense sandstone slabs which Roy salvaged.

Carol's decorative touches admirably complement the architecture. One bedroom has peony wallpaper and curtains of cream and coral, there are buttoned
velvet chesterfields, fiddleback chairs, and a number of particularly interesting
18th-century family portraits: one ancestor was Robert Chambers (of dictionary
fame) and a painting of his daughter, Lady Priestley, hangs on a wall.

From the sitting-room, doors open onto a paved courtyard, there are lawns
enclosed by hedges, a vegetable garden and a conservatory (Carol sometimes
serves breakfast here, with eggs from her own chickens, and fresh fruit).

She and Roy have always enjoyed meeting people, and entertaining, so those
visitors who order (in advance) a full dinner are, after an aperitif, treated to such
meals as salmon mousse, roast beef, a savoury which might be mushrooms on
toast, and lemon pie (wine included). Alternatively they can have a light supper
such as quiche and salad. Whichever you prefer, it will be served in the large and
attractive turquoise-tiled kitchen, by candlelight at an oval table.

Scaynes Hill is on the edge of Ashdown Forest, ancient woodland which in
Saxon times covered a vast area. This is a particularly good area for garden-lovers
because within a few miles are Borde Hill, Nymans, Wakehurst Place, Sheffield
Park, Leonardslee and, of more recent establishment, Denmans.

Visitors also enjoy outings to such towns as Horsham (old houses and byways),
the resorts of Brighton and Bognor, and mediaeval Lewes.

Both Gatwick Airport and Newhaven ferry are within half an hour.

208

OLD COURT

Newent, Gloucestershire, GL18 1AB   Tel: 0531 820522
North-west of Gloucester. Nearest main road: M50 (junction 3).

4 Bedrooms. £12.50–£20 (less for 3 nights). Bargain breaks. Some have own bath/shower/toilet. Tea/coffee facilities. TV. Views of garden.
Dinner. £9 for 3 courses (with choices) and coffee, at 7pm. Vegetarian or special diets if ordered. Wine can be ordered. **Light suppers** if ordered.
1 Sitting-room. With open fire, central heating, TV, record-player. Bar.
Large garden

A high wall and big garden give this handsome William-and-Mary house seclusion. One steps straight into a particularly fine hall – coral walls, white arches and a big chandelier, with the sun and moon revolving above the face of a grandfather clock which warns 'Time is Valuable'.

In the elegant dining-room, panelled in soft greens and with alcoves, a pretty skirted lamp hangs above the tables laid with Copenhagen china, heavy silver and crystal. Margaret Reece serves interesting, very English food: things like artichoke soup, pheasant casserole (with four vegetables, which may include such unusual combinations as sprouts and mushrooms braised together with mustard seed), and a raspberry soufflé, followed by cheeses. Much garden produce.

Architecturally, the sitting-room is outstanding. One end is curved; there are fluted pillars, prettily arched windows, and the plaster garlands on the ceiling have been picked out in soft colours. Margaret chose an acanthus wallpaper and velvet-covered Victorian sofas to complement this; and in the carved pine fireplace logs crackle on chilly evenings.

I particularly admired one of the bedrooms, the lofty walls of which are covered in a butterfly wallpaper. It has windows on two sides, armchairs and tables with crochet covers and a big indigo bathroom which is luxuriously carpeted.

Old Newent (only 5 minutes from the M50) is at its best when spring brings out the thousands of daffodils. It is close to the Forest of Dean (20 million oak, beech and other trees) where sheep graze and ancient rights allow miners and quarrymen to take coal and stone free. Drives and walks take you into the heart of the forest. Newent has a Victorian museum and a world-famous falconry centre where you can see flying displays, the young in their nests and lovely gardens. Within easy reach are the Wye Valley, Cheltenham, Bath, Malvern, the Cotswolds and the many beauty-spots in Wales.

Readers' comments: Excellent. Wonderful bedroom. A special and refined atmosphere but relaxed. Lovely house, excellent dinner. Very nice atmosphere, well presented menu. Fabulous meal.

OLD FARMHOUSE **C D**

Raskelf, North Yorkshire, YO6 3LF   Tel: 0347 21971
North of York. Nearest main road: A19 from York to Thirsk.

10 **Bedrooms.** £17 (less for 4 nights). Prices go up in March. Bargain breaks. All have own bath/shower/toilet.
Dinner. £11 for 4 courses (with choices) and coffee, at 7–7.45pm. Vegetarian or special diets if ordered. Wine can be ordered. No smoking.

2 **Sitting-rooms.** With open fire, central heating, TV.
Small garden
Closed in January.

Bill and Jenny Frost have established a reputation for very good food at their 18th-century guest-house, which has immaculate accommodation and decorative touches like a bouquet of silk flowers in the brick hearth whenever a log fire is not burning; a four-poster in one of the bedrooms; and, for sybarites, a particularly luxurious bathroom adjoining another.

But it is the outstanding dinners which bring most visitors here (for which reason advance bookings for bed-and-breakfast only are not usually accepted). At every course there are several choices, from which one might select (for example) deep-fried Camembert with cranberry compote as a starter; quail en croûte with gooseberry jelly; home-made coffee and Tia Maria ice cream; and finally the most interesting selection of a dozen English cheeses I have come across for some time, ranging from yarg (mild and low-fat, wrapped in edible nettle-leaves) to potted Stilton (buttery and port-laden); blue Wensleydale to snow-white Ribblesdale. Bread and preserves are home-made; local produce used wherever possible.

Nearby are the Hambleton Hills – splendid touring or walking country. It is a good base from which to explore both the North York Moors and the scenic coastline. York, Harrogate, the Dales, many stately homes and several spectacular abbey ruins (such as Rievaulx) are all within a comfortable drive, as are James Herriot's house, the Hambleton white horse, Newborough Priory, Beningbrough Hall and the 'mouse-man' workshops for oak furniture. Easingwold is a good hunting-ground for antiques.

A lovely but little-known part of the county, the Yorkshire Wolds merit exploration: gentle hills, Hornsea mere, fine churches, mediaeval Beverley and an outstanding coastline beyond.

Readers' comments: Wholehearted recommendation. High standard. Excellent and varied food, very amiable and faultless service. Spotless and comfortable accommodation. Quite outstanding. Our favourite: so friendly, and food is first class. Will go again. Excellent value in every way.

210

OLD FARMHOUSE HOTEL   C D S X

Lower Swell, Gloucestershire, GL54 1LF   Tel: 0451 30232
West of Stow-on-the-Wold. Nearest main road: A429 from Northleach to
Moreton-in-Marsh.

15 Bedrooms. £18.50–£35.50. Bargain breaks. Most have own bath/shower/toilet. Tea/coffee facilities. TV. Views of garden, country. No smoking. Washing machine on request.
Dinner. A la carte or £12.25 for 3 courses (with choices) and coffee, at 7–9pm. Vegetarian or special diets if ordered. Wine can be ordered. No smoking. **Light suppers** if ordered.
1 Sitting-room. With open fire, central heating. No smoking. **Bar.**
Large garden

A typical Cotswold stone house, dating from the 16th century, this small hotel has a series of pleasant downstairs rooms running into one another – from bar at one end to dining-room at the other. Here, as in the bedrooms, restful shades of pink, green or apricot predominate.

There is a particularly good pair of family rooms under the eaves, which children love; and two bedrooms with four-posters (in one, apricot moiré silk and, in the other, aquamarine clothe the bed). Most rooms are spacious and light, one of them with view of the stone-walled, sheltered garden. Some are in the former stables behind the house, together with a big sitting-room.

Erik Burger sets high standards in the kitchen: vegetables are not only fresh but freshly cooked for each customer, to accompany such dishes as whole poussins served with a creamy pepper sauce or pork fillet with apricots, brandy and cream.

Readers' comments: Very friendly, and comfortable. Excellent dinner.

Nearby Bourton-on-the-Water is too picturesque for its own good (it is thronged in summer) but **THE RIDGE** guest-house, Whiteshoots (tel: 0451 20660) is well away from all that. A gabled, Edwardian house, it is surrounded by lawns and fine trees, with hill views. Dining-tables are in a new conservatory overlooking a sunken garden; and among the several comfortable bedrooms is one on the ground floor. (Pamela Minchin provides only light suppers, if ordered.) From £13 to £17.50.

Readers' comments: Superb. Delightfully furnished, hospitable hostess. Have stayed three times.

OLD FORGE C PT X

Burgage Lane, Southwell, Nottinghamshire, NG25 0ER Tel: 0636 812809
North-east of Nottingham. Nearest main road: A612 from Nottingham to
Southwell.

5 **Bedrooms.** £18–£22 (less for 5 nights).
Prices go up in April. Bargain breaks. All
have own bath/shower/toilet. Tea/coffee
facilities. TV. Views of garden, country. No
smoking. Washing machine on request.
Light suppers if ordered.
1 **Sitting-room.** With open fire, central
heating, TV, record-player. No smoking.
Small garden

Flower baskets hang on the pale pink house where once a blacksmith lived and
worked; yet it was only about twenty years ago that there ceased to be a forge here.
The forge itself, at the back, is now two bedrooms, clematis growing over its roof;
and the great stone rim round which iron for wheels was hammered now lies idle
by the lily-pool in the little garden. This is overlooked by a small quarry-tiled
conservatory from which there is a view of historic Southwell Minster nearby.

Hilary Marston has filled the 200-year-old rooms with treasures such as a very
old 'log cabin' quilt from Boston (now used as a wall-hanging), Staffordshire
figures, a tapestry chair stitched by a great-aunt, and a brass bed with lace spread.

Each bedroom has its own character. One has a trellis-effect bedhead built in
and tulip-bud wallpaper; another is pink and flowery; a third – with a good view of
the Minster floodlit at night – has pale cottage-garden flowers.

Because there are 15 eating-places within 5 minutes' walk (Hilary recommends a
coaching inn, the Saracen's Head), full evening meals are not provided.

At the heart of the peaceful old town, surrounded by fields of red earth
reminiscent of Devon's soil, is the Minster, founded in Saxon times, with
remarkably fine stone carvings (in its Chapter House) of leaves from all the native
trees of England. Most visitors also want to see Newstead Abbey, founded in 1170
(it later became Byron's home), Belvoir Castle on its lofty crag, Lincoln's cobbled
lanes and dominating cathedral high up, the National Water Sports Centre (at
Holme Pierrepont) and the Robin Hood Centre in Sherwood Forest.

Nottinghamshire is, like certain other counties, stupidly ignored by most
tourists – which means it is less crowded for those who do appreciate its many
attractions (not least, a multitude of things appealing to children: farm parks,
shows about Robin Hood, 'adventure' parks, exhibitions about cave men's lives –
at Cresswell Crags, the National Mining Museum, canal trips and so forth). The
River Trent winds northward, flowing through Nottingham and past Newark – a
town dominated by ruins of the castle where King John died in 1216, and centred
on a big market square with 14th-century inns. Near it is Hawton's church, worth
a detour for its fine tower and 14th-century Easter sepulchre; to the north lies
Laxton where fields are farmed in individual strips, mediaeval-style. Eastwood is
where D. H. Lawrence grew up, in a mining cottage now open to the public.

Readers' comments: Made to feel very welcome, nothing too much trouble. Well
decorated, comfortably furnished, each room very individual. Warm welcome.
Well appointed rooms. Outstanding breakfast.

212

The Quay, Wareham, Dorset, BH20 4LP   Tel: 0929 552010
Nearest main road: A351 from Poole to Swanage.

4 Bedrooms. £18–£24. Prices go up in April. Some have own bath/toilet. Tea/coffee facilities. TV. Views of country, river.
Dinner. A la carte or £11.95 for 4 courses (with choices) and coffee, at 6.30–9pm. Vegetarian or special diets if ordered. Wine can be ordered. No smoking. **Light suppers** if ordered.
1 Sitting-room. With open fire, central heating. **Bar.**

Standing right on the quay by the River Frome, this 18th-century brick building was once a warehouse for grain that went by barge to Poole, and it still has much of its old character.

Derek and Rose-Marie Sturton run a restaurant on two floors, with good food served on flowery china in two dining-rooms furnished with cane chairs and attractive colours.

A typical meal might comprise, for instance, haddock Mornay, duckling, and raspberry mousse. There is a riverside terrace with seats, for cream teas and drinks (the terrace is lit up at night), and a bar with open fire. Upstairs are two floors with pretty, beamed bedrooms, their windows giving a view of the river, swans and the Purbeck Hills beyond. The local landscapes on their walls are for sale.

Wareham is a most interesting old town, a great mixture of history and of architectural styles. It is encircled by high earth banks built by the Saxons to fortify their village against Viking raids. The roads within this were laid out, Roman-style, on a grid. St Martin's church is Saxon and contains, rather oddly, a monument to Lawrence of Arabia (whose home at Clouds Hill is open to the public).

All around this area are marvellous places to visit – the following is merely a selection. Poole Harbour, the second largest and loveliest natural harbour in the world, the Blue Pool, Corfe Castle, Lulworth Cove, the Purbeck Hills; Arne – heathland nature reserve; Swanage, old-fashioned resort with sandy bay and architectural curiosities salvaged from London; Durlston Head – cliffs, birds, country park, lighthouse; Studland's beaches with Shell Bay beyond; Wool and Bere Regis (with Thomas Hardy associations); Bindon Abbey; the army Tank Museum at Bovington; Bournemouth, Compton Acres gardens, and any number of pretty villages down winding lanes.

As a change from driving you could take a boat trip from Poole (described elsewhere) or go on Swanage's little railway. And this is, of course, superb walking country with scenery made lovely by hills and valleys, wandering streams and villages of thatch and stone cottages to be discovered among the unfrequented lanes.

Readers' comments: Superb in every respect; a real find; haven't words to describe food, room and attention to detail; absolutely professional but very personal; welcoming and friendly, spotlessly clean, excellent food. Lovely situation, a personal touch. Food superb. Pretty bedrooms, high quality food. Unique place, very comfortable. Wonderful! Exceptionally friendly and welcoming. Very pretty dining-rooms. Full of character.

Black Bourton, Oxfordshire, OX8 2PF   Tel: 0993 841828
West of Oxford. Nearest main road: A40 from Oxford to Burford.

2 Bedrooms. £12.50. Prices go up in July. Both share own bath/shower/toilet. Tea/coffee facilities. TV. Views of garden, country. Washing machine on request.
Dinner. £9 for 4 courses (with choices) and coffee, at 7.30pm. Non-residents not admitted. Vegetarian or special diets if ordered. Wine can be brought in. **Light suppers** if ordered.
1 Sitting-room. With open fire, central heating, TV.
Small garden

No longer an inn, this 17th-century house is now the elegant home of Pat and John Baxter, filled with fine antiques and old prints. It has 'Gothick' windows in its thick stone walls, low beams in the sitting/dining-room and outside are views of the village and old houses, with the mediaeval church close by.

The bedrooms are very attractive: one is all-white (a crisp and light effect); another is a beamy room with antiques. They have board doors with old iron latches. Even the bathroom has been furnished with style – soft green carpet and William Morris wallpaper. The breakfast-room has pine chairs, scarlet cloths and a garden view. Only one family (or group of friends) is taken at a time.

Mrs Baxter provides the best of typically English food, asking her guests beforehand what they would like. Melon with port might be followed by a joint or a steak-and-kidney pie, and then perhaps brandy-chocolate cake – all served on pretty Blue Baltic china with good silver. Afterwards, when guests relax on the flowery blue-and-white sofas and armchairs in front of the log stove, the Baxters may join them for coffee. And only a minute or two away is the very pretty village of Clanfield (a tiny stream runs alongside the road) where, as an alternative, the Tavern serves meals of gourmet standard.

Black Bourton is well placed to explore the Cotswolds, Oxford and Abingdon, the Berkshire Downs, Woodstock and Stratford-upon-Avon. Favourite outings include Burford, Bibury, the Roman villa at North Leigh, Minster Lovell, Fairford's church, Filkins woollen mill, the Cotswold Wildlife Park – and the gardens at Pusey, Buscot House and at the house of *The Countryman* magazine. Antique shops abound.

Oxfordshire's long history (it was well populated even in prehistoric times) has left the fine landscape dotted with architectural and other relics of the past. Its mediaeval churches are outstanding because they were built when wool brought wealth. King Alfred was born at Wantage, Churchill at Blenheim (he is buried at nearby Bladon) and other names famous in English history during the centuries between. Much of the area's history is explained in the Vale and Downland centre in Wantage, and museums in other historic towns such as Wallingford, Abingdon (this one is in a fine building designed by one of Wren's masons), and of course Oxford which now has an audio-visual show on the subject. The county museum is at Woodstock.

Readers' comments: Comfort and service superb. Excellent food served with zest and style. Extremely comfortable and pleasant; delicious dinner. Extremely good value, very hospitable.

214

OLD JORDANS

Jordans, Buckinghamshire, HP9 2SW   Tel: 02407 4586
East of Beaconsfield. Nearest main road: A40 from London to High Wycombe.

32 Bedrooms. £18–£20 (less for 2 nights). Prices go up in April. Bargain breaks. Some have own bath/shower/toilet. Tea/coffee facilities. TV. Views of garden, country. No smoking. Washing machine on request.
Dinner. £7 for 3 courses (with choices) and coffee, at 7pm. Vegetarian or special diets if ordered. No smoking. **Light suppers** if ordered.
4 Sitting-rooms. With open fire, central heating, TV, record-player.
Large garden

A place of beehives and belfry, granary and lily-pool, flagstoned paths bordered by lavender and honeysuckle clambering over old walls. The house was a farm when Elizabeth I was on the throne, and a deed of purchase, 'signed' by thumbprints and dated 1618, hangs in one of the rooms. A brick-floored kitchen added in 1624 is now a dining-room, with Windsor chairs and elm tables, chintz curtains and a big inglenook with James I fireback and built-in bread oven.

The farm became a meeting-place for Quakers (including Fox and Penn), though many were arrested for gathering here; Penn's grave is at the 17th-century Quaker meeting-house just beyond the orchard. In 1910 the almost derelict farm was bought by the Quakers, repaired and turned into a guest-house.

Its Mayflower barn (built from the timbers of the historic *Mayflower* that carried the Pilgrim Fathers to America) is used for art exhibitions, concerts and so forth.

All told, this is a most unusual guest-house, open to all as a 'well from which to draw waters of peace'. Inside the house, winding corridors lead to simple but comfortable bedrooms and prettily decorated bathrooms. Board doors have wrought-iron latches and decorative hinges, each slightly different in design. Old furniture, pictures and other details in the sitting-rooms are all in character. Some carvings are from the *Mayflower*. It is run by a warden, Carole Hamer.

Meals are plain and wholesome: home-made soup, a roast or stew, gooseberry flan or pears in wine might be on the menu, followed by good coffee.

The neighbourhood is very interesting with beautiful scenery (typical of the chalk Chilterns, with beech woods on the hills, far views, and wooded valleys with tumbling streams). The village of Penn has a Norman church with the tomb of William Penn's grandchildren. Milton's cottage is at Chalfont St Giles, as is the Chiltern Open Air Museum, where ancient buildings (some 500 years old) have been saved from destruction and re-erected to provide a view of life in the Chilterns from past centuries. (You can park your car at the house, free, and taxi to and from Heathrow.)

Readers' comments: Have stayed many times, very pleased with standards and friendly service. Quite wonderful.

OLD MILL   D

Little Petherick, Cornwall, PL27 7QT   Tel: 0841 540388
South of Padstow. Nearest main road: A389 from Padstow to Bodmin.

6 Bedrooms. £16.50–£20.50. Prices go up in April. Some have own bath/shower/toilet. Tea/coffee facilities. Views of garden, country, river. Washing machine on request. **Dinner.** £8.95 for 4 courses and coffee, at 7pm. Vegetarian or special diets if ordered. Wine can be ordered. No smoking. **Light suppers.**
3 Sitting-rooms. With central heating, TV. Bar.
Small garden
Closed from December to February inclusive.

This picturesque 16th-century watermill (with a working water wheel) is beside a stream that winds its way into the Camel estuary, along a coastline celebrated for its many beautiful beaches (a number are protected by the National Trust).

Michael and Pat Walker have furnished the Mill very attractively. The beamy sitting-room has white stone walls, one with a mural of ploughing. William Morris sofas and Berber carpet contrast with the green slate of the floor. All around are unusual 'finds': an ancient typewriter and sewing-machines, clocks, and old tools such as planes and picks. The paved terrace by the stream is enclosed by suntrapping walls. Bedrooms are homely (very nice bathrooms); quiet ones at the back.

For dinner, at tables covered with homespun cloths, you may be offered such choices as chicken in a Stilton-and-pineapple sauce or lamb with ginger and orange; or there is a more conventional table d'hôte menu. Light suppers are available too.

Little Petherick is a pretty village with (just across the road from the Mill) a beautiful church; close to Padstow which is still agreeably antiquated. Narrow, crooked lanes lead down to Padstow's harbour, a pretty group of houses encircles the quay, and there are several outstanding buildings including the Court House where Sir Walter Raleigh dealt out judgments when he was Warden of Cornwall. The world-famous Hobby Horse street dance takes place on May Day here. There are idyllic, golden beaches around here (go to Treyarnon to see surfing). Near St Columb Major (impressive church) is an Iron Age fort called Castle an Dinas; St Mawgan is a pretty village in a woodland valley while, by contrast, St Wenn is a wild and windy moorland spot; by the lighthouse on Trevose Head you can see the whole coast from St Ives to Lundy Island. At Wadebridge, there is a new exhibition centre, housed in a converted railway station, dedicated to the life and work of Sir John Betjeman. He is buried at St Enodoc, just across the estuary.

On the whole, north Cornwall is far less touristy than the south, its greatest attractions being scenery (not only coastal but inland too) with fewer commercial entertainments, sights, etc.

Readers' comments: Beautifully furnished. Could not be more pleasant and helpful. Lovely setting. Very hospitable.

For explanation of code letters (C, D, H, PT, S, X) see page xxxiv.

OLD MILL HOUSE
C PT X

Lower Dolphinholme, Lancashire, LA2 9AX   Tel: 0524 791855
South of Lancaster. Nearest main road: M6 (junction 33).

3 Bedrooms. £15 (less for 3 nights in low season only). Some have own bath/shower. Tea/coffee facilities. Views of garden, country, river. No smoking. Washing machine on request.
Dinner. £9 for 3 courses (with choices) and coffee, at 7pm. Non-residents not admitted. Vegetarian or special diets if ordered. Wine can be ordered. No smoking. **Light suppers** if ordered.
1 Sitting-room. With open fire, central heating, TV, record-player.
Large garden

At the bottom of a steep little valley runs the River Wyre, and by the river stands the Old Mill House, over which – for all its three storeys – the mill itself once towered. A corn mill in the 17th century, it was used for weaving in the next century, being the world's first worsted mill, and wool was brought from as far away as Norfolk to supply it. In 1810, so that a 24-hour day could be worked, the then owner installed gas lighting, supplied by the first private gasworks outside London.

Nothing of all this industrial activity remains above ground level now, for the mill was demolished shortly after it closed, over a century ago. But interesting remains abound: the 15-foot-deep water-filled sump of the old gasometer, with a huge counterweight in the undergrowth beside it, the remains of the millpond and its race, overgrown steps and foundations. The new owners, Carol and Alan Williamson, are gradually extending the already big, formal gardens to take in these intriguing relics.

Not only those with an interest in industrial archaeology will enjoy exploring the wooded slopes of the grounds, which cover nearly four acres. They are a haven for wildlife (with official protection) and the river frontage provides fly fishing as well as pleasant views.

Overlooking the trim lawn, with walnut tree and herbaceous borders where the tall mill building once stood, are spacious bedrooms and, on the ground floor, an oval sitting-room with pale green wallpaper and carpet, and maroon leather chesterfields and armchairs. The dining-room is limited in size, and so Carol Williamson cannot seat a full house for dinner. Restaurants are a short drive away, but for those who eat in, Carol provides, for example, egg mayonnaise, roast pork in cider, and a gâteau. Most of the food is home-made.

It is hard to believe that the quiet hamlet of Lower Dolphinholme is only minutes from the motorway. It is close to the enjoyable city of Lancaster and the Forest of Bowland, about both of which there is more under other entries.

Only slightly further away are the Yorkshire Dales and, in the opposite direction, Morecambe Bay and the southern Lake District, which is much less overrun than the better known central area. But rural Lancashire deserves to be seen first, especially by those who think this is just a county of derelict cotton mills!

Prices are per person in a double room at the beginning of the year.

217

Thorpe, Derbyshire, DE6 2AW   Tel: 0033529 410
North-west of Ashbourne. Nearest main road: A515 from Ashbourne to
Buxton.

Views of garden, country.
Dinner. £8 for 3 courses (with choices) and
coffee, at 7pm. Non-residents not admitted.
Vegetarian or special diets if ordered. Wine
can be brought in.
1 Sitting-room. With open fire, central heating, TV.
Small garden

4 Bedrooms. £15 (less for 2 nights). Bargain
breaks. Some have own shower/toilet. TV.

**Closed from December to February
inclusive.**

Dovedale is one of the loveliest parts of the Peak District; and in this area there are
particularly fine views of it where the Manifold Valley runs down into the dale (at
the foot of Thorpe Cloud – one of several 1000-foot hills here).

On the edge of Thorpe village is a very prettily sited one-storey stone house in
traditional style, which stands where once an orchard of damson trees grew. This
is the comfortable home of Barbara Challinor and her husband; keen gardeners, as
is obvious from the herbaceous beds, stone terraces, rock garden and stream with
waterfalls in their sloping, landscaped grounds. (And it is their geese which
wander on the common beyond.) Barbara has a useful arrangement with the farm
next door: she provides bed-and-breakfast while dinner is served at the farmhouse
– straightforward soups, roasts and fruit pies, with home-baked bread. Bicycles
(either touring or mountain models) can be hired.

This part of the National Park is known as 'the White Peak' because the
underlying rock is limestone (further north, in 'the Dark Peak', the geology
changes). There is a network of paths around here by which to explore Milldale,
Wolfscote Dale and Beresford Dale – leading to other valleys further afield. The
celebrated Tissington Trail starts 2½ miles away.

But scenery is not the only attraction of the area. There are the stately homes of
Chatsworth and Haddon Hall to visit, the spa towns of Matlock and Bakewell, and
busy Ashbourne with a splendid church and antique salerooms.

It takes a long stay to do justice to the Peak District, a particularly scenic
National Park, but if you are pressed for time it would be possible to see some of
the finest parts by driving the following route. After walking in the beautiful park
of Ilam Hall (NT), continue to the head of Dovedale – a scenic route known as
Little Switzerland, with weird crags and pillars of rock, stone packhorse bridges
and a dramatic gorge – all familiar to Izaak Walton (who described them in his
Compleat Angler). Among the stone-walled fields and woodlands of Beresford Dale
is the pretty village of Hartington, its busy past as market and lead-mining town
now long gone. Arbor Law is a place of mystery – a circle of white stones erected on
a windswept site 4000 years ago and with burial mounds nearby. Beyond it lies
possibly the most perfect mediaeval stately home in this country (parts built by a
son of William the Conqueror): turreted Haddon Hall, with terraced gardens
descending to a sparkling river. Across high heather moors (with another stone
circle) lies Matlock which is in fact two towns, one a Victorian spa – there is a
mining museum worth visiting here. This is where the River Derwent has cut a
dramatic gorge through the limestone hills.

★ **OLD PARSONAGE FARMHOUSE**   **D**

Hanley Castle, Worcestershire, WR8 0BU   Tel: 0684 310124
South-east of Malvern. Nearest main road: A38 from Worcester to
Tewkesbury.

rear view

3 Bedrooms. £18.50–£19.75 (less for 7 nights). Prices go up in April. Bargain breaks. All have own bath/toilet. Tea/coffee and TV on request. Views of garden, country. Washing machine on request.
Dinner. A la carte or £13.50 for 4 courses (with choices of dessert) and coffee, from 7pm. Non-residents not admitted. Vegetarian or special diets if ordered. Wine can be ordered. No smoking. **Light suppers** if ordered.
2 Sitting-rooms. With open fire, central heating, TV, record-player. Bar.
Large garden
Closed from mid-December to mid-January.

It is not just the surrounding views of the Malvern Hills or the handsome 18th-century house of mellow brick which makes this worth seeking out: Ann Addison has a flair for both cookery and interior decoration, while Tony is a wine expert. He runs wine-tastings in the one-time cider mill adjoining the house.

You enter the house via a vaulted entrance hall (with Edwardian fireplace), then through double doors into the sandalwood sitting-room with its small library and television. On the right is the elegant, pale sea-green drawing-room with its arched Georgian windows and marble Adam fireplace. To the left is the sunflower-yellow dining-room which has the original brick hearth and bread oven.

Damask cloths and Rorstrand china from Sweden create an appropriate setting for the kind of meals Ann serves, such as mushrooms and herbs in puff pastry, chicken breasts with prawns in cream and brandy, bramble mousse, cheeses.

Upstairs are elegant bedrooms (for instance, one has waterlily fabrics complemented by daffodil walls, another has a vast bathroom with oval chocolate bath).

All around is superb countryside. Drive southward and you come to Upton-upon-Severn where a 14th-century bell tower still stands near the bridge: once it was part of a church, was given a 'pepperpot' cupola in 1770, and is now a heritage centre – the church itself was dismantled in the 'thirties. The town's historic byways and riverbank inns are well worth exploring.

Westward lie the Malvern Hills, with stupendous views from the Herefordshire Beacon (over 1100 feet high) and the remains of one of the greatest Iron Age forts in Britain. Near here is the village of Eastnor which has two castles, the moated one (15th-century) is real and ruined; the other (1812) is a romantic mansion, turreted in Norman style, which was designed by Smirke – architect of the British Museum – and has armour, tapestries, etc. inside.

Readers' comments: Very impressed. Warm and friendly welcome, helpful and charming. Extremely comfortable. High standard of imaginative food.

OLD PLACE
Cuckfield Road, Ansty, West Sussex, RH17 5AG   Tel: 0444 451464
West of Haywards Heath. Nearest main road: A23 from Brighton to Crawley.

2 Bedrooms. £15. Prices go up in spring. One has own bath/shower/toilet. Tea/coffee facilities. TV. Views of garden, country. No smoking.
Light suppers sometimes.
1 Sitting-room. With central heating, TV.
Large garden

A long track between banks of wildflowers leads to this half-timbered and tile-hung house, built in the year when Richard III was slain at the Battle of Bosworth. Another connection with that king: Selina Newman, who now lives here, is descended from Lord Hastings – beheaded by Richard III.

When the Newmans were renovating it, they discovered that an old brick outhouse had been the original toilet – very sociable, for it was complete with a three-holed bench! Upstairs and down are shapely Tudor fireplaces of stone, and over a large brick inglenook the original spit-rests still remain. Stairs are winding, oak doors have ancient latches, there is a 60-foot well.

From the windows are views of wooded hills and lawns (there is a swimming-pool, too), to be enjoyed from the sitting-room or from the bedrooms, the biggest of which has windows on three sides and a beamed ceiling. For the dining-room curtains and seats, Selina chose a particularly attractive William Morris fabric in blue to complement the huge refectory table and chairs specially made for the house from the old oak timbers of Lewes Theatre (now demolished). On many of the walls are watercolours by a well-known artist and playwright, James Forsyth, who lives in the next house; and a great armorial hatchment.

Breakfast only; for dinner, visitors go to nearby Cuckfield, a steep mediaeval village, where there is plenty of choice. Look for the cuckoo on the village sign, which is what gave the place its name – pronounced 'Cookfield' – and for the noble church which is worth a visit.

This is a good area for antique shops and for visiting outstanding gardens (such as Borde Hill, Sheffield Park, Nymans, Wakehurst and Leonardslee – all within a few miles). In Roman times the great forest of Anderida stretched for over a hundred miles along the Wealden ridge of north Sussex and traces still remain. Most of the oaks were, however, burnt in the furnaces of the Sussex ironmasters during the 17th century: the furnace ponds you discover here and there were created by them (they dammed streams to provide power for the hammers that forged their iron). How rich those ironmasters grew can be guessed from nearby Ockenden Manor, for example, the house of one of them. The largest surviving tract is Ashdown Forest where woods (much devastated in the hurricane of 1987) alternate with stretches of heath. There is a network of lanes and paths to explore, by car or on foot, between here and East Grinstead. The lane from Balcombe to Ardingly is especially pretty: all curves, rising and falling, with willow-fringed duck-pond along the way. Go to Turners Hill or Handcross for superb views. Westward is St Leonards Forest, with tales of smugglers and highwaymen; drifts of lilies-of-the-valley; and the high village of Colgate. Brighton is only 20 minutes away. Haywards Heath has a huge market.

Byford, Herefordshire, HR4 7LD   Tel: 098122 218
West of Hereford. Nearest main road: A438 from Hereford to Brecon.

3 Bedrooms. £12.50–£16 (less for 3 nights). Bargain breaks. Some have own shower/toilet. TV. Views of garden, country, river. No smoking. Washing machine on request.
Light suppers if ordered. Vegetarian or special diets. Wine can be brought in. No smoking.
1 Sitting-room. With central heating. No smoking.
Large garden
Closed from December to February inclusive.

An enormous cedar of Lebanon dominates the garden outside the Rectory, a handsome brick house which, though built in 1830, is Georgian in style – having big, well-proportioned rooms and great sash windows which make the most of the very fine views of hills and church. Audrey Mayson and her husband have put a great deal of loving care not only into the restoration of the big house but also the landscaping of the formerly neglected garden.

Themselves parents of a growing family, the Maysons welcome children and therefore run the house in an informal, caring way: comfortable and spacious, a place in which to relax completely.

The sitting/dining-room has pale green walls, deep pine-shuttered windows, pine-panelled doors, and their collection of unusual Escher pictures. There is a big family bedroom with sofa, and good views.

Audrey does not cook evening meals, although light suppers may be provided if ordered. Most visitors go either to the local Portway Inn or to one of the many restaurants in Weobley.

Byford is on the way to Wales, but there are many reasons to pause here for more than a stopover. Nearby are Hereford and its cathedral; Hay-on-Wye for its multitude of bookshops and for the Lost Street Museum, rows of old shops crammed with Victoriana; the hills of the Brecon Beacons; the lovely River Wye with footpaths alongside (salmon fishing and tuition available).

Because Monica Barker previously lived in India, **APPLETREE COTTAGE** (at nearby Mansell Lacy), built of half-timbering and brick in the reign of Henry VI, is full of exotic touches such as Kashmiri crewel bedspreads and curtains. These nevertheless assort well with pretty fabrics, antique oak furniture, and chairs covered in traditional tapestry or velvet Previously two cottages, then a ciderhouse, the building still has many of its original features, such as low beams and small, deep-set windows; and when Monica had to put in a new, twisting staircase, she had it wood-

pegged in the traditional way. By arrangement, she will cook such meals as cucumber and yogurt soup, steak pie (or nasi goreng, an Indonesian speciality) and meringues – using wholefood ingredients. The cottage stands at the foot of a hill popular with walkers and birdwatchers alike. (Tel: 098122 688.) From £14 to £17.

OLD RECTORY

Gissing, Norfolk, IP22 3XB   Tel: 037977 575
North of Diss. Nearest main road: A140 from Norwich to Scole.

3 Bedrooms. £18–£22. Prices go up in June. All have own bath/shower/toilet. Tea/coffee facilities. TV. Views of garden, country. No smoking. Washing machine on request.
Dinner. £14 for 4 courses and coffee, at 7.45pm. Non-residents not admitted. Vegetarian or special diets if ordered. Wine can be brought in. No smoking. **Light suppers** if ordered.
1 Sitting-room. With open fire, central heating, TV, piano, record-player.
Large garden

'Summer is i-cumen in
Lhude sing cuckoo . . .'

The song was composed by a 13th-century monk born in a village near here (Forncett St Peter), and accords well with the tranquil scenery in these parts.

Ian Gillam, a surveyor, collects unusual architectural drawings and prints, which now hang on the walls of this house – for instance, Voysey's own drawings of houses he designed, a Pyrenean orangery, the *fin-de-siècle* casino at Vichy.

The Rectory itself was built in 1874: a solidly handsome building with big sash windows in shuttered embrasures, its rooms now well furnished by Jill. She chose, for instance, an apricot and turquoise colour scheme for the large sitting-room with big chairs upholstered in cut velvet; and French provincial wallpapers and fabrics in one of the bedrooms, its bed covered with a brocade spread, and flowery friezes in another. She hunts at sales for old embroidered linens, or herself adds broderie anglaise to pillowslips and sheets, and makes frilled cushions.

Outside is a very large garden with terrace, conservatory and covered swimming-pool beyond which are lawns where visiting children enjoy her own family's swing and slide. Despite being a busy mother, Jill finds time to cook for visitors such meals as: iced lettuce soup; cod-and-prawn pie (there are almonds, grapes and wine in the sauce); a rich chocolate mousse; and cheeses.

Gissing (itself an interesting village) is well placed for visiting all of East Anglia because it is so central. The Norfolk Broads and the scenic, east coast are only ¾ hour away. Much closer attractions include the gardens of Bressingham.

A few miles eastward is 17th-century **GREENACRES FARM** at Wood Green, Long Stratton (tel: 0508 30261), right on the edge of a 30-acre common with ponds and ancient woods. Rooms are spacious and comfortable, some beamy; and there is a self-contained wing sometimes available on a b & b basis. In a huge games room, you can peer into the floodlit depths of a 60-foot well as old as the house itself. Joanna Douglas's dinners are homely two-course meals, such as

meatballs in tomato sauce and cheese-cake. (Bicycles on loan; tennis court.) From £14 to £16.

★ OLD RECTORY C(14) D
Patrick Brompton, North Yorkshire, DL8 1JN Tel: 0677 50343
East of Leyburn. Nearest main road: A684 from Bedale to Leyburn.

3 Bedrooms. £13.50–£16.50 (less for 7 nights). Some have own bath/shower/toilet. Tea/coffee facilities. TV. Views of garden, country. No smoking. Washing machine on request.
Dinner. £9.50 for 4 courses and coffee, at 7.30pm. Non-residents not admitted. Vegetarian or special diets if ordered. Wine can be brought in. No smoking. **Light suppers** if ordered.
1 Sitting-room. With open fire, central heating, TV. No smoking.
Small garden
Closed in December and January.

David and Felicity Thomas have furnished their home in keeping with its period (it was built early in the 18th century), complementing comfortable chintz sofas with a soft green colour scheme, the mahogany furniture of the dining-room with peach walls (the table is laid with Minton china and good silver). Bedrooms (on two floors, reached by a twisting staircase) are spacious and immaculate, some overlooking a walled garden with lawns beyond. There are alcoves, bay-windows and low doorways.

Felicity enjoys cooking. A typical dinner might comprise stuffed eggs, pork dijonnaise with wine sauce, and blackberry mousse, followed by cheeses.

The village is surrounded by small market towns (there's at least one market on the go every weekday), great mediaeval abbeys such as Jervaulx, two cathedral cities and two spa towns, waterfalls, famous crags and viewpoints, and the Dales – both Wensleydale and more rugged Swaledale are close by. Wensleydale (famous for cheese) is the broadest and most fertile of the Dales – heather-clad hills enclose fields marked by dry-stone walls, with stone cottages and prosperous 18th-century houses. Bolton, Richmond and Middleham have castles. The North York Moors and even the Lake District are accessible for a day's outing. Constable Burton Hall has a fine garden, Thorpe Perrow an arboretum. Antique sales and shops attract many visitors; and there is plenty of farm produce to buy or pick. In winter, there are activity weekends at the Old Rectory – painting, crafts, history, etc.

Bolton Castle well deserved the big restoration programme that has been going on and Bedale Hall is worth a visit for its small but very interesting museum of social history – there are folk museums, too, at Hawes and Reeth and, at Aysgarth Falls, the county's collection of 50 coaches and other horse-drawn vehicles. Working watermills can be seen at Little Crakehall and Bainbridge (at the former you can buy stone-ground flour; at the latter is a dolls' house centre).

Many of Yorkshire's great abbeys are world-famous. Less well known is Coverham Abbey in a beautiful riverside setting at Leyburn, and with lovely gardens. In it are effigies of early mediaeval knights.

Readers' comments: Delicious meal, pretty rooms. The best yet! Beautifully furnished, genuine welcome, superb dinner, wonderful hosts. Outstanding. Very pleasant rooms. Delightful owners. Wonderful hospitality, excellent food, most relaxing. A marvellous week. Most comfortable, so welcoming. House beautiful and food delicious.

223

OLD RECTORY　　　　　　　　　　　　　　　　　　C(12) **D H**

St Keyne, Cornwall, PL14 4RL　Tel: 0579 42617
South of Liskeard. Nearest main road: A38 from Bodmin to Plymouth.

8 Bedrooms. £18–£27 for 4-poster bedroom (less for 7 nights). Bargain breaks. All have own bath/shower/toilet. Tea/coffee facilities. TV. Views of garden, country. Washing machine on request.
Dinner. £10 for 3 courses (with choices) and coffee, at 7–8pm. Wine can be ordered. No smoking. **Light suppers.**
1 Sitting-room. With open fire, central heating. **Bar.**
Large garden

Throughout this house, there is an air of calm and dignity, with furnishings chosen to complement the early 19th-century architecture. Features like a fine fireplace of black marble, handsome staircase (with barley-sugar balusters and ruby glass in its windows) and panelled pine doors have fortunately survived the years intact.

There are handsome cushioned chairs around the tables in the dining-room (pale blue predominates in carpet and damask wallpaper) where, on fluted Wedgwood china, Ron and Kate Wolfe serve such 3-course meals as Stilton and celery soup, chicken in red wine, and chocolate fudge-cake.

In the sitting-room (which has glass doors to the garden) are capacious velvet sofas; and separated from it by a curtained archway is a turquoise and cherry bar. Bedrooms are equally distinctive. Two have lacy, four-posters; another, on the ground floor, would particularly appeal to anybody who finds stairs difficult.

St Keyne, being fairly high up, has panoramic views and is surrounded by varied scenery: moors, beaches, cliffs and woodland paths are all at hand. There are over 40 places to visit, which include unusual museums and collections, steam rail, fishing villages, gardens, seal sanctuary, tin mines, tropical bird gardens, waterfall, shire horse centre, watermills, river trips, craft centres and many National Trust houses.

Down on the coast, at the fishing harbour of Mevagissey, you can visit a folk museum and a miniature railway with over 2000 model trains. At St Austell you can choose between a vintage car museum, Polmassick vineyard, or tours round the china-clay workings, perhaps following this by a trip to the Wheal Martyn restored Victorian clay works operated by steam and waterwheels, or to Charlestown's shipwreck centre.

Readers' comments: Excellent cooking with quality ingredients; warm and welcoming. Charming atmosphere of true repose and Victorian elegance. Food exceptional.

224

★ **OLD RECTORY**   **C**
Standlake, Oxfordshire, OX8 7SG   Tel: 0865 300559
South-west of Oxford. Nearest main road: A415 from Witney to Abingdon.

4 Bedrooms. £17.25–£31.50 (less for 7 nights). Prices go up at Easter. Bargain breaks. All have own bath/shower/toilet. Tea/coffee facilities. TV. Views of garden, country, river. Washing machine on request.
Dinner. £15 for 4 courses and coffee, at 7.30pm. Non-residents not admitted. Vegetarian or special diets if ordered. Wine can be brought in. **Light suppers** if ordered. **2 Sitting-rooms.** With open fire, central heating. No smoking in one.
Large garden
Closed in December and January.

Once Magdalene College, Oxford, owned this house of Cotswold stone, the hall of which dates back to the 13th century. At the end of this is what an old inventory called 'the dark entry', leading to lawns with a seat beside the River Windrush (fishing and canoes available) and with tall beech hedges sheltering them. There are pine trees, a 500-year-old yew and a stew-pond (that is, one where fish were bred for the pot). The 15th-century dining-room had several big sash windows added later to take advantage of this view. Throughout, there are features of architectural interest: old ogee-arched fireplaces of stone, lattice-paned windows with stone mullions, odd angles and steps everywhere.

The house was in decay when Pat and Bob Claridge started on the long task of restoring and then furnishing it to a very high standard. Even the least expensive room (nicknamed 'the curate's quarters'!) is attractive; while others are really beautiful, the most luxurious being a suite with four-poster draped in a silky, pale blue fabric with a pleated pink canopy above, figured mahogany wardrobe, a delicately patterned Louisiana wallpaper, pink and gold bathroom and river view.

By arrangement, Patricia will serve dinner, a typical menu being prawn cocktail in a half-melon, chicken and chilli casserole, raspberry pavlova.

Around the village are lakes, and the beginning of the Cotswold Hills with sights such as Blenheim Palace, the Oxford colleges, historic Burford and Cogges Farm.

At Witney itself (a blanket-making town) is a great green with handsome lime trees and a wide main street, flanked with houses of Cotswold stone, and with a gabled, pillared and turreted Butter Cross built in the 17th century.

When and if the local Cotswold sights (which include the beautiful ruins of Minster Lovell Hall) are exhausted, it is easy to reach Bath, Stratford, Stonehenge, Cheltenham and even London from here. Garden-lovers appreciate Hidcote, Pusey, Kiftsgate, Sezincote and Mattocks' rose nurseries.

Readers' comments: Warm and friendly. Beautifully appointed. Superb breakfast. A delightful weekend. Sympathetically and beautifully restored. Faultless food and service. A marvellous break, so peaceful. Cooking superb. Hope to go back.

OLD RECTORY
Wetherden, Suffolk, IP14 3RE   Tel: 0359 40144
North-west of Stowmarket. Nearest main road: A45 from Stowmarket to Bury St Edmunds.

3 Bedrooms. £17–£20 (less for 2 nights). All have own bath/shower/toilet. Tea/coffee facilities. TV. Views of garden, country. Washing machine on request.
Light suppers only for elderly visitors.
1 Sitting-room. With open fire, central heating, TV, piano.
Large garden
Closed from December to February inclusive.

Readers who used the first edition of this book may have stayed with Pamela Bowden when she lived near Hadleigh. Now she has an equally elegant house here, into the decoration of which she has put the same tremendous amount of care.

The house, which dates from the 18th century, stands in extensive grounds (where sheep, horses and donkeys wander in summer). There is also a croquet lawn. One steps into a hall with stone floor, a piano in one alcove and pot-plants.

Up the deep pink and white staircase are elegant bedrooms – I particularly liked one decorated in apricot with an antique brass bed and comfortable armchairs. Fine paintings, interesting fabrics, graceful curtains and Persian carpets are features of this imaginatively renovated house. In the drawing-room is a wallpaper patterned with classical medallions; the raspberry dining-room has an Adam fireplace of pink marble and a most unusual table – immensely long, it was made in Renaissance Italy from a single piece of walnut. Pamela, a member of the Embroiders' Guild, has made many of the furnishings herself: cushions, curtains, bed-hanging and sheets with broderie anglaise, for example.

Bed-and-breakfast only. For other meals, Pamela recommends such local inns as the King's Arms at Haughley, the Bull at Woolpit or Trowel & Hammer at Cotton.

Central Suffolk, once forested, is now an area of wide open fields with prairie-size farms. Villages cluster around greens, big mediaeval houses like that at Parham are often moated – less for defence than to drain the site and provide a water-supply for the inhabitants (rainfall being low in this part of England). The area has had a turbulent history, hence the presence of so many castles (the one at Framlingham is outstanding, and so are the monuments in the church).

The many attractive villages include Debenham, threaded by a pretty stream and with rush-weaving to be seen; Eye, for the fine roodscreen in its church and the Minstrels' Gallery at the White Lion; Hoxne, scene of St Edmund's martyrdom at the bridge. Earl Soham, unusually leafy, has a great variety of architectural styles from every period; Saxtead Green, a working windmill; Heveningham, stately mansion in a park laid out by Capability Brown. Yoxford is called 'the garden of Suffolk' because of the abundance of spring flowers at every cottage.

From Wetherden, so centrally situated, it is easy to motor to the coast and Ipswich (beyond it the seaside resort of Felixstowe), and even to Cambridge, Norwich and Colchester in adjacent counties. In Stowmarket, a small market town, is Abbot's Hall which has a museum of rural life.

Readers' comments: The ambience was delightful, the house beautifully furnished, the breakfast excellent.

★ **OLD SCHOOL HOUSE**   C(12) **X**
St James' Street, Castle Hedingham, Essex, CO9 3EW   Tel: 0787 61370
South-west of Sudbury (Suffolk). Nearest main road: A604 from Halstead to
Haverhill.

3 Bedrooms. £18.50–£22.50 for a suite (less for 2 nights). All have own bath/shower/toilet. Tea/coffee facilities. Views of garden. No smoking. Washing machine on request. **Dinner.** £12.50 for 3 courses (wine, etc.) and coffee, at 7.30pm. Non-residents not admitted. Vegetarian or special diets if ordered. No smoking. **Light suppers** if ordered.
2 Sitting-rooms. With open fire, central heating, TV. No smoking.
Small garden

Garden-lovers in particular should go out of their way to stay here, for the Crawshaws have created – within a remarkably few years of taking over what was then a rough field – an elegant and lovely garden. Its several lawns are surrounded by shapely and brimming beds of shrubs and flowers, all grown from seed. Steps lead up to a lily-pool with koi carp, and at the end is hidden a neat vegetable garden which supplies the kitchen. And there's a population of little toads – hundreds of them – which come out at night.

Through the street door of the terracotta-and-white house, built in the 18th century, one steps straight into a quarry-tiled hall/dining-room. Between its ceiling beams is a trap-door, known as a coffin door – necessitated by the narrowness of the staircase – and a former inglenook is filled with flowers. There are Chippendale chairs around the dining-table, and silver candlesticks on it. Here, Penny may serve such dinners (if ordered in advance) as haddock soufflé in spinach leaves, rack of lamb and a choice of puddings – chocolate pots, lemon pie, etc. (pre-dinner drinks and wine included). Her breakfasts include such options as home-made trout fishcakes.

The sitting-room (brick-walled and with a copper-hooded fire), opens onto a paved terrace made colourful and appealing by a dozen huge plant-pots.

The principal bedroom is attractively decorated, with colourful quilted bedhead and spread, while the other has roses on walls and bed. The view from this room is of the public tennis court across the street which leads into the centre of the village (picturesque, and with interesting shops), over which the castle itself looms high. A cottage in the garden provides extra bedrooms and its own sitting-room – these rooms are especially attractive and quiet.

This is a very scenic part of Essex, near the Suffolk border, with a great deal to enjoy, crisscrossed by footpaths and bridleways. Audley End and a large number of other stately homes are in the neighbourhood, as well as many very pretty half-timbered villages and towns: Saffron Walden and Thaxted in particular (the latter has music festivals). Mole Hall Wildlife Park is another attraction. Colchester and Dedham Vale deserve at least one whole day. Cambridge is little more than half an hour away (it, and Suffolk villages such as Lavenham and Long Melford, are described under other entries.)

Readers' comments: Charming house and garden, excellent cooking.

OLD VICARAGE   S

Affpuddle, Dorset, DT2 7HH   Tel: 0305 848315

East of Dorchester. Nearest main road: A35 from Dorchester to Bere Regis.

3 Bedrooms. £15. Some have own bath/toilet. Tea/coffee facilities. TV. Views of garden, country. Washing machine on request.
Light suppers if ordered. Wine can be brought in.
Large garden with croquet.

Before Anthea and Michael Hipwell moved here, it was an ambassador's country home: a handsome Georgian house with fine doorways, windows and fireplaces – surrounded by smooth lawns and rosebeds within tall hedges of clipped yew, the old church alongside.

Anthea has a flair for interior decoration. Even the corridors are elegant, with portraits and flower-prints on walls of apple-blossom pink which contrast with the cherry carpet. In my bedroom, the curtains were of ivory moiré, the bedspread patterned with rosebuds.

Breakfast is served in the prettiest dining-room in this book. Taking as the starting-point her collection of aquamarine glass (housed in two alcoves) and a series of modern lithographs in vivid turquoise, Anthea decorated the walls to match, and chose a dramatic turquoise curtain fabric reproduced from a Regency design in Brighton's Royal Pavilion. Against this all-blue colour scheme, the pale furniture shows to advantage. As no evening meal is provided, many visitors go to the Brace of Pheasants at Plush, the Fox at Ansty or the Frampton Arms at Moreton.

The Old Vicarage is well placed for a stopover on the long journey (by A35) to the West Country; when arriving or departing on the Weymouth-Cherbourg ferry; or while learning to fish for trout at the nearby angling school (tel: 0305 848450).

The Hipwells lend walkers Ordnance Survey maps, and will advise them on sightseeing possibilities, including less obvious ones – such as the huge bric-à-brac market held at Wimborne every Friday, or little-known beaches (one favourite is at Ringstead, surrounded by National Trust land). In addition, there are such favourites as Hardy's cottage and T. E. Lawrence's; Kingston Lacy house (near which is Walford Mill crafts centre); Maiden Castle and Corfe Castle; Studland beach and the Purbeck Hills; and several garden centres – one specializing in old roses. And, at the end of the day, you are welcome to relax in the Hipwells' garden chairs under sun umbrellas.

There are a great many fine gardens in the county. Among lesser-known ones is Mapperton (near Beaminster), a Tudor manor house, which has pools, an orangery and fine views. In the same direction is more famous Parnham, also Tudor: as well as its large gardens, it has the workshop of Britain's most celebrated furniture designer, John Makepeace. And at Broadwindsor Crafts Centre you can see other craftsmen at work in a converted barn. For more gardens (and fine tapestries inside) visit 12th-century Forde Abbey near Chard.

Readers' comments: Very pleasant. Excellent service.

228

OLD VICARAGE

Higham, Suffolk, CO7 6JY   Tel: 020637 248

North of Colchester (Essex). Nearest main road: A12 from Colchester to
Ipswich.

4 Bedrooms. £16–£20 (less for 3 nights).
Prices go up in May. Bargain breaks. Some
have own bath/shower/toilet. Tea/coffee
facilities. TV. Views of garden, country,
river. No smoking. Washing machine on
request.
Light suppers sometimes. Wine can be
brought in. No smoking.
2 Sitting-rooms. With open fire, central
heating, TV. No smoking.
Large garden

One of the most elegant houses in this book, the Old Vicarage stands near a
tranquil village and is surrounded by superb views, with the old church close by.
Everything about it is exceptional, from the Tudor building itself (its walls
colourwashed a warm apricot), and the lovely furnishings, to the pretty south-
facing garden – which has unheated swimming-pool, tennis and safe river boats
(it's surprising that few families with children have discovered it, particularly
since the coast is near; Felixstowe and Frinton have sandy beaches).

Colonel and Mrs Parker have lived here for many years, and their taste is evident
in every room. Lovely colours, pretty wallpapers and chintzes, antiques, flowers
and log fires all combine to create a background of great style. In the breakfast-
room, eight bamboo chairs surround a huge circular table (of mock-marble), and
the walls have a trellis wallpaper the colour of watermelon. Bedrooms are equally
pretty: one green-and-white with rush flooring; another has mimosa on walls and
ceiling (its tiny windows are lattice-paned); the family room is in lime and
tangerine. There are lace bedspreads, Indian watercolours, baskets of begonias –
individual touches everywhere.

Bed-and-breakfast only; most visitors dine at the Angel, Stoke-by-Nayland.

Lynne, from the village, comes in to help and (herself a lively source of
information) is evidently as greatly impressed as the visitors themselves with all
that the Parkers do to help people enjoy their stay – from information on
sightseeing and eating-places, where to watch local wildlife, and so on.

Higham is very well placed for a great variety of activities and outings. One
could easily spend a fortnight doing something totally different each day. There
are Roman Colchester (lovely gardens on the ramparts), Constable's Flatford Mill
and Dedham, the seaside, racing at Newmarket, sailing, the mediaeval villages
and great churches of central Suffolk, tide-mill at Woodbridge, market and
Gainsborough's house at Sudbury, and lovely villages. Beth Chatto's garden,
Ickworth and East Bergholt Lodge attract garden-lovers. And everywhere superb
scenery, with few people on the roads.

Readers' comments: Lovely house, very calm, beautifully appointed, charming
staff. A firm favourite; superb and beautiful; hospitality outstanding. Perfect!
Delightful weekend; privileged to be there. Excellent in every way. Most beautiful
house. Very friendly. Thoroughly enjoyed it, superb. Very helpful. Food of
highest standard, attention to detail outstanding. Splendid home and hospitality.

229

C(7)

West of Richmond. Nearest main road: A684 from Leyburn to Sedbergh.

4 Bedrooms. £34.50 including dinner (minimum booking, 2 nights). All have own bath/toilet. Tea/coffee facilities. TV. Views of garden, country. No smoking. Washing machine on request.
Dinner. 5 courses and coffee, at 7.30pm. Non-residents not admitted. Vegetarian or special diets if ordered. Wine can be ordered. No smoking.
1 Sitting-room. With open fire, central heating. No smoking.
Large garden
Closed from November to mid-March.

At the head of lovely Swaledale, this house (filmed in the TV series 'All Creatures Great and Small') provides accommodation that is furnished with comfort and in character with the age of the house. King-size beds, good carpets, fruit and home-made biscuits in the bedrooms, and open fires all contribute to its comfort; and from every room there are fine views – for close by is Great Shunner Fell (2400 feet), the famous Buttertubs Pass, and Kisdon Hill. Good walking country.

Marjorie Bucknall's five-course meals are based on fresh produce; and all the bread (both white and brown) is home-baked. A typical menu might comprise tomato soup with basil, gratin of haddock and smoked salmon, roast beef and Yorkshire pudding, lemon cheesecake, home-made Swaledale cheese, and coffee with mints. At breakfast, orange juice is freshly squeezed and choices include figs and black pudding among other options.

If you want a daytime TV programme videoed for evening viewing, the Bucknalls will do it.

Muker is the largest of the villages of Swaledale. It houses a shop for woollens hand-knitted by a team of 40 farmers' wives and daughters, mostly from the wool of the breed of sheep to which the dale has given its name. From it, you can also visit the rest of the Yorkshire Dales, the Yorkshire Moors and the Lake District.

There is plenty of scenery to enjoy in Swaledale but, for a change, the nearest town is Kirkby Stephen, westward over the watershed of the Pennines in Cumbria. Its rather grand church contains the tomb of the man reputed to have killed the last wild boar in England. It is reached from the market square, where the area once used for bull-baiting is still marked, through the picturesque classical cloisters. There are some good walks along the River Eden, and castles to visit include the remains of one supposed to be the birthplace of Uther Pendragon, King Arthur's father. One could return to Muker via the Buttertubs Pass, having taken a look at Hardraw Force, the highest single-drop waterfall in England. Brass bands used to use the natural amphitheatre here for performances.

Readers' comments: Warm welcome, excellent value. Cannot praise too highly; rooms excellent, food superb, owners very attentive. Lovely people, went out of their way to make us feel at home; and the food . . . ! A delight; the Bucknalls are welcoming and perceptive; food excellent. Warm welcome, excellent food and value, we will visit again and again! Lovely house, superb views, quiet.

OLD VICARAGE   **C D PT**
Parc-an-Creet, St Ives, Cornwall, TR26 2ET   Tel: 0736 796124
Nearest main road: A30 from Redruth to Penzance.

8 Bedrooms. £14.50–£15.50 (less for 3 nights). Prices go up in June. Bargain breaks. Some have own bath/shower/toilet. Tea/coffee facilities. TV. Views of garden. **Dinner.** £10 for 4 courses (with choices) and coffee, at 7pm. Non-residents not admitted. Vegetarian or special diets if ordered. Wine can be ordered. **Light suppers** sometimes. **2 Sitting-rooms.** With central heating, TV, piano, record-player. Bar. Snooker, etc. **Large garden** with putting, badminton. **Closed from November to February inclusive.**

Although part of the once extensive grounds (on the outskirts of steep little St Ives) were sold off long ago to build modern houses all round, the trees in the remaining garden shut most of these (and the church) from view.

The house itself, built of silvery granite in the 1850s, is entered via a small conservatory and a great iron-hinged door of ecclesiastical shape, which opens into a hall with red-and-black tiled floor. Mr and Mrs Sykes have done their best to preserve this period ambience, furnishing the bar with crimson-and-gold flock wallpaper and all kinds of Victoriana. There's a piano here, which occasionally inspires visitors to join in singing some of the old songs of that period. In addition there is a sitting-room, and blue-and-white dining-room. Big windows (some with floor-length velvet curtains on poles) and handsome fireplaces feature throughout; and the Sykeses have put in excellent carpets, along with good, solid furniture – a 'thirties walnut suite in one bedroom, and velvet-upholstered bedheads. There is a refurbished Victorian loo, preserved in all its glory of blue lilies and rushes.

Jack Sykes, formerly an engineer, did all the modernization himself, even the plumbing; while Irene, who used to be a confectioner and later took a hotel management course, is responsible for the meals. She provides such dishes as Stilton-and-walnut mousse, haddock Wellington, and pineapple in kirsch with Cornish cream; then cheeses and coffee.

There are chairs and sun umbrellas in the garden; and a path leads down (in 10 minutes) to the sandy beach where there are beach chalets for hire. A bus will bring you uphill again. Another will take you out to the moors and rugged cliffs that lie between St Ives and Land's End, where attractions now include the Last Labyrinth – rock tunnels and a cosmic spectacle of the elements.

The colourful village of St Ives, famous for its artists' colony, is now a crowded tourist centre in summer. Beyond it lie (on the north coast) some splendid scenery, outstanding prehistoric remains, tin mines and lighthouses. The sheltered south coast has sandy coves like Porthcurno and Lamorna, the cliffside Minack theatre, wildflowers in abundance and historic fishing harbours (Mousehole and Newlyn in particular). The byways and curio shops of Penzance, as well as its subtropical gardens, are well worth exploring on foot and from here there are day-trips to the Isles of Scilly and to the castle on the little islet of St Michael's Mount.

Readers' comments: Beautifully restored; excellent in all aspects. Pleasant, and good value. Excellent in every way; superb home cooking.

★ **OLD VICARAGE**
Church Square, Rye, East Sussex, TN31 7HF   Tel: 0797 222119
Nearest main road: A259 from Folkestone to Hastings.

5 Bedrooms. £17–£24 for a suite (less for 7 nights). Prices go up in April. Bargain breaks. Some have own shower/toilet. Tea/coffee facilities. TV. Views of country. No smoking. Washing machine on request.
Light suppers if ordered. Vegetarian or special diets. Wine can be brought in.
1 Sitting-room. With central heating.
Small garden

This pink-and-white, largely 18th-century house is virtually in the churchyard, a peaceful spot since it is traffic-free and the only sound is the melodious chime of the ancient church clock (its pendulum hangs right down into the nave of the church). One steps straight into a very pretty sitting-room, yellow sofas complemented by Laura Ashley fabrics and prints. Curved windows, antiques and pot-plants complete the scene. Beyond is the breakfast-room.

The bedrooms are prettily decorated, mostly with pine furniture and flowery fabrics. Two have elegant four-posters. Those at the front have views of the church and its surrounding trees; others, of Rye's mediaeval roofscape. Henry James wrote *The Spoils of Poynton* while living here in 1896 with his fat dog, servants and a canary, before moving to nearby Lamb House. He said in a letter '. . . the pears grow yellow in the sun and the peace of the Lord – or at least of the parson – seems to abide here' (no pears now, but the rest is still true).

As only breakfast is served (and cream teas in the garden on sunny weekends), for dinner Julia Lampon recommends – out of Rye's many restaurants – the Landgate bistro, Flushing Inn or Old Forge. Julia will also do snack suppers (if ordered); and all guests are invited to a complimentary sherry with the Lampons in the evening.

There is a weekly sheep market and a general market. The Rye Heritage Centre features a sound and light show and an authentic town model. Romney Marsh (famous for its autumn sunsets and its spring lambs) attracts painters and birdwatchers. Rye itself was the setting for E. F. Benson's *Mapp and Lucia* stories. Benson lived in Georgian Lamb House after Henry James (it is now a National Trust property).

The town deserves a lingering visit to explore its cobbled byways, antique and craft shops and historic fortifications, for there are few places where a mediaeval town plan and original houses have survived so little altered. In addition there are in the area 20 castles, historic houses such as Kipling's Batemans, Ellen Terry's Smallhythe and (with fine gardens) Great Dixter, Sissinghurst and Scotney. Battle Abbey and Camber's miles of sandy beaches are other attractions.

Readers' comments: Charming house, pretty rooms, friendly welcome. Outstanding. Charm and helpfulness of the owners gave us a perfect weekend.

For explanation of code letters (C, D, H, PT, S, X) see page xxxiv.

OLD WHARF FARM

Yardley Gobion, Northamptonshire, NN12 7UE   Tel: 0908 542454

South-east of Towcester. Nearest main road: A508 from Milton Keynes to Northampton.

C D PT S X

3 Bedrooms. £15 (less for 7 nights). Bargain breaks. Views of garden, country, canal. No smoking. Washing machine on request.
Light suppers if ordered in advance. Wine can be brought in.
1 Sitting-room. With open fire, central heating, record-player.
Large garden with croquet.

In this idyllic waterside setting, many visitors sit fascinated to watch traditional barges being painted and restored in the dry dock which the Bowens have created in their orchard. The 18th-century house has had many lives – as farm, then inn, then wharfmaster's house and back to a smallholding before they took over. The Duke of Grafton helped to pioneer the canal system in this area and he used French prisoners-of-war to build the stables for horses to tow the boats along.

The wharf alongside is still in use, servicing colourful narrow-boats that use the Grand Union canal. The Bowens' boat can be hired by the day.

One enters through a tiled and beamed hall with an Orkney chair (made like the old straw beehives), interesting pictures and rugs. There's a deep green parlour for meals, with mahogany furniture, and a red-tiled sitting-room where old armchairs covered in William Morris fabrics are gathered round a log stove in the big inglenook. Board stairs lead to the bedrooms: one has a brass bed with ribbon-trimmed duvet and a grapevine peering through the window, while in a particularly pretty family room sugar-pink duvets match the walls. Lying casually about are such oddly assorted family treasures as the Bowens' own childhood teddybears and Bonzo, and the plush top-hat of showman C. B. Cochrane: John's father was a ballad singer in some of his variety entertainments. Other mementoes include a bust of John's father topped by the actual flying helmet he wore as an aviator in the First World War. Quadrophonic stereo is available for guests to use.

Outside there's a view of water-meadows, and a miscellany of animals ranging freely about, which children in particular enjoy: a donkey (which they can ride), goats, chickens, ducks, geese, pigs, some calves and two Jersey cows. The Bowens keep a herd of beef-cattle.

A rowing boat can be borrowed, for fishing, exploring or picnicking. Old farm machines, the original Victorian weighbridge (for carts delivering coal, etc., to the barges), and a rope-ladder up into a spreading willow all contribute to the scene.

Light suppers can be arranged if ordered, but most visitors go for meals to the Coffee Pot inn or the White Horse in the village (there are other choices of dining-places nearby). Tea and coffee are free – help yourself in the kitchen.

The southern part of Northamptonshire has agreeable countryside, easily reached from the M1 (use junction 15 for Yardley Gobion), with attractive stone villages among the folds of the hills. A special feature of the scene is water – rivers, canals, lakes and reservoirs abound (and on many of these watersports and boating are possible). The area was the scene of major battles in both the Wars of the Roses (15th century) and the Civil War (17th century). Sulgrave Manor is where George Washington's ancestors lived; other sights include the Waterways Museum at Stoke Bruerne, Turner's organ museum, and Castle Ashby and its park.

233

OLDFIELDS

102 Wells Road, Bath, Avon, BA2 3AL   Tel: 0225 317984
Nearest main road: A367 from Bath to Radstock.

14 Bedrooms. £17.50–£24 (less for 4 nights). Prices go up at Easter. Bargain breaks. Some have own bath/shower/toilet. Tea/coffee facilities. TV. Views of garden, country. Balcony (one).
1 Sitting-room. With open fire, central heating, record-player.
Small garden

Although this late Victorian house (or, rather, two) of honey-coloured stone stands just off a steep main road out of Bath, I spent a quiet night; and in a particularly attractive and spacious bedroom (pine-louvred doors to cupboards, a terracotta-and-cream colour scheme, sprigged Laura Ashley wallpaper, attractive modern pictures and lots of pot-plants). The big sitting-room is decorated in soft browns and mossy greens, with a marble fireplace (crackling fire in winter) and lace curtains from ceiling to floor at the high windows with their fine views of the city. But what I liked best about Oldfields were the owners, Anthony O'Flaherty and his wife Nicole, who are great fun. Breakfasts are generous (with herbal teas, if you like) with much emphasis on wholefoods.

Care is taken over every detail. Says Anthony: 'We buy muesli at a holier-than-holy wholefood shrine called Harvest, in a restored Victorian factory by the Avon, with the statutory Greenpeace poster alongside the statutory Employers' Public Liability notice. We buy butter from a Somerset farm, and eschew the miniscule foil-wrapped jobs. The bread from a local baker is unsliced wheatmeal which means more work at breakfast-time but it makes better toast: it's delivered to us the morning it is baked.'

Apart from Bath itself (which deserves at least a week-long stay with Wednesday reserved for the influx of antique dealers and Saturday for the 'flea market'), you can visit the cathedral city of Wells, the Cheddar Gorge and the lovely Mendip Hills, the sea at Weston-super-Mare, old market towns like Warminster, Chippenham and historic Bristol (a lively city, with plenty to interest tourists, theatre-goers etc.) And, of course, the beauties of Devon, the South Wales coast and hills, and the Cotswolds are not far away; also delectable villages like Lacock, Bradford-on-Avon, Biddestone and Castle Combe, as well as the gardens at Stourhead.

But one need not go even as far afield as this, for the tiny county of Avon is full of interest. Apart from its lovely landscapes there are, for instance, the old 1813 pump house at Claverton, its beam-engine often in action at weekends; 14th-century Clevedon Court and gardens; Dyrham Park, 18th century; Horton Court, partly Norman; nature trails (Poet's Walk, and a canal-side one); Priston's watermill, Timsbury's shire horse stables; prehistoric sites at Wellow and Worlebury.

Readers' comments: Wonderful! Exceptionally nice people. Warmth and charm. Spacious comfort.

THE ORCHARD

Bathford, Avon, BA1 7TG   Tel: 0225 858765
North-east of Bath. Nearest main road: A4 from Bath to Chippenham.

4 Bedrooms. £18.25–£20.25. Prices go up in March. All have own bath/shower/toilet. TV. Views of garden, country. No smoking.
1 Sitting-room. With open fire, central heating.
Large garden with croquet.
Closed from November to January inclusive.

All the pleasures of Bath are within about ten minutes by car (or bus), yet this little village perched on a hillside seems deep in the country. There are stunning views over the River Avon to the far countryside and all around is peace.

John and Olga London's home is a luxurious Georgian house standing in its own grounds. In the garden are specimen trees, such as a copper beech and a Judas tree; there are terraced lawns, and walls of creamy Bath stone – characteristic of many gardens in this conservation village. Sometimes one sees balloonists drifting by. The bedrooms are amongst the most elegant in this book, with private bathrooms and windows overlooking the garden; and the other rooms are equally handsome with attractive colour schemes and antique furniture. Even the landing is memorable: nicely framed etchings on russet walls, sparkling white paintwork. One bedroom (with very large bed and orthopaedic mattress), decorated in cream tones and furnished with pine and rush, has a huge bay window and armchairs from which to enjoy the view. There is an even bigger bed in a pinky-brown room, the velvety wallpaper complemented by a cream carpet. In a third room are peach fabrics, an antique settle and another big, south-facing window.

Breakfasts include freshly squeezed orange juice, home-made muesli, free-range eggs and locally baked wholemeal bread. For dinner, the nearby Crown Inn is excellent.

Most people stay here in order to visit nearby Bath for its Georgian elegance (including the Pump Room, Roman remains, abbey, enticing shops and exceptional museums (particularly outstanding is the museum of American history with 18 period rooms; others cover costume, industrial heritage, postal history, art, bookbinding, photography and decorative arts). You can stroll in the botanic gardens or go up Beckford's tower; visit Herschel's house or Sally Lunn's, admire the splendours of Prior Park or the classically simple chapel of the Countess of Huntingdon (with taped history of all Bath's buildings). Go only a little further afield to visit Bristol's historic quays (there are boat trips), and fine cathedral, to walk the Avon Gorge nature trail, or go on board the SS *Great Britain*. One of the newest attractions is the hands-on science centre called the Exploratory.

Readers' comments: House and appointments are a delight. Complete peace, beautiful surroundings, everything done perfectly. Went out of their way to make us feel welcome. Rooms fabulous. Delightfully furnished. Outstanding. A privilege to stay there. Excellent, could not be bettered, have stayed 3 times.

★ **ORCHARD COTTAGE** C(5) **D PT**
Back Lane, Upper Oddington, Gloucestershire, GL56 0XL Tel: 0451 30785
East of Stow-on-the-Wold. Nearest main road: A436 from Stow-on-the-Wold
towards Chipping Norton.

rear view

2 Bedrooms. £15–£17 (less for 3 nights).
Prices go up in March. Bargain breaks. One
has own bath/shower/toilet. Tea/coffee
facilities. Views of garden, country. No
smoking.
Dinner. £10.50 for 3 courses and coffee, at
7–8pm. Vegetarian or special diets if
ordered. Wine can be brought in. No smoking. **Light suppers** if ordered.
1 Sitting-room. With open fire, central heating, TV, record-player. No smoking.
Small garden
Closed in December and January.

A few ancient apple-trees are all that remain of the great orchard which gave this
18th-century cottage its name. Originally two tiny dwellings, the house has been
repeatedly modernized over the last two hundred years, most recently by its
present owner Jane Beynon. She has used soft colours in the rooms – for instance,
creams and pinks in a bedroom with lace bedspread; rush-seated and spindle-
backed chairs in the small dining-hall; and Doulton's 'Babylon' pattern bone china
on the table.

A typical dinner might comprise local trout pâté; lamb casseroled with aubergines, coriander and saffron (served in a ring of potato with browned almonds on
top, and accompanied by garden vegetables); syllabub of gooseberries and elderflowers, also from the garden. As an alternative to a cooked breakfast, she can
provide cold meats and cheeses in continental style.

The Cotswolds are not too well provided with bus services, so Jane is one of a
team of volunteers who drives a community minibus around eight villages and the
town of Chipping Norton once a week. She gladly takes visitors along, or will
provide routes for their own car tours. Late June is a good time to stay, when a
number of private gardens in Oddington are opened to the public.

Readers' comments: Hospitable, outgoing and kind. Every comfort. Cooking
first-class.

On a hill just south of Stow is **WYCK
HILL LODGE** (tel: 0451 30141),
built around 1800 as the lodge to a
nearby mansion. Phyllis Berry has furnished the house with button-back
chairs and other Victoriana in the L-
shaped sitting-room, oak furniture in
the dining-room, which has a huge
picture-window from which to enjoy
the terraced garden (with pool) and
views to the far hills. From the green-
houses come the plentiful pot-plants
that are in every room. Bedrooms are
on the ground floor. By special arrange-

ment, Phyllis will prepare such meals
as Cotswold trout with hollandaise
sauce, chicken cooked with paprika,
and papaya meringues or a chestnut
gâteau. From £16 to £18.

236

★ **ORCHARD HOUSE**   C PT
High Street, Rothbury, Northumberland, NE65 7TL   Tel: 0669 20684
South-west of Alnwick. Nearest main road: A697 from Morpeth to Wooler.

6 Bedrooms. £16.50–£18.50 (less for 7 nights). Some have own shower/toilet. Tea/coffee facilities. TV. Views of garden, country. Washing machine on request.
Dinner. £10 for 4 courses and coffee, at 7pm. Non-residents not admitted. Vegetarian or special diets if ordered. Wine can be ordered. No smoking.
1 Sitting-room. With central heating. Bar.
Small garden
Closed from December to February inclusive.

Rothbury, a pleasant little market town with some interesting shops, stands in the very centre of Northumberland, so many of the pleasures of that large and underestimated county are within an easy drive: the Roman wall to the south, Holy Island to the north, and in between countryside which can change from open moorland to woods and arable fields within a few miles, with picturesque villages and historic monuments for punctuation. Castles and peel towers (fortified farmhouses) remind one of border raiders.

Orchard House is Georgian. It stands well aside from Rothbury's bustling main street. Jeff and Sheila Jefferson took it over several years ago when Jeff left the RAF after years as an engineer (some of them spent in Malaysia) and have turned it into a comfortable and unpretentious place to stay. Like many people who provide good accommodation in relatively unknown spots, they have found that guests who stayed a night or two while passing through have returned for a longer holiday.

Sheila's four-course menus are out of the ordinary and varied, the only fixture being roast beef every Sunday. Otherwise you might get (for instance) French onion soup, pork scallopine, strawberry meringue and cheese (local produce is used whenever possible). Coffee is included, and there is free tea on arrival. In the lounge is a cabinet well stocked with miniatures of drinks for you to help yourself and enter in a book.

The sight closest to Rothbury is Cragside, the mansion which Norman Shaw (best known, perhaps, for his government buildings in London) designed for Lord Armstrong, the armaments king. It is one of the most complete late-Victorian houses there are. Among the oddities are a Turkish bath and a hydraulic lift, but its main distinction is that it was the first house in the world to be lit by electricity. The elaborately landscaped grounds are also notable.

Brinkburn Priory, Alnwick Castle, Wallington Hall and gardens are all near. At Cambo is a garden centre specializing in cottage-garden and windy-site plants.

Readers' comments: Very impressed. A delightful couple, friendly and helpful. Outstanding food; rooms sparkling clean and spacious. Excellent food – first-rate value. Comfortable, spotless; we thoroughly endorse all you say. Excellent in every way. Exceptionally helpful, excellent food, very good value. Very good food, everything of the highest standard. Marvellous food and accommodation. Thoroughly endorse all you say: excellent.

237

OTLEY HOUSE

Otley, Suffolk, IP6 9NR   Tel: 047890 253
North-west of Woodbridge. Nearest main road: A12 from Ipswich to
Saxmundham.

4 Bedrooms. £16–£23. Prices go up in March. Bargain breaks. Some have own bath/shower/toilet. TV. Views of garden, country. No smoking. Washing machine on request.
Dinner. £14 for 4 courses (with choices) and coffee, at 7.30pm except on Sundays. Non-residents not admitted. Vegetarian or special diets if ordered. Wine can be ordered. No smoking.
2 Sitting-rooms. With open fire, central heating, TV, piano. No smoking in one.
Large garden with croquet.
Closed from November to February inclusive.

It's a story frequently told about houses in this book: lovely old buildings, once occupied by a large family with many servants, prove too big and expensive for today's needs, and fall into sad neglect – until someone sees their potential for a new life sustained by paying guests who occupy rooms surplus to family needs.

When the Hiltons moved to mainly 18th-century Otley House, it was very run down and the grounds (once tended by seven gardeners) so overgrown with brambles that, when clearing them, they fell into a pool before realizing it was there. Within a few years all this was transformed. High French windows now open onto immaculate lawns and the two lakes that were part of a moat round the house. Wild ducks frequent these and a small island with marguerites and astilbes.

The sitting-room's wood block floor is scattered with oriental rugs, and on its off-pink walls hang some of the Hiltons' collection of watercolours. Many of these, like other objects around the house, come from Denmark – Lise's home country. The large hall (with handsome details such as arches and panelled doors) houses early Chinese porcelain which she has restored, and one of Michael's ship models.

Chippendale chairs surround the long mahogany dining-table with its crystal chandelier and family silver where Lise serves such meals as salmon mousse or a herby Danish pâté to start with; chicken in tarragon sauce; Danish lemon mousse or chocolate mousse with Grand Marnier; then Stilton. After the formal dinner, a grand piano awaits – or the billiard room, with big leather armchairs around a fire

Up the curving staircase with barley-sugar balusters are very attractive bedrooms, one with stripped pine four-poster and fabrics printed with old vegetable dyes; another that has windows in two of its cobalt blue walls, and pink carpet.

From Otley, beautiful stretches of the coast are only a few miles away and near the house itself is moated Otley Hall, with mediaeval wall paintings.

Readers' comments: Delighted. Dinner excellent, room well above average; first-class. Impeccable standard of cooking. Relaxed excellence, meticulous attention to detail and concern for every guest. Immaculate. Delicious food.

★ **OVERCOMBE HOTEL**   **C D H P T S X**
Horrabridge, Devon, PL20 7RN   Tel: 0822 853501
North-west of Yelverton. Nearest main road: A386 from Plymouth to
Tavistock.

rear view

11 Bedrooms. £18–£19 (less for 7 nights).
Prices go up in October. Bargain breaks.

Some have own bath/shower/toilet. Tea/coffee facilities. TV. Views of garden, country. Balcony. Washing machine on request. **Dinner.** A la carte or £10.50 for 4 courses (with choices) and coffee, at 7.30pm. Vegetarian or special diets if ordered. Wine can be ordered. **Light suppers** if ordered. **2 Sitting-rooms.** With open fire, central heating, TV. **Bar.** **Small garden**

Conveniently placed for one to explore Dartmoor and the coast, the Overcombe Hotel (now run by Brenda and Maurice Dumell) consists of two houses joined in one to make a very comfortable small hotel. You can relax in either of the sitting-rooms, according to what you want – a bar in one, TV in another, log fires, pleasant views. From the bay window of the dining-room, one looks across to the moors. The walls are hung with local paintings, some of which are for sale.

There is always a selection of dishes on the menu with such choices as pear and parsnip soup, salmon in filo pastry, apple mousse and cheeses.

Visitors come here for a variety of reasons (the least of which is that it's a good staging-post if you are on that long slog to furthest Cornwall). The Dartmoor National Park attracts people touring by car, anglers, riders, golfers and – above all – walkers (for them, Maurice organizes special two- to seven-day bargain breaks, with experienced guides accompanying visitors on walks of eight miles or more, and illustrated after-dinner talks about the moors). Plymouth is near; and among visitors' favourite outings are Cotehele, Buckland Abbey and Saltram House (all National Trust), Morwellham Quay and the Shire Horse Centre.

Further east lie the delectable South Hams: flowery valleys, sands, mildest of climates. To the west is the Cornish coast: dramatic cliffs, sandy coves and some harbours so picturesque (Polperro, Looe, etc.) that popularity threatens to ruin them. But go inland, and you will still find undisturbed villages and market towns.

Plymouth was heavily bombed, which means that its shopping centre is very modern. But the old quarter, the Barbican, which Drake and the Pilgrim Fathers knew so well, survived, and it is to this that visitors throng. Here are the old warehouses and the harbours full of small boats, the narrow alleys with beguiling little shops and restaurants, the mediaeval houses now turned into museums, the fish market and, high above, the 17th-century citadel. Plymouth has an outstanding aquarium, Drake's Island out in the Sound (to be visited by boat), the naval dockyard and the famous clifftop – the Hoe – with its unique seascape, memorials and flowers.

Other local sights: the 15th-century cottage where Drake's wife grew up (at Saltash); the gardens at Bickham House (Roborough) and at the Garden House (Buckland); and an unusual museum with 800 paperweights (Yelverton).

Readers' comments: A wonderful stay. Made us very welcome and could not have been more delightful hosts. Excellent food, fresh vegetables daily. Comfortable and warm. We will go again. A relaxed, easy atmosphere; we could recommend this hotel to any of our friends.

PARADISE HOUSE

88 Holloway, Bath, Avon, BA2 4PX   Tel: 0225 317723

Nearest main road: A367 from Bath to Radstock.

C(5) PT

9 Bedrooms. £20–£30 (less for 5 nights). **From £18 to SOTBT readers only, up to Easter.** Prices go up in July. Some have own bath/shower/toilet. Tea/coffee facilities. TV. Views of garden, country.
1 Sitting-room. With open fire, central heating.
Large garden with croquet.

It stands half way up a steep, curving road which was once indeed a 'hollow way': a lane worn low between high banks by centuries of weary feet or hooves entering Bath from the south: the last lap of the Romans' Fosse Way. It is now a quiet cul-de-sac in the lee of Beechen Cliff, with panoramic views over the city, the centre of which is only 7 minutes' walk away – downhill. (As to uphill – take a taxi! Or else a bus to the Bear Flat stop.) Look the opposite way and all is leafy woods.

The house itself was built about 1720, with all the elegance which that implies: a classical pediment above the front door and well-proportioned sash windows with rounded tops in a façade of honey-coloured Bath stone.

David and Janet Cutting took it over several years ago and have restored it impeccably throughout, stripping off polystyrene to reveal pretty plasterwork ceilings, for instance, and gaudy tiles to expose a lovely marble fireplace in which logs now blaze. They stripped dingy paint off the panelled pine doors and put on handles of brass or china. They have furnished to a very high standard indeed, with both antique and modern furniture, elegant fabrics, and well chosen colours, predominantly soft greens and browns. The sitting-room is especially pretty, with Liberty fabrics and wallpaper, pictures in maple frames and a collection of Coalport cottages. There is also a Jacuzzi.

The bedrooms, given as much care as the rest, vary in size and amenities.

At the back, beyond a verandah with ivy-leaf ironwork, is quite a large walled garden (a suntrap in the afternoon), with lawns, fish-pool, a rose-covered pergola and marvellous views of the city and hills all around. This secluded setting extends behind the mediaeval Magdalen Chapel next door, which was once a hostel for lepers banned from the city. In 1982 David and Janet acquired the adjoining Georgian house, which they then completely restored, furnished and decorated to the same elegant standards as the main house. (Lock-up garages for a small fee.)

As to Bath itself – which attracts more visitors than any other place in England except London – the attractions are so varied that they can hardly be compressed into one paragraph. Just wandering among the Georgian perfection of its streets and squares, which spread from the historic centre right up the sides of the surrounding hills, and in its award-winning gardens, is a pleasure in itself, and it would take many days to explore them all (the best method is to take a bus to each hilltop in turn and walk back downhill, with far views succeeded by discoveries of lovely houses, streets, alleys or gardens all the way).

Readers' comments: Top-class! Truly excellent. Ideal, with excellent facilities. Superbly equipped, very attractive. Outstanding hotel. Extremely comfortable. Beautiful home; made us very welcome. Lovely house and garden.

PARKFIELD HOUSE

C S

Hogben's Hill, Selling, Kent, ME13 9QU   Tel: 0227 752898
South of Faversham. Nearest main road: A251 from Faversham to Ashford.

5 Bedrooms. £14 (less for 2 nights). Prices go up in April. TV. Views of garden, country. No smoking.
1 Sitting-room. With open fire, central heating, TV. No smoking.
Small garden

There were Hogbens on this hill in 1086 (they are named in the Domesday Book) . . . and there still are!

It is Mr and Mrs Hogben who own Parkfield, a largely modern house with a pretty garden, as well as the small joinery works alongside – John Hogben's principal activity. It is worth staying at Parkfield House simply to listen to him talk about Kentish ways and history (especially his stories of past Hogbens, who were blacksmiths, farmers, wheelwrights and smugglers). Next door there used to be an inn called Ye Olde Century in memory of a John Hogben who lived there until he was 101.

The house, built in 1820, had become run down until about 30 years ago when Mr Hogben renovated and extended it. Now it is immaculate and very comfortable.

Although only bed-and-breakfast guests are taken (they can dine, very well indeed, at the old village inn – the White Lion), there is a sitting-room for their use in the evening, with television and big, velvet armchairs in which to relax by a log fire.

And if you want something special for breakfast (fish, fresh fruit, ham, cheese) Mrs Hogben will get it – and will do packed lunches.

Selling is in a very beautiful and tranquil part of Kent, well situated for touring, walking and sightseeing. It is, of course, the cathedral which brings most visitors to nearby Canterbury: one of Britain's finest and most colourful, with many historical associations, the site of Becket's martyrdom (commemorated in some of the finest stained glass in the world), the splendid tomb of the Black Prince, and much more.

The ancient walled city still has many surviving mediaeval and Tudor buildings, the beautiful River Stour, old churches and inns, Roman remains, a very good theatre, and lovely shops in its small lanes. It is in the middle of some of Kent's finest countryside, with a coast of great variety quite near (cliffs, sands or shingle; resorts, fishing harbours or historic ports) and ten golf courses. Howlett's Zoo and mediaeval Faversham are very popular, and the whole area is full of fine gardens and garden centres. Both Leeds and Dover castles are within easy motoring distance. One could spend a fortnight here without discovering all there is to see in one of England's most beautiful and most historic counties, rich in towns with antique shops and fields of pick-your-own fruit.

In blossom-time there are car 'trails' marked out among the orchards.

Readers' comments: Excellent in all respects, exceptional hospitality. Excellent service, well cared for. Warm welcome. Spotless. Attractive bedroom.

★ **PEACOCK FARM GUEST-HOUSE**   C D H PT X
Redmile, Leicestershire, NG13 0GQ   Tel: 0949 42475
West of Grantham (Lincolnshire). Nearest main road: A52 from Nottingham to
Grantham.

10 Bedrooms. £14–£17 (less for 7 nights). Bargain breaks. Some have own shower/toilet. Tea/coffee facilities. TV. Views of garden. Washing machine on request. **Dinner.** A la carte or £10 for 3 courses (with choices) and coffee, at 7.15pm. Vegetarian or special diets if ordered. Wine can be ordered. **1 Sitting-room.** With open fire, central heating, TV, piano. No smoking. **Bar.** **Large garden**

This guest-house with restaurant (built as a farm in the 18th century and later a canal bargees' inn) is ideal for a break when doing a long north-south journey on the nearby A1, particularly with children – or as a base from which to explore the many little-known attractions of Nottinghamshire and adjacent counties.

It is in the outstandingly beautiful Vale of Belvoir, with the Duke of Rutland's Belvoir Castle (full of art treasures) rearing its battlemented walls high above a nearby hilltop: an unforgettable sight. The topiary yew peacock on the front lawn, started in 1812, was inspired by the peacock in the crest of the Duke.

The Needs have created a happy family atmosphere here. Some rooms are simple and comfortable (en suite rooms are very nicely equipped), and two are ideal for families: a self-contained pine cabin and a coach house outside the main building. Children can safely play in the garden which has a large lawn, hammock, swings, small covered swimming-pool, playroom, pool-room, bicycles, barbecue, horse, goat and dogs. All around are wheatfields. Indoors are snooker and table tennis.

Food (much of it cooked by daughter Nicky) is above average, with home-made bread and soups, herbs from the garden and much local produce. Starters may include stuffed tomatoes or pan-fried sardines; main courses, salmon or trout with sorrel sauce or game pie; puddings, chocolate and rum nut loaf.

There are many popular sights in this region: Belvoir Castle, Belton House, Stapleford Park, Rutland Water and Wollaton Hall in its park; also Holme Pierrepont Hall, Doddington Hall, and Newstead Abbey (Byron's home). Eastwood has D. H. Lawrence's birthplace. Lincoln (cathedral), Southwell (minster), Sherwood Forest (Robin Hood display) and Nottingham are also near – the last a much underrated city. I recommend the arts museum in the castle and others at its foot (the lace museum is fascinating), river trips and walks through the Georgian quarter. The historic market towns of Stamford (in particular) and Newark are of great interest. One can shop for local Stilton, crafts and Nottingham lace to take home – Melton Mowbray is famous for pies and other pork delicacies. Well worth a detour is Burghley House, near Stamford.

PEAR TREE COTTAGE

C(2) D PT

Church Road, Wilmcote, Warwickshire, CV37 9UX   Tel: 0789 205889
North-west of Stratford-upon-Avon. Nearest main road: A34 from Stratford to
Birmingham.

7 Bedrooms. £15–£17 (less for 7 nights).
Prices go up in April. All have own bath/
shower/toilet. Tea/coffee facilities. TV.
Views of garden, country. Washing machine
on request.
2 Sitting-rooms. With central heating, TV.
Large garden

Mary Arden, Shakespeare's mother, grew up in the big half-timbered house which
overlooks this cottage of much the same date, and it is quite possible that
Shakespeare visited here when calling on his grandparents across the way. Now
there is a museum of rural life in the Arden house.

Pear Tree Cottage, too, is half-timbered. From its flowery garden one steps into
a hall with stone-flagged floor, oak settle, other antiques and bunches of dried
flowers. The floor is of blue lias, once quarried at Wilmcote, and to be seen also in
Stratford's famous Clopton Bridge and the steps of St Paul's Cathedral in London.

In the beamed sitting-room, the yellow and green armchairs and colourful
Staffordshire pottery figures show well against rugged stone walls. There is a little
breakfast-room with country Hepplewhite chairs; and bedrooms (reached by steps
and turns all the way) have very pleasant colour schemes – in one is a specially
made Windsor bedhead. From the shower room of another there is a perfect view
of Mary Arden's house: an ideal, if unusual, place from which to photograph it!

Outside are two gardens, a stream, a pool with pink waterlilies, stone paths and
seats under old apple-trees. Although Margaret Mander does not serve evening
meals, there are two kitchens in which guests can prepare their own snack suppers.
Most people stroll to the nearby Swan or Mason's Arms for dinner.

The cottage is right in the middle of 'Shakespeare country' with the Cotswold
Hills to the south. Oxford, Worcester and Warwick are all within easy reach.

There is an attractive cross-country drive from Wilmcote to visit Charlecote
Park, an Elizabethan house on a terrace overlooking the River Avon. The outside
is more beautiful than the interior (much altered in Victorian times) and in the
gatehouse is a museum of sporting life.

In the other direction, a rural drive will bring you to Coughton Court – another
gatehouse, with Gunpowder Plot and Civil War associations and good furniture
and paintings in its rooms. Beyond this lies the elegant old town of Alcester where
two rivers meet, and Ragley Hall – a classical stone mansion on a hilltop (one of its
treasures is a great, new mural in *trompe l'oeil* covering the wall of its big hall).

To the south the River Avon meanders on its way. Shakespeare is known to have
frequented the inn at Bidford-on-Avon (which has a 14th-century bridge) and at
Welford-on-Avon are a great many thatched and half-timbered cottages.

The countryside in this part of Warwickshire is pleasant rather than dramatic,
but there are attractive woodland walks and picnic spots.

Readers' comments: Ideal in all respects. Have always received most kind and
courteous attention and a wonderful breakfast. Thoroughly enjoyed every stay.

PEAT GATE HEAD

Low Row, North Yorkshire, DL11 6PP   Tel: 0748 86388

C H S

West of Richmond. Nearest main road: A6108 from Richmond to Leyburn.

rear view

6 Bedrooms. £32.50 with dinner (less for 2 nights). Prices go up in April. Some have own shower/toilet. Tea/coffee facilities. Views of garden, country, river. No smoking. Washing machine on request.
Dinner. 4 courses and coffee, at 7pm.

Vegetarian or special diets if ordered. Wine can be ordered. No smoking.
2 Sitting-rooms. With open fire, central heating, TV, piano. Bar. No smoking in one.
Large garden

It sometimes seems that anywhere north of Leeds now calls itself Herriot country, what with almost countless books, films, and television series. Though the author actually practises to the east of the county, much filming of his books was done in the Yorkshire Dales, and Peat Gate Head is just along the moor road (with watersplash) where the opening of every television episode was recorded.

Alan Earl had long loved Peat Gate Head, a 300-year-old Swaledale farmhouse built of the local limestone, and when his job as a history lecturer ended with the closure of the training college where he worked, he decided to buy it and to turn his enthusiasm for cooking to good use by opening it as a guest-house. From several choices at each course one might select, for instance, salmon mousse, chicken breasts in orange-and-tarragon sauce, and queen of puddings.

The beamed house is agreeably furnished. There is a vast stone chimneypiece in the dining-room, and in the sitting-room a wood-burning stove pleasantly scents the air. Two bedrooms are on the ground floor (one with own shower and toilet).

Outside the door, a summerhouse on the lawn looks across a sweep of Swaledale, a textbook illustration of a valley, from the river running along the flat bottom, through stone-walled fields, to open moorland. From the bedrooms on the opposite side of the house, you are at eye level with peewits and curlews. Richmond and other castles, especially Barnard Castle, are extra attractions, along with waterfalls and the Dales scenery. There is more on these in other pages of this book.

Readers' comments: Made us so welcome and entertained us non-stop; delicious meals; peaceful atmosphere. Great charm, most acceptable dinner, massive breakfast. Very good value, most entertaining too. Three unforgettable days . . . the quality of everything. A fine man, a character! Took a great deal of trouble. Excellent cuisine. Food interesting, well cooked and presented. Delightful premises; high standard of comfort. Totally relaxed mood.

For explanation of code letters (C, D, H, PT, S, X) see page xxxiv.

244

★ **PENNINE LODGE**   C(10) **D H PT**
St John's Chapel, County Durham, DL13 1QX   Tel: 0388 537247
West of Stanhope. Nearest main road: A689 from Stanhope to Alston.

5 Bedrooms. £16.50 (less for 3 nights). Bargain breaks. All have own bath/shower/toilet. Tea/coffee facilities. TV. Views of garden, country, river. No smoking.
Dinner. £8.50 for 3 courses and coffee, at 7pm. Non-residents not admitted. Vegetarian or special diets if ordered. Wine can be ordered. No smoking.
1 Sitting-room. With central heating, TV. No smoking.
Large garden
Closed from November to mid-March.

Pennine Lodge was built in the 16th century, and it has the long and narrow shape typical of a Weardale farmhouse. Just below the windows of the corridor which connects the bedrooms is the upper River Wear, rushing over a small waterfall backed by trees, a beautiful spot. The rooms themselves are full of interest, with lots of timber and stone, antiques and bric-a-brac: in one a grandfather clock (silent!), in another a real Durham quilt.

Guests dine in a long, low-ceilinged room next to the garden, with a stone inglenook at one end. There are three courses: a starter (or else cheese), with a main course which is quite likely to be a casserole of pheasant or other game from the Raby estates, and, for example, rhubarb pie and cream. All is home-made by Yvonne Raine, including jams and bread; afternoon tea is available. She has also researched, and sometimes cooks, local mediaeval recipes.

Raby Castle is one of the best of its kind, and High Force is England's highest waterfall. Killhope Wheel is a huge waterwheel with lead-mining displays.

Readers' comments: It's so good I've been back repeatedly. Lovely position, comfortable without being pretentious. Delightful old house, competent and delightful hostess, food excellent. Beautiful setting. Really excellent.

★ A few miles eastward is **BRECKON HILL** at Westgate (tel: 0388 517228), an old farmhouse which has been neatly renovated by Lyn and John Say. At the end of a rather steep drive, it is very peaceful, and there are impressive views of the dale from the gardens and from most of the bedrooms (one on ground floor). Lyn provides such meals as mushroom soup, pork in white wine (with fresh vegetables) and lemon surprise pudding. £16.50.

Readers' comments: Rooms delightful; magnificent views of Weardale. Facilities first class. Quiet and peaceful. Views magnificent and hospitality second to none. Food excellent.

Shipham, Somerset, BS25 1TW   Tel: 093 484 2659
North of Cheddar. Nearest main road: A38 from Bristol to Taunton.

18 Bedrooms. £16–£21 (less for 2 nights). Bargain breaks. Some have own shower/toilet. Tea/coffee facilities. TV (for hire). Views of garden, country. Washing machine on request.
Dinner. A la carte or from £8 for 3 courses (with choices) and coffee, at 7pm. Vegetarian or special diets if ordered. Wine can be ordered. No smoking. **Light suppers** if ordered.
2 Sitting-rooms. With open fire, central heating, TV. Bar.
Large garden
Closed in December and early January.

Built in the 15th century as farm cottages, Penscot became an inn on the village green, and still retains much of that character. It is a long low building, white-walled and with low beams and log fires inside. The atmosphere is informal and comfortable. Bedrooms are simple, the sitting-room well provided with plenty of deep armchairs and doors to the garden where one can sit in the sun. There is a small conservatory with a flourishing vine and hanging baskets of flowers.

There are two dining-rooms. The one (non-smoking) for residents has pine alcoves and Scandinavian-style chairs. Here the Tildens serve a set meal such as home-made soup, chicken casserole with local vegetables, and cheesecake. In a converted barn there is an à la carte menu too: mainly conventional food such as trout, duck, steaks etc., with many vegetarian dishes.

Most of the bedrooms are quite simple but two (on the ground floor) have special features. One very attractive room has a four-poster, plus an extra bed; and the other would be ideal for a family as there is a children's room adjoining.

From peaceful Shipham there are far views to Bridgwater Bay and the Welsh hills. It lies on the edge of the beautiful Mendip Hills (and half way along the walkers' Mendip Way which winds from the coast to Wells). In the neighbourhood are facilities for riding, golf, caving and painting. Plenty of sightseeing, too: castles, stately homes, gorges, woods, viewpoints, vineyards, museums, wildlife, gardens, the Wookey Hole caves and innumerable churches of architectural interest. There are many gardens, including those at Longleat and Cricket St Thomas; and antique shops. The Tildens have produced a book of local walks.

Readers' comments: Delightful. Tasty home cooking. Every comfort, good service, happy atmosphere. Good food and welcoming atmosphere. Nice to see everyone smiling. Warm welcome, enjoyable atmosphere and food, very good value. Delightful rooms; food was great; personal attention. So friendly, so peaceful. Gracious hosts, food wonderful. Cheerful, willing staff made us feel so welcome.

PETHILLS BANK COTTAGE   C D

Bottomhouse, Staffordshire, ST13 7PF   Tel: 05388 555 (changing in spring to 0538 304277)

South-east of Leek. Nearest main road: A523 from Leek towards Ashbourne.

3 Bedrooms. £17–£18 (less for 2 nights). Bargain breaks. All have own bath/shower/toilet. Tea/coffee facilities. TV. Views of garden, country.
Dinner. £11.50 for 4 courses (with choices) and coffee, at 7.30pm. Non-residents not admitted. Wine can be brought in.
1 Sitting-room. With open fire, central heating. No smoking.
Small garden

This 18th-century farmhouse, much modernized, stands in landscaped gardens on the crest of a hill, at the edge of the Peak District. The thick and rugged stone walls are exposed to view in a snug sitting-room which was once a cowshed – now soft lighting falls on pinky-beige chesterfields of buttoned velvet, and from the big window there is a view of the Martins' rock garden. In the dining-room are carved Dutch chairs upholstered in green velvet and a log stove on a tiled hearth.

One particularly pretty bedroom, on the ground floor, has its own verandah overlooking the hills, silky draperies and a private sitting-room with pink-and-blue sofa. Up an open-tread stair are more bedrooms, one in a former hayloft. Each has its own style: for instance, bamboo sofa in a room of brown velvet and cream; louvred cupboards, onyx 'Vanitory' and briar rose patterns in the other. Bathrooms are very good.

Yvonne's dinners (available on only some evenings) include such dishes as pasta, trout en croûte, chocolate cheesecake, cheese with fruit. Breakfasts are outstanding – particularly the array of fruits such as figs, mango and melon.

To many people, the name of Staffordshire suggests nothing but industrial ugliness. Wrong! The moorlands of the county form part of the Peak District National Park; while to the south is an 'area of outstanding natural beauty' – Cannock Chase where mediaeval kings once hunted forest game, lush pastures for dairy cows, and a network of rivers and canals with waterside paths.

At Three Shires Head by the bubbling River Dane the county meets Cheshire and Derbyshire, and you will encounter few other travellers if you follow the river along the wild Cheshire border. From the dramatic, rocky summit of the Old Man of Mow (near Biddulph) you can look right across Cheshire: on top of the crag is an 18th-century folly tower. Biddulph's church is worth a visit for its Flemish stained glass; and go to nearby Rudyard, a pretty village, for the scenic reservoir set among woods, crags and caverns. All this is north-west of Leek – while south-east lie lovely valleys and gorges (of the rivers Churnet and Manifold), picturesque villages including Ilam, Longnor and Wetton, windy heaths and woodland walks.

Even the industrial parts of the county have interest because much of the Potteries' past has been conserved. This is where Arnold Bennett wrote his 'five towns' novels and there is a museum devoted to him, at Stoke.

Readers' comments: Made most welcome, well looked after. Warm and cheerful hostess. Excellent cook. Nothing was too much trouble. Very attractive lounge, extremely attentive service. Warm and friendly, very helpful. Fine attention to detail. Excellent in every way and very good value. Breakfast here surpasses all others. Outstanding menu, cooking excellent. Charming hostess.

PHEASANT INN C D H

Stannersburn, Northumberland, NE48 1DD   Tel: 0660 40382

North-west of Hexham. Nearest main road: A68 from Corbridge to Jedburgh.

11 Bedrooms. £17–£20. Bargain breaks. Some have own shower/toilet. Tea/coffee facilities. TV. Views of garden, country. No smoking. Washing machine on request.
Dinner. A la carte or £9.50 for 4 courses (with choices) and coffee, at 7–9pm. Vegetarian or special diets if ordered. Wine can be ordered. No smoking. **Light suppers** if ordered.
1 Lounge bar. With open fire, central heating.

This is everything one wants a country inn to be – nearly four centuries old, stone-walled and low-beamed and in particularly lovely countryside. The Kershaws are determined to keep it unspoilt. The bedrooms, however, are modern, in a former hemel (farm implements store) and barn; many of them are on the ground floor. They are arranged round a square of grass where the farmyard must have been, to one side of the inn building.

The main bar (where very good snacks are served) is big and beamy, with a stone fireplace and some agricultural bygones, such as hay-knives and peat-spades; and a stuffed pheasant appropriately sits on a sill of one of the small windows. A smaller bar houses a pool table.

The dining-room is light and airy, with raspberry-coloured walls and pine furniture. Food is freshly prepared – one interesting starter is avocado with grapefruit and Stilton; trout comes with a sauce of yogurt and herbs; venison appears often.

Stannersburn is in the southern part of the Border Forest Park – 200 square miles of hills and moors that stretch from Hadrian's Wall to Scotland. Within this area is Kielder Forest with Kielder Water in the middle. The immense forest of various conifers was first planted in the 1920s, there are scenic drives through it, and the lake is a great man-made reservoir – the biggest in Europe.

Eastward lies Otterburn, scene of an epic conflict in 1388, when Percy ('Hotspur') led the English against the Scottish Earl of Douglas – as related in the 'Ballad of Chevy Chase'. Among the attractions of this area is the Otterburn mill, no longer working but with bargains in knitwear and tweeds. Other local villages include Elsdon (once the Norman capital of Redesdale), its historic houses – one of them a fortified parsonage – surrounding a huge village green; Harbottle, with the remains of a castle; and Alwinton, where hill farmers gather for agricultural shows.

Although the area is a National Park – England's least known? – it is largely unexploited, though there are one or two such things as 'open' farms to visit. The energetic can go in for watersports on Kielder Water, the contemplative may be rewarded by the sight of roe deer or red squirrels.

Readers' comments: It's super. A very good welcome. Delicious breakfast. Such a wonderful start to our holiday. Delightful country inn. Mr Kershaw and his family could not have been more friendly and courteous, our room was delightful and spotlessly clean, and the food was truly delicious – we look forward to a return visit.

248

★ **PICKFORD HOUSE**   C D PT S X
Bath Road, Beckington, Somerset, BA3 6SJ   Tel: 0373 830329
South of Bath (Avon). Nearest main road: A36 from Bath to Warminster.

4 Bedrooms. £12–£13 (less for 4 nights). Bargain breaks. Some have own bath/shower/toilet. Tea/coffee facilities. TV. Views of garden, country. No smoking. Washing machine on request.
Dinner. A la carte or £7 for 3 courses and coffee, from 7.30pm. Non-residents not admitted. Vegetarian or special diets if ordered. Wine can be ordered.
2 Sitting-rooms. With open fire, central heating, TV, piano, record-player. Bar.
Garden.

Sometimes parties of friends take the whole of this hilltop house for a gourmet weekend together – for Angela Pritchard is a cordon bleu cook (and cookery teacher) while Ken is a great wine enthusiast. (Every year, they go to a different region of France or Germany to bring back little-known wines and local recipes.)

On such weekends, the guests are invited to enjoy a Somerset cream tea to be followed later by a candle-lit dinner of 6 courses with appropriate wines. On the next day, they explore the area's attractions (on their own or with the Pritchards at the helm), which include Bath, Wells and innumerable stately homes, before another gourmet meal. On Sunday morning, there is the heated swimming-pool behind a wall in the garden or picturesque Beckington in which to pass the time before a traditional roast lunch.

Even on everyday occasions Pickford House food is exceptional. Angela offers the choice of a 4-course dinner or what she calls a 'pot-luck' one of 3 courses. An example of the former: mushroom roulade, lamb en croûte, mulberry mousse (made from garden fruit) and cheeses. And of the latter: fish au gratin, liver-and-bacon casserole, bananas baked with Kirsch.

As to the house itself, this is one of a pair that were built from honey-coloured Bath stone for spinster sisters in 1804. The furnishings are comfortable with two modern bedrooms in the old school house (one with kitchen adjoining). In addition to the principal sitting-room, there is a family room which has television and toys to keep children occupied; and outside is a large walled garden with views across the Frome Valley.

As Director-General of the Navy's supplies and transport, Ken played a vital role in the Falklands War.

Visitors dining at Pickford House are sometimes offered a free pre-dinner drive around little-known sights in the vicinity, and the Pritchards will advise on other sightseeing, book you into the local theatres, or help in other ways.

The area is not only very beautiful but full of historic interest. Go to Bath, of course, for its Georgian crescents and streets, elegant shops, abbey, Roman temple, baths and museums (especially the museum of American history). Wells has an outstanding cathedral and bishop's palace; Glastonbury, the famous Tor as well as abbey. Castle Combe claims, with good cause, to be the prettiest village in England and is probably the most photographed. Devizes, Bradford-on-Avon, Frome and Malmesbury are each worth a leisurely visit.

Readers' comments: Very friendly; particularly good value.

PILLMEAD HOUSE

North Lane, Buriton, Hampshire, GU31 5RS   Tel: 0730 66795
South of Petersfield. Nearest main road: A3 from Petersfield to Portsmouth.

C D H PT

2 Bedrooms. £15. Both have own bath/shower/toilet. Tea/coffee facilities. TV. Views of garden, country. No smoking. Washing machine on request.
Dinner. £10 for 3 courses (with choices) and coffee, at 7pm. Non-residents not admitted. Vegetarian or special diets if ordered. Wine can be brought in. No smoking.
1 Sitting-room. With open fire, central heating. No smoking.
Large garden

Sarah Moss used to run a kitchenware shop of distinction, and so she is particularly well equipped with things to produce, for instance, home-made pasta or ice cream. She grows much of the produce that is used in the kitchen for such meals as cucumber soup followed by roast lamb with fresh vegetables and then blackberry ice cream with home-made shortbread, for example.

The house overlooks a valley, its lawn and rock garden descending steeply among terraced beds of roses and lavender. Visitors can enjoy a view of the Queen Elizabeth country park and Butser Hill while drinking their after-dinner coffee.

The sitting-room's bow windows, too, make the most of the view. This is a pretty room, with pink wildflower curtains and sofas, and tapestry chairs.

Upstairs, white walls contrast with moss-green carpets. One bedroom, cottage-style, has peach fabrics and patchwork cushions; in another primrose predominates, with a patchwork bedspread and cushions.

Adjoining the house is a building that was once a schoolroom. John now uses it in connection with his work, which is renovating old buildings, a subject on which he is a mine of information. Pillmead House is itself of interest: its lozenge-paned windows and brick-and-flint walls are typical of many houses in this area, but the Tudor chimneys – very elaborate, and 8 feet high – came from a mansion.

Readers' comments: Excellent: our second visit.

There really are toads at **TOAD'S ALLEY** in South Lane on the other side of Buriton, home of interior designer Patricia Bushall (tel: 0730 63880). They can sometimes be seen heading to the stream which lies between the garden and the crest along which walkers follow the South Downs Way. The secluded house comprises three tiny farmworkers' cottages built in the 15th century, with brick-floored hall and low-sloping ceilings upstairs. A sitting-room for guests is attractively furnished, like the other rooms, with  pale colours. (Bed-and-breakfast only; both the village inns do good evening meals and are only two minutes' walk away.) From £13.50 to £17.

★ **PIPPS FORD**   C(5) **D H PT**
Needham Market, Suffolk, IP6 8LJ   Tel: 044979 208
North of Ipswich. Nearest main road: A45 from Ipswich to Bury St Edmunds.

6 Bedrooms. £15–£25 (less for 4 nights). Prices go up at Easter. Bargain breaks. All have own bath/shower/toilet. Tea/coffee facilities. Views of garden, country, river. No smoking. Washing machine on request. **Dinner.** £15 for 4 courses (with some choices) and coffee, at 7.15pm (during winter, Monday–Thursday, dinner with less choice is half-price). Vegetarian or special diets if ordered. Wine can be ordered. No smoking. **Light suppers** if ordered. **3 Sitting-rooms.** With open fire, central heating, TV, piano, record-player. **Large garden** with croquet, tennis and swimming-pool. **Closed from mid-December to mid-January inclusive.**

On a stretch of the River Gipping that has been designated an 'area of outstanding natural beauty' stands a large Tudor farmhouse. Raewyn Hackett-Jones has made patchwork quilts or cushion-covers for every room and searched out attractive fabrics (Laura Ashley, French ones and so on) for curtains or upholstery. She puts flowers in each bedroom. Many of the beds are collectors' pieces: a four-poster, a French provincial one and several ornamental brass beds. Oriental rugs cover floors of wood or stone. Even the bathrooms attached to each bedroom are attractive. One is spectacular, with a huge oval bath. Some bedrooms are in newly converted stables, with sitting-room.

This is a house of inglenook fireplaces, sloping floors, low beams and historic associations, for it once belonged to Tudor chronicler Richard Hakluyt. There are three sitting-rooms and in one, visitors can enjoy the family's huge collection of records. Meals are served in one of two flowery conservatories, grapes overhead.

Breakfasts are exceptional. From an enormous choice, you could select exotic juices; home-made sausages or black pudding; home-made yogurt, croissants or cinnamon toast; waffles, crumpets, muffins: kidneys, mackerel, fishcakes.

Popular dinner dishes include kidneys in a sauce of mustard, sherry and cream; pears and Stilton in filo pastry; a roulade of salmon, turbot and spinach; pork with ginger and orange sauce; tropical fruits with *fromage frais* and blackcurrant sauce.

Beyond the garden, there is coarse fishing in the river, where cricket-bat willows grow, and a Roman site. Interesting places to visit by car are Constable country, Aldeburgh, Southwold and Ipswich. The area is full of pretty villages and ancient churches.

Readers' comments: Most impressed; made very welcome; food absolutely super; most hospitable place; relaxed and informal, thoroughly happy and comfortable; delightful house, beautifully furnished; food and service outstanding; one of the best holidays ever; friendly good humour. A fitting climax to our wonderful trip with 'SOTBT'. Charming and talented hostess, food beautifully garnished.

251

Piddletrenthide, Dorset, DT2 7QX   Tel: 03004 358
North of Dorchester. Nearest main road: A352 from Dorchester to Sherborne.

10 Bedrooms. £16. Prices go up in April.
Bargain breaks. All have own bath/shower/
toilet. Tea/coffee facilities. TV. Views of
garden, country, river.
Dinner. A la carte, at 7pm. Wine can be
ordered. **Light suppers** if ordered.
1 Sitting-room. With open fire, central
heating. **Bars**.
Small garden

A mass of colourful flowers against white walls caught my eye when passing
through the village, and I stopped to visit this pretty inn. At the back, one crosses a
footbridge over the tiny River Piddle (after which the village is named) to enter the
pleasant beer-garden of the inn, parts of which date back to the 18th century. To
one side of this is a modern wing of ground-floor bedrooms in pink-and-white or
other fresh colour schemes; and to the other a solar-heated swimming-pool
enclosed for privacy by wood fencing. There are also bedrooms (rather larger)
inside the inn.

The bars are all you might expect of a busy village inn; the dining-room, with
turquoise leather chairs, is set apart from their bustle (there is also a barbecue in
the garden).

Here Dennis Fox and his family provide typical English pub food such as prawn
cocktail or soup, steak or salmon.

Nearby Dorchester is the 'Casterbridge' of Hardy's novel (and his birthplace, a
cottage at Higher Bockhampton, the garden of which can be visited). The town is
still full of farmers doing business, inns selling local beer and handsome buildings
of Portland stone with which he was familiar. It was here that the Bloody Assize
took place (when Judge Jeffreys condemned to death so many who took part in the
1685 Monmouth Rebellion), and also the 1834 trial of the Tolpuddle Martyrs,
transported for their attempts to set up a trade union.

West of the village is Cerne Abbas, famous for its white giant cut into the green
turf of the hills, a pagan fertility symbol, and for the ancient abbey remains behind
its small streets of Tudor houses. Nearby Sydling St Nicholas has an old smithy
and a church with a multitude of gargoyles and monuments. To the south is
Stinsford, a mecca for Hardy enthusiasts because his heart is buried here (his ashes
are in Westminster Abbey). Puddletown's church has fine monuments,
Athelhampton a battlemented mansion surrounded by a series of lovely gardens,
and Tolpuddle the same great sycamore under which the martyrs met.

The church at Bere Regis is remarkable for its carved roof and life-size apostles.

For another day's outing, head in the direction of picturesque Milton Abbas
(described elsewhere) and its abbey church; and Blandford Forum, an elegant
18th-century market town with good opportunities to buy books and paintings. If
you go from here to Shaftesbury, avoid the direct road in favour of scenic lanes at
the end of Cranborne Chase because there are fine views from the downs here.

Readers' comments: Lovely setting. Welcoming owners. Very good and filling
breakfast.

POLETREES FARM
Brill, Buckinghamshire, HP18 9TZ   Tel: 0844 238276
West of Aylesbury. Nearest main road: A41 from Aylesbury to Bicester.

2 Bedrooms. £14. Bargain breaks. Tea facilities. TV. Views of garden, country.
1 Sitting-room. With open fire, central heating, TV.
Large garden

There is clematis round the porch, baskets brimming with begonias and lobelias hang on the walls, and all around are roses, apple-trees and views of fields: a scene of total peace. But in the 16th century this was a coaching inn on the principal road (Roman in origin) from Oxford to Buckingham. Now that road is nothing but a grassy track, for the traffic goes another way.

Inside, stone walls, oak beams and an inglenook with a rare 15th-century window beside it – tiny oak mullions and wood-pegged shutters – have survived the centuries, though some features were plastered over or boarded up until the Coopers did restoration work. The water for the house still comes from a spring.

So ancient is the area that King Lud – that prehistoric (or mythical?) figure for whom London's Ludgate is named – is reputed to have hunted boar here when all was forest. Hence the name of a nearby village, Ludgershall; which is where Wycliffe started his great work of translating the Bible into English.

Anita has furnished her ancient home well. In the dining-room a thick blue carpet is complemented by chair and curtain fabric of flowery blue and bedrooms are pleasantly decorated too, with handsome walnut furniture. She caned the bedheads herself. On a wall of one room is a collection of keys – all from the old Brill railway, closed in 1926; and also what looks like a huge horseshoe but is in fact an ox shoe, from the time when oxen were used to draw carts.

Apart from livestock (sheep, cattle, ducks, geese – and a donkey) the farm produces a rather unusual 'crop' – turf, sold to garden centres. And in the garden is another pleasant surprise, a swimming-pool. (Bed-and-breakfast only.)

Buckinghamshire is one of the loveliest counties around London: in the south are the Chiltern Hills, with dense forests of beech – a handsome sight; and in the north the broad Vale of Aylesbury threaded by little streams – it is here that most of the stately homes and fine churches are to be found: great mansions include Ascott (outstanding furniture and paintings), Claydon (with Florence Nightingale museum), Hughenden (Disraeli's home), Stowe (by Vanbrugh) and Waddesdon (the Rothschild house of French Renaissance splendour).

The Thames runs along the southern edge of the county – with beauty-spots like Boulter's Lock, Bray (famous for punting), the spectacular reach by Cliveden (stately home, now an expensive hotel), Marlow, Medmenham and Hambleden.

Brill itself is of interest. It has a hilltop windmill, rare duck decoy (NT), good buildings of the 15th to 17th centuries, and a mediaeval gatehouse, Boarstall Tower is nearby.

Readers' comments: Fantastic weekend! Very friendly; felt totally at home. Comfortable, and lovely breakfasts. Would recommend Poletrees time and time again.

POND COTTAGE

Brandsby Road, Stillington, North Yorkshire, YO6 1NY   Tel: 0347 810796
North of York. Nearest main road: A19 from York to Thirsk.

2 **Bedrooms.** £11.50–£12.50. Tea/coffee facilities. TV. Views of garden, country. Washing machine on request.
Light suppers if ordered. Vegetarian or special diets.
1 **Sitting-room.** With central heating, TV. No smoking.
Small garden. Badminton, croquet.

In a barn adjoining this tiny primrose-yellow cottage is a treasure-trove of domestic bygones – from kitchen tools to antique bottles and cans, woodware to chamber-pots. For the Thurstans are antique dealers, specializing in 'kitchenalia' and pine furniture.

The 18th-century house itself is furnished with antiques, and its shelves and nooks are filled with curios. There are collections of coronation mugs and Staffordshire dogs in the low-beamed sitting-room, where high-backed wing chairs are grouped around an inglenook fireplace. This is a house of twists and turns, unexpected steps and low windows. Its pleasant bedrooms overlook a terrace with stone troughs of flowers, a croquet lawn and a natural pond. The only drawback is the distance of the bath from the guests' bedrooms, a minor inconvenience considering the modest price charged.

Dianne serves only breakfast because (the citizens of nearby York being great diners-out) the area is very well supplied with eating-places.

Stillington is almost equidistant from the city of York, the coast, the North York Moors and the Dales – each described elsewhere in this book, and offering totally different holiday experiences needing many days to explore. It is in the middle of the great Vale of York, a fertile area watered by the River Ure and its tributaries, unspoilt by industry. All around are traces of history, from prehistoric man and later the Romans to the Civil War, and onward. The nearest stately home is Sutton Park which has art treasures and furniture once in Buckingham House (precursor of Buckingham Palace) and gardens laid out by Capability Brown; the nearest market town is cobblestoned Easingwold.

The area is scattered with pretty villages, built of warm red brick and yellow stone and roofed with clay pantiles. A typical one is Coxwold, where Laurence Sterne was the incumbent. His house, called Shandy Hall after the house in his most famous book, is open to the public during the summer months. Now run by a trust, its rescue from neglect was the work of a single enthusiast for the author, and it is filled with his collection of Sterne memorabilia. The brick skin conceals a much older structure, and there is a curious Tudor wall-painting uncovered during restoration.

York itself, one of the most-visited cities in the country, hardly needs description: the newest draw, among its many attractions, must be the recently completed restoration work in the minster, which has put right the extensive damage caused by the lightning strike of a few years ago.

Readers' comments: Wonderful! Enjoyed very much. A warm welcome. Delightful house, hospitable and sensible hostess, cosy and comfortable, delicious and plentiful breakfasts. Will go again. A brilliant discovery.

The Green, Warmington, OX17 1BU   Tel: 029589 682 (*evenings best*)
North-west of Banbury (Oxfordshire). Nearest main road: A41 from Banbury to Warwick.

2 Bedrooms. £16 (less for 5 nights). Prices go up in May. One has own shower. Views of village green or garden.
Dinner. £10 for 3 courses and coffee, at 7pm (not on Sundays). Wine can be ordered or brought in.
1 Sitting-room. With open fire, central heating, TV.
Small garden
Closed from November to March inclusive.

This village, though near the A41, is so tucked away that, beauty-spot though it is, few tourists find it. Around a sloping village green with duck-pond and waterlilies, dominated at one end by a Tudor manor house, are ranged rows of charming cottages built from warm local stone, roses and honeysuckle climbing up their walls. Mrs Viljoen's home is one of these.

She has furnished its small rooms with great elegance. Gleaming antique furniture and silver contrast with the rugged stones of the sitting-room walls and hearth. She has chosen browns and lemon to harmonize with the colour of the stone. One pretty bedroom is all blue – from the silk spread and the cover of the armchair to the flowery Victorian wallpaper.

At the back is a tiny garden with a seat among roses and nasturtiums climbing up the walls.

Vi asks visitors to say what kind of food they like. A typical menu might include home-made soup, chicken with almond sauce, and a tart of her own fruit, or home-made ice cream.

Vi Viljoen is a Tourist Board guide – so is well qualified to advise visitors on sightseeing.

Pond Cottage has appeared on the cover of *Forever Ambridge* by Norman Painting (who plays Phil Archer in the radio series), a resident in the village. Within a few miles of it are the castles of Broughton and Kenilworth; Sulgrave Manor (home of George Washington's ancestors); sixteen stately homes belonging to the National Trust, a number of antique shops, and also fine gardens. Some visitors enjoy the motor-racing at Silverstone, and the great Royal Show (July) at the National Agriculture Centre. The Cotswolds, Althorp, Oxford and Blenheim are also easily accessible.

Readers' comments: A delightful stay. A pleasure to see so many lovely things in the house. Welcomed us like friends, and made our wedding anniversary dinner a feast. Delicious food, extremely good value. Most friendly and helpful; food memorable; pretty garden. Lovely little place. Delightful little cottage. Most enjoyable and relaxing. Charming house, warm welcome. Like staying with a friend, every need anticipated.

For explanation of code letters (C, D, H, PT, S, X) see page xxxiv.

POOL HOUSE HOTEL   C
Hanley Road, Upton-upon-Severn, Worcestershire, WR8 0PA
Tel: 06846 2151
South of Worcester. Nearest main road: A4104 from Pershore towards
Ledbury.

rear view

9 Bedrooms. £16–£23.50 (less for 2 nights). Prices go up in April. Bargain breaks. Some have own bath/shower/toilet. TV. Views of garden, country, river. No smoking. Clothes-washing on request.
Dinner. A la carte or £9.75 for 4 courses (with choices) and coffee, at 7pm. Vegetarian or special diets if ordered. Wine can be ordered. No smoking. **Light suppers** if ordered.
2 Sitting-rooms. With open fire, central heating, TV. Bar.
Large garden with croquet.

I have included this hotel for its superb river-bank setting, with gardens that make the most of this. Herbaceous borders wander among lawns with fruit trees, sloping down to the waterside. The 18th-century house is simply furnished. I thought bedroom 2 particularly attractive: it has a rose-and-white colour scheme and a good view of the river. Jill Webb's flower arrangements are a feature of the house.

Meals are traditional: home-made soup or a prawn cocktail might be followed by roast beef (with fresh local vegetables) and a rhubarb-and-raisin crumble, for instance. Beyond the peach dining-room is a hexagonal TV room with big armchairs and a door leading to the garden; and then a sitting-room with log fire.

From the house one enjoys views of the Malvern Hills. Not far off is the River Avon, the Cotswolds, 'Shakespeare country' and the lovely Wye Valley. Other sightseeing possibilities include Tewkesbury Abbey, Cheltenham spa, Worcester Cathedral (and the Royal Worcester factory), Hereford and Gloucester (two more cathedrals). Upton itself is a delightful old market town, as is Ledbury. The Malverns have a spring garden show, Hidcote is near, and Pershore Agricultural College grounds are well worth visiting. Racing, fishing, cricket and birdwatching at the waterfowl sanctuary are other pursuits which bring visitors here.

In Upton-upon-Severn itself (a small town that needs to be explored on foot and by boat), there are plaques dotted about on sites of historic events – the most photographed one describes how, on the spot, Cromwell was acclaimed in 1651 'with abundance of joy and shouting' after his victory at the Battle of Upton. The town's history, which goes back to Saxon times, is displayed in its heritage centre (in the old cupola-topped church tower). You can go as far as Tewkesbury on the pleasure-cruiser, or simply stay in Upton to make the most of its little shops, bistros and byways. The 'Three Counties' agricultural show takes place nearby.

Readers' comments: Most helpful. Food and accommodation excellent. Very enjoyable week's stay. The loveliest garden; friendly people. Beautiful setting.

When writing to me, if you want a reply please enclose a stamped addressed envelope.

★ **PORTWELL HOUSE**   **C D H PT**
Market Place, Faringdon, Oxfordshire, SN7 7HU   Tel: 0367 240197
Nearest main road: A420 from Oxford to Swindon.

7 Bedrooms. £16–£17 (less for 4 nights).
Bargain breaks. All have own bath/toilet.
Tea/coffee facilities. TV. Washing machine
on request.
Dinner. £8 for 3 courses (with choices) and
coffee, at 7–8pm. Non-residents not admitted. Vegetarian or special diets if ordered.
Wine can be ordered.
1 Sitting-room. With central heating.

David and Margo Manning run a small and friendly guest-house.

The curiously wedge-shaped house is well over 300 years old. Inside, all is fresh
and neat. Up two winding staircases are bedrooms (each with bathroom) which
have colourful curtains and duvets, comfortable chairs from which to watch
television and, in some cases, views of the weekly market below. There is a
ground-floor bedroom too, and a sitting area with pot-plants, aquarium, armchairs
and books. A typical dinner might be prawn cocktail, steak and apple pie.

Faringdon is a pretty town – a place of mossy roofs, old inn signs, swinging
lamps and clocks on brackets, with a colonnaded buttermarket. Brickwork, stone
and colourful stucco give the streets variety, and there is an ancient church
half-hidden behind great yews (one of many in this area). A good centre for public
transport and for many sports, it is at the heart of an area full of interest with plenty
to explore. In the spring, the grounds of nearby Faringdon House produce a
wonderful display of flowers. This was the home of Lord Berners (the model for
Lord Merlin in *The Pursuit of Love*), who also built the Folly Tower on the nearby
hill. In his will, he asked to be stuffed and placed on top of it, but his executors
thought otherwise. Unlike some areas, this is not tourist-ridden in August.

In the surrounding Vale of the White Horse there are plenty of good canalside
walks (with revitalizing little inns along the way); Uffington church, which has
memories of Tom Brown (of *Tom Brown's Schooldays*); the prehistoric white horse
itself, cut out of the turf on the chalk downs; and adjacent earthworks with far
views. The old Ridgeway Path runs here, with Wayland's Smithy close by. Great
Coxwell has a superb tithe barn; Coleshill and Buscot Park are two National Trust
properties, and Ashdown and Littlecote are not much further. Then there are the
wilder reaches of the Thames – Lechlade, the source, and Kelmscott (William
Morris's lovely house). The theatres of Oxford, Swindon and Newbury are
accessible. Pusey gardens, Blenheim, the Cotswold Wildlife Park, old Burford
and the Lechlade garden centre (for fuchsias) are top attractions. In fact, from here
you can easily reach a number of interesting areas described elsewhere: Hungerford, Cirencester, Marlborough and the Chilterns, for example.

Readers' comments: Kindness, attention and hospitality. Pleasant and comfortable;
the best bargain for a long time. Excellent standards, friendliness, very happy
atmosphere. Outstanding. Excellent in every way. Cannot praise too highly, warm
welcome. Attractive, roomy bedrooms. Excellent atmosphere.

Prices are per person in a double room at the beginning of the year.

257

★ **PRESTON FARM** C(4) S
Harberton, Devon, TQ9 7SW Tel: 0803 862235
South of Totnes. Nearest main road: A381 from Totnes to Kingsbridge.

3 Bedrooms. £12.50–£15. Prices go up in March. Some have own bath/shower/toilet. Tea/coffee facilities. TV. Views of garden, country. Washing machine on request.
Dinner. £7.50 for 4 courses and coffee, at 6.45pm (on six nights a week). Non-residents not admitted. Vegetarian or special diets if ordered. Wine can be brought in. No smoking.
1 Sitting-room. With open fire, central heating, TV, record-player.
Small garden
Closed from November to mid-March.

It's unusual to find a working farm with its house right in a village (a very quiet one), but there used to be several such clustered together in Harberton. The Steers' house, built in 1680, has been in the same family for generations. All the rooms are comfortable, and there is good home cooking at dinner, with the dishes as varied as pancakes stuffed with salmon au gratin, chicken Marengo, roasts, pies, baked Alaska, treacle pudding. The ingredients are mostly home-grown or local. One bedroom is in 'Country Diary' fabrics; all have pretty, co-ordinated fabrics. Breakfast comes on 'help-yourself' platters – conventional bacon and eggs or more unusual things like hog's pudding or smoked haddock.

Harberton is a picturesque cluster of old cottages with colourful gardens, set in a valley. Its 13th-century church has a magnificent painted screen and stained glass windows. The local inn is of equal antiquity. Preston Farm was once a manor house, which is why rooms are spacious.

Most visitors head for historic Totnes and its castle, or to Dartmouth and Salcombe, for example, via country lanes. Dartmoor lies to the north, the coast to the south, and neither is far off. Modbury is one of many picturesque towns near here, its Georgian or slate-hung houses clinging to a steep hill. Buckfastleigh (with abbey built in 1938; notable stained glass) is where the Dart Valley steam trains go, along a lovely route. At Dartmeet, one of the most famous of beauty-spots, two rivers join – there is a pretty 'clapper' bridge of stone slabs nearby. Totnes itself has, in addition to the 13th-century castle, steep lanes beside the River Dart; historic buildings such as the Guildhall; arguably the finest rood-screen in England, in St Mary's church; and a quaint Butterwalk.

A little further is Widecombe-in-the-Moor with its huge old church, its September fair and 'Uncle Tom Cobleigh an' all'. Exeter, Plymouth and Torbay are easily accessible by car. River trips, Dartington Hall, the Shire Horse Centre, innumerable gardens and garden centres add to the interest of this area, as do its many antique shops, markets and fairs (e.g. every Tuesday in Totnes).

Readers' comments: Far more than we had hoped for; made most welcome; meals were excellent, good variety and generous helpings. Warm welcome, excellent accommodation, superb cooking. Absolutely marvellous. Everything perfect – especially the fish pie! Very comfortable; delicious meals; perfect company. Excellent accommodation, super meals, everything delightful. First-class in every way. Happy atmosphere. A delight to be there – visited twice. Wonderful value.

PRIORY COTTAGE

C(5) D S

Butley Low Corner, Suffolk, IP12 3QD   Tel: 0394 450382
East of Woodbridge. Nearest main road: A12 from Ipswich to Lowestoft.

3 Bedrooms. £12.50–£14 (less for 2 nights). Bargain breaks. Tea/coffee facilities. Views of garden, country, river. No smoking. Washing machine on request.
Dinner. £10 for 4 courses (with choices) and coffee, at 7pm. Non-residents not admitted. Vegetarian or special diets if ordered. Wine can be brought in. No smoking.
1 Sitting-room. With open fire, central heating, TV, record-player. No smoking.
Large garden

Cats, cats and more cats (lifelike pottery ones) inhabit every room of this country cottage, some for sale. On arrival, visitors are greeted by a Muscovy duck who has made the well-head his own throne; all around is a prettily landscaped garden.

The entrance hall has an unusual floor of polished 'pamment' tiles, sofas and arrangements of dried flowers. There are velvet chairs in the pale green L-shaped sitting-room, and a log stove. In the dining-room (pine table, dresser and Windsor chairs) Rosemary Newnham serves dinner – if ordered in advance – which may comprise sherry, soup or mousse, a casserole or pie, fruit fool or meringues, and cheeses. Alternatively, there are several inns and restaurants in the area: at one inn, Suffolk folk songs can be heard on Sundays.

Upstairs, rooms with clear bright colours, flowery wallpaper friezes, pine doors and beds, and louvred built-ins are neat and cheerful: some have views of Butley Creek and the bird reserve on Havergate Island. I particularly liked the blue-and-white one which has a prettily draped bed and linen trimmed with broderie anglaise. A small box of chocolates greets new arrivals.

The cottage is in an area designated as being of outstanding natural beauty, and completely unspoilt. It is virtually on the Suffolk Coast Path (50 miles of footpath and bridleway) which wanders through forests where deer roam and along a shore much frequented by migrant wildfowl and by small yachts. Beyond the elaborately carved gatehouse of Butley Priory lies Orford – celebrated for its oysterage and for its huge polygonal castle (early Norman). Further up the coast is the old-fashioned resort of Aldeburgh (made famous by Britten's opera, 'Peter Grimes'), with an internationally famous music festival centred on the Maltings at nearby Snape and with events in numerous churches too. From the waterfront here are views of small craft bobbing on the estuary and, at times, avocets and oystercatchers combing the marshy banks at low tide. Inland lies Framlingham and another outstanding castle. South of the sailing centre of Woodbridge is the only big resort, Felixstowe: sedate and orderly, with well-tended flowerbeds along the seafront.

The sunny, breezy coast here has been much eroded (entire towns have vanished into the sea after floods or storms) and so the principal road lies some way inland (through heaths and across estuaries), with only lanes penetrating to the shore, which means the area is undisturbed by traffic or crowds. There are any number of outings: horse-drawn wagon rides, walks with a naturalist, a cruise in a motor launch, a cordon bleu picnic with champagne, clay-pigeon shooting and much else.

★ **PRIORY FARMHOUSE**   **C D S X**
Hodsock Priory Estate, Blyth, Nottinghamshire, S81 0TY
Tel: 0909 591768/474299
North of Worksop. Nearest main road: A1 from Newark towards Doncaster.

4 Bedrooms. £13.50–£14.50 (less for 7 nights). Some have own bath/shower/toilet. Tea/coffee facilities. Views of garden, country. No smoking. Washing machine on request.
Dinner. £5.50 for 3 courses and coffee, at 6–8pm. Non-residents not admitted. Vegetarian or special diets if ordered. Wine can be brought in. No smoking.
1 Sitting-room. With open fire, TV. No smoking.
Small garden

No priory ever existed here; but during the Gothic Revival, when the ancient mansion of Hodsock was extended (1823–33), it was fashionable to give houses ecclesiastical names. The architect, Ambrose Poynter, was both a pioneer of the Gothic Revival style and a founder of the Royal Institute of British Architects.

In its 1000-acre grounds there are secluded walks and fine views of the mansion, its 15th-century gatehouse, and the gardens. No road disturbs the peace – only woodcocks, pheasants and owls.

The guest-house is adjacent to the mansion, of which there is an imposing view as you approach along the narrow drive that stretches across the landscaped park.

Pat Buckley and Sylvia Mellars, the friends who together run the guest-house, live elsewhere but both grew up on the estate and are knowledgeable guides as to what to see in the neighbourhood. Rooms are light and pleasant, predominantly cream and brown; not elegantly furnished but comfortable and immaculate. Meals, too, are homely: for instance, soup, chicken, fruit crumble and cheeses – with much emphasis on fresh local vegetables and fruit.

Because Nottinghamshire is not one of the famous tourist areas, visitors feel they are making their own private discoveries when they come across – for instance – the longest tree-lined driveway in Europe (Clumber Park's two miles of limes in double rows), or the outdoor sculptures in the gardens at Rufford Park, or Sherwood Forest, which has a very well-conceived Robin Hood centre.

Readers' comments: Extremely pleasant and friendly, nothing is too much trouble.

In the nearby village of Firbeck is **YEWS FARMHOUSE** (tel: 0909 731458), mainly 18th-century, which faces a big croquet lawn bounded by a haha, beyond which graze Jacob sheep against a backdrop of woodland and stream. It is furnished principally with antiques: in one of the twin-bedded rooms, old carved oak bedheads stand against a Wedgwood blue wall. Catherine Stewart-Smith serves such dinners as home-made soup; lamb noisettes with at least three fresh vegetables; chocolate mousse

rear view

with cognac or whisky ginger syllabub, and cheeses (aperitif and wine included). From £18 to £25.

PROSPECT HILL HOTEL
Kirkoswald, Cumbria, CA10 1ER Tel: 076883 500
North of Penrith. Nearest main road: A6 from Penrith to Carlisle.

rear view

9 Bedrooms. £18–£25 (less for 3 nights). Prices go up in March. Bargain breaks. Some have own bath/shower/toilet. Tea/coffee facilities. Views of garden, country. Washing machine on request.
Dinner. A la carte, at 7.15–9pm. Vegetarian or special diets if ordered. Wine can be ordered. **Light suppers** if ordered.
2 Sitting-rooms. With open fire, central heating, TV. **Bar.**
Large garden
Closed in February.

A group of 18th-century farm buildings close to a village that feels remote (though the M6 is only 9 miles away) has been turned into a hotel with great individuality by Isa and John Henderson (he was formerly a television designer).

They reconstructed a rare gin case, a half-round room within which ponies walked round and round powering wheels to grind grain.

A collection of old farm implements is displayed on the sandstone walls in the bar (once a byre, with low-beamed ceiling and flagged floor).

Every bedroom is individually decorated, and traditional materials have been used. Many rooms still have walls of rugged stone, and a number have brass bedsteads with patchwork quilts. Homespun curtains, thick carpets and country colours like peat or moss are all in keeping with the character of the place. The former coach house has been turned into an annexe where one room is ideal for a family. There is a glassed-in porch with cane furniture and a terrace.

A typical dinner: leek-and-mushroom soup, lamb steak with honey and rosemary, strawberry shortcake and good, plentiful coffee. There is a vegetarian menu. Breakfast includes such things as green figs and smoked haddock.

John has produced his own leaflets of walks, from evening strolls to half-day hikes with notes about where deer can be seen, a spectacular waterfall in a gorge, riverside paths, a forest nature reserve with hide for watching badgers and hares or wildfowl, caves, old quarries and castle ruins. The neighbourhood is full of ancient villages, the prehistoric stones of 'Long Meg' and a traditional pottery still using a Victorian steam engine. Kirkoswald is a good choice for a winter break.

Maps, bicycles and gumboots can be hired.

Readers' comments: Comfortable and well organized; good cuisine; excellent amenities, nothing was too much trouble; very good in all respects; well decorated rooms; good and thoughtful service; value for money. Attractively converted and with good food. Thoroughly enjoyed our stay, food excellent. Full marks for service, cuisine and superb farmhouse conversion and lovely surroundings.

PULLENS FARM C
Lamberhurst Road, Horsmonden, Kent, TN12 8ED   Tel: 0892 722241
East of Tunbridge Wells. Nearest main road: A21 from Tonbridge to Hastings.

3 Bedrooms. £14.50–£16. Prices go up in March. Bargain breaks. Tea/coffee facilities. TV. Views of garden, country. No smoking. Washing machine on request.
Dinner. £10 for 3 courses (with choices) and coffee, at 7.15pm. Non-residents not admitted. Vegetarian or special diets if ordered. Wine can be brought in. No smoking.
1 Sitting-room. With open fire, central heating, TV. No smoking.
Large garden
Closed from November to February inclusive.

To get heavy wagons up the hill, extra horses were needed to pull. They were supplied by this farm, which thus got the name 'Pullings'. It is one of the oldest houses in this book, dating from about 1400 – only a few years after Chaucer wrote the *Canterbury Tales*. It has all the features so characteristic of early mediaeval houses – beams, brick inglenook, oak-mullioned windows with lattice panes, sloping floors, latched doors of matchboard. . . .

To this the Russells have added glass doors which open onto a small patio with vine and jasmine where one can sit after dinner (as an alternative to the velvet recliner chairs drawn up to the log fire). Sally's meals comprise such straightforward English dishes as home-made mackerel pâté, stuffed pork chops with vegetables from the garden or greenhouse, and apple pancakes.

Bedrooms are furnished in cottage style – there is a pretty blue one at the front, another with ceiling of boards and a view of a stream, and a large, light family room with beamed walls and brick fireplace. Beyond the big garden lies the cereal farm. (Once there were hops but imports of continental lager are killing the once-famous hop-growing region in Kent.)

For children, there are bicycles and a climbing frame in the large garden. There is also plenty for them to enjoy in the vicinity. Bewl Water, a huge lake with boat trips and adventure playground on the shore, the brass-rubbing centre and evocative heritage centre at Tunbridge Wells, rare breeds farm at Hildenborough, steam train at Tenterden, animated model scenes in an old oast house at Lamberhurst, and narrow-boat trips up river from Tonbridge.

In Kent, museums are almost as numerous as oast houses. Examples: at Staplehurst, vintage farm machines; Rolvenden, vintage cars; Cranbrook and Tenterden, social history; Headcorn, air warfare; Tonbridge, antique domestic appliances; Tunbridge Wells, arts; Paddock Wood, hop-growing.

The list of gardens is just as long: Benenden has an 18th-century walled garden; Staplehurst, an outstanding herb one. Go to Lamberhurst, The Owl House, Scotney Castle and Sprivers at Horsmonden; and, last but not least, to Sissinghurst.

Finchcocks is a baroque house with a museum of keyboard instruments (and occasional concerts). Goudhurst is a steep and lovely village of former weavers' cottages, worth exploring on foot, and has a church with fine monuments.

It is difficult to write briefly about Kent without making breathless lists of all there is to see and do, for few counties are so full of interest.

RACEHORSE COTTAGE
C(8) D S

Nepcote, West Sussex, BN14 0SN   Tel: 0903 873783

North of Worthing. Nearest main road: A24 from Worthing to Dorking.

2 **Bedrooms.** £13 (less for 2 nights). Tea/coffee facilities. TV. Views of garden and country. Washing machine on request.
Dinner. £8 for 3 courses and coffee, at 7.30pm. Non-residents not admitted. Vegetarian or special diets if ordered. Wine can be ordered.
1 **Sitting-room.** With open fire, central heating, TV, record-player.
Small garden

The flint-walled hamlet of Nepcote is almost part of 18th-century Findon village, celebrated for its three racing stables (and very ancient church). This explains the name of the cottage, for which the previous owner chose a roadside position where he could watch the strings of horses and their jockeys go by on their way to the surrounding South Downs for daily exercise. He built it in traditional Sussex style: its upper storey weatherboarded, the doors panelled.

It is a pleasant, unpretentious home with an L-shaped sitting/dining-room with open fire, trim bedrooms that have velvet bedheads and views of the Downs. There is a small garden and glasshouse from which come the fresh vegetables and fruit that Jean Lloyd serves her guests. She is a keen cook and prepares such meals (if ordered in advance) as ramekins of eggs with Stilton and cream or melon with kiwi fruit; gammon with Cumberland sauce; and blackberry bombe or loganberry flan. Bread, muesli and jams are home-made. The Lloyds usually dine with their guests.

The area round here is not only scenic but full of gardens, stately homes, Roman remains and castles to visit. Walkers enjoy wending their way from Nepcote right up to Cissbury Ring, a beech clump outlining a prehistoric hill fort.

South coast resorts within easy reach include sedate Worthing (a considerable number of retirement homes are here) and Brighton (celebrated for its oriental Pavilion and sophisticated pleasures – 'London by the sea').

An attractive route to follow for a very full day-long drive would be via Worthing (pausing at the museum for its explanatory display of the geology and vegetation that give Sussex its varied character) to Highdown Tower, from the terraced chalk gardens of which are far coastal views, and then to Poling, with a Norman church built of stone from Normandy, the Isle of Wight, Dorset and Sussex. Past Arundel (castle, Catholic cathedral and wildfowl reserve) is Amberley's open-air musem in former chalk pits – you can see a smithy, pottery, woodturner and early engines or follow a wildlife trail to look for butterflies. Nearby Parham is a magnificent Tudor mansion, full of treasures and surrounded by equally superb gardens (in the little church the squire had his own boxed-in pew complete with coal fire!). Onward to Shipley (home of Hilaire Belloc, which has a windmill in its grounds – sometimes open and working, with an exhibition about him), Leonardslee (landscaped gardens with ponds), Cowfold (the church has fine windows and a huge brass, and a mile away is Britain's only Carthusian monastery, 1883) and Henfield (good local museum; 18th-century watermill to the south). The last lap can take in Bramber where, beneath Norman castle ruins, is a museum of pipe-smoking; and Steyning for a very ancient church.

RECTORY FARM   C D

Sulgrave, Northamptonshire, OX17 2SG   Tel: 029 576 261
North-east of Banbury (Oxfordshire). Nearest main road: A43 from Oxford to
Northampton.

5 Bedrooms. £13–£16 (less for 7 nights).
Tea/coffee facilities. Views of garden, country. Washing machine on request.
Dinner (when available). £7 for 3 courses
and coffee, at 7pm. Wine can be ordered. No
smoking.
1 Sitting-room. With open fire, central heating, TV.
Large garden

The stars-and-stripes flies over Sulgrave, its design inspired by the stars and bars
in the family coat-of-arms over the porch of the manor house. For this was the
home (built in the reign of Elizabeth I) of Lawrence Washington – ancestor of
George Washington, some of whose possessions are on show at the house, which is
now a museum.

Rectory Farm is equally old, and it overlooks the manor. Under its thickly
thatched roof are walls of golden stone – the same stone which gives the Cotswolds
their particular charm continues into Northamptonshire. Yet, when the famous
Cotswolds are over-busy with tourists, this little-known area remains undisturbed, even though it is not far west of the M1. Winding lanes go up and down,
passing picturesque villages like Moreton Pinkney, ancient churches and some
outstanding buildings – Canons Ashby, for example.

Rectory Farm is, both inside and out, in harmony with this scene. Downstairs
are stone-flagged floors and a stone fireplace, deep-set windows giving a view of the
walled garden at the back. An old rocking-horse stands in the hall, a dresser laden
with china in the sitting-room. Up a substantial oak staircase are the bedrooms –
doors and floors alike have become crooked with age. Rebecca Trace has furnished
these in appropriately cottagey style: walls are in pale colours, curtains sprigged,
most furniture is of stripped pine. One has a view of the adjoining farmyard: the
Traces keep a few sheep, chickens and horses.

For dinner you may be offered a home-made soup, pâté or egg dish to be
followed, perhaps, by roast beef or chicken in a sweet-sour sauce of green peppers
and pineapple (accompanying vegetables are likely to be from the garden).
Puddings tend to the traditional: fruit pies, soufflés or mousses, for instance.

Sulgrave is well placed for visiting both Oxford and Stratford-upon-Avon, but I
recommend it also as a base from which to explore less well-known beauty-spots
(in Northamptonshire, particularly). It is close to the Grand Union Canal and its
pleasure-boats – the River Nene, too. At Badby is not only a hilly village of
thatched cottages but also a very lovely bluebell wood. Towcester – a steeple-
chasing centre – has the Saracen's Head inn which Dickens described in *The
Pickwick Papers*:

'The candles were brought, the fire was stirred up . . . In ten minutes' a
waiter was laying the cloth, the curtains were drawn, everything looked (as
everything always does, in all decent English inns) as if the travellers had been
expected, and their comforts prepared, for days beforehand.'

RED HOUSE C(6) PT

Sidmouth Road, Lyme Regis, Dorset, DT7 3ES   Tel: 0297 442055
Nearest main road: A3052 from Lyme Regis to Exeter.

3 Bedrooms. £17 (less for 7 nights). Prices go up in May. All have own bath/toilet. Tea/coffee facilities. TV. Views of garden, sea.
Small garden
Closed from December to February inclusive.

Delightful old Lyme has many claims to fame – the profusion of fossils (including dinosaur bones) found along its beaches; the landing of the rebel Monmouth in 1685 to start his abortive rebellion; and more recently *The French Lieutenant's Woman*, the author of which, John Fowles, lives locally.

When Geoffrey Griffin retired, he and his wife Elizabeth, a journalist, decided to move here and (inspired by reading previous editions of *Staying Off the Beaten Track*) run a bed-and-breakfast house. It wasn't any olde worlde cottage that they fell in love with but this dignified 'twenties house that had been built for Aldis (inventor of the famous signal-lamps which bear his name) on a superb site with a 40-mile sea view south-east as far as Portland Bill. It is a house with handsome features – iron-studded oak doors, leaded casements and window-seats, for example. On sunny mornings (occasionally even in late autumn), you can take breakfast on the wide verandah and enjoy sea breezes while you eat – at your feet, sloping lawns with colourful rhododendrons, camellias, fuchsias and wisteria. On chilly mornings, breakfast is served in an attractive room with a fire.

The bedrooms are excellent. Mine was 20 feet long, very comfortably furnished in period with the house, with a thick carpet. By contrast, there is an even larger family room in scarlet-and-white. Each bedroom is equipped with armchairs, TV, a refrigerator, flowers and books – the aim being to provide individual bed-sitters for guests, as there is no communal sitting-room, only a large landing which has seats and a supply of leaflets, maps and local menus.

This is a perfect base from which to explore the locality. Sandy beaches with their shrimp-pools are ideal for children. There are excellent walks (in Marshwood Vale or along the coast) including nature trails; drives along lanes of primroses, bluebells and subtropical wildflowers in the downs; Hardy villages; National Trust houses. You can watch or take part in sea-sports and cider-making.

'They went to the sands, to watch the flowing of the tide, which a fine south-easterly breeze was bringing in with all the grandeur which so flat a shore admitted. They praised the morning; gloried in the sea; sympathized in the delight of the fresh-feeling breeze . . . "I am quite convinced that the sea air always does good".' Thus spoke Henrietta to her sister Anne, in Jane Austen's *Persuasion*; and at Lyme today the same sands, sea and air are still working their magic.

Readers' comments: Just perfect, equal to the best hotels, excellent value. Kindness itself, so caring. The best ever. Good value. Splendid views and pleasant gardens. Comfort and charm. Could not have been kinder, a marvellous place.

★ **REGENCY HOUSE**   **C D PT X**
Neatishead, Norfolk, NR12 8AD   Tel: 0692 630233
North-east of Norwich. Nearest main road: A1151 from Norwich towards
Stalham.

5 Bedrooms. £15–£19 (less for 3 nights).
Prices go up in July. Bargain breaks. Some
have own bath/toilet. Tea/coffee facilities.
TV. Views of garden, country.
Light suppers if ordered.
Small garden

Former Manchester bank-manager Alan Wrigley was so touched by the friendliness of Neatishead people towards a newcomer that, after a few years here, he began planting wayside trees as a 'thank you': the total has already reached 3000. He and his wife Sue, previously a *Daily Express* reporter, run not only this 18th-century guest-house to an immaculate standard but also the village stores adjoining it, in the heart of the Norfolk Broads area – now a national park.

The breakfasts are outstanding: standard issue is 2 sausages, 4 rashers of bacon, 6 mushrooms, 2 whole tomatoes, 2 slices of fried bread and as many eggs as you request! But if you prefer it, Sue will produce a vegetarian breakfast instead. This is served in a fresh, white room with stoneware crockery on tables that were specially made by a local craftsman. On the walls are photographs of bygone Neatishead. Bedrooms have Laura Ashley fabrics (the bed in no. 6 is king-size and its bathroom is pine-panelled) and, in some cases, garden views. (As to dinner, there are three good places in the village to choose from, and others at popular Horning – such as the Swan. The nearby White Horse serves a local speciality, wild duck. Sue will provide snack suppers if these are ordered in advance.)

Pretty little Neatishead, at the centre of the Norfolk Broads, fortunately does not attract the crowds which sometimes ruin Horning and Wroxham.

There is a staithe (mooring) here for fifteen boats – and the Wrigleys have a 14-foot dinghy which visitors can use for fishing. Pleasant picnic-spots are by the waterside at, for instance, Barton Turf. Some families choose to divide themselves between cabin cruisers (for the younger generation) and Regency House (for older members, who prefer to sleep on shore and boat with their family only by day). There is good cycling around here, too; wildlife and birdwatching; and plenty of sightseeing in mediaeval Norwich and elsewhere. The sandy beaches are easily accessible, too. Rose nurseries, and the gardens at Blickling, Hoveton Hall and Burnt Fen interest flower-lovers; antique-hunters head for Holt and Norwich.

The Broadland Conservation Centre is worth seeking out at Ranworth (which also has a very fine church interior): a nature trail leads to a thatched, floating building with an exhibition about the Broads and their wildlife, and a hide from which to watch the waterfowl. Sue will give you leaflets with maps of two interesting walks – the Weavers' Way and Marriott's Way.

Readers' comments: Welcoming, friendly, good breakfast. Large rooms, lovely furnishings. Amazing breakfasts, generous hospitality. The best b & b we've stayed in.

266

RICHMOND LODGE

Mursley, Buckinghamshire, MK17 0LE   Tel: 029672 275   (tel: 029672 0275 from March 1991)

South-west of Milton Keynes. Nearest main road: A421 from Bletchley to Buckingham.

3 Bedrooms. £15–£20. Some have own bath/shower/toilet. Tea/coffee facilities. TV. Views of garden, country. No smoking. Washing machine on request.
Dinner. £10 for 3 courses and coffee, at 7pm. Non-residents not admitted. Wine can be brought in. No smoking.
1 Sitting-room. With open fire, central heating, TV. No smoking.
Large garden

Just before the First World War, this house was built as a hunting lodge for a wealthy London butcher who frequented the area when buying beef-cattle and decided to make his weekend retreat in this high, windswept spot. The whole atmosphere is still one of sedate, solid comfort; and even the garden retains its original Edwardian formality. From an immaculate lawn, with a stately blue cedar, there are views right down the Vale of Aylesbury with a glimpse of Waddesdon Manor, High Wycombe and Dunstable Downs.

Chris Abbey used to be a hotel manager and so her standards are very professional. Spotless rooms have well-chosen fabrics: for its view of the lily-pool, I thought the jade and strawberry bedroom the most attractive. Chris sometimes serves breakfast on a sunny patio where there are fuchsias and clematis. For dinner (if this is ordered in advance) she might cook you salmon mousse, pork chops with a celery and pineapple sauce, and (she loves doing puddings) summer pudding.

Buckinghamshire is a county of contrasts – leafy in the south, rising up into the Chiltern Hills where great beech trees flourish on the chalky soil, and then turning into a great fertile plain northwards (the Vale of Aylesbury). Here the landscape is threaded with little rivers. This is not an area for many spectacular views – that from Richmond Lodge is exceptional – but rather for the pleasures of making small, private discoveries of its beauties which include a wealth of ancient and interesting churches, for instance, and quite a lot of stately homes. These include several National Trust mansions, and 18th-century Stowe, now a school but open to the public – its landscaped gardens with classical buildings and six lakes are world-famous. To the south you will find such varied diversions as the Goat Centre at Stoke Mandeville (with other farm animals and products too), the Glass Market at Wooburn Green (craft demonstrations), shire horses at Chalfont St Giles, chair museum at Wycombe – 'the furniture town', 14th-century court house at Long Crendon, the exceptional model village at Bekonscot (oldest in the world, it is peopled by 1200 miniature inhabitants) and the churchyard of Stoke Poges with grave of Thomas Gray. Elizabethan Chenies Manor near Amersham has lovely gardens, recently planted with thousands of Dutch bulbs. Near Milton Keynes are beautiful Fenny Lodge (18th-century waterside house now full of modern crafts) and Stacey Hill Museum of rural bygones. Numerous rivers and the Grand Union Canal provide waterside walks.

On the other side of the A5 is Bedfordshire – Woburn Abbey and safari park are here, Stockwood's gardens and craft workshops, Whipsnade Zoo, and the historic grounds of Wrest Park with 18th-century gardens that include a painted pavilion.

RIVER PARK FARM　　　　　　　　　　　　　　　　　　**C S**

Lodsworth, West Sussex, GU28 9DS　Tel: 07985 362

West of Petworth. Nearest main road: A272 from Petworth to Midhurst.

4 Bedrooms. £13.50 (less for 3 nights). Tea/ coffee facilities. Views of garden, country. No smoking.
Dinner. £6 for 2 courses (with choices) and coffee, at 7pm. Non-residents not admitted. Wine can be brought in. No smoking.
1 Sitting-room. With central heating, TV.
Large garden
Closed from October to Easter inclusive.

The farm (of 340 acres of corn, bullocks, sheep and poultry) is in a secluded position among woods where, if you are up early enough, you may encounter deer. There is a 4½-acre lake with plentiful carp and ducks, and in front a pretty garden. The house itself, built in 1600, is old and beamy with comfortable bedrooms along twisting passageways, and outside are golden roses and wisteria clambering around the door. Altogether it is a pretty and tranquil spot, full of nooks and crannies – amazing, visitors think, because it is so close to London.

Pat Moss does not do full-scale dinners (available elsewhere locally) but has a list of homely dishes like shepherd's pie or macaroni cheese, and for puddings like banana split she uses rich Jersey cream from the farm's own cows. Bread is home-baked and eggs free-range. There are flowers in every room. Pat also makes and sells marmalade and dried flowers. Coarse fishing and table tennis available.

People come for the local walks and birdwatching (Pat has pinned up bird-identification charts and gives visitors field notes on the crops and wildlife in each season, with map, and her own daily nature notes); or to visit the many outstanding sights in this neighbourhood; or the polo or point-to-points at Cowdray; or to see the local game of stoolball played at Midhurst. There are many small country towns around here, streams running down into the River Rother, woodlands and picturesque villages with greens and duck-ponds, old inns and ancient churches, Arundel Castle, wildfowl reserves, Goodwood House and Roman remains. Turner knew and loved this area, staying at Petworth House where many of his paintings can be seen. It's a good area for antique shops, too. Garden-lovers head for West Dean and Denmans; and there is the open-air Weald and Downland Museum.

An attractive drive would be via Petworth, still with many 18th-century byways and, of course, one of the country's grandest mansions through the huge deerpark of which one can motor, to see some of the finest mosaics outside Italy in the big Roman villa tucked away among pretty lanes at Bignor. Near here is another hidden village, Bury, with thatched cottages beside the winding River Arun. On the way from here to Chichester is Boxgrove Priory, the tremendous and ancient church of which still survives.

Readers' comments: Warm hospitality, generous home cooking. Enjoyed ourselves so much that we have twice visited for a week. Marvellous setting and house, kind hosts, good food. Outstanding. Very relaxed atmosphere. Comfortable, quiet. Warm, relaxed, friendly atmosphere and lovely farm.

For explanation of code letters (**C, D, H, PT, S, X**) see page xxxiv.

ROCK HOUSE

X

Alport, Derbyshire, DE4 1LG   Tel: 0629 636736
South of Bakewell. Nearest main road: A6 from Bakewell to Matlock.

3 Bedrooms. £14. Some have own bath/ shower/toilet. Tea/coffee facilities. Views of garden, country. No smoking. Washing machine on request.

Light suppers if ordered.
1 Sitting-room. With gas fire, central heating, TV. No smoking.
Small garden

The rock for which the Stathams' house is named is a great crag of tufa (a type of volcanic stone, perforated like Gruyère cheese, which was formed 300 million years ago) rearing up alongside it.

Only a few yards from the 18th-century house two rivers join, splashing over weirs constructed long ago to contain trout downstream – you can watch these drifting in water so transparent that the locals call it 'gin-clear' (its purity is due to the limestone bed over which it runs). Lathkill Dale is a National Nature Reserve: Tony and Jan are first-rate sources of information about the wildlife and history of this most beautiful of valleys. They will lend maps, tell you the best riverside walks, and where to find river pools (created for washing sheep).

The front door opens straight into the stone-flagged sitting-room, its walls now painted mushroom, with grey buttoned velvet armchairs, where you will be served tea on arrival. Glass doors lead through to the breakfast-room.

By pre-arrangement, Jan may serve supper platters, beautifully presented (but most visitors go to the nearby Druid Inn or other pubs). Breakfast possibilities include muffins, poached fruit, Staffordshire oatcakes, home-made jams and some vegetarian dishes. All bedrooms are well furnished.

Alport is well placed for touring either the wild and dramatic 'Dark Peak' (the stone there is millstone grit) or the more benign 'White Peak' (limestone), a fertile and verdant region. It is close to Chatsworth House and park with garden centre (the autumn colours there are glorious), Dovedale, and Hardwick Hall – a great Tudor mansion, Castleton (remarkable caves), the market town of Bakewell where the original Bakewell puddings are still to be had, Haddon Hall (mediaeval), the spa of Buxton, Melbourne's stately home, the Crown Derby porcelain museum, historic trams at Crich, the canal at Cromford, a cable car to the heights outside Matlock, Kedleston Hall (designed by Adam), and Alton Towers for its gardens and leisure park. Many mansions have fine gardens. This part of Derbyshire has some of England's finest river valleys.

Readers' comments: Very comfortable and a warm welcome. Breakfast excellent, rooms large and comfortable. Beautiful house, much pampering, what breakfasts! One of our favourites, lovely house; thoughtful and friendly people. A charming house with lovely walks all round, and delicious breakfasts.

ROCK WINDMILL

C D

The Hollow, Washington, West Sussex, RH20 3DA Tel: 0903 892941
North of Worthing. Nearest main road: A24 from Horsham to Worthing.

2 Bedrooms. £14 (less for 7 nights). Prices go up in April. Tea/coffee facilities. TV. Views of garden, country. Washing machine on request.
1 Sitting-room. With central heating, TV, record-player.
Large garden

The composer John Ireland lived here until his death in 1962: much of his music was inspired by the surrounding landscape (for instance, the *Downland Suite*, *Equinox* and *Amberley Wild Brooks*). It had ceased to function as a mill long before – and the sails have gone – but part of the original building (1820) remains, further modernized in recent years: the octagonal sitting-room, for instance, which is now decorated in a restful celadon green and has modern leather armchairs. This opens onto a garden with swimming-pool (heated to 80°F). Bedrooms are in a modern extension, neatly furnished with pine and cane fitments.

Janice Langley provides only breakfast but she or David give visitors lifts to the Frankland Arms (immortalized in Hilaire Belloc's 'West Sussex Drinking Song' which is sometimes sung at the pub), where there is very good food and from which it is a pleasant walk back to the mill. Or drive to Barn Owls, Coldwaltham.

Chanctonbury Ring is within sight and accessible by steep footpath from the village: a striking landmark, it consists of beech woods within the earthworks of an Iron Age hill fort; superb views all round. In this part of the lovely South Downs are such attractive villages as Findon (flint-walled cottages and three racing-stables), Steyning (mediaeval gabled houses and an outstanding church), Bramber (castle ruins, and a museum of pipes) and Ashurst (well preserved and with far views). The River Adur runs through this area to the sea at the small port of Shoreham, and everywhere there are good walks to be found – the long-distance South Downs Way goes by Washington on its way from Hampshire to Beachy Head (80 miles), and this is one of its most scenic, hilltop stretches. The nearest coastal resort is Worthing; the stateliest homes are Petworth and Parham.

Bedroom at Northleigh House (see page 203)

ROOKERY FARMHOUSE   **C**
Castle Carlton, Lincolnshire, LN11 8JF   Tel: 0507 450357
West of Mablethorpe. Nearest main road: A157 from Louth towards
Mablethorpe.

3 Bedrooms. £13–£15. Prices go up in
April. All have own bath/shower/toilet. Tea/
coffee facilities. Views of garden, country.
No smoking. Washing machine on request.
Dinner. £9.50 for 4 courses and coffee, at
7–8pm. Non-residents not admitted.
Vegetarian or special diets if ordered. Wine
can be brought in. No smoking. **Light
suppers** if ordered.
2 Sitting-rooms. With open fire, central
heating, piano, record-player.
Large garden

Sweet peas and roses climb up the mellow brick front of the house, built in 1776,
on which a sundial tells the hours. Bees and butterflies hover over catmint,
hanging baskets fill the verandah with colour, and at the back a garden wanders
from one level to another: herbaceous beds, a tree peony, tai haku cherry and, in
spring, drifts of daffodils and irises. Often there are spectacular sunsets to enjoy
when relaxing here after dinner.

Inside the house, there are antiques; pot-plants on tiled window-sills; and a
piano in the high-ceilinged dining-room which was once a barn – its original brick
walls are still exposed; board-and-latch doors; low beams. In a book-lined 'snug',
are comfortable velvet chairs and everywhere are pictures and fresh flowers. One
(single) bedroom and a shower are on the ground floor.

Annemarie Gosse (Danish-born) makes the most of the excellent vegetables and
fruit which Lincolnshire's rich fenland soil produces – growing a great deal
organically herself. She bakes her own bread and croissants; honey, trout and
sausages are all local. A typical dinner might start with crab, followed by pigeon or
rabbit pie and then home-made ice cream with fruit sauce, and cheeses. Alternatively, you can have a simple supper (such as fish pie and treacle tart). The Gosses
often dine with their guests and Peter (formerly a history teacher) is a mine of
information on the local history of the area (which has special Australian and
American connections) and on its wildlife too.

The flat Lincolnshire coast has its own character: bracing breezes have swept
the sands up into high dunes at certain points, the tides go out so far that the sea is
sometimes almost out of sight, and it is still shallow when you do get to it. The
North Sea constantly sweeps Yorkshire soil down here, creating (at Gibraltar
Point) salt marshes frequented by seals, migrant birds and birdwatchers – a very
different spectacle (with fine views over The Wash) from that offered by the
over-jolly resorts, from Cleethorpes to Skegness. Inland, distinctive red cattle
graze and the sails of windmills still spin.

If you drive north along the coast, you will come to a nature reserve with
natterjack toads, Donna Nook (a good hunting-ground for seashells), Cleethorpes
– from the promenade of which one can watch the procession of ships heading for
the Humber, and the huge fishing port of Grimsby. It is worth pressing on to see
the 600-year-old sculptures of ruined Thornton Abbey with its remarkable
gatehouse. Alternatively, drive south to Gibraltar Point and return via Wainfleet
All Saints (a port until the sea receded).

Readers' comments: Enjoyable experience. Warm welcome. Excellent dinner.
Vast, delicious breakfast.

ROSE-IN-VALE HOTEL   C D H S
Mithian, Cornwall, TR5 0QD   Tel: 087255 2202
East of St Agnes. Nearest main road: A3075 from Newquay towards Redruth.

17 Bedrooms. £29.95 including dinner (less for 2 nights off season). Prices go up in June. Bargain breaks. All have own bath/shower/toilet. Tea/coffee facilities. TV. Views of garden, country. Some have balcony.
Dinner. 4 courses (with choices) and coffee, at 7–8pm. Vegetarian or special diets if ordered. Wine can be ordered. No smoking.
3 Sitting-rooms. With open fire, central heating, TV, piano. **Bar.** Games room. Solarium.
Large garden with croquet, badminton.
Closed from November to February inclusive.

This handsome 18th-century mansion was originally the home of a local mine captain. A regular visitor to the Nankivel family here was the artist, John Opie, who grew up nearby and painted Joyce Nankivel, 'the belle of Mithian'.

The Arthurs, who honeymooned here several years ago, made many discoveries after they took over and began making improvements.

In what is now the bar at the back, they uncovered a most unusual stone fireplace with a fringle (bread oven) built into what had been an inglenook fireplace in an old cottage adjoining the 18th-century house. They have added fire-baskets welded by Tony himself: he says his past experience as an engineer has come in handy! He installed central heating himself, too.

There are two large sitting-rooms, now fully refurbished to a high standard, with fine details preserved, such as sash windows with folding shutters. The curving staircase has a decorative window. In a modern extension at the back is a third sitting-room and a very long dining-room with huge windows giving a view of the lawns and rosebeds, with a primrose-banked stream behind. There is a small, sheltered swimming-pool heated by solar panels which, in a good summer, keep the water temperature at 78°. Some smaller, modern bedrooms open onto this, but for one with outstanding views from its four windows choose no. 1 upstairs with a four-poster, in the main house. There is also a family suite.

The Arthurs have a good chef – Philip Sims was once at the Imperial Hotel, Torquay, and now lectures part-time at Camborne Catering College. He prepares such à la carte specialities as fish mousse in crab sauce; game or local fish as a main course – or perhaps duck in a sauce of Grand Marnier served with little pancakes containing orange segments and zest; and delicious puddings like an iced soufflé of peaches, surrounded by a purée of raspberries and cream. Take your mother here for the mid-March weekend when he does a special Mothering Sunday luncheon.

Beyond the sheltered valley and quaint village of Mithian are the well-known surfing beaches of St Agnes and Perranporth (a quieter one is at Trevellas), seal sanctuary, country park, and six National Trust houses (with gardens).

Readers' comments: Hospitality beyond reproach; extremely high standard. Very pleasant; comfortable but not luxurious; friendly and helpful owners. Very pleasant – return visit planned. Food excellent. Top marks. Welcoming and cheerful. Service, comfort and cuisine excellent. Charming owners.

ROWE HOUSE   D PT
Horton-in-Ribblesdale, North Yorkshire, BD24 0HT   Tel: 072 96 212
North of Settle. Nearest main road: A65 from Settle to Ingleton.

6 Bedrooms. £16.50–£22 (less for 4 nights). Prices go up in March. Bargain breaks. Some have own bath/shower/toilet. Tea/coffee facilities. TV. Views of garden, country.
Dinner. £10.50 for 4 courses and coffee, at 7pm. Vegetarian or special diets if ordered. Wine can be ordered.
1 Sitting-room. With open fire, central heating, TV.
Large garden
Closed from December to February inclusive.

In the 18th century this started life as a wealthy wool merchant's shooting-lodge – hence some of the impressive details such as the very handsome window and decorative ceiling of the staircase, and a fireplace of local marble in the sitting-room. It stands just above the banks of the River Ribble and over it looms the great bulk of Penyghent – one of the famous 'Three Peaks' (each some 2000 feet high). All around is the spectacular scenery of the Yorkshire Dales National Park and only a few miles away is Lancashire's less celebrated but just as fine Forest of Bowland (moors, woods, valleys and rivers).

Bob and Ann Jones now run the lodge as a guest-house, with simply but agreeably furnished bedrooms and much emphasis on good cooking (Bob qualified at a catering college), using their own eggs, honey, fruit and vegetables. A home-made soup or pâté might be followed by roast pork, perhaps, and then a pudding such as walnut-and-treacle flan or sherry trifle, and cheeses. There is a garden which Bob has been steadily improving.

Lying so far to the east of the National Park, Ribblesdale's charms are sometimes overlooked but this means it may be less crowded than more famous parts such as Wharfedale, for instance. From Settle runs a famous scenic railway (to Carlisle), saved by a mere whisker from closure a few years ago – there is a station at Horton, and there are also several preserved steam railways in the region.

The history of this area is one that goes back through aeons of geological time, when two million years ago this part of the Pennine rocks cracked and the whole landscape slipped, creating such striking features as the roadside cliff known as Giggleswick Scar and a great gap through the high hills which enabled invaders or traders, railways or roads, to penetrate the high and lonely places around. Eventually villages grew up on the valley floors, some developing into little market towns. One sees extraordinary cliffs or terraces of stone among the greenery, while down below are warrens of subterranean tunnels and pockets which bring pot-holers here: the biggest underground cave is Gaping Gill (larger than a cathedral), entered through an opening on Ingleborough Hill.

The long-distance Pennine Way – it goes from Derbyshire all the way to Scotland – wanders across the hilltops; for the less energetic, there are breathtaking car drives to follow (for instance, to Hawes and then over the Buttertubs Pass).

The Lake District to the west, and pretty little Dentdale to the north are accessible – Dent is an exceptionally attractive little cobbled town.

★ RUTLAND COTTAGES   C S X

Cedar Street, Braunston, Leicestershire, LE15 8QS   Tel: 0572 722049
South-west of Oakham. Nearest main road: A6003 from Oakham to Kettering.

5 Bedrooms. £15–£16 (less for 3 nights). Prices go up in April. Bargain breaks. Some have own bath/shower/toilet. Tea/coffee facilities. TV. Views of garden, country. No smoking in some.
Light suppers if ordered. Vegetarian or special diets. No smoking.
2 Sitting-rooms. With open fire, central heating, TV, piano. No smoking in one.
Small garden

A 17th-century bakehouse is the home of John and Connie Beadman (she taught music); and in addition they own nearby cottages let either for self-catering or on a bed-and-breakfast basis. All b & b guests take breakfast together in the beamed dining-room of the house. Those who do not want to cook their own dinner (in their cottage) can eat at the Old Plough in this pretty conservation village of golden stone, or Connie will provide sandwich suppers. (Packed lunches can also be provided; tea and coffee are free.)

Guests have the use of the Beadmans' huge and beautifully furnished sitting-room (it has a see-through stone fireplace in the middle, and a 'curfew window' through which the village watchman could check that the baker's fires had been properly extinguished for the night). Its windows open onto a heather garden with a view of stately cedars beyond.

Bedrooms in the cottages are more homely, but guests have the advantage of self-contained accommodation including fully equipped kitchens.

John and his sons are keen bell-ringers, willing to take visitors on guided tours up into the bell-towers of local churches. This is a good area for walks or cycling (maps on loan), and other country pursuits, and for sightseeing too: the historic schools at Uppingham and Oundle, the mediaeval town of Stamford, castles at Rockingham and Belvoir as well as Oakham, the stately homes of Burghley and Belton – at the former, horse trials take place each September. The former county of Rutland (now absorbed into Leicestershire) still has its own rural museum.

Man-made reservoirs when naturalized can be as beautiful as any lake. Rutland Water, greater in area than any reservoir in northern Europe, is particularly fine. There are paths around its wandering perimeter, pleasure boats on it, a nature reserve and trail, and areas devoted to watersports. The road around the south side is the more scenic one. At Normanton, a classical church on a causeway seems almost to float on the water (it is now used as a water museum); the village of Upper Hambleton is picturesquely sited too, on a spur of land projecting into the reservoir. The excellent Bay Tree Garden Centre has pre-Christmas events and a good restaurant.

Other places of interest in the area include 16th-century Lyddington Bede House – a Tudor almshouse, and Tolethorpe Hall where the founder of the Congregational church was born (Shakespeare's plays are performed in an open-air theatre here). There is a collection of steam locomotives in the iron-mine sidings at Cottesmore. At Burrough Hill you can see a fine panorama from the site of a huge Iron Age fort; or go to the country park at Syston for lake and river.

Readers' comments: Most friendly. Cottage excellent.

274

★ ST CHRISTOPHER'S

C(12) **D PT S X**

Boscastle, Cornwall, PL35 0BD   Tel: 08405 412

North of Camelford. Nearest main road: A39 from Bude to Wadebridge.

9 Bedrooms. £14–£15 (less for 3 nights). Prices go up in June. Bargain breaks. Some have own shower/toilet. Tea/coffee facilities. Views of country, sea.
Dinner. £8 for 3 courses (with some choices) and coffee, at 7pm. Non-residents not admitted. Vegetarian or special diets if ordered. Wine can be ordered. No smoking.
Light suppers if ordered.
1 Sitting-room. With open fire, central heating, TV, record-player. No smoking.
Small garden
Closed from November to February inclusive.

This 18th-century house is in an unspoilt harbour village (a conservation area) and now belongs to Brenda and Brian Thompson who used to run a local restaurant.

One enters it through a slate-floored hall with roughcast walls. There is a large sitting-room, well furnished with damask wallpaper and a big velvet sofa. It is heated by a log-burner and adjoined by a cottage-style dining-room. Bedrooms have well-chosen colour schemes: no. 2, for instance, which is L-shaped, is decorated in celadon and white, with cane chairs.

A typical dinner might comprise a mushroom-and-wine savoury, then tenderloin of pork in a cream sauce, syllabub and cheeses. There is an extensive wine list.

This is a splendid area for scenery, birdwatching and wild flowers, and secluded beaches as at Trebarwith Strand and Bossiney Cove. National Trust houses and other 'sights' abound.

All along this coast are picturesque fishing villages such as Boscastle, Tintagel and Port Isaac, but the scenery inland deserves to be explored too. An interesting day's drive might start at Tintagel (with a visit to the romantically sited seashore castle and Celtic monastery ruins up 300 steps; King Arthur's Hall – his story told in stained glass; and the Old Post Office, in a 14th-century house) and go to the Delabole quarry where grey-blue slate has been hewn for four centuries. From the viewing platform, workers at the bottom of the vast hole, 500-foot deep, look like pinheads. The road continues to Port Isaac (no fun for a car driver, so explore its steep lanes and harbour on foot) and Pentire Point where a clifftop walk has splendid views of the Camel estuary. Then back via Wadebridge.

On another day one might go in the opposite direction via Boscastle (visiting the harbour, the many craft workshops and a museum of witchcraft), then inland to Camelford for the North Cornwall Museum of social history, which includes a reconstruction of an old moorland cottage and, for the really vigorous, a walk up to the county's highest point, Brown Willy. Blisland is an unusual village with 18th-century houses, a green and a church with a flamboyant interior; and Pencarrow a lovely 18th-century house with portraits by Reynolds and others, exceptional furnishings, and gardens at their best when camellias and rhododendrons are in bloom. In the same direction is the National Trust's equally fine but very different Lanhydrock House, memorable for such features as an immense ceiling with biblical scenes in the plasterwork.

Readers' comments: Very good. Pleasant welcome and good food. Excellent hospitality, very relaxing. Very good value. Excellent food with plenty of variety.

Boxgrove, West Sussex, PO18 0DY   Tel: 0243 773173
East of Chichester. Nearest main road: A27 from Chichester to Worthing.

1 Bedroom. £14. With own shower/toilet. Tea/coffee facilities. TV. View of garden. Washing machine on request.
Small garden

There is an increasing trend, of which this is a good example, to provide accommodation which is a mix of bed-and-breakfast with self-catering. Visitors have their own self-contained suite (including cooking facilities) but breakfast and service are provided.

In the case of St Hugh's, the accommodation is in a separate annexe in the garden. A spacious bedsitting-room – well and newly furnished – opens onto a private patio with cushioned chairs. There is an excellent shower room; and cooking facilities are hidden away in pine fitments. For breakfast, visitors enter the house and its dining-room (lined with ancestral portraits of Cornish farmers). No dinners: Edwina Tremaine recommends the Nicodemus restaurant in nearby Chichester or the Anglesey Arms at Halnaker.

Boxgrove itself deserves a visit because, when other great monastic churches were being destroyed by Henry VIII, the one here was saved by the protests of the Lord of the Manor and is now the parish church: its great Norman nave is quite outstanding. Walkers can follow the rural track of the Romans' Stane Street which was once the main route from Chichester to London: it goes across the Downs and passes near the Roman villa at Bignor. At West Dean (where the great house is now a college for arts and crafts) is a superb park with botanical gardens; with the Weald and Downland Museum near – an open-air collection of very ancient buildings rescued and re-sited here. Goodwood House is famous not only for its fine furniture and art treasures but for the racecourse. There are interesting villages such as Chilgrove and (for sea views) Selsey, the Hartings, yellow-painted Cocking, and Apuldram from the waterfront walks of which flocks of migrant ducks and geese can be seen. Turner painted seascapes at Birdham. The cathedral city of Chichester and its lovely natural harbour have been described elsewhere.

On what was a famous Battle of Britain airfield, Tangmere, there are now working models of aircraft and a flight simulator; Amberley's chalk pits house an outdoor museum of old industries; and at Arundel is a toy museum – as well as one of England's finest castles. The Wildfowl Trust has one of its major reserves near here, with a comfortable viewing gallery by one of its lakes; and Denmans Garden at Fontwell includes a school of garden design, water gardens and glasshouses.

From Littlehampton you can go by boat up the River Arun to Arundel or Amberley. Though small, the maritime museum at Littlehampton is an interesting one to visit.

Readers' comments: Wholly recommended, beautifully furnished.

ST JAMES'S HOUSE   C PT
The Green, Thirsk, North Yorkshire, YO7 1AQ   Tel: 0845 524120/522676
Nearest main road: A19 from Middlesbrough to York.

4 Bedrooms. £14–£18 (less for 7 nights). Bargain breaks. Some have own shower/toilet. Tea/coffee facilities TV. No smoking. **1 Sitting-room.** With central heating, TV.

No smoking. **Small garden** **Closed from November to mid-March.**

Barry Ogleby being an antique dealer, it is not surprising that every part of his 18th-century house is well endowed with period pieces. You may sleep in a room with a bedstead of prettily turned spindles or in a genuine Victorian four-poster; and in corridors as well as rooms there are such interesting pieces as inlaid blanket-boxes or unusual chairs. On the ground floor is a particularly convenient family room, looking onto flower beds, winding paths and lily-pool.

Only two minutes' walk from the quiet green, a conservation area, is Thirsk's busy market place and many restaurants (only breakfast is served by Liz Ogleby, who recommends the Carpenters' Arms for other meals). This is where the world's most famous vet, writing under the name of James Herriot, has his surgery. There are local guides who will accompany you on car tours, pointing out sites associated with Herriot, his books or the films; one shows videos en route.

In the immediate vicinity are the stupendous view from Sutton Bank, Castle Howard (famous even before 'Brideshead Revisited'), thriving Ampleforth Abbey and its school, the pretty villages of Coxwold and Kilburn – the latter associated with 'the mouse-man' and his furniture, the former with Shandy Hall (home of Laurence Sterne). A few miles away is Northallerton, a town of fine houses, with characterful villages all around. Fountains Abbey, Newburgh Priory, the white horse of the Hambleton Hills, Byland Abbey, Helmsley (old market town), arboretum at Bedale and Harlow Car gardens are other attractions.

There are landscaped gardens at Duncombe Park, Helmsley – a town dominated by great castle ruins on a huge earthwork. Seventeenth-century Nunnington Hall not only has fine rooms but a display of miniature rooms too. Sion Hill Hall, at Kirby Wiske, is not historic – except in style – but is notable for its displays of period furniture. What was once the home of Thomas Lord – of cricketing fame – is now Thirsk's museum of local history and of cricket. In an area of spectacular abbeys, do not overlook some of the smaller gems such as Mount Grace Priory (with 23 monastic cells) or Saxon St Gregory's Minster at Nawton.

Readers' comments: A warm welcome. Comfortable, quiet room; good breakfast. Friendly hostess, very good house, beautifully furnished. Breakfasts are something special.

ST MARY'S HOUSE C D H X

Kintbury, Berkshire, RG15 0TR Tel: 0488 58551
West of Newbury. Nearest main road: A4 from Marlborough to Newbury.

5 Bedrooms. £14.50–£20 (less for 4 nights). Some have own bath/shower/toilet. TV. Views of garden, country, river. Clothes-washing on request.
Dinner. From £8 for 4 courses (with limited choices) and coffee, at 7–8.30pm. Non-residents not admitted. Vegetarian or special diets if ordered. Wine can be ordered or brought in. **Light suppers** if ordered.
2 Sitting-rooms. With wood stove, central heating, TV. Bar.
Small garden

Old-fashioned roses and a grapevine up the walls add to the picturesque look of this unusual house. Its pointed windows are lozenge-paned, and little dormers punctuate the roof: it used to be a school from 1856 until 1963.

Some bedrooms are on the ground floor, one of them (with particularly handsome bathroom, chaise longue and flowery chintzes) opening onto a paved terrace with lavender hedge. Others are up a spiral iron staircase (strictly for the nimble), including a family room – with rocking-horse – under the rafters of the roof. The sitting-room is furnished with antiques, and the dining-room with a great, 17th-century refectory table surrounded by leather chairs. Alcoves of books, pointed arches, three outsize sofas around a lacquer table in front of the handsome fireplace, and great copper vats of logs all add to an interior of outstanding distinction.

Margaret Barr prepares (if given adequate notice) such meals as fish mousse, chicken in a variety of exotic sauces, and meringues or fruity desserts, followed by cheese. Alan has a well-stocked wine cellar to complement her cooking.

The lovely Kennet & Avon Canal is only a hundred yards away, for Kintbury lies midway between Hungerford and Newbury – towns described elsewhere in this book (along with the rest of Berkshire). Only a few miles south are the Hampshire Downs; and, westward, Wiltshire's Vale of Pewsey, both of which are also scenic areas which take days to explore. Northward is a region rich in prehistoric remains – hill forts, barrows, ancient tracks and so forth. The valley itself is quite different: woodland, commons and meadows as the backdrop to villages of flint, brick and thatch with narrow lanes and some richly decorated churches. Birdwatchers and walkers love the whole area (as do anglers). Favourite outings include Littlecote House, Avebury (prehistoric ring), Marlborough, Newbury (racecourse), Bowood House and Highclere Castle.

Picturesque Hungerford is famous for its scores of antique shops (many open even on Sundays). And, of course, most visitors go to Windsor not only for its famous castle and Eton College but also for the outstanding 'Royalty and Empire' show (in the old station, Tussauds have animated an event at Queen Victoria's diamond jubilee) and the safari park.

Readers' comments: Lovely atmosphere, first-class dinner.

278

SANDY PARK HOUSE

C(5) S

Sandy Park, Devon, TQ13 8JV   Tel: 06473 2377

North-west of Moretonhampstead. Nearest main road: A382 from Bovey Tracey towards Okehampton.

4 Bedrooms. £16–£18. Tea/coffee facilities. TV. Views of garden, country, river. No smoking. Washing machine on request.
Dinner. £15 for 4 courses (with choices) and coffee, at 7.30pm. Non-residents not admitted. Vegetarian or special diets if ordered. Wine can be ordered. No smoking. **Light suppers** if ordered.
1 Sitting-room. With open fire, central heating, TV, record-player. Bar.
Small garden
Closed from November to February inclusive.

It was in a Polish catering college that Wanda Weatherhead learnt to cook the kind of imaginative dishes she serves here: such meals as smoked trout with soured cream, followed by pork chops and mushrooms cooked in foil, then mango and passionfruit ice cream, with cheeses to follow. Dinner is served at tables clothed with crimson Paisley cloths (the velvet-upholstered chairs match these, and the pale yellow wallpaper is a perfect background).

Throughout the mainly 18th-century house there are equally attractive colour schemes and sparkling white paintwork – from the sitting-room of soft brown and buff shades to bedrooms with colours such as shell pink and beige, or pale lemon. On the walls are outstanding landscapes by Richard's father (the artist Ian Weatherhead), in a cabinet his grandfather's collection of big Toby jugs, and everywhere baskets of beautifully arranged dried flowers. This is a house of great charm and originality. (Breakfast is continental, unless you pay extra.)

Sandy Park is a hamlet at the head of the Teign Valley over the rolling meadows and occasional granite outcrops of which loom the heights of Dartmoor. Just up the road is Castle Drogo, built by Lutyens in a dramatically scenic setting – on the very edge of a granite headland, covered in heather, which overlooks the river. It is as imposing as any mediaeval fortress. The interior is equally bold, with unadorned granite walls and arches, tapestries, and mullioned windows that give views of terraced lawns and topiary on a monumental scale.

The little market town of Moretonhampstead has good buildings (including unusual granite almshouses built in 1637) and, on its outskirts, the high site of an Iron Age fort (known as Cranbrook Castle) from which to look down 1000 feet to the River Teign below. Nearby are pretty North Bovey – village green, thatched cottages, church perched on a knoll – and Postbridge, famous for its 'clapper' bridge of three stones that each span 15 feet (and for several prehistoric walled pounds for livestock in the vicinity).

Westward lies Chagford, tucked well away, which has a particularly fine river setting with a high viaduct spanning the wide waters of the Teign as they curve beneath wooded hills. Gidleigh, in addition to its castle, has innumerable prehistoric circles in its vicinity – the best is at Scorhill. At Sticklepath is a museum of rural industry; and all the highest points of Dartmoor are within a few miles. Okehampton, a market town, is known as the northern capital of the moor (its castle is beautifully sited above a river).

Readers' comments: Extremely comfortable, good food.

279

★ **SAXELBYE MANOR HOUSE** C D

Saxelby, Leicestershire, LE14 3PA Tel: 0664 812269
North-west of Melton Mowbray. Nearest main road: A6006 from Melton
Mowbray towards Derby.

3 Bedrooms. £13 (less for 4 nights). Tea/
coffee facilities. TV. Views of garden, country. Washing machine on request.
Dinner. £8 for 4 courses and coffee, at 7pm.
Non-residents not admitted. Vegetarian or
special diets if ordered. Wine can be ordered
or brought in.
1 Sitting-room. With open fire, central heating, TV, piano.
Large garden
**Closed from November to March
inclusive.**

In this little hamlet is an especially attractive farmhouse, tucked within a garden
where willows and fuchsias flourish. Parts of it are 800 years old. Margaret Morris
has furnished it with a fascinating collection of Victoriana (even in the cloakroom):
little velvet chairs and chaises longues, old prints and pot-plants in abundance.
Narrow passages lead to a grand staircase constructed four centuries ago in the old
stone stairwell. There's even a big Victorian bath in the huge bathroom. She
provides traditional 4-course dinners as well as bed-and-breakfast, all at a very
modest price. One might, for instance, eat prawn cocktail, the farm's own lamb
with four vegetables, sherry trifle and a cheeseboard that includes Stilton and
other local cheeses.

On the farm are cows, sheep and beef-cattle. It provides not only free-range eggs
for breakfast but very good, tested milk.

Melton Mowbray is a pleasant market town (from which you can go home laden
with its famous pork pies and other products of the pig), and is well placed for
visiting other historic Leicestershire towns such as Loughborough and Oakham
(as well as Grantham and Stamford in Lincolnshire, and Nottingham for its castle
and other historic buildings). Belvoir Castle and Rutland Water are well worth a
visit. The tiny county of Rutland still keeps its identity even though it was
incorporated into Leicestershire decades ago. Go to Bottesford (for its church
monuments), Burghley (for views), Uppingham (famous 16th-century boys'
school) and Wing (a mediaeval maze). There is also a steam railway.

For a scenic day tour of the best parts of the county, head south to explore first of
all such picturesque old villages as Barkby (fine stone tracery in the 13th-century
church), Queninborough, and Gaddesby where there is an extraordinary church
monument – a life-size hero of Waterloo on his dying horse. Around Little Dalby
are green hills where cows graze – among these lush dairy pastures was made the
first Stilton cheese; and from the 700-foot top of Burrough Hill (Iron Age
earthworks still visible) are superb views. Villages on the way to Uppingham are
built of glowing ironstone, and against the golden cottage walls roses clamber up in
profusion (Brooke's church deserves a visit). Lyddington is particularly pretty,
with wall-paintings in the church; and in its Bede House, where the bishops of
Lincoln used to hold audience, is a splendid hall with oak ceiling and carvings.

Readers' comments: Have stayed repeatedly. Another wonderful Gundrey house!
Meals and lovely bedroom were first class. Nothing was too much trouble. Lovely
room, wonderful meal. Good cook, charming hostess.

Water Street, Chesterton, Cambridge, CB4 1NZ   Tel: 0223 355550
Nearest main road: A1303 from Cambridge towards Newmarket.

rear view

3 Bedrooms. £15–£17 (less for 7 nights).
Prices go up in April. Tea/coffee facilities.
TV. Views of garden, river.
1 Sitting-room. With central heating, TV.
Small garden

Willow baskets hang overhead as you enter the archway (built for coaches) which
leads to a pretty courtyard and this 16th-century cottage. The basketmaker is Jane
Greening, in whose home there are now particularly attractive bedrooms where
once bargees lodged. For Water Street runs along a bank of the River Cam, at one
time a busy waterway for trade. Now it is a quiet backwater except when a regatta
or raft race is taking place. You can walk the towpath right into Cambridge (it is
1½ miles to Magdalene College); or cross a footbridge to Stourbridge Common.
(The less energetic can take a bus into Cambridge: one of Water Street's
attractions is that here, unlike the city centre, it is easy to park one's car.)

   Jane has put her own artistic touches everywhere, from the blue-and-white
fingerplates on pine doors to interesting pottery and paintings on brick walls. She
serves only breakfasts (recommending the garden restaurant of the riverside Pike
and Eel Inn for other meals). There is a small sitting-area upstairs.

   Cambridge itself takes days to explore, and then there is a lot to see in the
vicinity. Anglesey Abbey, for instance, which was really a priory only, founded in
1135. The buildings were completely transformed in this century by a wealthy
connoisseur who filled them with art treasures and around them created one of the
really great gardens of England.

Readers' comments: Could not have been better looked after.

On this side of Cambridge is Swaffham
★ Bulbeck and the **OLD RECTORY**
(tel: 0223 811986) which was built in
1818 for the Rev. Leonard Jenyns, a
distinguished naturalist who was
offered but declined a place on the
Beagle expedition, recommending instead his pupil Charles Darwin – who
was a frequent visitor to the Rectory.

   Jenny Few-Mackay frequents salerooms to seek out all the Victoriana
which furnishes the house in the style
of Jenyns' time: one room has a handsome brass bed from which, through
big windows, to enjoy the view of
hayfields. There is a large garden. Unless you order a simple supper, the best
place for dinner is the Hole in the Wall
at Little Wilbraham (or the Black
Horse inn in Swaffham Bulbeck).
From £13.50 to £18.50.

SEVERN TROW
Church Road, Jackfield, Shropshire, TF8 7ND Tel: 0952 883551
South-east of Ironbridge. Nearest main road: A442 from Telford to Bridgnorth.

4 Bedrooms. £15–£17 (less for 7 nights). Prices go up in April. Bargain breaks. One has own bath/shower/toilet. Tea/coffee facilities. Views of garden, country, river. No smoking.
2 Sitting-rooms. With open fire, central heating, TV, piano, record-player. Bar. No smoking.
Small garden

Through the deep Ironbridge gorge, scenic birthplace (in 1709) of the industrial revolution, flows the lovely River Severn on its way to the distant sea. As early as the 17th century it was a trade route, with flat-bottomed sailing barges called trows bearing goods downriver to the port at Bristol. After unloading, boats had to be hauled back up again by teams of men walking the 120-mile towpath. The Severn Trow, standing on the river bank, provided them with beer, dormitory lodgings and (on the top floor) a cubicled brothel.

When the railways came, river traffic declined and the house was for a while used as a church hall for village events, eventually losing even that function. Abandoned and derelict, it was eventually bought by Jim and Pauline Hannigan whose own strenuous work has transformed it.

To original features which gave the house unique character, they have added very attractive furnishings. There are now carpets on floors of red and black quarry-tiles, good sofas in the sitting-room where an old pine dresser serves as a bar, and in the dining-room an outstanding and very colourful mosaic floor and tiled fireplace fender made at the Jackfield factory close by (now a museum).

There are iron grates and stoves, board doors, exposed rafters, and a particularly decorative cast-iron kitchen-range. The arched entrance, big enough to accommodate a cart, once linked malt-store to brew-house, the latter is now another sitting-room with beer-vat openings still set in the brick walls.

Upstairs are excellent bedrooms with light colour schemes such as yellow and white, and interesting furnishings – a net-draped brass bed, for example, and a cupboard converted from an oriental-style, satin-domed commode.

Very substantial breakfasts are provided but no evening meal. However, Jim will drive visitors to and from any of Ironbridge's two dozen eating-places (or they can eat in the village's own inn, the Black Swan).

The Ironbridge gorge brings visitors from all over the world, for in this dramatically scenic area one can recapture the earliest history of the Industrial Revolution. Here, where Abraham Darby pioneered coke-smelting, were made the first iron wheels, rails, locomotives, boats and structures – the most famous of these being the world's first iron bridge (1779), still gracefully spanning the gorge. It is best to start one's visit in the 1840s wharfside visitor centre where an audio-visual show explains what you will then see: a museum of the River Severn, the Museum of Iron, Darby's original furnace, the toll house exhibition, and Blists Hill's 50 acres where gas-lit streets, rail yards, a candle factory and much else recreate a Victorian world. Finally there are the original Coalport china works.

Readers' comments: Most comfortable, wonderful welcome. Has to be seen to be believed.

SHEARINGS
Rockbourne, Hampshire, SP6 3NA   Tel: 07253 256
North of Fordingbridge. Nearest main road: A354 from Salisbury to Blandford Forum.

Bargain breaks. All have own bath or shower. Tea/coffee facilities. Views of garden, stream. No smoking. Washing machine on request.
Dinner. £12.50 for 3 courses or £16.50 (with aperitif and wine) and coffee, at 8pm. Non-residents not admitted. Vegetarian or special diets if ordered. Wine can be ordered or brought in. No smoking. **Light suppers** if ordered.
2 Sitting-rooms. With open fire, central heating, TV, piano.
Small garden

3 Bedrooms. £19.50 but with a 10% discount to SOTBT readers (less for 7 nights).

Closed from mid-December to end of January.

The house, with thatched roof and porch, overlooks a clear stream and has its own footbridge. It was built in the 16th century (from oak beams that are even older), and when Colin and Rosemary Watts came here they took great care to decorate and furnish it appropriately. One pink-carpeted sitting-room has rosy cretonne sofas facing the inglenook fireplace; another, with chintz-covered chairs, is for television. Most meals are eaten in the beamy kitchen/dining-room. (Bedrooms are rather simply furnished.)

The garden at the back is particularly pretty: sloping lawn, brick summerhouse, a suntrapping brick patio. Here there is an annexe to the house that could be particularly suitable for youngsters, with upstairs bedsitter.

Mr and Mrs Watts are interesting people to meet – she, musical and artistic; he, a retired brigadier. Rosemary is an excellent cook – of such meals as iced cucumber soup, beef, éclairs, cheeses.

The village itself is picturesque, and has a Roman villa.

Readers' comments: Excellent. Made very welcome. Truly beautiful and peaceful. Top marks. Treated like personal guests.

On Castle Hill at Woodgreen is **COTTAGE CREST** (tel: 0725 22009) where the Cadmans provide bed-and-breakfast. Bedrooms are some of the most beautiful and well-equipped in this book. A great brass bed with pink-and-white lacy linen is in one; it has an L-shaped room with windows on two sides from which to enjoy superb views of sunsets over the River Avon in the valley below. There is also a garden suite with private sitting-room facing this view. One can sit on a paved terrace with a little pool, or take a zigzag path down to a lower garden, to look

for badgers or walk straight into the New Forest. (Dinners available at the local Horse and Groom inn; or in Fordingbridge, at the riverside de George, Shepherd's Spring or Hourglass.) £15.

★ **SHIELDHALL** CDS
Wallington, Northumberland, NE61 4AQ Tel: 0830 40387
West of Morpeth. Nearest main road: A696 from Newcastle to Otterburn.

6 Bedrooms. £13.50–£17.50 (less for 3 nights). All have own bath/shower/toilet. Tea/coffee facilities. TV. Views of garden, country. No smoking. Washing machine on request.
Dinner. £7.75 for 3 courses (with choices) and coffee, at 6.30pm. Vegetarian or special diets if ordered. Wine can be ordered. No smoking. **Light suppers** if ordered.
2 Sitting-rooms. With open fire, central heating, TV, piano. Bar. No smoking.
Large garden
Closed from November to March inclusive.

18th-century stone buildings enclose a courtyard where white fantails strut, the former barns to left and right providing very well-equipped ground-floor bedrooms for visitors – each with its own entrance. Meals are taken in a beamed dining-room in the centre, furnished with antiques and an inglenook fireplace (a typical dinner might be home-made soup, a roast or lasagne, and blackcurrant tart – with produce from the smallholding); and to one side is a sitting-room for visitors. From a patio with chairs one enjoys a serene view.

Stephen Robinson-Gay is an accomplished cabinet-maker, happy to show visitors the workshop where he makes or restores furniture. Many of the bedrooms have examples of his work. For instance, beyond the arched doorway of the mahogany room is a colonial-style bed with very fine inlay, and in the oak room a four-poster with carved canopy, copied from a Flemish bed in Lindisfarne Castle (on Holy Island), complete with a secret cupboard to hold a shotgun – necessary bedside equipment in the troubled times of three centuries ago.

Celia is a fount of information on local history and what to see. Close by is one of the National Trust's biggest houses, Wallington Hall (very fine grounds), with others not far afield – Cragside, Belsay and a great number of castles. Capability Brown was born in the area, there are Pre-Raphaelite associations, and the whole region is one of impressive landscapes – from the hills and valleys of the Cheviots to the dramatic coastline more fully described elsewhere.

Flemish bed at Shieldhall

★ **SHIP INN**   **C D H PT S**

West Street, Oundle, Northamptonshire, PE8 4EF   Tel: 0832 273918
East of Corby. Nearest main road: A605 from Peterborough towards
Northampton.

:ear view

14 Bedrooms. £17.50–£22.50. Bargain breaks. Some have own bath/shower/toilet. Tea/coffee facilities. TV. Views of garden, country, river. Balcony. Washing machine on request.
Dinner. A la carte, at 7–10pm. Vegetarian or special diets if ordered. Wine can be ordered. **Light suppers** if ordered.
1 Sitting-room. With central heating, TV. **Bars** with piano.
Small garden

The traditional English inn is something of an endangered species, as 'improvement' applies its deadening uniformity. Fortunately, the Ship Inn has escaped modernization and here you will still find low beams (hung with tankards), panelling, inglenook and oak seats. The bar is usually full of locals who come for such traditional pub meals – home-cooked – as whitebait, beef-and-ale pie, and fruit crumble; or for a snack such as jacket potato with toasted Stilton.

Bedrooms are in two separate buildings alongside the inn. Those at the front are the less expensive, pleasantly furnished, and with a sitting-room for residents only: something which inns rarely provide. I particularly liked a quiet room overlooking a small courtyard garden (this, too, is for residents only). The breakfast-room is here.

Behind this extends a wing with more luxurious bedrooms (originally the coach house), which Dorothy Langridge has furnished with pretty fabrics draping the bedheads. As these overlook a patio bar, with carpark beyond, they have been triple-glazed for quiet.

Oundle, quickly reached from the A1, stands comparison with more famous Cotswolds towns: the underlying rock is the same golden limestone, so the architecture is similar and just as fine. The famous public school is on a par with some Oxford colleges. And if you eat or drink at the Talbot Hotel, you will find remnants of Fotheringhay Castle incorporated – notably the great staircase down which Mary Queen of Scots went to her execution and, at the top, there is still the barrier behind which she had been confined on an upper floor for so many years.

From here historic Rockingham Forest is easily reached – its woodlands dotted with fine churches and villages. Rockingham Castle (Norman and Tudor), stately homes such as Deene Park, Elton Hall and Boughton House (superb furnishings). Lilford Park (birds and animals), Wicksteed Park at Kettering, the country park of East Carlton and the Nene Valley steam railway are good outings for families with young children.

As to the arts, go to Kettering for its art gallery, Corby for concerts and Lamport Hall for art treasures (as well as fine gardens). All these are well known but add to your list the most unusual art gallery of all, in a barn at Ashton (weekends only). Here you will see paintings through which psychiatric patients resolved their emotional problems and – in some cases – discovered they were artists of high professional calibre. The thatched village of Ashton is also where world Conker Championships are held every October.

Readers' comments: Well furnished; enjoyable bar meal.

285

SHOTTLE HALL FARM

C D

Shottle, Derbyshire, DE5 2EB   Tel: 077 389 276

North-west of Belper. Nearest main road: A517 from Ashbourne to Belper.

9 Bedrooms. £17–£19. Prices go up in April. Some have own bath/shower/toilet. Tea/coffee facilities. TV. Views of garden, country. No smoking.
Dinner. £9.25 for 4 courses and coffee, at 7.30pm. Vegetarian or special diets if ordered. Wine can be ordered. **Light suppers** if ordered.
2 Sitting-rooms. With central heating, TV. Bar.
Large garden

The house is over a century old and has all the solid Victorian quality of that period: big rooms, fine ceilings and doors, dignity in every detail. Not only the bedrooms but even the bathrooms are large and close-carpeted, with paintwork and everything else in pristine condition. As well as a sizeable sitting-room, there are two dining-rooms – one is used for breakfasts because it gets the morning sun. From both, the huge windows have views of hills and of the fertile valley stretching below the house – much of it is the Matthews' land. There are a rose garden and lawns – and not another house in sight.

Philip is a former county chairman of the National Farmers Union and an extremely interesting person with whom to discuss agricultural politics, Common Market affairs and so forth. Occasionally, vintage cars rally here. Her guests enjoy Phyllis's straightforward home cooking. A typical dinner menu might include: salmon mousse, chicken in apricot sauce, meringue with raspberries, English cheeses, and coffee with cream. Phyllis collects antique cheese dishes; and has other antiques for sale.

Shottle is in the middle of a rural area of fine landscapes. Close by are the Derbyshire Dales and the Peak District (described elsewhere). The Matlocks are a hilly area with pretty villages to be found. The old spa of Matlock Bath has interesting places to visit (stately gardens, wildlife park, model village, a museum of mining, and the tower, terraces and caverns of Abraham's Heights). Cromford is both attractive and historic, with Arkwright's first mill, old waterside buildings, a good bookshop etc. There are six stately homes and innumerable good walks.

Around Derby, magnates built themselves great houses such as Wingfield Manor where Mary Queen of Scots was imprisoned, the very splendid Sudbury Hall which now houses a museum of childhood, Melbourne Hall where Lord Melbourne lived (the formal gardens are particularly fine and the Norman village church is outstanding), Kedleston Hall – a magnificent Adam house, and Calke Abbey (1701), the contents of which remained scarcely disturbed over the last century. In the Matlock direction is mediaeval Carnfield Hall. The traffic of Derby itself is worth braving to visit the cathedral, Elizabeth Wollaton Hall (now a natural history museum, in lovely grounds), the city museum with Derby porcelain among much else, and 18th-century Pickford's House.

Readers' comments: Lovely room, excellent dinner: a winner. Good and friendly. Wonderful! Delightfully warm and friendly couple. Superb cook. Thoroughly enjoyed our stay, charming and friendly people. Very impressed; could not have been more helpful. Superb. Very friendly and comfortable.

286

SHOULDER OF MUTTON INN   C D S
Kirby Hill, North Yorkshire, DL4 7JH   Tel: 0748 2772
North of Richmond. Nearest main road: A66 from Scotch Corner to Brough.

5 Bedrooms. £15.50 or £29 including dinner (less for 3 nights). Prices go up in May. Bargain breaks. Some have own shower/toilet. Tea/coffee facilities. TV. Views of country. Washing machine on request. **Dinner.** A la carte, at 7.30–9pm. Vegetarian or special diets if ordered. Wine can be ordered. **Light suppers** if ordered.

The Shoulder of Mutton is the sort of ivy-covered village inn to stay in if you like talking to the locals in a beamy, stone-walled bar in the evening – in fact, holiday-makers have been known to flee here from the formal atmosphere of a nearby hotel of the grander kind. There is no sitting-room, however, but a pool room. Now run by Hylton and Shirley Pyner, the inn has been extended to create a restaurant where you can order such dishes as steaks, guinea-fowl (in a sauce of asparagus, mushroom and cream), or plaice stuffed with smoked salmon and prawns. They have decorated rooms with attractive fabrics, Turkey carpets, and jolly Victorian pictures; and there is a log stove in the bar.

Kirby Hill is a small village, complete with green and old church. As the name suggests, it stands on a hill giving impressive views of the valley, which extends as far as the North York Moors. It is in a quiet spot close to the A1 and also to the historic town of Richmond, with its Georgian theatre and Norman castle. The Shoulder of Mutton is popular with race-goers, for Catterick is also within a few miles. You can do day trips to Hadrian's Wall, Durham Cathedral, York and the superb coastline of Northumberland and North Yorkshire.

Barnard Castle, a few miles away, is a small town which deserves half a day or more of one's time. Best known for the market cross in the centre and the riverside castle from which it takes its name, it is a good place to shop for antiques, and there is a choice of restaurants. Perhaps the most surprising thing there is an old textile mill by the river, which is now a supermarket-size remainder bookshop: there is no knowing what you will find there at knockdown prices, from a history of horror films to obscure technological works or classical authors.

Another surprising attraction of Barnard Castle is the Bowes Museum, just outside the town (not at nearby Bowes). This château-style pile was built in the 19th century by a distant relative of the Queen Mother's family (the Bowes-Lyons) to house the family's big collections of ornate French furniture, musical instruments, minor old masters, and ceramics, as well as toys, model ships, butterflies – and a two-headed calf. There is also a silver automaton of a swan which does its fish-swallowing performance every hour, and travelling exhibitions are mounted periodically. It is not what you would expect to find in such a spot.

Inland are some pleasant villages, many with good pubs: specially recommended is the Fox & Hounds at Cotherstone. Sample if you can Cotherstone cheese, a genuine local speciality which is excellent but elusive in shops.

Readers' comments: Super position, nice people. Idyllic; view from our corner room was magic; good food and attentive owners. Exceptional value, superb meal. Very welcoming, food splendid, enjoyed the Monday singalong!

287

SISSINGHURST CASTLE FARM   C D PT S X

Sissinghurst, Kent, TN17 2AB   Tel: 0580 712885

East of Tunbridge Wells. Nearest main road: A262 from High Halden towards Tunbridge Wells.

3 Bedrooms. £15–£18 (less for 5 nights). Prices go up in April. Bargain breaks. Some have own bath/shower/toilet. Tea/coffee facilities. Views of garden, country. No smoking.

Dinner. £10 for 3 courses and coffee, at 7pm. Vegetarian or special diets if ordered. Wine can be brought in. No smoking. **Light suppers** if ordered.

1 Sitting-room. With open fire, central heating, TV.

Large garden

'Hydrangea petiolaris will grow under trees and ramble over an old stump', wrote Vita Sackville-West to her tenant at the Castle Farm. 'I asked the Director of Kew and he specially advised this.' In the same note she said: 'I can give you a lot of columbines – ask Vass [her gardener] for them.' James Stearns (grandson of that tenant, who still farms here) treasures this note from one of England's most famous gardening ladies, creator of the adjacent gardens at Sissinghurst Castle (now NT). It was in fact James' great-uncle, an estate agent, who first introduced the Elizabethan castle to Vita.

The farmhouse, which dates from 1855, was once a mansion inhabited by a substantial family – hence the row of servants' bells which still survives, along with such period features as panelled sash windows, fretted woodwork and the galleried staircase. Here hang two fine paintings lent by Nigel Nicolson (son of Vita and Harold Nicolson) who still lives in a wing of the castle. Furniture is a homely, pleasant mixture of old pieces; and one bedroom, with windows on two sides, has a good view of the castle. Beyond the croquet lawn are leafy woodlands.

Pat Stearns is an accomplished cook, particularly fond of Delia Smith recipes. A typical meal might comprise cucumber and cream cheese mousse; lamb threaded with garlic, rosemary and mint; summer pudding – most of the puddings are prepared by her mother-in-law who lives in a cottage nearby; and local cheeses.

It is worth climbing to the top of the tower at the splendid brick castle to look across the Weald towards the North Downs: below are woods, lakes, oast houses, Castle Farm's fields of cereals and bullocks – and, of course, the world-famous gardens, with outbuildings and remnants of a moat. The castle was virtually a ruin when Vita and her husband, Harold Nicolson, rescued it in 1930. The gardens were planned as a series of 'rooms' and so although they extend to 6 acres the overall effect is intimate: a major part of their charm. Vistas open up unexpectedly, in every month there is something different in flower – from cottage-garden to rare species. One of the most popular of the gardens contains nothing but old-fashioned roses. Inside the castle you can see rooms where the two pursued their profession as writers.

Near here is the picturesque little market town of Cranbrook (with cathedral-like church), and beyond its steep main street the biggest working windmill in the country, built before the Battle of Waterloo. Beyond Northiam, a village of weatherboarded houses, is Great Dixter – both house and gardens were designed by Lutyens. Fourteenth-century Bodiam Castle (NT) is surrounded by a moat, and after this comes the seaside resort of Hastings, described elsewhere.

★ SLOOP INN

Bantham, Devon, TQ7 3AJ   Tel: 0548 560489
West of Kingsbridge. Nearest main road: A379 from Kingsbridge to Plymouth.

5 Bedrooms. £19–£20. Prices go up during summer. Bargain breaks. Some have own bath/toilet. Tea/coffee facilities. TV. Views of country, sea, river. Washing machine on request.
Dinner. A la carte, at 7–10pm. Vegetarian or special diets if ordered. Wine can be ordered.
Closed from mid-December to mid-January inclusive.

It goes without saying that this 400-year-old inn by the sea has a history of smuggling.

One of its owners was in fact a notorious wrecker, luring ships (by means of false lights) onto rocks in order to plunder them. Since the law was that 'if any man escape to shore alive, the ship is no wreck' – and so plundering it would be theft, wreckers were murderous wretches too. Neil Girling can tell you many stories of the smugglers and point out places in the village where they hid their kegs of French brandy. Once, the Sloop minted its own coins (some are now in the interesting museum at Kingsbridge) with which to pay for goods and services – the coins were usable only to buy drinks at the Sloop: good business!

The inn is unspoilt: everything one hopes that a lively waterfront inn will be but rarely is, low-beamed, stone-flagged and snug. Some walls are of stone and some panelled.

One of its several bars is made from old boat-timbers. Here you can take on the locals at a game of darts or table-skittles after enjoying an excellent bar meal; or stroll down to the sandy dunes to watch the sun set over the sea. Bathing, building sandcastles and exploring rock-pools delight children; and there is surfing. Many of the unpretentiously furnished bedrooms have a view of the sea or River Avon. There is a yard and well at the back with seats.

Soups are home-made and ham home-cooked; smoked salmon, crabs and steaks are all local produce; granary bread is served. Fish is, of course, particularly good and fresh. All portions are generous.

Bantham is one of Devon's most ancient villages (the remains of prehistoric dwellings were laid bare in an 18th-century storm, and there was a Roman camp here later). Once, its main livelihood was pilchard-fishing but there are no more pilchards now.

The whole area is remote, peaceful and unspoilt with good walks through particularly beautiful countryside or along the coastal footpath; and yet the historic cities of Plymouth and Exeter are within reach, and the great resort of Torquay. In early spring, wildflowers are everywhere and the blue waves are already beginning to be dotted with boating enthusiasts. This is a rich farming area ('the fruitfullest part of Devonshire'), with villages of well-kept colourwashed cottages thickly thatched.

On the other side of the Avon is Bigbury where a strange, long-legged 'tram' takes people across the sea to Burgh Island.

Readers' comments: Food very good. A most enjoyable stay.

SNOWFORD HALL FARM   C

Hunningham, Warwickshire, CV33 9ES   Tel: 0926 632297

East of Leamington Spa. Nearest main road: A423 from Coventry to Banbury.

4 Bedrooms. £12–£14 (less for 3 nights). Some have own shower/toilet. Tea/coffee facilities. TV. Views of garden, country. No smoking.

Dinner. £10 for 4 courses and coffee, from 6.30pm. Non-residents not admitted. Wine can be brought in. No smoking. **Light suppers** if ordered.

1 Sitting-room. With central heating, TV, piano. No smoking.

Large garden

A very long drive through fields leads to this spacious 18th-century house at the heart of a 300-acre farm (cattle and crops) with fine views around it. One enters through an interesting hall with old china on a big dresser and polished wood floor. The huge sitting-room is very attractively furnished. Here and there around the house are many things made by Rudi Hancock herself, a skilled craftswoman – samplers, for example, and corn dollies; and furniture which she has restored.

Dutch-born, she was previously a cookery teacher and so (except at harvests, when she has no time to cook evening meals) you can expect a good dinner, if booked in advance. She uses many home-grown vegetables and fruit, and makes her own jam.

The most interesting of the bedrooms has a very unusual and decorative Dutch bed of solid mahogany, handsomely carved.

Snowford Hall is near Leamington Spa and its environs, described elsewhere, and such sights as Kenilworth Castle, Coventry Cathedral and Draycote water country park. Packwood House has an exceptional garden, and the National Centre for Organic Gardening is near. Southam is an old market town; Stoneleigh a mediaeval village (with the great National Agricultural Centre outside it). The National Exhibition Centre is within easy reach, so are Warwick University and Rugby School. And all around are some of England's finest landscapes.

Hunningham is close to the ruler-straight Fosse Way which goes all the way from Devon to Lincolnshire, built by the Romans to link their most important forts. Though not even a 'B' road now, it still survives the centuries, so well was it engineered, on the line of a prehistoric trail which was an important trade route linking the mines of the south-west to ports that traded with Scandinavia. Now trade travels by other roads and the Fosse Way sees little traffic.

Leamington gained the prefix 'Royal' when the young Queen Victoria stayed there only a year after coming to the throne. Fine 18th- and 19th-century squares and terraces give the town a discreet charm. There are some outstanding gardens in the area – including the public Jephson Gardens in Leamington and those of the Mill House by the river at the foot of Warwick Castle.

Readers' comments: Lovely rooms; gorgeous, silent countryside. Wonderful reception, beautiful house, plenty of very good food, wholly pleasurable. Very comfortable.

Prices are per person in a double room at the beginning of the year.

★ **SOMERSET HOUSE**   **C(9) D PT S X**
35 Bathwick Hill, Bath, Avon, BA2 6LD   Tel: 0225 466451
On A36 from Bath to Warminster.

9 Bedrooms. £20. To SOTBT readers only: £18 midweek to 21 February, for stays of 2 nights or more. Prices go up in September. Bargain breaks. All have own bath/shower/toilet. Tea/coffee facilities. Views of garden or city. No smoking. Laundry facilities.
Dinner. £16.50 for 4 courses (with choices) and coffee, at 7pm. Vegetarian or special diets if ordered. Wine can be ordered. No smoking.
2 Sitting-rooms. With open fire, central heating, TV, piano. Bar. No smoking.
Large garden

The Seymours moved to this handsome Georgian mansion from a smaller house down the steep hill. Above the Doric-columned portico is a decorative iron verandah; wisteria and roses climb up the walls of honey-coloured stone.

The entrance hall (marble-tiled and with a Greek key border round the ceiling) leads to a sitting-room, with conservatory (opening onto lawn), grand piano, fire and abundant books and records. There is one bedroom on the ground floor. The dining-room is below stairs (it, too, has an open fire), furnished with pine dresser.

On the first floor is another sitting-room with a particularly pretty plasterwork ceiling and very old Venetian glass chandelier. The original panelled shutters flank the high sash windows; outside is the long verandah, with fine city views.

Bedrooms are large and pleasantly furnished, many with antique fireplaces (one has an antique loo) and attractive views. Some have Laura Ashley fabrics.

Malcolm (once director of a regional tourist board) is a mine of information on what to see in the neighbourhood. Throughout the year he arranges weekends with special themes: Georgian Bath, Herbs for Health, Brunel. (Ask for programme.) Jean, formerly a teacher, enjoys cooking recipes appropriate to each of these occasions, assisted by other members of the family.

At breakfast, few people opt for the full cooked version because there is such an array of home-baked breads (nutty, spicy or fruity), preserves, muesli, freshly squeezed fruit juice and so forth; often haddock, kidneys, Cumberland sausage or muffins are offered. As to dinner, when nothing more exotic is afoot, Jean may produce something like (for example) game soup, her own 'rolypoly, gammon and spinach' recipe with home-grown vegetables, and apples in cider served with home-made ice cream.

Perhaps the greatest glory is the garden. Every tree flowers at a different season, and the centrepiece is a great 300-year-old Judas tree – at its purple best in May. All around, between beds of peonies and columbines, is a 7¼-inch rail track installed by a former owner. Adjoining is a herb and fruit garden. All within a 12-minute walk of the city centre.

Readers' comments: The best establishment I've stayed at, where people count; the cooking reinvigorates the taste-buds. Superb comfort and food. Excellent accommodation; the most interesting and nicest food we have ever experienced. Particularly delighted. A favourite. The Seymours make guests welcome; one meets interesting people there. We stay regularly. Comfortable; very good food.

SOUTH FARM
East Meon, Hampshire, GU32 1EZ   Tel: 073 087 261
West of Petersfield. Nearest main road: A272 from Winchester to Petersfield.

3 Bedrooms. £16–£18 (less for 2 nights). Prices go up at Easter. Bargain breaks. Some have own bath/toilet. Tea/coffee facilities. TV. Views of garden, country, river. No smoking. Washing machine on request.
Light suppers if ordered.
1 Sitting-room. With open fire, central heating, TV.
Large garden

The approach to the farm is delightful. There are specimen trees on a lawn (ash, viburnum, chestnut), an old granary and a grapevine under glass. In the 500-year-old house is a brick-floored dining-room with huge inglenook, rush ladderback chairs and a big oak table. The very large sitting-room has carved furniture and chinoiserie curtains in gold-and-blue. Bedrooms have been very agreeably furnished by Jane Atkinson: one with poppy fabrics, for instance; in another are purple-and-white clematis curtains and a lace bedspread. An oak-panelled room has William Morris's chrysanthemum fabric. All are outstanding.

The house is full of flowers because Jane, a professional flower-arranger, regularly has large deliveries from Covent Garden market. You can dine at the Izaak Walton inn in East Meon if you want more than a light supper.

The Meon Valley amid the South Downs has churches that go back to Saxon times, flint-walled houses, and prehistoric burial mounds. To the south are woodlands, remnants of the once-great Forest of Bere, and then comes Portsmouth Harbour. Despite heavy traffic on roads into the port, this is well worth a visit – to see Nelson's *Victory*, Henry VIII's *Mary Rose* and his Southsea Castle, Victorian forts up on the hills and Norman Portchester Castle down by the waterfront. There are boat trips and ferries to the Isle of Wight; excellent museums (don't miss the Royal Marines one); Dickens's birthplace; much ceremonial on Navy Days; and waterfowl on the wilder shores of the two natural harbours here. Queen Elizabeth Forest contrasts with all this (drive to Georgian Buriton, go up Butser Hill, or visit the recreated Iron Age village).

The clear chalk streams, with occasional watermills, have made this lovely area well known for its watercress and its trout: the River Itchen is famous among anglers, and its valley is outstandingly beautiful – to drive or walk along it from Itchen Stoke is an unforgettable experience, pausing at Ovington's mediaeval inn on the way. Old and New Alresford are on opposite banks of the River Alre: in the latter, colourful Broad Street, with 18th-century houses, is well worth visiting (and in its churchyard are the graves of French prisoners from the Napoleonic wars). At the north end of Broad Street are a millstream and dam built in the 12th century; and also a lovely footpath through watercress beds and past a black-and-white thatched mill spanning the river. Other villages worth seeking out include Tichborne – famous for a *cause célèbre* in 1871 when an Australian imposter laid claim to the estate here; and for the Tichborne Dole, flour given to villagers since 1150.

SPION KOP   C(5) D S X
Spring Lane, Ufford, Suffolk, IP13 6EF   Tel: 0394 460277
North of Woodbridge. Nearest main road: A12 from Ipswich to Lowestoft.

3 Bedrooms. £13–£15 (less for 4 nights). Bargain breaks. Some have own bath/shower/toilet. Tea/coffee facilities. TV. Views of garden, country. Washing machine on request.
Dinner. £8 for 3 courses (with choices) and coffee, at 7pm. Non-residents not admitted. Vegetarian or special diets if ordered. Wine can be brought in. **Light suppers** if ordered.
1 Sitting-room. With open fire, central heating, TV, record-player.
Large garden

When Colonel Walters returned from the Boer Wars he built himself a house reminiscent of his years on the veldt, with an almost conical roof of thatch and a wide-eaved verandah. Its site must have reminded him of the hill on which 300 British died at the hands of the Boers, for he named it after this.

The Fergusons have added their own distinctive touches to what was already a very unusual house. Along the verandah (hung with brimming baskets of lobelias and begonias) are life-size marble nymphs – the Four Seasons – with more among the flowerbeds. Indoors, along with much other Victoriana which surely would have delighted the colonel, are bronzes and paintings of turn-of-the-century beauties well displayed against the pale pink walls of sitting- and dining-rooms, through the lattice windows of which (or from the glass sun-room) there are wooded valley views more typical of Devon than of Suffolk. There is a meadow brilliant with kingcups and wild orchids in spring.

Bedrooms are spacious and elegantly furnished; and Susan's meals are delicious. One example – a herby soup with croûtons was followed by pork in a sauce of mushrooms, cream and wine (with vegetables cooked to perfection); raspberry meringues; cheeses, and a glass of wine included.

Readers' comments: Superb food. Like being pampered by a special friend.

About 50 houses, mostly in Suffolk, are in a scheme under which one-third of whatever you pay is given to Oxfam. The participating proprietors choose a particular project to support (for example, in one year it was a college in Kampuchea to train young men in irrigation systems), and between them over £9000 a year is raised. The scheme was originated by Rosemary and Robin Schlee, at whose own very lovely home – with equally lovely garden – visitors are also welcomed. I looked at this and two others nearby (Four Elms at Ufford, and No. 29 Ipswich Road, Woodbridge) and was very impressed with their high standards and – at the latter – a spectacular view of the Deben estuary from one of the bedrooms. All charge similar prices to Spion Kop (other, simpler houses in the scheme charge less); and all have been inspected. On departure, every visitor is given a special receipt for the one-third that goes to Oxfam. Phone Mrs Schlee to book in at any: her number is 03943 2740.

SPORTSMAN'S ARMS   **C**
Wath-in-Nidderdale, Pateley Bridge, North Yorkshire, HG3 5PP
Tel: 0423 711306
West of Harrogate. Nearest main road: A59 from Harrogate to Skipton.

7 Bedrooms. £20–£25; **£18 to SOTBT readers only.** Bargain breaks. Some have own shower/toilet. Tea/coffee facilities. TV. Views of garden, country, river. No smoking. Washing machine on request.
Dinner. £10–£15 for 4 courses (with choices) and coffee, at 7.30pm. Vegetarian or special diets if ordered. Wine can be ordered. **Light suppers** if ordered.
2 Sitting-rooms. With open fire. Bar.
Small garden

A delightful place, in a delightful setting: Wath is a hamlet tucked away beside the River Nidd.

A pine-panelled bar leads to the dining-room (and, beyond this, sitting-rooms) which has palms, pink-and-grey colour scheme and bentwood chairs, reflected by the light of cut-crystal candle-lamps in the big mirror of a carved Victorian sideboard. Jane Carter has chosen blue/green/beige colour schemes for bedrooms in which curtains and bedspreads match. Huge Victorian baths have been retained. Ray, who used to be catering lecturer, cooks all the meals, assisted by a team of enthusiastic young people. A typical summer dinner: salad with scallops and sweetbreads; salmon filled with prawns, and hollandaise sauce; and summer pudding with cream. The cooking is exceptional, and much produce is local. Wines are outstanding and reasonably priced.

Lovely Nidderdale, being outside the National Park area, is less frequented than some other dales. It has some very old reservoirs created by damming the River Nidd, now well naturalized and full of ducks, geese, herons and other birds (200 species have been recorded, including some rare migrants). The effect is reminiscent of the Lake District. How Stean is a romantic gorge with a stream cascading into a rocky cleft 70 feet deep (good home-made cakes at the modest café nearby). From the churchyard at Middlemoor, high up at the head of the dale, there are spectacular views down the length of it.

From here one can easily motor to a number of Yorkshire's spectacular abbeys – Bolton, Jervaulx, and Byland. Also Harewood Hall, Newby Hall and garden, and half a dozen castles; as well as the strange natural formations of Brimham Rocks.

Readers' comments: Food fabulous, staff well trained and friendly. Food very good, and staff appeared to be one largish happy family. Delightful; good food, excellent value. Could not be faulted; food, rooms and surroundings all outstanding in every detail. Very friendly. Superb cuisine. First rate.

294

★ **SPURSHOLT HOUSE**   **C D S**
Salisbury Road, Romsey, Hampshire, SO51 6DJ   Tel: 0794 512229
North of Southampton. Nearest main road: A31 from Bournemouth to
Winchester.

3 Bedrooms. £12.50–£14 (less for 5 nights). Bargain breaks. Some have own bath/shower/toilet. Tea/coffee facilities. Views of garden, country, river. No smoking. Washing machine on request.

Light suppers if ordered.
1 Sitting-room. With open fire, central heating, TV. No smoking.
Large garden

The house had originally been built for one of Cromwell's generals. It came into the hands of the Palmerston family who lived at Broadlands; and in the 1830s was extended for occupation by Lord and Lady Cowper. Emily Cowper became one of Lord Palmerston's many mistresses (the prime minister was nicknamed Cupid!); and then, after her first husband's death, his wife.

The result of those additions is the imposing mansion one sees today, surrounded by a magnificent garden. There are paved terraces with urns of geraniums, overlooking a lawn, impressive topiary, and a view of Romsey Abbey. Beyond flowerbeds, yew hedges enclose a succession of further pleasures – one garden leading into another, rose beds followed by apple-trees, and a lily-pool. There is a tennis court too, and dovecote with fantails.

Rooms have been furnished by Anthea Hughes in keeping with the character of the house. A few have stained glass originally in the Palace of Westminster. One bedroom is oak-panelled, and all contain antiques. Two have open fireplaces, extra-large beds, elegant sofas and garden views; another two are more basic.

Downstairs is a dining-room handsomely furnished in Victorian style, just as Palmerston might have known it; and a spectacular sitting-room with Knole sofa in silvery damask, a turquoise love-seat and a carved fireplace.

Bed-and-breakfast only, though sandwiches can be provided for supper if ordered. For a full dinner, Anthea recommends the Manor House restaurant or a number of local inns.

The house is close to Broadlands, ancestral home of the Palmerston family and later of Lord Mountbatten; and to the fine abbey church of Romsey, built by the Normans. The abbey of Mottisfont, a few miles away, was converted into a stately home during the 18th century (it stands in fine riverside grounds notable for their old roses; and inside is a big *trompe l'oeil* drawing-room painted by Rex Whistler). The quiet river here is the Test, crossed by numerous hump-back bridges and world-famous among anglers for trout. Following its meandering route one can detour to King's Sombourne, which has an arts centre, and Middle Wallop for its museum with exhibits from a century of army flying. By walking to the top of Danesbury's Iron Age hill fort, one can enjoy tremendous views. For another day tour, go to Salisbury; also to Winchester (yet another cathedral), pausing en route at Farley Mount for wooded walks in the nature reserve and hilltop views.

STANSHOPE HALL

C S

Stanshope, Staffordshire DE6 2AD   Tel: 033527 278
North-west of Ashbourne (Derbyshire). Nearest main road: A515 from
Ashbourne to Buxton.

3 Bedrooms. £17.50–£23.50 (less for 3 nights). Prices go up in April. Bargain breaks. Some have own bath/shower/toilet. Tea/coffee facilities. TV. Views of garden, country.
Dinner. £14.50 for 3 courses (with choices) and coffee, at 7.30pm. Non-residents not admitted. Vegetarian or special diets if ordered. Wine can be ordered. No smoking.
1 Sitting-room. With open fire, central heating, piano, record-player.
Large garden

Built in 1670 by Cromwell's quartermaster, Jackson, the hall has seen many changes. It was greatly extended in the 1780s and when, at nearby Ilam, a great mansion burnt down in the 19th century, salvaged fireplaces were re-installed here. Later a theatrical designer made it his home, embellishing it with all sorts of *trompe l'oeil* effects. The murals with peacocks and trees in the sitting-room are in the manner of Rex Whistler, while in the entrance hall a stairway and arches of Hopton stone contrast with painted marbling.

Upstairs, in one bedroom Indian cotton hangings with tassels match bedspreads and curtains, and there are other unusual fabrics elsewhere. Another bedroom has a little double box-bed painted with flowers, urns and pilasters: one goes up steps to get into it.

Not only the ambience but also the food provided by Naomi Chambers and Nick Lowie is out-of-the ordinary. A typical menu: carrot and ginger soup or pancakes stuffed with leeks and cream cheese, followed by lamb in red wine and honey, then either gooseberry ice cream or Bakewell tart.

BEECHENHILL FARM, just outside Ilam, is a long low house built from limestone two centuries ago. Perched on a south-facing hillside, it overlooks grazing sheep and cows. Sue Prince has painted roses on walls and drawers; and her breakfasts have won an award (there is always plenty of fruit and, in winter, porridge). No dinners, but there are local inns. There's a pretty garden with pond, hanging baskets of flowers, and ducks. Pleasant bedrooms, one of which is a light and spacious family room. (Tel: 033527 274.) From £14 to £18.

296

THE STEPPES

Ullingswick, Herefordshire, HR1 3JG Tel: 0432 820424

North-east of Hereford. Nearest main road: A417 from Ledbury towards Leominster.

Prices go up in March. Bargain breaks. All have own bath or shower/toilet. Tea/coffee facilities and refrigerators. TV. Views of garden, country. No smoking. Washing machine on request.

Dinner. 4 courses (with choices) and coffee, at 7.30pm. Non-residents not admitted. Vegetarian, special diets, or à la carte if ordered ahead. Wine can be ordered. No smoking. **Light suppers** sometimes if ordered.

1 Sitting-room. With open fire, central heating. No smoking. **Bar.**

Large garden

5 Bedrooms. £33.50–£39 including dinner. B&b (at short notice only) £17.50–£23.

This is one of the prettiest old houses in this book, very attractively furnished by its owners Henry and Tricia Howland. Part of the house is mediaeval, most of it 17th century. Originally, the ground floor was one great hall (the old flagstoned floor is still intact).

The dining-room has a great inglenook fireplace with its original log-irons, and there is a bread oven adjoining its chimney. In the thick walls are original built-in cupboards, and between some rooms 'borrowed lights' (that is, internal windows) with their original glass. The red-and-black tiles of the dining-room are also old.

The beamed dining-room, with a patterned rug on the tiled floor and some dried hop-bines draped across the fireplace, has great character. There are corn dollies on the white walls, flowers on each table, and a melodiously chiming clock.

The ancient dairy and cider-making cellars have been skilfully restored and now form the lounge and cellar bar, which includes half a dozen kinds of local cider, from clear-and-sparkling to rough-and-heavy. In the sitting-room, flowery chairs and pale velvet curtains contrast with the rugged stone fireplace. Quaint pastry dolls hang on some walls – made by Tricia (a few for sale).

Each bedroom has a different and colourful style – raspberry-pink wall and rosebud fabrics in one, crisp blue-and-white in another; built-in pine storage fitments, pretty lace curtains or deep-pile carpets contribute to the individual character of each one. Each has its own shower. A few steps from the house, in one of the original farm outbuildings, there are two newly converted bedrooms with en suite bathroom. Views are of rounded hills, sheep or cows, hop kilns and the old garden where lilac spreads its fragrance in early summer.

Tricia cooks a wide range of very imaginative dishes and ensures that not one is repeated during a guest's stay. One local speciality which she serves is cheese-and-cider soup (chilled and creamy); another unusual starter is grapefruit with mint ice. The main course might be boned duck with a stuffing of beef, onions, bacon and herbs, or turkey saté (served with peanut sauce and cucumber relish – a Thai recipe). A pudding such as zabaglione, or raspberry meringue gâteau may follow.

Readers' comments: Thoroughly enjoyed it. Superb. 5-star food! Attentive and comfortable. Local food specials and the puddings were excellent. A wonderful few days; delicious and individual cooking served on lovely china. One of the prettiest houses, wonderful garden. First-rate, quiet, cordon bleu cooking. Enchanting house, superb food. Excellent in every way.

297

★ **STOKE FARM**   C S

Broad Chalke, Wiltshire, SP5 5EF   Tel: 0722 780209

West of Salisbury. Nearest main road: A354 from Salisbury to Blandford
Forum.

2 Bedrooms. £18. Both have own bath/
shower/toilet. Tea/coffee facilities. TV.
Views of garden, country. No smoking.
Washing machine on request.
Dinner. £11 for 3 courses (with some
choices) and coffee, at 7pm. Non-residents
not admitted. Vegetarian or special diets if
ordered. Wine can be brought in. **Light
suppers** if ordered.
1 Sitting-room. With open fire, central
heating, TV, record-player. Billiards, etc.
Large garden with croquet and tennis.
**Closed from November to February
inclusive.**

A gracious house at the heart of a 1000-acre farm overlooking the Ebble Valley,
this is very typical of many other such farms set among the rolling downs of
Wiltshire: a mixture of arable fields and of pastures for beef-cattle and dairy-cows.

One approaches the house past mossy rickstones, old cattle-troughs now filled
with flowers, and tree-stumps overgrown by periwinkles. A lovely magnolia
covers the front wall. Inside, the early Victorian features have been retained –
panelled doors, arches and window shutters. My bedroom had windows on three
sides with pretty 'cottage-garden' curtains and views across fields of cows to the
hills. Late in the year, the pens immediately below are full of calves. Throughout
the house, soft colours predominate, with carefully arranged flowers, baskets of
trailing plants and interesting paintings well lighted (one is by Cecil Beaton, who
used to live in the village). There are good carpets and attractive wallpapers
everywhere, even in the bathroom. In the big sitting-room, deep armchairs are
grouped around a log fire, a record-player and well stocked bookshelves. Last but
far from least, Janet Pickford is an excellent cook. Meals are served in a
dining-room that still has the old built-in bread oven, often with local trout and
pheasant on the menu.

Many guests go walking. The Pickfords have produced their own map of local
footpaths, all well waymarked in this region, which lead down to watercress beds
in the valley or up to the Ridgeway which was once a drove road for oxen being
taken to market.

I first stayed here in order to visit nearby Salisbury and its cathedral. In addition
there is plenty to see in the area – Elizabethan Breamore House, attractive villages
(like Downton, Fordingbridge or Tilshead), the Celtic fort on top of Figsbury
Hill, Old Sarum with the ruins of its Norman castle on another hilltop, the Roman
villa at Rockbourne, Wilton's historic carpet factory and Wilton House, for
example. Other leading sights: Stonehenge, the New Forest, two shire horse
centres, and plenty of gardens (garden centres too).

Readers' comments: The best b & b in England! Everything about Stoke Farm
would be difficult to fault. Very pleasant and helpful. Wonderful! Most comfortable; huge towels, wonderful bathroom. Great kindness. Superb house, lovely
antiques.

For explanation of code letters (**C, D, H, PT, S, X**) see page xxxiv.

STONE HOUSE HOTEL

C D H S X

Sedbusk, North Yorkshire, DL8 3PT Tel: 0969 667571
North of Hawes. Nearest main road: A684 from Hawes to Sedbergh.

15 Bedrooms. £20–£30 (less for 3 nights). Bargain breaks. Some have own bath/shower/toilet. Tea/coffee facilities. TV. Views of garden. No smoking. Washing machine on request.
Dinner. A la carte or £12.50 for 4 courses (with choices) and coffee, at 7–8pm. Vegetarian or special diets if ordered. Wine can be ordered. No smoking. **Light suppers** if ordered.
3 Sitting-rooms. With open fire, central heating. Bar.
Large garden with lawn tennis.
Closed in January.

P. G. Wodehouse, with a new novel near completion, was still searching for a good name to give his principal character. On holiday here, he sat watching village cricket – and in to bat went the Stone House gardener, *Jeeves*. Problem solved!

To this day, Stone House looks exactly right for a house-party with Bertie Wooster and Jeeves drawing up in a sports car at the front door. It was built in Edward VII's reign as a country gentleman's retreat, and some of the oak-panelled rooms, the leather club chairs, 'Spy' cartoons and racehorse shoes on the wall, the billiard table, and the library with books from floor to ceiling, are unchanged.

The present owner, Peter Taplin, is an incurable collector, and on show are his many vintage slot-machines (with a supply of pre-metric pennies with which to operate them), hundreds of old 'Dinky' cars, and antique thimbles. He and Jane have furnished the house well: red chinoiserie fabric on the bar's armchairs; comfortable cushioned seats in the dining-room (which has an aquarium built into one wall); and light, immaculate bedrooms with sprigged fabrics (four are on the ground floor), their stone-mullioned windows overlooking paved terraces, neat box borders and far views. Some bedrooms have their own conservatory/sitting area, opening onto the garden.

Peter used to be a butcher, so it is not surprising that Stone House has a good reputation for straightforward English food – roast beef and Yorkshire pudding naturally being pre-eminent, perhaps preceded by crofter's soup and followed by old-fashioned trifle.

Jeeves would have approved!

For details of the Wensleydale area, see other entries. There are waterfalls (Hardraw and Aysgarth), folk museum and market at Hawes, the Settle railway and the Buttertubs Pass – both very scenic. It is easy to reach Swaledale from here – totally different scenery from Wensleydale.

Prices are per person in a double room at the beginning of the year.

299

★ **STOURCASTLE LODGE** C PT X
Gough's Close, Sturminster Newton, Dorset, DT10 1BU Tel: 0258 72320
South-west of Shaftesbury. Nearest main road: A357 from Blandford Forum to
Wincanton.

4 Bedrooms. £16.50–£19.50 (less for 7
nights). Bargain breaks. Some have own
shower/toilet. Views of garden. Washing
machine on request.
Dinner. £11 for 3 courses (with choices) and
coffee, at 7.30pm. Vegetarian or special diets
if ordered. Wine can be brought in.
1 Sitting-room. With open fire, central heating, TV. No smoking.
Small garden

Gourmets seek out this secluded town house, for peace as well as good food.
Although just off the market place, Gough's Close is traffic-free and quiet: a
narrow lane opening out into a green and pleasant place, with the River Stour
beyond. The Lodge, which was built in 1739, has been agreeably furnished by Jill
Hookham-Bassett, with soft greens and pinks predominating. Everything is very
spick-and-span, the bedrooms cottagey in style, and many rooms have views of the
secluded garden where one can take tea.

Ken and Jill, who achieved a gold star for cooking when she trained at Ealing
Technical College, also run a catering service, so food here is well above average. A
typical dinner might be: kedgeree, chicken cooked in a tarragon and mushroom
sauce, and charlotte Malakoff (made with cream and almonds). An unassuming
house with a lot to offer in the way of hospitality.

From the Lodge, it is easily possible to explore not only Dorset but parts of
Wiltshire and even Somerset too.

Mediaeval Sherborne's superb 15th-century abbey of golden stone deserves a
lingering visit because of its remarkable fan-vaulting, colourful roof-bosses and
other outstanding carvings, as well as a glass reredos engraved by Laurence
Whistle. There are two castles: one, Norman and perched on a steep mound; the
other, built for Sir Walter Raleigh and surrounded by park and gardens – it
contains a series of very fine rooms and art treasures.

Readers' comments: Friendly; eager to help and please. Tastefully furnished house
and spotlessly clean. Jill's cooking was superb. Delightful. Made to feel welcome
and at home. Room charming.

STRAWBERRY COTTAGE at
Packers Hill, Holwell, is even older, a
cottage of thatch, stone and brick, with
modern furnishings of high standard.
There is a comfortable TV room which
is well supplied with tourist literature.
The cottage is situated in quiet countryside near Sherborne. Vivienne
Powell does b & b only (tel:
096323 629). From £15.50 to £17.50.

Stowford, Devon, EX20 4BZ   Tel: 056683 415
South-west of Okehampton. Nearest main road: A30 from Okehampton to
Launceston.

6 Bedrooms. £17–£19.50 (£27.50 including
dinner). Bargain breaks. Some have own
bath/shower/toilet.   Tea/coffee   facilities.
TV. Views of garden, country.
Dinner. A la carte or £14 for 4 courses (with
choices) and coffee, at 7–9pm. Vegetarian or
special diets if ordered. Wine can be
ordered. **Light suppers** if ordered.
1 Sitting-room. With open fire, central heating, TV. **Bar.**
Large garden
Closed in January.

This former country rectory is now a comfortable hotel, dignified by its 18th-
century features such as the fine windows, handsome front door, a graceful
archway inside and impressive staircase. The large garden is at its best in May.

The hotel has a reputation for good food. With over 20 years' experience
of running first a catering service for businessmen and then a restaurant in
Winchester, Jenny Irwin has accumulated a wide repertoire of recipes. Typical
dishes she may serve – in a dining-room with a particularly fine Victorian fireplace
– include kidneys in sherry, mocca roulade, and Cambridge tart (made with mixed
peel and glacé cherries).

Bedrooms are large, light and airy. Everywhere is a profusion of pot-plants; and
on some walls are delicate watercolours by her father-in-law, Sydney Irwin.

Nearby is Lydford which, a thousand years ago and more, was a place of note
(its tin was exported to the Mediterranean). In Saxon times it even had its own
mint; and seven coins from the time of Ethelred the Unready are displayed at the
Castle Inn. The neat, square castle was built in 1195 for use as a 'stannary' prison
(the tin-miners had their own 'stannary' laws and courts – *stannum* is Latin for tin),
with a pretty little church beside it. Lydford is also famous for its gorge – one can
walk by foaming waters with oak woods hanging overhead to the roaring 200-foot
waterfall known as the White Lady. Lichens, mosses and ferns give the scene a
subtropical look as the waters hurtle around smooth black boulders.

Within about 30 miles are Princetown (high and bleak, famous for Dartmoor
Prison, which was built by Napoleonic prisoners, and for prehistoric stones
nearby), Plymouth, the sandy resort of Bude with rocky Tintagel beyond, Exeter,
lovely Salcombe, Looe and Clovelly, and Dartmoor.

From here one can explore the 400 square miles of Dartmoor's wild hills, its
forest and woodlands, granite tors, archaeological sites and moorland villages. As
well as the famous Dartmoor ponies roaming free, there is a great deal of wildlife.
Granite quarries, stone slab bridges, waterfalls, ruins of tin mines, thatched
cottages – all contribute to the variety of the scene. There are guided walks with
experts to explain what one sees, or National Park leaflets to consult if you go on
your own (available at 9 information centres).

When one has had one's fill of scenery, there are plenty of other things to do.
Southward lies Tavistock, where Francis Drake grew up. It has its origins in
Saxon times but became wealthy only when first, tin-mining and then, the cloth
trade brought prosperity. Drake's home, Buckland Abbey (with the Drake Naval
Museum) now belongs to the National Trust (it is near the pretty village of
Buckland Monachorum – Buckland of the monks).

★ **STRATFORD LODGE**   C(8) **PT X**
   4 Park Lane, Castle Road, Salisbury, Wiltshire, SP1 3NP   Tel: 07223 25177

8 Bedrooms. £16–£18 (less for 3 nights). Prices go up in April. Bargain breaks. All have own bath/shower/toilet. Tea/coffee facilities. TV. Views of garden. Balcony. No smoking. Washing machine on request.
Dinner. £12 for 3 courses (with choices) and coffee, at 7pm. Vegetarian or special diets if ordered. Wine can be ordered. No smoking.
2 Sitting-rooms. With open fire, central heating, piano, record-player.
Small garden

In a quiet byway overlooking a park stands a fine Victorian house, now a handsomely furnished guest-house. Jill Bayly has taken a lot of trouble to find good furniture in keeping with the style of the house. The sitting-room has much Victoriana and a large array of African violets; the pale green dining-room, mahogany tables laid with pretty rosy china (napkins to match) and wildflower curtains at the windows. Bedrooms are attractive, particularly one with a cane and carved bedhead on a bed with cover to complement the apricot walls. In another room, pale pink, a brass bed has a lace spread. After dark one can go on sitting in the garden which is enclosed by flowering shrubs, because Jill brings out candle-lamps. Beyond it is the vegetable plot which provides fresh produce.

Jill has a varied repertoire of dishes for dinner (only light suppers on Sundays and Mondays, served in the conservatory), and she cooks to a high standard. A typical menu: pears baked with Roquefort cheese; duckling with a sauce of port and black cherries; syllabub made with Tia Maria or apple strudel with clotted cream; then cheeses. Breakfasts, too, are generous, with options such as kedgeree and marmalade which she makes herself.

Salisbury is also known as New Sarum (new in 1220!) because the first town was elsewhere, on the hill now known as Old Sarum which began as an Iron Age fort – you can still see traces of a Norman cathedral up there. When it was decided to rebuild on a better site, two miles away by the water meadows, the new cathedral, with the tallest spire in England, was surrounded by grass and big walls to keep the township that followed at a respectful distance. Thus the cathedral can be well viewed all round, unlike some which have buildings crowding right up to them. Inside are fine tombs, the oldest working clock in the country, some fan vaulting, and immense cloisters. Historic houses surround the precincts, some open to the public. There is a big market in the town's central square on Tuesdays and Saturdays.

★ **FARTHINGS**, at 9 Swaynes Close (tel: 0722 330749), is quite central (there's a view of the cathedral spire over rooftops) yet very quiet, and it has a garden with brimming flowerbeds. All rooms are immaculate, and pleasantly furnished. Gill Rodwell serves breakfast only (choices include, croissants and much else). Exceptional value. From £12 to £14.

STRATHAVON

8 Charlotte Street, Bath, Avon, BA1 2NE   Tel: 0225 23068
Nearest main road: A4 from Bath to Bristol.

7 Bedrooms. £16.50 (less for 2 nights in autumn and winter). Bargain breaks. TV. No smoking. Washing machine on request. **Dinner.** £12 for 3 courses (with choices) and coffee, at 7–9pm. Vegetarian or special diets if ordered. Wine can be ordered. No smoking. **Light suppers** if ordered.
1 Sitting-room. With central heating, TV. No smoking.
Small garden
Closed in January.

It is difficult to locate a good but inexpensive hotel in the centre of Bath, so the Strathavon is quite a find. It is in a terrace of 18th-century houses, with a very small garden at the back and a road at the front (bedrooms at back are quiet). Rooms are conventionally furnished, and immaculate.

What makes the Strathavon special, however, are Tom Waugh's outstanding gifts as a chef. I have eaten at many of Bath's innumerable restaurants but – price-for-price – never better than at the Strathavon. Small though this little hotel is, he is able to offer many choices at each course by the sensible expedient of asking visitors to make their selection by midday (he will post the menu to you). That way he can shop for and prepare every dish freshly for each person – things like a particularly good seafood Mornay as a starter, chicken breast stuffed with spinach, and delicious fresh fruit desserts.

Many of Bath's major attractions are within a short stroll. In the city centre there is much to see: the abbey, the Roman temple and baths, the botanical gardens, the shopping arcades and much else. Wells is near, as are Stourhead and Corsham.

Readers' comments: Cannot praise it too highly. Food excellent, and imaginative.

A little further out is **PARKSIDE**, an Edwardian villa (11 Marlborough Lane, tel: 0225 429444). From the bay window of the comfortable sitting-room (with simulated coal fire) balloonists from the adjacent Royal Victoria Park can often be watched gliding by. Also nearby are the beautiful botanic gardens. The dining-room opens onto a garden with paved terrace (presided over by a teak lady from Thailand), lawn and pergola. I particularly liked bedrooms 2 and 3, on the second floor, because they are so big and airy.

Katy Putler produces not only such dinners as melon, lamb chops, blackberry parfait, and West Country cheeses but specializes in vegetarian dishes, using organic produce. Breakfast options include wholefood cereals with fruit salad, and a raw mix of celery, carrots, cucumber and onions as a refreshing change from the bacon-and-egg routine. From £15 to £17.

303

★ **STREET FARMHOUSE**   **C D X**
South Warnborough, Hampshire, RG25 1RS   Tel: 0256 862225
South-east of Basingstoke. On A32 from Odiham to Alton.

3 **Bedrooms.** £14–£16. Prices usually go up in May. Bargain breaks. Some have own shower. Tea/coffee facilities. TV. Views of garden, country. Washing machine on request.
Light suppers only. Vegetarian or special diets if ordered. Wine can be brought in.
1 **Sitting-room.** With open fire, central heating, TV, record-player.
Large garden. Heated swimming-pool.

Two 16th-century cottages were combined into one to make this attractive house, beamed and with inglenook fireplace, in an ancient village through which a stream runs. Wendy Turner's choice of furnishings admirably complements the old house. There are prettily carved chairs in the pale green dining-room; pine doors have been stripped and brick walls exposed; buttoned chairs in rust-colour covers are gathered around a log stove in the sitting-room. Bedrooms are very pleasant – for instance, furnished with chest-of-drawers of woven cane, with very good armchairs and colour schemes. One bathroom has an oval bath in peach, and a bidet. Standards throughout are high. Snack suppers only; for other meals Wendy recommends the Royal Oak in Lasham (Britain's gliding centre) or the Hoddington Arms in Upton Grey.

North Hampshire (quickly accessible along the M3) is an area often overlooked by people hurrying on to Winchester, Southampton or the New Forest. But anyone who lingers here will find plenty of interest, not least because this is Jane Austen country (her house is at Chawton, and scenes from the area feature in her books). Farnham still has streets much as she knew them, and a hilltop castle. Not far away is Selborne where Gilbert White wrote his natural history (1789) and one can still see countryside that he saw. Both his and Jane Austen's homes are open to the public – his has a museum about Captain Oates and Scott's Antarctic expedition and it is surrounded by National Trust woodlands. Nearby Odiham, too, retains the appearance of an 18th-century market town, with ruined castle nearby; and there are pretty villages – Greywell, Upton Grey (houses encircling a pond), Sherborne St John (with a Tudor mansion, the Vyne – NT, and moated Beaurepaire), Basing (castle ruins). Silchester was once a great Roman fort with a road running to Salisbury – now this is a mere track in a region of woods, streams and fields. The several fast roads in the area mean that most traffic has been siphoned off to leave the lanes peaceful. South of Basingstoke are the North Downs (running into Surrey) with splendid viewpoints.

Westward lie Litchfield, a flowery village in an area of prehistoric remains; Wherwell, a real showpiece – all timber and thatch, with fine views of the famous River Test; streamside Hurstbourne Tarrant; and Highclere – castle and hilltop grave of Lord Carnarvon (who discovered Tutankhamen's tomb in 1922); Burghclere (Stanley Spencer paintings in a chapel); the two beautiful Clatford villages with pretty river bridges.

In marked contrast to all these quiet pleasures are Farnborough's air show and Aldershot's military tattoo. And if you want to go further afield there are a number of famous tourist spots within easy reach – Windsor, for instance, and of course London itself.

★ SUGARSWELL FARM

Shenington, Warwickshire, OX15 6HW   Tel: 0295 88512
South of Stratford-upon-Avon. Nearest main road: A422 from Stratford to
Banbury.

3 Bedrooms. £18–£25 (less for 7 nights).
Bargain breaks. All have own bath/toilet.
Tea/coffee facilities. TV. Views of country.
No smoking. Laundry facilities on request.
Dinner. £14 for 3 courses and coffee, at
6.30pm. Non-residents not admitted. Wine
can be brought in. No smoking. **Light
suppers** if ordered.
1 Sitting-room. With open fire, central heating, TV. No smoking.
Large garden

Rosemary Nunnely is a cook of cordon bleu calibre – her greatest delight is
preparing meals. Visitors who stay with her are likely to get something very
different from ordinary 'farmhouse fare': on the day of my first visit, she had
prepared seafood gratin followed by fillet steak (home-produced) in a sauce of
port, cream and garlic, with home-made lemon sorbet to finish. Rosemary uses
wine and cream in many of her dishes, rum in such specialities as Jamaican torte.

The house is modern but made from old stones taken from a demolished
cottage. It has big picture-windows, and a striking staircase with 18th-century
portraits. Sofas are grouped round a huge stone fireplace in the sage green
sitting-room. The hall, like the dining-room, has terracotta walls. Guests sit on
Chippendale chairs to dine; there is good silver on the table, and one side of the
dining-room consists of a glass wall filled with Rosemary's collection of Crown
Derby.

Upstairs are elegant bedrooms – one with a sofa from which to enjoy woodland
views beyond the fields where cows graze, and a very large bathroom decorated in
bright mulberry.

Included in the price is the gift of a touring map of the region, showing how to
get to (for instance) Warwick, Stratford, the Cotswold towns, Woodstock
(Blenheim Palace), Oxford, Silverstone (car races) and Sulgrave (the Washington
ancestral home) or such stately homes as Upton House (horse trials in autumn) and
Farnborough Hall. In Shenington itself is an outstanding garden, at Brook
Cottage.

As to the curious name Sugarswell, Rosemary explained its origin: shuggers
(mediaeval slang for robbers) made a settlement here, which their more respectable neighbours destroyed. Vestiges can still be seen from the air.

Readers' comments: Lovely home, superb cooking. A marvellous place. Time-
capsule of the good life! Excellent: very good food and well-appointed bedrooms.
Charming hostess, comfortable and delightful accommodation, delicious food.
Very pleasant rooms and good views. Comfortable accommodation, superb
cooking. A lovely place to stay. An outstanding cook. Accommodation excellent.
And from the former manager of a 5-star hotel: We have been back nine times.

For explanation of code letters (C, D, H, PT, S, X) see page xxxiv.

SWALCLIFFE MANOR

C(7) D

Swalcliffe, Oxfordshire, OX15 5EH   Tel: 029578 348

West of Banbury. Nearest main road: A361 from Banbury to Chipping Norton.

3 Bedrooms. £17.50–£27.50. Prices go up in March. All have own bath/shower/toilet. Tea/coffee facilities. Views of garden, country. Washing machine on request.
Dinner. £16 for 4 courses (with choices), sherry and coffee, at 8pm. Non-residents not admitted. Vegetarian or special diets if ordered. Wine can be brought in.

2 Sitting-rooms. With open fire, central heating, TV, piano, record-player. Table tennis in games room.
Large garden
Closed from December to February inclusive.

Certainly the most striking entrance of any in this book is here: one passes through a 13th-century undercroft, the vaulted stone ceiling supported on massive circular pillars. Beyond is the former great hall of the house, with a vast fireplace. Judith and Francis Hitching (he is the author of several books on prehistoric mysteries) have furnished this with antiques and oriental rugs, a grand piano, and a carved mediaeval chest which contrasts well with pink walls. Traces of ancient wall-paintings can be seen, Tudor roses much in evidence.

The drawing-room is completely different, for in the 18th century an extension was added in Georgian style. This classical room, decorated in pale green, has Corinthian pilasters and a very pretty fireplace of green marble in a pine surround carved with acanthus leaves. Through high sash windows, set in deep panelled embrasures, is a view of the croquet lawn and a former studio now used as a games room for children. This is part of a large garden which includes a suntrapping stone terrace, a Saxon font planted with daisies, swimming-pool (unheated) and a sunken garden with a parterre of flowers grown in Tudor times: Judith put much research as well as hard effort into re-creating this.

A gifted cook (once nominated 'Gourmet of the Year' by a London newspaper), she will cook whatever her visitors prefer, or devise the menu herself – in which case you might be served scallops cooked with ginger and leeks; very good roast meat or game, in which this area excels (accompanied by vegetables from the garden, and herby sauces); then her own Swalcliffe pudding – a sponge with gooseberries, sultanas and honey. Food is served on flowery Portmeirion pottery.

Upstairs, bedrooms open off a broad gallery, full of pictures and antique toys. The one Georgian bedroom overlooks thatched roofs in the pretty village; while older ones have small stone-mullioned windows with church views. Pointed stone arches of the 13th-century frame baths or bathroom entrances.

Readers' comments: Charming. Nice people, interesting house, good food. Lovely welcome, splendid dinner. Excellent.

306

TALLY HO INN

C(8) D PT S X

Hatherleigh, Devon, EX20 3JN   Tel: 0837 810306
North of Okehampton. Nearest main road: A386 from Okehampton to
Torrington.

3 Bedrooms. £18–£20. Bargain breaks. All have own bath/shower/toilet. Tea/coffee facilities. TV. Views of garden, country. Washing machine on request.
Dinner. A la carte, at 7–9.30pm. Vegetarian or special diets if ordered. Wine can be ordered. **Light suppers.**
Small garden

The 15th-century inn overlooks the market place in this small historic town which was first recorded in a charter issued by King Ethelred in 981. One thousand and two years later, Gianni and Annamaria Scoz bought it, and today their cosy bar with its wooden beams and huge open fireplaces immediately conveys the feeling of hospitality and well-being that is the essence of the place.

Annamaria looks after the food which ranges from a good selection of bar snacks to a full à la carte dinner menu for the little restaurant. Essentially Italian (although there is also traditional English food for those who prefer it), this menu could not be bettered in any city trattoria – for a modest country pub in mid-Devon, it is quite outstanding. There is a choice of continental or full English breakfast, with a glass of freshly squeezed orange juice to help you decide.

A recently installed small brewery (with wood-panelled ceiling and copper-clad vessels), which can be viewed through a large picture-window in the courtyard, now means that home-brewed ale is also available.

Above the bar and restaurant, three delightful bedrooms have been professionally created by one of the Scoz's three daughters, and are object lessons in how to bring modern comforts to an ancient building with sensitivity. Mellow stripped pine furniture blends happily with soft cream walls, delicate floral prints, velvet curtains and simple doors of pine that are stained a deep warm brown. In the sumptuous bathrooms, the water flows through shining brass pipes.

Gianni is rightly proud of a thatched barbecue he has built in the small garden behind the inn where summer evening meals may be enjoyed. Private fishing in season, Dartmoor and Exmoor close at hand, and the north Devon coast just a short drive away.

Where two rivers join, a small settlement grew up, known to the Saxons as 'hawthorn glade' – the origin of Hatherleigh's name. It expanded when the industrious Normans took it over; and from miles around farmers used to attend its markets. Later the townsfolk were given the perpetual right to gather gorse for cooking-fuel on Hatherleigh Moor (which earned them the nickname 'pot-boilers'), commemorated in an old jingle:

> 'I, John of Gaunt
> Do give and grant
> Hatherleigh Moor
> To Hatherleigh poor
> For evermore.'

Go there in November for the fiery carnival with flaming torches and tar-barrels.

★ **THORNLEY HOUSE**   **D PT X**
Allendale, Northumberland, NE47 9NH   Tel: 0434 683255
South-west of Hexham. Nearest main road: A69 from Newcastle to Hexham.

3 Bedrooms. £15–£17.50 (less for 4 nights). Prices go up in March. Bargain breaks. Some have own bath/shower/toilet. Tea/coffee facilities. TV. Views of garden, country. Washing machine on request.
Dinner. £8.50 for 3 courses and coffee, at about 7pm. Non-residents not admitted. Vegetarian or special diets if ordered. Wine can be brought in.
2 Sitting-rooms. With central heating, TV, piano, record-player.
Large garden
Closed from November to late March (except for Christmas breaks and New Year).

Allendale Town is a large village in a sheltered valley amid some of the most open scenery in England – deserted grouse moors and breezy sheep pastures which stretch for uninterrupted miles, punctuated only by isolated farmhouses and the occasional relic of the lead mining which once made this area important. On the outskirts of the village is Thornley House, a large and solid inter-war house in a big garden with woods and fields around it. Rooms are spacious and light, with views of the wooded roads into the village and of the Pennines.

Eileen Finn is a keen cook, and though guests are offered conventional fare (vichyssoise soup, breaded chicken, salad, and chocolate mousse, for example, served on Wedgwood china), she needs only a little encouragement to cook a dish from Mexico, where she lived for eight years, or from another of the many countries to which she has paid long visits. Mementoes of her journeys abound in the house: batik pictures from Kenya, onyx figures and chess sets from Mexico, Chinese paintings (one on cork), rugs from Turkey and elsewhere (and others she has made herself). As well as being a linguist (she has a degree in Czech) and passionate world traveller, she is an able pianist, and there is a Steinway grand in one of the two sitting-rooms. Visitors may be taken on guided walks on occasion. Otherwise, they can make their way through woodland to the village, or to investigate the remains of the lead-mining industry which, for 300 years or more, made the north Pennines into a sort of northern Klondike.

Allendale is Catherine Cookson's country. She lives nearby and many of her Mallen stories are set here. It is one of the loveliest parts of the north country, wild and rocky, in parts comparable with some Swiss scenery. Allen Banks, where two rivers converge, is a beauty-spot. Not far off is the Killhope pass (nearly 2000 feet high) with a great wheel once used for crushing ore when these hills were mined for lead. A long process of restoration (by Durham County Council) is approaching completion: the result will be one of the most interesting 'working museums' in the country. In Allendale Town, on every New Year's Eve costumed 'guizers' parade with blazing tar-barrels on their heads – vestige of a half-forgotten pagan fire-rite. At Allenheads a few miles away, an award-winning heritage centre houses a small display about the history of the area, shops and a café. At Hexham is a great Norman abbey, well worth visiting, a garden centre and a lively market every Tuesday. The Roman Wall and Kielder Forest are not far off.

Readers' comments: Very welcome. Delightful venue. Very comfortable.

THORNTON MANOR

Ettington, Warwickshire, CV37 7PN   Tel: 0789 740210
South-east of Stratford-upon-Avon. Nearest main road: A429 from Warwick to
Stow-on-the-Wold.

3 Bedrooms. £13–£16 (less for 3 nights).
Prices go up in April. Bargain breaks. Some
have own shower/toilet. Tea/coffee facilities
in kitchen. Views of garden, country. No
smoking. Washing machine on request.
Light suppers sometimes.
1 Sitting-room. With log stove, central heating, TV, piano, record-player.
Small garden

A stately home in miniature, this stone manor house, E-shaped in plan, declares its
date, 1658, on a doorpost. Through an iron-studded oak door with decorative
hinges, heavy bolts and locks, one enters a great hall dominated by a large stone
fireplace with log stove. Overhead are massive chamfered beams; and the furniture
is in keeping with this scene.

Through the leaded panes of deep-set, mullioned windows in the breakfast-
room (and in a bedroom above it) there are views of the garden, woods and the
fields of this farm, which is well tucked away at the end of a long drive. Little
humps in the grass show where there was once a village in view until, in the 13th
century, the Black Death killed off all its 60 inhabitants. Ancient outbuildings
include an old pigeon-house from the days when the birds were farmed as an
important source of food.

Gill Hutsby (who occasionally sings at the Royal Shakespeare Theatre) has used
old-fashioned furniture and rosy cretonnes in the bedrooms. There is a kitchen for
guests' use (Gill does not often provide evening meals because there are local inns
and Stratford has many restaurants), and also a tennis court. Visitors can fish for
trout in the Hutsbys' lake or enjoy coarse fishing in the River Dean. Stratford-
upon-Avon (best visited out of season) has not only Shakespeare's birthplace but
also Hall's Croft (his daughter's home), the fine mediaeval church with his tomb,
and Harvard House (after which the American university was named).

Also at Ettington is **GROVE FARM**
(tel: 0789 740228), a house found at the
end of a brick path, with grapevine
beside it and an old pump. It is full of
character, with unusual furniture and
trifles Meg and Bob Morton have collected: from a spectacular carved sideboard to an old imp's head built into
one wall, an elm manger to a collection
of knobkerries. The chased silver
pheasant-gun belonged to Bob's grandfather and the old dough-chest to
Meg's (he was a baker). Bedrooms
under the sloping eaves are simple:
they have old-fashioned furniture and
Turkey carpets on board floors. Meg
serves only breakfast: for other meals, I

found the bar food at the Houndshill
Inn more than adequate. Meg collects
elderly horses; they are to be seen grazing in the fields beyond which are deer
woods and a panoramic view of the
Cotswolds as far as Bourton-on-the-
Water. From £12.50 to £15.
Readers' comments: Warm, friendly
welcome. Most impressed.

Stone-in-Oxney, Kent, TN30 7JU   Tel: 023383 251
North of Rye (East Sussex). Nearest main road: A268 from Hawkhurst to Rye.

3 Bedrooms. £14 (less for 7 nights). Views of garden, country.
Light suppers if ordered.
1 Sitting-room. With open fire, central heating, TV, piano.

Large garden
Closed from November to February inclusive.

This 17th-century house is full of works of art and unusual antiques (collected by Jimmy Hodson's father, a sculptor before he took to sheep-farming here) and also oriental pieces (Elise's family lived in India for many years). The blue bedroom, for instance, has not only a carved mediaeval table but geisha-girl prints and Numdah rugs; a Jacobean chest has Indian paintings above it; in the oldest room, with mullioned windows, are carved marquise chairs from Paris and a Kashmir chainstitch rug. The Hodsons have retained one very curious feature – a concealed iron winch above the staircase, which they think was used when hiding contraband (Romney Marsh was notorious for smuggling).

One breakfasts at a polished refectory table with rush chairs in a particularly interesting room – hop-bines are strung across the inglenook, with a copy of a statue of the Virgin Mary in Notre-Dame; there's a carved oak sideboard and brass rubbings from the local church. In the beautiful sitting-room are unusual chests and other antiques; the old iron fireback carries the royal coat-of-arms.

The garden is equally attractive, especially a paved terrace, brimming with fuchsias and roses.

As dinner is not served (only snack suppers), Elise provides visitors with menus gathered from good local inns and restaurants – and with a series of postcards on which she has detailed routes recommended for sightseeing tours.

Being midway between Rye and Tenterden (each described elsewhere), Tighe Farm is ideally placed for exploring historic and beautiful parts of both Sussex and Kent. Guests usually visit Smallhythe (Ellen Terry's Tudor house), Sissinghurst and Great Dixter gardens, Bodiam Castle, Tenterden and its steam railway, Camber sands and the Romney Marsh churches.

Readers' comments: Very welcoming and helpful. Excellent room, peaceful. Have stayed three times: so welcome; peaceful; a stately home in miniature. Made very welcome. Mrs Hodson very helpful. Very good value for money. Wish we had stayed longer. Surpassed our expectations. Made more than welcome. Fresh and polished to a glow. Shall stay here frequently.

TILED HOUSE FARM
C(10) S

Oxlynch, Gloucestershire, GL10 3DF   Tel: 045382 2363
West of Stroud. Nearest main road: A38 from Gloucester to Bristol.

3 Bedrooms. £11–£13. Some have own bath/shower/toilet. Tea/coffee facilities. Views of garden, country. No smoking.
Light suppers if ordered. Vegetarian or special diets. Wine can be brought in. No smoking.
1 Sitting-room. With open fire, central heating, TV, piano, record-player. No smoking.
Large garden
Closed from November to March inclusive.

Long ago, this was the first house in the area to have the innovation of tiles to replace thatch on the roof, hence its name. A paved path flanked by rickstones leads to the front door of the 400-year-old house. The ceilings are low and stairs steep. In a big sitting-room with huge stone fireplace, the original bacon-hooks in the beams and gun-racks above the hearth still remain. The green and white colour scheme contrasts with a polished woodblock floor.

The dining-room overlooks a farmyard sometimes full of much-photographed pedigree cows, from which stairs go up to some of the bedrooms (and a very nice bathroom), the largest of which has timber-framed walls. There is also a self-contained ground-floor suite with good bathroom; here a strange little 'gothick' window was uncovered in a thick stone wall when renovations were being done.

In nearby Quedgeley there are five restaurants; but for visitors not wanting to go out Diane Jeffery will make a light (and inexpensive) supper of, for instance, tuna mousse, then lasagne with salad and garlic bread, followed by apple pie. Vegetables are organically grown.

Visitors to this far west part of the Cotswolds find not only superb scenery but countless picturesque villages, inns and stately homes.

Readers' comments: First-class accommodation and superb breakfast.

At the foot of the National Trust's Haresfield Beacon is **LOWER GREEN FARMHOUSE** (tel: 0452 728264), a house of stone walls, leaded and mullioned windows, beamed ceilings. The light and spacious family bedroom is particularly attractive, with views across the Severn to the Forest of Dean (superb sunsets). By arrangement, Margaret Reed will cook straightforward English meals (preceded by sherry), such as pâté, chicken in cider, apple pie and cheeses. In the garden is a stone barbecue, pool

with yellow irises and a 40-foot well. From £13 to £14.

Readers' comments: Can't recommend too highly. Excellent cook and hostess.

★ **TREGONY HOUSE**   C(7) **PT**
Tregony, Cornwall, TR2 5RN   Tel: 087 253 671
East of Truro. Nearest main road: A3078 from St Mawes towards St Austell.

rear view

6 Bedrooms. £27.50–£30.25 including dinner (less for 7 nights). Some have own bath/shower/toilet. Tea/coffee facilities. TV. Views of garden, country. Washing machine on request.
Dinner. 4 courses (with some choices) and coffee, at 7pm. Special diets if ordered. Wine can be ordered.
1 Sitting-room. With open fire, central heating, TV, record-player. Bar.
Garden
Closed from November to February inclusive.

Behind a yellow façade is a house partly dating from the 17th century; later, additions were made – so the dining-room, for instance, is low-beamed and thick-walled while the hall and sitting-room have 18th-century elegance, particularly since the addition of well-chosen fabrics, a pomegranate wallpaper in the hall, rounded alcoves crammed with books, and interesting antiques.

All the bedrooms have their own individual character and comfortable style. They are furnished with antiques, velvet bedheads, electric heaters and pretty flower arrangements. Two double rooms with bathroom in between make a self-contained suite – suitable for families.

In the dining-room (furnished with oriental rugs, oak tables and Windsor chairs) Barry and Judy Sullivan serve such imaginative meals as spinach roulade, apricot and walnut stuffed lamb, and Calvados apple mousse (plus local cheeses). Herbs, raspberries etc. come from the cottage-garden at the back, where you can have tea.

Because Tregony, although interesting, is not one of Cornwall's show villages, it remains uncrowded even in high summer. From it you can quickly reach the warm south coast of Cornwall, with all its coves, beaches, harbours and scenic drives in the Roseland peninsula, an area of outstanding natural beauty, with numerous stately homes and gardens to visit too. Truro and St Mawes are interesting towns, and a feature of the region are the old beam engines (for mines).

The wilder north coast, too, is easily accessible. On the way there, you might like to pause at Goscott Historic Farm (with interpretation centre, and walks in ancient woods); or at the geological and mining museums at Camborne; or at Treskillard's shire horse farm. A good place at which to enjoy the views along this dramatic coastline is Tehidy Country Park; for those who want the company of an expert naturalist, there are guided walks in the woodlands here. Visitors are encouraged to watch the milking and feed the cows at Peloe Dairy Farm (near Camborne).

Readers' comments: Food marvellous: imaginative and beautifully cooked. Warm and friendly. Interesting food; comfortable, friendly. Outstanding; excellent, imaginative meals attractively presented. A very happy week; accommodation excellent, comfortable, tastefully decorated; delicious food; friendly and hospitable.

312

TREWERRY MILL

Trerice, Cornwall, TR8 5HS   Tel: 0872 510345
North of Truro. Nearest main road: A30 from Redruth to Bodmin.

6 Bedrooms. £13.50–£16. Prices go up in July. TV. Views of garden, country. No smoking. Washing machine on request.
Dinner. £5 for 3 courses (with choices) and coffee, at 6.30pm. Non-residents not admitted. Vegetarian or special diets if ordered.

Wine can be ordered. No smoking. **Light suppers.**
2 Sitting rooms. With open fire, central heating, TV. Bar. No smoking.
Large garden
Closed from November until Easter.

Trerice, owned by the National Trust, is an Elizabethan manor house of stone, with lattice-paned windows (one has 576 panes) and elaborate plaster ceilings. The watermill was built in 1639 to provide flour for the household; now it is a guest-house, the wheel stilled but a stream still flowing by. Ponds attract wildfowl.

One passes through a stone-flagged hall to two sitting-rooms, the first overlooking a lawn with millstone tables where home-made cakes are served at teatime, and the second with big leather armchairs around a log fire and a window through which there is an inside view of the waterwheel. Bedrooms are small and neat (there is one large family room), and the dining-room is simply furnished with oak tables and chairs. Here Ethel Grateley serves, for instance, turkey soup, local plaice in cheese sauce, home-grown vegetables and fruit crumbles – all for a very modest price.

Readers' comments: Food plain but well cooked, bedrooms very comfortable, garden a delight. A lovely, restful weekend. A great success. Delightful place. Hosts extremely competent and concerned about the welfare of their guests. Fabulous value for money.

Undercroft at Swalcliffe Manor (see page 306)

TUDOR FARMHOUSE HOTEL

C(5) **D X**

Clearwell, Coleford, Gloucestershire, GL16 8JS   Tel: 0594 33046
South-west of Gloucester. Nearest main road: A466 from Monmouth to
Chepstow.

9 Bedrooms. £19–£25 (less for 3 nights).
Prices go up in April. **Special weekend
terms for SOTBT readers, except at bank
holidays.** All have own bath/shower/toilet.
Tea/coffee facilities. TV. Washing machine
on request.
Dinner. A la carte or £11.50 for 3 courses
(with choices) and coffee, at 7–9.30pm.
Vegetarian or special diets if ordered. Wine
can be ordered. **Light suppers** if ordered.
1 Sitting-room. With open fire, central heating. Bar.
Small garden. Conservatory.

Parts of this house date back to the 13th century, and panelled walls are almost as
old. Oliver Cromwell stayed here while hunting in the Forest of Dean – Clearwell
is one of the prettiest villages on the edge of the forest – and may well have warmed
his toes at the same inglenook fireplace round which big, flowery sofas are now
grouped.

In the dining-room, rugged stone walls contrast with tables attractively laid with
delicately sprigged china.

The house, still surrounded by fields with horses, now belongs to a young and
lively professional couple (Sheila and James Reid). The table d'hôte dinner may
start with a home-made soup, pâté or quiche; perhaps followed by beef cooked
with Guinness and orange, or pork with cider and apples. Puddings are traditional
favourites (crumbles, mousses, pineapple upside-down cake, etc.); and then there
is a choice of cheeses.

The full à la carte menu changes monthly and has become very popular in the
local area.

To reach the pleasantly decorated bedrooms you ascend either a spiral stair or a
wide oak one; or go to a converted barn just outside, past an ancient stone
cider-press now planted with flowers. There are low, iron-studded doors, leaded
window-panes, stone mullions. Three spacious family rooms in the stone barn are
particularly attractive (rather like little self-contained cottages).

Clearwell has Roman iron mines and a network of caves you can visit; a
neo-Gothic castle; and mysterious Puzzle Wood – extraordinary and huge
boulders from which trees sprout. Newland's impressive church is known as 'the
cathedral of the forest'. Not only is there the beautiful forest to explore (in
autumn, the colours are at their best) but also the nearby Wye Valley and the gorge
at Symonds Yat, South Wales' beauty-spots (including Tintern Abbey's spectacular 12th-century ruins), and the market town of Ross-on-Wye. Newent's falconry
centre, England's oldest house (part-Saxon), the forest's heritage exhibition and
its steam railway, Lydney Park gardens and deer park, tours of the Stuart crystal
glass factory, bird gardens, a model farm, a great maze, and a tropical butterfly
garden are just some of the other sights which make it worth staying here for at
least a week if you can.

Readers' comments: First-class accommodation, food superb, made us very
welcome.

314

UPPER BUCKTON   C S X

Leintwardine, Herefordshire, SY7 0JU   Tel: 05473 634
West of Ludlow (Shropshire). Nearest main road: A4113 from Knighton
towards Ludlow.

3 Bedrooms. £18 (less for 2 nights). Views of
garden, country, river. No smoking.
Washing machine on request.
Dinner. £10 for 4 courses (with choices) and
coffee, at 7pm. Special diets if ordered.
Wine can be brought in. No smoking. **Light
suppers** if ordered (by late arrivals).
1 Sitting-room. With open fire, central heating, TV. No smoking.
Large garden

Yvonne Lloyd is an accomplished cook, serving such starters as bananas and
bacon with curry sauce or stuffed mushrooms; then roasts, salmon or chicken with
orange and almonds; vacherins or chocolate roulade. Such meals are presented on
Doulton's 'Old Colony' china with Harrods silver. It is largely her reputation for
good food which brings visitors here – that, and the peace and quiet of this
18th-century house (at the centre of a 300-acre sheep and cereal farm) in which
antiques furnish the comfortable rooms.

All bedrooms are named after local sites (mine was Coxall, with a view of Coxall
Knoll where there was an Iron Age fort). Yvonne has a decorative touch, with a
taste for ribbon-and-posy fabrics in one room (used even on the scalloped and
quilted bedhead), poppies in another, for instance. All the frilled or pleated
valances are made by her.

Outside is a verandah on which to sit with pre-dinner drink or after-dinner
coffee to enjoy the view towards the high ridge of the Wigmore Rolls. A lawn
slopes down to a clear stream fringed by hostas, to one side a tall and graceful birch
and to the other a high, feathery ash and the mound where once a Norman fort
stood. To keep children in particular happy, a granary has been equipped with
table tennis, darts and snooker; there are also a croquet lawn and other games.

This is very good country for walking and birdwatching, or for leisurely drives,
and only a little further afield are the Shropshire hills, Radnor Forest, Elan Valley
and Offa's Dyke. There are many picturesque black-and-white villages (typical of
this area), and castles (relics of the centuries of border warfare with Wales):
Ludlow, Stokesay, Croft, Powys, Montgomery. Museums cover all manner of
special interests from cider-making to industrial archaeology, farming to local
history. The Severn Valley steam railway is popular with children as much as
adults.

I particularly enjoyed an evening drive high up where the buzzards fly, the still
higher hills a distant blue. The sun went down on the glorious colours of gorse and
rose bay willowherb which adorned the ever-varied shapes of hills and valleys. The
following day, we drove along lanes flanked by the blowsy hedges and golden fields
of a hot summer's day: whenever the road rose up there were head-turning
panoramas of landscape laid out like a relief map, and when it plunged down again
there would be high wayside banks brilliant with drifts of wildflowers.

Readers' comments: Outstanding location, imaginative and generous cooking, most
comfortable. Marvellous hosts, lovely house, food excellent. Warm, attractive
rooms, delicious meal, we felt completely at home. Gracious country living.

315

Manor Road, Towersey, Oxfordshire, OX9 3QR   Tel: 084421 2496
East of Thame. Nearest main road: A4129 from Thame to Princes Risborough.
(*see picture on front cover*)

9 Bedrooms. £15–£24. Bargain breaks. Some have own bath/shower/toilet. TV. Views of garden, country. No smoking.

2 Sitting-rooms. With central heating, TV. No smoking.
Large garden

A building of whitewash and thatch overlooking a duck-pond at the front, Marjorie and Euan Aitken's house is one of the prettiest in this book. They uncovered 15th-century beams with the original carpenters' identification marks; came across Elizabethan coins; restored the wood shutters which (window-glass having yet to be invented) were all that kept out wintry blasts five centuries ago; found a secret priest-hole where, in the days of religious persecution, a Catholic priest might have to hide for days when the search was on. In one huge chimney, there were still the iron rungs up which small boys were forced to clamber to clear the soot. In what is now the quarry-tiled breakfast-room, an old kitchen-range and adjoining copper boiler have been preserved, together with the rack on which spits for roasting whole sheep were kept, and the special hooks used for drying the farmer's smocks by the fire. In the hall is a pump (still working). Six of the bedrooms are in a newly converted barn where there is a huge beam with the date 1790 written on it.

Marjorie, who used to be an antique dealer, has filled every room with fascinating trifles – Victorian jugs and jam-pots on the sprigged brown tablecloth at breakfast, shelves of old bottles (found discarded in the garden), beadwork pincushions and watch-cases, a huge marble washstand in the downstairs cloak-room, naive Staffordshire figures, old brass scales (which she uses) and tin toys.

The Aitkens not only tell visitors about the well known sights nearby (which include Claydon House, Ryecote Chapel, West Wycombe's 'hellfire' caves, the horses' home of rest, etc.) but introduce them to other sides of local life. For instance, you may go and see the sorting and grading of sheep fleeces, join in bell-ringing, pick up bargains at local markets or auctions, chat up balloonists as they glide by only a few yards above the farm. And, of course, their sheep, ducks, chickens and geese are an entertainment in themselves.

Bed-and-breakfast only; there is excellent pub food within short walking distance. Guests who bring their own snacks will be provided with plates, tea, etc.

Readers' comments: Charming home, warm hospitality: we arrived as guests and left as friends. Much impressed by warm welcome, delightful house and excellent breakfast. Wonderful couple – it always feels like going home! Charming people, absolutely delightful house. Superb breakfast. Absolutely excellent.

★ **UPTON HOUSE**   **D**

Upton Snodsbury, Worcestershire, WR7 4NR   Tel: 090560 226
East of Worcester. Nearest main road: A422 from Stratford-upon-Avon to
Worcester. *(see picture on back cover)*

3 Bedrooms. £18.50–£30. Bargain breaks. All have own bath/shower/toilet. Tea/coffee facilities. TV. Views of garden, country. No smoking.
Dinner. £17.50 for 4 courses and coffee, at 7.30 or 8pm. Non-residents not admitted.

Vegetarian or special diets if ordered. Wine can be brought in. **Light suppers** if ordered.
1 **Sitting-room**. With open fire, central heating.
Large garden with croquet.

Part 14th-century, part Tudor and part 18th-century, this building is full of individuality. It has been furnished in character, with antiques collected by Hugh and Angela Jefferson. They decided to take guests to help with the cost of educating four children, then found how much they enjoyed entertaining them.

Their colour schemes are fresh and imaginative. In the dining-room, chairs covered in watermelon satin contrast with primrose walls (this room has a vast fireplace); in the sitting-room, sofas covered in pink or blue brocade are grouped round another log fire. A feature of this room is the pretty little bay window with wide sill, through which one looks across the lawn (surrounded by trees and rosebeds) to half-timbered cottages and the Norman church, the clock of which chimes every quarter-hour.

The pink bedroom, low-beamed, has sweet peas on curtains, a moss-green carpet and violets on the Royal Albert bone china for early-morning tea. The peach room has an elegant Victorian bathroom. The blue room is almost as attractive.

Some visitors eat at the Boot (at Flyford-Flavell) or award-winning Brown's (Worcester), but menus at Upton House are good – a typical meal might comprise seafood vol-au-vent, stuffed lamb, chocolate truffle cake and cheeses.

It is hoped to get the old cider-mill at the back restored in due course. Meantime, if you want to see cider being made in the traditional way (in October) there is another mill nearby which you can visit. Children enjoy exploring the orchard, and meeting the ducks. From Upton House one can readily visit the Bredon and Malvern Hills (Hereford and the Wye Valley beyond them); such Cotswold beauty-spots as Broadway or Chipping Campden; and, in the other direction, Stratford-upon-Avon in Warwickshire. Worcester (cathedral and china factory), Spetchley gardens and several garden centres are other options. When in Worcester (best explored on foot) seek out the Commandery for Civil War exhibits, 15th-century Greyfriars, the guildhall and lovely riverside gardens.

Readers' comments: Excellent. Comfort and friendliness.

★ **VAULD FARMHOUSE**   C(5) **PT X**
Vauld, Herefordshire, HR1 3HA   Tel: 056884 898
North of Hereford. Nearest main road: A49 from Hereford to Leominster.

6 Bedrooms. £12.50–£18 (less for 7 nights). Some have own bath/shower/toilet. Tea/coffee facilities. TV. Views of garden, country. Washing machine on request. **Dinner.** £10 for 3 courses (with choices) and coffee, at 7.30–9pm. Non-residents not admitted. Wine can be brought in. **Light suppers** if ordered.
Sitting-rooms: see text.
Large garden with ornamental pond.

'Sleepy hollow', the locals call this area where the ancient farmhouse lies hidden, its creamy, black-timbered walls lopsided with age (it was built in 1510). Past a lake and a stone cider-press, one steps through the front door into a great room with stone-slabbed floor, half-timbered walls, log fire and colossal beams overhead.

Those who book the granary suite (which has its own stone staircase from outside) have a private sitting-room, with deep velvet armchairs, bedroom, bathroom and a gallery with another bed; and, through windows with unusual crisscross glazing bars, a view of the lake. Other visitors may prefer the ground-floor oak room with a very impressive four-poster (this, too, has its own entrance and bathroom). Additional accommodation is also available in the recently converted, 17th-century timber-frame barn which is situated directly opposite the farmhouse. Here, there is also a guests' sitting-room with television, and a dining-area. In summer, meals are sometimes served outside on a terrace.

If you order dinner, Jean Bengry will prepare a meal using much local produce, for this is an area of fruit-farms; and she keeps her own poultry and goats. A typical menu: chicken liver and mushroom pâté, turkey in hazelnut sauce or beef in ale, trifle and local cheeses – served on willow-pattern china at a lace-covered table.

Readers' comments: Excellent accommodation, fine food, friendly folk. None of us wanted to leave. Nothing was too much trouble. Made us completely at home.

Also in this area is **MAUND COURT** at Bodenham (tel: 056884 282), an old red sandstone house at the heart of a large mixed farm. Some of the bedrooms overlook the swimming-pool, heated to 76°. Although there are good eating-places in the area, Pauline Edwards will, by arrangement, provide such dinners as prawns in sherry sauce, pheasant and profiteroles. There is a beamed dining-room and a sitting-room with an oak-beamed fireplace. Plenty of local maps on loan. Guests can also enjoy the large garden, patio and croquet lawn. From £15 to £17.

Readers' comments: Very pleasant and welcoming, a hearty breakfast, we will go again. Friendly and welcoming atmosphere, excellent breakfast.

318

★ **VILLAGE FARM**   C(10) S
Sturton-by-Stow, Lincolnshire, LN1 2AE   Tel: 0427 788309
North-west of Lincoln. Nearest main road: A1500 from Gainsborough towards Lincoln.

3 Bedrooms. £12–£16 (less for 3 nights). Prices go up at Easter. Bargain breaks. Some have own bath. Tea/coffee facilities. TV. Views of garden. No smoking.
Dinner (not on Sundays). £8 for 4 courses (with choices) and coffee, at 7pm. Non-residents not admitted. Vegetarian or special diets if ordered. Wine can be brought in.
1 Sitting-room. With open fire, central heating, TV, record-player.
Large garden with hard tennis court.
Closed from November to March inclusive.

In the middle of this usually quiet village stands an early Victorian house, now pleasantly furnished by Sheila Bradshaw – at the heart of a 350-acre farm where pedigree cattle and sheep are raised. For the sitting-room she chose a pale green carpet, pink velvet curtains held back in tasselled loops, and flowery chintzes; among many Victorian heirlooms are things of her own making – canvaswork or patchwork cushions, for instance. She is a keen Women's Institute member, a handbell-ringer, loves flower-arranging and has made a big sampler depicting the house itself. Her husband's family farmed in Sturton for many generations back: among his enthusiasms are Shetland ponies and growing orchids.

Guests eat in the dining-room, seated around a large Victorian dining-table. A typical menu: smoked mackerel, farm lamb, apricot brûlée and cheeses. Upstairs are very attractive bedrooms: one, with matching Sanderson wallpaper and fabrics, has a sloping ceiling and odd windows; in the peach-and-cream one is a rocking-chair; one of the prettiest has pink Laura Ashley sprigged linen and a Philippine cane chair. In the garden is a vast walnut tree; to one side are pantiled barns. Coarse fishing and rough shooting available.

The Wolds, the coast and the Humber Bridge are easily reached. Nearby sights include Doddington Hall, a country park, Gainsborough Old Hall, Tattershall Castle, Pennell's nursery gardens and Stow's cathedral-like church. The Red Arrows aerobatic team is based near here. Lincoln and its cathedral are also close.

Readers' comments: Very helpful, a lovely week. Sheer magic! Comfort, views and value – all very good.

An alternative in Lincoln itself is a quiet Edwardian house (5 minutes' walk from the centre), **CARLINE GUEST-HOUSE**, 3 Carline Road (tel: 0522 530422). Immaculate and comfortable. Gill and John Pritchard provide bed-and-breakfast only. Unusually well-equipped; and very moderate prices for rooms with TV, own bathroom, etc. – eggs from their own hens. From £12.65 to £16.

Readers' comments: Every conceivable amenity.

319

VINE FARM

C(8) **H S**

Waterman Quarter, Headcorn, Kent, TN27 9JJ   Tel: 0622 890203
South-east of Maidstone. Nearest main road: A274 from Maidstone towards
Tenterden.

3 Bedrooms. £17.50 (less for 3 nights). All
have own bath. Tea/coffee facilities. Views
of garden, country. No smoking. Washing
machine on request.
Light suppers if ordered.
1 Sitting-room. With open fire, central heating, TV. No smoking.
Large garden
Closed from November to April inclusive.

Nothing could be more typical of Kent than this white weatherboarded house,
originally the home of a Tudor yeoman. It is surrounded by flowerbeds, lawns,
landscaped ponds, paved court, well, pots of flowers and 50 acres where sheep
graze. Hens and ducks roam the courtyard of the 16th-century barn.

One enters through the big brick-floored kitchen, its ceiling low and beamed.
In the sitting-room, Victorian armchairs of buttoned velvet and a large old
chesterfield surround an inglenook with log stove. Through small-paned casements in the pink walls, hollyhocks peer in; and there are views of the fields
beyond – a busy scene at lambing time. The dining-room is similarly furnished
with antiques, family portraits and pretty chintz curtains. Here Jane Harman
serves breakfasts, and light suppers such as home-made soup, sandwiches with
salad, and lemon mousse.

Bedrooms have antiques, festoon blinds of Designers Guild or Laura Ashley
fabrics, and bedheads of brass curlicues or ladderback mahogany. There is one
ground-floor room (with its own scarlet and white bathroom); and in the attic is a
suite, with armchairs and a private dressing/bathroom (the stairs to it are strictly
for the nimble).

The garden is particularly attractive, thanks to Jane's enthusiasm for gardening,
with such features as a patio of local Bethersden marble where breakfast
is sometimes served, and a landscaped fish-pond. Coarse fishing and riding
available.

The name Waterman Quarter, incidentally, tells a story. Once this quarter used
to be subject to floods when the river overflowed. It was the waterman's job to fly a
warning flag when the river was in spate.

Within easy reach are many of Kent's spectacular mansions and castles (Knole,
Leeds and Hever, for example, Scotney with its lovely gardens, and Sissinghurst
with gardens created by Vita Sackville-West), and historic cities (such as
Canterbury and Maidstone) and towns (Tenterden, Cranbrook). The country
lanes are particularly beautiful in apple-blossom time (usually May) or even
earlier, when the cherry-trees are in flower. In September, the hops are gathered
and taken to the oast houses for drying – a few allow visitors. There are several
good garden centres.

**When writing to me, if you want a reply please enclose a stamped
addressed envelope.**

320

★ **WALLACE FARM** C PT

Dinton, Buckinghamshire, HP17 8UF   Tel: 0296 748660

South-west of Aylesbury. Nearest main road: A418 from Aylesbury to Thame.

3 Bedrooms. £14–£16 (less for 3 nights). Some have own bath/shower/toilet. Tea/coffee facilities. TV. Views of garden, country. Washing machine on request.

1 Sitting-room. With open fire, central heating, TV.

Large garden

When the Cooks took over this 16th-century house, they brought with them some unusual furniture collected when they lived abroad – a Chinese wedding-chest of scarlet leather, for instance, and one from the Philippines with mother-of-pearl inlay. An Indonesian dowry chest has carvings of bride, groom and dragons. Jackie has an eye for what is decorative and unusual, whether old or new – such as the hand-painted bathroom tiles which feature rare breeds of British animals.

Bedrooms differ in style – a small room in crisp white, for instance, and a very large one in pale green and pink with old pine furniture including a dresser loaded with books.

There is a tiled breakfast-room with a big, sturdy oak table and a log stove (for dinner, visitors usually go to local inns: the Bugle Horn, Stone; the Bottle and Glass, Gibraltar; the Seven Stars, Dinton); by one stone hearth, an original bread oven has survived the centuries; and the guests' sitting-room has shuttered casement doors on two sides, opening onto a terrace with seats, croquet lawn, orchard, and cows seen grazing across a haha. Also in the grounds are ponds (with coarse fishing), Jacob sheep, ducks and geese. Bicycles on loan.

This peaceful spot is roughly equidistant to Heathrow Airport and London. There is a 'Travel Card' available for only a few pounds which covers the cost of rail to London (1 hour) and unlimited bussing about on arrival, so that visiting London can alternate with tranquil country days.

The nearest town, Aylesbury, has a lively market, a 15th-century inn belonging to the National Trust, and historic houses in its byways. Other towns well worth visiting include Old Amersham – a particularly charming main street, very wide and flanked by historic buildings; Georgian Beaconsfield; Buckingham (a splendid beech avenue leads from it to Stowe, the Vanbrugh mansion that is now a famous school, grounds open to the public); High Wycombe (centre of furniture-making, with Disraeli's home – Hughenden – nearby); riverside Marlow; and Eton.

Dinton itself is a pleasant old village with stocks and whipping-post on its green, a Tudor manor house and mock ruins (look for fossils in its stones). Another attractive village is Bradenham, preserved by the National Trust.

Readers' comments: Beautiful house. Would like to return.

WALLETT'S COURT   C PT

West Cliffe, Kent, CT15 6EW   Tel: 0304 852424
North-east of Dover. Nearest main road: A258 from Dover to Deal.

7 Bedrooms. £20–£30 (less for 5 nights). Very good bargain breaks. All have own bath/shower/toilet. Tea/coffee facilities. TV. Views of garden, country, sea. Washing machine on request.
Dinner. A la carte or £16 for 3 courses (with choices) and coffee, at 7–9pm. Vegetarian or special diets if ordered. Wine can be ordered.
1 Sitting-room. With open fire, central heating, piano.
Large garden

Built on cellars that date back to Norman times is a magnificent 17th-century manor house. But it is not just the building, or even the surrounding scenery (protected by the National Trust), which bring visitors here: Chris Oakley is an exceptional chef who has worked with the Roux brothers, at Le Gavroche.

The huge sitting-room with carved oak beams and two fireplaces, one of stone and one of brick, has deep-set, pine-shuttered sash windows with window-seats; buttoned velvet chairs and antiques furnish the room. In the elegant dining-room, tables are laid with bronze cutlery and Royal Worcester china decorated with game birds. Dining chairs are upholstered in pink, there is a log fire, brass-rubbings decorate the walls and on elaborately carved woodwork are the date 1627 and the initials of the Gibbon family (its most celebrated member was the author of *The Rise and Fall of the Roman Empire*). Bedrooms in the house are excellent (some with large, buttoned, velvet armchairs; all with antiques), bathrooms elegant. Other bedrooms, small and with modern pine, are in a converted barn. (The patchwork spreads were made by Lea Oakley.) There are murals; handsome newel-posts on the stairs; mellow brickwork exposed here and there. The Norman cellars are used for snooker and table tennis.

As to the meals, these are very special and people come from far afield to dine at Wallett's Court (non-residents admitted on Saturday; no meals on Sundays). The Saturday dinners often include such choices as game terrine with citrus salad followed by turbot with lobster sauce, a sorbet, haunch of venison in claret, and a wide choice of puddings. With the coffee come petits fours. Weekday dinners, though less extensive, are of similar quality.

The peaceful countryside along this coast, facing the Dover Straits, is only three miles from Dover, its castle and its harbour (for day trips to France). One can walk along the famous white cliffs here, and there is a fine garden (the Pines) with waterfall and Nemons' statue of Churchill. St Margaret's Bay is where cross-Channel swimmers start from, and further along are Walmer and Deal – both with castles, a string of which (Norman through to Victorian) dot this coastline as it faces Europe. To the south, near Folkestone, there is an exhibition on the Channel Tunnel. The white cliffs are in fact the end of the North Downs, one of the region's most beautiful features, with many good drives or walks among the hills and historic villages (Canterbury is quite near).

Readers' comments: The calm atmosphere delighted, the antiquity amazed.

WALLTREE HOUSE FARM   C
Steane, Northamptonshire, NN13 5NS   Tel: 0295 811235
North-west of Brackley. Nearest main road: A422 from Banbury to Brackley.

8 Bedrooms. £17.50–£18.50. Prices go up in April. Some have own bath/shower/toilet. Tea/coffee facilities. TV. Views of garden, country. Washing machine on request.
2 Sitting-rooms. With open fire, central heating, TV.
Large garden

Quite a surprise to find, at the end of a long farm lane, a park-like setting in which this handsome Victorian farmhouse stands.

Pauline and Richard Harrison have transformed the house and its outbuildings to provide a large number of bedrooms, so that this is virtually a farm hotel now. Those in the former granary are very modern in style: Stag furniture in some, rosy fabrics, much bamboo and pine, very good bathrooms. One family suite is virtually a cottage, so well-equipped is it. You can be sure of ample warmth on 365 days in the year, for Richard installed a special straw-burner which means all his central heating costs him nothing but the labour of gathering straw from his fields after each harvest.

If you would like to try microlight flying – or just sit and watch from the comfort of bamboo armchairs in a big octagonal sun-room – you can do so at the back of the farm, for it overlooks a mini-airfield, in use only by day.

It was at Brackley that the barons negotiated Magna Carta before its sealing at Runnymede later in 1215. Today the attractive town lies around a particularly wide, mile-long main street flanked by trees and little lanes, and adorned by a very fine 18th-century town hall, historic school, old inns and quaint almshouses. The church is worth a visit for its windows and monuments are of particular interest.

The whole county is full of good things and quiet beauty, yet so many visitors merely pass through it on the way to more celebrated places of interest. It is a green county, and a county of stone – which means there are fine buildings to be found. It is a historic county, too, where many epic events took place. If you were to travel from Oxford through Northamptonshire to Peterborough you would be in a limestone area where the villages are just as lovely as those of the Cotswolds and there are scenic uplands nearly all the way. The stone varies in colour – grey, honey-gold, reddish brown – which adds to the interest of the scene. North-amptonshire is nicknamed the 'county of spires and squires', so expect fine churches and fine houses – the latter very numerous and dating from every century from the 14th onwards (a complete architectural history of England) but with the Tudor period most fully represented. The churches are notable for the number of Saxon ones that have survived. Just over the Oxfordshire border is Banbury, celebrated for its cakes and cross.

Book well ahead: many of these houses have few rooms. Do not expect dinner if you have not booked it or if you arrive late.

WALNUT COTTAGE

C(14) H PT

Old Romsey Road, Cadnam, Hampshire, SO4 2NP Tel: 0703 812275
West of Southampton. Nearest main road: A31 from Romsey to Ringwood.

3 Bedrooms. £15.50–£17 (less for 2 nights). Prices go up in April. Bargain breaks. All have own bath/shower/toilet. Tea/coffee facilities. TV. Views of garden. Washing machine on request.
2 Sitting-rooms. With open fire, central heating, TV.
Small garden

The road no longer leads anywhere (its days ended when a nearby motorway replaced it). The little white cottage, with brimming window-boxes and a red rambler-rose by the door, stands in a pretty garden (with an old well) which traps the sun. One bedroom opens onto this.

All the rooms have been attractively furnished by Charlotte and Eric Osgood, who did much of the work themselves (even the tiling of the showers, and the flowery china door-knobs on each bedroom door). There are two sitting-rooms with pale carpets, cretonne armchairs, flowers on the window-sills and interesting objects on the shelves. One has windows on all three sides. In the dining-room are Regency chairs, cupboard and mirror; a diminutive iron grate, as old as the cottage, has been preserved (though the only fireplace still in use is in the larger sitting-room). Here Charlotte serves breakfast on Royal Doulton vineleaf china, but for other meals, she recommends a thatched and whitewashed inn a few yards down the lane (the 12th-century Sir John Barleycorn).

The cottage is on the edge of the New Forest (it was originally occupied by foresters). Romsey and Broadlands are very near; Beaulieu, Breamore House, Bucklers Hard (historic waterside village), Salisbury, Winchester and Bournemouth only a little further. From Southampton (with Spitfire and maritime museums – and sometimes the *QE2*) there are trips to the Isle of Wight, and London is less than two hours away. The nearby motorway (M27), its hum just within earshot, makes many distant sights easy to reach.

The Osgoods not only lend maps and cycles free, but have photocopied useful hints for a selection of car outings in the area, describing the route for each, listing sights, and also recommending the best inns for lunches, good bookshops etc. They have also mapped out a 'Howards' Way' tour; and can tell you where to buy trout, venison, local fruit etc.

This is a good choice for an October break, when the forest colours are superb; but book well ahead if you want to go in September when Southampton's boat show and Beaulieu's 'auto jumble' sale are on. May is a good month for the many superb gardens such as Exbury, Furzey, Spinners and Compton Acres. Southampton's 'Ocean Village' has an audio-visual of maritime history.

Readers' comments: Beautifully located . . . most helpful people. Delightful couple, charming rooms, comfortable; superb breakfasts. Excellent: a charming couple. Very impressed by their care and attention. A spacious and comfortable bedroom; helpful hosts. Their interest in the comfort and pleasure of their guests has to be experienced to be believed. Faultless accommodation and welcome. Felt at home at once. Marvellous!

WARDEN'S HOUSE   D
Lode Lane, Wicken, Cambridgeshire, CB7 5XP   Tel: 0353 624165
South of Ely. Nearest main road: A1123 from Huntingdon towards Soham.

1 Bedroom. £12.50 (less for 4 nights). Tea/coffee facilities. Views of garden, country. No smoking.
Large garden

rear view

Many who visit historic Ely and its superb cathedral prefer somewhere rural to stay overnight. This comfortable house with garden, tucked away behind high beech hedges on the edge of Wicken Fen (Britain's very first wildlife reserve), provides the answer. It is the home of naturalist Tim Bennett – head warden of the Fen – and his wife Cindy (an amateur botanist), an interesting couple with whom to stay before spending a day exploring this fen, one of the few areas of true wilderness that are still left. (Bed-and-breakfast only, using humanely produced eggs, bacon etc.; there's a discount if you want only continental breakfast. Pub meals in the village at the Maid's Head.)

The fens' history is well explained in the National Trust's interpretation centre at Wicken. Once, vast areas of peaty, waterlogged land provided the perfect habitat for many wildlife species; but most has been drained for farming. Only at Wicken can you see an ancient remnant (600 acres), used in the traditional way. In one part, hay is mown and this encourages a diversity of wildflowers. The wetter sedge fields provide material for thatch, and here other plants flourish. Carr (small thickets) shelter birds among the shrubs, ferns and mossy undergrowth. Very ancient streams still thread the Fen, and also a lode (a waterway once used by barges). It is a problem now to keep the Fen from drying out, so a restored wind-pump feeds water in. You can go from a demonstration garden identifying Fen plants to woodland, ponds, areas rich in wildflowers, old brick-pits now flooded and colonized by water-plants, a stack of 4000-year-old oak trunks dug from bogs, through glades to a tall 'hide' from the top of which are far views beyond a mere with wildfowl and a sunny bank that attracts a host of butterflies.

★ The original **SPINNEY ABBEY** founded in 1220, outside Wicken, was closed down by Henry VIII, became a private house (where Cromwell's son lived after the Stuarts were restored to the throne) and was later pulled down. Its stones were used to build a new house in 1775. This is now the home of Valerie Fuller (and of her inherited collection of Victorian stuffed birds), who has roomy and comfortable bedrooms, a sunken bath in one bathroom and, from the farm lands, views into

Wicken Fen. B & b only. (Tel: 0353 720971.) From £12.50 to £13.

325

WATER HALL FARMHOUSE

C D

Ifield Wood, Charlwood, West Sussex, RH11 0LA Tel: 0293 20002
West of Gatwick. Nearest main road: A23 from South London to Brighton.

6 Bedrooms. £18–£23. Prices go up in April. Tea/coffee facilities. TV. Views of garden, country. No smoking.

1 sitting-room with open fire, central heating, TV.
Large garden

There are several houses in this book (in Surrey or Sussex) sufficiently close to Gatwick Airport for it to be convenient – and usually cheaper – to leave your car with them while abroad and taxi to and from the airport (some – such as this – even provide the taxi service themselves).

This one is the nearest: it takes about 10 minutes to get to Gatwick from here. Despite the aircraft, I slept peacefully: they do not fly through the night.

The farmhouse (parts of which are nearly five centuries old) is a traditional Sussex building, its upper storey hung with scalloped tiles up which creepers grow. There are tubs of bright busy Lizzies outside, and flowerbeds. Beyond the stone-walled and tiled hall is a sitting-room with antiques, a silvery damask wallpaper and comfortable chairs; and a breakfast-room the French doors of which open onto a lawn, more flowerbeds and beyond these fields of grazing horses (the house is full of horse pictures, among others).

Bedrooms, with double-glazed windows, are neat and pleasantly furnished: in one, for instance, an old spinet now does duty as a dressing table. I particularly liked a large blue room (called 'George's') because it has windows on three sides.

Rosalind Tilson serves only breakfast but I dined well at Limes Bistro in Charlwood just over a mile away.

The airport is not, in fact, the only reason for staying here: it is a good centre from which to explore the North Downs in one direction and the Weald in another. (It is, incidentally, a very suitable spot to which to take children for they will enjoy the Gatwick Zoo Park, the plane-viewing platform at the airport and the Bluebell Line steam railway, for example.) In the immediate vicinity are a number of old villages interesting to visit: Rusper for its church memorials to the Broadwoods (of piano fame, and associated with the folk-song movement led by Cecil Sharpe); Worth, on the edge of woodlands, which has a Saxon church and a memorial to a 17th-century worthy which boasts that he was 'discended from ye right ancient and long before ye Norman Conquest . . .'. One of England's greatest agricultural shows is held at Ardingly each June; and a little further afield is Lindfield, so famous a beauty-spot that it is best avoided in high summer: houses from every period, some colour-washed, some half-timbered.

★ THE WATERMILL

C PT S(off-peak)

near Hildersham, Cambridgeshire, CB1 6BS   Tel: 0223 891520
South-east of Cambridge. Nearest main road: A604 from Haverhill towards Cambridge.

1 Bedroom. £15. With bath/toilet. Views of garden, country, river. No smoking. Washing machine on request.

Light suppers only. Vegetarian or special diets if ordered. Wine can be brought in.

A track through fields, past a windmill without sails and by a narrow stretch of the River Granta, suddenly comes to this very large watermill – last used (for grinding wheat or sawing wood) in 1904. Its present owner, engineer David Hartland, is engaged in the long task of restoring the 7-ton waterwheel. One day he hopes it will generate enough power to run a heat-pump for the house. He has amassed a collection of old photographs and drawings illustrating the history of the mill, which dates from the 11th century (the present buildings are early 19th century).

Guests are accommodated in one-time stables (converted in the 'thirties, when a door from Cambridge Castle was salvaged and installed here). Breakfast is brought to their roomy bedroom, or served on the lawn by the river when the weather is sunny. The unusual bedroom (white plank walls, sloping ceiling) is furnished in cottage style: sprigged fabrics, and rugs on the floorboards. The oak bedstead dates from the 18th century. The room has views of lawn, weeping willows and the millstream, the sound of which lulls one to sleep. Boating available; and trout fishing free.

Cambridge is only a few miles away. If your time is limited, the best selection of colleges to visit is perhaps King's, Corpus Christi, Queen's and Trinity – and there are also the Botanic Gardens, the great art treasures of the Fitzwilliam Museum, the lawns and gardens of 'the Backs' and an unusual house, Kettle's Yard, with beautifully arranged modern art and artefacts just as the owner left them. A boat or punt on the River Cam is a particularly enjoyable way of seeing the Backs (of colleges).

Some other sightseeing options include the Imperial War Museum's outpost at Duxford, Saffron Walden, Newmarket, Ely, and also a number of stately homes such as Audley End, Wimpole Hall and Chilford Hall with vineyard. At Hinxton you can see flour being ground (and buy it) at a 17th-century watermill recently restored. Good, inexpensive pubs and restaurants abound.

Readers' comments: Superb – a lovely weekend. Enjoyed very much. Warm welcome. Comfortable room. Most welcoming hostess, lovely room.

WAVENDEN HOUSE

Compass Cove, Dartmouth, Devon, TQ6 0JN   Tel: 0803 833979

Nearest main road: A379 from Dartmouth to Kingsbridge.

3 Bedrooms. £13–£15 (less for 7 nights). Prices go up in May. TV. Views of garden, country, sea. No smoking. Washing machine on request.
Dinner. £10 for 4 courses (with choices) and coffee, at 7.30pm. Non-residents not admitted. Vegetarian or special diets if ordered. Wine can be ordered or brought in. No smoking.
1 Sitting-room. With wood stove, central heating, TV, record-player. No smoking.
Large garden

So beautiful is the coastal scenery here (owned by the National Trust) that today no-one is allowed to build on it: Wavenden is the only house there to enjoy the superb view of the River Dart's wide estuary, jagged headlands and, across the water, 15th-century Kingswear Castle.

When Ken and Lily Gardner moved here, it was a rather ugly 'twenties bungalow which they rebuilt so sensitively that even environmentalists have congratulated them on enhancing the previous scene. And the garden too, sloping down to the shore (where you can bathe or fish), has been improved by them, with grassy terraces, primrose banks and well-landscaped flowering shrubs.

There is a large two-level dining- and sitting-room, with huge glass doors through which to enjoy the view, and also a big fireplace of polished black slate (with wood burner). Through these doors one steps onto a paved sundeck with reclining chairs from which to watch every kind of craft go by.

From every bedroom, furnished in Laura Ashley style, are glimpses of the sea and garden, colourful even in early spring because the climate here is so mild.

Ken (who used to be an award-winning investigative journalist) and Lily have always been accomplished cooks, so Wavenden is a good choice for gourmets (a typical dinner might include creamed mussels as a starter, game casserole and treacle tart). Local fish goes into their seafood chowder and other dishes.

It is a good choice, also, for walkers because the Devon Coastal Path and a network of National Trust footpaths lie just beyond the gate. In a hedge are traces of the first cross-Channel telegraph cable (about 1870).

In hilly Dartmouth itself is a picturesque Butterwalk with houses supported by granite pillars; 17th- and 18th-century buildings; and, on a hill high above, the imposing Royal Naval College.

Readers' comments: Delicious and bountiful fare. The location, the welcome, the comfort, the food, the decor – everything was superb value. Lovely views, and atmosphere generated by the Gardners. Excellent food.

Holne, Ashburton, Devon, TQ13 7RX   Tel: 03643 273
West of Newton Abbot. Nearest main road: A38 from Exeter to Plymouth.

4 Bedrooms. £13–£15 (less for 7 nights). Some have own bath/shower/toilet. Tea/coffee facilities. Views of garden, country. Washing machine on request. **Dinner.** £7 for 4 courses and coffee, usually at 7pm. Vegetarian or special diets if ordered. Wine can be brought in. **1 Sitting-room.** With central heating, TV. Games room (snooker, table tennis). **Small garden**

Tucked away in a fold of the gentle hills south of Dartmoor is this small farm where sheep and hens are kept; donkeys, goats and rabbits too.

Sue Townsend has furnished the bedrooms very prettily, and she equips them with supplies of fruit-squash and biscuits as well as tea. There is a family unit of two rooms and a shower, and a ground-floor suite. A comfortable sitting-room is available to guests.

Four-course dinners are served in the dining-room. After a starter such as melon or pâté, the main course will probably be a roast, poultry or steak pie, perhaps followed by fruit pie or flan, always accompanied by Devonshire cream, then cheese and coffee. Sue tries to cater for every guest individually. There is no charge for washing and ironing facilities, mealtimes are flexible, the welcome warm, and many extra services provided (loan of maps, hair-dryer, free tea on arrival). From the farm, which has a small swimming-pool, there are views of the moors.

One of the local beauty spots is 60-foot Becky Falls in oak woodlands threaded by nature trails. At Bovey Tracey are exhibited local crafts of high quality in a granite watermill. There is a vineyard and a rare breeds farm and the National Trust has 200 acres of riverside park.

Other local NT properties include mediaeval Bradley Manor with its own chapel, and the 16th-century Church House at Widecombe. Ugbrooke House by Adam contains a collection of armour and uniforms, Trago Mills the largest model railway in the county. Yarner Wood is a national nature reserve with a trail through heathland and woods.

Chudleigh has something for everyone: vintage cars, Victorian rock gardens with an 80-foot cliff and a cave, a model circus and, in a mill with working waterwheel, 17 craft workshops.

Readers' comments: We were pampered, the situation is an absolute dream. Loud praises of all aspects, especially the food. The very best: nothing is too much trouble. One of our favourites; Sue is one of the best cooks; food beautifully presented. Very enjoyable; warm welcome, good food, comfortable. Sensational cook. Caring hostess. Beautiful setting.

WEST HOUSE

C(5) D PT

12 West Street, Warminster, Wiltshire, BA12 8JJ Tel: 0985 213936
Nearest main road: A36 from Salisbury to Bath.

2 Bedrooms. £16–£18. Both have own bath/shower/toilet. Tea/coffee facilities. TV. Views of garden. Washing machine on request.
Dinner. £12 for 4 courses (with wine) and coffee, at 8pm. Non-residents not admitted. Vegetarian or special diets if ordered. **Light suppers** if ordered.
2 Sitting-rooms. With open fire, central heating, TV, piano, record-player.
Large garden
Closed from November to February inclusive.

A very graceful sitting-room extends from front to back of the 18th-century stone house: soft pink sofas and armchairs contrast with a celadon carpet, their colours complemented by those of chinoiserie curtains with pheasants. White-shuttered windows are at each end. On the walls of this and other rooms are some of the sporting prints and early English watercolours which Charles Lane collects (and writes about). A fine staircase leads to charming bedrooms: I particularly liked one with rosebud wallpaper matching the pastel-coloured patchwork spread on the cane-headed bed. Flowers are put in each room.

The large entrance hall serves as a second sitting-room – handsomely decorated with a peach-coloured wallpaper, comfortable sofas, good paintings and a marble fireplace over which hangs a large antique mirror. There are two white alcoves filled with china and porcelain, including some of Charles Lane's quite extensive collection of ornamental elephants. The TV is also here and guests are welcome to sit with the family.

In the equally attractive dining-room, Celia Lane uses cordon bleu recipes with fresh ingredients for such meals as Stilton and onion soup, crown of lamb with apricot stuffing, and one of the best raspberry pavlovas I've ever tasted.

At the back are two large walled gardens with old-fashioned roses, herbaceous beds and an immense tulip tree (it flowers late in July).

Charles is, incidentally, a descendant of the celebrated Jane Lane whose story is told elsewhere (see **King's Lodge**, Warwickshire).

The Lanes love to tell their guests of good places to explore – not just the famous sights (Salisbury, Bath, Glastonbury and Wells) but delightful spots such as Shaftesbury, Frome, Devizes or Bruton, for instance. Close by are Longleat with its Elizabethan mansion and famous lions, Avebury ring, Stonehenge, Wilton House, Stourhead and many beautiful but lesser known gardens. Near picturesque Bradford-on-Avon is 15th-century Westwood Manor with a topiary garden. Corsham has, in addition to its well-known stately home, a museum devoted to Bath stone, which is housed in a quarry.

Around Warminster, there are plenty of antique shops, as well as good walking country.

Readers' comments: A true 'house guest' atmosphere prevailed and nothing was too much trouble. Charming owners. Most comfortable and informal.

WESTERN HOUSE   C S X
Cavendish, Suffolk, CO10 8AR   Tel: 0787 280550
North-west of Sudbury. On A1092 between Long Melford and Clare.

4 Bedrooms. £12–£13. Tea/coffee facilities.
Views of garden. Only one has basin.
Light suppers if ordered. Vegetarian or
special diets.
Large garden

Twice made redundant, Peter Marshall decided he had had enough of industry
and – his children now being grown up – would instead make a living from his best
asset: his attractive 400-year-old house in the historic village of Cavendish.

He and his wife Jean (who teaches singing) are vegetarians, so at one end they
started a wholefood shop, full of the good smells of dried fruit and fresh herbs, and
refurnished several bedrooms to take bed-and-breakfast guests. Breakfast is
served in the bedrooms. Options include all kinds of good things (such as their
own muesli, eggs, mushrooms, tomatoes and home-made bread) but no bacon.
They will recommend good restaurants of all kinds in the village, at Long Melford
or in Sudbury.

Each beamed bedroom, reached via zigzag corridors, is very pretty, and
spacious – well equipped with chairs, table etc. One at the front (double-glazed,
because it looks onto the main road through the village) has a fresh white-and-
green colour scheme extending even to the sheets.

One of the nicest features is the large and informal garden where paved paths
wander between old-fashioned flowers, elderly fruit trees, and plant troughs.

Cavendish is one of a string of mediaeval villages described elsewhere. Clare is
close, so is Sudbury town and Long Melford – very long indeed, lined with
dignified houses and antique shops. Its church and its great mansions (Melford
Hall and Kentwell Hall) are well worth seeing. So are Kersey, Georgian Ickworth
Hall (grounds by Capability Brown; paintings by Velasquez, Gainsborough and
Reynolds), East Bergholt, Dedham (Alfred Munnings exhibition), the Roman-
Norman city of Colchester (with castle), Castle Hedingham, a steam railway and
Beth Chatto's garden.

Although Suffolk is heavily cultivated, you can still find ancient woodlands with
oxlips, and meadows where wildflowers thrive untouched by weedkillers; and you
can hear curlews in the Breckland area. From Sudbury runs the 24-mile 'Painters'
Way', a footpath beside the River Stour (as well as shorter walks along beautiful,
abandoned railway lines).

The fields are a pattern of colours (for crops, not grazing, predominate): barley
and wheat turn to ripe gold at the end of summer, the former often destined for
beer-making; stretches of bright yellow in early summer may be either mustard or
rape (grown for its seeds, rich in oil for margarine); occasionally, there are fields of
blue linseed flowers to be seen. A lot of sugar beet is grown. And now lupins are
being tried as a crop for animal feed.

Readers' comments: Excellent, with very good breakfasts. Much enjoyed it; and the
shop is excellent. Extremely comfortable; warm welcome. Absolutely excellent,
high standard.

WESTERN HOUSE

Winchelsea Road, Rye, East Sussex, TN31 7EL   Tel: 0797 223419
On A259 from Hastings to Folkestone.

3 Bedrooms. £12.50–£15. Prices go up in April. All have own bath/shower/toilet. Tea/coffee facilities. TV. Views of garden, country.
Large garden

The mediaeval port of Rye was perched high on a thumb of land (almost an island) projecting into the sea. But centuries ago the sea receded, leaving behind dry land which became ideal pasturage for sheep. It is here, at the foot of Rye town, that tile-hung Western House was built in the 18th century, commanding far views – you can even see Hastings in clear weather – from its paved terrace (with working pump) where tea may be taken, or from the huge lawn surrounded by brilliant flowerbeds set against mellow stone walls. On summer evenings, the terrace is lit by an old Victorian street-lamp.

Artist Ron Dellar is the present owner of Western House, and his paintings fill the dining-room walls. Up the staircase, and in the bedrooms are all manner of finds he has amassed over the years: African masks, a parrot in a glass dome, an 1820 box of paints ('Constable was alive then', he comments), Rupert Bear books, antique toys. Melanie, his wife, sells Victorian lace, linen, baby-gowns and books which are laid out in the big entrance hall. Ron's own prints of Rye are on sale too.

This is a house of character, as befits its long history. A boat-builder lived here and, later on, Members of Parliament. Among its visitors (in 1913) was the impressionist artist Pissarro; and Ron has incorporated him in a mural featuring Rye church which he painted for one of the bedrooms. All these rooms are attractively decorated, with interesting wallpapers and fresh flowers, and some have good views of the marshes across which you can walk to Winchelsea. There's a moated Martello tower out there, giant marsh-frogs croak throatily, you may see herons or marsh harriers flying overhead. (Although the house is on the road to Winchelsea I slept undisturbed.)

Dinner is not usually served because Rye has so many good inns and restaurants such as the Old Forge, Runcible Spoon or Flushing Inn.

The Cinque Ports (seven, in spite of the name) stretch along the south-east coast and in the centuries before the Navy existed their seamen would serve the king in time of war. In return, they were given trading privileges which made them rich – hence the number of fine old houses and churches still to be found in most of them, from Sandwich in Kent to Hastings in Sussex (and Rye is the jewel of them all). Their history is told in Hastings museum.

In this scenic and historic area, there is plenty to enjoy within a short drive. Brickwall House at Northiam, for instance, where the formal gardens surrounding the Jacobean house include an 18th-century bowling alley, a chess garden, and a sunken topiary garden; or the park and terraces of Tudor Hareham Hall at Etchingham. Along the coast, at the resort of Bexhill, is a costume museum.

Readers' comments: We were particularly delighted. View magnificent.

332

WESTLEA   C(2) **H PT S**
29 Riverside Road, Alnmouth, Northumberland, NE66 2SD
Tel: 0665 830730
South-east of Alnwick. Nearest main road: A1068 from Newcastle to Alnwick.

7 Bedrooms. £15–£18. Prices go up at Easter. Bargain breaks. Some have own shower/toilet. Tea/coffee facilities. TV. Views of garden, country, estuary. Balcony. Laundry facilities.
Dinner. From £8 for 4 courses (with some choices) and coffee, at 6.30–7pm. Non-residents not admitted. Wine can be brought in. No smoking.
1 Sitting-room. With central heating, TV, video, record-player.
Small garden

This is a very comfortable modern guest-house facing the Aln estuary, immaculately kept by Janice Edwards. One attractive bedroom (wildflower fabrics and cane bedheads) opens onto the sunny front garden; others vary in size and style but all, even if small, are well equipped. The upstairs sitting-room has a balcony from which to enjoy the river view. Just a few yards from the house are good, sandy beaches.

Breakfasts are imaginative; and for dinner (4 courses) there may be such dishes as beef, salmon, Cheviot lamb (with Northumbrian baked suet-puddings) or game pie. For the way she runs Westlea, Janice received a local Hospitality Award in 1989. (The Edwards are willing to collect guests without their own transport from the nearby railway station.) As many visitors come repeatedly for long holidays, booking well ahead is essential.

Nearby Alnwick is the seat of the Duke of Northumberland (and the historic Percy family whose deeds feature in so many of Shakespeare's plays), who lives in Alnwick Castle – ruined but then restored in the 18th century. This area is a good place in which to follow riverside walks; to explore the dramatic coastline and its many castles – particularly Warkworth at daffodil-time; to visit Craster for its succulent kippers (the ancient smoke-house is a listed building); and to walk to the romantic clifftop ruins of Dunstanburgh which Turner painted many times; or little Amble for its sandy beaches and island of eiderducks. Alnmouth itself is a picturesque yachting resort and has one of England's oldest golf courses (1869).

Visitors enjoy trips to the Farne Islands to watch seals and puffins, to Holy Island and to the Scottish borders. At Bamburgh is the Grace Darling museum as well as a theatrically sited castle and golden sands. Although scenery – free from crowds – is the area's greatest attraction, there are plenty of other interesting things to see, such as the wild white cattle, a rare survival, at Chillingham; the farm park at Embleton; or the World Bird Research Station (very tame birds in 17th-century buildings, and an arboretum).

Blyth has one of the county's several good railway museums, there are a great many country parks, and this is a good area in which to seek out craft workshops.

Readers' comments: A most enjoyable week. Nothing was too much trouble for Janice Edwards. Hearty meals, beautifully cooked and presented. Kind and helpful. Excellent food and an amazing choice for breakfast.

Whashton, North Yorkshire DL11 7JS   Tel: 0748 2884
North-west of Richmond. Nearest main road: A66 from Scotch Corner to
Brough.

8 Bedrooms. £18–£20 (less for 7 nights).
Bargain breaks. All have own bath/shower/
toilet. Tea/coffee facilities. TV. Views of
garden, country, river.
Dinner. £10 for 3 courses (with choices) and
coffee, at 7pm. Non-residents not admitted.
Vegetarian or special diets if ordered. Wine
can be ordered.
1 Sitting-room. With open fire, central heating. Bar.
Small garden
Closed from 20 December to 20 January.

Far more handsome than the average farmhouse, 18th-century Whashton Springs
has great bow windows and other detailing typical of this fine period in English
architecture. Around it is a large, mixed farm run by two generations of Turnbulls. It is high among wooded hills, with superb views of the Dales and of a stream
with mediaeval bridge below.

Every bedroom is different. One, for instance, has flowery fabrics, broderie
anglaise on the bedlinen, pretty Victorian antiques and a bow window; another, a
four-poster with William Morris drapery and buttoned velvet chairs. Others in a
converted stable-block are more modern in style (velvet bedheads, flowery duvets
and pine furniture); most of these overlook a courtyard where tubs and stone
troughs brim with pansies and petunias; one has a garden view. Another outbuilding houses the pottery studio of the Turnbulls' daughter-in-law, Jane.

Fairlie Turnbull and her daughter Christine provide dinners except on Thursdays, always with some choice. A typical example: cheese soufflé, home-bred roast
lamb, and brandysnaps. Or, a typical Yorkshire ending to a meal, Wensleydale
cheese served with fruitcake. (The meals are very good value – with wine
included.)

The many gardens of this region are at their best in spring, and the famous sights
(York, Durham, Richmond and the Dales) less crowded. One can even drive
across to the Lake District from here. It's an area not only of spectacular scenery
but of dramatic or romantic ruins (great abbeys and castles). Walkers seek out
waterfalls and caves, fells and crags, for which the Yorkshire Dales are famous.
The little cobbled villages and old inns seem hardly to change at all with the years.

Whashton's nearness to the A1 means many people use it as a one-night stopover
on their London–Edinburgh journey, but it deserves better than this because
there are so many good reasons to linger. Swaledale alone takes days to explore,
and so does Teesdale (both described elsewhere). It is a region of contrasts. Lonely
moors rise to 2000 feet (this is where to listen for curlews and plovers, and to
wonder at lives passed in such few isolated farms as there are), while every dale
differs – Wensleydale is wide and either pastoral or wooded; Swaledale winds
between steep hills; some others are like deep clefts – Arkengarthdale, Coverdale,
Bishopdale, for instance. Heather moors, houses of 18th-century dignity, the
distinctive curly-horned sheep; all contribute to the individuality of this area.

Readers' comments: Very comfortable. Made very welcome. High praise. Lovely
surroundings and easy access to many places.

★ WHEATHILL FARM
C(5) S

Church Lane, Shearsby, Leicestershire, LE17 6PG   Tel: 0533 478 663
North-west of Market Harborough. Nearest main road: A50 from Leicester to
Northampton.

4 Bedrooms. £14–£16 (less for 2 nights).
Prices go up in June. One has own shower.
Tea/coffee facilities. Views of garden, country. No smoking. Washing machine on
request.
1 Sitting-room. With open fire, central heating, TV, record-player. No smoking.
Large garden with croquet and boules.
Closed in December and January.

In 1823, the owners of this cottage (part Saxon, part mediaeval) put a new façade
on the front: brick, with trim white paintwork. But behind this the old beamed
rooms remained unchanged, with huge inglenook housing a log stove, and a
twisting stair.

Sue Timms has a decorative touch, and uses pretty fabrics or beribboned net in
cottage-style bedrooms, one downstairs (and even in one of the bathrooms too).
The house is full of unusual heirlooms, including a 100-year-old pot-plant which
originally belonged to a lighthouse-keeper (her great-uncle) on the wild Farne
Islands off the Northumberland coast. Outside is an attractive garden with
lily-pool and lake, and fields of Wheathill's cows.

For evening meals, Sue recommends the local village pub which serves food that
is both inexpensive and freshly cooked.

Shearsby is, like many others around here, a particularly pretty village, not far
from Georgian Market Harborough (its lively markets date from 1200) and at the
centre of rich grazing country – a tranquil region threaded by waterways with, at
Foxton, ten locks packed in a tier to raise boats up a 75-foot incline.

Further north is the scenic Charnwood Forest area – a mixture of heath, crags,
ridges and remnants of oak forest with fine views from its hilltops. Within a short
distance are Anstey's mediaeval packhorse bridge, the pretty little spa town of
Ashby de la Zouch, a particularly interesting church at Breedon-on-the-Hill, and
Loughborough which has a carillon of 47 bells in a high tower in the park. Other
sights include Birdland, Twycross Zoo and Stanford Hall.

Sitting-room at Wheathill Farm

WHICHAM OLD RECTORY

C S

Silecroft, Cumbria, LA18 5LS   Tel: 0229 772954
West of Millom. Nearest main road: A595 from Broughton-in-Furness to
Whitehaven.

3 Bedrooms. £13 (less for 2 nights). Tea/
coffee facilities. TV. Views of garden, country, sea.
Dinner. £7 for 3 courses (with some choices)
and coffee, at a time to suit guests. Non-
residents not admitted. Vegetarian or special
diets if ordered. Wine can be brought in.
Light suppers if ordered.
1 Sitting-room. With open fire, central heating, TV, piano.
Large garden
**Closed from mid-December to mid-
January.**

So many people head for the heart of the Lake District that the outlying areas of
the National Park remain uncrowded and uncommercialized. The south-west
corner in particular is often overlooked, even though it is within an easy drive of
famous beauty-spots and has its own particular attractions – uncrowded beaches,
for example, and a mild maritime climate. The last accounts for the peaches and
other fruit that flourish in the garden of the Old Rectory – some appearing on the
dinner-table, or going into the wine which guests usually sample.

The house is typical of those Victorian rectories built for Trollope-size clerical
families with domestic staff in proportion. David Kitchener – an ex-RAF supply
officer and an accomplished woodworker – has put a lot of work into the spacious
house, some of it to display intriguing family possessions – Victorian dish-covers,
an ancient cast-iron pressure cooker – and other interesting bric-à-brac: a big
model of a dhow he bought when on service in the Middle East, a fairground flare,
woodwork from a Warwickshire church, a collection of kukris and other weapons.

He and Judy Kitchener also find time to grow most of the vegetables which she
uses in her enthusiastic cooking. There is always a home-made soup, with
alternative first courses, then for example coq au vin (which may be half a chicken
per head), with at least three vegetables, to which guests help themselves, and a
sweet such as raspberry mousse, to which the garden is likely to have contributed
too. The freshly baked bread is David's speciality.

All the bedrooms overlook the lawn, next to which is a small semi-circular
conservatory which David has built onto the end of the stable, so that guests can
enjoy the garden even when a sea breeze is blowing. The energetic can take a
footpath to the top of Black Combe (2000 feet) for views of Scotland and Wales.
The less energetic can explore the beach at Silecroft, with its sands and rock-pools.
Up the coast are mansions and gardens, a narrow-gauge railway, and old seaports.
Eastward are pleasant market towns, Morecambe Bay and the seabird reserve of
Walney Island. Inland is, of course, the Lake District.

For – almost literally – a cross section of Lake District scenery, one could drive
up the Duddon Valley (or Dunnerdale), which was a favourite of Wordsworth's.
From Duddon Sands (at sea level, of course), the road follows the river through
increasingly rugged scenery. At the top, Hardknott Pass takes one westward to the
coast, Wrynose Pass into the central Lake District.

WHITE BARN

Crede Lane, Bosham, West Sussex, PO18 8NX   Tel: 0243 573113

West of Chichester. Nearest main road: A259 from Chichester to Portsmouth.

rear view

4 Bedrooms. £19. Prices go up in April. Bargain breaks. All have own bath/shower/toilet. Tea/coffee facilities. Views of garden. **Dinner.** From £13 for 4 courses (with choices) and coffee, at 7.15pm. Non-residents not admitted. Vegetarian or special diets if ordered. Wine can be brought in. No smoking. No dinners in August. **1 Sitting-room.** With open fire, central heating, TV. No smoking. **Small garden**

As interesting architecturally as any house in this book, White Barn is no barn but a very modern house indeed (single storey), designed by architect Frank Guy, and standing in the seclusion of a former orchard.

The dining-room is impressive: its principal features are a roof of exposed boards, a vast glass wall on one side (opening onto a red-tiled terrace where dinner is sometimes served).

This room is open to the big kitchen with its scarlet Aga cooker, pans hanging from brass hooks, and solid beech work-counter with old brass grocery-scales.

Then there is an oddly-shaped sitting-room, built all around the circular brick hearth on which a modern log stove stands. Its huge sofas face a narrow window 20 feet high. Throughout there are white walls and glossy scarlet doors.

Few visitors prefer a separate table for meals but join all the others at a huge pine refectory table, laid with flowery Portmeirion pottery, where Susan Trotman serves such appetite-whetting meals as stuffed mushrooms or Italian cheese croûtes with a piquant red pepper sauce, before, perhaps, chicken breasts sautéed in cream and white wine (and an abundance of fresh vegetables), followed by a pavlova topped with home-made lemon curd and Jersey cream (or a steamed treacle pudding).

Bedrooms open onto the garden, or overlook it. One is an imaginatively planned family suite: the room with children's bunk beds is like a cabin.

Not far away is the Saxon harbour of Bosham (its church is depicted in the Bayeux tapestry), thronged with little boats. Chichester, described elsewhere, lies in one direction and the historic naval waterfront of Portsmouth in the other – where you can visit HMS *Victory*, the *Mary Rose*, the dockyard museum, old bastions and byways, Southsea Castle, and the ring of high Victorian forts. The colossal, ironclad HMS *Warrior* is an attraction. There are many Roman sites.

Readers' comments: Very comfortable, food superb. Excellent value, memorable – not to be missed! Wonderful. Warm and welcoming. A memorable stay; outstanding. Food is out of this world. Top class! Comfortable, restful, very good food in ample quantity. Charming, cheerful, considerate. Meals superb.

WHITE HOUSE

Grindon, Staffordshire, ST13 7TP   Tel: 0538 304250
East of Leek. Nearest main road: A523 from Leek towards Ashbourne.

3 Bedrooms. £16–£18 (less for 3 nights). Prices go up in March. Bargain breaks. All have own bath/shower/toilet. Tea/coffee facilities. TV. Views of garden, country. No smoking.

1 Sitting-room. With open fire, central heating, TV.
Small garden

In the 17th century, this sparkling white cottage was a little inn, in a beautiful part of the Peak District (1000 feet up, it overlooks the very lovely valley of the River Manifold). Philomena Bunce used to teach crafts and needlework, and every bedroom reflects this – the pretty colour schemes and the hand-made cushions, patchwork quilts, lampshades and padded bedheads are her work.

Outside is a very pleasant garden with seats on a paved area with roses and cottage flowers. Drink in hand, one can watch the sunlight fading and, over a mossy wall, cows ambling on their way to be milked, while the swifts dart low.

For breakfast, Philomena offers several out-of-the ordinary options, such as kippers delivered from Craster in Northumberland or a Staffordshire oatcake (like a pancake) topped with a tasty mushroom, mustard and egg mixture. Bread is home-baked. Visitors dine at the nearby Cavalier Inn or can choose a restaurant of their choice from the range of local menus which are kept in the house.

Apart from visiting the Peak District, Dovedale and the Manifold Valley from here, you can explore lesser-known Derbyshire and the much underrated north of Staffordshire. In the south the scenery is pastoral, with calm rivers. Derby city has an 18th-century quarter and other historic buildings, many parks, and Kedleston Hall – an Adam mansion. Alton Towers – an exceptional leisure park – is near.

Six towns make up the 'Ceramic City' of Stoke-on-Trent containing Coalport, Spode, Wedgwood and other well known potteries. Closer are the many antique and mill shops of the interesting town of Leek, surrounded by moorlands. Lichfield has a cathedral and Denby pottery; Tutbury, Smedley knitwear mills (bargains!). The M6 will take you south to Dudley and one of the region's most popular attractions – the open-air Black Country Museum of bygone industries.

Readers' comments: Furnishings outstanding; highest standard of comfort, good food and warm welcome. Our stay one of the pleasantest ever. Absolutely superb – perfection! A wonderful find, and very reasonably priced. One of the best weekends we can remember; perfect comfort, lovely surroundings, delectable meals. A gem! Made to feel part of the family. Excellent, comfortable, friendly.

WHITE HOUSE C(5)

North Road, Widmer End, Buckinghamshire, HP15 6ND   Tel: 0494 712221
North-east of High Wycombe. Nearest main road: A404 from High Wycombe
to Amersham.

1 Bedroom. £15 (less for 3 nights). Has own bath/shower. Tea/coffee facilities. TV. View of garden, country. No smoking. Washing machine on request.
Large garden

Hot in pursuit of a Buckinghamshire debutante, the Prince of Wales in 1931 persuaded his aide-de-camp, who lived in a 16th-century cottage conveniently near, to build on an extra wing for the Prince's use. It is in the Prince's self-contained but modest suite that visitors are today accommodated; and those who drop in at the village inn may encounter elderly locals who still remember the Prince's activities.

(By a coincidence, the present owner – Jane Vaughan – also has family reminiscences of the indefatigable Prince who, up in Yorkshire, had courted yet another girl, Jane's great-aunt.)

From the bedroom, with its view of grazing sheep, one descends via a staircase of exposed beams and brickwork to the breakfast-room in the old part of the cottage. No dinners (only light snacks if ordered in advance) but there is a good inn, the Hit or Miss at Penn Street; the Royal Standard at Forty Green; and plenty of restaurants in the old quarter of Amersham.

The nearby Hughenden Valley has – although only an hour from London – such fine scenery that much of it is owned by the National Trust, including the great house at its centre which was Disraeli's home. At West Wycombe there is much to see and most is very unusual, including an underground cave system open to the public, and the 18th-century church with so immense a golden ball on top of its tower that parties were held in it by Sir Francis Dashwood – leader of the 'Hell Fire Club' which held orgies in the caves and in the ruins of Medmenham Abbey. His magnificent Palladian mansion is surrounded by parkland which Capability Brown laid out.

Then there are Penn, where William Penn lived, and Jordans, associated with the Pilgrim Fathers (see entry for **Old Jordans**); Milton's Cottage at Chalfont St Giles; and High Wycombe's chair museum (from the Chiltern beech woods originated the Windsor chair, and the town is still a centre of furniture-making).

In this Chilterns area of outstanding natural beauty, it is the gentle drive through beech woods and along country lanes to the old Roman road at Ellesborough – the Upper Icknield Way – that Jane recommends most. There are fine views of Chequers, the country home of Britain's Prime Ministers, and the route passes close to the 17th-century home of parliamentarian John Hampden.

339

WHITESTONE FARMHOUSE

C D PT S

Staintondale, North Yorkshire, YO13 0EZ Tel: 0723 870612

North of Scarborough. Nearest main road: A171 from Scarborough to Whitby.

rear view

4 Bedrooms. £10.50 (less for 3 nights). Prices may go up in April. Bargain breaks. Tea/coffee facilities. TV. Views of garden, country, sea. No smoking. Washing machine on request.

Dinner. £6 for 4 courses and coffee, at 6.30pm. Non-residents not admitted. Vegetarian or special diets if ordered. Wine can be brought in. No smoking.

2 Sitting-rooms. With open fire, central heating, TV, record-player.

Small garden

'I like my guests to feel they are having a dinner-party every night!' says Pat Angus, which is one reason why many return.

That and the position of the stone-built farmhouse just south of Robin Hood's Bay (famous for its three-mile sweep, and the constant erosion which has caused many cottages to tumble into the sea) and near National Trust coastal scenery, all with spectacular views.

There is a glass-walled sun-lounge so that you can see meadows with goats, cows and lambs in one direction and the sea in the other – from the comfort of the large curved sofa or an armchair. A steep staircase leads up to neat bedrooms which enjoy similar views.

Adjoining the farmland are woods and Heyburn Wyke nature reserve – roe deer occasionally wander in from the reserve. There are footpaths down to the rocky shore and along a disused rail track; the long-distance Cleveland Way passes by on its far journey to the North Yorkshire Moors.

As to Pat's dinner-parties, here is an idea of the kind of thing she prepares for her guests: fruit juice; tomato stuffed with walnuts, raisins, cheese and chives in mayonnaise – served with a salad and home-baked wholemeal roll; turkey breast in breadcrumbs with cranberry sauce and four vegetables; sherry trifle. Exceptional value.

Staintondale's attractions include not only the coast but also the North York Moors. To the north is Whitby (described elsewhere) and to the south Scarborough – a huge mixture of resort, fishing harbour and historic town, with superb scenery around (both cliffs and sandy bays). Some of it is now garish; but the harbour and fishmarket are as they always were, and dramatically positioned on a headland are the remains of a Norman castle overlooking Scarborough's superb bay. Staintondale's shire horse centre is a popular outing.

Anne Brontë died and is buried at Scarborough. She wrote about 'the deep, clear azure of the sky and ocean, the bright morning sunshine on the semicircular barrier of craggy cliffs surmounted by green swelling hills, and on the smooth, wide sands, and the low rocks out at sea – looking, with their clothing of weeds and moss, like little grass-grown islands – and above all, on the brilliant, sparkling waves. And then the unspeakable purity and freshness of the air!'

Readers' comments: A lovely atmosphere, food excellent in content, presentation and quantity. A caring couple. Wonderful value for money.

340

★ **WHYKE HOUSE**   **C PT S X**
13 Whyke Lane, Chichester, West Sussex, PO19 2JR   Tel: 0243 788767
Nearest main road: A27 from Worthing to Portsmouth.

rear view

4 Bedrooms. £15 (less for 7 nights). Some have own bath/shower/toilet. Tea/coffee facilities. TV. Views of garden. No smoking. Washing machine on request.
1 Sitting-room. With central heating, TV. No smoking.
Small garden

In an ordinary suburban cul-de-sac, very close to the historic centre of Chichester (and overlooking a grassy Roman site at the back, where children now play) is an unusual bed-and-breakfast house, ideal for families.

Here Tony and Lydia Hollis cook their guests' breakfasts (and service their rooms), give advice on sightseeing, then depart to their own home next door. There is a fully equipped kitchen which guests are then welcome to use to prepare other meals, if they do not wish to go to Chichester's many restaurants and cafés (the Nags is popular). Unlimited tea etc. is provided. Guests can also use the sitting-room and back garden (with croquet), glimpsed in the drawing. It is almost like being in a home of your own, with complete freedom.

The furnishings throughout have great individuality. Family antiques mingle with Russian folk art, local paintings (you may meet the artist) with soft furnishings made by Lydia – who also has a flair for painting furniture decoratively. Adjoining the sparkling white kitchen is a dining-room with green bamboo wallpaper and furniture 'scumbled' in green by Lydia; the baby's highchair is a century-old heirloom, so is the grandfather clock.

For some older guests, the ground-floor bedroom and shower are particularly convenient. Guests can be met by car at the station.

Other entries describe the cathedral city of Chichester (latest addition to its treasures is the collection of modern art in 18th-century Pallant House) and its environs, which include Arundel Castle, Fishbourne Roman palace, Bosham waterfront village, Goodwood House, the open-air museum of ancient buildings and West Dean gardens. Tony, once in the antiques trade, is a good adviser on the best shops locally.

At Earnley, as well as the butterfly house, children will enjoy the rabbit and bird sanctuary. Vineyards open to the public are at Lyminster (tastings in a 15th-century barn, and a collection of farming bygones), Singleton (the winery is in an old station), and Nutbourne (where there is a watermill mentioned in the Domesday Book).

Readers' comments: The Hollises are so kind and helpful. Very comfortable; the Hollises are charming and very helpful; unpretentious and suited to young families. What good value. Comfortable and enjoyable. Comfortable, quiet, convenient; most welcoming. Pleasant weekend, comfortable; so helpful and welcoming; a real treat to stay. So welcoming, well organized. Relaxed, comfortable atmosphere. Friendly and helpful. The location was perfect.

★ **WILLOW DALE** **PT**

17 Carr Hill Lane, Briggswath, Sleights, North Yorkshire, YO21 1RS
Tel: 0947 810525
South-west of Whitby. Nearest main road: A169 from Whitby to Pickering.

3 Bedrooms. £14–£16 (less for 3 nights). Bargain breaks. All have own bath/shower/toilet. Tea/coffee facilities. TV. Views of garden, country. No smoking. Washing machine on request.
Dinner. £8 for 3 courses and coffee, at 7pm. Wine can be brought in. No smoking.
1 Sitting-room. With central heating, record-player. No smoking.
Small garden
Closed from December to February inclusive.

Bountiful Roman goddesses Flora and Pomona adorn the sitting-room door, with swags of fruit; the front hall has stained glass; there are big sash windows throughout and handsome fireplaces of marble or decorative tiles: all redolent of the Edwardian era when this house was built. Surrounded by gardens, it looks down over the quiet Esk Valley (yet busy Whitby is quite close).

Judy Potts has boldly decorated the dining-room (which has a log fire) with a striking gold Chinese wallpaper and tasselled pelmet, while in the sitting-room are comfortable leather chairs and sofa. One bedroom has a brass bed, festoon curtains, rosebud bedlinen and pink corduroy sofa (and a really beautiful shower). The mulberry room has a frilled four-poster and an excellent bathroom with bidet.

Visitors help themselves from a drinks tray before dinner – which might, for instance, be smoked trout, chicken (with stuffing, broccoli, red cabbage Austrian-style, and jacket potatoes with cream cheese), Malvern pudding (an egg-custard and apple dish), then cheeses with celery.

Whitby is both fishing port and seaside resort, overlooked by the dramatic ruins of its 13th-century abbey on a high headland. The old part of the town is a place of steep byways, craft workshops and Captain Cook's house. There are sandy beaches further along. Briggswath is on the edge of the North York Moors; a steam railway line goes across the moors to Pickering.

Readers' comments: Most comfortable, good attention to detail. Dinner plentiful and imaginative. Peaceful. Excellent in every way.

On the other side of Whitby is 17th-century **CROSS BUTTS FARM** which has a big bedroom that is handsomely panelled – it has an immense four-poster, seven feet wide, with barley-sugar posts. Long hours went into the making of its crochet bedspread. Other rooms are attractive: Eileen Morley has used rosebud fabrics and broderie anglaise, for instance. Willow-pattern curtains match the china on a dresser that stands against one of the stone walls. For dinner,

many visitors go to the Magpie. The farm is near sandy beaches. (Tel: 0947 602519.) £15.

★ **WINDMILL HOUSE**   **C PT S X**

Winterbourne Monkton, Wiltshire, SN4 9NN   Tel: 06723 446
South of Swindon. Nearest main road: A4361 from Swindon to Devizes.

3 Bedrooms. £13–£15 (less for 7 nights). Views of garden, country. Washing machine on request.
Dinner. £7 for 3 courses (with choices) and coffee, at 6.15pm. Non-residents not admitted. Vegetarian or special diets if ordered. Wine can be brought in. No smoking. **Light suppers** if ordered.
1 Sitting-room. With open fire.
Small garden

All but the base of the windmill vanished long ago and this, the miller's house, has been greatly modernized – although in some rooms the old walls made of chalk blocks are visible, one bearing the date 1711. All around are fields, with far views of Silbury Hill, the Ridgeway path, and Wansdyke (all prehistoric remains). This is a very ancient part of England; and the mill itself had a long history: wheat was ground there as far back as the 13th century.

A narrow spiral stair leads up to bedrooms that are simply furnished but comfortable, and the dining/sitting-room (with log stove) is unpretentious. Outside is an unheated swimming-pool. But what most impresses the walkers, game-shooting parties, and others who come here is the food. Penny Randerson, who used to be an industrial chemist, comes from a family of chefs, which may be why meals are of an order to compare with some many-starred hotels. Although one-night visitors are offered a set menu (with choices at each course), those staying longer can order ahead from her considerable repertoire of such dishes as pigeons en cocotte, seafood gratin, cheese fondue (unusually prepared with cherry brandy), filet Chateaubriand, pork chops ardennaise, and many more. Bread is home-baked, vegetables from the garden, and there are always flowers on the table).

After a visit to Swindon to see historic locomotives in the railway museum (and its section devoted to Brunel), as well as the restored village of Victorian railwaymen's cottages, one could go to Lydiard Tregoze where there is a classical stone mansion in a great park, its rooms (which have elaborately decorated ceilings) filled with antiques and paintings. The colourful effigies in the ancient church here are well worth seeing. Beyond lie Malmesbury and its abbey and Tetbury, a particularly attractive old market town.

If you go south, in less than two miles you come to the prehistoric stone circles which surround Avebury village – they are even older than Stonehenge, their purpose unknown, and their construction method a mystery too, since each weighs up to 40 tons. The village has a Norman church, great thatched barn (with museum of rural life) and an old manor house.

The road westward from here passes Silbury Hill and one of Wiltshire's many white horses cut into the chalk of the downs on the way to Calne and 18th-century Bowood House – its grounds most colourful when rhododendrons and then bluebells are in flower. Capability Brown laid these out.

When writing to me, if you want a reply please enclose a stamped addressed envelope.

WINDRUSH
S

Little Comberton, Worcestershire, WR10 3EG Tel: 038674 284
West of Evesham. Nearest main road: A44 from Evesham to Worcester.

2 Bedrooms. £10.50. Tea/coffee facilities. TV. Views of garden, country.

1 Sitting-room. With central heating, TV. **Small garden**

Two little thatched cottages from the 17th century have been combined as one, with a particularly pretty garden created around them – lobelias and geraniums planted in an old tree-stump, the weathered grey of rickstones providing a good foil to colourful blooms. Rooms are low-beamed, and the inexpensive little bedrooms furnished in appropriately cottagey style. Altogether, a really 'old world' effect.

At the back are fruit trees and vegetables, with Mr Lewis a willing guide to all aspects of the garden in which he has worked for nearly 40 years.

Breakfast only, but there is good food to be had at The Mill (Elmley Castle) and the Fox and Hounds (Bredon), for instance.

Evesham is a riverside market town at the centre of the fruit-growing Vale of Evesham (this is at its prettiest in spring blossom-time). A ruined abbey with bell tower, 18th-century and older houses, fine churches, and the old Almonry (now housing a museum) all contribute to its charm. Around it are innumerable pretty villages. Offenham still has that rarity, a maypole; Elmley Castle, no castle now but plenty of half-timbered cottages, a deer park and mediaeval sculpture in the church; Bredon, a huge 14th-century tithe barn to hold the grain which served as taxes paid to the church. Above looms Bredon Hill – 1000 feet high – dominating an otherwise gentle landscape of placid rivers, apple orchards and pastures where cows graze. There are prehistoric and Norman earthworks, a castellated 'gothick' folly, and from the summit a view of at least eight counties. Around the hill is an apple-blossom trail marked out for drivers to follow in the spring.

There are boat trips available on the River Avon; and within a short car-ride the showpiece village of Broadway, Malvern (spa town) and historic Pershore, famous for its plums. Other popular outings include Winchcombe, Sudeley Castle, Beckford Silk Mill, Broadway Tower, Snowshill Manor, Hailes Abbey, Tewkesbury Abbey, the sunken gardens at Kemerton and the 'minimum labour' garden at Bredon Springs.

Readers' comments: Beautifully preserved; garden a joy to behold. Mrs Lewis is charming and friendly. A gem of a find.

Prices are per person in a double room at the beginning of the year.

★ **WINDRUSH HOUSE**   **C**(12)
Hazleton, Gloucestershire, GL54 4EB   Tel: 0451 60364
West of Northleach. Nearest main road: A40 from Cheltenham to Oxford.

4 Bedrooms. £16–£18. Bargain breaks. Some have own shower/toilet. TV. Views of garden, country. Washing machine on request.
Dinner. £13.50 for 4 courses and coffee, at 7.30pm. Wine can be ordered or brought in.
Light suppers if ordered.
2 Sitting-rooms. With open fire, central heating, TV, piano, record-player.
Large garden

The greatest attraction of this small guest-house built of Cotswold stone is Sydney Harrison's outstanding cooking (though she serves dinner on only three days a week). Not only is everything impeccably prepared – vegetables delicately sliced and lightly cooked, bread home-baked, breakfast orange juice freshly squeezed – but she has a repertoire of imaginative dishes that puts many an expensive restaurant in the shade. With your breakfast porridge you will be offered whisky. And all the food is served on Royal Worcester porcelain. On nights when dinner is not served, she recommends the Fosse Bridge or Frog Mill.

Sydney's friendly welcome is manifest the moment you arrive, and a free glass of sherry awaits you in your room.

As to the house itself, this is furnished with much attention to comfort, and in tranquil colours. All the rooms are immaculate, and the furnishings (conventional in style) are of high quality.

The house stands in a quiet spot some 800 feet up in the Cotswold Hills, where the air is bracing and the views are of far fields and grazing sheep. It is on the outskirts of a rambling village of old stone farmhouses with a small church nearby – part of it early Norman.

Hazleton – under two hours from London – is close to beautiful Northleach, which has a mediaeval church of great splendour and an excellent museum of country life; Cirencester, a lovely market town with the outstanding Corinium museum, crafts, another church as grand as a cathedral and a great park; Burford; and Cheltenham, with all the elegance of a spa, particularly at the Montpellier end of the great Promenade (another good museum and fine church). The beauty of the Cotswold Hills needs no describing, nor its showpiece villages like Bourton-on-the-Water, Bibury and Stow-on-the-Wold. There is a Roman villa at Chedworth, butterfly and bird gardens, folk and farm museums, wildlife and rare breeds parks, stately homes and gardens, castles (such as Sudeley), abbeys and walks. Riding can be arranged.

Readers' comments: Food absolutely outstanding, even for a spoiled Swiss! Absolute calm. First-rate; inventive menu; highly recommended. Excellent food and genial hosts. Food outstanding; what a find! Superb cooking. The best meal we'd had – highly recommended. Excellent in every way, especially food and wine. The best cook we've found in England. Excellent food; very comfortable; welcoming. Our third visit. Excellent cook and hostess; very comfortable. One of the nicest people; outstanding cook. Very comfortable.

WINDYRIDGE   C(8) **PT S X**

Wraik Hill, Whitstable, Kent, CT5 3BY   Tel: 0227 263506
North of Canterbury. Nearest main road: A299 from Faversham towards
Ramsgate.

rear view

8 Bedrooms. £14.50–£17.50 (less for 7
nights). Prices go up in May. Bargain
breaks. All have own shower/toilet. Tea/
coffee facilities. TV. Views of garden, country, sea.
Dinner. £8 for 3 courses (with choices) and
coffee, at 6.30pm. Vegetarian or special diets
if ordered. Wine can be ordered or brought
in. **Light suppers** if ordered.
4 Sitting-rooms. With open fire, central
heating, TV. Bar. No smoking in one.
Large garden

The architectural eccentricities of this house are due to the fact that a demolition
contractor once lived here, and in the course of expanding what was originally a
small cottage he built in all kinds of curios – even gargoyles from a chapel, and rare
Norman panes of purple glass. Some iron-framed windows came from a prison.
Two-foot-thick walls have a mixture of granite slabs, bricks and low stone
archways combined in an odd assortment.

Nanette Fitchie and her husband now run Windyridge as a guest-house. At one
end of the very big sitting/dining-room, sofas and cretonne wing chairs face a great
stone fireplace with log stove (there are three more sitting-rooms elsewhere) while
beyond the tables at the other end a steep, open-tread staircase rises to the
bedrooms – and also to a verandah with telescope from which to enjoy the
panoramic sea views. Even without its aid, one can often see from this high
vantage-point the distant shores of Essex and, at night, the twinkling lights of its
liveliest resort, Southend-on-Sea. There is a particularly good family room with
curtained annexe for children.

Beyond a sun-room with cushioned bamboo chairs, a rambling garden descends
towards the sea where the sandy beaches are separated by the Swale from the Isle of
Sheppey – this waterway is a haven for wildfowl.

Nanette serves such dinners as chilled cucumber soup, pork chops, home-made
passioncake and cheeses.

Of all counties, Kent – fertile and wealthy – has played a greater part in English
history than any other because its coast is only 20 miles from Europe (to which it
was once joined) and because of its proximity to London.

Once, Whitstable enjoyed an important role in all this and was busy with
travellers who came by coach from Canterbury to embark there for a sea journey to
London (which says much about the sad state of road transport to the capital
at that time). Then in 1830, the world's first passenger train took over this route
from the coaches: you can see its locomotive (Robert Stephenson's *Invicta*) in
Canterbury.

But it was only in this century that Whitstable really prospered as a seaside
resort. It still has rows of black-and-white weatherboarded fishermen's cottages to
give it character, and old inns such as the Sun (where you can eat well). Eastward
lie Herne Bay, an old-fashioned Victorian resort, and Reculver's twin towers –
Norman, but within the remains of a great Roman fort, overlooking the sea.
Westward, historic Faversham is particularly worth exploring.

Readers' comments: Very friendly owners, excellent food.

★ **WOLD FARM** C D PT S
Old, Northamptonshire, NN6 9RJ   Tel: 0604 781258
South-west of Kettering. Nearest main road: A43 from Northampton to
Kettering.

6 Bedrooms. £15 (less for 3 nights). Some
have own bath/shower/toilet. Tea/coffee
facilities. TV. Views of garden. Washing
machine on request.
Dinner. £10 for 4 courses, wine and coffee,
at 7pm. Vegetarian or special diets if
ordered. Wine can be brought in. **Light
suppers** if ordered.
2 Sitting-rooms. With open fire, central
heating, TV, record-player. Billiards.
Garden

This 18th-century house has particularly attractive and spacious rooms, and two
delightful gardens with rose pergola, golden pheasants and swing-seat. A garden-
house has recently been converted to provide more bedrooms, one of which is on
the ground floor. Throughout the house are attractive fabrics and wallpapers; one
bedroom in Japanese style, another with rosebuds, and a third using 'Country
Manor' pattern on walls, bed and curtains. In the sitting-room are alcoves of
Hummel figures, in the dining-room a carved 17th-century sideboard, and in the
breakfast-room a dresser with the exhortation: 'Nourish thyself with lively
vivacity'. Window-seats, antiques and white-panelled doors add further character
to the rooms. Throughout, standards are of the highest.

The house is at the heart of a beef and arable farm.

For dinner, Anne Engler serves – in an oak-beamed dining-room with inglenook fireplace – such meals as a quiche or fish salad followed by a roast joint and
then perhaps profiteroles or lemon meringue pie, and cheeses – with a sherry, wine
or beer included. Anne (once a 'Tiller girl') is a most warm and welcoming hostess.

A feature of the rolling agricultural landscape round here is the network of 18th-
and 19th-century canals, and the reservoirs (now naturalized) that were built to
top up the water in these. At Stoke Bruerne a waterways museum tells the whole
story of the canals, and you can take boat trips. The many stately homes include
Althorp (childhood home of the Princess of Wales) and Boughton House (mod-
elled on Versailles). There are Saxon churches at Brixworth and Earls Barton. The
county is famous for its high-spired churches and for its many historical associations: it has two 'Eleanor Crosses' erected in the 13th century by Edward I
wherever his wife's coffin rested on its journey to burial in Westminster Abbey;
Fotheringhay is where Mary Queen of Scots was executed; Cromwell defeated
Charles I's army at Naseby in 1645 (good bar food at the Fitzgerald Arms, and a
museum of the battle). In the Nene Valley is a scenic steam railway.

Looking at all the things there are to see and do – interesting to children and
adults alike – it seemed to me that staying here would be a very good all-weather
alternative to a traditional seaside holiday for the family. There's a live museum of
roundabouts and organs, for instance, near Northampton; several water gardens
and bird gardens; and Wicksteed Park is famous for its playground amusements.

In autumn, Blakesley village has a soap-box 'grand prix' and Ashton world
conker championships.

Readers' comments: Cooking outstanding. Very thoughtful attention.

De Courcy Road, Moult Hill, Salcombe, Devon, TQ8 8LQ
Tel: 054884 2778
South of Kingsbridge. Nearest main road: A381 from Salcombe to Totnes.

rear view

6 Bedrooms. £18–£24 (less for 7 nights). Prices go up in May. Some have own bath/shower/toilet. Tea/coffee facilities. TV. Views of garden, country, sea. Balcony (some). Washing machine on request.
Dinner. £13 for 5 courses (with choices) and coffee, at 7.30pm. Vegetarian or special diets if ordered. Wine can be ordered. **Light suppers** if ordered.
1 Sitting-room. With open fire, central heating, piano, record-player.
Small garden

One of the most spectacular sites in this book is occupied by a turn-of-the-century house which seems almost to hang in the air, so steep is the wooded cliff below it. One looks straight down onto the pale golden beach of South Sands (a small cove), and the blue waters of Salcombe estuary with the English Channel beyond. Rocky headlands stretch into the distance. To make the most of this exceptional view, some bedrooms have balconies and the elegant L-shaped sitting-room has huge windows that open onto a paved terrace (sometimes meals are served on a verandah). One can walk through the garden to a steep woodland footpath which goes down to the sands – but what a climb up again! – and from there take the ferry to Salcombe. Sometimes visitors can borrow a boat.

Bedrooms, on two floors, have different styles. No. 1 is all pink and white. No. 2 has a sensational bay window framing a view of the estuary. No. 3, a single, is very pretty: Laura Ashley festoon blinds and wallpaper, pine panelled doors. No. 4, with bamboo furniture and a turquoise-and-cream colour scheme, has a balcony; as does No. 5, with four-poster and outsize bathroom. No. 6 is level with a small lawn.

In the dining-room (handsomely furnished with velvet chairs, white-gold Minton china and linen napkins), Pat Vaissière serves candlelit dinners that use much local produce – such as cheese-filled eggs, lamb with apricot-and-almond stuffing, chocolate rum trifle, and cheeses. Rolls are home-baked.

Salcombe is Devon's southernmost resort, and arguably its most beautiful one. Even orange and lemon trees grow here which, together with palms, remind one of parts of the Mediterranean. The estuary is very popular for sailing, garden-lovers come to see Sharpitor (NT), walkers make for the viewpoints of Bolbery Down and Bolt Head. All along the coast from here to Plymouth are picturesque waterfront villages, such as Bantham and Newton Ferrers, described elsewhere. In the opposite direction are Kingsbridge (old market town), the long stretch of Slapton Sands (nature reserve, with lagoons), picturesque Dartmouth (of outstanding historical interest – two castles, quaint quays, elaborately carved woodwork on buildings, the Royal Naval College, river trips, two ferries).

Readers' comments: Outstanding standards. They go out of their way to provide that little bit extra at every turn. Made to feel so much at home. Worth coming for the food alone! Lovely site; delighted. Superb comfort, food and hospitality.

WOODCOTE MANOR

C S

Bramdean, Hampshire, SO24 0LL   Tel: 0962771 793
East of Winchester. Nearest main road: A272 from Winchester to Petersfield.

TV. Views of garden, country. No smoking. Washing machine on request.
Dinner. £12 for 3 courses and coffee, at 8pm. Non-residents not admitted. Wine can be ordered or brought in. No smoking. **Light suppers** if ordered.
2 Sitting-rooms. With open fire, central heating, TV, piano, record-player. No smoking.
Large garden

3 Bedrooms. £15–£20. Bargain breaks. All have own bath/toilet. Tea/coffee facilities. **Closed from November to March inclusive.**

In July 1554, Philip II of Spain arrived (in the pouring rain) at Winchester for his marriage to Mary Tudor. She had spent the previous night at this house; and must have been more tense than most brides, for there had been a Commons' petition against the Spanish marriage, and a plot to depose her before it could take place. (Nor was she popular with Philip's courtiers either, who called her 'old and flabby, no eyebrows . . . it would take God himself to drink this cup.') Today's visitors who occupy her room may sleep more happily than she did that night.

Woodcote Manor is one of the most outstanding houses in this book. At its heart is a 14th-century building to which additions were made in Tudor and Jacobean times, with alterations in the 18th century, and a further – very handsome – extension made in 1911. Caroline McLaughlan and her family live in one part of the house, and it is her husband's paintings which hang on many of the walls. Her mother Marguerite Morton lives in the other part, and she also takes paying guests.

One enters a great hall, panelled and with elaborately plastered ceiling. On the floor of black and white marble tiles stands a huge mediaeval table which was made for the refectory of a monastery; an 18th-century Flemish cradle now nurses pot-plants. The panelled sitting/dining-room is lined with books; leather chairs are grouped round the fireplace. From this room there are good views of the grounds (which include a grass tennis court and a swimming-pool in a walled garden). The garden is opened to the public every Easter, when wild daffodils in the woods are at their best and the trees just coming into leaf; it has a number of copper beeches and a 'handkerchief tree'.

A very long sitting-room has tall sash windows and window-seats deep-set in its pale blue walls; a marble fireplace; and Florentine cabinet with birds and flowers inlaid. Crystal sconces light the room, which has velvet sofas and a grand piano. At the back is a large dining-room dominated by a panel of Dutch oak carved with a scene of the Israelites escaping from Egypt.

A handsome staircase leads up to bedrooms including the one used by Mary Tudor before her wedding. Oak-panelled, it has a splendid fireplace that was specially installed for her visit. There is a very attractive attic suite with leaded casements which would be ideal for a family. Caroline has chosen attractive contrasts of colours and textures – white flokati rugs on polished oak floors; white cane bedheads with aquamarine walls and redcurrant curtains.

As to dinner, this is always based on the farm's own produce. A typical menu: spinach soup, roast pheasant, blackcurrant sorbet, cheeses.

349

★ **WOODMANS GREEN FARM**
Woodmans Green, West Sussex, GU30 7NF Tel: 042876 250
North of Midhurst. Nearest main road: A3 from Guildford to Petersfield.

3 Bedrooms. £14–£16. Bargain breaks. Some have own shower/toilet. Tea/coffee facilities. TV. Views of garden, country. No smoking. Washing machine on request. **Dinner.** £10 for 3 courses (with choices) and coffee, at 7.30pm. Non-residents not admitted. Vegetarian or special diets if ordered. Wine can be brought in. No smoking. **Light suppers** if ordered. **2 Sitting-rooms.** With open fire, central heating, TV, piano, record-player. No smoking. **Large garden.** Heated swimming-pool.

This Tudor house has interesting features of the period, which include a particularly grand staircase, stone-mullioned windows in the gable, low doorways (on which Mary Spreckley drapes swags of dried flowers) and, in the farmyard, an unusual roofed and brick-walled midden.

Mary Spreckley has furnished the rooms with style. Bedrooms are attractive and in the elegant sitting-room, where pale colours predominate, are chinoiserie chintz sofas, a Steinway grand piano and handsome iron firebacks.

By arrangement, Mary – who is a very good cook – will prepare either a full dinner (such as carrot-and-orange soup, chicory-stuffed chicken with blue cheese sauce, and apple flan with cream) or a light supper (such as cauliflower cheese).

This very attractive area around Haslemere, Petersfield and Petworth is a good base from which to visit Chichester, Fishbourne Roman palace, Petworth House, and the Weald and Downland open-air museum of ancient buildings.

Readers' comments: Friendly atmosphere, cooking imaginative and attractively served; very pleasant indeed.

A large woodland garden screens **CUMBERS HOUSE** at Rogate (tel: 0730 821401) from the road, and beyond are fine downland views. Each bedroom is spacious, has large casement windows, and is pleasantly furnished. In the green-and-grey sitting-room there are pretty trifles around and guests are welcome to play on the mellow, well-tuned Schiedmeyer piano. Prue Aslett serves excellent breakfasts: bread is home-baked; eggs are home-produced. Non-smokers preferred. There are many good eating-places nearby. £16.

rear view

Readers' comments: Full of praise – maximum stars! Delightful hospitality.

YEW TREE COTTAGE   C(5)

Baybridge, Hampshire, SO21 1JN   Tel: 096274 254
South-east of Winchester. Nearest main road: A33 from Winchester to
Southampton.

2 Bedrooms. £15–£17.50. Prices go up in
March. Bargain breaks. Tea/coffee facilities.
TV. Views of garden, country. No smoking.
Washing machine on request.
Dinner. £12 for 3 courses and coffee. Non-
residents not admitted. Vegetarian or special
diets if ordered. Wine can be ordered or
brought in. No smoking. **Light suppers** if
ordered.
1 Sitting-room. With open fire, central heating, TV. No smoking.
Small garden

Tucked away in pretty countryside is a little lattice-paned, thatched cottage dating
from the 17th century. There are – of course! – roses round the door and
wood-smoke curling up from the chimney whenever a fire is alight in the big
inglenook which dominates June Coombe's little sitting-room. This has carved
bergère chairs, low beams and, beyond it, a small staircase winding up to two
pleasant blue-and-white bedrooms with furniture painted by her daughter and a
shower room between them. Mrs Coombe does not take more than one family (or
party) at a time, and they have sole use of sitting- and dining-room. She used to be a
professional cook, so dinner here is well above average with menus such as trout
pâté and salad, chicken breasts in wine, cream and mushrooms; and peaches with
raspberry sauce.

Nearby Winchester was England's capital in the days of King Alfred (indeed, it
had been a considerable town long before that, during the long Roman occupation). Kings were crowned – and buried – here. The Norman cathedral
dominates all, its most famous bishop – William of Wykeham – being the founder
of one of England's great public schools, Winchester College (which can be
visited), and of Oxford's New College. There are the remains of two castles here,
the Bishop's Palace, and a new 'Crusades Experience' with animated models,
sounds and so forth. The byways in the heart of the city are full of ancient
buildings, in one of which Jane Austen lived at the end of her life. Main streets are
partly colonnaded, there is a statue of King Alfred, pleasant gardens and walks to
take you along the riverside or the remaining walls. And at 8pm a bell sounds
curfew every day. As well as several museums there is a Great Hall housing what
was once reputed to be King Arthur's round table. And all around are, as Keats
said, 'the most beautiful streams I ever saw, full of trout'.

St Swithin, best known for a weather legend, was Bishop of Winchester in the
9th century when the town was capital of the kingdom of Wessex – the most
important of all England's kingdoms then. A century after his death, his remains
were moved from the cemetery he had chosen into the cathedral – whereupon,
although it was July, a prolonged and heavy rainstorm occurred. Hence the
superstition which lingers on, that if it rains on St Swithin's Day it will go on
raining for forty days: improbable, even for an English summer!

Eastward, in the Petersfield direction, is rolling downland and, in one of the
valleys, the very lovely village of East Meon, threaded by a clear stream and with a
fine church. Northward lies the loveliest valley of all where the River Itchen
wanders; and the pleasant old town of Alresford.

West Knighton, Dorset, DT2 8PE   Tel: 0305 852087
South-east of Dorchester. Nearest main road: A352 from Dorchester to Wareham.

2 **Bedrooms.** £12.50–£14.50 (less for 7 nights). Prices go up in March. Tea/coffee facilities. TV. Views of garden, country. No smoking. Washing machine on request.
Dinner. £10.50 for 3 courses and coffee, at 7.30pm. Non-residents not admitted. Vegetarian or special diets if ordered. Wine can be brought in. No smoking. **Light suppers** if ordered.
1 **Sitting-room.** With open fire, TV. No smoking.
Large garden

In every room of this picturesque cottage, all whitewash and thatch, are terracotta sheep or pigs, little houses or trees – which both Furse and Rosemary Swann make in their studio at the back. (There is a garden-house with a display of them for sale.) 'Becoming redundant was one of the best things that happened to me', says Furse, who changed career in mid-life (he previously taught English).

The great beam over one of the inglenook fireplaces carries the date 1622. Rooms are low and white-walled, the staircases narrow and steep, floors stone-flagged, windows small and deep-set. Until 50 years ago, the cottage was divided: a carter living in one end, a shepherd at the other.

The Swanns have filled the house with an immensely varied collection of treasures, from 19th-century glass paintings of bulls to modern abstracts, pictures of Borzoi dogs by Weschke and prints by Munch to a portrait of 'Mrs Darling' (in *Peter Pan*) by a great-uncle. There is a collection of green Bristol glass and another of Breton plates, a splendid samovar of Polish brass, odd-shaped pebbles from the nearby beach at Ringstead, rag rugs and Victorian raised-cotton bedspreads, metal animals by an award-winning sculptor whose work they spotted in India . . . in every room there is a visual feast. Bedrooms are equally attractive (the bathroom is on the ground floor).

The large garden is a romantic spot, with flagged paths wandering among cottage flowers, hedges separating one secret spot from another.

Rosemary produces not only imaginative dishes of her own (for instance, pork tenderloin with water chestnuts in a sweet-sour cream sauce, or trout fillets with ginger and dill) but also a number of specialities from Sweden, where she lived for many years. Furse prepares breakfasts, which can include such unusual options as scrambled eggs on anchovy toast; and he makes all the jams.

Next door is the 18th-century New Inn where you may enjoy a drink with the locals – among them a long-retired postman who knew Thomas Hardy when he owned the house opposite Yoah Cottage; in his days as an architect, Hardy restored West Knighton's church.

In this western part of Dorset, a lovely area, you will find Hardy's birthplace, 'Egdon Heath', an exciting coastline, the market town of Dorchester, archaeological sites and a great many literary associations in addition to 'Hardy country'.

Readers' comments: Most beautiful and characterful. Warm and welcoming, most interesting people. Comfortable and extremely well fed.

ALPHABETICAL DIRECTORY OF HOUSES AND HOTELS IN
WALES

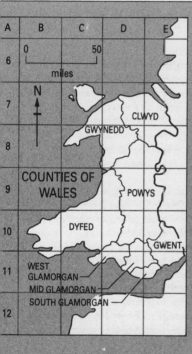

COUNTIES OF WALES

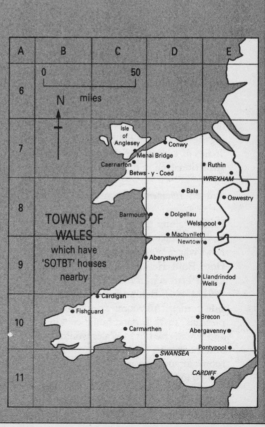

TOWNS OF WALES
which have 'SOTBT' houses nearby

★ **BRON HEULOG**   C D PT X
Waterfall Road, Llanrhaeadr-ym-Mochnant, Clwyd, SY10 0JX
Tel: 069189 521
North of Welshpool (Powys). Nearest main road: A490 from Welshpool to
Llanfyllin.

3 Bedrooms. £11.50–£12 (less for 7 nights). Tea/coffee facilities. TV. Views of garden, country. Washing machine on request.
Dinner. £6.50 for 3 courses and coffee, at 6–8pm. Non-residents not admitted. Vegetarian or special diets if ordered. Wine can be brought in.
1 Sitting-room. With open fire, central heating, TV, piano, record-player.
Large garden

There is an especially lovely drive through hills, moors and woods from Bala to the Tanat Valley. Here, on the way to the country's highest waterfall is this handsome stone house of 1861 which, as its name (*bron*) suggests, is on a hillside.

Lorraine Pashen has filled it with her collection of antiques, oil-paintings and Blüthner grand piano: the curving staircase is almost an art gallery. One bedroom, with prettily draped bedhead, looks onto the unusual tortuosa willow (as depicted on willow-pattern plates). Lorraine's dinners include dishes like avocado mousse, sweet/sour pork, and home-made rum-and-raisin ice cream, served on Wedgwood's Florentine china in a blue and gold dining-room with crystal chandeliers and 17th-century portraits.

Llanrhaeadr, surrounded by the Berwyn Mountains, is very near the English border, Offa's Dyke and the Shropshire towns of Shrewsbury and Oswestry. Of its famous waterfall George Borrow wrote: 'I never saw water falling so gracefully, so much like thin beautiful threads, as here.' In the opposite direction lie Lakes Vyrnwy and Bala (described elsewhere) and Llangollen (on the way to which, call at Llanarmon's curious church with two pulpits), home every July to the world-famous international *eisteddfod*. Salmon leap beneath its 14th-century bridge over the Dee (one of the 'seven wonders of Wales'), castles crown the peaks surrounding the vale. In the richly carved church of St Collen's are buried the 18th-century 'ladies of Llangollen' whose black-and-white house, Plas Newydd, was a tourist attraction even in their day. From here one can take a canal boat or steam train.

Readers' comments: Rooms, food, hostess a delight. Best meals I had.

Further along the beautiful and little-known Tanat Valley is Pen-y-Bont-Fawr where Welsh is regularly spoken. Here Enid Henderson and her niece live at 17th-century **GLYNDWR** (tel: 069174 430). Behind is a pretty riverside garden. All rooms are simple but pleasant, there is good home cooking, and where else but in Wales would you find bedrooms with their own bathrooms at such reasonable rates? From £10.50 to £11.50.

Readers' comments: Superb meals, cosy and warm.

BRONANT

CDSX

Bontnewydd, Gwynedd, LL54 7YF   Tel: 0286 830451
South of Caernarfon. Nearest main road: A487 from Porthmadog to
Caernarfon.

3 Bedrooms. £12–£15 (less for 2 nights).
Prices go up in June. Bargain breaks. Tea/
coffee facilities. Views of garden, country,
sea. No smoking. Washing machine on
request.
Light suppers if ordered. Vegetarian or
special diets. Wine can be brought in. No
smoking.
2 Sitting-rooms. With open fire, central
heating, TV, organ. No smoking.
Large garden

On the north side of the Lleyn peninsula (looking over the Menai Strait to
Anglesey) is Bronant, a handsome Victorian house, kept in immaculate order by
Megan Williams and her nieces who run a tea-room here. Their traditional Welsh
teas are really authentic: the gingerbread, *bara brith* (speckled bread) and Welsh
cakes regularly take first prizes at county shows. Bedrooms are spacious, with
Welsh tapestry bedspreads in rich colours and views of sheep, pine trees and
mountains. Some windows have stained glass depicting apples and pears,
appropriate to a house where good, natural food excels.

The peninsula is one of the most Welsh parts of Wales, with the native language
still very much alive. It has wild and dramatic scenery inland, sandy beaches along
its shores – many secluded. Past Trefer (near where a 1700-foot mountain looms
above the sea, deserted quarries cut into its sides) are the secret valley of Nant
Gwrtheyrn, a shadowy place of old legends, and the Lleyn's highest peak – Yr Eifl.
Porth Nefyn is a particularly long and lovely bay with a safe, sandy beach and
clifftop walks; and still further west you can find the 'whistling sands' of Porth Oer
(at times, the grains of sand squeak when you walk on them). Right at the end of
the Lleyn is Mynydd Mawr, a National Trust headland with coastal views
comparable to those of Cornwall's Land's End. Over two miles of choppy waters
lies Bardsey Island (known to pilgrims as the isle of 20,000 saints).

Along the south coast, in a wilderness of subtropical flowers, are the little manor
house (part mediaeval) of Plas-yn-Rhiw; another great bay – Porth Neigwl,
otherwise known as Hell's Mouth because of the treacherous rocks on which so
many ships foundered; and Abersoch, a busy little harbour, near which is the
showpiece village of Llangian. Seek out the old part of Pwllheli to find a Georgian
arcade and canopied Victorian shops in sharp contrast to the popular modern
attractions of this resort. Penarth Fawr is a rare survival, a stone hall house –
basically one great room in which family and servants all dwelt together in the 15th
century. A mossy stone path leads to the clear waters of St Cybi's well, behind
Llangybi village; and at Brynkir you can see traditional Welsh cloth being woven
in the watermill.

The Lleyn's most famous village is, of course, Portmeirion, an Italianate
waterside fantasy designed by Sir Clough Williams-Ellis in 1925. Every
architectural style, and every colour of the rainbow, seems to be represented here:
Sir Clough himself described it as a 'gay, light opera sort of a place'. There are
paths and gardens from which to enjoy the scene.

Finally, beyond Porthmadog (harbour, maritime museum, narrow-gauge railway up the mountains, pottery and other crafts) are sand dunes and caves.

BRONIWAN

Rhydlewis, Dyfed, SA44 5PF   Tel: 023975 261

CDSX

East of Cardigan. Nearest main road: A487 from Cardigan to Aberystwyth.

3 Bedrooms. £17 (less for 4 nights). Bargain breaks. Some have own bath/shower/toilet. Tea/coffee facilities. TV. Views of garden, country. No smoking. Washing machine on request.
Dinner. £7 for 3 courses (with choices) and coffee, at 7–7.30pm. Non-residents not admitted. Vegetarian or special diets if ordered. Wine can be brought in. No smoking. **Light suppers** if ordered.
1 Sitting-room. With open fire, central heating, TV, piano, record-player. No smoking.
Large garden

On a rocky hillside (*bron*) stands an ivy-clad, grey stone house, sheltered by beech trees and looking across to the Frenni Fawr Hills were Pwyll, prince of Dyfed, fell in love with a lady in gold brocade riding a pale horse and made her his bride: 'The countenance of every maiden he had seen was unlovely compared with her countenance.'

It was built in 1867, with much use of pitch-pine (this is a distinctive wood, imported from America in Victorian times), for doors and the panelling of its big bay windows. Outside a decorative white iron fence encloses the front garden.

Carole and Allen Jacobs combine farming with teaching English. They have Aberdeen Angus beef-cattle, sheep, hens and a vegetable garden – all of which supply their table and in the care of which visitors are welcome to join if they wish (there is a donkey too). The rooms are very pleasantly furnished with, for instance, striped wallpaper, Welsh tapestry bedspreads, modern watercolours and old Staffordshire pottery figures. On chilly evenings they light a log stove which stands in the stone fireplace. Below the terrace is a barn now equipped as a playroom with paints, books, games and a record-player.

A typical dinner: watercress soufflé, New Quay mackerel in oatmeal (with garden vegetables and a salad of cucumber and yogurt), pears in white wine.

Broniwan is well placed for a holiday full of varied interest. In one direction is the long sandy coastline around great Cardigan Bay, dotted with such pleasant little fishing villages as Aberaeron and Llangrannog and with seals to be seen; while inland are hill walks among gorse and heather where butterflies and buzzards fly. There are old market towns along the banks of the River Teifi, waterfalls (and fishermen in coracles) at Cenarth and a mill at Cwm Cou. The ruins of Cilgerran Castle are perched high on a rocky spur above the river gorge: Turner was one of many artists to paint the great circular towers and gatehouse which still stand, along with crumbling but massive outer walls built by the Normans – Owain Glyndwr devastated it when he led his great revolt in 1405.

Cardiganshire is the place to go if you like wide open spaces. The windswept moors, where skylarks soar, rise up towards 2000-foot peaks and along the way are views to far horizons. It is a great area for birdwatchers who may spot kestrels, red grouse and even the rare kites. This is one of the least populated parts of Britain, except in the leafy valleys or at resorts along the coastline of cliffs, coves and golden beaches. There is no industry to mar the scene but plenty of craft workshops.

356

BWLCH COCH

CDSX

Llanwrthwl, Powys, LD1 6NY   Tel: 0597 810985

West of Llandrindod Wells. Nearest main road: A44 from Leominster to
Rhayader.

6 Bedrooms. £16–£19.50 (less for 6 nights).
Bargain breaks. Some have own bath/
shower/toilet. Tea/coffee facilities. TV.
Views of garden, country. No smoking.
Washing machine on request.
Dinner. £11 for 3 courses (with choices) and
coffee, at 7–8pm. Vegetarian or special
diets if ordered. Wine can be ordered. No
smoking. **Light suppers** if ordered.
1 Sitting-room. With open fire, central heating. Bar. No smoking.
Large garden.
**Closed from December to March
inclusive.**

If ever a house lived up to the title of this book, Bwlch Coch ('the red pass') is it.
High over the mountains, Cistercian monks making their way from the distant
abbey of Strata Florida to that of Abbey Cwmhir established a long footpath which
became known as the Monks' Trod – a delight to walkers today because, ascending
to open moorland at 1600 feet, it passes through an area of true wilderness with
superb views as you go. Rare birds nest here (there is an RSPB sanctuary) and the
wind blows free where once there were oak forests – felled by the monks to provide
grazing for black-faced sheep. Along their route, six centuries ago, the monks
built this halfway house at which to rest overnight.

Jenny Standen has greatly extended it and filled it with family treasures: flower
paintings by her artist grandmother, a portrait of a great-great-aunt, and one of
ancestor James Paine (related to Tom Paine – author of *The Rights of Man*). In the
sitting-room with its floor of massive slabs, ancient and blackened cooking-pots
still hang over the log fire. Upstairs are sloping floors and low, tiny windows. But
there is also a modern extension where, lying in bed, you can look through sliding
glass doors to a view of the heather-clad hills.

Jenny's dinners comprise such dishes as courgette soup, beef cooked in beer,
and blackcurrant crumble.

Readers' comments: Full of atmosphere, excellent bedrooms, wonderful scenery. A
perfect gem, will go there again.

18th-century **ARGOED FAWR**,
Llanwrthwl (off the Newbridge road),
was once owned by James Watt, of
steam-engine fame. It is now the home
of Maureen Maltby; and although old
features have been retained – such as a
ham rack, great salting table, slab
floors and slate hearths – every room is
comfortable and immaculate; the bathroom is excellent. Breakfast choices
often include kidneys, black pudding
and Ayr haddock. Supper is a help-
yourself buffet of such things as

chicken, salmon, quiches and pâtés.
Spring water. (Tel: 059789 451.) £8 to
£14.

Readers' comments: Delightful. Nicest
ever visited. Breakfast fit for a king!

CEFN
Tyn-y-Groes, Gwynedd, LL32 8TA Tel: 0492 650233
South of Conwy. Nearest main road: B5106 from Conwy to Llanrwst.

2 Bedrooms. £14. All have own bath/toilet. Tea/coffee facilities. TV. Views of garden, country, mountains, river.

1 Sitting-room. With central heating. **Large garden** **Closed from November until Easter.**

Up the River Conwy, one can head for the hills and this well secluded, white, 17th-century house (*cefn* means ridge). It is surrounded by lawns with camellias and magnolias, from which to enjoy superb views of Snowdonia and of the valley below (there is also a glass-roofed verandah, and a summer house). The huge sitting/dining-room (with slate inglenook fireplace) has pink-cut velvet sofa and chairs, white walls and big beams; casements open onto the verandah. There are handsome bathrooms and most bedrooms are exceptionally spacious and well decorated, with thick carpets, superb views and armchairs. (*Detailed directions are essential, as is booking well ahead.*) B & b only.

Conwy, still surrounded by mediaeval walls, lies to the north of the Snowdonia National Park, its great 13th-century castle (there are 29 towers around its ramparts) dominating the estuary. The valley that runs inland, following the River Conwy, goes to the mountain village of Betws-y-Coed, described elsewhere, and onward high up to a vast slate mine where one can go on an underground tram (or take a coach to the high dam and power station of Stwlan). One of Wales' famous, little single-track trains runs up this valley, a beautiful route and a relaxed way to journey along it. The train departs from Llandudno, the biggest of many resorts along the sandy north coast, which has a cable railway to the viewpoint of Great Orme Head Cove (one can walk down through Happy Valley, planted with rare flowers and trees). There are two historic bridges along the way, one by Telford (1826) and the other by Robert Stephenson (1848).

The River Conwy is at first wide and calm, later sparkling and boulder-strewn. On the east side is one of Britain's most famous gardens, Bodnant, its 90 acres sloping down towards the waterside. At Llanrwst (where there is a bridge by Inigo Jones and Tudor Gwydir castle among other points of interest), one can head eastward to see the ancient and diminutive cathedral of St Asaph, a deer park, and Cefn Caves where once prehistoric men and beasts lived. Or, if you follow the road along the west side of the river, you will come to the tiny spa of Trefriw and its woollen mill; and to Llanbedr-y-cennin, which has a cosy 13th-century inn with good views. There are fine drives to some of Snowdonia's most dramatic viewpoints, via such mountain villages as Capel Curig, Pen-y-Gwryd, Beddgelert and Llanberis (from which a rail track goes to the top of Snowdon). Bethesda is in a particularly spectacular part.

358

THE CLOISTERS　　　　　　　　　　　　　　　C(10) **D PT S**
Llanvihangel Crucorney, Gwent, NP7 8DH　Tel: 0873 890738
North of Abergavenny. Nearest main road: A465 from Abergavenny to
Hereford.

Tea/coffee facilities. TV. Views of garden,
country. No smoking. Washing machine on
request.
Dinner. £12.50 for 4 courses (with choices)
and coffee. Non-residents not admitted.
Vegetarian or special diets if ordered. Wine
can be ordered. No smoking. **Light suppers**
if ordered.
1 Sitting-room. With open fire, central heating, TV, record-player. Bar.
Large garden

2 **Bedrooms.** £15 (less for 5 nights). Bargain
breaks. All have own bath/shower/toilet.

**Closed from November to February
inclusive.**

Despite the monastic-sounding name, this house in the Brecon Beacons National
Park has a very different history. It began life as the cottage of the coachman who
drove the gentry of Llanvihangel Court, a great Tudor mansion close by. In later
centuries it was extended but still has such ancient features as leaded panes in
stone-mullioned windows.

It is a particularly pretty house, approached by a flagstone path through
brimming flowerbeds. In the garden at the back Lynda McCarthy occasionally
serves a barbecue meal (swordfish as well as meats).

From the sitting-room, with cretonne sofas facing a log fire, a white staircase
ascends to one of the attractive bedrooms, apricot and white with handsome
built-in cupboards of mahogany. Another staircase (steep, and with walls of
rugged stone) rises from the dining-room to a second bedroom which is almost a
private suite, for adjoining the room itself (brass bed, Victorian furniture and
cottage-garden curtains) is a sitting area with sofa-bed and very good bathroom.

Lynda, who enjoys cooking and uses vegetables from the garden, serves such
dinners as a pâté made from mackerel and sour cream, lamb guard-of-honour with
onion sauce, and fresh fruit brûlée. Vegetarian dishes too. Meals are served in a
stone-walled dining-room with log stove and a dresser of china, on embroidered
tablecloths laid with blue-and-white Spode.

Only a few yards away is the famous Skirrid Inn; at 900 years old, the most
ancient in Wales and possibly in Britain. Upstairs was a courtroom and from a high
beam above the great oak stair it is known that at least 200 sheep-stealers brought
to trial here were hanged: the first such record is dated 1110. Did Shakespeare get
his idea for Puck (in *Midsummer Night's Dream*) when visiting this inn? For
centuries it was customary to leave a brimming 'pwycca jug' on the doorstep to
appease a mischievous neighbourhood spirit. The Skirrid was where the Welsh
hero Owaîn Glyndwr rallied his troops before battle, and the mounting-stone from
which he got onto his horse still stands outside. Within, the flagstone floor and
ancient beams are still just as in his time.

Readers' comments: Decor, setting and service superb. Excellent value.

For explanation of code letters (C, D, H, PT, S, X) see page xxxiv.

CWMTWRCH   **C D H X**
Nantgaredig, Dyfed, SA32 7NY   Tel: 0267290 238
North-east of Carmarthen. Nearest main road: A40 from Carmarthen to
Llandeilo.

6 Bedrooms. £18. Prices go up at Easter.
Bargain breaks. All have own bath/shower/
toilet. 3 have tea/coffee facilities. TV. Views
of garden, country. Washing machine on
request.
Dinner. £11.50 for 4 courses (with choices)
and coffee, from 7.30pm. Vegetarian or
special diets if ordered. Wine can be
ordered. **Light suppers** if ordered.
2 Sitting-rooms. With open fire, TV,
record-player. No smoking. **Bar.**
Large garden

The name of this farmhouse-turned-hotel means 'valley of the wild boar'. Nothing
so wild now disturbs the peace of this civilized spot where Jenny Willmott and her
husband have transformed a group of old farm buildings with great sensitivity.
The dining-room (an excellent restaurant) has stone walls painted white, slate
floor, boarded roof above, and grey Paisley cloths on the tables. At one side, her
kitchen is open to view; on the other is a glass wall overlooking the courtyard, pots
of begonias and busy Lizzies, and sheep fields beyond. The food is exceptional.
Stuffed mushrooms (with garlic and cheese), followed by individual fish pies
(salmon etc. under puff-pastry) or very tender venison, with vegetables imaginatively cooked; and a flan of grapes with sponge and almond topping were among
the varied choices when I stayed. There are a small bar and two sitting-rooms: all
with interesting and lovely objects, paintings and pottery (for sale). Bedrooms (full
of character) are in the house or (at ground level) in former stables.

Readers' comments: Excellent. Charming owners. Superb cooking. Marvellous.
Most comfortable, made to feel at home. Food excellent.

Also in this area is Llanpumsaint and
FFERM-Y-FELIN or 'mill farm' (tel:
0267 253498 after 7pm), the 18th-
century home of Anne and David
Ryder-Owen: a place of particular
interest to birdwatchers. David, a keen
ornithologist, can tell you where to spot
pied fly-catchers, buzzards and even
the rare red kite. Beyond the dining-
room is a sitting-room so large that it
has a fireplace at each end; pink buttoned velvet sofas and a walnut piano
contrast with rugged stone walls. Anne

serves such meals as corn-on-the-cob,
wild trout with home-grown vegetables, and apple crumble.

This would be a good place for a
family holiday: the children's bedroom
(with toys) has a picture-window overlooking the lake and its waterfowl, and
there is a pet donkey as well as other
livestock. Prospective visitors can borrow a video of the farm and vicinity.
Non-smokers preferred. From £14 to
£16.

★ **CYFIE FARM**   **C**

Llanfihangel, Powys, SY22 5JE   Tel: 069184 451
North-west of Welshpool. Nearest main road: A490 from Welshpool to
Llanfyllin.

toilet. Tea/coffee facilities. TV. Views of
garden, country. Washing machine on
request.
Dinner. £8 for 3 courses (with choices) and
coffee, at 6.45–7pm. Non-residents not
admitted. Vegetarian or special diets if
ordered. Wine can be brought in. **Light
suppers** if ordered.
2 Sitting-rooms. With open fire, central
heating, TV, record-player. No smoking.
Small garden

3 Bedrooms. £13–£18 (less for 7 nights).
Bargain breaks. All have own bath/shower/

Close to the English (Shropshire) border is a picturesque hillside longhouse of
stone with a very pretty garden: as romantic a place as you could wish, and near
scenic Lake Vyrnwy. Outside is an old pump, trellis porch and busy Lizzies bright
against the old stonework. From a slate-paved terrace, one looks down into the
Meifod Valley far below.

Inside, all is low beams, narrow stairs, nooks and crannies (except in the
stable suite, a more modern conversion, with its own sitting/dining-room).

This is a beautifully kept house, which Lynn Jenkins has furnished attractively,
with pleasant fabrics and wallpapers, pewter plates arrayed on an old Welsh
dresser in the dining-room, pot-plants and antiques in the sitting-room. She is an
excellent cook of traditional meals using farm produce. Visitors have been known
to stay three weeks at Cyfie – not once but repeatedly – in this surprisingly
little-known part of Wales. Some take part in the activities of the 200-acre
stock-rearing farm or simply walk the nearby hills which are full of wildlife.

Lake Vyrnwy is not only picturesque but surrounded by 5000 acres of woods.
At the foot of grouse moors one finds Pistyll Rhaeadr, the country's highest
waterfall. There is another lovely lake at Bala, ringed by mountains; and the sea
coast is only an hour away. Small villages, inns and agricultural shows add to the
interest of this very scenic area. Motoring is a traffic-free pleasure, alternating
between roads that feel as if on top of the world – heather, gorse or bracken all
around – and lanes that plunge deep into valleys.

Readers' comments: An island of peace and relaxation. Delightful hosts. Charm and
comfort.

Sitting-room at Cyfie Farm

DEWIS CYFARFOD C(8) **D H X**
Llandderfel, Gwynedd, LL23 7DR   Tel: 06783 243
North-east of Bala. Nearest main road: A494 from Corwen to Bala.

5 Bedrooms. £18–£23 (less for 7 nights). Bargain breaks. All have own bath/shower/toilet. Tea/coffee facilities. TV. Views of garden, country, river. Washing machine on request.
Dinner. £10 for 2 or £14.50 for 4 courses (with choices) and coffee, at 7.30pm. Vegetarian or special diets if ordered. Wine can be ordered.
1 Sitting-room. With open fire, central heating.
Large garden

On the way to beautiful Lake Bala is one of the most attractive houses I found in Wales, Dewis Cyfarfod – 'the chosen meeting-place'. Drovers used to meet at this spot where road and river converge, a convenient place to water their livestock. Now the pair of 17th-century cottages is the elegant home of Peter and Barbara Reynolds, furnished with antiques and pretty chintzes, good paintings and well-chosen colour schemes. The spacious sitting-room has groups of comfortable armchairs, a log fire, and panoramic valley views through its picture-windows, with the chance to spot squirrels, foxes and a great variety of birds. In one bedroom, William Morris's 'strawberry thief' fabric complements a white wall-paper with cherries, and other rooms are equally pretty – one with a walnut bed and wildflower fabric, another (in a ground-floor cottage close by) with an oyster and charcoal colour scheme. One bathroom is particularly sumptuous (two basins, royal blue and gold fittings), another has swags of flowers painted by Barbara.

The Reynolds also own a celebrated restaurant in Chester (Abbey Green), and so it is not surprising that meals here comprise such feasts as celery and lemon soup, beef braised with oranges and wine (accompanied by savoyard potatoes, Polish cauliflower and mange-tout peas), *fromage frais* with strawberries and then farmhouse cheeses – unless you prefer a light supper. One can eat on the terrace in fine weather, surrounded by pots and baskets brimming with flowers, or in the elegant dining-room; with silver, crystal and candles on the table.

Along the same road is a 13th-century watermill, **MELIN MELOCH** (tel: 0678 520101). From the tapestry armchairs in the sitting-room (quarry-tiled floor and four-foot thick stone walls) one gazes up past a series of galleries to the roof beams. Through an arch by the fireplace is a great table flanked by pews, where Beryl Fullard serves such meals as melon with port, lamb and five vegetables, apple crumble and cream. A trout pool in the garden provides fish for the table. Bedrooms – one on ground floor – are attractive, and there is a spacious family suite. Everywhere are lovely

arrangements of dried flowers and 'finds' such as a milkchurn and mangle colourfully repainted by Richard in between landscaping the large sun-trapping garden. From £13.50 to £16.

Readers' comments: Spectacular. Food and location excellent.

★ **DYSSERTH HOUSE**   **C(10) D PT S**
Powis Estate, Powys, SY21 8RQ   Tel: 0938 552153
South of Welshpool. Nearest main road: A483 from Welshpool to Newtown.

rear view

4 Bedrooms. £14–£17. Prices go up in June. Bargain breaks. All have own bath/shower/ toilet. Tea/coffee facilities. Views of garden, country, river. No smoking. Washing machine on request.
Dinner. £12 for 4 courses (with choices) and coffee, at 7.30–8pm. Non-residents not admitted. Vegetarian or special diets if ordered. Wine can be ordered or brought in. No smoking. **Light suppers** if ordered.
1 Sitting-room. With open fire, central heating, TV, piano, record-player.
Large garden
Closed from December to February inclusive (except for shooting parties).

A crag of red rock and a moat provided strong defences for 13th-century Powis Castle, from which the princes of Powis ruled much of Wales. The management of their descendants' estates was in the hands of Paul Marriott until he retired. His 18th-century manor house is close to the castle (now NT).

The house is furnished with fine antiques and Maureen's well chosen wallpapers and fabrics – delicate clematis paper in one bedroom, blue brocade on the walls of the dining-room, for instance. There are good paintings everywhere. Across a paved terrace with rosebuds one can enjoy the view to the Severn.

Dinner (by arrangement) may be a candlelit meal of avocado and prawns, Welsh lamb, meringues and cheeses.

On the other side of Welshpool, at
★ Trelydan, is mediaeval **BURNT HOUSE** (tel: 0938 2827). Above a big, open-plan sitting/dining-room with ample sofas are attractive bedrooms. For instance, one has a pink wall with exposed timbers and pretty walnut beds and its bathroom is outstanding – handsome textured tiles around the built-in bath. A coffee-and-white room has a view of the Berwyn Mountains beyond a lawn with big beds of brilliant nasturtiums. Tricia Wyke used to cook cakes professionally and so, after perhaps home-made pâté and pork fillet in a sauce of cream and sherry, one may be offered a spectacular gâteau or meringue confection. £14.

Readers' comments: Lovely views, welcoming hostess, excellent cook. Delightful, cooking admirable.

EYARTH STATION   C D H X
Llanfair-Dyffryn-Clwyd, Clwyd, LL15 2EE   Tel: 08242 3643
South of Ruthin. Nearest main road: A525 from Ruthin to Wrexham.

6 Bedrooms. £16–£16.50 (less for 7 nights). Bargain breaks. All have own bath/shower/ toilet. Tea/coffee facilities. TV. Views of garden, country. Washing machine on request.

Light suppers only. Wine can be brought in. **2 Sitting-rooms.** With open fire, central heating.
Large grounds

I, like many people, had underestimated the county of Clwyd. No national park here, but superlative scenery nevertheless in the range of the Clwydian Hills running south. Ruthin is an attractive little town with half-timbered houses and a craft centre (at its castle, really good mediaeval banquets are held).

Just south of here, a disused railway station is now an unusual – and unusually excellent – guest-house. It has been imaginatively converted and furnished by Jen Spencer. Outside, all is white paint and flowers. Ground-floor bedrooms have such touches as broderie anglaise festoon blinds and canopied bedheads with dolly-mixtures fabrics; some (more simply furnished) are in what were the porters' rooms. Excellent bathrooms (even a bidet). What was once the waiting-room is now a very large sitting-room (one of two) with a balcony just above the fields: big sofas, modern marble fireplace with log stove and thick carpet make this particu-larly comfortable. The conservatory/dining-room – once the station platform – overlooks (as does one bedroom) a small, well-heated swimming-pool which gets the afternoon sun. Jen offers only snacks for supper: crusty rolls and pâté, quiches and salads.

Northward, Denbigh's high castle overlooks the Vale of Clwyd all the way from Ruthin to the sea. At Dyserth, waterfalls drop a spectacular 60 feet, there is a ruined castle, and a stately home (Bodelwyddan Castle) with fine gardens – it was nominated National Heritage Museum of the year in 1989. It is an outstation of London's National Portrait Gallery.

At Rhuddlan is an even more impressive castle, the parliament house of Edward I and the viewpoint of Bon Hill. Holywell had a shrine to which even kings came as pilgrims; many visitors still come to the beautiful friary at Pantasaph (and to the cave museum of military vehicles with tableaux of war scenes).

Mold is worth visiting for the animal frieze in its ancient church, and its theatre; and Nannerch for the watermill crafts centre. Above Cilcain rises a great peak with Jubilee Tower on top, a landmark for miles around, and a country park. Llanarmon-yn-Ial has an unusual church, with effigies.

As to the landscape on the way to all these towns and villages, Gerard Manley Hopkins wrote: 'There can hardly be in the world anything to beat the Vale of Clwyd.' One route which shows the area at its best is via the Horseshoe Pass.

★ **FFALDAU**
Llandegley, Powys, LD1 5UD Tel: 059787 421
East of Llandrindod Wells. Nearest main road: A44 from Kington to Rhayader.

3 Bedrooms. £15–£18. Bargain breaks. Some have own bath/shower/toilet. Tea/coffee facilities. TV. Views of garden, country. Washing machine on request. **Dinner.** £14 for 2 or £16 for 3 courses (with choices) and coffee, at 7–9pm. Vegetarian or special diets if ordered. Wine can be ordered. **Light suppers** sometimes. **2 Sitting-rooms.** With central heating, TV, piano. Bar. **Large garden**

Set back from the road is one of the prettiest mediaeval houses in this book: roses climb up stone walls of palest apricot, rustic seats overlook colourful beds of heather. Beyond the lawns are grazing sheep and distant hills. At night, the garden is illuminated.

Ffaldau ('sheepfold') began life around 1500 as a longhouse: people lived at one end, livestock at the other. When the Knotts took over, the ceilings leaked, floors had rotted, and all around was a litter of railway wagons and hen-houses. Not only have they transformed the house and garden but – with no previous experience – they run a restaurant which has an ever-widening reputation for fine food (even bar meals are exceptional, and at breakfast there may be Loch Fyne kippers).

Old features have been retained and restored, from a wig-cupboard built into one thick wall, to a characterful old iron grate with Prince of Wales feathers in its decoration. Upstairs one can see the cruck construction of the house: the great tree-trunks used to support the roof. Mullioned windows are set into the stone walls, slabs of slate floor the hall, a log stove stands on an old inglenook hearth.

All this is complemented by the taste of Sylvia and her daughter Sara who made the swags of dried flowers and chose waitresses' floral dresses to match the pink linen and walls of the dining-room, where candles with nosegays deck each table. Bedrooms are named for wildflowers – honeysuckle, rose, anemone – and on the landing is a sitting area well stocked with books.

As to the food, there is a full menu from which to choose such imaginative dishes as a tartlet of smoked tuna in sour cream and horseradish, followed by veal fillet with a sauce of green peppercorns, Grand Marnier and orange and then one of Sara's puddings such as a brandy-snap cup filled with ginger and raisin ice cream and hot brandy.

Nearby Llandrindod Wells has the faded charm of a one-time spa (indeed, you can still 'take the waters' there) and stands in an area of great beauty, little troubled by traffic or tourists. One can drive almost without sight of another car among hills like dusty velvet, with mountain sheep occasionally silhouetted on the skyline.

Readers' comments: Excellent cooking, most welcoming and obliging, most tastefully furnished. Thoroughly enjoyed good hospitality. Good cooking; caring and informal.

HIGHGATE FARM   C

Betws Cedewain, Powys, SY16 3LF   Tel: 0686 625981
North of Newtown. Nearest main road: A483 from Welshpool to Newtown.

Tea/coffee facilities. Views of garden, country. Washing machine on request.
Dinner. £7 for 3 courses and coffee, at 6.30pm. Non-residents not admitted. Vegetarian or special diets if ordered. Wine can be ordered. No smoking.
2 Sitting-rooms. With open fire, central heating, TV, piano, record-player. No smoking. **Bar.**
Large garden

3 Bedrooms. £15–£17 (less for 2 nights). Bargain breaks. All have own shower/toilet.   **Closed from December to March inclusive.**

A priest's hole (in the ceiling of what is now a shower room) tells its own story, of the days when the Catholic religion had to be practised in secret. For this was a part of Wales in which recusancy flourished: in 1678, the Earl of Powis was imprisoned for five years in the Tower of London during the anti-Catholic mania whipped up by Titus Oates.

This fine black-and-white house, five centuries old, stands among rolling hills with distant views across its gardens. Whitticases have farmed here for generations. When Gwyn, latest in the line, took over, he stripped away ugly accretions to reveal the big stone fireplace and ceiling beams which are now the main features of the sitting-room. Through a little bar, one reaches a large panelled dining-room with inglenook fireplace and old Welsh dresser where Linda serves such meals as leek soup (with fresh-baked rolls), their own lamb, and blackberry-and-apple pie.

She has a decorative touch, making swags of dried flowers and choosing colourful wallpapers (pink tulips on one, crimson cabbage-roses on another) to complement the exposed timbers of walls in bedrooms that are handsomely furnished with mahogany antiques, for instance.

Highgate's grounds have much to interest visitors. A series of old millponds in a dell, with waterfalls, have been stocked with pintails, black-necked swans and bar-headed geese. Gwyn breeds and shows shire horses. And there are all the farm animals too – sheep, calves, Charolais bulls, chickens. Children, and adults, can participate in some of the farm activities. Riding, shooting and fishing are available.

As to the surroundings, Gwyn is glad to help visitors plan attractive routes to follow and discover how very fine and unspoilt this part of Wales is – not overrun by tourists despite its accessibility from the Midlands and even London. Newtown (new in 1321!) is a pleasant market town, so are Welshpool and Llanidloes.

Montgomery's ruined castle is romantically perched on an ivy-clad crag; in the town itself are Tudor and 18th-century buildings and a 13th-century church which houses particularly splendid effigies under an elaborate canopy. Northward is Powis Castle – a palatial and battlemented building with terraced gardens and parkland below, which provide an appropriate setting; and there is a wing devoted to Clive of India. Near a canal aqueduct is flowery Berriew, full of black-and-white houses and threaded by a bubbling river, which repeatedly wins 'best kept village' awards – marble effigies in this church too. Beyond it lies Llanfair Caereinion from which one of Wales' little steam railways sets out into the rolling countryside.

LLWYNDÛ   C

Llanaber, Gwynedd, LL42 1RR   Tel: 0341280 144
North of Barmouth. Nearest main road: A496 from Barmouth to Harlech.

Tea/coffee facilities. TV on request. Views of garden, country, sea. No smoking. Washing machine on request.
Dinner. £7.50 for 3 courses (with choices) and coffee, at 7–7.30pm. Non-residents not admitted. Vegetarian or special diets if ordered. Wine can be ordered. **Light suppers** if ordered.
1 Sitting-room. With open fire, central heating, TV, record-player.
7 Bedrooms. £15 (less for 7 nights). Bargain breaks. Most have own bath/shower/toilet.
Large garden
Closed in December and January.

In the year that the youthful Shakespeare wrote *The Taming of the Shrew*, an even younger man made his way from remote Llwyndu to London, to study law in the Inner Temple. It was 1597, and this house had already seen generations of his family grow up. Peter Thompson, whose home it now is, researched the history of the house and its inhabitants for a university dissertation: he even has some of their very early wills.

This, therefore, was a house of considerable consequence in the neighbour-hood, and handsomely built. The walls are immensely thick and the living-room huge; one ceiling-beam is over two feet thick, and great blocks of granite form the fireplace. New discoveries continue to come to light – for instance, a 16th-century oak-mullioned window which had long been blocked up.

The bedrooms have, in most cases, views (and sounds) of the sea waves – and excellent bathrooms (one with oval bath and bidet, for example). One room has a dressing-room, another its own stone stair to the garden; some are in a newly converted granary. Everywhere are attractive furnishings, and great pieces of driftwood from the beaches stand here and there like sculpture.

Peter is a very keen cook, preparing for visitors such meals as parsnip-and-apple soup, lamb in a mushroom and cinnamon sauce, rhubarb-and-banana pie.

As to the name of the house, which means 'black grove', this refers to a one-time feature of the region – groves of sycamores planted because they alone would withstand the salty breezes from the sea.

Readers' comments: House has tremendous character. Lovely food, great value. Delightful situation, friendly welcome.

On the south bank of the Mawddach estuary is **HERONGATE**, at Arthog (tel: 0341 250 349), the simple and in-expensive but pleasant home of Pat Mallatratt whose late husband's paint-ings line the walls of the small sitting-room. Herons, oystercatchers and tame sheep seeking titbits can be seen from the bay windows. The house is in a small, isolated terrace built by a Victorian entrepreneur as part of a grander plan that never materialized.

(B & b only: one can dine in Dolgellau.) From £11 to £12.

OLD RECTORY C D

Aberyscir, Powys, LD3 9NP   Tel: 0874 3457

West of Brecon. Nearest main road: A40 from Brecon to Sennybridge.

3 Bedrooms. £12.50–£14 (less for 7 nights).
Prices go up in June. Tea/coffee facilities.
TV. Views of garden, country, river.
Washing machine on request.
Dinner. £6.50 for 4 courses (with choices)
and coffee, at 7pm. Vegetarian or special
diets if ordered. Wine can be brought in.
1 Sitting-room. With central heating, piano,
record-player.
Large garden

Well tucked away in the hills, this Victorian stone house, standing in large grounds, has been furnished by Elizabeth Gould to high standards of comfort and solid quality – but prices are modest. A horse, ram and squirrel greeted our arrival, and there is poultry too. I particularly liked the pink bedroom which has windows on two sides and very lovely views of the Brecon Beacons. Dinners include generous quantities of such dishes as smoked haddock ramekins, beef Stroganoff and Elizabeth's Malibu dessert – coconut liqueur combined with tropical fruits and whipped cream. Afterwards, there are velvet chairs and a chaise longue in the attractive, green sitting-room from which to enjoy the views through big sash windows or watch Elizabeth use her New Zealand spinning wheel. (Bicycles and pony rides available.)

The Brecon Beacons are the highest mountains in South Wales, with several peaks over 2000 feet. Ice Age glaciers scored deep valleys in the red sandstone; to the south, the underlying rock is limestone or millstone grit, producing different scenery and a multitude of cave systems, gorges and waterfalls.

The Eppynt Hills to the north are softer (at their feet runs the lovely River Wye) but even here you can enjoy panoramic views all the way to Carmarthen.

Scenery is the main but not the only attraction of the area. There are plenty of castles to visit: for instance, at Y Gaer, (near Brecon), was the Romans' largest inland fort, and mediaeval castles are at Builth Bronllys and Crickhowell among other places. Brecon has a Norman cathedral, and in many villages are churches with fine rood screens. Zulu War relics can be seen in the museum of the South Wales Borderers Regiment which fought at Rorke's Drift; and everywhere one finds craft workshops (Welsh tweeds and flannels are particularly good buys).

However, it is outdoor activities which bring most people here. There is superb walking country, even if you do not want to tackle the mountain paths. Forest trails are well waymarked; and there are guided walks, too. Vast areas around Builth are relatively unexplored (the Tourist Information Centre there has a leaflet of walks). For the intrepid, caving, climbing, hang-gliding and watersports await; less taxing is angling – and brass-rubbing.

Good day trips by car along scenic routes include the Usk reservoir (visiting the Black Mountain bird park on the way), and also the Llyn Brianne reservoirs (perhaps picnicking in the Gwenffrwyd bird reserve, or following a riverside nature trail to the cave of outlaw Twm Catti, before arriving at the dam viewpoint).

The Elan Valley has a chain of lakes and five dams extending over nine miles; a short detour brings you to yet another stupendous dam at the Claerwen reservoirs.

Readers' comments: Outstanding value, lovely scenery, food and people.

PANTYFEDWEN

C S

Pontrhydfendigaid, Dyfed, SY25 6EN Tel: 09745 358
South-east of Aberystwyth. Nearest main road: A485 from Aberystwyth to
Tregaron.

3 Bedrooms. £14–£17. Prices go up in
March. Bargain breaks. Views of garden,
country. Washing machine on request.
Dinner. £10 for 3 courses (with some
choices) and coffee, at 7pm. Non-residents
not admitted. Vegetarian or special diets if
ordered. Wine can be brought in. **Light
suppers** if ordered.
2 Sitting-rooms. With open fire, central
heating, TV, piano, record-player.
Large garden
Closed in December and January.

In the Strata Florida ('flowery vale'), just beyond very lovely abbey ruins, is the
17th-century home of two teachers, Ceri and Siân Davies. The name of the house
means 'a hollow with birch trees'. Behind its sparkling white façade are ancient
inglenook fireplaces, a curious spiral staircase of stone and other ancient features
preserved when the house was recently modernized.

Siân has used attractive fabrics, Berber carpets or white flokati rugs on board
floors and furniture in keeping with the house (refectory tables, for example, with
pretty pine and rush chairs). Handsome modern armchairs of pale velvet face a
huge stone hearth with log stove. Up a coral staircase are bedrooms decorated in,
for instance, a creamy colour scheme or blue and white. There is also a child's
room with toys. One bathroom is luxurious (two dark brown basins, bidet etc.)

As to meals, which include home-grown vegetables, a typical dinner might be
leek soup, carbonnade of beef and orange mousse.

This is a very scenic area and on the coast is the lively resort of Aberystwyth.

A few miles eastward is Lledrod and
★ **BRYNARTH FARMHOUSE** (tel:
09743 367), where a very pretty group
of white stone buildings, three centuries old, encloses a big courtyard
with lily-pool, flowering shrubs and
benches of stone and timber inviting
one to linger – or sometimes to enjoy a
steak from the stone barbecue. Inside
the guest-house is a sitting/dining-area
where the slate-tiled floor and stone
walls are complemented by old pews
and a chunky pine table. There is a
small bar adjoining this. Brenda Ball
serves such meals as ratatouille, lamb
fricassée (with egg and lemon sauce),
and plum or apple pies. Attractive bedrooms have panelled bedheads and
wardrobes, flowers painted on their
doors and stone walls (all have baths or
showers). From £15 to £16.

PARK HALL   **D S**

Cwmtydu, Dyfed, SA44 6LG   Tel: 0545 560306

North-east of Cardigan. Nearest main road: A487 from Cardigan to
Aberystwyth.

5 **Bedrooms.** £16.95 (less for 7 nights).
Prices go up during summer. Bargain
breaks. All have own bath/shower/toilet.
Tea/coffee facilities. TV. Views of garden,
country, sea. Washing machine on request.
Dinner. A la carte or £12.95 for 5 courses
(with choices) and coffee, at 8pm. Vegetarian or special diets if ordered. Wine can be
ordered.
2 **Sitting-rooms.** With open fire, central
heating, TV, piano, record-player. Bar.
Large garden

In a wooded valley protected by the National Trust is one of the most interesting
'finds' that I made in Wales. A quite exceptional guest-house has been created in
this turn-of-the-century mansion which is decorated with flair, using much
Victoriana – the table linen and silver, the brass beds (one four-poster), the leather
chesterfields and even the bath with brass claw feet are in period. Antique lace has
been used quite a lot, and Laura Ashley Victorian-style fabrics as well as
patchwork, Welsh tapestry bedspreads, and a wallpaper of sweet peas in a
bathroom. From pine-panelled bay windows, there are views of Cardigan Bay
between the hills and of the picturesque valley running down to it. Chris
Macdonnell's dinners are of a high order. A popular starter is, after soup such as
vichyssoise, a prawn and avocado salad; main courses can include salmon poached
in vermouth; with such puddings as profiteroles – and then cheeses. Dinner is
served in a large, new conservatory which overlooks the sea. Afternoon teas and
light lunches are also available.

Cardigan's ancient bridge straddles the Teifi, a salmon river. There are a castle,
abbey ruins at St Dogmael's, and a park of native wildlife. Upriver (at Cilgerran)
you may see coracle fishing – a coracle regatta is held each August – and there is a
romantic castle ruin; at Henllan, beautifully sited, or Llanbydder are little woollen
mills open to visitors; and at the valley's 'capital', Lampeter, one can visit St
David's College or attend the horse fairs in May. In the opposite direction is
Aberystwyth, a resort and university town, with fine gardens around its castle
ruins and a good museum. Some of Britain's finest beaches are along this coastline.

Readers' comments: Impossible to find criticism. Very friendly, superb accommodation. Excellent value. We will return.

On Cardigan Bay is a picturesque cove
over-popular in high summer – Llan-
granog, but set aside from the throng
here is quiet **HENDRE FARM** (tel:
023978 342), unpretentious but very
comfortable and with good home cooking by Bethan Williams, using the
farm's own fruit, vegetables and other
produce: a good choice for a traditional
farmhouse holiday. From £13 to £17.

PLAS TREFARTHEN

Brynsiencyn, Isle of Anglesey, Gwynedd, LL61 6SZ   Tel: 0248 73379
South-west of Menai Bridge. Nearest main road: A4080 from Rhosneigr to
Menai Bridge.

8 Bedrooms. £13–£16. Some have own bath/toilet. Tea/coffee facilities. TV. Views of garden, mountains, river. No smoking. **Dinner.** £7.50 for 3 courses (with some choices) and coffee, at 6.30pm. Non-residents not admitted. Vegetarian diets if ordered. Wine can be brought in. No smoking.
1 Sitting-room. With open fire, central heating, piano, record-player.
Large garden

It had seemed an ordinary day. True, the house is a handsome 18th-century mansion at the heart of a 200-acre farm, and its waterfront site is outstanding (there are superb views across the Menai Strait to Snowdon). But suddenly the experience became exceptional for me . . . in fact, unique. Standing by her piano in the dining-room, Marian Roberts began to sing impromptu (to my husband's accompaniment). Her voice soared effortlessly, true and clear, to the highest notes. I have rarely heard such a lovely and unaffected sound from any singer.

Marian, after repeatedly winning the highest accolades at the international *eisteddfods* each year, now spends much of every winter on tour, singing in America, Australia and elsewhere. But in summer she is a 'bed-and-breakfast lady', welcoming visitors to Plas Trefarthen and – yes – quite often singing to them.

In the sitting-room, a big picture-window makes the most of the view across the water to Caernarfon Castle. The green brocade walls and a big Welsh dresser display souvenirs of Marian's travels; musical mementoes are gathered in the dining-room. Bedrooms are roomy – the pink one has an outsize bathroom and windows on two sides; the pine-fitted one has the best views of Snowdon. There are also attic rooms with large skylights.

Marian serves full dinners on some nights (home-made soup, Welsh lamb and apple tart, for instance) and will provide light suppers on others, by arrangement.

The house stands in an area of outstanding natural beauty. Unlike the rest of Wales, Anglesey's 300 square miles are rocky but not mountainous: they have other charms. The island is still a centre of Celtic culture.

Around Anglesey there is a great deal to see: a huge nature reserve of dunes at Newborough (wildfowl and wading birds); Holy Island reached by a causeway, from which there are views to the Isle of Man and Ireland, glimpses of seals or seabirds on South Stack, and vast caves on North Stack; Cemaes Bay for good bathing and clifftop walks; Amlwch, a resort surrounded by fine coastal scenery; the picturesque fishing village of Moelfre; Penmon with mediaeval remains and trips to Puffin Island; and weekly markets at Llangefni. One of Anglesey's claims to fame is the village with the longest name in Britain: Llanfairpwllgwyngyllgogerychwyrndrobwillantysiliogogogoch.

★ **TALBONTDRAIN**   C PT(limited) S

Uwychygarreg, Powys, SY20 8RR   Tel: 0654 702192
South of Machynlleth. Nearest main road: A489 from Machynlleth towards
Newtown.

6 Bedrooms. £13–£15 (less for 7 nights).
Some have own bath/shower/toilet. Views of
garden, country. No smoking. Washing
machine on request.
Dinner. £8 for 2 courses and coffee, at
7.30pm. Non-residents not admitted.

Vegetarian or special diets if ordered. Wine
can be brought in. No smoking. **Light suppers** if ordered.
1 Sitting-room. With open fire, central heating, piano. No smoking.
Large garden

Hilary Matthews abandoned a London career as a social worker to restore this
remote, slate-floored house, high in the hills, furnishing it very simply – for people
who travel light – but with attractive colours and textures. Inexpensive guided
walking holidays are an extra attraction here (no car is needed: Hilary will pick you
up at Machynlleth station and drive you up her long, twisting lane); and she
provides particularly well for children. She serves such 2-course meals as bacon-
and-leek flan with vegetables, followed by nectarines in a creamy sauce. Occasionally she does fungus identifying (and cooking) weekends. Her breakfasts
feature Welsh specialities: I recommend 'Glamorgan sausage', a type of cheese
croquette. Some guests enjoy her excellent pianola as an after-dinner treat.
Talbontdrain (its name means 'thorn tree at the end of the bridge') is in a varied
area of woodland, waterfalls, moors and sheep pastures; utterly peaceful. Around
the house are goats, bees, big tubs of petunias, wagtails and chickens; inside are
warmth and comfort.

The market town of Machynlleth, at the head of the Dyfi estuary, did not grow
up in the higgledy-piggledy way of many mediaeval towns but was laid out
systematically in the 13th century, with its main streets forming a 'T'. The Welsh
patriot Owaîn Glyndwr gathered his supporters (in 1404) where the 16th-century
Parliament House now stands; other historic buildings include the Mayor's
House, Royal House – Glyndwr's home, and the 5-arched bridge over the river.
The town is particularly well provided with craft shops, and has on its outskirts the
exceptionally interesting Centre for Alternative Technology in a disused quarry –
where you can see everything from aerogenerators to organic vegetable gardens,
solar cells to fish-farming.

A great many scenic roads converge here, and all around are interesting villages
and other sights. Derwenlas has attractive cottages on the estuary; Ffwrnais
(meaning 'furnace'), a watermill which once powered ironmaking and a very
beautiful waterfall; in the Dyfi National Nature Reserve is a mile-long nature trail,
at Corris a railway museum, in Tre'r ddol a chapel with a museum of religion in
Wales; Clywedog reservoir has the highest dam in Britain.

Readers' comments: Friendly; good food and company; extremely comfortable.
Beautifully situated.

372

★ **TREGYNON**   **C H X**

Gwaun Valley, Dyfed, SA65 9TU   Tel: 0239 820531

South-east of Fishguard. Nearest main road: B4313 from Fishguard to Narbeth.

All have own bath/shower/toilet. Tea/coffee facilities. TV. Views of country. Smoking discouraged. Washing machine on request. **Dinner.** A la carte or £10.50 for 3 courses (with choices) and coffee, at 7.30pm. Vegetarian or special diets if ordered. Wine can be ordered. No smoking. **Light suppers** if ordered.

2 Sitting-rooms. With open fire, central heating, piano, record-player. Bar. Smoking discouraged.

8 Bedrooms. £18.50–£22.50 (less for 2 nights). Prices go up in July. Bargain breaks.

Large grounds

In the heart of the Pembrokeshire Coast National Park is something quite exceptional. Of all the places I have stayed in Wales, this remote 16th-century, country farmhouse hotel has some of the most spectacular scenery around it, including an Ice Age ravine with waterfall, ancient oak woods, countryside where badgers and polecats or buzzards and red kites are sometimes spotted, wild moorland and a prehistoric fort. From nearby peaks of the Preseli Mountains, one can sometimes see Ireland and Snowdon. Not far away are some of the sunniest sandy beaches in the country, renowned for their pure air.

The meals, too, are exceptional with emphasis on wholefood. Peter Heard grows vegetables organically, keeps a variety of livestock, and has his own trout ponds. Speciality breads, sausages, traditionally smoked ham, cheeses and Tregynon's own spring water contribute to the very special experience of eating here. You can relax afterwards by a log fire in the beamed sitting-room which has a massive stone inglenook and button-backed chesterfields of raspberry and grass-green velvet, with a snug stone-walled bar adjoining it. Some bedrooms are in the house, others in converted stone outbuildings – spacious, pretty and well equipped.

The National Park extends round almost the entire coast from Cardigan Bay to Carmarthen Bay (there is a coastal path all the way) and inland to mountains.

Readers' comments: Excellent host. Varied and original menus of excellent quality (best ice cream we have ever tasted). Nothing seemed too much trouble.

For anyone tracing their family history, I recommend a stay at inexpens-
★ ive **MOUNT PLEASANT FARM** at Penffordd (tel: 0437 563447) because Pauline Bowen is an expert on the subject, while Peter collects vintage cars and bygones. A warm, hospitable couple, their small, beamed farmhouse of rugged stone has been immaculately modernized and is very comfortable. Good home cooking and, from the comfort of big armchairs of pink velvet, fine views of the Preseli Mountains

– superb when heather is in bloom. £12.50.

Readers' comments: Exceptional value.

★ **TY GWYN**   C DH PT S X
Betws-y-Coed, Gwynedd, LL24 0SG   Tel: 06902 383
On A5 from Betws-y-Coed to Llangollen.

13 Bedrooms. £17–£32.50. Bargain breaks. Some have own bath/shower/toilet. Tea/coffee facilities. TV. Views of garden, country, river. Balcony (one). Washing machine on request.
Dinner. A la carte or £12.50 for 3 courses (with choices) and coffee, at 7–9.30pm. Vegetarian or special diets if ordered. Wine can be ordered. **Light suppers.**
1 **Sitting-room.** With central heating, TV, tape-recorder. **Bar** with open fire.
Small garden

A former coaching inn, Ty Gwyn ('white house'), although on a road, has quiet bedrooms at the back. Sheila Ratcliffe has a flair for interior decoration, and every bedroom – small or large – is beautiful, many with en suite bathrooms (prices vary accordingly).

The most impressive is an attic suite with four-poster and sitting-room; the most convenient for anyone disabled, a pretty ground-floor room. A mountain rises up sheer at the back, where one tiny room has stone walls contrasting with a cane bedhead. Even in the ancient, beamed bar (fire glowing in the old black range, copper pots, carved oak settle) Sheila's colourful patchwork cushions are everywhere. There is also a very comfortable sitting-room and another where she sells antiques and old prints. Flagstone floors have Turkey carpets; all around are stone walls and old country charm. Every ledge or sill is laden with brass kettles, Sheffield plate, baskets, tankards, dried flowers . . .

Cooking is done by chef Martin, the Ratcliffes' son, whose specialities include exotic dishes like lamb flamed in crème-de-menthe or pork in an apple and ginger sauce (the table d'hôte menu is simpler). These meals are served in a picturesque dining-room: antique furniture, crochet, crystal and silver on the tables. Even the bar snacks include such imaginative options as shark with garlic butter, bulghar wheat and walnut casserole or homely rabbit pie.

Four wooded valleys meet at this village, with a high plateau looming above it. Walkers use it as a centre to explore in every direction, the serious ones making for Snowdon but most for the riverside paths, the Gwydyr Forest, any of several lakes or waterfalls, or the Fairy Glen (the hotel has route cards, graded for difficulty).

Also in Betws is a small, partly 14th-century watermill: **ROYAL OAK FARMHOUSE** (tel: 06902 427/632). Although so central, the mill is hidden in a little valley with a deep salmon pool close by. The lattice-paned windows, great stone fireplace, carved oak settle and small but very pretty bedrooms give this inexpensive guest-house great character (very good bathroom, incidentally). Elsie Houghton serves only breakfast, but there are good eating-places in Betws. From £11 to £12.

Equally attractive (and with en suite bathrooms) is **ROYAL OAK FARM COTTAGE** (tel: 06902 760) run by Elsie's daughter-in-law Kathleen. From £12.50 to £13.50.

★ **TŶ'N RHOS**   C(6) **D H PT**(limited) **S**
Llanddeiniolen, Gwynedd, LL55 3AE   Tel: 0248 670489
North-east of Caernarfon. Nearest main road: A487 from Bangor to
Caernarfon.

11 Bedrooms. £18–£21 (less for 2 nights).
Prices go up in March. Bargain breaks. All
have own bath/shower/toilet. Tea/coffee
facilities. TV. Views of garden, country.
Washing machine on request.
Dinner. £11 for 4 courses and coffee, at
7pm. Non-residents not admitted. Vegetarian or special diets if ordered. Wine can
be ordered. No smoking. **Light suppers** if
ordered.
1 Sitting-room. With open fire, central
heating.
Large garden

These days things are very different at this farm compared to its early beginnings
(the name means a moorland smallholding). It is now almost a hotel, run in a very
professional way by Nigel and Lynda Kettle. A wing of modern, well equipped
bedrooms and en suite bathrooms has been added, to a standard even the most
fastidious reader would approve. It is nevertheless still a working farm, which
supplies produce for the table (and cheese to take home). Lynda is an excellent
cook of such meals as beef soup, salmon with hollandaise sauce, and chocolate
sponge with brandy sauce – served in a dining-room with, at one end, big glass
windows that slide open upon a tranquil scene of lawn and lakes; and at the other, a
sitting area for pre-dinner drinks.

The farm itself is of interest before one goes sightseeing further afield, as visitors
are encouraged to watch what goes on. There are usually calves, pigs, sheep, hens,
ducks and a sheepdog to be seen. The farm makes its own yogurt, cream and
cheese. Fly fishing is available; and a vegetable garden supplies the kitchen.
Guests can also relax in the traditionally furnished sitting-room with log stove.

One is in the heart of Snowdonia here, with Caernarfon in one direction and
Bangor in the other. The rugged grandeur of the mountain passes is in complete
contrast to the tranquil countryside around the farm, with wildflowers and birds in
abundance. The island of Anglesey is soon reached; some of its sandy beaches
sheltered and others open to Atlantic breakers, ideal for surfing. The Lleyn
peninsula is a beautiful area to explore. There are preserved railways – steam
at Ffestiniog, rack-and-pinion up to Snowdon's summit; innumerable craft
workshops (including harp-making); and, of course, some sensational castles –
Caernarfon in particular, but also Beaumaris, Penrhyn, Conwy and Harlech.

One of the finest day drives would be through the Llanberis Pass to Capel Curig
and then to the 'alpine' village of Betws-y-Coed beyond which are Dolwyddelan
Castle, Ffestiniog power station (guided tours), a mountain interpretation centre
at Gloddfa Ganol and the cavernous slate mine at Llechwedd (you are conveyed by
train through Victorian scenes underground).

Readers' comments: Fabulous, comfortable, warm and welcoming. Super food.
Bedrooms beautifully and tastefully furnished. Absolutely superb.

Prices are per person in a double room at the beginning of the year.

TY'R YWEN
Lasgarn Lane, Trevithin, Gwent, NP4 8TT   Tel: 049528 200
North of Pontypool. Nearest main road: A4042 from Newport to Abergavenny.

2 Bedrooms. £15. Both have own bath/shower/toilet. Tea/coffee facilities. TV. Views of garden, country, sea, river. No smoking. Washing machine on request.
Dinner. (Must be pre-booked.) £7 for 3 courses and coffee, at 7pm. Non-residents not admitted. Vegetarian or special diets if ordered. Wine can be brought in. No smoking. **Light suppers** if ordered.
1 Sitting-room. With open fire, central heating, TV.
Large garden

Over the 1200-foot Garn Wen mountain by a rough and lengthy track – superb views of the Brecon Beacons, but not a drive for the timid! – is a 16th-century longhouse, Ty'r Ywen ('house of yews'), which young Susan Armitage and her husband laboured for three years to transform from a derelict state to the present very attractive home. Each guest room has a four-poster (one has two), made by David with pretty draperies by Susan, and the en suite bathrooms are luxurious (one has a bubble-bath). Across the inglenook fireplace is a massive two-foot beam. In the huge dining-kitchen, fiddleback chairs surrounding two refectory tables, Susan serves (with the help of their vegetable garden, bees and Jersey cows) such meals as: melon salad, chicken legs with stuffed courgettes and blackcurrant gâteau. David, a hospital engineer, drives a vintage car to and from his work, the long track notwithstanding.

Gwent was among Wales' ancient kingdoms, and one of its monarchs, Caractacus (son of Shakespeare's 'Cymbeline'), put up a fierce fight against the Romans – until captured in AD 51 and sent to Rome in chains. The Normans, too, found it difficult to subdue – which is why there is such a large number of castles. Nevertheless, the Welsh eventually yielded to foreign (English) influence here more than in other parts, hence the large number of anglicized place names.

One of the county's most outstanding beauty-spots is the woodland Wye Valley (it winds from the fortified clifftop town of Chepstow north to old Monmouth), with Tintern Abbey's imposing and romantic ruins by the riverside. Walkers can follow Offa's Dyke on the opposite bank. From Chepstow west to Newport, one can drive along an attractive road first laid down by the Romans to link their strongholds at Venta Silurum near Caerwent (walls and gates visible) and Caerleon (there are a huge amphitheatre and barrack remains still to be seen); and then head north through the picturesque Usk Valley to mediaeval Raglan Castle beyond the market town of Usk – it, too, has a castle, other mediaeval buildings, and the stately home of Lord Raglan (of Crimean fame – or notoriety: it was he who was responsible for the tragic Charge of the Light Brigade).

Near Caerwent is Caldicot. Its castle (where mediaeval banquets are held) has a country park around it and in the River Severn near here you can sometimes see salmon being caught in conical baskets.

Monmouth is particularly worth a lingering visit. Its web of streets is full of old buildings, it has the Norman castle where Henry V was born (ruined now, but 17th-century Castle House and its decorative ceilings have survived), a Nelson museum, and a unique fortified Norman bridge.

WYNNSTAY INN

Llansilin, Clwyd, SY10 7QB   Tel: 0691 70355

West of Oswestry (Shropshire). Nearest main road: A5 from Shrewsbury to Llangollen.

CDS

4 Bedrooms. £12.50 (less for 3 nights). Prices go up in May. Bargain breaks. Tea/coffee facilities. TV. Views of garden, country.
Dinner. A la carte or £6 for 3 courses (with choices) and coffee, at 6.30pm. Vegetarian diets if ordered. Wine can be ordered. **Light suppers.**
1 Sitting-room. With open fire, central heating, TV. **Bars.**
Small garden

The long, stone inn has been standing here two hundred years and many of its features seem hardly to have changed. There are two black, iron cooking-ranges, a tapestry settle in the dining-room, cretonne armchairs and old oak pews in the beamed bars. Roses and clematis grow up its walls. It even has a ghost story to tell.

Michael Gilchrist's food is plain, good and ample: half a duck, for instance.

I particularly liked bedroom no. 3 and, although the inn itself may be old, bathroom equipment is good and new.

The inn stands among fields and rocky, wooded hills, well sited in the days when the road outside was a busy coaching route: in the time of Charles II it was the highway from Chester to Cardiff. The area is full of mediaeval buildings, and historic – even prehistoric – connections (the village church was burnt down during the 15th-century rebellion of Owaîn Glyndwr, Wales' national hero, and it still carries Cromwellian bullet-holes). Even though this is so lovely a region and so accessible, its mountains, valleys, streams and waterfalls are little frequented.

For a particularly scenic drive, take the road to Llanrhaeadr and the highest waterfall in England and Wales, then onto the beautifully sited village of Llanarmon with mediaeval inn, and Glyn Ceiriog to explore cavernous slate mines (guided tours and a museum), and the memorial institute with stained glass and furniture presented by Welsh emigrants to Argentina.

'The pass on the hill', which is what
★ **BWLCH Y RHIW** means, exactly describes the splendid situation of this early Victorian house perched high above the Tanat Valley just outside the village of Llansilin. From its flowery, paved terrace there are superb views. The big quarry-tiles of the kitchen are original: one passes through here to reach the large, beamed breakfast-room which has a particularly handsome table, 'country Chippendale' chairs and a Welsh dresser full of willow-patterned china. The stone inglenook fireplace still has the original bread oven built in, and a great brass hood. All rooms are spacious and the best

rear view

of the bedrooms enjoys a view of the valley. Brenda Jones provides only breakfasts. (Tel: 069170 261.) From £14 to £15.

CANCELLATION INSURANCE

On booking, you make a legally binding contract. I therefore recommend the following cancellation insurance, on which a special discount has been negotiated for you. Here are the details. (The application form is overleaf and can be photocopied if you may need more than one this year.)

From the date of booking and payment of premium to the end of the holiday, the policy reimburses the cost of irrecoverable travel or accommodation charges if the Insured is unable to travel as arranged due to:

(a) The death, injury, illness or compulsory quarantine of the Insured, a friend with whom the Insured intends to travel, or of the Insured's husband or wife, parent, brother, sister or child, or a close business associate. (This cover will also operate in the event of the death, severe accidental bodily injury or serious illness of any other relative of the Insured Person.)
(b) The Insured Person or any person with whom the Insured Person intends to travel being summoned for Jury Service or as a Witness in a Court of Law during the period of the holiday.
(c) Hi-jack occurring during the period of insurance.
(d) Redundancy (qualifying for payment under current Redundancy Payment Legislation) provided that such notice of redundancy is announced to the Insured Person after the insurance has been effected and has been advised to the insurers within fourteen days of such announcement.

In addition the insurers will indemnify the Insured Person in respect of:

(e) Reasonable additional travelling expenses incurred by the Insured Person and other Insured Persons travelling with the Insured Person in returning to the home address in the United Kingdom where such return journey is urgently required through the death, serious illness or severe injury of one of the Insured Person's relatives or a close business associate where such relative or close business associate is resident in the United Kingdom.

Premiums payable
Value of booking or part, £100 = Premium £3.50. Rising by £3.50 each £100 or part thereafter.

ORDER FOR 1992 EDITION

Name (capitals _____

Address (UK only or BFPO) _____

_____ Postcode _____

Please send me _____ copies of STAYING OFF THE BEATEN TRACK 1992 as soon as it is published in November 1991

I enclose a cheque/PO for £_____ made payable to EXPLORE BRITAIN. Price per book is £7.95 including postage and packing

Please send this form, together with a cheque/PO to Explore Britain, Alston, Cumbria, CA9 3SL

APPLICATION FOR CANCELLATION INSURANCE (SOTBT)

Name (capitals) _____

Address _____

_____ Postcode _____

Period of holiday from _____ to _____

Value of booking _____ Premium _____

Failure to disclose any facts which are material to the risk and which may influence the Company's acceptance and assessment of the proposal could lead to the contract being void and of no effect.

If you are in any doubt relating to facts which you consider may affect the risk, please disclose them to the Company.

Date _____ Proposer's signature _____

Please send proposal plus cheque/P.O. to:–
Rothwell & Towler, Insurance Brokers, 1 Union Street, Penzance, Cornwall, TR18 4SG. Telephone: 0736/65711

APPLYING FOR INCLUSION IN STAYING OFF THE BEATEN TRACK

Many proprietors ask for their houses to be included in this book, and – although not all can be accepted – such applications are welcomed, particularly from areas not already well covered; *provided that* the b & b price is within the book's limits (see page xxix). Ideally, either dinner or light snacks should be available in the evening. There is no charge for an entry but, compiling the book being expensive, nearly all proprietors make a contribution at the end of each year (no bills are issued). Every house has to be visited first and it may be some time before this takes place. Brochures, prices, etc. should be posted to: Elizabeth Gundrey, 19 Fitzjohns Avenue, London NW3 5JY. No phone calls please.